JESUIT ACCOUNTS OF THE COLONIAL AMERICAS

Edited by Marc André Bernier, Clorinda Donato, and Hans-Jürgen Lüsebrink

In recent years scholars have turned their attention to the rich experience of the Jesuits in France's and Spain's American colonies. That attention has brought a flow of new editions and translations of Jesuit accounts of the Americas; it is now time for a study that examines the full range of that work in a comparative perspective. *Jesuit Accounts of the Colonial Americas* offers the first comprehensive examination of such writings and the role they played in solidifying images of the Americas.

The collection also provides a much-needed re-examination of the work of the Jesuits in relation to Enlightenment ideals and the modern social sciences and humanities – two systems of thought that have in the past appeared radically opposed, but which are brought together here under the rubric of modern ethnographic knowledge. Linking Jesuit texts, the rhetorical tradition, and the newly emerging anthropology of the Enlightenment, this collection traverses the vast expanses of Old and New World France and Spain in fascinating new ways.

MARC ANDRÉ BERNIER is the Canada Research Chair in Rhetoric at l'Université du Québec à Trois-Rivières.

CLORINDA DONATO is the George L. Graziadio Chair of Italian Studies and professor of French and Italian at California State University, Long Beach.

HANS-JÜRGEN LÜSEBRINK is the chair of Romance Cultural Studies and Intercultural Communication at Universität des Saarlandes.

JESUIT ACCOUNTS OF THE COLONIAL AMERICAS

INTERCULTURAL TRANSFERS, INTELLECTUAL DISPUTES, AND TEXTUALITIES

Edited by
Marc André Bernier, Clorinda Donato, and Hans-Jürgen Lüsebrink

Published by the University of Toronto Press, in association with the UCLA Center for Seventeenth- and Eighteenth-Century Studies and the William Andrews Clark Memorial Library utorontopress.com

Reprinted in paperback 2022

ISBN 978-1-4426-4572-1 (cloth)
ISBN 978-1-4875-4977-0 (paper)

Publication cataloguing information is available from Library and Archives Canada.

This book has been published with the help of a grant from
the UCLA Center for Seventeenth- and Eighteenth-Century Studies.

We wish to acknowledge the land on which the University of Toronto Press operates. This land is the traditional territory of the Wendat, the Anishnaabeg, the Haudenosaunee, the Métis, and the Mississaugas of the Credit First Nation.

University of Toronto Press acknowledges the financial support of the Government of Canada, the Canada Council for the Arts, and the Ontario Arts Council, an agency of the Government of Ontario, for its publishing activities.

Canada Council for the Arts | Conseil des Arts du Canada

Funded by the Government of Canada | Financé par le gouvernement du Canada

Contents

Acknowledgments

We wish to acknowledge the many people whose work has made possible the publication of this volume and the organization of the two seminars in Los Angeles and Trois-Rivières. We wish to thank as well Peter Hanns Reill, Director of the UCLA Center for Seventeenth- and Eighteenth-Century Studies of the William Andrews Clark Library, for both financial and moral support of this project from start to finish. We are equally grateful to the Canada Research Chair in Rhetoric (Université du Québec à Trois-Rivières), the Cercle interuniversitaire sur la République des Lettres (Université Laval), the Deutsche Forschungsgemenschaft, the Universität des Saarlandes, and the Fonds de recherche Société et Culture du Québec, without whose generous support this project would not have been possible. We extend sincere gratitude to the attentive re-reading of Dr. Isabelle Lachance, research professional for the Canada Research Chair in Rhetoric, Rebecca Addicks, research assistant to the Graziadio Chair of Italian Studies at California State University–Long Beach (CSULB) at the time of manuscript preparation, currently a Ph.D. student in English at the University of California, Riverside, and Dr. Claudia Gosselin†, Emerita Adjunct Professor of French, CSULB. Additionally, Alejandro Alvarez, Laurence Moscato, and Manuel Romero, current research assistant to the Graziadio Chair of Italian Studies and Masters student in Italian at CSULB, deserve profound gratitude for their editorial and translation expertise. The volume has also profited immeasurably from Ellen Wilson's editorial eloquence and discerning eye, without which both the form and content of this volume would be seriously lacking.

JESUIT ACCOUNTS OF THE COLONIAL AMERICAS

Introduction

MARC ANDRÉ BERNIER, CLORINDA DONATO,
HANS-JÜRGEN LÜSEBRINK

The links between the Jesuit Relations and the newly emerging anthropology of the Enlightenment, which is the key issue examined in this volume, did not attract international research interest until fairly recently. For a long time, the thought and work of the Company of Jesus appeared radically opposed to Enlightenment ideals and the progress of modern social sciences and humanities. Subsequent, notably, to the work of Michel de Certeau (1974) and Michèle Duchet (1985), and with the publication of more recent collective works such as those edited by Manfred Tietz and Dietrich Briesemeister (2001), Karl Kohut and Maria Christina Torales Pacheco (2007), Perla Chinchilla Pawling and Antonella Romano (2008), and the study of Niccoló Guasti (2006), these relationships between the Jesuits' work and modern ethnographic and anthropological knowledge – complex and contradictory in certain regards – have been rethought and placed into new perspectives. The proceedings of two seminars organized at the Center for Seventeenth- and Eighteenth-Century Studies of the William Andrews Clark Library (University of California, Los Angeles), and its former director, Peter Hanns Reill, as well as the Université du Québec à Trois-Rivières, which gave birth to the present volume, testify to this effort to rehabilitate the Jesuits' work from an interdisciplinary perspective. Shared by literary scholars, historians, art historians, and anthropologists, the desire for a re-examination using various tools, methods, and fields of investigation forms the basis of the studies collected in this volume.

The initial part of this volume aims to explore the forms of reception of seventeenth- and eighteenth-century Jesuit writings and their impact on both sides of the Atlantic. This avenue of analysis presupposes considering the transatlantic cultural space of the seventeenth century and, even more so, the century of the Enlightenment, as a transcultural literary field where phenomena of migration, translation, and transfer have played a significant but largely underestimated role in literary and historical disciplines longtime restricted to national spaces. The anthropological and ethnographic works of the Jesuits – notably those expelled after 1767 from the Spanish colonies in South America and installed in Italy and the German-speaking countries – bear the trace of these transcultural dimensions that pose particular challenges for research: they were written in Spanish, Italian, German, and Latin, translated in all the major European languages (chiefly English and French), and read and commented on in the most diverse cultural milieux in Europe and the Americas. The various histories, chronicles, *relaciones*, *relations*, and *récits* collectively constituting *Jesuit Accounts* have been examined here as products of what were often competing or complementary models. These models and the images of the New World they have produced are probed here as a function of Jesuit training and the multifarious impulses of official mission, personal mission, national agenda, and gender, as well as the evolving reception of the history, geography, and customs of the cultures being described; more importantly, the ways in which different generations and groups have accepted or rejected those images over time have also been evaluated.

Second, it became necessary to place the Jesuits' ethnographic and anthropological production within the controversies and disputes that set them against authors such as Buffon, Raynal, De Pauw, and Robertson, who were connected with encyclopedism. Far from a simple ideological quarrel opposing the "religious party" to the "enlightened party," these debates allow us, first and foremost, to highlight a divide – still rarely studied – between empiricism and theoretical spirit, direct experience of the field and cultural and geographical distancing.

Finally, the textual, and particularly the rhetorical, structures specific to the Jesuit Relations will be considered in the third and last part of this volume. The latter have, in fact, often been read as mere historical documents; they have not been analysed with regard to their rhetorical, stylistic, and generic structures. Jesuits accounts had of course, without any doubt, a predominantly ideological bias, but the issue now is to examine them with a view to grasping the specificity of their rhetorical, and in a wider sense generic, logic.

* *

The first part of this work plumbs a field of inquiry that has long received backburner status in Iberoamerican studies in Europe, Latin America,

Canada, and the United States alike: pre- and post-expulsion Jesuit accounts of the New World and their role as an important medium of intercultural transfers between the New World and the Old. Although Renaissance exploration has received lavish attention, late seventeenth- and eighteenth-century views have been largely ignored, even though Italy had become the home to a high percentage of the Jesuits expulsed from Latin America in 1767, where some continuity with Renaissance exploration narratives might have been expected. Instead, the ignominious condition of exile and expulsion imbued the post-expulsion narrative with a nostalgic hindsight. The juxtaposition of pre- and post-expulsion texts in this collection makes it possible to tangibly measure the effect that the end of the Jesuit empire had on the Jesuit worldview, as well as on the Jesuits' view of themselves in the world, moulded on the precepts of Ignatius Loyola. Alternating between case studies of particular accounts across the breach of expulsion and the ideas and precepts set forth by Ignatius Loyola in the *Constitutions of the Society of Jesus,* written a few years before his death in 1556, the Jesuits were to fulfill an apostolic mission, being "ready to live in any part of the world where there was hope of God's greater glory and the good of souls." Adherence to this precept, coupled with the instructive and educational platform of the order, made the documentation of missionary work and its dissemination an integral part of the Jesuit calling. Early Jesuit discourse recounting missionary life reflects both this apostolic mission and contemporary discourse models in France and in Spain. Over time, however, these models give way to new forms, a need fueled to a large extent by the nature of the New World material that required innovative rhetorical solutions and strategies, especially in light of the 1767 expulsion, after which many of the Jesuit narratives about Latin America were written.

Introducing Part I, "Intercultural Transfers," Girolamo Imbruglia establishes the genealogy of eighteenth-century Jesuit civilizing methods as evolving out of evangelizing and socializing practices melded "in the crucible of the Jesuit mission experience in South America." The ensuing civilizing discourse ultimately encapsulated and incorporated into its fold new members in an ever-expanding, Jesuit-built empire predicated upon the Jesuit mission, a structure where spiritual and temporal power converged in the permanent missions of Paraguay, prompting a public debate on Jesuit methods and goals. Imbruglia's reflections serve to illuminate the vision informing the Jesuit accounts examined thus far, while at the same time establishing a transition to the following sections – Part II, "Intellectual Disputes," and Part III, "Textualities." Indeed, the disputes that pit Jansenist theology against Jesuit doctrines of power extracted from sacred history become the content of the transatlantic literary, anthropological, and political responses outlined in the second section of this set of essays.

The competitive desire of expelled Jesuits to participate in the Republic of Letters as discerning intellectuals who are aware of the value of the knowledge contained in their accounts is acutely perceived in Italian Jesuit Filippo Salvatore Gilij's 1780–1784 *Saggio di storia americana* ("Essay on American History") analysed by Clorinda Donato. Following in the footsteps of Joseph Gumilla in the Orinoco Valley, Gilij's goals in documenting his reflections nonetheless depart sharply from Gumilla's 1745 empire-building, pre-expulsion *Orinoco Enlightened*, which melded Jesuit and Spanish aspirations. With its reference to the entire sweep of the American continent rather than a circumscribed region, the title of Gilij's essay alone is indicative of a work that promoted itself as an intellectual assessment of the Americas. He argues for methods that tell the truth in opposition to the aggrandizing of former Spanish accounts, locating himself as an Italian whose writing rests on a solid tradition of historical erudition and intellectual transfer. Alexander von Humboldt profited greatly from the knowledge contained in Gilij's text, for he could read Italian. Those who couldn't, however, would have to wait until 1967, when the first Spanish translation was published. The ongoing politics of knowledge transfer and transmission of Jesuit sources taken up here remind us of the need to interrogate the content of these texts in tandem with the conditions leading to their publication, translation, and dissemination.

Eileen Willingham's analysis of Jesuit historian Juan de Velasco's 1789 *Historia del Reino de Quito en la América meridional* ("History of the Kingdom of Quito in South America") concerns one of the major – and largely neglected – contributions of the Jesuits to the historical anthropology of South America. The account reimagines empire as Creole, in the image and likeness of the elite Creoles of Velasco's own lineage. Velasco imbued the merging of indigenous and European ancestry with a mythical significance that continues to resonate today as the founding narrative of Ecuador. Written during Velasco's exile in Faenza, Italy, the *Historia* countered the degrading accounts of anti-American European historians. Though first written in Spanish, plans to translate it into Italian immediately ensued, for in Italy, the major land of Jesuit exile, earning the favour of a well-placed cardinal ensured for those Jesuit accounts a wider audience, and for their exiled authors, the patronage that might restore their lost status. Similar incentives can also be attributed to Francesco Xavier Clavigero, whose work, *Historia Antigua de México,* which first appeared in Italian in 1780 in Cesena, was translated into the language of exile by the author himself.

Beatriz de Alba-Koch's contribution teases from Clavigero's narrative the intertwined strands of personal and patriotic narration that constitute one of the unique features of Jesuit accounts written from Italy. Uprooted from their missions, physically distant from Spain for many years, especially if born as Creoles in the colonies, these Jesuit authors now had to negotiate the cultural politics of Italian ecclesiastical intrigues, vying, through the medium of Italian, for a share of the market. Yet Italy also offered a number of advantages to these Jesuits, not the least of which was a European vantage point from which to counterattack the discourses of the *philosophes*: Cornelieus De Pauw, George-Louis Leclerc, Comte de Buffon, Guillaume-Thomas Raynal, and William Robertson. It also provided exposure to Giambattista Vico's theories of providential history and Cesare Beccaria's treatise on crimes and their punishments. Alba-Koch discusses how Clavigero's vision succeeded in establishing a Creole identity through attachment to the Nahua peoples and their past, while allowing him to lay equal claim to his Spanish origins. This was accomplished through a narrative that justified native leaders and Cortés alike through a fusion of eyewitness testimony and European philosophy. At the same time, however, this article points to those historical moments when Clavigero struggled with providential rationalization, imagining, instead, different outcomes if there had been greater agency among the indigenous peoples.

Hans-Jürgen Lüsebrink's article uses Austrian Jesuit Martin Dobrizhoffer's *Account of the Abiponi* as a springboard for engaging the modernity of Jesuit accounts through postmodern scrutiny. Lüsebrink has telescoped the critical gaze of those who have defended Jesuit accounts through the centuries into a thought-provoking reflection on the nuanced methods required for understanding the intercultural transfer present in these accounts. Capturing echoes of Clavigero, Lüsebrink articulates Dobrizhoffer's counter-discourse to European Enlightenment critiques of Jesuit secrecy and obscurantism in Paraguay by demonstrating how this discourse is predicated on modern methods of comparative ethnography. The scientific accuracy of Dobrizhoffer's view, based on knowledge of indigenous languages, lends authority to his debunking of the *philosophes*, while making available a body of information about the Abiponi that continues to inform both the contents and methods of social scientists today.

Taking a step back from the knowledge transferred to query the genesis of written Jesuit genres, Perla Chinchilla Pawling's contribution, "From Sacred Rhetoric to the Republic of Letters: Jesuit Sermons in

Seventeenth-Century New Spain," charts the emergence of Jesuit knowledge into the public sphere. Through an analysis of the printing press as catalyst for social transformation in post-Tridentine Europe, she points out the effects wrought on Jesuit conversion practices as they moved from orality to literacy, a movement that made possible the intellectual Jesuit network to which both sections of this volume bear ample witness.

The last contribution in this section on knowledge transfer also concludes the first part of this series. For seventeenth-century French Jesuits, as a rule, the North American experience was based on the classical experience of language or, if one prefers, a concept of discourse that, in this "âge de l'éloquence" (see Fumaroli 1980), viewed the arts of persuasion as the ideal method for conquering hearts and minds. Sara Melzer's contribution, accordingly, focuses on French colonial thought during the early modern period only after emphasizing the debt the Jesuits' accounts of North America owed to this classical experience of speech. Indeed, in light of the absence of a clearly formulated official document by political authorities in the Kingdom of France, Sara Melzer prefers to retrace the basic tendencies of a colonial strategy. One can, in fact, use the writings of the Jesuit fathers to define a classical and French conception of the colonial enterprise, one that was not reduced to the sole use of force. On the contrary, this manner of viewing colonization called incessantly for North America's aboriginals to be culturally integrated into the empire, an achievement that was to come about through persuasion and seduction. Evangelical mission and "civilizing mission," in this view, were overlapping concepts, so that French domination became a matter of acculturation rather than subjugation. In other words, far from seeking to maintain the differences between Amerindians and Europeans in order to subjugate the former to the latter, French policy aimed instead to make the French and the "savages," as the minister Colbert himself wrote, "a same people and a same blood" (Colbert 1930–1931, 67). Now an ambition like this, which opened the door to marriages between natives and Europeans, presumed a cultural policy and an art of persuasion whose main result was domination by France with a concurrent acceptance of assimilation.

* *

The first chapter of Part II, "Intellectual Disputes," addresses the seething debate surrounding Jesuit power in the missions in Paraguay. Fomented by the *philosophes* and ultimately prompting the expulsion, the dispute over Jesuit power inspired the Brazilian ex-Jesuit poet José Basilio de Gama's 1769 epic poem, *O Uraguay*. Wiebke Röben de Alencar Xavier's analysis of Gama's compositional choices breaks new ground for future work, for the poem resides within a literary corpus examined for the first time here in the wider scope of transnational Jesuit activity. As with Velasco's *Historia,* from the nineteenth century forward, *O Uraguay* became a seminal text in the establishing of a Brazilian national literary canon by poeticizing the lives and deeds of the peoples inhabiting the banks of the Uruguay River. However, instead of charting the mythically peaceful union of two distinct strands, Jesuit and indigenous, Gama's poem is filled with scenes of strife and warring conflict pitting Jesuits, natives, and Portuguese soldiers against each other in the Guarani missions of Paraguay. Seen in the light of the interdisciplinary, eighteenth-century Atlantic intertextualities described in this volume, the lusophone context reveals itself as a fresh site for charting the Jesuit debate.

In the second contribution treating disputes, Ute Fendler explores the anthropological dimensions of the debate by tracing the evolution of Jesuit perceptions of themselves and the Indians in their missions over time as a function of their shared living, cut off in space and time as they were from Europe. Intellectual disputes over the purported barbarity of the Indians becomes nuanced as the missionaries begin to recognize how the Indians' intellectual capabilities linked them to the rest of mankind. Fendler identifies in these accounts the developing awareness among the Jesuits of their status as "frontier men," mediating between two worlds where perceptions transform the place of encounter into a site where new knowledge about the Indians is formed and from which it can be transmitted. In her contribution, Karen Stolley takes on the "why" of the expulsion, the intellectual dispute that continues to resonate today as we seek to fill the gaps in expulsion history resulting from the gag order imposed by the Spanish crown on the Jesuits who were expelled. Yet through comparative readings that juxtapose official Spanish reports of Jesuit opulence and imperial designs with Jesuit accounts of not only misery, isolation, and danger, but also commitment through following the *via crucis,* Stolley exposes how exile has been transformed into a narrative homecoming in the accounts, where nostalgia for what has been lost is palpable.

Finally, it was not only fictional writing that could become the exaggerated, or even deformed, echo of an art of eloquent speech that appeared, with its seductive turns and studied detours, to be emblematic of Jesuit culture. As Isabelle Lachance shows, this rooting of Jesuit identity in a tradition of oratory was vigorously affirmed as well by polemicists hostile to the missionary work of the Company of Jesus. Accordingly, the *Factum du procès entre Jean de Biencourt, sieur de Poutrincourt et les pères Biard et Massé* (1614) offers a negative image of the Jesuits in New France that had already been fixed in the French mind by the *Catéchisme des Jésuites* (1602) attributed to Étienne Pasquier, with the difference that the *Factum* delights in exaggerating one feature: the mouth. In fact, if omnipresent images of the Jesuit mouth caused Loyola's disciples to be reduced, both maliciously and conveniently, to an order of insatiable eaters and drinkers taking advantage of relaxed morals, this synecdoche had the added advantage of associating them with the figure of the rhetorician and the sophist cultivating treacherous and ambiguous speech. However, by making rhetoric an art of pompous or deceitful verbiage, the *Factum* poses, above all, the problem of the legitimacy of the alliance between Christian faith – in reformed theology, the moving spirit of an impassioned conscience – and a theory of discourse where religious belief runs the risk of being lived and preached amidst the illusory brilliance of an eloquence rooted in ancient, pagan tradition. Thus, Father Biard's reply, which can be read in his *Relation de la Nouvelle-France* (1616), undertakes to restore the link between oratorical art and religious faith in the name of a free will whose exercise, Isabelle Lachance concludes, very specifically involves a deliberative capacity where the use of persuasive speech attests to the freedom to act.

Although comparison supplied evidence with a heuristic dimension, it was also the expression of an art of speaking and narrating which, in the Jesuit Relations on the subject of New France, demonstrated that the function of these texts was to influence their readers, thereby contributing to the emergence of a public space and opinion in the eighteenth century. Such at least is the view espoused by Klaus-Dieter Ertler who, in developing this idea, correctly insists on the importance of taking into account the poetics and rhetoric of the narrative fact in the methods used by the Jesuits to convey experience when they wrote about North America. Particularly important in this context is the emphasis placed on rendering sensory experience, notably in favour of a writing that sought at times to depict the outside world, and at times to give visible shape to spiritual life. To privilege the mediation of the senses and to show the workings of divine inspiration were precepts that had already been outlined in Loyola's *Spiritual Exercises*; these precepts generally encouraged the promotion of sensory experience while inviting the authors of the *Relations* to make themselves both the subject and the object of their own stories, with their personal experiences serving as examples lived *ad majorem Dei gloriam.* Now, Klaus-Dieter Ertler argues in the end, it is precisely this theatrical rhetoric of apologetics that the *philosophes* would contest during the second half of the eighteenth century in the name of an ethnological science that thereafter distrusted narration and descriptions characterized by the literary and rhetorical concern with recounting the particular adventures of individuals who saw themselves as so many *milites Christi*, or "soldiers of Christ."

Finally, the reader moves on to a study of *Description de la Louisiane* (1697) by the Récollet priest Louis Hennepin, in which Catherine Broué questions the silence of this disciple of Saint Francis regarding the Jesuits' missionary work in North America. Here again, the image Catherine Broué seeks to restore is a negative one. In fact, if the Récollet priest saw fit to not so much as mention the Jesuit presence in New France, it was to better reject the Company's conception of a missionary effort founded on the authority of public discourse and to favour instead a doctrine where the conversion of native peoples was based on subjection through occupation and colonization. Here again, we see, it was precisely the Jesuits' classical and humanistic hope in the exercise of speech that became the favourite target of their adversaries. The Récollet priest, therefore, draws the attention of the twenty-first-century reader in particular to the main reason for an interest in the Jesuit accounts of the Americas: the memory of an indelible experience where the oratorical tradition inherited from the Ancients entrusted eloquent speech – not weapons – with the business of presiding over a unique meeting between peoples within this first globalized space opened by the Age of Discovery.

* *

The third part of this work, "Textualities", unites contributions that, by focusing on the Jesuits' writings about North America, highlight the importance of taking the rhetorical dimension of these writings into account. As we know, contemporary university research has strongly emphasized the extent to which rhetoric, far from being "a trite technique of manipulation or pretence" or "a technique of speaking too well to be honest," was, for the Jesuits of the early modern period, "the creative driving force of their ethics, spirituality, exegesis, anthropology, and theology" (Fumaroli 1999, 91–2). The work of seventeenth- and eighteenth-century missionaries in New France is additional testimony to this, with rhetoric in their case supposing not only a theory and practice of persuasive discourse, but also a specifically classical and humanistic confidence in men's capacity to act upon the course of history solely by virtue of speech.

As a theory, rhetoric has sought since ancient times to understand speech as a force that is affirmed through an energy capable of acting on others and the self, one having the ability to change ideas and acts, wishes and desires. Rhetoric, therefore, views the exercise of language as a civilizing force, that is, a power inviting recourse to persuasion, even seduction, in order to better contain excessive violence and abuses of physical restraint in keeping with Cicero's famous formula: "cedant arma togae" (Cicéron 1881a, viii), let arms yield to public speaking. Fundamental in Jesuit culture, reference to Cicero thus allows for an optimistic conception of language, one where the glorified memory of the Ancients' oratorical model defines the terms of a rhetorical humanism in which constant parallels drawn between ancient ideal and modern experience further energize an imagination that is both comparatist and critically based. Indeed, far from reducing itself to a mere philosophy of language, the oratorical culture of the fathers of the Company of Jesus also welcomed a kind of anthropological comparative method, where incessant parallels between the Ancients and the moderns, so central to the Jesuit imagination, promoted the exercise of a critical view based on comparison, as is testified by the great 1724 work of Joseph-François Lafitau, *Mœurs des sauvages amériquains, comparés aux mœurs des premiers temps* ("Customs of the American savages, compared with the customs of ancient times").

But if one cannot consider rhetoric a mere theory of language or doctrine, it is because it deploys as well a practice of discourse that places the enterprise of seduction at the heart of the exercise of speech. This more strictly literary dimension of oratorical tradition determines a narrative regimen in which lived experience, historical testimony, and travel accounts are related and re-related as both an epic rich in models to imitate and a story of adventure that recounts the conversion of hearts and the transformation of societies. To teach, to delight and to move: in Cicero's thought, the union of these three concepts – *docere, delectare,* and *movere* – was the essential component of all eloquence (Cicero 1966, Book 2: 115); for the Jesuits, this Ciceronianism flourished in a form of writing that aimed to make experience palpable, thus variously presenting scenes from everyday life to teach a moral lesson, colourful images to delight the senses, and scenes of horror to stir the passions. The Ciceronian precept that taught the importance of writing so as to "bring before the eyes" ("ante oculos ponere" [Cicero 1881b, ii]) overdetermines the spirit that informs the *Spiritual Exercises* of Ignatius Loyola, founder of the order, for whom inner experience was to lead, not to silence and incommunicability, but to a representation that achieves and exalts the work of contemplation through the intermediary of the senses. To derive hope from the expressive powers of language, to regard comparison between centuries and peoples as a heuristic principle, and to consider the pleasures of discourse to be the condition of effective action and shared speech: when evoked in rapid succession these three aspects of the Jesuit imagination correspond also to the three major perspectives explored in turn by the six contributions in this section devoted to the rhetorical and stylistic structures of the Jesuit accounts, especially those on North America.

In fact, the first contribution in this section, Pierre Berthiaume's article "L'héritage de José de Acosta" not only recalls the extent to which missionary work in North and South American must be viewed from a pan-American and transatlantic perspective, as these studies as a whole suggest, but it also relates how the Jesuit experience in New France was rooted, perhaps to an even greater degree, in that humanistic confidence in the effectiveness of eloquent speech that informed the overall spirit of the Company. This, at least, is one conclusion that can be drawn from Berthiaume's study comparing the *De Procuranda Indorum salute O predicacion del evangelio en las Indias* (1588) by Father José de Acosta (1540–1600) and the *Relation de la Nouvelle-France* (1616) by Father Pierre Biard (1567 or 1568–1622). The Spanish Jesuit, in Berthiaume's view, associates the missionary enterprise with the practice of *encomiendas* or "reductions," which placed the Amerindians under a political and administrative supervision in order to Europeanize their customs and therefore better ensure their conversion. Contrary to this policy of force, Pierre Biard founded the work of conversion, instead, upon an attitude that valued the effectiveness of the verb, thereafter calling upon example, along with eloquence of speech and gesture, to be the cornerstone of missionary work in New France.

This imagination, both literate and militant, which prevailed among the Jesuits, even commanded, as Marie-Christine Pioffet maintains, an "imaginary map in two hemispheres," itself designed using rhetorical and theological considerations where antithetical couples – Christianity and paganism, civilization and savagery – oppose and confront each other. For Paul Lejeune, for example, the description of New France oscillates between a present-day *terra doloris* and a "celestial Jerusalem" of the future (Lejeune [1637] 1972, 33). On the one hand, Lejeune sees North America as a desolate, God-forsaken landscape with its "horrible" ice floes (Lejeune [1634] 1972, 13) drifting down the St. Lawrence River and its forests "capable of terrifying the most experienced travelers" (Lejeune [1662] 1972, 13). Accordingly, to describe the New World was to produce various images all derived from a commonplace of rhetoric, the *locus horribilis*, a vast repertoire of literary motifs whose development made Canada the perfect antithesis of those smiling, civilized rural landscapes where the shepherds of ancient pastoral tradition romped and revelled. By resorting to this figure par excellence of misery and dereliction, sadness and savagery, not only did the Jesuits depict Canadian nature as a thing of fear and terror, but they also transformed it into a theatre where the glory of their own courage and martyrdom stood out more sharply still. On the other hand, because the Jesuits performed on such a hostile stage, their work shone all the brighter in that it was placed within a temporal perspective that destined it for triumph, with the conversion of the savages and the civilizing work of the French called on to transform "all our forests in order to make Cities of them," thereby turning "a land of Savages into a Conquest for Jesus Christ and for France" (Lejeune [1662] 1972, 40–1). In this context, Marie-Christine Pioffet concludes, the *locus horribilis* appears as a uchronian fiction.

Also reflecting a dual exterior/interior sense, Margaret Ewalt's treatment of Spaniard Joseph Gumilla's 1741 *El Orinoco ilustrado* ("Orinoco enlightened") demonstrates how Gumilla used the medium of the book to bring public attention to the greatness of the Orinoco and to how it might be harnessed in the future physical and spiritual economy of a Jesuit-Spanish empire. Gumilla has translated the brio of Pelleprat's seventeenth-century inventorying of wonders into a lesson of engagement, encouraging the use of these exceptional resources to build new sites of knowledge and spirituality. He is among the first to attribute such enlightenment or *illustración* to the spiritual leadership of the Jesuits, who had developed the linguistic and intercultural skills necessary to make the enterprise a success. Together these two essays reveal the role of early Jesuit New World accounts in reflecting and shaping emerging sensibilities and the tools needed to usher in the era of empire imagining. Gumilla's vision of a Jesuit mandate in the Orinoco Valley is thus replicated in accounts of the Kingdom of Quito, as well as in those dealing with Mexico and Paraguay studied in other contributions to this volume.

The joint expertise of Marc-André Bernier and Réal Ouellet analyses the exterior and interior effects of the Caribbean New World on French missionary Pierre Pelleprat. His 1655 account of the Jesuit missions in the Antilles reveals both Pelleprat's sense of adventure as he inventoried New World wonders (Ouellet), as well as the foreboding sense of the necessary moral shift in sensibilities to accommodate this new spectacle of nature (Bernier). Furthermore, as Andréanne Vallée reminds us, this tendency to transform New World travel narratives into fiction is particularly evident in Claude Le Beau's *Avantures* (1738). For this literary adventurer, who was a lawyer at the Parliament of Paris, incarcerated in Bicêtre, then deported to New France, literary invention and the rewriting of Jesuit texts were one and the same. In fact, by drawing from a multitude of anecdotes, descriptions, and illustrations of everyday life from Jesuit sources, Joseph-François Lafitau in particular, Le Beau incessantly reworked these borrowings into an original narrative of adventure. Of course, this literary and rhetorical dimension of Jesuit writings on New France had not, we have seen, been neglected in their *Relations*. In his *Instructions pour l'histoire* (1677), the Jesuit Father René Rapin likewise insisted on recalling that the Memoirs, the accounts, and, more generally, the writing of history, should "be a perpetual narration" insofar as nothing seemed more important for these genres "than to tell a good story" (Rapin 1677, 47). But in the end, although this literary and oratorical propensity was a definite component of Jesuit tradition, concerned, as always, with acting on readers' hearts and minds, it is nonetheless true that everything in Le Beau's work tended to highlight it. Now, it is precisely in this important crossing of boundaries into a fictional and profane universe that the dual objective of the Jesuits' writings on North America, to instruct and delight, is most clearly seen, given that the generic hybridization between these writings and a novel of adventure provides further evidence still of the ambition to seduce and entertain that is a hallmark of Jesuit anthropology.

The goal of the arts of persuasion and the Jesuits' employment of them, however, was not merely to serve policy: they included a specifically epistemological dimension as well, a fact highlighted by Hans-Jürgen Lüsebrink, who examines, in the postface closing this volume, the links between comparison as an oratorical process and the act of comparison as an instrument of cultural and anthropological knowledge. In rhetorical tradition, we know, comparison is primarily a figure of style where two objects are placed into relationship, but in such a way that pleasure is introduced into discourse, thereby making the practice of discourse a further invitation to examine the similarities and differences between the two objects. This explains why comparison is a figure where the art of pleasing and the cognitive process mix and mingle, and where the rhetorical process supposes, in effect, a knowledge of the world that rests upon a comparative approach. As such, comparison was to enjoy a huge success throughout the eighteenth century, inspiring writing that was at once oratorical, comparatist, and critical, as Lafitau's *Mœurs des sauvages amériquains* so eloquently illustrates. In imitation of Plutarch's *Parallel Lives* or even of Herodotus, whose historical works paved the way with their comparisons of various peoples, but in imitation, too, of the very numerous parallels between the Ancients and the Moderns that had multiplied in Europe since Sully's *Parallèle de César et de Henri le Grand* (1615), the Jesuits' model of ethnographic writing supposed a continuous comparison that aimed to examine and explain the relationships and differences among several cultures. In short, comparison here became not only a method inspired by rhetorical tradition, but owing to the constant use of parallels between classical antiquity, modern travel accounts, and personal observations, it further appeared as the very foundation of a comparative anthropology. The result, Hans-Jürgen Lüsebrink argues, was that oratorical tradition for the Jesuits blossomed into a global vision of societies and cultures, becoming the basis of a new conception of the history of humanity thereafter conceived as a differentiated process of transformation that could be apprehended by means of an intercultural approach.

BIBLIOGRAPHY

Certeau, Michel De. 1974. "Le dix-septième siècle français." In *Les Jésuites. Spiritualité et activités. Jalons d'une histoire*, 71–109. Paris: Beauchesne.

Chinchilla Pawling, Perla, and Antonella Romano, eds. 2008. *Escrituras de la modernidad. Los Jesuitas entre cultura, retórica y cultura científica.* México, D.F.: Universidad Iberoamericana.

Cicero. 1881a. *Seconde Philippique.* In *Œuvres complètes de Cicéron*, ed. M. Nisard. Paris: Firmin-Didot et Cie.

–. 1881b. *Remerciement à César pour le rappel de Marcellus.* In *Œuvres complètes de Cicéron*, ed. M. Nisard. Paris: Firmin-Didot et Cie.

–. 1966. *De l'orateur*, ed. Edmond Courbaud. Paris: Société d'édition Les Belles Lettres.

Colbert, Jean-Baptiste. [1667] 1930–1931. Lettre du Ministre Colbert à Talon, 5 April. In *Rapport de l'Archiviste de la Province de Québec* 10: 67.

Duchet, Michèle. 1985. *Le partage des savoirs. discours historique et discours ethnologique.* Paris: La Decouverte.

Fumaroli, Marc. 1980. *L'âge de l'éloquence. Rhétorique et "res literaria" de la Renaissance au seuil de l'époque classique.* Genève: Librairie Droz.

–. 1999. "The Fertility and the Shortcomings of Renaissance Rhetoric: the Jesuit Case." In *The Jesuits: Cultures, Sciences and the Arts, 1540–1773*, ed. John W. O'Malley, 90–106. Toronto: University of Toronto Press.

Guasti, Niccoló. 2006. *L'esilio italiano dei gesuiti spagnoli: identità, controllo sociale e pratiche culturali, 1767–1798.* Roma: Edizioni di storia e letteratura.

Kohut, Karl and Maria Cristina Torales Pacheco, eds. 2007. *Desde los confines de los imperios ibéricos: los jesuitas de habla alemana en las misiones americanas.* Madrid: Iberoamericana/Frankfurt am Main: Vervuert.

Lejeune, Paul. [1634] 1972. *Relation de ce qui s'est passé en la Nouvelle France en l'année 1633.* In *Relations des jésuites.* Vol. 1. Montréal: Éditions du Jour [facsimile of Québec: A. Côté, 1858].

–. [1637] 1972. *Relation de ce qui s'est passé en la Nouvelle France en l'année.* In *Relations des jésuites.* Vol. 1. Montréal: Éditions du Jour [facsimile of Québec: A. Côté, 1858].

–. [1662] 1972. *Relation de ce qui s'est passé en la Nouvelle France, ès années 1660. et 1661.* In *Relations des jésuites.* Vol. 5. Montréal: Éditions du Jour [facsimile of Québec: A. Côté, 1858].

Rapin, René. 1677. *Instructions pour l'histoire.* Paris: Sébastien Mabre-Cramoisy.

Tietz, Manfred and Dietrich Briesemeister, eds. 2001. *Los Jesuitas españoles expulsos: su imagen y su contribución al saber sobre el mundo hispanico en la Europa del siglo XVIII.* Madrid: Biblioteca Ibero-Americana.

PART I

INTERCULTURAL TRANSFERS

chapter one

A Peculiar Idea of Empire: Missions and Missionaries of the Society of Jesus in Early Modern History[1]

GIROLAMO IMBRUGLIA

Empire between Evangelization and Civilization

In the Spanish conquest of South America, religion played an essential role. The Spanish kings considered the spiritual conquest of native populations indispensable and complementary to successful political and military subjugation. This spiritual conquest had different forms, according to its protagonists: bishops, Dominicans, Franciscans, and Jesuits. Among these groups, the experiences of the Jesuits were certainly the most original. Today we know quite a lot about the experiences of Jesuits in America and about their mission practices and organization, but we know less about their own perceptions and framings of these experiences (see Rieter 1995; Ganson 2003). Yet the Jesuits themselves offered the necessary clues, already at the end of the sixteenth century, when they adopted the term *reducciones* as the moniker for their missions in South America. This name, by itself, reveals that those missions were conceived as places in which "savage" people were to be *reducti*, conducted towards human life; that is, transformed into Christian subjects who had learned to live according to the rules of political society. The Jesuit missions, therefore, served two deeply intertwined ends: the first being to spread the word of the Christian gospel to heathens, the other being to transform the savage South American societies into polities amenable to European styles of governance. In this sense, Jesuit evangelizing also entailed "civilizing" South American tribal societies. Thus, though the word "civilization" did not get coined until the eighteenth century, its essence was already found precisely in the Jesuit goals and in the comportment of their missions (see Benveniste [1954] 1966, 336–45). Indeed, Jesuit narratives and analyses of their experiences contributed to the cultural process by which Europeans constructed typologies of societies, placing their own, of course, at the apex.

The first positive recognition of the Jesuit contribution to civilizing came in the eighteenth century, from Enlightenment *philosophes* who argued that the Jesuits had chosen the best strategy for civilizing non-European peoples. For instance, D'Alembert wrote that, in their missions, the Jesuits "bring happiness, it is said, to the peoples there who obey them and whom they have managed to subdue without the use of violence" ("y rendent heureux, à ce qu'on assure, les peuples qui leur obéissent et qu'ils sont venus à bout de soumettre sans employer la violence" [D'Alembert 1765, 24–6]). Therefore, in nations where people were savage or oppressed, he wished that there were "some Jesuits as apostles and guides" ("des jésuites pour apôtres et pour maîtres" [24–6]). Their experiences could be useful in the task of designing new policies for the various European empires, and their examples could be imitated by empires that needed to be reformed. D'Alembert was not the only Enlightenment thinker to see the practical value of the Jesuit practices. In mid-eighteenth-century Spain, in the debate about the crisis of the Spanish Empire in America, *élites* and the government itself judged Jesuit practice a suitable model for colonial state administrations. For example, Bernardo Ward, writing his recommandations to the Spanish Board of Trade (Junta de Comercio) in 1762, observed that in its relationship with colonial America, Spain had to follow "a general system of discipline" ("un sistema general de policía"), and that particularly with savage peoples it was necessary to "establish a good discipline and, through good economic government, to reduce the Indians to civilian life, treat them with kindness, and gentleness, as well as to encourage industry" ("establecer una buena policía y por medio de un buen govierno economico, reducer á los Indios á vida civil, tratarlos con benignidad, y con dulzura, animarlos á la industria" [Ward 1779, 255 and 232]).[2] Here the Jesuit practice of missions was clearly being echoed; it was to become an important tool in the European imperial and colonial perspectives of the nineteenth century. As has been perceptively remarked, "it is telling [...] that Kant derided justifications of European imperial incursions as 'Jesuitism'" (Muthu 2003, 281; also see Osterhammel 2006).

But here I am going to discuss another aspect of the missions, the theories that underlay the practices, acting as apologies, explanations, and determinants of policy. Never confined to the Catholic Church and its many institutions, the development and discussion of these theoretical frameworks marked an important moment in the process of secularization. The developmental process begins with the origins of the Society of Jesus itself, in its early commitment to traditional, itinerant preaching; that is, to the sort of preaching with millenarian impulses that had inspired the earliest Christian apostles. The goal of preparing for the imminent arrival of the end of time would be transformed rather quickly into one of evangelizing; that is, into the activity of spreading the gospel so that lives could be lived in a manner that would enable redemption whenever the end of time did arrive. Because the behavioural prescriptions of the New Testament had become the normative ideals of European society, the duty to spread the gospel was easily transformed in the South American context into one of spreading European social and political forms: thus the well-known relation between evangelizing and civilizing in the context of the *reducciones*. Therefore, to understand the genealogy of "civilization" as one among many forms of the relationship between European culture and extra-European societies, it is necessary first to understand the ways that ideas of evangelization changed from the sixteenth century to the eighteenth century (see Curto 2005, 3ff.).

The investigation of the Company of Jesus as a religious order combined with inquiry into its missions uncovers the ambiguity of the Jesuit strategy: on the one hand, the missionaries sent out by the Company paid great attention to the different social and cultural situations in which they were intervening; but on the other hand, they were conscious of being part of a centralized religious order, which had strong ideological and political unity (see Pizzorusso 1995; Abe 2003, 69ff.; Broggio 2005). We should therefore say that the Jesuit strategy always had three different dimensions: the religious, the anthropological, and the political, and that it was through the construction of their "empire" that these three facets were brought together. The idea and practices of empire and the modern idea of civilization (taken as the practices of evangelization and of socialization according to fixed rules) are thus inextricably linked, born together and from each other, in the crucible of the Jesuit mission experience in South America.

If one observes the Company as a systematic whole, one notices that it was fully aware that it was creating a new sort of "empire," essentially different from known forms, contemporary or classical (see Pavone 2004; Ditchfield 2007). The Jesuit innovation lay not just in the determination to achieve universal domination, an impulse that was immediately grasped by perceptive observers like Montaigne, but in the very structure of this domination, which relied on spiritual conquest by non-violent means, at least in theory.[3] This new category of empire could be applied as a conceptual tool both to internal problems of organizational operation and to external ones faced in the missions of America. The Jesuits did not hesitate to use the category in precisely these ways.

We find the best representation of the Jesuits' ideal in the *Imago primi saeculi* (Tollenaer 1640, e.g., 249–79), edited by Jesuit historian Jean Bolland for the first centenary of the Company. The *Imago* presents the activity of the mission and the spirituality of the missionary as the essential features of the Company and of its history. Therefore, the life of the Company was said to have two characteristics: inside the Society, Jesuit practice imitated the apostolic life of the primitive Church; outside, the Society modelled itself on the category of empire – in particular that of the Romans (165).[4]

This life outside, with its *imperii propagatio*, or Jesuit imperial expansion, was unique: ranging over more of the globe than any other empire, and – this was the salient point – of a nature completely "other" from any known empire ("diversa sane a Regnis atque Imperiis ratione"; see Richardson 1991). Where all previous empires had brought in their wake destruction, new taxes and subjugation ("civitates subiugare"), the new Jesuit empire propagated Christian freedom: "[T]hey by severity of laws, the Society of Jesus contends for power with constant and generous meekness" ("[I]lli rigore legum, haec mansuetudine beneficiisque certat perpetuis"). The Jesuit goal was to incline, not to force, human wills: "[I]t is much more difficult to subdue will than to take cities by storm, to tame souls than fortresses, to conquest men than walls" ("[L]aboriosus est voluntates quam urbes espugnare, animos quam oppida debellare, homines quam moenia superare" [Tollenaer 1640, 250–1]).[5] Nevertheless, the *Imago* admitted the use of violence, of the sort it called "benignant violence" ("amica violentia") in certain situations: the military and coercive violence to which the Company sometimes had to turn, it was argued, did not cancel the extraordinary character of the Jesuit conquests because the end of that violence was civilizing and Christianizing peoples who, in turn, were "glad of their obedience" ("hac servitude sua laetos" [394]). The ends – civilizing and Christianizing – altered the very quality of violence, turning it into something beneficial instead of malignant or malevolent. The paradoxical aspect of this discourse lay in the fact that the actual history of the Jesuit missions showed that the Company had united the spiritual with the temporal, thus denying its own assertions of principle. The Jesuit pretension to empire would become one of the principal themes of the anti-Jesuit polemic of the seventeenth and eighteenth centuries (see Pavone 2005).

Viewed from the perspectives of the long-term history of the Company of Jesus and of the more general history of the European colonizations, this particular imperial theme provides not so much grist for polemical mills as opportunities to give deeper meaning to the modern category of empire and to acquire a more nuanced understanding of the relations, constituted through the operations of that category, between European and non-European cultures (see Pagden 2001).[6] It would seem, in fact, that the centralized, political form of empire functioned as a primary determinant of the relationship with Otherness in the long history of the development of modern European identity.

Although it lies outside the realms of my present theme, it is impossible not to be struck by the fact that the nineteenth-century empires attempted to unite the political authority of the civilization process with an ideology, in particular with a liberal ideology. In other words, they united conceptually that which the greatest empire of Ancien Régime Europe, the Spanish one, had separated into the two categories: military conquest and spiritual conquest – the latter having been explicitly entrusted to the Jesuits (see Pagden 1995; Armitage 2000).

In both the characteristics of the Company of Jesus I am emphasizing – the apostolic life inside the Society and the capacity of conquest – an essential role was played by the concept of mission, to which my paper is dedicated.

Mission and the Society of Jesus

The concept of "mission" played a fundamental role in the genesis and history of the Society of Jesus, not only by providing a vehicle for the translation of the founders' inspirations into a Tridentine-era organization, but also by creating a role for the Society that was expertly tailored to an era shaped by geographical explorations. Both religious and secular sixteenth-century literatures pointed out that the discovery of new populations in America had ushered in a new religious and social era in the history of the world. Columbus's experiences in America were the "prologue" to a period of radical renewal of Christian life, driven in part by a revival of the role of itinerant, apostolic preaching in the Church. Augustine's idea, stated in the *City of God* and repeated by the Scholastics, that profane history only existed alongside the sacred one, was no longer true; the messianic perspective of sacred history, which was based upon the enthusiastic expectation of a world soon to be entirely Christian and which had disappeared from the Christian European horizon, regained its original force. Even as the expectation of universal Christianity collapsed, forcing a revised understanding of the way that sacred history might actually play out in the world, the fractured condition of the human world heightened feelings that a time of collective regeneration or rebirth, the *novissima tempora,* was near, or already here. The duty of evangelization was now charged with apocalyptic sentiments and Saint John's Apocalypse sounded true in a new way: it was now indeed possible that *all* the globe would be ruled by "only one priest" ("unus pastor"). This reframing of history, begun with the return of Christopher Columbus from his first voyages to the Americas, would circulate for a long time thereafter, even among the Jesuits (see Imbruglia 1989).

The appearance of many new religious orders after 1500 is a sign of the many challenges that confronted the Church as it tried to deal with a novel religious geography. Some Catholic reformers chose to reaffirm the monastic tradition and cloistered, contemplative, communal life. Ignatius chose a different path, encapsulated in the fourth vow of obedience to the Holy Father.[7] In the conditions of the sixteenth century, with the Protestant reforms that fractured the Church and the recently acquired knowledge that there were whole societies of humans who had never had a chance to hear the Gospel, obedience to the pope translated into the duty to go out, preach, and teach. The members of the Company of Jesus were not to engage in monastic life. Laínez remarked that he had heard someone say of a group of Jesuits: "They will reform some country" ("Ils vont reformer quelque pays" [see Laínez (1547) 1897]).[8] Indeed, going out into the world to preach and teach was the true nature of the Company. Jerome Nadal reiterated the point in different words: "He who desires constant prayer, solitude, he who enjoys retiring and fleeing mankind and will not search him out in order to help him, is not fit for our vocation" ("Quien quiere siempre oración, soledad, a quien agrada el rincón y huir de los hombres y el trato con ellos para aprovecharlos no es para nuestra vocación" [Nadal (1554) 1962, 5: 325]).[9]

Probably, the reason for the extraordinary success of Jesuit spirituality came from its capacity to link the ancient tradition of Christianity with consciousness of the radical novelty of the sixteenth-century European world. The Company of Jesus understood that the discovery of extra-European populations had transformed Europeans, rendering them in part strangers to their own recent past. It also understood that those discoveries would stimulate a revisiting of the remote religious past of Christianity, and that the Humanistic traditions and historical methods of the Renaissance, which had restored to Europeans their classical past, might also be applied productively to the task of recovering primitive Christianity (see Huppert 1970). The Company of Jesus, therefore, situated itself halfway between Humanistic tradition and ecclesiastic tradition; since the rediscovery of the remote past of Christianity required an apocalyptic eye, the Company existed and acted on the border between sacred history and profane history. This mediating position constitutes yet another element able to explain the Company's great fascination.[10]

The messianic dimension was well represented at the birth of the Company, in the ideas of both the young Ignatius of Loyola and Francesco Borgia (see Pastore 2005). Borgia actually connected the birth of the Company explicitly to the works of Joachim da Fiore, daring to represent Ignatius's new foundation as a sign of the *novissima tempora* (see Milhou 2001).[11] Soon, however, the Company distanced itself from such views, and Ignatius formally recanted the scatological point of view (see Pastore 2005, 173–8). At this point in the development of the Society of Jesus, in the last two decades of the sixteenth century, the spirit of prophecy was defeated. The strategy of evangelization was invested with this revision; it was no longer animated by this apocalyptic dimension, but it remained a duty for the order. The clearest example of the discussion about this issue came from Peru, where the earliest Jesuit missionaries had had a millenarian perspective, but where, by the end of the sixteenth century, in response to the anti-millenarian spirit of the Tridentine rules, the Society of Jesus had acquired a new identity. It was the general Aquaviva who, by obligating Jesuits to live committed to the Tridentine Church and in obedience to their general, brought the new identity into being.

Mission and Universal History: José de Acosta

The discussion about the idea of mission addressed three basic questions: Who were the missionaries most qualified to carry out the tasks of the missions? Who were the people to be evangelized? What were the ways of accomplishing mission goals (see Schröder 1999; Cuturi 2004)? Answers to these three questions depended on definitions of the relationships of religion to both politics and anthropology, as well as on the more delicate issue of the relationship between the two kinds of history – sacred and profane. The significance of Acosta's experience lay in the fact that his answers to the specific challenges of missionizing in Peru also offered solutions to these fundamental philosophical problems. His ideas, like others from the Jesuits, derived strength from their systematic structure (see Morales 1998, 3ff.).

Not long before 1572, when José de Acosta arrived in Peru, the Spanish crown requested that the Society of Jesus be charged with the task of bringing the remaining unconquered American native populations into submission (see Egido, Burrieza Sanchez, and Revuelta Gonzalez 2004). Conquest by military means had proved insufficient and ineffectual. The Jesuits realized that to fulfil their new charge, they would have to change the strategies that had served them so well in other locations. They could not model their missions after the parishes of Europe, or take on the activities of parish priests because Ignatius's *Constitutions* prohibited any sort of permanent mission, which, of course, a parish would be; Jesuit missions were to last only for a prescribed period (see Loyola 1556, 9 [VI, 3: § 588]). Such temporary missions were proving useful within Europe as instruments for improving the Christian life of communities already familiar with the gospel; they helped to ensure that the Tridentine standards of religious life were being respected, or uncovered heresy. But among people who had never heard Christ's word they were useless. Thus, because they were addressing different conditions, Jesuits thought that in their missions in the Americas they had to develop new forms and practices tailored to the sorts of human beings and cultures that were their targets. Jesuits recognized that the task of bringing such peoples to Christianity and transforming their societies into Christian worlds would require time, as well as continuous control over and direction of local missions.

It is an important fact, therefore, that the Company arrived in America only after the Valladolid Disputation of 1550, between the Dominican Bartolomeo de Las Casas (1484?–1566) and the Humanist theologian and philosopher Juan Ginés de Sepúlveda (1489–1573), over the question of whether American natives were capable of self-governance: in other words, the disputants had to define for themselves the human nature of American populations. Sepúlveda maintained that American peoples were *barbari simpliciter*, barbarians in essence. Las Casas, in contrast, argued that they were *barbari secundum quid*, barbarians only in some respects; they might lack certain cultural and technological characteristics of Europeans, but they nevertheless had "principles which are common to all men" ("semientes y principios a todos los hombres comunes y de nunguno carece"); in other words, they were barbarians in the same way "we are to them" ("nosotros somos a ellos" [Las Casas (1559) 1909, 13: 550 and 695]). From his Aristotelian perspective, Las Casas concluded that traditional evangelization was possible in America. The gospel could be preached to them in the same way it had been delivered to Mediterranean populations. Of course, Sepúlveda, who thought of American peoples as essentially different, of a wholly barbarous nature, disagreed.

But Sepúlveda's argument also drew on another significant element: the recognition that traditional apostolic evangelization had possessed a powerful auxiliary, legitimizing aid in miracles, and that this auxiliary seemed to be lacking in the missions of the Americas (see Sepúlveda 1997, 1: § 16). Sepúlveda concluded, therefore, that the only kind of evangelization that could work in sixteenth-century America was evangelization *manu militari*. The Valladolid discussion ended in an impasse that would not be resolved until the end of the century when Acosta, by arguing for practices legitimized by something other than violence, found a way out of the conundrum (see Lopetegui 1942; Burgaleta 1999; Imbruglia 1994, 61ff.; MacCormack 1994). He succeeded in avoiding Scylla and Charybdis, the extremes of Las Casas and Sepúlveda, because of the way he linked the seemingly opposing visions together: though all American peoples were human beings, they and their societies nevertheless possessed special qualities that required adaptive preaching strategies. To support his position, Acosta developed a general vision that we might almost define as "universal history." He classified all the peoples of the world into three groups: those with fully developed civilization (of course the word "civilization" was not used by Acosta himself, as it had yet to be coined, but I think it can be adopted here without anachronism); those with weak civilization, and those without civilization. It is noteworthy that, according to Acosta, people without civilization were nevertheless human beings. The institutions and practices of the Mediterranean nations provided his yardstick for measuring and grouping "Oriental" cultures as well as American ones. A society belonged to the highest human order (the one I have called "full civilization") if it had political laws and hierarchy, God and rites, and culture, especially writing. Around the Mediterranean Sea could be found many societies with different, indeed opposite, characteristics, with rival religions and politics (Hebrew, Muslim, "heretic," and Catholic societies). But all these societies had in common the standards of civilization heretofore sketched. Most important, these societies could be described in Scholastic-Aristotelian terms: their people were political animals. In this sense, according to Acosta, the Mediterranean and European nations, together with China and Japan, represented the highest level of culture.

American societies, particularly the Incan and Aztec, occupied a second level, the one I have called "weak civilization": they had developed the concepts and practices of political hierarchy; they had ideas of divinity, embodied in deities whom they honoured with rites; and, though their cultures were very "primitive," they had writing. Acosta saw continuities between the institutions of these non-European societies and those of Mediterranean cultures. In this respect, the Aztec and Incan peoples could be considered examples of Las Casas's barbarians *secundum quid*; the Aristotelian standards of humanity and society served to define their nature. Consequently, Acosta thought, the message of Christ's word might be preached among these "new" peoples in the same way that the apostles had preached it to the Mediterranean peoples during the first centuries of Christianity: that way of preaching we have called "apostolic."

The third and lowest level of human society in Acosta's schema was represented by South American "savages," who lived without civilization. According to Acosta, the savage communities (he called them *behetria*, using a medieval Spanish term) were social groups completely different from Mediterranean ones, lacking permanent settlements and social authorities, parental, political, or religious ("disobedient to their parents" ["parentibus non oboedientes"]). They also, consequently, lacked the hierarchical institutional structures associated with "civilization": "[T]hey do know neither the right political State, nor magistrates, nor laws; they wander as beasts" ("[R]empublicam nullam habent propriam, neque Magistratus, neque leges, ritu ferarum [...] vagantur"). These groups lived "without laws, without kingship, without God" ("sine lege, sine rege, sine Deo" [Acosta (1588) 1670, 1: viii and 100]).[12] Their social forms could not be made to fit Aristotelian or Scholastic categories. Yet, Acosta noted, as unlikely as it might seem, the members of these societies managed to live together peacefully. They had an energy that engendered community. I would like to quote a text by Leibniz in which the problem posed by Acosta's theory is well exposed:

> It is perfectly true [...] that Canadian savage people live in society without political and judiciary powers; that there are conflicts between different nations, but not inside a single nation. As I have said, it is a political miracle, which would have been unknown to Aristotle, but which is not in contradiction to Hobbes' theory ("Verissimum est, [...] Americanos illius tractus [Canada] sine omni magistratu et tamen quiete cohabitare; rixas, odia, bella, non aut vix, nisi inter diversae nationis linguaeque homines, illic evenire. Id, poene dixerim, miraculum politicum est, Aristoteli incognitum, Hobbio non animadversum" [quoted in Landucci 1972, 110–11]).[13]

To explain the mysterious social force binding these societies, Acosta turned to the concept of *libido* and provided a remarkable expression: "[T]hey use desire as reason" ("[L]ibido pro ratione utuntur" [Acosta (1588) 1670, 1: 10]). He thought that these societies possessed a dynamic, which would be able to move them from this lowest of human social conditions to the next higher level: that is, to the one of basic civilization as evidenced in Incan Peru.[14]

As Acosta's work demonstrates, the Jesuits were aware that the world of *sauvagerie* was radically different from the Mediterranean one, and they recognized that they had to find "a new way or ground for evangelizing among new kinds of men" ("novo generi hominum novam evangelizandi rationem" [Acosta (1588) 1670, 1: 16]). It was impossible to look to European historical experience for models either for evangelizing these people or for bringing them under the authority of European political administrations. In fact, the gospel had to be preached *non evangelice*, in a non-evangelizing fashion; "culture" was to provide the means through which "men from the forest" or "savage men" ("homines sylvestres") were to be transformed into rational individuals. Acosta added another identifiably "Jesuit" element to this strategy: if the indigenous populations were willing to be civilized, they were to be treated with gentleness; otherwise, for "their own salvation" ("pro sua salute"), they were to be entrusted "legitimately" ("non illiberaliter") to wise men who, with violence if necessary, would persuade them to live "as human beings and not as beasts" ("humane et non bestialiter"). Men would pass from a natural state to civilized life by "learning to fear" ("timere et terrere").[15] Dread and reverence were aspects of social life not to be eliminated but rather to be used for civilizing ends.

Missionaries

The *Imago primi saeculi Societatis Jesu* clearly echoed Acosta's ideas in its presentation of the relationship between *sauvagerie* and religion among peoples of the sort found in the Americas; first, such people had to be taught the rules of human society, and, afterwards, they could be introduced to those of religion: "[T]hey have to be forced to live in a human way before religion and religious matters could be taught them" ("[P]rius ad humanum ritum traducendi sunt, quam Religione et caelestium rerum scientia imbui possint"). As we have seen, the Jesuits were aware that miracles functioned well as a tool for evangelizing. Where miracles were not occurring, preachers had to impress their listeners in other ways. In these conditions, the "miracle" came to be represented by the preacher, whose extraordinary life could inspire the confidence of the people by its example. Nadal had already said that the legitimacy of the missionary derived from "his faith and exemplary life" ("puritatem vitae et exemplum, et charitatis fervorem" [Nadal 2003, 825]). But for this kind of miracle to be effective and convincing, preachers had to acquire the languages and the customs of the target societies: "The Christian preacher has to live according to the local traditions, in order to be judged worthy of trust by those whom he is going to evangelize" ("Evangelicus concionatur illam instituere debet vivendi rationem qua dignus judicetur ab iis, inter quos versatur, qui audiatur" [De Nobili 1971, 82]).[16]

These words encapsulate the essence of the strategy of "adaptation," by means of which the Society acquired the ability to make effective contact with non-European societies, to understand them, as it were, not as outsiders but (almost) as insiders. Usually, it is said that the theory of adaptation was developed for India, Japan, and China – ancient societies with, as we have seen, hierarchies, religions, cultures, politics: that is, with full civilization. But Acosta's vision of a universal history allowed this model of evangelizing to apply to any human society in the world. Even more, with roots deep in the spirituality of the Company, adaptation ultimately provided a basis for spiritual conquest and empire.

The Jesuit could adapt himself to the world into which he was sent to live, not because he expected to find there elements of continuity with his original cultural world, but for exactly the opposite reason: because he had been taught to forget his origins. The idea of adaptation derived from the fact that Jesuits were trained, from the time of their entry into the order, to set aside their individual, historical, and native identities. At the end of his religious formation, the Jesuit missionary was no longer a European priest; he was but a Christian (see Imbruglia 1992). Within this peculiar empire, the Jesuit could lose his first identity (Italian or French, nobleman or bourgeois, and so on) and emerge with his new "universal" and apostolic identity. Then, from this condition of *homo universalis*, he could assume a local identity, becoming Chinese, or Japanese, or Indian. In a sense he could wear this new mask in the world because he had lost his original one. The Jesuit in his foreign mission provides another example of late Renaissance, or better, of Mediterranean Baroque ways: literally, he was living "honest dissimulation" ("onesta dissimulazione"), but what was important here was not the dissimulation but rather the honesty. Yet, thanks to his imitation of Christ, the Jesuit did not consider himself an actor in profane history; he belonged to sacred history. The models for Jesuit adaptation came not from European history, but from experiences with non-European social systems and traditions. Thus adaptation entailed a real intercultural transfer, between European culture and alien wisdoms and societies. The loss of identity that a Jesuit experienced as a novitiate, becoming a "new" religious man, happened within the net of the Society of Jesus. Thus Jesuits who came across new cultures were able to cope with strangeness and challenges, precisely because, as Jesuits, they also always moved within *their* own Jesuit cosmos – the Jesuit "empire," wherein the individual's relationship with fellow Jesuits and with the Society's hierarchy was moulded according to the ancient ideal of the Church of Jerusalem, and the individual's life was lived in imitation of Christ.[17] From this point of view, the lack of miracles did not represent a difficulty for the Jesuit missionaries: they themselves, along with their lives and their works, were the "new" miracle which God had allowed.[18] In this way, at the end of the sixteenth and in the first decades of the seventeenth centuries, the missionary strategy based upon adaptation resolved the problem of the absence of miracles in the contemporary world with a solution that, in the deeper sense, actually depended on the persistence of their absence in perpetuity.

The Missions of Paraguay

In 1639 Ruiz de Montoya published his *Conquista espiritual hecha por los religiosos de la Compañia de Jésus en la provincias de Paraguay, Parana, Uruguay y Tapi* ("The spiritual conquest made by the religious of the Society of Jesus in the Provinces of Paraguay, Parana, Uruguay, and Tapi"), which proudly described the Jesuit strategy and its achievements: "[L]os redujó la diligencia de los Padres á poblaciones grandes y á vida politica y humana" ("[T]he assiduity of the Jesuits forced them to live in communities according to political and human laws" [Montoya (1639) 1892, 29]). The societies that the Jesuits were creating – the *reducciones* – were being built on a hierarchical, institutional, and social model, in which individual life was organized and controlled in communities designed to sustain agriculture; land and labour both were divided. In a sense, the Jesuits were using the Incan model for their *reducciones,* without "servicio personal." In so doing, they were assuming that the forms they were imposing entailed a developmental step up for the Paraguayan peoples, and also that a political society could be brought forth through "conquista spiritual."[19]

Here we can see the circle that links together anthropology, religion, and politics in the missionary theory of the Society of Jesus. Montoya's description was perfectly consistent with the principle Jesuit theories about natural human sociability, as presented, for instance, by Luis de Molina (see Höpfl 2004, 192ff.). According to Molina's theology, mankind needed divine grace in order to be saved, but God's grace, nevertheless, "was worked in the lives of individuals through the exercise of their natural mental faculties" ("facienti quod est in se Deus non denegat gratiam"), especially the will. This theory, called "semipelagianism" or "pelagianism," opened up a path towards the rescue and rehabilitation of human nature from the negative assessments associated with the Augustinian tradition.[20] The charge of semipelagianism was one of the major reproaches that Pascal and other Jansenists uttered against the Jesuits.

Intellectual Disputes

At the end of the seventeenth century, at least in some part, the Jesuits renounced the theoretical framework that had supported their mission practices, even though life in the missions continued unchanged and the appraisal and support by the kings of Spain remained unaltered. There are many reasons to explain this change. Certainly the disputes within the Church – for instance, the one about the nature of Chinese rites – greatly influenced the arguments of both the Jesuits and their opponents. But in the decades of the crisis of the European conscience (to call to mind the famous book by Paul Hazard), the disputes between the new culture of the radical (pre-)Enlightenment and among the various Christian churches also brought momentous consequences. Here, I should like to highlight two of these disputes: the first with Jansenism on the subject of propaganda and miracles, and the second on the issue of utopianism.

Missions, Propaganda, and Miracles

The first dispute is not often discussed as a factor in the processes that transformed Jesuit missionary strategies. In 1656, after Pascal's *Lettres provinciales* were published, theological and ecclesiastical questions were being debated across Europe for the first time in French, not in Latin. Of course, we cannot speak here yet of Habermas's public opinion (*Oeffentlichkeit*), but even so, with the *Lettres provinciales,* discussions about religious matters, together with the philosophical and critical discussions of those decades, brought forth the conditions which led to the creation of public opinion as an area different from that of propaganda. I mean by this that the *Lettres provinciales* were not only a tool of propaganda, but were also one of the starting points of the history of public opinion, in the sense that the authority Pascal acknowledges in his conflict with the Society of Jesus is not an institutional power (this was the case of Jesuit discourse, which was but false and violent propaganda), but rather the individual, critical conscience:

> You trust in your strength and impunity, but I believe I possess the truth of innocence [...]. When force combats force, the stronger destroys the weaker: when argument is opposed to argument, true and convincing reasoning confounds that which is based on vanity and lies: but violence and truth have no power over each other ("Vous croyez avoir la force et l'impunité, mais je crois avoir la vérité de l'innocence [...]. Quand la force combat la force, la plus puissante détruit la moindre: quand on oppose les discours aux discours, ceux qui sont véritables et convaincants, confondent et dissipent ceux qui n'ont que la vanité et le mensonge: mais la violence et la vérité ne peuvent rien l'une sur l'autre" [Pascal 1963b, Letter 12: 429]).[21]

The Jesuit theories of probabilism, ethics, and adaptation were all being examined in a larger public forum and were being held up to public derision (see Knebel 2000). In their controversy with Pascal and other Jansenists, the Society of Jesus understood very well that ideas of vital importance were at stake. The Jesuit theological, ethical, and political system looked at Christian doctrine and history with modern (or modernizing) eyes, while the Jansenist approach involved observing and preserving the ancient constitution and ancient doctrines with rigour. Both Jansenists and Jesuits had a common purpose: to persuade the new, seventeenth-century man, the "libertin[e] [...] seek[s] only to doubt religion" ("liberti[n] qui ne church[e] qu'à douter de la religion"); but their apologetics were different and their ideas about both preaching and salvation were at variance.[22] The Jesuits' "new kind of preachers" ("nouvelle sorte de prédicateurs") had a peculiar style of denouncing the corruption of moral and religious life, which Pascal described in some famous pages (see Pascal 1963b, Letter 10: 416). Pascal heard a Jesuit say that

> if we suffer any laxity in others, it is rather from complaisance than from design. We are forced to do this. Men are so corrupt nowadays that, since we

> cannot make them come to us, we must therefore go to them. Otherwise, they would leave us; worse, they would backslide entirely ("si nous souffrons quelque relâchement dans les autres, c'est plutôt par condescendance que par dessein. Nous y sommes forcés. Les hommes sont aujourd'hui tellement corrompus, que ne pouvant les faire venir à nous, il faut bien que nous allions à eux. Autrement il nous quitteraient; ils feraient pis, ils s'abandonneraient entièrement" [Pascal 1963b, Letter 6: 394]).

The core of Pascal's criticism aimed at this sort of "condescension," which he believed stemmed from Molina's probabilism, the confutation of which was the great theme of the *Lettres provinciales.* Probabilism, Pascal argued, was based upon the assertion that "only the fear of punishment [...] and thus to be saved without ever loving God" ("la seule crainte des peines [...] et ainsi être sauvé sans avoir jamais aimé Dieu en sa vie") was sufficient. This Jesuit theology of accommodation was a "strange theology of our time" ("étrange théologie de nos jours"), which affirmed that the world, which had been "redeemed by Christ, will be discharged from loving him" ("racheté par Christ, sera déchargé de l'aimer" [Pascal 1963b, Letter 10: 417]). Any preaching based upon this "strange theology" was based, therefore, not on the perspective of the "true conversion of heart" ("veritable conversion de cœur"), but on a point of view that gave greater value to the material interests of men (see Letter 10: 416). The condescension exercised by the Jesuits towards men was also a condescension for the Society itself: "Your main object is to maintain the credit and glory of your Company" ("Vous avez pour principal objet de maintenir le crédit et la gloire de votre compagnie" [Letter 12: 426]); commitment to power, not to human salvation was the motto (devise) of the Society.

At the end of the seventeenth century, the Society of Jesus decided to reply to the Jansenist attacks and started publishing both the so-called *Mémoires de Trevoux* and the *Lettres édifiantes et curieuses.* The latter publication, presented in French in order to reach the largest possible European audience, was an instrument of propaganda and a defence of the strength and theological orthodoxy of the Jesuit "empire," portrayed in a new light.[23] By this time, the Company of Jesus itself was finding the model of adaptation less useful than it once had been. The essence of the change, I would say, was that the narratives of Jesuit conquests and of life in the missions began being rich in miracles, in the traditional sense, while descriptions of the behaviour of the missionaries receded into the shadows.

We have seen that Acosta's idea of mission among South American savage people and its realization by the Jesuit missionaries were both based upon the assumption that this class of mankind had an internal energy that could assure its "progress" towards the social and cultural conditions represented by the Incan State. The assumption had required that European standards of evangelization be adapted to the indigenous rules of life and that some extra-European cultural elements be included in order for the civilizing process, upon which spiritual conquest ultimately depended, to occur. It had been easy to conclude that the new permanent missions of Paraguay could imitate the villages founded by the Incan conquest and imitate the Incan organization of labour. But, in many of the *Lettres édifiantes et curieuses* that described the *reducciones* of Paraguay, the fact that such adaptation strategies had been used was not emphasized; now missionary practice would draw for its models not from the history of extra-European societies, but from that of Europe itself; the model henceforth was to come from sacred history, not from profane history. The difference between the two varieties of history and the need for linking them on behalf of the Catholic perspective had been articulated already by Bossuet in his *Discours sur l'histoire universelle.* Sacred history was the story of the truth, which was uncovered through ecclesiastical history on the one hand, and through profane history on the other hand: the latter, however, was nothing but a chaos of events which acquired sense only when that chaos was made part of sacred history (see Ricuperati 1999).

The certainty of belonging to the trajectory of sacred history and of knowing, therefore, that actions were being directed by God's will could come only through the witness of miracles. Thus miracles were now necessary, in the missions and in the world. From the sixteenth-century era of challenges to the integrity of the Church, to the seventeenth-century epoch of the saints, a major step had indeed occurred in Christian history, as the Jesuits acknowledged: "The age which we are living is an age of saints, because apparently God gives gifts and occasions of becoming a saint in a much larger way than in precedent ages" ("Saeculum hoc, quo vivimus, saeculum esse Sanctorum, propterea quod Deus dona sua, et praeclaras parandae sanctitatis rationes videatur largius quam superioribus aetatibus communicare"). "God is truth" ("Deus est veritas"), but human history is the proof, even the guarantee, of that truth: "You ask how do I know that God has done something extraordinary: but how do you know that he has not done it?" ("Quaeris unde mihi constat fecisse Deum quidquam memoratur: unde tibi constat non fecisse?" ['Introductio,' in Bolland and Henschen 1643, 1: xxi]).

In the *Acta sanctorum* (1643), Johan van Bolland, Godfried Henschen, and Daniel van Paperbroeck showed that it was possible to write *sacred* history. It was true that miracles "broke with the normal ways" ("consuetum rerum humanarum modum"), but that did not mean that their reality could be denied: "Facts are not to be denied because they could not logically or naturally happen" ("Cave igitur neges facta, quia fieri non potuerint aut debuerint"). Believing narratives of miracles or of the lives of saints required the same *fides humana* required for accepting the histories Livy or Thucydides wrote as truths about Roman or Greek societies (see xxxiv–xxxix). In other words, Jesuit historiography argued the same kinds of trust and faith were required whether the arguments to be accepted were from profane history or sacred history. This point of view was another aspect of the anthropological semipelagianism that we have seen in Molina's theory of man. The grace of God could find correspondence in the will of man. Sacred history gave intelligibility to profane history: between them there was continuity. Jansenists had confuted this point of view. Antoine Arnauld's *Art de Penser*, for example, had argued that only in sacred history could a fact theoretically possible also be necessary; in profane history this argument was false because the logic of sacred history and the logic of human nature were different; consequently, the two histories, sacred and profane, were radically disconnected (see Pascal 1963a, 230). For Jansenists, the city of God was drastically separated from the city of man. For the Jesuits, on the contrary, this idealization was not only possible but also useful. It was a great weapon of propaganda, which the *Lettres édifiantes et curieuses* could not help using.

In this new-style propaganda, the missions of Paraguay still played an important role at the centre of a new intercultural transfer, but now they were embedded into a more traditional ecclesiastical discourse based upon the need for the divine intervention of miracles. Now probabilism supported the moral possibility of miracles; thus it reinforced the Jesuits' claim to represent the "new miracle," while coincidentally maintaining the Society's independence from any other power, profane or even sacred. In this way, the Society proved itself able to renew its forms of propaganda. Nevertheless, the new, open, and free space of public opinion would be a domain which was and had to be extraneous to its way of thinking all through the eighteenth-century, and the ancient, twofold, original spirit of the Society of Jesus that had fascinated the culture of the Renaissance – its millenarianism united with its will to work in the world – would be weak and unable to speak to the new culture of Enlightenment.

Missions, History, Utopianism

It was impossible for the Jesuits to adopt a primitivist ideal of the state of nature, of the sort articulated by Montaigne in his *Essays*. The theme or myth of the good savage had always been extraneous to the culture of Catholicism, and even the intense rehabilitation of human nature offered by Molina could not embrace it: the fall of Adam meant the fall of any natural man (see Pagden 1986). Primitive society had always been represented as society without political obligation, and after Montaigne, the image would be adapted by philosophers, such as Locke, arguing for the existence of civil society prior to the state: an impossible utopia for the Jesuit, who could not think of a society or a community functioning without fear, obedience, and hierarchy. The other type of ideal society, represented by More's *Utopia*, was also incompatible with the model of society underlying Jesuit thought. The cause of this incongruity is well stated in a letter attributed to Tirso Gonzalez, General of the Society of Jesus (1687–1705): "Do they pretend to form ideal republics, whose citizens would all be lords exempt from serving and working for others? Do they want these Indians, now masters of their property, to be able to dispense with all help?" ("Est-ce qu'ils prétendent former des républiques idéales, dans lesquelles ceux qui les composent seraient tous seigneurs exempts de servir et de travailler pour les autres? Veulent-ils que ces Indiens, devenus les maîtres de leurs biens, puissent se passer de tout secours?" [quoted by Ibañez Echevarry 1780, 1: 199–200]). Very likely, this letter is a forgery, but it is useful, nevertheless, because its argument is so clear that I think it requires no further comment. The Jesuit idea of natural law as well as Jesuit political culture rested on a social ideal completely different from the one described in these texts on utopias: the ideal of a religious state without the freedom of a civil society, and equally without the freedom of a republican state. Neither the political utopia nor the primitivist one was suitable for the Jesuit idealization of their missions; both belonged, in the age of pre-Enlightenment, to the secular, radical, philosophical tradition. The autonomy of human and social life, as it had been described in More's *Utopia* or idealized in the descriptions of savage societies, was the "issue" ("enjeu") of this debate.

In the search for proof of the keen attention paid by Christian culture to utopian discourses and the dangers they posed, it is interesting to observe a surprising rejection of the ancient biblical tradition of government by theocracy. This tradition, the *antiquitates judaicae*, was a model to which Christianity could turn in its search for utopian perfection. But it had become a dangerous model for two reasons. First, it could support the notions of society found in the stateless, communitarian utopias. As Jean Le Clerc (1716) noted in his *Historiae ecclesiasticae prolegomena*, theocracy could resemble the social organization of More's *Utopia*: "In the theocratic system of Moses you are not in search of an utopian model, where (to speak in a platonic way) the most extraordinary laws are compulsorily performed by its citizens" ("In lege ergo Mosaica, non est quaerenda idea quaedam ut Platonico more loquar, perfectae Reipublicae, in qua civibus consummatissima virtus, ad quam se componeret, proponatur"). Laurence Mosheim, the great German Lutheran historian, was also keenly aware of this ambiguity and stated his fear that, within this tradition, somebody could find "an imaginary republican State, as imagined by Plato or More" ("fictam rempublicam, qualem Platonis aut Mori" [Mosheim 1722, 11]). Second, theocratic government had been discussed by the "atheist" philosophers Hobbes and Spinoza. The latter, for example, had applied theocracy, a religious political form, to human political philosophy, using theocracy not as the myth upon which Christianity was founded but rather as a framework from which to reflect on politics and a secularized vision of liberty. It is not amazing to read in the anonymous *Analyse du traité théologi-politique de Spinosa* that "human politics has not imagined anything as wonderful as this theocracy" ("la politique humaine n'a rien imaginé de si merveilleux que cette théocratie" [(Boulainvilliers), 1767, 99]). And also, it is not amazing that the Jesuits did not accept this path to utopia.

To idealize their missions, the *Lettres édifiantes et curieuses* adopted more than one approach. Their propagandistic goals required the translation of the experience of missions into a model of utopia, but this model could not be taken from the secularized traditions of More, Locke, or Spinoza. Theocracy was too ambiguous, as we have just noted. But in specifically Christian history, there was another case of idealized society: the early apostolic community of Jerusalem. It is true that the Calvinist Grotius had used the model when he said in the early seventeenth century that the best example of people living "with mutual charity" ("inter se in mutua quadam eximia caritate" [Grotius 1758, 2:56]) came from the Christians of Jerusalem ("qui Hierosolomis primi existerunt"). In this case, however, the compromised orthodoxy of the writer could not invalidate the tradition, for, as we have seen, this myth of the apostolic church was one of the foundational myths behind the Society's self-image: the Jesuits lived in imitation of Christ and the Society in imitation of the apostolic community for the Society. Both ideas were thus more than extrinsic ecclesiastical traditions; they functioned as the inner reasons of their faith and of their life. Still, as we are seeing, those myths were losing their energy.

The *Lettres édifiantes et curieuses* had said that in Paraguay "the gentleness, faith, selflessness, union and charity that reign among these new followers, never ceased to remind me of the Church in that happy time when Christians, detached from the things of the world, had but one heart and one soul" ("la douceur, la foi, le désintéressement, l'union et la charité qui règnent parmi ces nouveaux fidèles, me rappelaient sans cesse les souvenir de ces heureux temps de l'Eglise, où les Chrétiens, détachés des choses de la terre, n'avoient tous qu'un coeur et qu'une ame");[24] "[s]ince goods are held in common, ambition and greed are unknown vices, and among them one sees neither division nor prosecution" ("[c]omme les biens sont communs, l'ambition et l'avarice sont des vices inconnus, et l'on ne voit parmi eux ni division, ni process"); "[o]ne sees in that place neither poor people nor beggars, and all enjoy an equal abundance of the things necessary for life" ("[o]n n'y voit ni pauvres ni mendians, et tous sont dans une égale abondance des choses nécessaires à la vie").[25] The missions in Paraguay represented a miracle in the history of the world: a reconstruction of the forms of the primitive Church, functioning successfully in the era of the new commercial society.

In the eighteenth century, a synthesis of all these elements – the description of the experience of missions, the presentation of savage people, the discussion about the role of the missionary, and finally the need to resort to utopian ideals for reasons of propaganda – was made by the greatest Italian Catholic intellectual of the eighteenth century, the abbot Ludovico Antonio Muratori (see Niccoli 1976, 161ff.). In *Cristianesimo felice nelle missioni dei padri Gesuiti nel Paraguay* (1743), Muratori wrote that he "loved" ("amava") those missions because in them he found the primitive Church (see Muratori [1754] 1983). But, according to him, the Paraguayan missions were superior in many aspects to many European nations, not because of an "almost unceasing miracle" ("miracle presque continuel"), as the *Lettres édifiantes et curieuses* had said, but because the Jesuits had successfully exploited the notion of utility, linking it to religious sentiments. Jesuit Paraguay was a good example of religious utilitarianism in practice: a society of reason, perhaps, but certainly not the image of the city of God.

In the unfolding of these various points of view, the discussion about the idea of mission arrived at a contradiction. On the one hand, the mission had become an example of a path of historical development linking history to utopia: the utopia was an existing one to which it was possible to travel, as d'Anville, who confirmed the narratives of the *Lettres édifiantes et curieuses*, remarked in his 1733 publication, *Observations géographiques sur la carte du Paraguay*. On the other hand, already seen in the writings of Muratori, the mission had been offered as an example of a reverse historical developmental path aligned with the operation of utility in the world: the one that moved not from the imperfect world to the perfect utopia, but rather from utopia to practical human history: to the story of the development of human civilization.

Conclusion

A few years after the publication of Muratori's book, Montesquieu, who had been interested in the Society of Jesus and its history since his youth, offered, in his *Esprit des lois* (1748), a new and enlightened interpretation of the Jesuit missions (see Montesquieu 1964b, 912n537). He compared them to the classic republics, setting aside considerations of religion in his assessment and analysis; he laid special emphasis on the fact that, through centralization, republics linked the needs of commercial society with those of democracy; he outlined an original anthropological theory of the social stages, and in particular of the savage people; and finally, he provided a completely secular answer to the question of the right to civilization, grounding his argument upon reason and the superiority of European ingenuity ("industrie"), rather than on religion (see Montesquieu 1964a, vol. 4, § 6: 542). The three questions from which our discourse moved originally found entirely new answers in his work. European civilization henceforth was going to have new political, social, and cultural foundations and forms.

NOTES

1 I wish to thank Clorinda Donato and Laurence Moscato for translating significant portions of this text. I am particularly grateful to Ellen Wilson for her careful reading and perceptive suggestions.

2 Ward was member of the Junta de Comercio.

3 Montaigne 1962, 1231, on the Collegio Romano: "Observing the position this college occupies in Christianity is amazing; and I believe there never was a brotherhood and body among us that enjoyed such status, nor one that would produce, finally, the effects that these will, if they continue with their enterprise. They will soon possess all of Christianity. It is a breeding ground for great men of every kind. Of our members, this is the one that poses the most threat to the heretics of our time" ("C'est merveille combien de part ce colliege tient en la chretianté; et croi qu'il ne fut jamais confrerie et cors parmi nous qui tint un tel ranc, ny qui produirait enfin des effaicts tels que fairont ceus ici, se leurs desseins continuent. Ils possedent tantost toute la chretianté. C'est une pepiniere de grans hommes en toute sorte de grandeur. C'est celui de nos mambres qui menasse le plus les hérétiques de nostre tamps").

4 The internal political structure of the Society was a monarchy tempered by aristocracy (see Tollenaer 1640, 145).

5 This colonization of the conscience of a people in name of the universal tenets of Tridentine Catholicism has been studied in the Italian perspective by Prosperi 1996.

6 As it is known, the bibliography is immense; I quote only the studies relevant to my argument.

7 See the discussion in O'Malley 1993.

8 Laínez (1502–1565), who descended from Jewish origins, was one of the original companions of Ignatius in Paris, at the time the Company was conceived. He was chosen as papal theologian to the Council of Trent; he became, in 1558, the second general of the Company of Jesus, after Ignatius.

9 Jerónimo Nadal (1507–1580) played an essential role in the foundation and subsequent history of the Jesuits. See also Nadal 1994 and 2003.

10 See "D'Érasme à la Compagnie de Jésus. Protestations et intégration dans la Réforme catholique au XVIe siècle," in Bataillon 1991, 3: 279–303; and Pastore 2004.

11 The manuscript was widely circulated throughout Europe. Andrès de Ovieda became a Jesuit in 1541 and was patriarch of Ethiopia.

12 See Del Pino Díaz 1995.

13 The letter is from Leibniz to Friedrich Wilhelm Bierling (1710).

14 Acosta [1590] 1977, 1: 25: "There are great and apparant coniectures, that these men for a long time had neither Kings nor common weales, but lived in troupes as they do at this day in Florida, the Chiriguanas, those of Bresill, and many other nations, which have no certaine Kings, but as occasion is offered in peace or warre, they chose their Captaines as they please. But some

excelling others in force and wit, began in time to rule and domineere as Nembrot did; so increasing by little and little, they erected the Kingdomes of Peru and Mexico" ("Hay conjecturas muy claras que por gran tempo no tuvieron estos hombres reyes ni repúblicas concertadas, sino que vivían por behetrías, como ahora los Floridos y los Chiriguanás y los Brasile, y otras naciones muchas que no tienen reyes ciertos sino conforme a la ocasión que se ofrece, en guerra o paz, eligen sus caudillos como se les antoja. Mas con el tempo algunos hombres, que con fuerza y habilidad se aventajaban a los demás, comenzaron a señorear y mandar como antiguamente Nemrot, y poco a poco creciendo vinieron a fundar los reinos de Perú y de México"). See MacCormack 2007, 164.

15 See MacCormack 1985. To learn about directive and coercive authority as one of the main structures of Jesuit politics, see Höpfl 2004, 209ff.

16 See also De Nobili 2000. On the strategy of adaptation in Oriental societies, see Rubiès 2005, 237ff., and Minuti 2006.

17 See this suggestion in Mongini 2005, 178–80.

18 The case of Ignatius was paradigmatic in this respect. See Ribadeneira, *Flos sanctorum* (1599–1610), quoted by Levy 2004, 121, writing about Ignatius that "the greatest miracle in my judgment is that God the Father elected the father [e. g. Ignatius] to institute, govern and expand a Society that amongst Catholics and heretics, and among the infidels, in such short time has reaped much fruit in the world. And the miracle is so great and so manifest that if the other miracles were to be lacking, this one alone should suffice to know and esteem the sanctity that God gave to this father."

19 Important documents can be found in Morales 2005.

20 See the old, but interesting PhD thesis by Mercier (1960).

21 See also Pascal 1963b, lettre 12: 424: "[B]eing alone as I am, with no strength and with no human support against such a large body, and being sustained only by truth and sincerity" ("[É]tant seul comme je suis, sans force et sans aucun appui humain contre un si grand corps, et n'étant soutenu que par la vérité et la sincérité").

22 The quotation is from Pascal 1963b, lettre 4: 384. See also Pitassi 1991 and Gregory 2000.

23 For more about the Jesuit system of networks, see Rétif 1951; Harris 1996, 293–303; and Friedrich 2008.

24 See Bolland and Henschen 1643, 2: 46 and 4: 32.

25 This text by Florentin de Bourges, a Franciscan friar, is quoted in Bouchet [1716] 1843, 142. It gives the paradigmatic image of the missions of Paraguay that circulated in the *Lettres édifiantes et curieuses*. See Paschoud 2008, 7.

BIBLIOGRAPHY

Abe, Takao. 2003. "What Determined the Content of Missionary Reports? The Jesuit Relations compared with the Iberian Jesuit Accounts." *French Colonial History* 3: 69–83.

Acosta, Jose de. [1588] 1670. *De promulgando evangelio apud Barbaros, sive de procurando indorum salute.* Reprint, Lyon: Laurent Anisson.

Acosta, Jose de. [1590] 1977. *Historia natural y moral de las Indias.* Reprint, Valencia: Valencia Cultural.

–. [1604] 1880. *The Natural and Moral History of the Indies,* ed. Clements R. Markham, trans. Edward Grimston. Reprint, London: Hakluyt Society.

Armitage, David. 2000. *The Ideological Origins of the British Empire.* Cambridge: Cambridge University Press.

Bataillon, Marcel. 1991. *Erasmo y España. Estudio sobre la historia espiritual del siglo XVI.* Genève: Droz.

Benveniste, Émile [1954] 1966. "Civilisation. Contribution à l'histoire du mot." In *Problèmes de linguistique générale,* 1: 336–45. Paris: Gallimard.

Bolland, Jean, and Godefroid Henschen, eds. 1643. *Acta sanctorum.* Antwerp: Jacob de Meurs.

Bouchet, Antoine. [1716] 1843. Lettre du Père Bouchet au Père J. B. D. H. [Jean-Baptiste Du Halde], 14 February. In *Lettres édifiantes et curieuses,* 2: 142–53. Paris: Société du Panthéon littéraire.

[Boulainvilliers, Henri de]. 1767. *Analyse du* Traité Théologi-politique *de Spinosa.* London: s.n.

Broggio, Paolo, ed. 2005. *Evangelizzare il mondo: le missioni della Compagnia di Gesù tra Europa e America (secoli XVI–XVII).* Roma: Carocci.

Burgaleta, Claudio M., SJ. 1999. *José de Acosta (1540–1600). His Life and Thought.* Chicago: Loyola Press.

Curto, Diogo Ramada. 2005. "The Jesuits and Cultural Intermediacy in the Early Modern World." *Archivum Historicum Societatis Jesu* 74: 3–22.

Cuturi, Flavia, ed. 2004. *In nome di Dio. L'impresa missionaria di fronte all'alterità.* Roma: Meltemi.

D'Alembert, Jean le Rond. 1765. *Sur la destruction des Jésuites en France.* S.l.: s.n.

De Nobili, Roberto. 1971. *On Adaptation,* trans. of *Narratio fondamentorum quibus Madurensis Missionis institutum coeptus est et hucusque consistit,* ed. Savarimuthu Rajamanickam. Polayamkottai: De Nobili Research Institute.

–. 2000. *Preaching Wisdom to the Wise: Three Treatises by R. de Nobili, S.J. Missionary and Scholar in the 17th Century India,* trans. and eds. Anand Amaladass and Francis X. Clooney. St. Louis: The Institute for Jesuit Sources.

Del Pino Díaz, Fermín. 1995. "Los caníbales chiriguanos, un reto etnográfico para dos mentes europeas: Acosta y Polo." In *Visión de los otros y visión de sí mismos,* eds. F. Del Pino and Carlos Lázaro Avila, 57–89. Madrid: CSIC.

Ditchfield, Simon. 2007. "Of Missions and Models: The Jesuit Enterprise (1540–1773) Reassessed in Recent Literature." *Catholic Historical Review* 93: 325–43.

Egido, Teófanes, Javier Burrieza Sanchez, and Manuel Revuelta Gonzalez. 2004. *Los Jesuitas en España y en el mundo hispánico.* Madrid: Pons.

Friedrich, Markus. 2008. "Circulating and Compiling the *Litterae Annuae.* Towards a History of the Jesuit System of Communication." *Archivum Historicum Societatis Jesu* 77: 3–40.

Ganson, Barbara. 2003. *The Guaraní under Spanish Rule in the Rio de La Plata.* Palo Alto, CA: Stanford University Press.

Gregory, Tullio. 2000. "Apologeti e libertini." *Giornale critico della filosofia italiana* 79: 3–35.

Grotius, Hugo. 1758. *De jure belli ac pacis.* Lausanne: Bousquet & Cie.

Harris, Steven. J. 1996. "Confession-Building, Long-Distance Networks, and the Organization of Jesuit Science." *Early Science and Medecine* 1: 287–318.

Höpfl, Harro. 2004. *Jesuit Political Thought: The Society of Jesus and the State, c. 1540–1630.* Cambridge: Cambridge University Press.

Huppert, George. 1970. *The Idea of Perfect History: Historical Erudition and Historical Philosophy in Renaissance France.* Urbana: University of Illinois Press.

Ibañez Echevarry, Bernardo. 1780. *Histoire du Paraguay sous les Jésuites et de la royauté qu'ils y ont exercée pendant un siècle et demy.* Amsterdam: Arkstée et Merku.

Imbruglia, Girolamo. 1989. "L'*Historia do Futuro* del gesuita Vieira e il processo di secolarizzazione della storia universale." *Archivio di storia della cultura* 2: 185–97.

–. 1992. "Ideali di civilizzazione: la Compagnia di Gesù e le missioni (1550–1600)." In *Il nuovo mondo nella coscienza italiana e tedesca del Cinquecento,* eds. Adriano Prosperi and Wolfgang Reinhard, 287–308. Bologna: Il Mulino.

–. 2004. "Il missionario gesuita nel Cinquecento e i 'selvaggi' americani." In *In nome di Dio: L'impresa missionaria di fronte all'alteratà,* ed. Flavia Cuturi, 61–73. Roma: Meltemi.

Knebel, Sven K. 2000. *Wille, Würfel und Wahrscheinlichkeit. Das System der moralischen Notwendigkeit in der Jesuitenscholastik, 1550–1700.* Hamburg: Meiner Verlag.

Laínez, Diego. 1897. *Lettera al Polanco,* 1547. In *Monumenta ignatiana,* 4: 113. Madrid: Excudebat typographorum Societas.

Landucci, Sergio. 1972. *I filosofi e i selvaggi. 1580–1780.* Bari: Laterza.

Las Casas, Bartolomeo de. 1909. *Apologetica historia Sumaria [...] de las gentes destas Indias occidentales,* 1559. Madrid: Biblioteca de Autores Españoles.

Le Clerc, Jean. 1716. *Historia ecclesiastica.* Amsterdam: David Mortier.

Levy, Evonne A. 2004. *Propaganda and Jesuit Baroque.* Berkeley: University of California Press.

Lopetegui, León. 1942. *El padre J. de Acosta.* Madrid: Consejo Superior de Investigaciones Cientificas.

Loyola, Ignazio di. 1556. *Costituzioni della Compagnia di Gesù,* part VI. Available at: http://www.undicesimaora.net/biblioteca/Costituzioni_Ignazio_Loyola.pdf. Accessed 15 December 2010.

MacCormack, Sabine. 1985. "'The Hearth Has Its Reasons': Predicaments of Missionary Christianity in Early Colonial Peru." *The Hispanic American Historical Review* 45: 443–66.
–. 1994. "Ubi Ecclesia? Perceptions of Medieval Europe in Spanish America." *Speculum* 69: 74–100.
–. 2007. *On the Wings of Time: Rome, The Incas, Spain and Peru.* Princeton, NJ: Princeton University Press.
Mercier, Roger. 1960. *La réhabilitation de la nature humaine (1700–1750).* Villemonble: La Balance.
Milhou, Alain. 2001. "El manuscrito gesuita-mesiánico de Andrés de Oviedo (1550) a Francisco de Borja." *Caravelle* 76–7: 345–54.
Minuti, Rolando. 2006. *Orientalismo e idee di tolleranza nella cultura francese del primo '700.* Firenze: Olschki.
Mongini, Guido. 2005. "Censura e identità nella prima storiografia gesuita (1547–1542)." In *Nunc alia tempora, alii mores: Storici e storia in età postridentina,* ed. M. Firpo, 169–88. Firenze: Olschki.
Montaigne, Michel de. 1962. *Journal de voyage en Italie.* In *Œuvres complètes.* Paris: Biliothèque de la Pléiade.
Montesquieu. 1964a. *Esprit des lois.* In *Œuvres complètes.* Paris: Éditions du Seuil.
–. 1964b. *Mes pensées.* In *Œuvres complètes.* Paris: Éditions du Seuil.
Montoya, Ruiz de. 1892. *Conquista espiritual hecha por los religiosos de la Compañia de Jésus en la provincias de Paraguay, Parana, Uruguay y Tapi,* 1639. Bilbao: Imprenta del Corazon de Jesus.
Morales, Martin M., SJ. 1998. "Los comienzos de las reducciones de la provincia del Paraguay en relación con el derecho indiano y el Istituto de la Compañia de Jesús. Evolución y conflictos." *Archivum Historicum Societatis Iesu* 67: 3–129.
–. 2005. *A mis manos han llegado: Cartas de los PP. Generales a la antigua provincia del Paraguay (1608–1639).* Madrid and Rome: Institutum Historicum Societatis Iesu.
Mosheim, Johann Lorenz von. 1722. *Vindiciae antiquae Christianorum disciplinae adversus celeberrimi viri J. Tolandi Nazarem.* Hamburg: Joseph C. Kisner.
Muratori, Ludovico A. [1754] 1983. *Relation des missions du Paraguay,* ed. Girolamo Imbruglia. Reprint, Paris: Maspero.
Muthu, Sankar. 2003. *Enlightenment against Empire.* Princeton, NJ: Princeton University Press.
Nadal, Jerónimo, SJ. [1554] 1962. *Exhortationes in Hispania.* In *Epistolæ et monumenta,* ed. Michael Nicolau, SJ. Rome: MHSI.
–. 1994. *Contemplatif dans l'action. Écrits spirituels ignatiens (1535–1575),* ed. François Évain, SJ. Paris: Desclée de Brouwer.
–. 2003. *Adnotationes,* in *Annotations and Meditations on the Gospels,* ed. Walter S. Melion. Philadelphia: St. Joseph University Press.
Niccoli, Ottavia. 1976. "Metodo storico e propaganda politica: *Il Cristianesimo felice nel Paraguay* di L. A. Muratori." *Rivista di storia e letteratura religiosa* 12: 161–87.

O'Malley, John W., SJ. 1993. *The First Jesuits.* Cambridge, MA: Harvard University Press.

Osterhammel, Jürgen. 2006. *Europe, the "West" and the Civilizing Mission.* London: German Historical Institute.

Pagden, Anthony. 1986. *The Fall of Natural Man: The American Indian and the Origins of Comparative Ethnology.* Cambridge: Cambridge University Press.

–. 1995. *Lords of All the World: Ideologies of Empire in Spain, Britain and France c. 1500–c. 1800.* New Haven, CT: Yale University Press.

–. 2001. *Peoples and Empires: A Short History of European Migrations, Exploration, and Conquest, from Greece to the Present.* New York: Modern Library.

Pascal, Blaise. 1963a. "Préface sur le *Traité du vide.*" In *Œuvres complètes.* Paris: Éditions du Seuil.

–. 1963b. *Lettres provinciales.* In *Œuvres complètes.* Paris: Éditions du Seuil.

Paschoud, Adrien. 2008. *Le monde amérindien au miroir des "Lettres édifiantes et curieuses".* Oxford: Voltaire Foundation.

Pastore, Stefania. 2004. *Un'eresia spagnola. Spiritualità conversa, alumbradismo e Inquisizione (1449–1559).* Firenze: Olschki.

–. 2005. "I primi gesuiti e la Spagna: strategie, compromessi, ambiguità." *Rivista storica italiana* 117: 158–78.

Pavone, Sabina. 2004. *I gesuiti dalle origini alla soppressione, 1540–1773.* Roma: Laterza.

–. *The Wily Jesuits and the Monita Secreta: The Forged "Secret Instructions" of the Jesuits; A History and a Translation of the "Monita."* St. Louis, MO: The Institute of Jesuit Sources.

Pitassi, Maria-Cristina. 1991. *Apologétique 1680–1740. Sauvetage ou naufrage de la théologie?* Genève: Labor et Fides.

Pizzorusso, Giovanni. 1995. *Roma nei Carabi. L'organizzazione delle missioni cattoliche nelle Antille e in Guyana (1635–1675).* Rome: École française.

Prosperi, Adriano. 1996. *Tribunali della coscienza: inquistori, confessori, missioanri.* Torino: Einaudi.

Rétif, André. 1951. "Brève histoire des *Lettres édifiantes et curieuses.*" *Neue Zeitschrift für Missionswissenschaft* 7: 37–50.

Richardson, John S. 1991. "Imperium Romanum: Empire and the Language of Power." *Journal of Roman Studies* 81: 1–9.

Ricuperati, Giuseppe. 1999. "J.-B. Bossuet et l'histoire universelle." *Storia della Storiografia* 35: 27–62.

Rieter, Frederick J. 1995. *They Built Utopia: The Jesuit Missions in Paraguay 1610–1768.* Potomac, MD: Scripta Humanistica.

Rubiès, Joan Pau. 2005. "The Concept of Cultural Dialogue and the Jesuit Method of Accommodation: Between Idolatry and Civilization." *Archivum Historicum Societatis Iesu* 74: 237–80.

Schröder, Ingo W. 1999. "From Parkman to Postcolonial Theory: What is New in the Ethnohistory of Missions." *Ethnohistory* 46: 809–15.

Sepúlveda, Juan Ginés de. 1997. *Democrates secundus sive de iustis belli causis.* In *Obras Completas*, ed. Angel Losada and Alejandro Coroleu. Mexico: Colegio de San Luis.

Tollenaer, Jean de, SJ. 1604. *Imago primi saeculi Societatis Jesu.* Antwerp: Balthasar Moreti.

Ward, Bernardo. 1779. *Proyecto economico en que se proponen varias providencias, dirigidas á promover los interesse de España, con los medios y fondos necesarios por su plantification.* Madrid: Joachin Ibarra.

chapter two

The Politics of Writing, Translating, and Publishing. New World Histories in Post-expulsion Italy: Filippo Salvatore Gilij's 1784 *Saggio di Storia Americana*

CLORINDA DONATO

Post-expulsion Italy became home to thousands of Jesuits who had been abruptly exiled from their South American missions in 1767. These Jesuits, mainly Spaniards (many of Catalan origin), Austrians, Germans, and Italians as well, faced and suffered similar losses and traumas of resettlement back in Europe. Corsica, under Genoese rule in 1767, had agreed to house the newly exiled Jesuits; yet in 1768, Corsica passed from Genoese to French rule and the Jesuits were shuttled off once again to new destinations throughout the Italian peninsula. Once in Italy, they found themselves immersed in a rapidly evolving cultural context in which the role and status of Italian literature in Europe was being hotly disputed. This debate held a particular resonance for the Spanish Jesuits, for it was the purportedly corrupting influence of Spanish culture on Italy that formed the main bone of contention. Thus the stakes were high for Italian and Spanish Jesuits who were now together in Italy, geographically displaced from the Spanish empire. Thrust into a postcolonial context in the Italian peninsula, the relationship between Italian and Spanish Jesuits changed. The unity that had once prevailed through conjoined dedication to the tenets of Ignacio Loyola's order broke down over national lines once the order had been officially dissolved and the former Jesuits realigned themselves as a function of national pride and traditions, taking up the cultural dispute in their writings. The current situation reverberated with preceding debates that had been fueled by the writings of several erudite Jesuits in Italy, both pre- and post-expulsion. The consequences and outcomes of this complex universe of cultural, linguistic, and literary alliance formations can be understood through a study of the life of Italian Jesuit Filippo Salvatore Gilij and of his extended essay on the history of America, *Saggio di Storia Americana*.

Filippo Salvatore Gilij's *Saggio di Storia Americana, o sia Storia Naturale, Civile e Sacra Dei Regni e delle Provincie Spagnuole de Terra Ferma nell'America Meridionale* ("Essay on American History, or Natural, Civil, and Sacred History of the Spanish Kingdoms and Provinces of the South American Continent"), published in four volumes in Rome between 1780 and 1784, has ranked among the most inexplicably overlooked texts in the field of eighteenth-century Iberoamerican studies. Recognized for its anthropological, linguistic, and scientific excellence today, and noted among eighteenth-century men of erudition including cultural and literary historian Girolamo Tiraboschi and explorer Alexander von Humboldt, who knew Italian, Gilij's *Saggio di Storia Americana* only came to the attention of postcolonial scholars following its translation into Spanish in 1987. While the histories of any number of exiled Jesuits residing on Italian soil have been the subject of scholarly attention, Gilij's has been overlooked within this context of post-expulsion narratives. His text slipped under the radar for reasons that can be traced to Gilij's Italian origins, for Gilij's Italian cultural roots and his unique position as an Italian Jesuit who was "exiled" to his place of origin made him an insider in the cultural debate about Italy's role and place on the map of European culture. Gilij's *Saggio di Storia Americana*, then, must be read from the perspective of Italy so as to fully appreciate how it differs from other Jesuit accounts of the post-expulsion period and to evaluate its innovative contents, as well as its symbolic value for both the Vatican and the Spanish Crown.

Filippo Salvatore Gilij was born in Legogno, a small town near Norcia, in Umbria, Italy, 16 July 1721. Gilij entered the Jesuit order 16 July 1741. He probably did his novitiate in Spain, in the Collegio of San Hermenegildo of Seville. In February of 1743, he embarked for America from Cadiz, arriving in Cartagena of the Indies. He continued on to Santa Fe de Bogotá in an expedition presided over by Father Joseph Gumilla, author of the 1741 *Orinoco Ilustrado y defendido.* It is easy to imagine that Joseph Gumilla had hand-picked the young prelate Father Gilij to carry on his work in the Orinoco, noting his unique linguistic abilities and his desire to converse with the Indians. In Bogotá he studied at the Javeriana University and was ordained in 1748. In February 1749, he traveled to El Meta, arriving in Orinoco where he would live for eighteen and a half years, until the expulsion. He was twenty-seven years old, and he dedicated himself to fulfilling the mission of evangelization. In the Orinoco Medio, or Middle Orinoco, he founded and managed the frontier mission of the Reducción de San Luis Gonzaga de la Encamarada, at the South-East edge of the Orinoco, in the actual Bolívar State. There he worked with a variety of indigenous groups, primarily the Tamanacos and the Maipures, whose languages he learned and analysed in grammar books and dictionaries. He remained in the Orinoco until July 1767, the year of the expulsion of the Jesuits from the Spanish-run missions, and returned to Italy. In 1768, post-expulsion, he returned to Europe where he worked and wrote until his death in Rome on 10 March 1789 (see Guasti 2006, 466–7).

In 1767, in the midst of the Orinoco, the suppression of the Jesuits in the Kingdom of Spain came as a surprise to Father Gilij. He headed toward the Guaira, where Franciscan fathers took him in from 4 August 1767 until 5 March 1768, when he was sent to Corsica with the other Jesuits who had been removed from South America. A 1784 letter about Gilij's return to Italy that was addressed to the Spanish Crown by Floridablanca, in the interest of procuring a pension for him, relates that once he had arrived in Corsica, "he could not resist the temptation of going to Rome to visit his family after so many years away, for which he renounced receipt of his pension, and [has] continued in this way to live as a dependent of his relatives" ("no pudo resistir a la tentación de venir a Roma, a ver sus parientes después de tantos años de ausencia, por lo que dejó de percibir la pension, y así ha continuado hasta ahora, viviendo a cargo di sus parientes" [Guasti 2006, 468: n. 31]). Once he returned to the Roman provinces, however, he was immediately recruited into the service of the popular Jesuit missions in Italy, becoming spiritual director in Macerata and rector of Monte Santo; in 1773 he was working as rector and prefect of study in Orvieto, close to his place of birth in the Umbrian hills. In that same year Clement XIV suppressed the Jesuits, serving the final blow to the order whose public humiliation had begun some fourteen years prior in 1759, when Pombal banned the Jesuits in Portugal. The 1773 suppression of the order in Italy provoked the closure of the domestic missions. Thus Gilij moved to Rome, where he began writing his history of America for the dual purpose of pleasing the Vatican, in its desire to present a scientific face to the world, and of pleasing the Spanish Crown, so as to recapture his lost pension and to possibly receive the double pension that the King of Spain was now offering to those Jesuits who wrote scientifically inspired works about their years in South American missions. Gilij memorialized the work he performed at the Middle Orinoco mission he had founded, dedicating the last decade of his life to writing and promoting his *Saggio di Storia Americana.*[1]

In a volume that focuses on the textualities, intellectual disputes, and intercultural transfers of Jesuit discourse about the colonial world, Filippo Salvatore Gilij and his *Saggio* provide a unique case for consideration. Indeed, the double profile of Filippo Salvatore Gilij, a Jesuit under Spanish control and a Jesuit of Italian origin, raises a number of fresh questions about disputes and knowledge transfer in Jesuit post-expulsion accounts. For what is transmitted about America and how in Gilij's *Saggio di Storia Americana* can only be fully understood by examining the text through the double lens of Italian and Spanish interests during the post-expulsion period, especially after 1773, the year Clément XIV also banned the order in the pontifical states.

As a Jesuit of Italian origin, Gilij was among the very few for whom exile was synonymous with a cultural and linguistic homecoming. Aspiring to become a Jesuit as a youth of nineteen, like so many young men throughout Europe, Gilij had elected to subordinate his cultural origins to the discipline of the Jesuit religious order when he became one of the lucky few selected for evangelizing service at a foreign mission.[2] Post-expulsion, however, this privilege turned to stigma in a climate of fractious, ever-evolving factions of Jesuit supporters and detractors in Italy and Spain, as the Vatican and the Spanish Crown negotiated over the final fate of the Jesuits. Shuttled from Corsica to Genoa when Corsica transferred from Genoese to French rule in 1768, the bewildered Jesuits became the pariahs of Europe, now without status or sources of income. Thus the financial burden of settling some 4,500 Jesuits constituted a significant bargaining chip in negotiating a final place of exile in an Italian environment that was increasingly hostile to Spanish influence. In order to sweeten the deal for the Vatican, so that it would be more amenable to establishing Italian sites of exile for the expelled Jesuits, the Spanish Crown offered living allowances to each displaced Jesuit. Numerous cities along the Italian Adriatic would subsequently agree to provide hospitality to the Jesuits, as would Rome and Genoa, where a number of Spanish Jesuits also settled.

The Spanish Crown would eventually double the amount of support for those Jesuits who agreed to memorialize their experiences as published findings in scientifically oriented accounts that would be of interest to a Europe whose thirst for encyclopedic knowledge gave no signs of abating. A new role for the expelled Jesuits that held the promise of rehabilitation through a new form of service to the Crown inspired hundreds of the expelled Jesuits residing in Italy to take up the challenge.

The Crown hoped that by emphasizing knowledge transfer provided by the Jesuits, attention would be deflected from the ongoing negative fallout of the *Leyenda Negra* which had spiked once again throughout Spain in the wake of the hostile readings of Jesuit activity by the *philosophes.* Substituting *Leyenda Negra* with positive, "enlightened" documents about the Spanish presence in the New World coincided with the politics of the Holy See as well, as it, too, sought to present a newly minted face as a progressive and science-friendly institution in which spiritual goals and economic growth could be promoted as compatible objectives. In order to accomplish this, however, Rome needed to perform the delicate balancing act of distancing itself from Spain without thoroughly alienating the Spanish Crown. This meant Italian letters were to be rehabilitated through a critique of Spain that could be defended scientifically as a rational balance sheet of pros and cons that the Spaniards might even agree with, since, it has been recently argued, many Spaniards were highly self-critical and agreed with a number of the aesthetic concerns that had assailed them.[3] Not surprisingly, Spain and its Jesuit defenders would interpret this enlightened critique as yet another example of egregious scapegoating, one they would strive to attack and expose.[4] Here the publishing industry played a unique role, for the many publishing houses of the Adriatic and Genoa, where Spanish Jesuits had settled, began to produce a prodigious number of Jesuit accounts, the vast majority by Spanish Jesuits seeking the favour of the Crown. This business was lucrative but did not advance the agenda to relaunch the Italian cultural and literary program. The publishing house of the Vatican, Luigi Perego Erede Salvioni, was thus enlisted in this enterprise, producing Gilij's four-volume text over the span of 1780–1784, but publishing as well a new edition of one of the most controversial compendia of the eighteenth century, Italian Jesuit Girolamo Tiraboschi's *Storia della letteratura italiana.*

First published in thirteen volumes over a ten-year period, 1772–1782, with several new editions following closely on its tails to meet demand, Tiraboschi's compendium, the first history of Italian literature, offered a picture of Italian literary excellence. This was achieved through an exhaustive, systematic compendium of Italian culture that covered not only literature, but also covered art, philosophy, theology, and law, as well as history, politics, and cultural institutions. Tiraboschi's *Storia* became a powerful document of cultural unification that presented Italian culture positively, but also addressed threats to its brilliance. Thus Tiraboschi also took serious aim at Spain as an inferior, regrettable influence from which Italian writers were encouraged to take their distance. Literature and culture became unifying features of identity, mapped on to the "geographical expression" that was Italy as defined by Tiraboschi himself. Indeed, in the preface to his literary history, Tiraboschi defined those writers to be addressed in his compendium in the following way: "We refer to as ours all of those who lived in that expanse of country that is now known as Italy" ("Nostri diciamo tutti coloro che vissero in quel tratto di paese che or dicesi Italia" [Tiraboschi 1787–1794, 1: xiv]). While the relationship between Tiraboschi's *Storia della letteratura italiana* and the Jesuit accounts published in Italy post-expulsion deserves more attention, the contours of the situation locate the evolving identity of the Italian Jesuits vis-à-vis the Spaniards and, in particular, the status of Filippo Salvatore Gilij.[5] Ironically, this was not the first time that Spain had been implicated in the flaunting of Italy's literary legacy; in 1476 Lorenzo il Magnifico had partnered with Angelo Poliziano to create the first anthology of Italian literature in the Tuscan vernacular, the *Raccolta Aragonese*, which sang the praises of Tuscan as the most viable language of culture and, ultimately, empire. Though the *Raccolta* was limited to the literature of Tuscany for reasons of both time and place, the commingling of literary and political aspirations of unification of the entire peninsula sustained the vision of writers from Dante to Manzoni in what is known as Italy's "language question" ("questione della lingua"). Already, then, in the first collection of Italian literature, the pen as weapon of preference constructs Florence's cultural and rhetorical virtuosity in exactly the same way that Latin represented the hegemony of Roman culture. Lorenzo de' Medici spoke of the propitious literary might of the *Raccolta* as symbolic of Florence's political potential against the Aragonese, who controlled Naples.

Tiraboschi's history of Italian literature, so many centuries later, was interpreted by Spaniards as an insult and a direct challenge to the presence of Spanish Jesuits in Italy. Indeed, the text became a *cas célèbre* of Jesuit dispute, in which a Catalan Jesuit residing in Genoa, Saverio Llampillas, pit himself against the Italian Jesuit Girolamo Tiraboschi. Llampillas wrote in Italian an apology of Spanish literature in reaction to Tiraboschi's critique. Both the second edition of Tiraboschi's *Storia*, published in Modena in 1778, as well as an edition of Tiraboschi's *Storia* published by the same Vatican publisher who had published Gilij, carried a lengthy *Eloge* of Tiraboschi, summarizing the controversy; in the revised, corrected, and augmented second edition published in Modena in 1794, the entire controversy was moved from the eighth volume to the paratextual material, as explained below:

> Friar Saverio L[l]ampillas truly rose up against this work with the intent of censuring it with his Saggio Apologetico della Letteratura Spagnola, which had begun being published in Genoa in 1778. Cavalier Tiraboschi defended himself with a letter addressing Llampillas' essay which was published in Modena in 1778, and then reprinted in Volume VIII, pt. II of the *Storia della Letteratura Italiana* in the second edition published in Modena, p. 533 and following ("L'Abate Saverio Llampillas insorse veramente a censurare quest opera, col suo Saggio Apologetico della Letteratura Spagnola cominciato a stamparsi a Genova nel 1778. Il Cavalier Tiraboschi si difese con una lettera intorno al detto saggio impresso in Modena nel 1778, e poi ristampata nel Tomo VIII, pt. II della *Storia della Letteratura Italiana* nella seconda edizione di Modena p. 533 e segg" [Ciocchi 1794, 9: n. 5]).

It was in this climate that Gilij began to write his history of America. Now back in Italy, his views about missionary life were vetted in exchanges with influential circles of Italian Jesuits that he could frequent for the first time. These men had made names for themselves in the cultural and literary debates that rocked Italy during the first half of the eighteenth century. The debates had become particularly heated during the eighteen and a half years that Gilij lived in South America. Among the Jesuits who assumed the role of Italian arbiters in this debate, Saverio Bettinelli and Girolamo Tiraboschi stand out as those who acquired European fame as literary luminaries; through their writings, they debated the explosive question of Italian literary decadence. Wary of the *philosophes* and their virulent attempts to dismantle and poach upon Italy's literary legacy, Bettinelli and Tiraboschi nevertheless sought solutions to this literary morass by directly invoking Spain, which appeared (to many Spaniards) to rehabilitate Italian letters at the expense of Spain, though Tiraboschi adamantly rejected criticism that he was categorically singling out Spain. He explained that he was looking at the history of literature scientifically and objectively, focusing on works and genres, rather than single authors. Indeed, the modernity of this approach was misunderstood by many of his contemporaries.[6]

Gilij skillfully positioned himself and his text to extract the maximum benefit from the debate spearheaded by Bettinelli and Tiraboschi; at the same time, the content of his *Saggio*, considered today the first scientific study of indigenous languages in which new theories about origins and provenances were born, met the criteria for scientific content desirable to the Spanish Crown and to Pius VI's Vatican, both of which were seeking to rehabilitate their stodgy and retrograde images with a modern patina of credibility as sources and conduits of knowledge in the world. Gilij played each of the different cards he was dealt in the best way possible so as to obtain a positive outcome for himself and his text. Gilij's relationship with Pius VI's Vatican, the Spanish Crown, and the special avenues of promotion open to him through his status as an Italian Jesuit are easily distilled from the publishing history of Gilij's *Saggio*, its paratext, its contents and their organization, and finally Gilij's correspondences with Girolamo Tiraboschi, which reveal how Gilij worked to form alliances with other ex-Jesuit, Italian intellectuals with whom he shared a specific world view and set of beliefs.

Viewed through the lens of this unique Italian/Spanish cultural moment, Gilij's paratextual material reads like a program for Italian intellectual authority in the field of New World accounts. This material opens with a dedication to Pope Pius VI, successor to Clement XIV, less than two years following Clement XIV's quandary over pressure to eliminate the Jesuits, which was so intense that contemporary historians attribute his untimely death to a gradual "poisoning" from within over guilt associated with the closure of the order (see Sismondi [1807–1815] 1815–1818, 16: 338). Post-expulsion, Clement XIV became the preferred victim of ex-Jesuits throughout the world. As Niccolò Guasti has shown in his monograph on the Italian exile of Spanish Jesuits, a voluminous amount of anti-Clement literature was published and disseminated throughout Europe by the exiled Jesuits now living in his backyard (see Guasti 2006, 232). The virulence of their invective precipitated Clement's precarious mental state, such that he became extremely ambivalent about his own motives for imposing the closure of the order. Nowhere is this ambivalence clearer than in his deathbed refusal to appoint a group of Jesuit-hating cardinals. His unwillingness to comply with the final wish of the anti-Jesuit faction left maneuvering room for pro-Jesuit groups to lobby for a pope who, at the very least, would be neutral. Thus ambiguously situated with respect to the Jesuit question, Count Giovanni Angelo Braschi, Pius VI, was believed by some to be a supporter and by others a detractor of the Jesuit cause. The ambiguity of his position served him and people like Gilij well. Pius VI was able to chart an able path, satisfying the Spanish Crown on the one hand, while favouring former Jesuits in Rome, such as Gilij, whose scientific work would be published by the Vatican Press, a salient example of the ways in which Pius worked with the anti-Counter-Reformation Jesuits to promote a science-friendly Catholicism.[7]

In the dedication, Gilij compares himself to Pliny, who had dedicated his own history of the natural world to Tito Vespasiano. Recognizing Pliny's importance as a model for a divulgatory work with political implications, Gilij establishes his right to share Pliny's glory as an erudite, enlightening figure. Gilij is shedding light on a part of the world that was unknown to Pius VI, and had been documented through the work of his mentor, Gumilla:

> Pliny offered Europe, Asia and a small part of Africa to his prince. I, before my Sovereign, place, albeit not without trepidation, America. Not all of America, (since neither zeal nor life could support such an effort) but indeed that part of America where, through divine intervention, I lived as a missionary for many years ("Ma quella di Plinio, comecchè di forastiere cose tratti ancor essa, e meglio di me indubitatamente le tratti, non mai però a quella parte di mondo si stese, a cui la mia mercè di tempi più prosperi, è pervenuta. Egli l'Europa, e l'Asia, egli parte scarsa dell'Africa propose al suo principe. Io innanzi al mio Sovrano metto, benchè non senza timore, l'America. Non già tutta [poichè nè lena mi reggerebbe, nè vita] ma quella, in cui per divina disposizione stetti missionario molt'anni" [Gilij 1780–1784, 1: vii–viii]).

The "sovereign" referred to by Gilij is the pope, not the king of Spain, yet Gilij uses the rhetoric of possession reserved by explorers for the Spanish Crown. Gilij's verbatim use of such language is hopeful. Like a new Columbus, Gilij delivers lands and souls to an Italian "sovereign"; thus behind the rhetoric of respectful admiration and dedication, Gilij's sense of the importance of his *Saggio* as breaking new ground is apparent. While in the past such works would be dedicated to reigning sovereigns, Gilij explains that it is far more important to dedicate such a work to the successor of Saint Peter, for through his work, represented by his *Saggio*, he, Filippo Salvatore Gilij, is delivering directly into the Pope's hands a new group of Catholics: "[T]he Orinoquians, a people hardly known at all in Italy, prostrate themselves before you, full of that salutary faith, which unites their hearts to the Church, to their sovereigns, to their pastors and to this Holy See, the center of true belief" ("Gli Orinochesi, gente appenachè nota all'Italia, vi si prostrano innanzi, di quella salutari fede ripieni, che unisce alla Chiesa, unisce a' loro sovrani, e pastori, congiunge a questa santa Sede, al centro della vera credenza, i loro cuori" [Gilij 1780–1784, 1: ix]).

Noteworthy in this vein is the letter written by Pier Luigi Galletti, Bishop of Cirene, immediately following Gilij's dedicatory letter to the Pope authorizing publication. Galletti's letter provides intellectual grist to the normally formulaic letter of ecclesiastical approbation. Galletti was a rising Vatican star whose erudition had been duly noted by open-minded, anti-Jesuit Catholic luminaries such as Pope Benedict XIV (1675–1758) and Cardinal Domenico Silvio Passionei (1682–1761) in the previous generation. When Giovanni Angelo Braschi became Pope Pius VI in 1775, he quickly promoted Galletti with the honorific title "Bishop of Cirene" and rewarded him with handsome emoluments to go with it. Not one to sit on his laurels, Galletti reviewed manuscripts for the publishing arm of the Vatican, offering scholarly and censorial oversight in literary matters (see Salvioni 1793, 1–2).[8] His letter of approval is therefore of far greater importance than a simple censorial pass. It constitutes a professional endorsement from a highly placed and well-respected man of Catholic letters. Galletti was upholding the literary policies of Pius VI regarding the publication of works of former Jesuits now living in Rome, in which an attempt was being made to carve out an Italo-Vatican editorial presence in matters related to the New World. Galletti's letter hints at a possible controversy and a sense of rivalry over Gilij's having written a work covering the same natural history and peoples as Joseph Gumilla's 1741 *El Orinoco ilustrado.* Though Gumilla was Gilij's predecessor in Orinoco, the Bishop's letter emphasizes the originality of Gilij's work:

> To those who know of the work of the famous P. Gumilla containing the history of the Orinoco, which he wrote in his native language, Spanish, and then, thanks to the applause with which the public received it, it was translated into French, and it might seem that the diligent and erudite gentleman, Father Filippo Salvatore Gilij has undertaken a superfluous task by illustrating the region already written up by Gumilla. But that is certainly not the case; for if one compares Gilij's work with Gumilla's, it will soon become apparent that although the illustrious and well-deserving Spanish missionary can pride himself on having been the first to provide us with news about such a vast country, our author now has the esteem to have been able to meld together those insights and new discoveries that were missing from the above-mentioned Gumilla, whose work Gilij has sagaciously corrected at key points so as to render accurate a work of this kind. Having then carefully checked this work, commissioned to me by Rmo P. Maestro del S.P.A. I am convinced that there this work will encounter no difficulty in being published, since it contains nothing against our holy faith or our good morals ("A coloro, che hanno notizia dell'opera del celebre, P. Gumilla contenente la storia dell'Orinoco, ch'egli scrisse nella sua natìa lingua Spagnuola, e poi per l'applauso, con cui il pubblico la ricevette, tradotta fu

nell'idioma Francese, parrà, che il diligente ed erudito signor abate Filippo Salvadore Gilij abbia a nostri giorni intrapreso un superfluo assunto col ritrattarne. Ma non è certamente così; poichè se si confronterà questo di lui lavoro con quello, ben subito si scorgerà, che se l'insigne e benemerito missionario Spagnuolo ha il vanto di essere stato il primo a darci notizie de sì vasto paese, hà ora il nostro autore il pregio di averne potuto ragionare con quella copia di cognizioni, e di nuove scoperte, che mancano nel suddetto Gumilla, quale altresì egli corregge opportunamente in punti assai importanti per rendere accurate un'opera di questo genere. Avendola io adunque per commissione del Rmo P. Maestro del S.P.A. riveduta attentamente, sono persuaso, che e non vi dovrà essere difficultà per la pubblicazione, poichè nulla contiene contro la, santa Fede, o i buoni costumi, che anzi è molte volte edificante, e che sarà per essere molto grata e dilettevole a quei, che se ne provvederanno. Da S. Callisto il 17. Agosto 1780, P.L. Vescovo di Cirene" [Gilij 1780–1784, 1: ix]).

Gilij capitalized on the French critique, underscoring in his own preface how he could offer new insights and discoveries about the Orinoco region that were missing from Gumilla. The flawed nature of some of Gumilla's claims had been widely disseminated through Marc-Antoine Eidous's 1758 French translation, in which a detailed rendering of these errors was given in an essay-like translator's preface (Eidous's "Avertissement du traducteur" in Gumilla's *Histoire naturelle*). In his letter, the Bishop has foreshadowed Gilij's own comments about Italian accounts of the New World with respect to the Spanish ones, a subject that broached a centuries-old dispute in the documenting of the New World. It also stands as evidence of a newer, albeit related, escalating debacle that pit Spanish letters against Italian letters. The dire consequences of Spanish cultural and literary isolation imposed by the Spanish Crown in the seventeenth century were now building to a crescendo in a European context that had taken up the mantra of Spanish literary decadence heralded by the Père Bouhours in his 1687 *Manière de bien penser dans les ouvrages de l'esprit*, which categorized Italian language, literature and culture as solidly belonging to a defunct past, inaugurating French as the language and literature of the future. Moreover, Bouhours attributed to Italian literature a very precise responsibility for having spread the bad taste of the seventeenth century throughout Europe. Bouhours's treatise pitting the Ancients (Spain and Italy) against the Moderns (France) is considered one of the most destructive salvos fired against Italy in France's quest for cultural hegemony at the end of the seventeenth century. Italians and

Spaniards were immediately placed on the defensive, writing apologies for their literary traditions and their beneficially formative influence.[9]

In addition to Tiraboschi and Bettinelli, another Jesuit would play a prominent role in this debate: Ludovico Antonio Muratori, Tiraboschi's predecessor as librarian to the Este family in Modena. Muratori took up the mantle in 1703 to write *Primi disegni della republica letteraria d'Italia* ("First designs of a literary republic") followed by his *Riflessioni sul buon gusto* ("Reflections on good taste"). The examples cited here constitute but a very few samples of the proliferation of writing on this topic that emanated from the academies and learned societies of Italy. These literary clubs, of which the most famous was the Arcadia, had been accused by Muratori as bearing the brunt of the responsibility for the sorry state of affairs in Italian literature by promoting within their ranks the practice of bad taste and bad poetry through prizes and public ceremonies.[10] Ultimately, therefore, Italy was in competition with its own past. Among the ranks of Italian intellectuals, the desire to move beyond their poetic legacy prompted lively discussion in learned correspondences throughout the century.[11] An Italian Jesuit like Gilij offered a way out.

To be sure, this debate about the state of Italy's literary patrimony, citing the influence of Spanish letters as desultory, launched by a Frenchman, added yet another bone of contention to the mounting critique at the end of the eighteenth century of Spain as a colonizing power. This critique filled the pages of Raynal's *Histoire des deux Indes* as well as the *Encyclopédie méthodique*, culminating in Masson de Morvilliers's article "Espagne," in which the self-fashioned French geographer asks: "What do we owe Spain?" ("Que doit-on à l'Espagne?" [1782–1788, 565]). There were even a few Spaniards, such as the neoclassical poet Manuel José Quintana, who looked at his country through an Italian filter when he edited and published the *Introducción Histórica a la Colección de poesías castellanas* ("Historical introduction to the collection of Castillian poems"). Here he dubbed the work of Góngora and of Quevedo "monstrous extravagances" ("extravagancias monstruosas") while renewing the ranking of Tasso among the all-time classics next to Homer, Sophocles, Virgil, Horace, Racine and Pope (see Muñiz Muñiz 1999).

In the heated exchanges that characterized this debate within Italy, national sentiment was continually being stoked in one camp or the other. This situation was further exacerbated by the preponderance of erudite Spanish and Italian Jesuits who had been expelled from America in 1767 and given refuge in Faenza and Ferrara in Northern Italy. As these Jesuits gradually recovered from the physical, psychological, and spiritual impact of relocation to the Italian peninsula, they began to assess the wealth of experience amassed in missions spanning America. They began to write histories of their experiences, of the Indians among whom they lived, and the flora, fauna, and customs of the places they had lived and worked. Most of these ex-Jesuits wrote in Italian, having acquired the language during their exile; if they wrote in Spanish, their works were immediately translated into Italian and dedicated to an Italian cardinal or influential ecclesiastical figure, which facilitated future publication and distribution; however, the same did not hold true for Gilij. Once written and published in Italian it would not be translated into Spanish until the 1987. The reasons for this oversight will be explored further on in this paper.[12]

Jesuits always found themselves caught in the ambivalence of religious and political discourses, especially during the establishment of the missions for Spain in America. The missions of the Society of Jesus were not, and might not be permanent: they were meant to last only for a certain length of time. Jesuits could break this ecclesiastical law, because they had the political support of the king of Spain. Between the Spanish king and the Roman tradition, they chose to obey the former. Once on Italian soil, numerous problems emerged. Italian Jesuits affirmed their loyalties to the Vatican, while Spaniards gravitated toward the king of Spain. Jesuits of each stripe sought to gain political clout by pleasing both the Vatican and the King, while some tried to pit one against the other (see Baldini and Brizzi 2010). For Italian Jesuits, the appeal to the Vatican accompanied a sense of Italian nationalism, which manifested itself in literary taste and commentary, leading to comparisons of the Italian and Spanish accounts of discovery and conquest. Filippo Antonio Gilij embodies this position in his 1790 *Saggio di Storia Americana*, in which he roundly criticizes the Spanish chroniclers of the encounter as hyperbolic and partial, incapable, due to their literary tradition, of writing history objectively. Gilij explains that he has therefore taken on this task in the Italian tradition so as to restore the transmission of information and the removal of ignorance as the basis of historical writing, rather than amusement, of which he accused the Spanish historians.

One of the threads of Italian reaction to the Père Bouhours critique was a defense of the Italian literary tradition based upon concurrence with the French in their critique of Italian literary decadence that was attributable to Spanish corruption of Italian models. With so many Spanish Jesuits exiled in Italy and the literary policies promoted by both the Vatican and the Spanish Crown, it is not surprising to discover that the debate flares with renewed vigor, dividing along national lines in defense of Spanish or Italian cultural quality in written treatises, histories, and testimonials about the New World (see Guasti 2006, ch. 5: 451–533, "Ex Gesuiti e governo spagnolo: un opportunism reciproco" ["Ex-Jesuits and the Spanish government: reciprocal opportunism"]). Gilij's *Storia* offers an intriguing case of a Jesuit cultural artifact that is argued as promoting both the Italian/Vatican agenda as well as that of the Spanish Crown in its broader outlines. Gilij's preface in particular expresses his intention to rehabilitate Italian letters through the *Saggio*. Gilij immediately interjects the Italian thread in his preface by referring to Italy's centuries-long passion for receiving news of the New World, lamenting, however, the paucity of information that arrived and the quality of what little did come through. Concerning the information available, Gilij took an extremely critical stance, citing the Spanish goal of amusing the reader as the sole criterion for writing books about America:

> They [these books] are all considered good as long as they entertain. But besides the damage they do, these books do not remove the readers' ignorance, which should be the goal of those who write histories. Instead, these books increase and infinitely stimulate the readers' ignorance ("Tutti sono buoni, purche divertano. Ma questi libri, oltre al danno, che spesso apportano, l'ignoranza non tolgono de' lettitori, che pur dovrebbe aversi in mira de chi scrive storie; l'accrescon anzi, e la fomentano infinitamente" [Gilij 1780–1784, 1: xiii–xiv]).

Gilij then recalls the three centuries that have passed since the moment when Columbus left from Italian shores in search of America. Gilij inscribes the voyage among the great voyages of antiquity, laying claim to Columbus's voyage for Italy while noting the glorious role that Italians played in the discovery of the New World. He praises the purity of the sources that relayed the news of the discoveries – for example, Oviedo and Gomara – and the Italian telling of the discovery in the texts of Giovan Battista Ramusio (see Àlvarez Peláez 2000). Having recalled the purity of the first accounts, Gilij turns once again to the modern accounts, criticizing, this time, the writings of the *philosophes*, such as Denis Diderot's *Supplement au Voyage de Bougainville* or Guillaume Raynal's *Histoire des deux Indes*, which sought to understand the wisdom of indigenous systems of knowledge while imagining how the Western world might benefit from them. Gilij's pride in his Jesuit training as a missionary and his first-hand experience as an educator and proselytizer provoke a reaction that thoroughly dismisses those "who hold up for our edification *Cannibals* and *Esquimos,* and such stolid nations [...]. Lo and behold a *Casique* who climbs to the podium, a few, self-appointed nude people, to instruct us" ("e ci sì dan per maestri i Canibali, gli Esquimèsi, e si fatte stolide nazioni [...] Ed ecco montare in cattedra un *Casìche,* un regolo di poche nude personi, per erudirci" [Gilij 1780–1784, 1: xvi]). Yet Gilij's endorsement of his work as a missionary and his accomplishments should not be read as a disparaging assessment of the Indians of the Orinoco, but rather as a recognition of their intelligence and therefore ability to become civilized and educated. This view is further emphasized by Gilij in his Preface, when he discusses his approach to studying the abundant Indian tribes that inhabited the territory where he established his mission and the surrounding areas. Rather than perpetuate the reaction to and documenting of marvel at possession, Gilij's interest lay in the penetrating of the secrets of indigenous languages, customs, and habits in the interest of understanding who these people were. The human subject interested Gilij as it had his intellectual forebear, Ludovico Antonio Muratori, whose 1743 work, *Il cristianesimo felice nelle missioni dei padri della Compagnia di Gesù nel Paraguai,* on the Jesuit missions of the Guaraní in Paraguay offered a balanced assessment of the economic interests of vying groups of Spaniards, Criollos, and Jesuits. Muratori recognized the intellectual capacity of the Guaraní, citing their many accomplishments. He also noted, however, that the education policies of the Jesuits limited access to Spanish language education. As John J. Crocitti has noted, Muratori considered the Guaraní underutilized, and interpreted as ethnocentrically biased the European denigration of the cognitive capacity of indigenous peoples (see Crocitti 2002).

Had Gilij not passed away in 1789, his *Saggio* might have garnered the recognition it clearly deserved in its time. He also worked tirelessly to publicize and disseminate his work, which was written in the genre of the *Saggio,* or essay, rather than the letter, history, or account. In contrast with the writings of Clavigero and Gumilla, for example, which began circulating beyond Jesuit circles almost immediately thanks to swift translations and new editions, Gilij's *Saggio* lay dormant after his death in 1789. It was available only to those who could read Italian, among whom we find Alexander von Humboldt, who profited from it greatly in preparation for his own explorations and their rendering in his *Personal Narrative of Travel to the Equinoctial Regions of the New Continent during the Years 1799–1804.* It was not translated into Spanish until 1987, almost two centuries after first being published in Italian. It has only now begun retroactively to attract the attention of scholars, in particular anthropologists and linguists, who have been finding scientifically sound material for research, thanks to Gilij's comparative methods and the continual mode in which he interrogated his material throughout the four volumes.

Gilij's *Saggio di Storia Americana* also functions as a response to mentor Joseph Gumilla's 1741 *El Orinoco Illustrado* (reprinted in 1745 and in 1791 respectively) some forty years later. In order to understand Gilij's critique and rewriting of Gumilla, it is important to read them through the difference in their status as Jesuits – Gumilla, a Spaniard, writing pre-expulsion, and Gilij writing post-expulsion from within Italy at the behest of the Spanish Crown, yet in at least equal measure to please the Pope with the return of an Italian voice to New World accounts and narratives. The two accounts, when taken together, demonstrate the evolution in Jesuit thinking about indigenous populations that Réal Ouellet and Mylène Tremblay delineated in their readings of travel narratives and beyond. They noted the emergence of the "reasonable Indian" in Antoine Simon Le Page du Pratz's work as an intellectual being who critiqued his own culture and society. Though Pratz was merely placing his own critique of Indian culture in the mouths of the Indians themselves, this third "reasonable Indian," who expanded the possibility of European-constructed Indian identities beyond the peaceful and savage Indian into a potential European interlocutor, in Gilij's account, is now seen as intellectually independent in his critique of European religion and belief systems and a master of language and rhetoric (see Ouellet and Tremblay 2001). Indeed, Gilij's heavy focus on language, conversation, and discourse (the entire third volume of his work is devoted to these topics as they relate to the indigenous populations that inhabited the missions) can be linked to the trajectory of language and language questions that were being debated when Gilij first left Italy as a boy of nineteen in 1741, questions whose relevance had not abated when he returned in the 1770s. Astute student of culture that he was, Gilij's text shows a profound awareness for the many issues regarding language, usage, and its implications for both the Italian and Indian languages he so diligently studied and documented. Gilij immediately differentiates between the use of Spanish and Italian as a means of cultural transfer about the New World. He faults Spanish accounts as being flawed due to the almost universal tendency for exaggeration among Spaniards. These of course were the flaws commonly attributed to Italians and to the Italian language by the French in their European politics of cultural hegemony of Europe. Here, Gilij is using one of the most common critiques against the Spanish that the French habitually made against the Italians: the inferior rational quality of the language. He is also adamant about maintaining linguistic purity in his text. He explains that all Spanish terms will be rendered in Italian, reflecting as well debates that were common among academies throughout Italy, including the Accademia dei Pugni[13]:

> Everyone can see that I promote a use of language assisted by reason in my History, one that is common to all ancient writers, but which has been cast aside today. I always give foreign words Italian endings; I don't know why only the Spaniards or the French are allowed to make the many Indian words their own, providing them with endings in accordance with the genius of their own languages. Must we not apply the same right to ourselves, do the same in our language? What could be more annoying, or of greater bother, just to give you an example, than to find in a book: The Maipures went with the Otomacos! Come on. Let us simply say, say more correctly and without barbarism, The Maipuri went with the Ottomachi; in this way we imitate the ancient Italians, the Latins, and the Spaniards, and let's imitate, if we like, the French. Italians have too great a bias in favour of foreign languages. In order to curb this tendency, I will always provide in my lists of words, the Italian equivalent of the Orinocan word. I will give the names of rivers and waterfalls in the three languages as well as compile a catalogue of the nouns referring to the Orinocan nation in three languages so that the lovers of foreign expressions will be happy and everyone else can choose freely ("Vedrà ognuno in questa mia storia promosso un uso il quale, benchè assistito dalla ragione, e commune a tutti gli antichi ascittori, a' dì nostri vien dismesso, senza fondamento de molti, i quali scrivono de' paesi forastieri. Io do sempre a' vocaboli stranieri l'Italiana terminazione; nè so capire, perchè essendo agli Spagnuoli, o Francesi permesso di render proprie tante Indiche voci, terminandole secondo il genio della lor lingua, non dobbiamo noi, usando lo stesso diritto, fare il medesimo nella nostra lingua. Che cosa più increscevole, a cagion di esempio, e di maggior intoppo in leggendo, che il trovar ne' libri: *Andarono I Maipures cogli Otomacos! Eh via. Dicasi pure, e si dirà più propriamente, e senza barbarismo; Andarono I Maipuri cogli Ottomachi*; e imitiamo gli'Italiani antichi; imitiamo i Latini, e gli Spagnuoli; imitiamo se così ci piace, i Francesi. Ma è troppo il pendio, che hanno pe' forastieri linguaggi gl'Italiani. Per consolare anche questi, io oltre alle voci Spagnuole, e Indiane, che spesso nella mia storia si troveranno nelle piccole note a piè di pagina; tesso sul bel principio un catalogo de' nomi delle Orinochesi nazioni in tre lingue. In tre lingue altresi do i nomi de' diversi fiumi, e delle cascate dell'Orinoco; e cosi rimarranno i geniali di forestierismo contenti, e, agli altri sarà libera la scelta" [Gilij 1780–1784, 1: xiii–xiv]).

Scholars increasingly recognize Gilij as the pioneer in the study of South American languages, indeed, the person who, according to the linguist L. Campbell, had the greatest impact on early South American linguistics. His interest in languages and his ability to learn them rapidly gave him a broad platform for comparison. This led to his recognition of sound patterns and to his development of the evolutionary tree of South American languages. Indigenous languages of the region were divided into nine, interrelated families, which he called "mother languages" ("lingue matrici"). As a number of linguists have observed, his linguistic insights precede those of Sir William Jones. They also provided a baseline study for the linguistic work of Spanish Jesuit Lorenzo Hervas y Panduro whose studies focused on the languages of Mexico.[14] However, working as they do with the Spanish translation of Gilij's work (see Gilij 1987), and being specialists of South American indigenous languages and historically, Spain (as colonizer) and the Jesuits (as a Spanish-founded and -based order), these linguists have missed the underlying Italian subtext that so strongly informs Gilij's linguistic considerations to the same degree that it has informed the cultural policies and strategies of the Italian Vatican and the Italian Jesuits that we have outlined above.

Lourdes Giordani has noted how Gilij's *Saggio di Storia Americana* is rife with "vivid descriptions and conclusions that enable the critical reader to grasp the socio-cultural complexity of the region (e.g., its multiethnic character), the contradictions of mission life, and the uncertainties that develop and linger in the minds of those who dwell in such a zone of constant intercultural exchange and in the contact zone. Indeed, the *Saggio* can be considered the most relevant extant text for the study of native societies inhabiting the Middle Orinoco in the 18th century" (Giordani 1995, para. 6). Margaret Ewalt's work on Gumilla allows us to reflect further on the unique relationship that the Jesuit fathers forged with the indigenous populations through the promotion of inculturation, which "allowed missionaries to participate in a unique space of accommodation, mediation, and reciprocity with Amerindian philosophers" (Ewalt 2006, 14). The Spanish Crown was particularly beholden to the Jesuit missions in the Middle Orinoco run by Gumilla and Gilij, for, during the period they were there until the expulsion in 1767, conquest and colonization of this area were in their infancy, resulting in a largely uncolonized population that demonstrated a high degree of cultural and linguistic pluralism about which Gilij wrote in his *Saggio*. European and Carib Indian raids were still the rule rather than the exception; thus the Spanish Crown was far from achieving its usual degree of territorial and sociopolitical consolidation and depended more heavily on the Jesuit missions in Orinoquia that they did on missions in other parts of South America.

Against this backdrop of strife and negotiation, Gilij carved out a distinct place in the history of Jesuit accounts in South America by charting the linguistic diversity of the indigenous populations among whom he resided. This focus may have been a strategy for survival as well as for carrying out, to the extent possible, both his conversion duties as a Jesuit and his economic stewardship of the mission. In a region as volatile and unsettled as the Middle Orinoco, understanding linguistic difference and nuances of meaning became important to differentiate between the indigenous populations of the region as well as to understand the disputes and questions that may have been important for Gilij to settle or circumvent (Sweet 1994, 88). Gilij's detailed discussion of these disputes is a continual reminder to the reader that the Orinoco region was far from being settled and was still, very much, a contact zone. Gilij's primary interlocutors were the several tribes of indigenous peoples among whom he resided. His nuanced view of their languages, culture, appearance, and habits chapter after chapter in his four-volume work are striking in that they demonstrate Gilij's profound understanding of the peoples he lived with and his respect for their cultures and intellect. His text constitutes a new chapter in thinking about the intellectual capacity of indigenous populations and the need to learn their languages to probe the complexity of their cultures. The benefits of Gilij's thinking for future generations have been of paramount importance for linguists, as we have already stated; yet they would prove to be of almost immediate importance to Alexander von Humboldt, who relied heavily on the Jesuit accounts for information about the New World as he prepared to embark on his journey to transverse the southern half of the Americas. Charles Minguet's 1969 monograph *Alexandre de Humboldt historien et géographe de l'Amérique espagnole, 1799–1804*, enumerates the many textual influences that shaped Humboldt's view of the colonial world, including the Jesuit accounts of Joseph Gumilla and Filippo Salvatore Gilij. Indeed, Gumilla and Gilij are of particular importance due to their documenting of the peoples, customs, and languages of the Middle Orinoco, about which Humboldt wrote extensively. However, Minguet's analysis is limited to identifying specific instances in Humboldt's text where Gumilla and Gilij are cited in reference to particular occurrences that corroborate Humboldt's findings some forty years later.

Closer reading and comparison of Gumilla, Gilij, and Humboldt sheds light on the more systemic range of this Jesuit influence on Humboldt's thinking, particularly in the area of the world view, belief systems, and thought processes of the indigenous peoples Humboldt encountered both inside and outside the missions; and while Humboldt generally disdained mission life, the enforced strictures of Catholic doctrines, and the Western World as destructive of indigenous cultures, he respected Jesuit thought, which he could also place in historical perspective. By the time Humboldt traveled through Latin America with Aimé Bonpland at the turn of the century, the Jesuits had been gone for nearly forty years. He often stayed at missions that had been run by the Jesuits pre-expulsion but had now been taken over by other Catholic orders. His direct experience and observations provided a set of data that he compared to what he had gleaned through the reading of Jesuit accounts published in the 1780s. Here, Gilij's discussion in the third volume of his *Saggio di Storia Americana* on the sophisticated rhetorical and reasoning skills of the shamans is reflected in Humboldt's consideration of both linguistic and conceptual problems with the Spaniard's hell, or *infierno*, when attempts were made to explain it to the Indians. Humboldt was critical of the mission life, yet fascinated by the extent to which the European and indigenous cultures clashed or melded. He concluded that the compatibility index of these disparate groups was largely a function of their ability to truly communicate. Indeed, Humboldt stayed in these missions, charting closely and analysing the miscommunication that kept the Indians and the Europeans from truly understanding each other. A striking case of intertextuality can be found if we compare with Gilij the following observation in Humboldt's *Relation historique du Voyage aux régions équinoxiales du Nouveau Continent* about the inability of the Chaymas, an Indian tribe in today's Venezuela, to communicate with the missionaries:

> It was a rather difficult task to explain dogmas to the neophytes, especially the ones who only had a very imperfect knowledge of the Spanish language. The similarity of sounds in Spanish confuses the poor Indians and puts the most whimsical ideas into their heads. For example, I saw a missionary labouring with great earnestness to prove that infierno (hell) and invierno (winter) were not one and the same thing but as different as heat and cold. The Chaymas know no other winter than the season of rains, so consequently they imagined that the "hell of the white man" was a place where

> the wicked are exposed to frequent showers. The missionary harangued in vain; it was impossible to efface the impression caused by the similarity between the two consonants (Humboldt [1852] 1995, 87).

Humboldt also noted that the majority of the Indians paid little more than lip service to the Christian faith. This also echoes Gilij's experiences in his attempts to Christianize the indigenous populations of the middle Orinoco. As we read Humboldt, we can hear Gilij's musings in the *Storia* about languages and conversion, especially in the astuteness of the shamans when it came to dismissing the notion of hell. Like Humboldt, Gilij focused a great part of his energies on Indian languages, of which he learned and wrote grammars for three. He was adamant about relating information about religion in the language of those he was trying to convert, declaring the pointlessness of trying to teach them about God in Spanish, indicating instead his experience in using their own languages to convert them. Rather than the monologue of the seventeenth-century preacher of fire and brimstone, of which there were any number of Jesuits in Baroque Italy, Gilij was far more interested in dialogic models that crossed boundaries of both class and gender. Gilij differentiates between speaking with servants, women, and the shamans with whom he shared a profound intellectual affinity. The rhetorical and dialogical models employed by Gilij in his *Saggio* deserve a far more careful treatment than we can provide here. However, implicit and explicit references to Italian models both as personal, internalized archives, and as a bridge to communication with an Italian readership abound. Gilij's attachment to Italian Renaissance models of discussion and dialogue and his admiration for the genius and subtlety of much indigenous conversation may well derive from a comparison of that conversation with the most sophisticated dialogic models found in the Italian rhetorical and behavior manuals of the Cinquecento, including Pietro Bembo's *Prosa della Volgar Lingua* (1525) and Baldissar Castiglione's *Il Cortigiano* (1528), while his recounting of anecdotes related to relationships between men and women, in which cleverness is used to momentarily circumvent marital taboos, immediately recalls Boccaccio's *Decameron* (see Gilij 1780–1784, 2: 92). Throughout the volumes, Gilij draws comparisons between the reality of indigenous habits and lifestyle and those of the Italians, such as when he compares the proximity of two indigenous languages to the similarity between the Neapolitan and Roman dialects to emphasize that communication was possible across related language systems (see 3: 117). Anthropological understanding of the inverse relationship between nudity and clothing for the Italians and the indigenous peoples was explained through a sophisticated set of cultural comparisons that never derided or mocked the indigenous peoples' practices. For example, Gilij explains in the second volume how the Indian women, when handed a piece of cloth by the missionaries to cover their genitalia, used it instead as a decorative scarf, underscoring the distance between sexual signs for Europeans and Indians, but most importantly the extent to which Gilij understood this distance and sought to communicate it as a system of sexual semiotics worthy of respect and understanding (see 3: 49). He also recognized the superior linguistic competence of the shamans, about whom he said that "[n]o one speaks languages better than they do" ("Niuno meglio di essi parla le lingue" [3: 95]). This comment subtly reveals the esteem that Gilij held for the cognitive, linguistic, and communicative abilities of the shamans, for the abilities he attributes to the shamans are those that were attributed to the Jesuits by their supporters and detractors alike. Indeed, the erudition and sophistication of the Italian Jesuits had already been observed in the seventeenth and eighteenth centuries for its intrinsic value, as well as for its disinterested political status with respect to Portuguese and Spanish colonial history (see Kamen 1967, 81).[15] Here, Gilij's *Saggio di Storia Americana* offers a provocative coda to this notion. Post-expulsion, in his newly imposed and embraced capacity as historian, Filippo Salvatore Gilij writes the history of America in a voice that can only be defined as that of an Italian Jesuit. The Italian voice that defends the tools of the peninsula's culture, erudition, and tradition in the wake of the expulsion is certainly too disinterested politically to defend the Spanish empire or to even write for a Spanish audience. Even a cursory reading of Gilij's four-volume text leaves an indelible impression of an Italian account, inspired by a postcolonial mentality that sees the Spanish empire in its rearview mirror. It comes as no surprise, then, that the Spanish Crown did not commission a Spanish translation of Gilij's *Saggio*, nor were they interested in the dissemination of an American history told from an Italian perspective.

NOTES

1 On the history of the popular missions in Italy, see Guidetti 1988, in particular pt. 2, "Missioni e missionari durante la soppressione (1773–1814)."

2 This desire and yearning for adventure and a better life that motivated young Italian men seeking acceptance into the Jesuit order is amply documented in a volume that publishes their letters; see Del Rio 1996.

3 Matthieu Raillard (2009) offers a provocative perspective on the infamous article by armchair geographer Nicolas Masson de Morvilliers, whose negative cultural assessment of the Spanish empire in his article "Espagne" created a public outcry upon its publication and circulation in Spain in 1783. Raillard views it as yet another example of "Spain's hybridized cultural identity" in which, Raillard argues, as has David Gies, national character and a sense of intrinsic inferiority plays itself out in numerous texts. Having an outsider, and a Frenchman, no less, point such a glaring and public accusation against Spain struck a new note on a chord that had heretofore been played only internally.

4 Following the publication of Masson de Morvilliers's article "Espagne," numerous writers responded to defend Spain. These are the same years in which Gilij was publishing his *Saggio*, and the sensitivity over the critique against Spain's literary patrimony is particularly evident in the most famous of the responses to the Masson de Morvilliers's polemic; see Forner 1786.

5 See Guasti 2006, 421: n. 107, for a discussion of the rapidly evolving historiography on the diversity of Jesuit identity both pre- and post-expulsion, which challenges the views of earlier historians who viewed the Jesuit personality as homogenous across nations. As we have stated earlier in the case of Gilij, these changes became far more pronounced post-expulsion and broke along national boundaries.

6 For further consideration of Tiraboschi and the cultural politics of his *Storia della letteratura italiana* within the context of the Republic of Letters, see Dainotto 2007. A succinct version of these same ideas may also be found in Dainotto 2006.

7 See Guasti 2006, 293, for a thorough discussion of the interaction between former Jesuits and elite Italian leaders, especially the Pope, in building the foundation for a scientifically and technologically forward-looking Church that could become a "player" in new economic enterprises involving the New World.

8 It would appear that the publisher himself prepared this volume, for no author is indicated, but the dedication is signed "Lo Stampatore." Salvioni refers to him as a close friend to whom he wishes to pay homage in the first chapter. His *Notizie spettanti alla vita di Pier Luigi Galletti* also contains two of the author's previously unpublished manuscripts; Salvioni published Gilij's text as well.

9 See Waquet 1989 for an in-depth treatment of the relationship between French and Italian intellectuals from the time of Louis XIV to the second half of the eighteenth century, the period in which the French made a concerted effort to surpass Italian culture as the point of reference in Europe

for literary, rhetorical, and scientific innovation. An understanding of this race for cultural hegemony not only explains the concerted efforts made by France to dominate culture through language, but it also provides the background for the attacks against Spain that found Italy in the middle, torn between former cultural icon for Europe and now-tarnished model contaminated by Spain. A sequel to Waquet's seminal text charting the next fifty years, 1750–1800, would certainly need to address in no small measure the triangular relationship of France, Italy, and Spain.

10 On the cusp of the eighteenth and nineteenth centuries, poet and novelist Ugo Foscolo was one of the most vehement critics of the Arcadia and the bad taste in poetry fostered by Italian academies. He exhorted Italians to reconnect with their language and literary traditions and to eschew the stereotyping of Italian culture that was rampant in grand tour Italy. Pertinent in this regard is the following quote, taken from Foscolo's "Life of Pius VI." Foscolo considered him an unprincipled pope who had no interest in preserving Italian culture: "Pius was a patron of genius; but preferred the fine arts to literature or science – and he was neither a very learned nor a very impartial patron. His greatest weakness was in patronizing or tolerating the Arcadians – the name is not very celebrated, we believe, in this country. Yet all the curious are aware, that here has existed at Rome, for a hundred and fifty years, an academy or corporation of poets, under that fantastic appellation – and richly deserving all the ridicule with which it is pregnant. It was established at a time when such affectations were more easily tolerated, and for a good enough purpose; but for many years it had become a liability and a nuisance, filling Italy with its shepherds and affiliated societies. Any blockhead who could produce a sonnet and a sequin gained easy admittance into the Arcadia, the credentials and patent of the poet, a pastoral name, and a grant of lands in some romantic district of the ancient Arcadia. Even now, a visitor no sooner arrives in Rome, than he receives a visit from the Secretaries of this Academy, who offer him the Laurel and a copy of verses already prepared, which are to be recited in the name of the generous visitor. Now and then too, at their public meetings, they place the crown on the head of some traveler, who is vain and silly enough to play the hero in these farces: But those who submit to this coronation, are generally *improvisatori* by profession, who, to increase their cache at home, go to Rome to purchase this honour, much in the way that quacks in medicine purchase their degrees from some venal university" ([Foscolo] 1819, 279). Foscolo's essay first appeared without the author's name in the *Edinburgh Review* 62 (1819, 271–95). Despite some reservations, Foscolo was generally happy with Jeffrey's rendering of his text into English.

11 In a letter to Isodoro Bianchi, Giovanni Bianchi discussed the poetic compositions of a certain Abbot Ferri and the Abbot's delusions of poetic grandeur, both in regard to his own poetic aspirations that those he thought should be transmitted to young seminarians who Bianchi believed needed training in prose: "[A]lthough Abbot Ferri composes a great deal in Latin verses, and even more in vernacular verses, I don't believe that the Muses have befriended him, for in conversation the other day with a prominent individual, and telling him that it was necessary to accustom the young people in the seminary to write in prose, especially in Latin prose, and to leave behind the verse writing, especially in the vernacular. This person answered that he who criticized vernacular poetry was someone who didn't know how to compose poetry and that Abbot Ferri was one of the best professors in Italy when it came to Latin. The first proposition might be true, but the second can easily be considered doubtful, since any person might cast doubts upon that statement, that gentleman added that currently in Italy there are Italian poets who surpass Dante, Petrarca, Ariosto and the like, but let us leave this behind" ("[B]enche il Sig. Abe. Ferri componga molto e in versi latini, e in versi volgari massimamente, io credo che egli non abbia le muse troppo amiche, ed alcuni giorni prima parlando io qui con un personaggio, e dicendogli che bisognava assuefare i Giovani de' Seminari a scrivere in prosa, e specialmente latine, e tralasciare tanti versi e specialmente di poesia volgare. Questi mi rispose che chi biasimava la poesia volgare era segno che in essa non sapea comporre e che il Sig. Abe. Ferri nel Latino ere uno de' primi professori d'Italia. La prima proposizione può esser vera; ma la seconda facilmente sarà posta in dubbio, siccome ognuno porrà indubbio ciò, che m'aggiunse quel Signore, che ora in Italia ci sono de' poeti italiani, che superano il Dante, il Petrarca, l'Ariosto, e simili. Ma lasciamo queste cose" [Biblioteca Ambrosiana T-125, 21 June 1764]).

12 Among the many foundational texts of American history that were either written and first published in Italian or that immediately appeared in an Italian translation, we may include Francisco Javier Clavijero's *Storia Antica del Messico* ("Ancient History of Mexico"), published in Cesena in 1780; Juan de Velasco's *Historia del Reino de Quito en la América meridional* published in1789, written in Italy in Spanish and immediately translated and published in Italian; and Juan Nuix y Perpiñà's *Riflessioni imparziali sopra l'umanità degli Spagnuoli nell'Indie contro i pretesi filosofi e politici per servire di lume alle storie de'signori Raynal e Robertson* ("Impartial reflections on the humanity of the Spaniards in the Indies, against the presumed to be philosophers and politicians, for elucidating the histories of Raynal and Robertson") published in1782 (first Spanish edition). Juan Nuix y Perpiñà provides an example of Spanish nationalism as it began to develop among

the exiled Jesuits living in Italy, in particular the acute form of this national sentiment harboured by Spaniards of Catalan origin. Miguel Batllori, who has studied the Hispano-Italian culture of the exiled Jesuits, calls our attention to the particular case of the Catalan Jesuits' defence of Spain in his comments on Paul Hazard's observations about late eighteenth-century nationalisms: "Paul Hazard has noted that during the enlightenment, in a century in which European culture appeared under the banner of French hegemony as an inevitable reality, individual nationalisms were nonetheless extremely vibrant, and that Spanish nationalism could be located most especially among those Jesuits who had been exiled in Italy after their expulsion in 1767. However, what Hazard failed to notice was the paradox that among the most exuberant of the nationalists to be counted were the Catalans, who made up the largest percentage among those exiled coming from the crown of Aragon ("Paul Hazard ha notado que en un siglo en que la unidad de la cultura europea bajo la hegemonía francesa parece un hecho indudable, los nacionalismos están aún muy vivos, y que el nacionalismo español se centra precisamente en los jesuitias exiliados en Italia. Pero Hazard no ha advertido la paradoja de que entre los nacionalistas más exaltados se cuentan precisamente los catalanes y demás exiliados procedentes de la corona aragonesa" [Batllori 1966, 583]). The Catalan Juan Nuix (y Perpiña) fits Batllori's description perfectly. He rejected criticisms levied by the philosophers of the Enlightenment and justified the policy of the Spanish crown in its treatment of the Indians in its possessions in the Americas and in the Far East. In turn he criticizes the actions of the English, French, and Germans. He may have also wanted to criticize the actions of the Italians, but did not dare. As we know from a number of accounts, the expelled Jesuits, especially the Spaniards, found themselves in a compromised position. While publishing histories in Italian garnered favour for them with the Pope, they were at the same time concerned about gaining the support of the king of Spain, who had begun to emerge for them as an important point of national reference, nostalgic, as they now were, for Spain and the New World missions they had been forced to leave behind.

13 See Alessandro Verri's "Rinunzia avanti notaio degli autori del presente foglio periodico al Vocabolario della Crusca" ("Notarized renunciation of the Crusca dictionary by the authors of the present periodical") for a sarcastic assessment of the Crusca Academy's prohibition against Italianizing words from other languages. Verri, instead, proclaims the right to Italianize "le parole francesi, tedesche, inglesi, turche, greche, arabe sclavone" ("French, German, English, Turkish, Greek, Arabic, and Slavonic words" [Verri [1764] 1993, 48]) in much the same tone used here by Gilij to Italianize Indian words. One of the most strident polemics taken up by the Milanese

Accademia dei Pugni ("Academy of the Fists") in their periodical *Il Caffé* was the ironclad hold on linguistic usage wielded by the Crusca Academy, whose charge it was to censor any writing that veered even slightly from usage as practiced by the canonical authors of Florentine usage – in particular Dante, Boccaccio, and Petrarca.

14 See Pendleton 2003, 6. Pendleton draws from the work of Campbell, Darnell, Gray, and Fiering in his thesis. These four experts have discussed Gilij's contributions in their work.

15 J. S. Cummins notes that a Portuguese Jesuit missionary remarked "the Italians understand so much better than us things which so little concern them"; as late as the last decades of the eighteenth century, Lord McCartney commented that the Italian fathers in Peking were "more learned and liberal than the Portuguese who still retain a considerable share of ancient bigotry and rancour" (Cummins 1993, 66–67).

BIBLIOGRAPHY

Àlvarez Peláez, Raquel. 2000. "La Historia natural en tiempos del emperador Carlos V. La importancia de la conquista del nuevo mundo." *Revista de Indias* 60 (218): 13–31.

Anonymous. 1786. "*Nachrichten vom Lande Guiana, dem Orinocoflus und den dortigen Wilden.* Aus dem Italienischen des Abbt Philip Salvator Gilii auszugsweise übersetzt." *Allgemeine Literatur-Zeitung* 92 (2): 116–20 and 93 (2): 121–3.

Arvelo-Jiménez, Nelly, and Horacio Biord-Castillo. 1989. *Reflexiones antropológicas sobre el "Ensayo de Historia Americana."* Caracas: UCAB.

Baldini, Ugo, and Gian Paolo Brizzi. 2010. *La presenza in Italia dei gesuiti iberici espulsi. Aspetti religiosi, politici, culturali.* Bologna: Clueb.

Batllori, Miguel, SJ. 1966. *La Cultura hispano-italiana de los jesuitas expulsos. Españoles-Hispanoamericanos-Filipinos (1767–1814).* Madrid: Gredos.

Belton, Benjamin Keith. 2003. *Orinoco Flow. Culture, Narrative, and the Political Economy of Information.* Lanham, MD: The Scarecrow Press.

Cañizares-Esguerra, Jorge. 1998. "Spanish America in Eighteenth-Century European Travel Compilations: A New 'Art of Reading' and the Transition to Modernity." *Journal of Early Modern History* 2 (4): 329–49.

–. 2005. "How Derivative Was Humboldt? Microcosmic Nature Narratives in Early Modern Spanish America and the (Other) Origins of Humboldt's Ecological Sensibilities." In *Colonial Botany: Science, Commerce, and Politics in the early modern world*, eds. Londa Schiebinger and Claudia Swan, 148–68. Philadelphia: University of Pennsylvania Press.

Ciocchi, Carlo. 1794. *Lettera dell Ab. Carlo Ciocchi, Bibliotecario di S. A. S. il Sig. Duca di Modena, Al dottissimo Signor Abate Francescantonio Zaccaria Risguardante*

alcune più importanti notizie della Vita e dell'Opere Del Chiarissimo Sig. Cavaliere Abate Girolamo Tiraboschi, 5–15. Modena: La società tipografica.
Crocitti, John J. 2002. "The Internal Economic Organization of the Jesuit Missions Among the Guaraní." *International Social Science Review* 77 (1&3): 3–15.
Cummins, James S. 1993. *A Question of Rites: Friar Domingo Navarrete and the Jesuits in China.* Hants: Scholar Press.
Dainotto, Roberto Maria. 2006. "Girolamo Tiraboschi." In *Encyclopedia of Italian Literary Studies*, eds. Gaetana Marrone and Paolo Puppa, 1872–1873. London: Routledge.
–. 2007. "Republic of Letters. What is European Literature?". In *Europe (in Theory)*, ch. 3. Durham, NC: Duke University Press.
Del Rio, Domenico. 1996. *I gesuiti e l'Italia: storia di passion, di trionfi e di amarezze.* Milano: Corbaccio.
Ewalt, Margaret. 2005a. "Father Gumilla, Crocodile Hunter? The Function of Wonder in *El Orinoco ilustrado.*" In *El saber de los jesuitas, historias naturales y el Nuevo Mundo*, eds. Luis Millones Figueroa and Domingo Ledesma, 303–33. Madrid: Iberoamericana.
–. 2005b. "Frontier Encounters and Pathways to Knowledge in the New Kingdom of Granada," *The Colorado Review of Hispanic Studies* 3: 41–55.
–. 2006. "Crossing Over: Nations and Naturalists in *El Orinoco ilustrado.* Reading and Writing the Book of Orinoco Secrets." *Dieciocho* 29 (1): 1–25.
Forner, Juan Pablo. 1786. *Oración apologética por la España y su mérito literario, para que sirva de exornación al discurso leido por el abate Denina en la Academia de Ciencias de Berlín, respondiendo a la qüestion Qué se debe a España?* Madrid: Imprenta Real.
[Foscolo, Ugo]. 1819. "Life of Pius VI." *The Edinburgh Review* 62: 271–95.
Gilij [Gilii], Filippo Salvadore. 1780–1784. *Saggio di storia americana; o sia, Storia naturale, civile e sacra de'regni, e delle provincie spagnuole di Terra-Ferma nell' America Meridionale.* 4 vols. Roma: L. Perego erede Salvioni.
–. 1785. *Nachrichten von dem Lande Guiana; dem Oronocoflus, und den dortigen Wilden*, trans. Matthias Christian Sprengel]. Hamburg: Carl Ernst Bohn.
–. 1965. *Ensayo de Historia Americana*, 3 vols., trans. Antonio Tovar. Caracas: Academia Nacional de Historia.
Giordani, Lourdes. 1995. "Speaking Truths or Absurdities: The Religious Dialogues Between Father Gilij and His Indian Contemporaries (18th Century, Venezuela)." In *LASA95 Papers Pilot Project*, ed. Latin American Studies Association. Available at: http://lanic.utexas.edu/project/lasa95/giordani.html. Accessed October 2013.
González Echevarría, Roberto. 1972. "'Semejante a la noche' de Alejo Carpentier: *Historia / Ficción.*" *Modern Language Notes* 87 (2): 272–85.
–. 1990. *Myth and Archive: A Theory of Latin American Narrative.* Cambridge: Cambridge University Press.
González Oropeza, Hermann, SJ. 1989. "Felipe Salvador Gilij, boceto biográfico y bibliográfico." *Montalbán* 21: 9–20.

Guasti, Niccolo. 2006. *L'Esilio italiano dei Gesuiti Spagnoli: identita, controllo sociale, e pratiche culturali (1767–1798)*. Roma: Edizioni di Storia e Letteratura.

Guidetti, Armando, SJ. 1988. *Le Missioni popolari: I Grandi gesuiti Italiani. Disegno storico-biografico delle missioni popolari dei gesuiti d'Italia dalle origini al Concilio Vaticano II.* Milano: Rusconi.

Gumilla, Joseph. 1741. *El Orinoco ilustrado, historia natural, civil y geographica de este gran río, y de sus caudalosas vertientes; govierno, usos, y costumbres de los Indios sus habitadores, con nuevas, y utiles noticias de animales, arboles frutos, aceytes, resinas, yervas, y raíces medicinales.* Madrid: Manuel Fernandez.

–. 1745. *El Orinoco ilustrado, y defendido, historia natural, civil y geographica de este gran río, y de sus caudalosas vertientes; govierno, usos, y costumbres de los Indios sus habitadores, con nuevas, y utiles noticias de animales, arboles frutos, aceytes, resinas, yervas, y raíces medicinales.* Madrid: Manuel Fernandez.

Gumilla, Joseph. [1745] 1963. *El Orinoco ilustrado y defendido [...]*, ed. Demetrio Ramos. Reprint, Caracas: Fuentes para la Historia Colonial de Venezuela.

–. 1758. *Histoire naturelle, civile et geographique de l'Orenoque, et des principales rivieres que s'y jettent*, trans. Marc-Antoine Eidous. Avignon: Veuve de F. Girard.

Harris, Steven. 2005. "Jesuit Scientific Activity in the Overseas Missions, 1570–1773." *Isis* 96: 71–9.

Helferich, Gerard. 2004. *Humboldt's Cosmos: Alexander von Humboldt and the Latin American Journey that Changed the Way We See the World.* New York: Gotham Books.

Humboldt, Alexander von. 1850. *Aspects of Nature, in Different Lands and Different Climates; with Scientific Elucidations*, trans. Elizabeth Juliana Leeves Sabine. Philadelphia: Lea and Blanchard.

–. 1852–1853. *Personal Narrative of Travels to the Equinoctial Regions of America, during the Years 1799–1804*, trans. and ed. Thomasina Ross. London: Henry G. Bohn.

–. 1970. *Relation historique du Voyage aux régions équinoxiales du Nouveau Continent,* 1852, 3 vols. Stuttgart: F. A. Brockhaus.

–. [1852] 1995. *Personal Narrative of a Journey to the Equinoctial Regions of the New Continent,* trans. 1852, Jason Wilson. London: Penguin Books.

Isaacs, Jorge. [1867] 1991. *María*, ed. Donald McGrady. Reprint, Madrid: Cátedra.

Jardine, Nicholas, James A. Secord, and Emma C. Spary. 1996. *Cultures of Natural History.* Cambridge: Cambridge University Press.

Journal des savans, combiné avec les Mémoires de Trévoux. 1758. Amsterdam: Rey.

Juan, Jorge, and Antonio de Ulloa. 1748. *Relacion historica del viage a la America Meridional hecho de orden de S. Mag. para medir algunos grados de Meridiano Terrestre e, y venir por ellos en conocimiento de la verdadera Figura, y Magnitud de la Tierra, con otras varias Observaciones Astronomicas, y Phisicas: Por Don Jorge Juan, Comendador de Aliaga, en el Orden de San Juan, Socio correspondiente de la Real Academia de Ciencias de Paris, y Don Antonio de Ulloa, de la Real Sociedad de Londres; ambos Capitanes de Fragata de la Real Armada.* Madrid: Antonio Marin.

Kamen, Henry. 1967. *Rise of Toleration.* New York: McGraw Hill.

La Condamine, Charles Marie de. 1745. *Relation abrégée d'un voyage fait dans l'interieur de l'Amérique Méridionale. Depuis la côte de la Mer du Sud, jusqu'aux côtes du Brésil & de la Guiane, en descendant la riviere des Amazones.* Paris: Veuve Pissot.

Labat, Jean-Baptiste. 1722. *Nouveau voyages aux isles de l'Amerique. Contentant l'histoire naturelle de ces pays, l'Origine, les Moeurs, la Religion & le Gouvernement des Habitans anciens & modernes [...]. Avec une Description exacte & curieuse de toutes ces Isles.* Paris: Pierre-Francois Giffart.

Langer, Erick, and Robert H. Jackson, eds. 1994. *The New Latin American Mission History.* Lincoln: University of Nebraska Press.

Latour, Bruno. 1979. *Laboratory Life: The Social Construction of Scientific Facts.* Beverley Hills, CA: Sage Publications.

Lee, Michael Radcliffe. 2005. "Curare: The South American Arrow Poison." *Journal of College Physicians of Edinburgh* 35 (1): 83–92.

Masson De Morvilliers, Nicolas. 1782–1788. "Espagne." In vol. 1 of *Encyclopédie méthodique, ou par ordre des matières* ("Géographie moderne"), 554–68. Paris: Panchoucke.

Minguet, Charles. 1969. *Alexandre de Humboldt historien et géographe de l'Amérique espagnole 1799–1804.* Paris: Maspero.

Muñiz Muñiz, Maria de la Nieves. 1999. "Italia-Spagna: l'immagine riflessa." In *Italia e Italie tra Rivoluzione e Restaurazione,* ed. Mariasilvia Tatti, 161–80. Roma: Bulzoni.

Navarrete, Rodrigo. 2000. "Behind the Palisades: Sociopolitical Recomposition of Native Societies in the Unare Depression, the Eastern Venezuelan Llanos (Sixteenth to Eighteenth Centuries)." *Ethnohistory* 47 (3–4): 535–59.

Ouellet, Réal, and Mylène Tremblay. 2001. "From the Good Savage to the Degenerate Indian: The Amerindian in the Accounts of Travel to America." In *Decentring the Renaissance: Canada and Europe in Multidisciplinary Perspective, 1500–1700,* eds. Germaine Warkentin and Carolyn Podruchny, 159–73. Toronto: University of Toronto Press.

Pendleton, Ryan Lawrence. 2003. "Pre-Nagpra Native American Reburial Policy and Its Implications on Cultural and Linguistic Classification." PhD diss., Florida State University.

Pimental, Juan. 2001. "The Iberian Vision: Science and Empire in the Framework of a Universal Monarchy, 1500–1800." *Osiris* 15: 17–30.

Porter, Roy, and George Sebastian Rousseau. 1980. *The Ferment of Knowledge: Studies in the Historiography of Eighteenth-Century Science.* Cambridge: Cambridge University Press.

Pratt, Mary Louise. 1992. *Imperial Eyes: Travel Writing and Transculturation.* New York: Routledge.

Raillard, Matthieu. 2009. "The Masson de Morvilliers Affair Reconsidered: Nation, Hybridism and Spain's Eighteenth-Century Cultural Identity." *Dieciocho: Hispanic Enlightenment* 32 (1): 31–48.

Raynal, Guillaume-Thomas-François, Abbé. 1770. *Histoire Philosophique et politique, des etablissemens & du commerce des Europeéns dans les deux Indes.* Amsterdam: s.n.

Rivera, José Eustasio. [1924] 1998. *La vorágine,* ed. Montserrat Ordóñez. Reprint, Madrid: Cátedra.

Rodríguez, Manuel. 1684. *El Marañon y Amazonas. Historia de los descubrimientos, entradas, y reducción de naciones. Trabajos malogrados de algunos conquistadores, y dichosos de otros, así temporales, como espirituales, en las dilatadas montañas, y mayores rios de la America.* Madrid: Antonio Gonzalez de Reyes.

Salazar, José Abel. 1947. "El P. Gilij y su *Ensayo de Historia Americana.*" *Missionalia Hispánica* 4: 248–328.

Salvioni, Luigi Perego. 1793. *Notizie spettanti alla vita di Pier Luigi Galletti.* Roma: Presso Luigi Perego Salvioni.

Silva Cáceres, Raul. 1967. "Una novela de Carpentier." *Mundo Nuevo* 17: 33–7.

Sismondi, Jean Charles Léonard Simonde de. [1807–1815] 1815–1818. *Histoire des Républiques italiennes du Moyen Âge,* 16 vols. Reprint, Paris: Treuttel et Wuertz.

Smith, Adam. [1761] 1776. *An Inquiry into the Nature and Causes of the Wealth of the Nations.* Reprint, London: W. Strahan and T. Cadell.

Stepan, Nancy Leys. 2001. "Going to the Tropics." In *Picturing Tropical Nature,* 31–56. Ithaca, NY: Cornell University Press.

Suárez, María Matilde. 1974. "El contenido etnográfico del *Orinoco Ilustrado.*" *Montalbán* 3: 309–35.

Subirats, Eduardo. 1981. *La ilustración insuficiente.* Madrid: Taurus.

–. 2001. *Modernidad truncada de América Latina.* Caracas: CIPOST, Centro de Investigaciones Postdoctorales.

Sweet, David. 1994. "Reflections on the Ibero-American Frontier Mission as an Institution in Native American History." In *Where Cultures Meet: Frontiers in Latin American History,* eds. David J. Weber and Jane M. Rausch, 87–98. Wilmington, DE: Scholarly Resources.

Thorbjarnarson, John. 1995. "Trailing the Mythical Anaconda." *Americas* 47 (4): 38–46.

Tiraboschi, Girolamo. 1787–1794. *Storia della letteratura italiana.* 2nd ed., 9 vols. Modena: Società tipografica.

Vernes, Jules. 1898. *Le Superbe Orénoque.* Paris: J. Hetzel.

Verri, Alessandro. [1764] 1993. "Rinunzia avanti notaio degli autori del presente foglio periodico al Vocabolario della Crusca." In *Il Caffè, 1764–1766,* eds. Gianni Francioni and Sergio Romagnoli, 47–50. Torino: Bollati Boringhieri.

Waquet, Françoise. 1989. *Le Modèle français et l'Italie savante. Conscience de soi et perception de l'autre dans la république des lettres (1660–1750).* Rome: École française de Rome.

Wylie, Lesley. 2005. "Hearts of Darkness: The Celebration of Otherness in the Latin American *novela de la selva.*" *Romance Studies* 23 (2): 105–16.

chapter three

Imagining the Kingdom of Quito: Reading History and National Identity in Juan de Velasco's *Historia del Reino de Quito*

EILEEN WILLINGHAM

Jesuit historian Juan de Velasco's *Historia del Reino de Quito en la América meridional* (1789), which was not published in his lifetime, nonetheless has played a central role in creating and narrating his patriotic community. Velasco, who wrote in exile from Faenza, Italy, after the expulsion of the Jesuits from Spain and its territories in 1767, was a Creole whose family had migrated from Spain two generations before his birth in 1727.[1] In his radically non-canonical interpretation of Quito's history, Velasco fashions a patriotic past upon which his fellow elite Creoles could look with pride and honour. At the same time, the text defends his patria against foreign detractors. Velasco produces a narrative of authenticity and legitimacy in his *Historia*, which has served as a cornerstone of nineteenth- and twentieth-century nationalist thought in Ecuador. Nationalists have appropriated and transformed Velasco's account of a fabled Kingdom of Quito, united both in terms of its borders and its ideal ethnic makeup, a perfect balance between indigenous and European ancestry, whose noble past and organic geography are based not on illegitimate conquest but on peaceful affiliation. Nationalist historians have categorized Velasco's text as a wellspring of historical truth, claiming it as the foundational text of Ecuadorian historiography; yet Velasco's text has also been repudiated as false and therefore unworthy of the foundational text designation. Despite the fact that much of Velasco's "prehistory" was discredited, the text has nonetheless been reclaimed and re-signified as literature, folklore, geography, and the font of nationalist myth by scholars and others who have interacted with this text. Thus Ecuadorians have reinterpreted historical and archaeological evidence in an effort to retain Velasco's "parallel" Incas, the Scyris, as Ecuador's mythic ancestors, so as to better serve various ideological and patriotic agendas. This article will explore the late eighteenth-century conditions under which the *Historia del Reino de Quito* was produced, as well as its appropriation by various groups of Ecuadorian scholars and citizens from the nineteenth century to the present. Velasco has been invoked in discourses aimed at unifying the nation, in upholding its legal claims to territorial sovereignty, in "solving" the "Indian problem," and in defining the nation's essence. In short, Velasco's *Historia del Reino de Quito* has been drawn upon continually in conceptions and conceptualizations of national identity in Ecuador since news of its composition first reached Quito in 1791, announced in the pages of Eugenio Espejo's periodical *Primicias de la Cultura de Quito.*

As the author of a "history" or "historia," the genre that constitutes the principal form of literary production during colonial times, Velasco positions himself as a patriotic intellectual uniquely qualified to pronounce authoritatively on Quito's identity. Velasco strives to express his own subjective position and that of others like him, that is, elite Creoles and Jesuit missionaries. He seeks to identify Quito's social categories and to link his definitions of them to discourses of history, memory, and ideology. Velasco privileges the role of patrician Quiteños in national culture, whether these elites are ancient but noble Indians or contemporary Creoles, because of their superior knowledge of the American landscape and its inhabitants. Velasco maps out a poetic geography and political structure for the Kingdom of Quito, complete with ideal notions of ethnic proportions and power relations, with the Creoles managing society from above. While he seeks to fashion an ideal patriotic community by drawing on the prestige and weight of history to unite the Kingdom of Quito into a natural and inevitable whole, Velasco produces a contradictory discourse of inclusion within and exclusion from the patria. Both Velasco and later nationalists sought to define the patria/nation and fix its essential qualities and guidelines for membership. But Velasco's text already contains within it the seeds of instability regarding what constitutes the patria, and especially, who and what is included or excluded. How did Velasco's foundational text, with its elite Creole patriotic ideology, get transformed into a blueprint for national unity based on an idea repugnant to Velasco – that of Ecuador as the peaceful, mestizo nation?[2] The debates engendered by the text, which endows Ecuador with a mythical and ancient indigenous past, add up to a history of the construction of a nation, with its rhetoric of inclusion and exclusion.

Velasco struggles to construct a sense of Quiteño identity both for himself and others like him, as well as for his patria as a whole, by narrating a seamless history based on the common use of the same territory by a people who somehow share an essential legacy, whether biological or cultural. Velasco strives to describe his patria's cultural and ethical legacy, characterized by love of liberty, monotheism, legitimacy, authenticity, and the practice of just war, all grounded in what the Jesuit portrays as an Eden-like homeland. The common memory of this past is handed down through the practice of cultural traditions by the people, eyewitnesses, and certain approved historical sources. In Velasco's imagination one period of history flows into the next; one group takes over the other following initial resistance, which then yields to alliances and the amalgamation of the best qualities of each, as the borders become fixed and the people all become Quiteños. Velasco produces a Quiteño people and patria, "naturalizing" Quiteños from ancient times to the late colonial period as the authentic inhabitants of the Kingdom of Quito because of their long claim to the area and their access to a legacy of legitimate pre-Hispanic culture, government, and religion. If Velasco's narrative asserts that Spanish colonialism broke those bonds initially, he nonetheless maintains that Christian civilization offered the tools for both repairing those bonds and perfecting what the original inhabitants had achieved.

The *Historia del Reino de Quito* is Velasco's stirring narrative of his patria's unique and glorious past, replete with heroes, a dramatic plotline, and the exposition of his patria's moral and political destiny. Velasco's history of the Kingdom of Quito describes a cult of heroes who may claim legitimate, authentic ownership of a determined patriotic homeland. Velasco ties the arrival of the heroic and civilized Scyris (the indigenous people Velasco constructs as Ecuadorian Incas), to the establishment of both the Kingdom of Quito's boundaries and its civic history. In his narrative, Velasco attempts to rest unfavourable myths about his patriotic community, the Kingdom of Quito, and at the same time, he creates new stories of origin, descent, and historical destiny. To counter anti-American historians' representations of degenerate Creoles living in a forbidding landscape,[3] Velasco relates new patriotic myths about the Kingdom of Quito's ancient inhabitants: the native Quitus, seen as primitive but authentic, the "glorious" Scyris, Velasco's nobly construed Equadorian ancestors, followed by the Incas a few hundred years later, and the early Spanish conquistadors. Velasco endows the Scyris with exemplary traits: they practice a monotheist religion, inhabit an ideally organized aristocratic kingdom, and have achieved an admirable degree of cultural progress. In portraying the Scyris as civilized monotheists and wise governors, Velasco provides Quito with its own authentic and noble forebears, who compare favourably with the Incas, whom Velasco portrays as illegitimate outsiders. Furthermore, Velasco provides liberation myths for his patria so as to infuse it with moral purpose in his portrayal of the Scyris's resistance to "Peruvian" tyranny, their love of liberty, and their legitimate governance based on the rule of law. Through his portrayal of the heroic Scyris as freedom loving, brave, powerful, and defiant, Velasco topples the Incas from the exalted position they had long enjoyed in Spanish American historiography. In Velasco's patriotic discourse, Quito's cultural advancement under Incan rule was a direct result of the Scyris's shared origin with the Peruvians, or their later reunion with them on Quiteño soil in the fourteenth century. Finally, Spanish conquerors and Jesuit missionaries complete the patria-building process which the Scyris began by introducing Christianity and a more perfect civilization to the Amerindians, thus rounding out the Kingdom of Quito's profile. In the final analysis for Velasco, all these groups are Quiteños, whose heroic actions have defined both the geographical and moral contours of the patria.

Velasco's text cannot be separated from its subsequent reformulations in a variety of genres that have been targeted for a variety of purposes. Velasco relies on non-canonical sources for Andean history in his narration of a formerly glorious patria that had sunk into misery by the eighteenth century.[4] Velasco argues that it could have been saved by the Jesuit missions, through economic reforms, or by segregating society along ideal ethnic proportions, which in Velasco's view meant a proper proportion of Indians to Spaniards. Later, nationalists would cling tenaciously to Velasco's tale of a glorified Kingdom of Quito, whose borders are historically determined and inviolate, even as Ecuador's neighbours took over chunks of the patria's territory. Velasco, like his counterparts, Mexican Jesuit Francisco Javier Clavijero and Chilean Jesuit Juan Ignacio Molina, belonged to a cadre of writers intent on defining their communities both to themselves and to the world.[5] An analysis of histories, scholarly articles, literary histories, school texts, and speeches by Ecuadorian public intellectuals since Velasco's time provides evidence of the contentious nature of the struggle to define the essence of "Ecuatorianidad" or Ecuadorian-ness. In addition to seeing the *Historia* as an effective contribution to the charting of the region's early history, Velasco's eighteenth-century readers assigned it a proactive role as a useful manual for improving Ecuador's impoverished condition. The *Historia* also provided a sense of shared destiny among elite Creole Quiteños in America and among the exiled Jesuit community in Europe. While news of its composition had filtered back to Quito even before independence, publication of the first Ecuadorian edition of the *Historia del Reino de Quito en la América meridional* in the 1840s provided the fledgling nation with its own foundational narrative. Upon its publication in Quito, Ecuador's nineteenth-century men of letters zealously embraced Velasco's *Historia* as their own and as that of the Ecuadorian people. Historians fervently based their accounts of Ecuador's pre-Columbian past on Velasco's Scyri antiquity until advances in archaeology and source evaluation in the early twentieth century rendered much of his tale of the Scyri empire suspect. In the ensuing polemic, a mainly elite group of nationalist writers, the so-called Velasco "detractores" and "defensores," emerged and opened the text to new appropriations.

Early Readings

News of the work reached Quito relatively quickly upon its completion in Italy in 1789. In the second issue of the short-lived newspaper, the *Primicias de la Cultura de Quito*, on 19 January 1792, Eugenio Espejo published a letter from the Quiteño Pedro Lucas Larrea, whose brothers Ambrosio and Joaquín, both Jesuits, shared Velasco's Italian exile.[6] All three Larreas expressed their enthusiasm for Espejo's proposed Sociedad Patriótica. Pedro Lucas Larrea's letter includes news from his brother Joaquín that the two exiled Jesuits were at work translating the three volumes of Velasco's *Historia* into Italian, hoping to ensure its publication in Italy by dedicating it to an Italian Cardinal or some other person of esteem and influence. Ambrosio wrote that the work would be "much celebrated" and that he wanted to include in Velasco's book a copy of Espejo's letter, in which he proposed the founding of the Sociedad Patriótica. He announced his intention of sending a copy of his *Discurso* to several people, and most especially to Velasco, for insertion in the *Historia* so that Espejo's useful ideas about bettering the deteriorated condition of Quito might reach a wide audience. Joaquín testifies to their shared horror of the "enormous imputations, falsehoods and very denigrating images" ("enormes imposturas falsedades y denigrantísimos dibujos") made against America and the Americans by such writers as De Pauw, making clear that Quiteños both in Quito and in exile were reading – and reacting against – the anti-American philosophers and historians (Espejo [1791–1792] 1958, 38). Finally, Joaquín links Velasco to two other Jesuit patriotic historians, Clavijero and Molina, as admirable adversaries of these calumniators.

Pedro Lucas Larrea further elaborated on his plan for linking Velasco, Espejo, and the betterment of Quito by suggesting that Espejo write a treatise documenting the history and causes of the "frightful poverty that we suffer in this unhappy Province" ("la espantosa pobreza que padecemos en esta infeliz Provincia"), along with suggestions for remedying Quito's situation (Espejo [1791–1792] 1958, 38). Pedro offered to send this to his brothers for inclusion in the work by "our Countryman" ("nuestro Paisano") Velasco as well as in their subsequent Italian translation of it. He believed that the *Historia* would reach a wide audience, based on his brothers' praise of it, and that the book could make its way to Spain's "principal Ministers" or even the king himself, who would thus become informed of Quito's miserable state and see to its improvement. Espejo did not respond directly to this letter in the *Primicias*, but his inclusion of it suggests its importance in his project to stimulate Quito's development. This community targeted to receive this appeal for the renewal of Quito's economic and social fabric included Quiteños residing in both continents who were involved in the task of recognizing the Kingdom of Quito as a separate entity; a history that belonged to Quito alone and could be invoked for patriotic purposes held the promise of a powerful tool for justifying their position.

The impact of the *Historia* on Ecuadorian nationalism was delayed another forty years, until the appearance of the first edition published there between 1841 and 1844, under the direction of a leading nineteenth-century Quiteño intellectual, Dr. Agustín Yerovi. He made numerous changes, both in style and in content, in collaboration with other prominent Ecuadorian men of letters, most notably Juan León Mera.[7] Velasco's version of Ecuadorian history as presented in the *Historia* met with uncritical acceptance in the nineteenth century from Ecuadorian men of letters. As Velasco "detractor" Jacinto Jijón y Caamaño wrote in 1918, "[g]reat has been the influence exercised by the *Historia*" ("[g]rande ha sido la influencia ejercida por la *Historia*") both within and outside of Ecuador. He continues: "[L]ittle time had elapsed from the publication of the work in Quito when the History of the Schyris and the Duchicelas was universally accepted in our Patria" ("[P]oco tiempo había transcurrido desde la publicación de la obra en Quito, cuando la Historia de Schyris y Duchicelas era universalmente aceptada en nuestra Patria" [Jijón y Caamaño 1918, 35]). Indeed, histories soon appeared that embraced Velasco's Scyri antiquity. Liberal historian Pedro Moncayo relied on Velasco's version of prehistory in his *El Ecuador de 1825 a 1875, sus hombres, sus instituciones y sus leyes* (1885).[8] The late nineteenth-century literary historians

Pablo Herrera and Juan León Mera passed judgment on Velasco's literary capacities, and Mera even included a reference to the Scyris in his 1877 novel *Cumandá* and in several poems.[9] The first important historian of the new order in the Republican period, Pedro Fermín Cevallos, relied heavily on the *Historia* for his *Resumen de la Historia del Ecuador*, published in Lima in 1870.[10] This book in turn sparked Federico González Suárez, archbishop of Quito, to write his monumental *Historia General de la República del Ecuador*, published between 1890 and 1904, in reaction to what he saw as Cevallos's flawed account of prehistory.

In Pursuit of Scientific Truth

González Suárez brought a new standard to the study of history in Ecuador. He was one of the first Ecuadorians to apply the study of archaeology and other "auxiliary sciences" to history (philology, craniology, ethnology, and paleontology) and always insisted on adherence to a rigorous scientific standard of proof and truth in historical work. González Suárez conceived of history as a "moral science" that would impart lessons within a strictly Catholic framework. For history to be a true science, the moral aspect could not be ignored, he believed. The archbishop and his intellectual labours influenced generations of Ecuadorian scholars. His work generated scandal, especially his reading of Velasco, but his treatment of shameful priestly behaviour during the colonial era was also greeted with outcry. A staunchly conservative Catholic, he was wounded by attacks from certain sectors asserting that he was a Liberal, a traitor to his adopted class,[11] because he dared to question the accepted state of historical knowledge and because he documented moral laxity among colonial clergymen. However, he never tired of repeating that his adherence to the truth and to a scientific approach to the past would, in the end, vindicate him and his work.

González Suárez recounts in his autobiographical "Memorias íntimas" that his reading of Velasco as a child had led to his lifelong passion for history, even though his opinion of the Jesuit's work would undergo a complete reversal throughout his life, transitioning from uncritical reverence to skepticism:

> That work awoke in me the keenness for historical studies concerning our nation: I do not know what happened within me as soon as I had read the Ancient History of the Kingdom of Quito. I became restless and I felt spurred by an impatient curiosity to discover and to know [...]; in this way,

> not only the keenness but also the passion for historical studies and for archeological research sprang up in me ("Esa obra despertó en mí la afición a los estudios históricos relativos a nuestra nación: no sé qué pasó en mí cuando hube leído la Historia Antigua del Reino de Quito. Me puse inquieto y me sentí aguijoneado por una impaciente curiosidad de descubrir y de saber [...]; así nació en mí no diré sólo la afición, sino la pasión por los estudios históricos y por las investigaciones arqueológicas" [González Suárez, "Memorias íntimas," quoted in Tobar Donoso 1960, lxxx]).

His passion for knowledge of his country's past soon led to dissatisfaction with contemporary historiography, but his reading of Velasco changed from early grudging acceptance of the Scyris to complete refutation later in his career based on his mistrust of indigenous sources that Velasco relied on, new research in archives, philology, archaeology, and the contention that Velasco wrote from memory in exile. In the end, he concluded: "This is the only thing that can be admitted: the legend (no longer 'tradition') of the Caras and the Schyris of Quito does not rest on any foundation acceptable to critical history. This legend should therefore be eliminated from the Ancient history of Quito or from Ecuadorian Prehistory" ("Esto es lo único que puede admitirse: la leyenda de los Caras y los Schyris de Quito no descansa en fundamento ninguno aceptable por la crítica histórica. Debe, por lo mismo, esa leyenda eliminarse de la Historia antigua de Quito o de la Prehistoria ecuatoriana" [Tobar Donoso 1960, 251]). González Suárez allowed that if sufficient proof emerged from future archaeological finds and dispassionate historical investigation to corroborate Velasco's work, he would be willing to reinstate the legend. But, he cautioned, we cannot accept what Velasco writes about religion, writing, *tolas* (burial sites), expeditions, or conquests, as true, nor his knowledge of the early historians of Peru and Ecuador, nor his system of classifying Ecuador's indigenous peoples (see 251). The effect of this exhaustive list of the Jesuit historian's defects severely eroded his text's standing as Ecuador's foundational history.

Social scientist Jacinto Jijón y Caamaño was the most prominent of González Suárez's "disciples," as they are known to their adversaries. The scion of a wealthy, noble family, from an early age Jijón y Caamaño was able to dedicate both time and considerable financial resources to archaeological and historical investigation. He was instrumental in creating and fomenting the Sociedad Ecuatoriana de Estudios Históricos Americanos, later the Academia Nacional de Historia. Jijón considered debunking Velasco as his patriotic, scientific duty, one that grew out of his devotion to honour and truth. His 1918 article entitled "Examen crítico de la veracidad de la *Historia del Reino de Quito* del P. Juan de Velasco, de la Compañía de Jesús" ("Critical examination of the veracity of the *History of the Kingdom of Quito* from Fr. Juan de Velasco, of the Society of Jesus") appeared in the inaugural issue of the *Boletín de la Sociedad Ecuatoriana de Estudios Históricos Americanos.* Its polemical nature was apparent from the title, and the essay provoked passionate debate, as foreshadowed by the insinuations inherent in its style, not only because of Jijón y Caamaño's scientific arguments against the existence of the Scyris, but also because of his attacks on Velasco's character. Over the course of his career, his tone towards Velasco the man softened, but his judgments regarding the value of Velasco's history hardened, based on principles of impartial, thorough, and scientific investigation.

Jijón lamented the lack of history textbooks in Ecuador, a situation that led to reliance on Cevallos's *Compendio de la Historia del Ecuador* in schools, a book that devoted more attention to the "fabulous" history of the Scyris than to three centuries of colonial rule. In this way, Velasco's prehistory became the official history predicated by Ecuador's men of letters and passed on to its impressionable youth (see Jijón y Caamaño 1918, 35). Jijón calls for the eradication of this "pernicious fable [from] all serious books" ("fábula perniciosa [de] todo libro serio") – a call that had for the most part been heeded at the end of the twentieth century, except in the case of school texts, and in certain entrenched pro-Velascan circles. Like certain Spanish writers who fabricated historical documents, Jijón argues that Velasco no doubt manipulated or invented sources to cloak his patria in glory. Jijón emphasized his shock that priests could author such falsifications, but believes Velasco, motivated by nostalgia, and a wish to combat the European detractors of America and to boost Quito's place in relation to Cuzco, did just that. Aware of the explosive reaction his attack would surely produce, Jijón y Caamaño expresses his difficulties in burying "centuries of the patria's history," his devotion to the truth, and his impartiality (Jijón y Caamaño 1918, 62–3).

The Literary Velasco: History, Fiction, or Magical Realism?

Isaac Barrera, also a member of the Academia Nacional, wrote measured assessments of Velasco and the *Historia* throughout his long career as historian and literary critic. Barrera shifts the focus from strict adherence to scientific historical truth to a literary analysis of the *Historia.* Specifically, he points out Velasco's important achievement of having preserved the traditions of his native land in a written, comprehensive form. In his *Historia de la Literatura Ecuatoriana*, published 1944–1950, Barrera employs a literary approach in his appraisal, celebrating Velasco's confection of a luminous Scyri dynasty that could rival that of the Incas. While he concedes that colonial documents and the "auxiliary sciences" do not support the historical veracity of Velasco's narrative, he nevertheless exalts it in any case as a foundation for Ecuadorian nationhood. Barrera also registers the Ecuadorian people's reaction to the *Historia* as what he terms "psychological history" by noting the way in which this account of a glorious Scyri kingdom had filled a psychological void, by implying that the Quiteños' deep sorrow at the invasion of their land by the Incas resonated with contemporary Ecuadorians. The Scyri legends thus became arms in the defence against the hegemony of the Inca empire, which finds its implicit continuation in the modern Peruvian state. This literary history appeared soon after Ecuador's terrible humiliation at the hands of the Peruvians in 1941–1942, when Ecuador lost an enormous expanse of its disputed Amazonian territory to its neighbour to the south. Indeed, many pro-Velascans portray modern Peruvians as the successors to the invading Cuzqueños and argue that one of Velasco's most salient contributions lies in his recording of the territory's difference with respect to Peru. Barrera also recognized the importance of the text in mapping out a unified national territory, which Velasco had conceptualized as a result of his travels and historical investigations. The notion of national unity had been much debated in Ecuador before that time and has been much debated since, but for Barrera, the portraying of a nation linked by common geographical and territorial traditions is one of the Jesuit's greatest achievements.

In his *Historiografía del Ecuador* of 1956, Barrera raises "folklore" to a science: it is the science of popular tradition, which can preserve the traces of a country's historical origin. Against the scientific proofs offered by the "auxiliary sciences," which may or may not prove the existence of the Scyri empire, Barrera upholds the scientific value of folklore: "[S]cience has corroborated the validity of tradition and legend as sources that point toward a remote truth" ("[L]a ciencia ha comprobado la validez de la tradición y de la leyenda como fuente indicadora de una verdad remota" [Barrera 1956, 99]). Now Barrera sees Velasco's greatest contribution as the transmission of these "vague recollections preserved in the memory of the peoples and transmitted through numerous generations" ("vagos recuerdos conservados en la memoria de los pueblos y transmitidos por numerosas generaciones" [100]). These memories form the basis of the national narrative of Ecuador, an unbroken connection between past, present, and future (99). While on the one hand Barrera is unwilling to concede too much to the "auxiliary sciences" such as archaeology, or to methodical documentary analysis, he privileges the new science of folklore, which can disinter a nation's "profound" history while probing its collective psyche. Barrera rereads the work as an enchanting narrative, which confers upon Quito a precolonial past to rival the Incas' splendor. He also sees Velasco's narrative of the colonial era, ridiculed as fanciful and lacking credibility by Jijón and González Suárez, as one that recasts events of the period as evidence of long-standing Creole consciousness. Barrera's insight lies in enunciating the fact that while Velasco's *Historia del Reino de Quito* may not stand up to certain scientific proofs – except those of the science of folklore – the text remains "proudly ingrained in popular conviction" ("ufana en la convicción popular").

Other methods of preserving the viability of Velasco's work were also found. Certain writers began to sidestep the veracity issue altogether by embracing Velasco's text as literature. For instance, Benjamín Carrión, a leading figure for decades in Ecuador's cultural and political life, calls the *Historia* Ecuador's first novel in his 1958 literary history of Ecuador, *El nuevo relato ecuatoriano* (see 13–36). This theme was picked up and developed further by others, including the novelist-turned-historian Alfredo Pareja Diezcanseco:

> All history begins with myth, which is creative power. When the document – sometimes intentionally disfigured – is not enough, the peoples nourish the spirit and affirm their love of the mother earth in the extraordinary virtues of legend. And legend, it must be recognized, if poetical, sweet and magical, is nothing other than the truth pronounced with other words ("Toda historia empieza con el mito, que es el poder creador. Cuando el documento – algunas veces intencionalmente desfigurado – no basta, los pueblos se nutren del espíritu y afirman su amor a la madre tierra en las virtudes extraordinarias de la leyenda. Y la leyenda, ha de reconocerse, si poetizada, dulce y mágica, no es sino una verdad dicha con otras palabras" [Pareja Diezcanseco 1954, quoted in Estrada 1967, 169]).

This position would in its turn provoke a response from those who wished to separate "myth" from "history" and to remove the Scyris from the historical record as the founders of Ecuadorian nationhood. For example, Isaac Barrera sees Velasco's treatment of Ecuador's physical environment through the lens of what could be called "magical realism" ("real maravilloso"): Velasco may have been credulous, but

> that candid credulity harmonized with our exuberant nature, which speaks with disproportionate signs of mountain chains, of intricate jungles, of animals that because they are unknown border on the fabulous. It does not seem at all strange that in this wild and disconcerting nature ("esa credulidad cándida se armonizaba con nuestra naturaleza exuberante, que habla con signos desproporcionados de cadenas de montañas, de selvas intricadas, de animales que por desconocidos confinan en lo fabulosos. Nada extraño parecería que en esta naturaleza bravía y desconcertante" [Barrera 1944, 111]).

one would find the zoophytes (i.e., animal hybrids) that Velasco described in his volume dedicated to Quito's natural history. "Who cares if this is ingenuous?" Barrera seems to ask. American nature *is* fabulous, and Velasco's work simply gives voice to Ecuador's lush landscape.

The editor of a popular edition of selections from the *Historia* followed this lead, publishing in 1986 *Zoología fantástica,* a compilation of excerpts from Velasco's volume of natural history (that rereads parts of the *Historia* as precursors to twentieth century "fantastic" or magical realist literature), which forms a significant part of the work. The anonymous editor recognizes Velasco's particular blend of fact and fiction:

> [I]t is evident that Father Velasco's *Historia* mixes legends, myths, fantastic narratives, etc., with objective information whose scientific treatment could be deemed acceptable, especially if we take into account the time in which he was carrying out his work. Here, then, we have assembled examples of the most imaginative parts of his *Historia* (basically from the *Historia natural*) in which we can come face to face with fantastic fauna and flora that inaugurates amongst us "magical realism" already as a literary expression, originating no doubt in that marvelous reality that Juan de Velasco described by recurring to disproportion and to hyperbole ("[E]s evidente que la *Historia* del Padre Velasco mezcla leyendas, mitos, narraciones fantásticas, etcetera, con datos objetivos cuyo manejo científico podría admitirse, sobre todo si pensamos en los años en que fue realizando su trabajo. Aquí, entonces, hemos podido armar una muestra de lo más imaginativo de su *Historia* (básicamente de la *Historia natural*) en la que podremos enfrentarnos a una fauna y una flora fantásticas que inaugura entre nostoros, ya como

expresión literaria, el 'realismo magico,' originado, sin duda, en esa realidad maravillosa a la que Juan de Velasco tuvo que describir echando mano de lo desmesurado y de lo hiperbólico" [Velasco 1986, 1]).[12]

In this rereading of the Jesuit's history, Velasco is not only Ecuador's first novelist, but he is also its first practitioner of "lo real maravilloso" and "magical realism" ("realismo mágico") and, therefore, Ecuador's first short-story writer.

The editor of this collection and other critics over the course of the polemic advocate challenging the disciplinary boundaries that would pigeonhole Velasco's *Historia* strictly within the confines of narration as historical truth. In doing so, they open the text up to new analytical approaches that include the search for Ecuador's "first novel" in this foundational colonial text. Nationalists who embrace the literary Velasco at the expense of the historian would still hail him as "a man of letters, of everlasting glory" (Pareja Diezcanseco 1981, xcii).

Ecuador the Peaceful, Mestizo Nation

Throughout the twentieth century, Ecuadorians have debated Ecuadorian nationhood, identity, and culture in discourses that link race, history, and nation. Like thinkers across the continent, such as Mexican José Vasconcelos, Ecuadorian nationalists embraced the notion of racial and cultural *mestizaje* as the essence of Ecuadorian-ness (Silva 1992, 9–14; see also Miller 2004, 119–40). Velasco's Scyris have played a role in developing the myths surrounding Ecuatorianidad. Writers who proclaimed the unifying force of "mestizaje" in what they termed "Indoamerica" saw Indians as lacking in culture and in need of integration into national life, thus implying that Indians were un-cultural, ahistorical, and a passive sector of the nation. The impulse to tie Velasco's work to a purportedly integrative *mestizaje* in the service of defining "Ecuatorianidad" is ironic, given that Velasco believed Quito's eighteenth-century decadence could be attributed to insalubrious race mixing and an ideal of ethnic structuring that had gone awry. Velasco and his writing can be – and have been – manipulated to fit any ideological and patriotic framework.

In the wake of Ecuador's humiliation at the hands of Peru in the border conflict of 1941–1942, Ecuador's intelligentsia struggled to formulate new ways of theorizing the nation. A leading public intellectual, Benjamín Carrión, was one of the founding members of the Casa de la Cultura Ecuatoriana, which he envisioned as an arm in Ecuador's struggle to articulate its identity, both internally and internationally.[13] Carrión suggested conceiving of Ecuador as a small nation, undeniably weak in economic and military matters, but strong in its culture. Ecuador could be a shining light for all nations, known for its arts and craftsmanship and its proud democratic traditions, much like other small nations such as Greece, Belgium, and Israel in the Old World, and Mexico and Costa Rica in the New World. A defining characteristic of the Casa de la Cultura was its role in uniting elites of seemingly disparate politics, such as the leftist Carrión and Jijón y Caamaño, champion of the Ecuadorian Conservative Party. Thus as Fernando Tinajero (1986) has demonstrated, Ecuador's dominant classes presented a united front in defining the discourse on culture in the country, to the exclusion of other voices (see 68–9), turning to Velasco's Scyris to explain the country's origins and modern mission. Employing vague notions of Ecuador's glorious past, rooted in the Scyris' Kingdom of Quito, they found evidence of cultural continuity from prehistoric times, through the colonial period, and well into the twentieth century. These writers strove to explain Ecuatorianidad in terms of a cultural, spiritual, and ethnic *mestizaje* that had its roots in the founders of the nation, the Scyris. Whether this *mestizaje* is described as an antagonistic or pacific union, such thinking is closely aligned with exploration of the country's essential qualities, all of which first found expression in Velasco's *Historia*.

Quiteñidad: Defining the Nation's Essence

Many writers theorize continuity between the ancient inhabitants of the Quito region, as chronicled by Velasco, through the colonial period running from the sixteenth century to the nineteenth-century wars of independence known as the "Audencia y Presidencia," and later to the modern nation's sense of identity. The strand that unites them is *Quiteñidad*, a notion embraced by many Sierra-based intellectuals that implies that the nation's origins and essence share the same geographical and historical space: the modern city of Quito, site of the ancient kingdom. In this conception of the country's essence, the Scyris stand not only for past greatness, now lost but somehow recoverable, but also as direct ancestors of today's Ecuadorian people. For this reason, Velasco's *Historia* must be defended at all costs.

Ecuador's well-known *indigenista* thinker and activist, Pío Jaramillo Alvarado, published four editions of his sociological study, *El indio ecuatoriano*, between 1922 and 1954. His aim was to expose the miserable living conditions of Ecuador's indigenous population, their bondage to a system of forced labour, and their supposed lack of integration into national life, while suggesting ways of ameliorating their situation. In order to pinpoint the causes of their misery and to suggest remedies, Jaramillo Alvarado believed that he had to investigate the nation's history and "prehistory." He believed that the Indian "problem" was central to questions of nationhood and that direct correlations conditions in his day could be gleaned from studying the past. Jaramillo Alvarado accepts Velasco's history of the Scyris as a confederation of peoples that united for common defence. He marks this period as the germination of Ecuadorian nationhood. For Jaramillo Alvarado, the Kingdom of Quito, the last "autochthonous" Ecuadorian civilization, equaled or excelled Inca civilization. He based this evaluation primarily on the conception of property, since the Scyris practiced individual land ownership. While Jaramillo Alvarado argues that the Incas' benevolent "communism" may have been advantageous in some ways, he believes that the holding of property in common took away the Indians' individualism. In this way, Inca domination prepared the way for Spanish rule over the indigenous population, a control that was merely continued during republican times. According to *El indio ecuatoriano*, during these latter three periods Indians lost their sense of individuality and laboured under their masters in semi-slavery. Thus, Jaramillo Alvarado uses the *Historia* to paint a picture of utopian freedom and equality during Scyri times, which ended under the domination of foreign powers. For this reason, Jaramillo Alvarado believes that the legends upon which Ecuador's prehistory are based must be safeguarded, since they preserve both the memory of the Indians' origin and their original legislation, both factors in understanding the situation of contemporary indigenous people. Defence of Velasco's *Historia antigua* is vital in Jaramillo Alvarado's concept, since it chronicles this collective memory of the Indians, the basic unit of Ecuador's nationhood.

What is the essence of *Ecuatorianidad* or *Quiteñidad*? For pro-Velascans, it stretches back in time to the period of the Quitus and the Scyris and is characterized by freedom, an advanced culture, and other vague notions of greatness. The nation's essence, crystallized during its "prehistory," continues unchanged throughout the colonial and republican periods, although "defenders" may emphasize one era's importance over another in initiating the process. Whatever the exact nature of "Quiteñidad," many Ecuadorians agree that the nation may look to Juan de Velasco for the precious gift of recording its origins. The Scyri-based notion of Quiteñidad combines with the unifying power of *mestizaje* in the figure of the first Ecuadorian mestizo, Atahualpa, whom Velasco portrays as the apotheosis of Inca and Scyri culture, a morally pure Quiteño hero who inspires later generations with his exemplary wisdom, love of independence, just leadership, and brave conduct. In his veins coursed the noble blood of both his Inca father, Huayna Cápac, and his Scyri mother, Paccha. Velasco's text has contributed to the mythologizing of Atahualpa as the "initial representative of a nationhood in nascent evolution" ("representante inicial de una nacionalidad en evolución naciente" [José María Vargas, quoted by Estrada 1967, 179]).[14] According to historian Galo René Pérez, Atahualpa comes across as the maximum figure in the *Historia del Reino de Quito* because of his "very clear consciousness of the rights of his nation" ("conciencia tan despejada de los derechos de su nación" [Pérez 1972, 22]), which he defended along with his Quiteño generals against the Peruvian Inca, Huáscar. In addition, the *Historia*'s account of the Scyris and of Atahualpa's personality and deeds has been invoked as an arm in defending the nation from enemies both from within and without. Much ink has been spilled on the subject of Atahualpa's centrality to the birth of the nation – and on the topic of Peruvian perfidy in attempting to claim a Cuzqueño birthplace for Ecuador's national hero.

Benjamín Carrión wrote a historical novel, *Atahuallpa* (1932), full of picturesque details of Inca and Scyri life. Carrión contrasts the virile, steadfast Quiteño Atahuallpa with the effeminate, vacillating Huáscar (Carrión [1932] 1968, 112–14). Following Velasco closely, Carrión presents the Inca Huayna Cápac's division of his empire between these two sons as the restoration of Quito to its rightful owners. Carrión portrays Atahuallpa as forceful, decisive, fair, and above all, virile. Atahuallpa assumed control of his empire, and did not simply follow Cara or Inca traditions in a servile way. The Quiteño ruler was of a "more robust, virile culture" ("cultura más recia, viril" [115]) than Huáscar, and like many heroes of the Spanish renaissance, was a man of both arms and letters, educated both in war and in quipu traditions. According to Carrión's novel, the first Ecuadorian *mestizo* was "a rough and strong example of the mixture of two lines: that of the Caras, and that of the Incas" ("un ejemplar rudo y fuerte de la mezcla de dos estirpes: la de los caras y la de los incas" [115]).

Atahualpa, as depicted by Velasco and developed by twentieth-century writers, represents the pinnacle of Ecuatorianidad, especially during Ecuador's crisis of the 1940s. The figure of Atahualpa unites a variety of concerns. The portrait of Atahualpa that emerges manifests a markedly gendered concept of nationhood, as Atahualpa is repeatedly described as "virile." Virility is tied to notions of independence, wisdom, and a measured yet forceful temperament. By extension, the Reino de Quito could also be described in such terms. Its successor, the nation of Ecuador, shares these traits and is compared to the effeminate and decadent court of Cuzco, Peru. Adherence to the cult of Atahualpa also implies defence of the nation's "territorial integrity" in the face of incursions by Cuzco's heir, the modern Peruvian nation. Moreover, as the nation's "first" *mestizo,* Atahualpa is a transitional figure who spans both the ascendancy of the last Scyri-Inca period and the birth of the new "Indohispanic" bloc. Those who herald Atahualpa as the supreme representative of Ecuadorian nationhood see in him a heroic figure whose strength, determination, and independent spirit should be emulated by contemporary Ecuadorians.

Peruvian Treachery: Velasco and the Loss of the Amazon

In the context of the Velascan polemic, Peruvian crimes are not confined to the written page, but extend to the violent struggle over the territory disputed by Ecuador and its neighbour to the south. War has broken out a number of times and the 1941–1942 battles led to a profound crisis in Ecuadorian national thought, after Ecuador lost much of its Amazonian territory to Peru. The struggles continued well into the twentieth century, with hostilities continuing periodically throughout the 1980s and 1990s, before the two countries signed a peace accord in 1998. Ecuadorian nationalists have turned to Velasco's *Historia* to prove the nation's territorial contentions, reading in his pages both a clear denomination of Ecuadorian territory and an uncontestable right to Ecuadorian possession of this land, based on the Kingdom of Quito's Jesuit missions and explorations in the Amazonian territory.

In the midst of Ecuador's 1941–1942 border war with Peru, Velasco's history was invoked to ratify the continuity of Ecuador's borders from time immemorial. For example, in a speech entitled "El Historiador Juan de Velasco y el Oriente ecuatoriano" ("The Historian Juan de Velasco and the Ecuadorian Amazon"), pronounced in the Ateneo Ecuatoriano de Cultura in August 1941, José María Avilés Mosquera recognizes the thinkers and soldiers who have conceived of and defended the patria throughout its history:

> I want to proclaim the immortal greatness of Ecuador and evoke the memory of the forgers of our nationhood; I want to venerate, warmly and fervidly, not only those who fell in the battlefields, from the last of the Shirys

> of Carán, who in the plains of Atuntaqui struggled to detain the invader from the south, to the humble and brave soldier who only yesterday offered his life on the border, but also to all the thinkers, who with their insights contributed to the exaltation of Ecuador, because both the former and the latter symbolize the generous, vital fluid that flows, fecund, through the channels of our history ("[Q]uiero hacer votos por la inmortal grandeza del Ecuador y evocar el recuerdo de los forjadores de la nacionalidad; quiero rendir culto, cálido y fervoroso, no sólo a los que cayeron en los campos de batalla, desde el último de los Shirys de Carán, que en las llanuras de Atuntaqui se esforzaban por detener al invasor del sur, hasta el humilde y valeroso soldado que ayer no más ofrendó su vida en la frontera, sino también a todos los pensadores que, con sus luces contribuyeron al engrandecimiento del Ecuador, porque éstos como aquellos simbolizan la savia generosa que fecunda corre por los cauces de nuestra historia" [Avilés Mosquera 1921, 177]).

He portrays an Ecuador that is a victim of its own loyalty to its commitment to peace and to its noble sentiments, despite the smallness of the nation; moreover, he evokes the hordes of refugees who at that moment were fleeing border skirmishes, abandoning the jungle region to take refuge in the Andes, "refuge in the arms of their brothers and generous relief for their pain in the welcoming lap of the mutilated republic" ("amparo en los brazos de sus hermanos y alivio generoso para sus penas en el regazo acogedor de la mutilada república" [Avilés Mosquera 1921, 177]).

As other nationalists who were inspired by Velasco's account of Ecuador's ancient history, Avilés Mosquera traces the birth of Ecuador's nationhood to the fateful afternoon in 1532 when Atahualpa was taken prisoner. He identifies this event as the moment when Ecuador coalesced as a mestizo nation:

> On that historic afternoon two civilizations and two cultures, two races and two worlds, convene. From this fusion would emerge in the future, the peoples of America, the subject matter, environment, and synthesis of Father Juan de Velasco's *Historia.* Atahualpa represents at the same time the dynasty of the Shirys and of the Incas; in him is concentrated the entire history of the only somewhat civilized peoples in the southern part of pre-Columbian America. Pizarro is the authentic expression of Conquistador Spain of the sixteenth century, of that Spain used to risking it all ("En aquella histórica tarde se dan cita dos civilizaciones y dos culturas, dos razas y dos mundos.

De esta fusión surgirían en el futuro los pueblos de América, argumento, ambiente y síntesis de la Historia del P. Juan de Velasco. Atahualpa representa al mismo tiempo la dinastía de los Shirys y de los Incas, en él se concentra toda la historia de los únicos pueblos relativamente organizados en la parte Sur de la América pre-colombina. Pizarro es la expresión auténtica de la España conquistadora del siglo XVI, de esa España acostumbrada a echar la casa por la ventana" [Avilés Mosquera 1921, 180]).

This pivotal moment marks a historical transition for the nation: "In Cajamarca the ancient history of the Kingdom of Quito draws to a close and right there the modern one begins. The race [is] in full gestation and Indo-American Hispanism is germinating" ("En Cajamarca concluye la historia antigua del Reino de Quito y allí mismo comienza la moderna. La raza en plena gestación y germina la hispanidad indoamericana" [Avilés Mosquera 1921, 180]). In this conception of *mestizaje*, Hispanism or *Hispanidad* acts as a peaceful integrator of indigenous and European elements, leading to a "superior harmony."[15] It is in this vein that Avilés reads Velasco: as a truthful historian who "exalted Castilian glories" while at the same time defending the Indian "personality."

Avilés proclaims the importance of Velasco's demarcation of geographical space as the theatre where the historical events of the *Historia* would unfold. He cites a long passage in which the Jesuit designates the borders of the Kingdom of Quito. In a section entitled "Velasco Orientalista," Avilés declares:

> If Ecuador lacked the titles to defend its indisputable and self evident right over the Oriente [eastern Amazonian] region, it has more than enough [evidence] in the erudite history of Father Juan de Velasco [which was] written with documentation much earlier than when cunning Peruvian ambition attacked the territorial integrity of our patria ("Si al Ecuador le faltaran títulos para defender su indiscutible y diáfano derecho sobre la Región Oriental, tiene de sobra con la erudita historia del P. Juan de Velasco, escrita documentadamente mucho antes que la artera ambición peruana atentase contra la integridad territorial de nuestra patria" [Avilés Mosquera 1921, 187]).

Velasco's division of the Kingdom of Quito proves the legitimacy of contemporary Ecuador's border claims that are based on pre-Hispanic and Spanish conquests and expansion in the territory. Moreover, Avilés ties the border question to the expulsion of the Jesuits:

> It was not Velasco's duty to defend the territorial patrimony of the Royal Audience of Quito, guarded up to that point by his brothers, the Missionaries of the Spanish Marañón. The expulsion of the Jesuits from America was injurious to Ecuador because since that time, without the Cross of Christ, which holding his arms outstretched, gave permanence to our borders, all that had been gained in over 130 years of indefatigable missionary labor and 233 years of discoveries and conquests, was lost ("A Velasco no le tocó defender el patrimonio territorial de la Real Audiencia de Quito, guardado hasta entonces por sus hermanos los Misioneros del Marañón español. La expulsión de los jesuitas de América fue perjudicial al Ecuador pues desde entonces, sin la Cruz de Cristo, que con sus brazos extendidos daba permanencia a nuestros linderos, se perdió todo cuanto se había adelantado en más de 130 años de infatigable labor misional y 233 años de descubrimientos y conquistas" [Avilés Mosquera 1921, 188]).

For Avilés and others, Velasco's documenting of the missions and explorations in the Amazonian (Marañón) region validates the activities that lent proof and legitimacy to Ecuador's claims. In short, Avilés Mosquera's speech incorporates many of the crucial elements in the anguished interrogations into the nation's essence and cultural continuity in the midst of the 1940s border war.

In the struggle with Peru over Ecuador's border, Velasco's legacy has been invoked as a rallying cry and as evidence of Ecuador's legitimate claims to the Amazonian region. Many writers point to Velasco's delimitation of the Oriente's geography and his history of the region as proof of Ecuador's legal rights to the region. These nationalist writers hail Velasco's Scyris as virile defenders of their own territory, a trait many wish the Kingdom of Quito's successor state and its citizen would imitate. While for some, the *Historia* provides Ecuador with both a legal arm in its fight against Peru and a heroic example of a just yet potent ancestral state, many other scholars have turned away from Velasco's account of the past and question his narrative's contribution to debates over *Ecuatorianidad.* Almost a century after the first calls to remove the Scyris from Ecuadorian school texts, however, Ecuadorian archaeologist Ernesto Salazar noted in 1988 that their continued canonization in the schools up to that date responds to questions of territorial integrity and a yearning for a mythical past for Ecuador, on par with that of the Incas. As Salazar and others have pointed out, school texts and much of the debate stemming from Velasco's *Historia* about the country's essence place Ecuador's origins in only one part of the country, the Sierra region. Erika

Silva and others have documented the emergence of indigenous voices in the debate over what constitutes *Ecuatorianidad,* and Silva notes that Velasco's Scyris are invoked in contradictory discourses of the country's men of letters who have pointed to a glorious Indian past while excluding contemporary Indians from the picture. Others, such as Michael Handelsman, alert us to calls for a "plurinational" view of Ecuador that would include not only indigenous sectors but also Afro-Ecuadorians in debates surrounding Ecuatorianidad (Handelsman 1999, 1–9).

Conclusion

Jesuit Juan de Velasco's *Historia del Reino de Quito* has experienced more transformations than any of the zoophytes he describes in his volume on natural history. The text's eighteenth-century appraisers saw it as a useful manual for improving Quito's impoverished situation and as an effective contribution to the region's early history. As Velasco intended, it also provided a sense of a shared destiny among elite Quiteños, both in America and in Europe. The first inklings of doubt about his account of the glorious Scyri past certainly shook that foundation.

Velasco unites in the Kingdom of Quito's geographical space the glorious ancient past of the Scyri and Inca peoples, and the Creole present into one continuous historical narrative. In this narrative, Velasco rehabilitates the image of America against Eurocentric representations of the land and its people, upholds the legitimacy of the American subject to relate his own history, and extols the virtues of his patria. In so doing, he provides myths and markers of communal self-identity powerful enough to counteract negative portrayals, to fill in the historiographical gaps in Quito's history, and to furnish his intellectual heirs with a rich stock of patriotic legends and lessons on which to draw.

The construction of Ecuador's national identity, based on Velasco's mythical history of the Kingdom of Quito, has been a contentious process, and the struggle over identity and politics in the national sphere resonates with nationalist and postcolonialist debates and projects throughout Latin America. This exploration of historical representation and imagination may provide a way of re-evaluating Creole consciousness in the waning years of Spanish colonial rule. Velasco wrote the Kingdom of Quito's history in the *Historia del Reino de Quito en la América meridional* in Faenza, Italy, towards the end of his twenty-five-year period of exile there, a time that coincided with the end of his life. His narration is inscribed within a double frame, both in time and space: the Italy of his exile and the Quito of the first forty years of his life. From this double frame emanates a poetic geography tinged by nostalgia, haunted by the specters of decadence and distance, and, most importantly, evocative of causes both personal and collective. The struggle for patriotic representation began with Velasco, who, although he did not live to see his text published, may have had an inkling about how the *Historia*'s legacy would become that of furnishing the underpinnings of Ecuadorian nationalist thought that continues to shape the collective imaginary in contemporary Ecuador.

NOTES

1 After studying in Jesuit schools in Riobamba and Latacunga, Velasco became a Jesuit novitiate in 1744. He continued his studies in Quito, where he obtained his doctorate in Theology from the Colegio Máximo in 1753, the same year he was ordained. He made the Jesuit profession of the fourth vow in 1762. Velasco carried out his ecclesiastical duties throughout the Province of Quito, serving as educator and missionary. He taught in indigenous missions, and in the Jesuit Colleges of Ibarra and Popayán, where he provided instruction in philosophy and physics. During this time, Velasco traveled extensively throughout the region, studying Quichua, native traditions, and monuments; he also undertook botanical and ethnographic research. Velasco lived twenty-four years in exile in Faenza, where besides the *Historia del Reino de Quito,* he produced another work of history, *Historia Moderna del Reyno de Quito y Crónica de la Provincia de la Compañía de Jesús del Mismo Reyno*; a compilation of poetry written by himself and his companions in exile, *Colección de poesías varias, hecha por un ocioso en la ciudad de Faenza*; the fruit of his linguistic studies, the *Vocabulario de la lengua índica;* and a few unpublished religious tracts. Velasco died in Italy in 1792. See Larrea 1971 for Velasco's biography.

2 See Stutzman 1981 for an analysis of the rhetoric of *mestizaje* in Ecuador.

3 See Gerbi 1973, Brading 1991, and Cañizares Esguerra [1932] 1986 for Creole responses, especially by Jesuits, to denigration of America, its inhabitants, and its physical environment.

4 See Willingham 2001 and Bustos 1995 for Velasco's sources and Andrien 1995 for the Quito region's political and economic history in the late colonial period.

5 For Clavijero and Molina, see Cañizares Esguerra [1932] 1986. See also Higgins 2000 for Mexican Jesuits.

6 Espejo [1791–1792] 1958, 37–9 ("Avisos interesantes," letter in *Primicias* no. 2, 19 January 1792, from Pedro Lucas Larrea, dated 14 October 1791).

7 The next edition was published in 1927. For the *Historia*'s publishing history, see Pareja Diezcanseco 1981, xiii–xviii.

8 See Ayala Mora 1985, 16.

9 Herrera 1927, 36; Mera 1893, 175–7; and Mera [1877] 1976, 69–72. See Harrison 1996 for an analysis of nineteenth-century Ecuadorian poetry that relies on images of Scyris and Incas.

10 According to Ayala Mora, Cevallos was part of the land-holding elite that inherited power after the end of Spanish domination. In this early Republican period, after the independence struggles, "praised by the poets and narrated by its chronicler-actors, the republican era dawned with the urgency of advancing the recently founded and precariously united Ecuador. The need for a new historical synthesis then arose, one that would justify the independence struggle and would also justify a new order, established by and designed for the use of the "lords of the land," heirs of colonial regimes of control" ("cantado por los poetas y relatado por sus actores-cronistas, se abrió la época republicana con la urgencia de sacar adelante al Ecuador recién fundado y precariamente unido. Surgió entonces la necesidad de una nueva síntesis histórica que justificara la emancipación y justificara también un nuevo orden establecido y usufructuado por los 'señores de la tierra' herederos de la dominación colonial" [Ayala Mora 1985, 14–15]).

11 González Suárez had a humble beginning. He was brought up solely by his poor, religious mother and won a scholarship to study with the Jesuits, with whom he remained for ten years. See Jijón y Caamaño, "Prólogo," in González Suárez 1944, x–xv.

12 These texts from the *Historia natural* include: "What we are told about the land of the giants [...]. Amazons, serpents that resemble dogs, beasts that are fifty fathoms long, plants that are almost animals, and, in short, all manners of fauna, which compels us inevitably toward a marvellous vision of the world, a consequence of course of a marvellous world" ("[L]o que se nos cuenta de la tierra de los gigantes [...]. Amazonas, de serpientes que tienen mucho de perro, de bestias que miden cincuenta brazas de longitud, plantas que casi son animales, y en fin, de toda una fauna que nos conduce, irremediablemente, a una visión maravillosa del mundo, consecuencia, por supuesto, de un mundo maravilloso" [Velasco 1986, 5]).

13 For Carrión, the Casa de la Cultura and the crisis of the 1940s, see Silva 1992, 19–23; and Tinajero 1986, 65–9.

14 José María Vargas continues that whatever form the Reino de Quito took, it ended with the Inca invasion. Many Ecuadorians have taken Huayna

Cápac's splitting of the empire between his sons as the resurrection of the Reino de Quito, when in fact only two possibilities exist. Either Atahualpa was a sort of viceroy to Huáscar with a limited jurisdiction or the brothers were co-emperors, with Huáscar as primus inter pares. In any case, the Inca Empire remained whole.

15 Avilés Mosquera subscribes to the following notions of *raza* and *indigenismo*: "'Race,' as Alfonso Junco puts it so admirably, "does not mean arrogant exclusion, but loving fusion; it does not imply the materialist and pagan theory of an isolating racism, but the reverse: the spiritual and Christian doctrine of an integrative Hispanism, one that integrates 20 nations that extol the embrace of the Spanish and the indigenous, that integrates that eminent spiritual community that we call Hispanism. The common denominator, unitary sign that does not erase, but rather raises ethnic differences, local contributions and autochthonous values to a superior harmony. The voice of history and of language, the voice of religion and of culture. Because we are authentically Hispanists as we are authentically indigenists" ("'Raza,' como admirablemente escribe Alfonso Junco, "no significa exclusión altanera, sino amorosa fusión; no implica la teoría materialista y pagana de un racismo aislante, sino al revés, la docrina espiritualista y cristiana de un hispanismo integrador. Integrador de veinte naciones que cantan el beso de lo español y de lo indígena. Integrador de esa egregia comunidad espiritual que llamamos Hispanidad. Común denominador, signo unitario que no borra, sino levanta a superior armonía, las diferencias étnicas, las aportaciones locales, los valores autóctonos. Voz de la historia y de la lengua, voz de la religión y de la cultura. Porque somos auténticamente hispanistas como somos auténticamente indigenistas" [Avilés Mosquera 1921, 180]).

BIBLIOGRAPHY

Andrien, Kenneth J. 1995. *The Kingdom of Quito, 1690–1830: The State and Regional Development.* Cambridge: Cambridge University Press.

Avilés Mosquera, José María. 1921. "El historiador Juan de Velasco y el oriente ecuatoriano." In *Memoria,* 2: 176–88. Quito: SEIHGE.

Ayala Mora, Enrique. 1985. "Estudio Introductorio." In *La historia del Ecuador: ensayos de intepretación,* 9–52. Quito: Corporación Editora Nacional.

Barrera, Isaac J. 1918. "El Padre D. Juan de Velasco." *Boletín de la Sociedad Ecuatoriana de Estudios Históricos Americanos* 1 (2): 136–44.

–. 1944–1950. *Historia de la Literatura Ecuatoriana.* 3 vols. Quito: Ecuatoriana.

–. 1956. *Historiografía del Ecuador.* Mexico: Instituto Panamericano de Geografía e Historia.

Brading, David. D. 1991. *The First America: The Spanish Monarchy, Creole Patriots, and the Liberal State, 1492–1867.* New York: Cambridge University Press.

Bustos, Guillermo. 1995. "La producción de la escritura histórica en la Colonia tardía: la obra del jesuita Juan de Velasco." Master's thesis, Facultad Latinoamericana de Ciencias Sociales (FLACSO), Sede Ecuador.

Cañizares Esguerra, Jorge. 2001. *How to Write the History of the New World: History, Epistemology, and Identity in the Atlantic World in the Eighteenth Century.* Stanford: Stanford University Press.

Carrión, Benjamín. [1932] 1968. *Atahuallpa.* Reprint, Panama: Albon International.

–. 1958. *Nuevo relato ecuatoriano. Crítica y antología.* 2nd ed. Quito: Casa de la Cultura Ecuatoriana.

Cevallos, Pedro Fermín. [1870] 1972. *Resumen de la Historia del Ecuador, desde sus origen hasta 1845.* 3rd ed. Ambato, Ecuador: Casa de la Cultura.

Espejo, Eugenio. [1791–1792] 1958. *Primicias de la Cultura de Quito,* 2nd ed. Quito: Publicaciones del Museo de Arte e Historia de la Municipalidad de Quito.

Estrada, Julio Enrique. 1967. "Mito y nacionalidad," *Cuadernos de Historia y arqueología Casa de la Cultura* 17: 169–83.

Gerbi, Antonello. 1973. *The Dispute of the New World: The History of a Polemic, 1750–1900,* trans. Jeremy Boyle. Pittsburgh: University of Pittsburgh Press.

González Suárez, Federico. 1890–1904. *Historia general de la Repúlica del Ecuador.* 7 vols. Quito: Imprenta del Clero.

–. 1944. *Obras escogidas.* Quito: Imprenta del Ministerio de Gobierno and Ediciones del Instituto Cultural Ecuatoriano.

Handelsman, Michael. 1999. "Introducción." In *Lo afro y la plurinacionalidad: el caso ecuatoriano visto desde su literatura,* 1–9. Oxford, MS: University of Mississippi Department of Modern Languages.

Harrison, Regina. 1996. *Entre el tronar épico y el llanto elegíaco: simbología indígena en la poesía ecuatoriana de los siglos XIX–XX.* Quito: Ediciones Abya-Yala / Universidad Simón Bolívar.

Herrera, Pablo. 1927. *Ensayo sobre la historia de la literatura ecuatoriana.* Quito: Imprenta Nacional.

Higgins, Antony. 2000. *Constructing the Criollo Archive: Subjects of Knowledge in the Biblioteca Mexicana and the Rusticatio Mexicana.* West Lafayette, IN: Purdue University Press.

Jaramillo Alvarado, Pío. 1954. *El indio ecuatoriano.* 4th ed. Quito: Casa de la Cultura Ecuatoriana.

Jijón Y Caamaño, Jacinto. 1918. "Examen crítico de la veracidad de la *Historia del Reino de Quito* del P. Juan de Velasco, de la Compañía de Jesús." *Boletín de la Sociedad Ecuatoriana de Estudios Históricos Americanos* 1: 33–63.

–. 1944. "Prólogo." In *Obras escogidas,* Federico González Suárez, x–xv. Quito: Imprenta del Ministerio de Gobierno and Ediciones del Instituto Cultural Ecuatoriano.

–. 1951. *Antropología prehispánica del Ecuador: resumen.* Quito: La Prensa Católica.
Larrea, Carlos Manuel. 1971. *El Padre Juan de Velasco y su Historia del Reino de Quito.* Quito: Editorial Ecuatoriana.
Mera, Juan León. 1893. *Ojeada histórico-crítico sobre la poesía ecuatoriana desde su época más remota hasta nuestros días.* 2nd ed. Barcelona: Impr. de J. Cunill Sala.
–. 1976. *Cumandá o un drama entre salvajes,* 1877. Reprint, Madrid: Editorial Espasa-Calpe.
Miller, Marilyn Grace. 2004. *Rise and Fall of the Cosmic Race: The Cult of Mestizaje in Latin America.* Austin: University of Texas Press.
Pareja Diezcanseco, Alfredo. 1954. *Historia del Ecuador.* Quito: Casa de la Cultura Ecuatoriana.
–. 1981. "Prólogo" and "Criterio de esta edición." In *Historia del Reino de Quito,* ix–xlix. Caracas: Biblioteca Ayacucho.
Pérez, Galo René. 1972. *Pensamiento y Literatura del Ecuador.* Quito: Casa de la Cultura Ecuatoriana.
Robalino De Baldeón, Piedad. 1989. *Juan de Velasco.* Riobamba: Pedagógica Freire.
Salazar, Ernesto. 1988. *Mitos de nuestro pasado.* Quito: Museo del Banco Central.
Silva, Erika. 1992. *Los mitos de la Ecuatorianidad.* Quito: Abya-Yala.
Stutzman, Ronald. 1981. "*El Mestizaje*: An All-Inclusive Ideology of Exclusion." In *Cultural Transformations and Ethnicity in Modern Ecuador,* ed. Norman E. Whitten, 45–94. Champaign: University of Illinois Press.
Tinajero, Fernando. 1986. "Estudio Introductorio." In *Teoría de la cultura nacional,* 10–77. Quito: Banco Central del Ecuador and Corporación Editora Nacional.
Tobar Donoso, Julio. 1960. "Padre Juan de Velasco, S.I." In *Historia del Reino de Quito en la América meridional,* Juan de Velasco, xix–xcii. Puebla: Cajica.
Velasco, Juan de. 1995–1996. *Historia del Reino de Quito en la América meridional,* 1977. Reprint, Quito: Casa de la Cultura Ecuatoriana.
–. [1789] 1981. *Historia del Reino de Quito en la América meridional,* ed. 1789, Alfredo Pareja Diezcanseco. Caracas: Biblioteca Ayacucho.
–. 1986. *Zoología fantástica.* Quito: El Conejo.
Willingham, Eileen. 2001. "Creating the Kingdom of Quito: Patria, History, Language and Utopia in Juan de Velasco's 'Historia del Reino de Quito'" PhD diss., University of Wisconsin–Madison.

chapter four

For Love of Patria: Locating Self and Nation in Clavigero's Rendition of the Conquest of México

BEATRIZ DE ALBA-KOCH

In 1767, Francisco Xavier Clavigero and his Jesuit brethren were expelled from New Spain. The uprooting of Clavigero from the Spanish empire would convert him into a historian. By the following year Clavigero was established in Bologna, where he remained until his death in 1787, at the age of fifty-six.[1] During most of his exile in the Papal States, he dedicated himself to writing in Spanish and translating into Italian the work which would win him a place of honour within the Catholic Enlightenment, his magisterial *Historia antigua de México*, the first volume of which appeared in Cesena in 1780 under the title *Storia Antica del Messico.* In this work, and especially in its narrative of the Conquest, a counterpoint is sustained not only between Clavigero's religious convictions and his engagement with the premises of the "Age of Reason," but also between an articulation of his identity as a Criollo and an affirmation of his *mexicanidad.*

The *Historia* offers a "ligero bosquejo," or brief outline, of the discussion of America published by the *philosophe* Cornelius De Pauw in his *Recherches philosophiques sur les Américains* (1768). De Pauw was a renegade cleric who, according to Clavigero, maintained "an implacable hatred [...] towards the clergy of the Roman Church, and especially the Jesuits ("un odio implacable [...] a los eclesiásticos de la Iglesia romana, y sobre todo a los jesuitas" [Clavigero [1789] 1945, 513]).[2] Clavigero summarized De Pauw's depiction of the peoples of the New World concisely:

> Men barely differed from beasts in form only [...]. They are brutish and feeble and are subject to many outlandish diseases, the result of an unhealthy climate. But even if their bodies are thus, their souls are still more imperfect. They lack memory [...]. They do not know how to reflect on or organize

> their ideas; nor are they capable of improving themselves, because only coarse and vicious humours circulate in their brains. Their will is insensible to the stimulus of love or any other passion. Their laziness has submerged them in a savage life. Their cowardice was manifested in the conquest [...]. Drunkenness, lies and sodomy were common [...] throughout the New Continent. They lived without laws. The few arts they knew were very rudimentary. Agriculture, amongst them, was entirely abandoned, their architecture was very poor and their tools were even more imperfect. Throughout the New Continent there were only two cities: Cuzco [...] and Mexico [...], and these two were only miserable villages ("Los hombres apenas se diferenciaban de las bestias si no es en la figura [...]. Son brutos y débiles y están sujetos a muchas enfermedades extravagantes, causadas por el clima insalubre. Pero aun siendo así sus cuerpos, todavía son más imperfectas sus almas. Carecen de memoria [...]. No saben reflexionar ni ordenar sus ideas, ni son capaces de mejorarlas, ni aun de pensar, porque en sus cerebros sólo circulan humores gruesos y viciosos. Su voluntad es insensible a los estímulos del amor y de cualquier otra pasión. Su pereza los tiene sumergidos en la vida salvaje. Su cobardía se manifestó en la conquista [...]. La embriaguez, la mentira y la sodomía eran comunes [...] en todo el Nuevo Continente. Vivían sin leyes. Las pocas artes que conocían eran muy groseras. La agricultura estaba entre ellos enteramente abandonada, su arquitectura muy mezquina y más imperfectos todavía sus instrumentos. En todo el Nuevo Mundo no había más que dos ciudades: Cuzco [...] y México [...] y estas dos no eran más que dos miserables aldeas" [Clavigero [1789] 1945, 422–3]).

For Clavigero, this "monstrous portrait" ("monstruoso retrato" [Clavigero [1780] 1945, 423]) was the summation of much supposedly learned European commentary on the New World, and was all the more alarming because it was based on the climatological research of a naturalist of the stature of the *philosophe* George-Louis Leclerc, Comte de Buffon; moreover, he believed that De Pauw's vision was endorsed by respected sources such as William Robertson and the *Histoire des Deux Indes*.[3] Clavigero articulated his response to De Pauw, Buffon, and other detractors of the New World by composing nine essays or *disertaciones*, sustained by an extensive historiographical apparatus that precedes them in the text. While the *disertaciones* which close the *Historia* clearly illustrate the polemical orientation of the work, his rebuttal is also evident in the footnotes found throughout the text. Nonetheless, Clavigero was convinced that he had to begin by establishing his credibility as an authority on this subject, given that the French Enlightenment had already decided that neither clergymen nor Spaniards could be trusted to provide reliable testimony concerning the New World, but rather that the understanding of its continents should be entrusted to the presumed sophistication of the French *philosophe* (Brading 1973, 47; Cañizares-Esguerra 2001, 12–49).

Through the wide range of themes explored in the *disertaciones*, Clavigero contests the "jokes" ("bufonadas" [Clavigero [1780] 1945, 422]) of the detractors of America, concluding that the "nonsense" ("despropósitos" [455]) that he feels obliged to correct is not only the result of the ignorance of authors writing from their desks in Paris, Berlin, or Edinburgh, who had never set foot in America, but also in the final analysis is the "effect of a blind and excessive patriotism that has made them conceive an imaginary pre-eminence of their own country over all the countries in the world" ("efecto de un ciego y excesivo patriotismo que les ha hecho concebir ciertas imaginarias preeminencias de su propio país sobre todos los otros del mundo" [455]). However, if Clavigero combats this "blind and excessive patriotism" by proposing truth as his principal object (xxii), he is also motivated by patriotism as well as loyalty to his order. Although his love for his "patria" is articulated openly, his *esprit de corps* is only expressed between the lines.

The *Historia* is dedicated to the Royal and Pontifical University of México, the institution to whose custody were entrusted the collections of books, codices, manuscripts, and scientific instruments as well as educational programs that had previously been the responsibility of the Jesuits.[4] Declaring himself to be a "mexicano," without mentioning his affiliation with the Society of Jesus, Clavigero begins by indicating that he has dedicated himself to writing his *Historia* "to be useful to his country" ("por ser útil a su patria" [xvii]). He "friendily" complains "of the indolence and neglect of our elders with respect to our country" ("amistosamente de la indolencia o descuido de nuestros mayores con respecto a nuestra patria" [xviii]), lamenting the loss of many ancient indigenous documents and the knowledge of how to interpret them, as well as the abandonment of the teaching of indigenous languages, a task at which some of the Jesuit *colegios* had excelled. Asserting his modernity, he suggests that the university establish a museum, an institution that heretofore had not existed in New Spain, to "try to preserve the remains of the antiquities of our country" ("tratar de conservar los restos de las antigüedades de nuestra patria" [xviii]). He concludes his dedication by expressing his desire that his work be accepted "as a testimony of [his] most sincere love of country" ("como testimonio de mi sincerísimo amor a la patria" [xix]).

In his prologue, Clavigero again emphasizes his patriotic motivation, indicating that although the preparation of the *Historia* had been "not less tiring and difficult than expensive" ("no menos fatigosa y difícil que dispendiosa" [xxi]), he undertook it "to avoid the exasperating and reprehensible idleness to which I am condemned, to serve my country in the best possible way, and to restore the splendor of truth, which has been obscured by an incredible mob of modern writers of America" ("para evitar la fastidiosa y reprensible ociosidad a que me hallo condenado, para servir del mejor modo posible a mi patria, para restituir a su esplendor la verdad ofuscada por una turba increíble de escritores modernos de la América" [xxi]).

These declarations of patriotism, associated with ascribing a positive value to the pre-Hispanic Nahua culture, have attracted the attention of scholars today and of a wide readership since the publication of Clavigero's *Historia*.[5] However, the importance of the providentialism of Clavigero's narrative of the Conquest, where the ambiguity of his position is most apparent, has been overlooked or diminished.[6] Although he displays with unusual objectivity an ample range of evidence concerning the controversial events of the Conquest, in the context of the more thoroughgoing secularization associated with much of the European Enlightenment, his providentialism reveals that he was as concerned with the vindication of Catholicism as he was with defending the ancient "mexicanos," called Aztecs here for the first time.

"A history of Mexico written by a Mexican" ("Una historia de México escrita por un mexicano" [xvii]): so Clavigero begins his *Historia*, but "México" and "mexicano" did not – in the eighteenth century – have the same meaning as they do now. After the creation of an independent Mexican nation-state in the nineteenth century, Mexican nationalists normalized the term "mexicano," while depriving it of some of the ambiguity found in its use during the viceregal period; Clavigero understood his "nation" as a broader entity encompassed by the Spanish empire.[7] México, in addition to being the capital city of New Spain, was also, in the eighteenth century, a *reino* and a province. The *reino* of México comprised not only the eponymous province, but also included the provinces of Tlaxcala, Puebla, Oaxaca, and Michoacán, and constituted a small fraction of the territory of the viceroyalty of New Spain, which included most of Central America, the Philippines, Spanish possessions in the Caribbean, and the northern marches of California, Sonora, New Mexico, and Texas. Although the area ruled by the pre-Hispanic kingdom of "México" under Motecuhzoma II was but a small portion of the viceroyalty, Clavigero assigns great importance to this pre-Hispanic polity throughout the *Historia.* Thus he contributed to the acceptance of México as the natural synecdoche for the great diversity of the viceroyalty. "[M]exicano," then, had a range of uses in the eighteenth century: the term could refer to an indigenous ethnic group, the "Mexica," the best known of the Nahua peoples to Criollo scholars, but also to the inhabitant of a variety of political jurisdictions. Clavigero exploits this polysemy to celebrate his sense of attachment to a geographic space associated with a storied past. While he most commonly uses "mexicano" to refer to the Nahua, he also uses the term to describe himself, and other Criollos of New Spain he admired, such as Carlos de Sigüenza y Góngora (1645–1700) and sister Juana Inés de la Cruz (1648–1695). He refers to "Sor Juana," the famous poet and Hieronymite nun, as a most "ingenious Mexican" ("ingeniosísima mexicana" [428]). The scientist, antiquarian, and poet Sigüenza y Góngora is identified as a "Creole, born in the [...] Mexico City" ("Criollo, nacido en la [...] ciudad de México" [532]), and described as a "most learned Mexican" ("doctísimo mexicano" [xxxvi, 293, and 425]), a "great Mexican" ("gran mexicano" [294]) and a "most renowned Mexicano" ("famosísimo mexicano" [426]).

In *Novohispano* society, indicating one's *casta* or *calidad* was important in establishing entitlement to privileges that the crown had assigned to various components of the population. In legal documents, Criollos were known as *españoles americanos* or *españoles,* a practice that continued in independent México until the 1861 separation of church and state. Clavigero speaks of his lineage thus:

> We were born to Spanish parents and have no affinity or ties of kinship with the Indians, nor can we expect to gain anything from their misery. And thus no motive other than love of truth and zeal for humanity, makes us abandon our cause to defend that of others with less danger of error ("Nosotros nacimos de padres españoles y no tenemos ninguna afinidad o consanguinidad con los indios, ni podemos esperar de su miseria ninguna recompensa. Y así ningún otro motivo que el amor a la verdad y el celo por la humanidad, nos hace abandonar la propia causa por defender la ajena con menos peligro de errar" [503]).

Clavigero's "own cause" was to question the discrimination to which the civil and ecclesiastical hierarchy of the viceroyalty under the Bourbon kings had subjected the Criollos, by favouring peninsular Spaniards for benefices and important administrative posts. Claiming to cast aside his personal interests, Clavigero also distances himself rhetorically from the "mexicanos" in order to convince his readers of his objectivity. However, he is equally keen to distinguish himself from Europeans who had written about the Americas, insisting that unlike them, he has personal familiarity with his subject. He affirms that, having lived for thirty-six years in various provinces of the Mexican *reino*, he has mastered the "Mexican language" ("lengua mexicana" [xxi]) and has resided for "some years" ("algunos años") with the same "mexicanos" whose history he is writing. To underline his impartiality, he declares:

> What I say is based on a serious and painstaking study of their history, and on my close contact with Mexicans for many years [...]. Being their compatriot does not incline me in their favour, nor does the love for my nation or the zeal for honor of my nationals compel me to condemn them; so I will recount here what I know about them, both the good and the bad ("Lo que yo diré va fundado sobre un serio y prolijo estudio de su historia, y sobre el íntimo trato de los mexicanos por muchos años [...]. Ni la razón de compatriota inclina mi discernimiento a su favor, ni el amor de mi nación o el celo del honor de mis nacionales me empeña a condenarlos; y así diré lo bueno y lo malo que en ellos he conocido" [45]).

Here Clavigero privileges the Criollo as observer, suggesting that he is neither a partisan of the imperial policies of Spain (his "nation"), nor of the colonized (his compatriots), yet nonetheless is intimately familiar with the latter. This distancing, however, does not prevent him from passionately defending the "mexicanos" in his *disertaciones*. Thus, regarding their intellectual capacity, he asserts:

> I say to [De] Pauw and all of Europe that the souls of the Mexicans are in no way inferior to those of the Europeans, that they have a capacity for all the sciences, even the most abstract, and if their education was seriously attended to [...] they would see philosophers, mathematicians and theologians among the Americans who could compete with the most famous in Europe ("Protesto a Pauw y a toda Europa, que las almas de los mexicanos en nada son inferiores a las de los europeos; que son capaces de todas las ciencias, aun las más abstractas, y que si seriamente se cuidara de su educación [...] se verían entre los americanos, filósofos, matemáticos y teólogos que pudieran competir con los más famosos de Europa" [518]).

His defence of the "mexicanos" is coupled with a denunciation of the abject condition in which not only the majority of the Nahua find themselves, but also the descendants of the ancient noble houses, New Spain's indigenous peoples having been consigned to a subaltern position in viceregal society.[8] He observes that it is "very difficult, if not impossible, to make progress in science amidst miserable, servile, and continuously discomforting life" ("muy difícil, por no decir imposible, hacer progresos en las ciencias en medio de una vida miserable y servil y de continuas incomodidades" [518]). While lamenting the fate of the indigenous population, Clavigero suggests that the basis of social organization for New Spain should be class, not ethnicity. There is no doubt, he affirms, "that the policy of the Spaniards would have been wiser if, instead of bringing women from Europe and slaves from Africa, they would have married into the very same American houses, in order to create from all of them a single and individual nation" ("que hubiera sido más acertada la política de los españoles si en vez de llevar mujeres de Europa y esclavos de África, se hubieran enlazado con las mismas casas americanas, hasta hacer de todas una sola e individua nación" [213]). His promotion of *mestizaje* is framed by a decidedly elitist political vision.

Nonetheless, Clavigero's use of the term "mexicano" reveals his empathy with the oppressed indigenous peoples of New Spain, particularly since so designating oneself in the hierarchical *novohispano* context was to invite being associated with one of the poorest components of society. However, in this declaration of solidarity with the destitute, Clavigero is consonant with the rhetorical tradition that the Jesuits of New Spain had developed to respond to critics who pointed to the wealth and elitism of the order. Oriented originally towards the education of the sons of prosperous Criollos, enriched by productive estates using slave labour and on whose income they refused to pay tithes, the Jesuits were attacked repeatedly and severely for their commitment to the material welfare of their order. More than a century before their expulsion, the bishop of Puebla, Juan de Palafox y Mendoza, already questioned the right of the Society of Jesus to exist in its current form.[9] The Jesuits did not deny, nor seek to justify their privileges, but rather emphasized their pastoral merits, pointing to their work among the faithful and their missions to ethnic groups such as the Yaquis, who were among the most resistant to conversion of New Spain's peoples and poorly integrated into the viceroyalty's economy (see Brading 1991, 246–7).

The strategy adopted by Clavigero, of declaring an attachment to an indigenous past and the Nahua peoples without repudiating his Hispanic identity, was employed recurrently by Criollos keen to distinguish themselves from Iberian Spaniards. The *novohispanos* who were most prominent in the construction of this identity based on cultural reconciliation were clerics for the most part, and thus their sense of identity was profoundly religious. The religiosity of Criollo patriotism was linked closely to the veneration of the Virgin of Guadalupe, a highly popular devotion. Clavigero's *Breve ragguaglio della prodigiosa y rinomata immagine della Madona de Guadalupe del Messico* appeared in Cesena two years before his *Historia.* Here, in a discussion of the cult of the goddess Centeotl at the *cerro* of Tepeyac, Clavigero provides an observation on the veneration of the Guadalupana that demonstrates the limits of his cultural relativism:

> Today, at the foot of the same mount, stands the most celebrated shrine in all America. It is dedicated to the Mother of God, converting that place of abomination into a temple, where the Lord bestows an abundance of his grace on those peoples in that place so drenched in the blood of their ancestors ("Hoy está al pie del mismo monte el más célebre santuario de toda la América, dedicado a la Madre de Dios, convirtiéndose en propiciatorio aquel lugar de abominación y derramando el Señor abundantemente sus gracias en beneficio de aquellos pueblos en aquel lugar bañado con tanta sangre de sus antepasados" [Clavigero [1780] 1945, 157–8]).

This attitude towards the cult of the Guadalupe is consistent with his providential interpretation of the Conquest, the only section of the *Historia* where Clavigero openly identifies himself with his faith, alluding to "our religion" ("nuestra religion" [301 and 322]) and to "the pure and holy truths of our religion" ("las puras y santas verdades de nuestra religion" [310]).

The *Historia* celebrates the ancient kings of Tenochtitlan less than the rulers of Acolhuacan, whose capital, Texcoco, is praised as the "Atenas del Anáhuac" (115). The Kingdom of Acolhuacan or Texcoco was adjacent to Tenochtitlán, and second only to that great city within the Triple Alliance; Acolhuacan's most famous ruler was Nezahualcoyotl (1402–1472). No ruler discussed in the *Historia* is accorded more admiration than Nezahualcoyotl, "one of the greatest heroes of ancient America" ("uno de los mayores héroes de la América Antigua" [113]). Described as an enlightened absolutist *avant la lettre,* punishing his subjects as if he had been counseled by Cesare Beccaria, Clavigero's Nezahualcoyotl insists that the punishment be commensurate with the crime (113). An embodiment of that reconciliation of faith and reason that was a fundamental value of the Catholic Enlightenment, Nezahualcoyotl is also praised as the founder of a tradition of learning without precedent, thanks to "the higher lights of his understanding" ("las superiores luces de su entendimiento" [114]). Through his continual study of natural phenomena and their causes, he was able to conceive of a universe governed by a single deity, Clavigero contends, but did not arrive at this conclusion through revelation or by observing a miracle.

Early portrayals of Nezahualcoyotl as a learned man attributed his wisdom to a knowledge of the Christian God. This approach is comparable to the approach to pre-Hispanic indigenous culture espoused by the Inca Garcilaso de la Vega (see Brading 1991, 274). Garcilaso de la Vega, a Neoplatonic Humanist, affirms that before the Spanish invasion a knowledge of the Christian God was achieved in Tiwantinsuyo, the Inca empire, through direct divine illumination. Clavigero, however, as a man of the Enlightenment, was not attracted to such explanations that so privileged the role of the supernatural. Rather, he focuses on study, frequent observation, experimentation, and reflection as the sources of knowledge of God. Clavigero claims:

> But in nothing did Nezahualcoyotl delight more than in the study of nature. He acquired some knowledge of astronomy through the frequent observation of the trajectory of the stars. He applied himself to knowing plants and animals [...]. He investigated with curiosity the causes of the effects he admired in nature and this continued consideration made him realize the insubstantiality and falsehood of idolatry [...]. [H]e recognized no other God than the Creator of Heaven ("Pero en nada se deleitaba tanto Nezahualcóyotl como en estudiar de la naturaleza. Adquirió algunos conocimientos de astronomía con la frecuente observación que hacía del curso de los astros. Se aplicó a conocer las plantas y los animales [...]. Investigaba curiosamente las causas de los efectos que admiraba en la naturaleza y esta continua consideración le hizo conocer la insusbstancia y falsedad de la idolatría [...]. [É]l no reconocía otro Dios que el Creador del Cielo" [Clavigero [1780] 1945, 115]).

However, more prudent politician than zealot for the faith, Nezahualcoyotl kept his beliefs within the bosom of his family and did not eradicate human sacrifices, although he decreed that the only victims of these practices were to be prisoners of war.

Clavigero attributes to *tlatoani* Nezahualpilli, the son of Nezahualcoyotl, a language typical of monotheism: "Creador del Cielo," "Omnipotente Dios" and "Señor del mundo" (126) are among the expressions ascribed to him. Clavigero also notes that the grandsons of Nezahualcoyotl, the invaluable Spanish allies Carlos and Fernando Ixlilxochitl, were among the first Aztec nobles to convert to Christianity. The Jesuit historian's admiration for the Kingdom of Acolhuacan echoes that of the Texcocan scholar Fernando de Alva Ixtlilxochitl, whose papers, bequeathed to Sigüenza, and by him to the Jesuit *colegio* of México, were read there by Clavigero (xxviii). Alva Ixtlilxochitl portrayed his ancestor Fernando as a more pious version of Hernán Cortés, and affirmed that Fernando, not Cortés, was really the one responsible for bringing the military and spiritual conquest of the "mexicanos" to a successful conclusion.[10] However, Clavigero, careful to base his account of the Conquest on a diversity of sources, does not allow his enthusiasm for the family of Nezahualcoyotl to extend to embracing this claim.

In striving for objectivity in the presentation of the Conquest, Clavigero seeks to transcend the limitations of accounts which reflected the perspectives of soldiers, ecclesiastics, and indigenous or *mestizo* historians, who were typically motivated to write by a desire to justify themselves, to celebrate their order, or to defend the interests of their people.[11] In contrast, Clavigero offers a pluralistic vision of the Conquest: he admires equally the speeches celebrating the honour and patriotism of Cacamatzin, king of Acolhuacan (348–9), the dexterity in combat of the "famous Tlatelolcan" ("célebre tlaltelolca" [312]) Tzilacatzin, and Cortés' audacity in grounding his ships.[12] While the actions of the conquistadors and their allies as well as the responses of their enemies are recounted in accordance with their internal logic, and while Clavigero sees heroism on both sides of the struggle, his narration of the Conquest is shaped by his efforts to harmonize free will and divine design. For him, the Conquest was the consequence of human weaknesses and achievements, such as greed and technological advances in maritime navigation, both of which he sees as linked to the exercise of human free will, but he situates their effects in the context of a divinely determined struggle between good and evil.[13]

The structure of the *Historia* points to the central importance assigned by Clavigero to the Conquest, yet his definition of this event is tightly circumscribed: he sees it as beginning with the first expedition to the coast of México, led by Francisco Hernández de Córdoba in 1517, and ending with the triumph of Cortés and his allies on August 13, 1521, the day on which Cuauhtemoc, the last emperor, was captured and Tenochtitlan, the capital of the Aztec empire, surrendered. More pages of the *Historia* are devoted to the events of these four years than to Clavigero's account of eight centuries of the political history of the Valley of México. He justifies this emphasis on the Conquest by describing it as the "general upheaval of a whole world, and unquestionably the most rare and remarkable event in human history" ("el trastorno general de un mundo entero, que es sin disputa el más raro y notable suceso que se lee en la historia humana" [141]). Although for much of the *Historia*, Clavigero aligns himself with the relativist position regarding ancient cultures that was proposed two centuries earlier by the famed Dominican Bartolomé de las Casas in his *Apologética historia sumaria* (finished in 1552), the Jesuit historian is more of an apologist for Christianity and the Spanish presence in America than his distinguished predecessor. In the final analysis, unable to accept the religious beliefs of the ancient "mexicanos," Clavigero, unlike Las Casas, saw the Conquest as a just punishment for the fallacy and cruelty of their beliefs.

The Jesuit's presentation of the drama of military manoeuvres and political intrigue associated with the Conquest echoes Giambattista Vico's philosophy of history, according to which providence corrects the errors of humankind.[14] In the *Historia general de la América Septentrional*, Lorenzo Boturini Benaduci explained that Vico's approach was "a new system of natural law for nations, resting upon the two pillars of Providence and free will" ("un nuevo sistema del derecho natural de las gentes sobre las dos columnas de la Providencia y del libre alvedrío" [Boturini Benaduci (1746) 1990, 18]). Clavigero consulted Boturini's observations extensively, and although he does not cite Vico in the *Historia*, he probably had an opportunity to read the *Scienza nuova*, as this work was disseminated widely in the Papal States (Trabulse 1988, 52–3). Vico affirmed the complementarity of human agency and providence, contending that "[t]he world of nations is in fact a human creation," but that "without doubt this world was created by the mind of providence, which is often different, sometimes contrary, and always superior to the particular goals which people have set for themselves" (Vico [1725] 2001, 489). Providence works through the individual decisions of humankind; thus, Vico explained, "providence uses peoples' limited goals as a means of attaining greater ones" (489). He saw conquests as one of the "remedies" that providence could provide against "great civil maladies" (488). Clavigero, reluctant to demonize pre-Hispanic religion, nonetheless repudiates it while adopting a compassionate attitude towards its followers; this compassion is mingled with frustration in his narration of the Conquest, where he contends that the Aztecs failed to seize opportunities to rid themselves of the invaders.

That Clavigero understands the conquistadors as instruments of providence becomes evident in the discussion of Motecuhzoma II's efforts to satisfy the invaders with gifts, instead of responding to their intrusion with force. Here the ambiguities and contradictions in Clavigero's position are manifested in his exasperation with Motecuhzoma's ineffective strategy, though Motecuhzoma's approach greatly facilitated the establishment of Catholicism in the lands of the former Aztec empire, a development that the *Historia* is committed to celebrating. Clavigero comments: "The King thought his generosity would oblige the Spanish to leave, not realizing that the love of gold is a fire that rages ever more fiercely, and how the more plentiful the fuel that ignites it" ("Pensaba aquel rey obligar con su liberalidad a los españoles a la partida, sin advertir que el amor del oro es un fuego que tanto más se enciende, cuanto más abundante es el pábulo que se le suministra" [Clavigero [1780] 1945, 304–5]).

The apparent incapacity on the part of the "mexicanos" to understand the dimensions of Spanish greed is not portrayed as the result of innate stupidity or cowardliness, an interpretation favoured by European commentators such as De Pauw. For Clavigero, the only possible explanation for Motecuhzoma's error is a supernatural one:

> There is no doubt that on this and many other occasions [...] Moctezuma could easily rid himself of these few foreigners, but God kept them as instruments of his justice, using their weapons to avenge the superstition, cruelty, and other offenses with which those nations had incurred his wrath for so long ("No hay duda de que en esta y otras muchas ocasiones [...] pudo fácilmente Moctezuma deshacerse de aquellos pocos extranjeros; pero Dios los conservaba para instrumentos de su justicia, sirviéndose de sus armas para vengar la superstición, la crueldad y los otros delitos con que aquellas naciones habían provocado por tanto tiempo su indignación" [305]).

To exculpate himself from the accusation that he is here favouring the Spanish and abandoning the objectivity he promised to maintain, Clavigero adds:

> We do not claim with this to justify the intention and conduct of the conquistadors, but we have to recognize in the series of conquest, despite incredulity, the hand of God that led the empire to its own ruin and that God used men's own errors of judgment to achieve the lofty goals of his Providence ("No pretendemos con esto justificar la intención y la conducta de los conquistadores; pero tampoco podemos menos que reconocer en la serie de la conquista, a pesar de la incredulidad, la mano de Dios que iba disponiendo las cosas de aquel imperio a su ruina y se

servía de los mismos desaciertos de los hombres para los altos fines de su Providencia" [305]).

Thus the greed of the Spanish and the errors of Motecuhzoma unknowingly conspired to advance the cause of Catholicism. The imprisonment of Motecuhzoma by the conquistadors, accomplished without resistance from the emperor or his entourage a few days after the invaders arrived to the capital, proved more difficult for Clavigero to explain. The Jesuit was conscious that his readers on both sides of the Atlantic, like himself, were apt to find troubling the inadequacy of Motecuhzoma's defence of himself and his people in this situation:

> I am aware that readers will perceive, when reading and thinking about the circumstances of this extraordinary event, the same displeasure that I feel in writing [about them;] but in this and other events in our history, we must bow to the higher wisdom of Divine Providence, which took the Spanish as the instrument of its justice and mercy for those nations, punishing some for their superstition and cruelty, and enlightening others with the light of the Gospel ("Bien conozco que los lectores percibirán al leer y reflexionar en las circunstancias de este extraordinario suceso, la misma displicencia que yo siento al escribirlo pero es preciso adorar en este y otros sucesos de nuestra historia los altísimos consejos de la Divina Providencia, que tomó a los españoles por instrumento de su justicia y de su misericordia para con aquellas naciones, castigando en unos la superstición y la crueldad, e iluminando a los demás con la luz del Evangelio" [344]).

Another critical moment in this Conquest narrative is the burning at the stake of Cuahpopoca and his son, as well as fifteen other nobles on the orders of Cortés. These nobles were declared guilty of treason against Charles V because they had killed Captain Juan de Escalante and his party. Cortés profited from the incident to increase his power over his royal prisoner and the Mexica people: the public execution of the Mexica nobles was performed in front of Motecuhzoma's principal palace. Clavigero judges this initiative to have been rash, arguing that a violent reaction of the Mexica in this situation was to be expected. Thus their passivity when faced with this "unprecedented" event – accomplished by Cortés' "few men" – leads him to ask:

> But in truth, what were all his troops compared with the immense multitude of Mexicans who observed this great event, if God, ordering all things

> for the purposes of His Providence, did not halt the effects that naturally should be feared of this unprecedented attack, perpetrated by those few men? ("Pero a la verdad, ¿qué era toda su tropa comparada con la inmensa multitud de mexicanos que deberían ser espectadores de aquel gran suceso, si Dios, ordenando todas las cosas a los fines de su providencia, no impidiera los efectos que naturalmente deberían temerse del inaudito atentado de aquellos pocos hombres?" [346]).

Here again, ascribing the decisive role to divine intervention allows Clavigero to affirm his commitment to Catholicism, while simultaneously assuaging the injury to his patriotism arising from what appears to him to be an inadequate response on the part of the Mexica to the Spanish invasion.

The concept of "patria" is even more evident when Clavigero turns to the actions of the Mexica, but is also tied to expressions of frustration. This frustrated patriotism shapes his account of the refusal of Cuauhtemoc and his priests to surrender Tenochtitlan. The Mexica's refusal to capitulate came to be seen as an act of great heroism by intellectuals and politicians of the nineteenth century, particularly during the regime of Porfirio Díaz (Pastrana Flores 2004, 216 and 219–20). For Clavigero, however, it was but another manifestation of the "superstitious fear that dominated their spirits" ("el temor supersticioso que dominaba en sus espíritus" [408]). Thus, "the Spanish general was answered that there was no need for his proposals; that the war should continue while the time was ripe, that they were resolved to defend themselves until their last breath" ("se respondió al general español que no había lugar a sus proposiciones; que continuase en hora buena la guerra, que ellos estaban resueltos a defenderse hasta el último aliento" [408]). For Clavigero, this defiance was the result of a tragic combination of the superstition of the "mexicanos" and the duplicity of the Spaniards:

> If sentiments of honour and patriotism had held more sway than superstition in this determination, it would not have been so reprehensible, because although their ruin was the inevitable result of an ongoing war, they had no better fortune than peace. The experience of past events made them wary of promises; thus, dying, weapon in hand while defending one's country and freedom, should have presented itself more in accordance to the ideas of honour rather than prostituting one's homeland to those strangers' ambition and, by surrendering, condemning oneself to a sad and wretched servitude ("Si en este dictamen hubieran tenido más influjo los

> sentimientos de honor y el amor a la patria, que la superstición, no fueran tan reprensible; porque aunque previeran inevitable su ruina continuando la guerra, no tenían mayor fortuna con la paz. La experiencia de los pasados sucesos les hacía desconfiar de las ventajas que les prometían; y así debería representárselos como más conformes a las ideas del honor, el morir con las armas en la mano en defensa de su patria y de su libertad, que el prostituir su patria a la ambición de aquellos extranjeros y sujetarse, con su rendición, a una triste y miserable servidumbre" [408]).

Clavigero, then, would have wished to see the Mexica demonstrating more agency and patriotism; he was also frustrated that they did not take advantage of opportunities available to them to eliminate the leader of the invasion. On many occasions, he contends, the Mexica could easily have killed Cortés if they had desisted from seeking to capture him alive in order to sacrifice him to their gods. The determination of the Mexica to capture Spanish officers alive was "undoubtedly one of the things that facilitated the conquest to the Spanish" ("sin duda una de las cosas que facilitaron a los españoles la conquista" [392 and 405]). He closes his account laconically:

> The total occupation of the city and the conquest of the Mexican empire were accomplished on August 13, 1521 [...]. The Mexicans, along with all the other nations that helped in their ruin were, despite the Christian and prudent laws of the Catholic monarchs, abandoned to misery, oppression, and contempt, not only from the Spanish but even from the most vile African slaves and their infamous descendants, God avenging the cruelty, injustice, and superstition of their elders on the miserable posterity of those nations. [This is an] [i]ll-fated example of divine justice and of the instability of earthly kingdoms ("La total ocupación de la ciudad y conquista del imperio mexicano fue el día 13 de agosto de 1521 [...]. Los mexicanos, con todas las demás naciones que ayudaron a su ruina, quedaron, a pesar de las cristianas y prudentes leyes de los Monarcas Católicos, abandonadas a la miseria, la opresión y al desprecio, no solamente de los españoles sino aun de los más viles esclavos africanos y de sus infames descendientes, vengando Dios en la miserable posteridad de aquellas naciones la crueldad, la injusticia y la superstición de sus mayores. Funesto ejemplo de la justicia divina y de la inestabilidad de los reinos de la tierra" [417–18]).

Here Clavigero brings his reader to the present: almost three centuries of Spanish domination are telescoped in this final peroration. Far from the Franciscan triumphalism, which saw in the fall of Tenochtitlan the beginning of the evangelization of the Nahua, Clavigero underlines the poverty of the indigenous peoples and the failure of Spanish rule to remedy their situation.

Clavigero presents the suffering of the Mexica as a punishment merited in accordance with divine providence, but does not claim that the passage of time has alleviated their hardships, and reflecting the ambiguity characteristic of his interpretation throughout, allows the reader to ponder how providential the Conquest was from the indigenous perspective. Firmly attached to his faith and not anxious to defend a regime that had expelled him, he makes no effort to present a more nuanced portrait of racial interaction and intermingling in New Spain, to soften his portrayal of racial exploitation. Indeed, Clavigero underscores how low the indigenous peoples have fallen by pointing to the contempt with which he claims they are treated by slaves of African origin, "infamous by law" ("infames por derecho") according to the racial hierarchy or system of *castas* that governed eighteenth-century New Spain, and hence putatively inferior to *indios* (MacLachlan and Rodríguez 1990, 199). By emphasizing this calamity, however, he demonstrates his sympathy for the plight of the Nahua, a sympathy heightened by the expulsion of the Jesuits, a personal catastrophe for him. It is only in light of Clavigero's insistence on the misery to which the Nahua had been reduced that the full significance of his declaration that he is a "mexicano" becomes apparent.

NOTES

1 For biographical information on Clavigero, see Beristáin de Souza 1816, 353–7; González y González 1995, 111–29; and Ronan 1977. Clavigero's surname is widely given as Clavijero, but he preferred the spelling I use here.

2 On De Pauw and the reception of his work, see Gerbi 1993, 66–409; Cañizares-Esguerra 2001, 26–7, 32–5, and 234–5. Clavigero calls De Pauw a "fashionable and erudite philosopher, especially in certain areas, where it would be better if he were ignorant or, at least, did not talk" ("filósofo a la moda y erudito, principalmente en ciertas materias, en las que sería mejor que fuese ignorante o, a lo menos, que no hablase" [Clavigero [1780] 1945, 422]).

3 For an analysis of the pejorative lexicon used by De Pauw, see Marchetti 1986, 39–50; for Robertson's views, see Robertson 1851, 6: 1–3, 8–37, and 39–58.

4 Giovanni Marchetti argues that this recognition of the *novohispano* university was also a rebuttal of De Pauw's affirmation that the universities of America had not produced any illustrious scholars (Marchetti 1986, 68).

5 See Rodríguez 1998, 16–17; González y González 1995, 125; and Tanck de Estrada 1988.

6 David Brading maintains that the "intellectual achievement of Clavijero was complex, subtle and ambiguous." In re-evaluating the ancient indigenous cultures of the *reino* of México, "his patria was thus endowed with a distinguished, not to say, glorious past. So too, he advanced a powerful defence of New Spain's historiographical tradition, its privileged access to native manuscripts and codices. By eliminating all supernatural interference, he presented a persuasive image of Tolteca-Mexica society as a civilization" (Brading 1991, 460). Concentrating on this erasure of supernatural intervention, Fernando Cervantes contends that "[p]erhaps Clavigero's single most important achievement was to exorcize the devil from his *patria*'s past, to liberate the pre-Hispanic world from the nagging interpretative burden of Acosta and Torquemada." Cervantes observes that "in sharp contrast to all previous accounts of ancient Mexico, the *Historia antigua* adopted an unmistakeably secular historical approach" (Cervantes 1994, 149). This conception of the Jesuit's work is in many respects convincing, and emphasizes his patriotic and secularizing inclinations. However, Clavigero's secularizing proclivity, which led him to break with the historiographic tradition that had demonized indigenous religions, is not as unequivocal as Brading and Cervantes suggest, nor is it present throughout the *Historia.* On the redefinition of the natural, "preternatural," and supernatural in western European culture of the late seventeenth century, see Daston 1991.

7 For a discussion of Clavigero's understanding of the "nation," see Marchetti 1986, 132–5.

8 In a footnote he laments: "One cannot see without pain the gloom and destitution to which are reduced many of the most illustrious families of that kingdom [of Mexico]" (No se puede ver sin dolor el abatimiento y misera a que se hallan reducidas muchas familias de las más ilustres de aquel reino [de México] [Clavigero [1780] 1945, 213: n. 3]).

9 See Brading 2001, 67, and Méndez 2002.

10 See Alva Ixtlilxóchitl 1985, 291, as well as 1975, 462–6, 483–4, 494, and 515.

11 The rather transparently self-serving agenda of many of the narratives penned by ecclesiastics and soldiers had discredited much of this historiography in the eyes of European Enlightenment critics. See Cañizares-Esguerra 2001, 12–13.

12 Faithful to his commitment to impartiality, Clavigero is equally critical of commentators who had, in his view, exaggerated the merits of Cortés, as he is of scholars who had denigrated him, asserting that "any man, impartial and well versed in his military actions, must confess that, in bravery, perseverance, and military, consistency and prudence, [Cortés] can compete with the most famous generals, and that he had that kind of heroism that we recognize in the Alexanders and the Caesars, in whom one praises the magnanimity, despite the vices that sullied them" ("cualquier hombre imparcial y bien instruido en las acciones militares de aquél, deberá confesar que en valor, constancia y prudencia militar puede competir con los más famosos generales, y que tuvo aquella especie de heroísmo que reconocemos en los Alejandros y en los Césares, en quienes se alaba la magnanimidad a pesar de los vicios con que estaban manchados" [Clavigero [1780] 1945, 520]).

13 Clavigero provides a concise overview of his interpretation of the Conquest: "[I]t cannot be denied that amongst the Americans it was believed as by tradition that other men of very different condition would arrive to those kingdoms, that they would become lords of all the land. [...] It is impossible to know its first origin; but in the sixteenth century and even in the fifteenth and in the fourteenth, when after the invention of the compass men no longer feared losing sight of land, when Europeans, because of ambition and the insatiable thirst for gold, had begun familiarizing themselves with the dangers of the ocean, that malignant spirit, capital enemy of humankind that revolves around all the earth threatening mortals, could easily surmise the progression of the Europeans, the discovery of America and many of the great events that were to happen there, and it is not unlikely that he predicted it to nations entirely consecrated to his worship, to confirm them, with the same prediction of the future, in the erroneous belief in his divinity. But if the devil foreshadowed future calamities to fool those miserable peoples, God announced them to prepare their spirits for the Gospel" ("[N]o puede negarse que entre los americanos se creía como por tradición que aportarían a aquellos reinos otros hombres de muy diferente condición, que se harían señores de toda la tierra. [...] Es imposible averiguar su primer origen; pero en el siglo XVI y aun en el XV y en el XIV, después que con la invención de la aguja náutica no temían ya los hombres perder de vista la tierra, cuando los europeos, por la ambición y la sed insaciable del oro habían comenzado a familiarizarse con los peligros del océano, aquel maligno espíritu, enemigo capital del género humano, que gira por toda la tierra acechando a los mortales, pudo fácilmente conjeturar los progresos de los europeos, el descubrimiento de la América y mucha parte de los grandes sucesos que en ella debían acaecer, y no es inverosímil

que los predijese a unas naciones enteramente consagradas a su culto, para confirmarles, con la misma predicción de lo futuro, en la errónea creencia de su divinidad. Pero si el demonio pronosticaba las futuras calamidades para engañar a aquellos miserables pueblos, Dios las anunciaba para disponer los ánimos al Evangelio" [Clavigero [1780] 1945, 138–9]).

14 For a discussion of Clavigero's reading of Vico, see Trabulse 1988, 52–7, and Ballesteros Gaibrois 1990, xlviii. Cf. Brading 1991, 461.

BIBLIOGRAPHY

Alva Ixtlilxóchitl, Fernando de. 1975. *Obras Históricas*, 1891–1892, ed. Edmundo O'Gorman. México: Universidad Nacional Autónoma de México.

Alva Ixtlilxóchitl, Fernando de. 1985. *Historia de la nación chichimeca*, 1891–1892, ed. Germán Vázquez. Madrid: Historia 16.

Ballesteros Gaibrois, Manuel, ed. 1990. "Estudio preliminar." In *Historia general de la América Septentrional*, ix–liv. México: Universidad Nacional Autónoma de México.

Beristain De Souza, José Mariano. 1816. *Biblioteca Hispano-Americana Septentrional.* México: Calle de Santo Domingo y Esquina de Tacuba.

Boturini Benaduci, Lorenzo. 1990. *Historia general de la América Septentrional*, 1746, ed. Manuel Ballesteros Gaibrois. México: Universidad Nacional Autónoma de México.

Brading, David Anthony. 1973. *Los orígenes del nacionalismo mexicano*, trans. Soledad Loaeza Grave. México: SEP.

–. 1991. *The First America: The Spanish Monarchy, Creole Patriots, and the Liberal State 1492–1867.* Cambridge: Cambridge University Press.

–. 2001. "La patria criolla y la Compañía de Jesús." *Artes de México* 58: 59–70.

Cañizares-Esguerra, Jorge. 2001. *How to Write the History of the New World: Historiographies, Epistemologies, and Identities in the Eighteenth-Century Atlantic World.* Stanford, CA: Stanford University Press.

Cervantes, Fernando. 1994. *The Devil in the New World: The Impact of Diabolism in New Spain.* New Haven, CT: Yale University Press.

Clavigero, Francisco Xavier. [1780] 1945. *Historia antigua de México*, 1780, ed. Mariano Cuevas. México: Porrúa.

Daston, Lorraine. 1991. "Marvelous Facts and Miraculous Evidence in Early Modern Europe." *Critical Inquiry* 18 (1): 93–124.

Gerbi, Antonello. 1993. *La disputa del Nuevo Mundo: Historia de una polémica, 1750–1900*, ed. and trans. Antonio Alatorre. México: Fondo de Cultura Económica.

González Y González, Luis. 1995. *Obras completas.* México: Clío.

MacLachlan, Colin, and Jaime Rodríguez. 1990. *The Forging of the Cosmic Race: A Reinterpretation of Colonial Mexico.* Berkeley: University of California Press.

Marchetti, Giovanni. 1986. *Cultura indígena e integración nacional: La "Historia antigua de México" de F. J. Clavijero,* trans. Alberto Guaraldo and María del Rosario Rodríguez. Xalapa: University Veracruzana.

Martínez Rosales, Alfonso, ed. 1988. *Francisco Xavier Clavigero en la Ilustración mexicana, 1731–1787.* México: Colegio de México.

Méndez, María Agueda. 2002. "Poderes encontrados: Juan de Palafox vs. la Inquisición novohispana." In *Juan de Palafox y Mendoza: Imagen y discurso de la cultura novohispana,* ed. José Pascual Buxó, 93–103. México: Universidad Nacional Autónoma de México.

Pastrana Flores, Miguel. 2004. *Historias de la conquista: Aspectos de la historiografía de tradición náhuatl.* México: Universidad Nacional Autónoma de México.

Robertson, William. 1851. *Works.* London: Longman.

Rodríguez, Jaime. 1998. *The Independence of Spanish America.* Cambridge: Cambridge University Press.

Ronan, Charles E. 1977. *Francisco Javier Clavigero, S J. (1731–1787): Figure of the Mexican Enlightenment.* Roma: Institutum Historicum.

Tanck De Estrada, Dorothy. 1988. "Clavigero: Defensor de los idiomas indígenas." In *Francisco Xavier Clavigero en la Ilustración mexicana, 1731–1787,* ed. Alfonso Martínez Rosales, 13–30. México: Colegio de México.

Trabulse, Elías. 1988. "Clavigero, historiador de la Ilustración mexicana." In *Francisco Xavier Clavigero en la Ilustración mexicana, 1731–1787,* ed. Alfonso Martínez Rosales, 41–57. México: Colegio de México.

Vico, Giambattista. [1725] 2001. *New Science,* trans. 1725, David Marsh. London: Penguin.

chapter five

Between Ethnology and Romantic Discourse: Martin Dobrizhoffer's *History of the Abipones* in a (Post)modern Perspective

HANS-JÜRGEN LÜSEBRINK

The Return of the "Repressed": The Rediscovery of the Jesuit Accounts

From the founding of the Society of Jesus in 1540 until the year 1767, when it was prohibited in France and in the Spanish Empire, the order has been traditionally cast as an anti-model of Enlightenment discourse. In the eyes of Diderot and Voltaire, as well as in the eyes of Herder in Germany and Robertson in Scotland, Jesuits embodied the policies of secret-mongering and inquisitorial practices that were the very opposite of rational thinking and the enlightened struggle against obscurantism and clerical oppression.

However, when we examine non-canonical and peripheral voices, we encounter intellectual defenders of Jesuit activity as early as the late Enlightenment, not only among the clergy, but also among the representatives of the intellectual and social elites of the time. One such example is the Abbé Guillaume Thomas Raynal, a former Jesuit who had left the order in 1748 to become a journalist and the editor of the *Mercure de France.* Later on, in the 1770s, he would become the main author and editor of the *Histoire philosophique et politique des établissemens et du commerce des Européens dans les deux Indes* (1770), the first encyclopedic history of the European settlements outside of Europe. This work defended the accomplishments of the Jesuits, especially in Paraguay, as having fostered an egalitarian social utopia which had considerably improved the situation of the Indian population (see Raynal 1783, book 8: 105–232).

This new esteem for the Jesuits, and the (re)discovery of their ethnographical and anthropological works, came mainly from the periphery of the European and transatlantic Enlightenment, predominantly from

Italy, particularly from Bologna and Ferrara where many of the exiled Jesuits such as Francisco Xavier Clavijero published their works. They also came from Germany, or more precisely from the German-speaking countries, where several exiled Jesuits like Johann Jakob Baegert, the author of the *Nachrichten aus de Amerikanischen Halbinsel Californien* ("News from Lower California"), published in 1772, or Martin Dobrizhoffer, the author of the *History of the Abipones*, settled after their expulsion from South America by the Spanish king Carlos III in 1767. While in exile they published their manuscripts and received particular attention from German historiographers and anthropologists, such as the historian Matthias Christian Sprengel from the University of Halle (see Tietz 2001; Fitzpatrick et al. 2004, 149 and 438; as well as Lafone Quevedo 1896). Ultimately, the "rediscovery" of the South American Jesuits, and especially of the exiled Jesuits, came from within South America itself, where the construction of new, non-European views of the history, culture, and anthropology of South American societies used the Jesuit histories as important sources, considering them to be genuine predecessors in the quest to document indigenous social life and culture. Quite paradoxically, the work of some exiled Jesuits such as Clavijero and Baegert in Mexico, Juan Velasco in Ecuador, and Martin Dobrizhoffer in Paraguay and Argentina became important references for the constitution of new models of South American identity in the extremely varied discourses of ethnology, anthropology, historiography, linguistics, and politics.

Ethnography and Counter-Discourse

Alfred Métraux, one of the pioneers of modern anthropology in France, together with Claude Lévi-Strauss, emphasized the important role of the Austrian Jesuit Martin Dobrizhoffer and his *Account of the Abipones, an Equestrian people of Paraguay*, in an article published in 1942 on the contributions of the Jesuits to the anthropology of South America:

> During the whole 19th century it was one of the most often quoted sources of the new science of anthropology and sociology. Furthermore, it remains one of the few excellent monographs on any South American tribe. [...] His statements are precise and fairly complete. They have been amply verified by observations made among modern Indians of the Chaco. His account becomes invaluable when he deals with religion and social institutions. For

> no modern tribe of the Chaco have we such a wealth of detail on the ceremonies, etiquette, and beliefs. He devotes many pages to descriptions of social groups, such as military societies, which today have vanished (Métraux 1944, 52–3).[1]

In spite of the important place Dobrizhoffer occupies in the history of the ethnology and the anthropology of South American societies and cultures, relatively little research has been done on his work and its reception. This is due certainly to the fact that his main work, the *Account of the Abipones*, was published first in Latin and then in German (see Dobrizhoffer 1783a and 1783b), and that he received particular acclaim not in eighteenth-century France or England, but in Austria and other German-speaking countries during the 1770s and 1780s.

Martin Dobrizhoffer was born in Friedberg, Bohemia in 1718; he was ordained in 1736 and worked as a missionary in Paraguay between 1749 and 1767, first in the Guaraní reductions and then among the Abiponi people.[2] He returned to Europe in March 1768, after the prohibition of the Society of Jesus in the Spanish colonies in South America in 1767. Between 1769 and 1791, the year of his death, he lived in Vienna, as an "active preacher, pastor, and writer," and was a "favorite preacher at the court of Maria Teresa" (Jacobsen 1947, 184), where his jovial and entertaining personality was welcomed and appreciated, especially in his oral accounts of his South American experience. Dobrizhoffer's most prominent work, the above-mentioned *Account of the Abipones*, a three-volume description of the history, customs, and society of an indigenous people in Northern Paraguay, was originally composed in Latin, the written language he had mastered the best, and was almost simultaneously translated into German by Anton Kreil, a Freemason and professor of philosophy at the University of Pest (see Bachleitner n.d., 2), with the help of its author. It was published in Vienna in 1784 under the title *Geschichte der Abiponer, einer berittenen und kriegerischen Nation in Paraguay*. An English translation of Dobrizhoffer's work came out in London in 1822 thanks to Sara Coleridge (1802–1852), the daughter of Samuel Taylor Coleridge; that translation contributed to its positive reception in early nineteenth-century England, especially among the members of the Romantic movement (see Dobrizhoffer 1970).[3]

Dobrizhoffer's work was based on notes taken during his stay in South America, but ultimately its writing and publication were probably due to two other major circumstances. As Dobrizhoffer explains in the preface to his work, he was frequently asked questions about America and encouraged by people of distinction at the Imperial Court in Vienna to write down the answers in the form of a systematic book:

> In America, I was often interrogated respecting Europe; in Austria, on my return to it, after an absence of eighteen years, I have been frequently questioned concerning America. To relieve others from the trouble of inquiring, myself from that of answering inquiries, at the advice of some persons of distinction, I have applied my mind to writing this little history; an undertaking which, I am aware, will be attended with doubtful Success and infinite vexation, in this age, so abundant in Aristarchi, accustomed to commend none but their own, or their friends' productions, and to condemn, as abortive, those of all other persons ("Preface," in Dobrizhoffer [1822] 1970, 1: v).

The circumstances of his return from South America to Europe in 1768–1769 might also have been a reason for the writing and publication of the book. In fact, when Dobrizhoffer sailed from Buenos Aires to Spain, he found himself reunited with the four outstanding missionary writers of the El Chaco region, who all wrote and intended to publish works on the American Indian societies of the region: Fathers José Brigniel, José Sánchez Labrador, José Jolis, Francisco Miranda, and especially Florian Paucke, who had become a close friend of Dobrizhoffer since their common travels to South America in 1749. Their long journey from South America to Spain and their subsequent extended stays in Cádiz, as well as in a Franciscan convent in the port of Santa Maria in Italy, gave them extensive opportunities to speak about their experiences, to exchange notes, and to envisage possible publication projects.

Dobrizhoffer's discourse on Abipone ethnography is based on a radical criticism of the existing writings by European travellers, historians, and conquerors of Paraguay and of the El Chaco region. He conceived his work as an explicit counter-discourse to the existing European writings on Paraguay and the Rio de la Plata region, underscoring the fact that he had acquired a profound knowledge of these regions based not on readings and prejudices, but on direct empirical experience and observation, as well as through the learning of indigenous languages:

> A seven years' residence in the four colonies of the Abipones has afforded me opportunities of closely observing their manners, customs, superstitions, military discipline, slaughters inflicted and received, political and economical regulations, together with the vicissitudes of the recent colonies, all

> which I have described with greater fidelity than elegance, and for the want of this I am surely to be pardoned: for who can expect the graces of Livy, Sallust, Caesar, Strada, or Maffeus, from one who, for so many years, has had no commerce with the muses, no access to classical literature? [...] What I have learned among the Paraguayans in the course of eighteen years, what I have myself beheld in the colonies of the Indians and Spaniards, in frequent and long journeys through woods, mountains, plains, and vast rivers, I have set forth, if not in an eloquent and brilliant narration, certainly in a candid and accurate one, which is at least deserving of credit. Yet I do not look upon myself as a person incapable of making a mistake, and unwilling to be corrected (Dobrizhoffer [1822] 1970, 1: 16–17).[4]

He thoroughly examined the widely read travelogue of the French explorer Louis-Antoine de Bougainville (1729–1811), which contained an extensive chapter on the Rio de la Plata region:

> M. Louis-Antoine de Bougainville, in his work entitled *Voyage autour du monde,* must be read with caution. He loads the Jesuits with egregious praises, but by and bye relates a thousand things as contrary to truth as dishonourable to us and the Guarany colonies. [...] True it is, he wrote falsely about us and the Guaranies; but rather deceived by the narrations of others, than through envy or malice. He never even saw the Guarany towns from a distance. I wish he had seen them! He would have painted the Indians and their missionaries in fairer colours. A little while, and but a little while, he remained in Buenos Ayres, the port and threshold of Paraguay. There he drew the very worst notions, from the very worst sources, and gave them to Europe as the undoubted truth ("Preface," in Dobrizhoffer [1822] 1970, 1: 174–5).

Dobrizhoffer indicates in the foreword of his *Account of the Abipones* that he had found no less than twenty-six factual mistakes concerning the geography, the natural environment, and the inhabitants of Paraguay in Bougainville's travelogue. Consequently the introductory motto of the *Account,* taken from Plautus (*Truculentus* 2.6), underlines the importance of ocular proof and personal testimony: "An eyewitness represents more value than ten ear-witnesses. Those who only hear, say merely what they have heard; those who see, know it with certainty" (Dobrizhoffer [1822] 1970, 1: 21).

Other writers who had published on Paraguay and the Guaraní received a similarly critical and negative judgment in Dobrizhoffer's work: for example, Bernardo Ibañez's book on the Guaraní colonies, *Il passagero*

Americano, which he calls "bare and ridiculous prattle" (Dobrizhoffer [1822] 1970, 1: 21; kahles und lächerliches Geschwätz [Dobrizhoffer 1783b, 1: 21]). Other sources were held up as positive models, in particular those by fellow Jesuits, such as Ruiz de Mantoya's *La conquista espiritual*, the work of Father Nikolaus del Techo, the letters of Father Anton Sepp to his brother, those of Father Charlevoix in their original French version, and the writings of Dominikus Muriel, published in Venice in 1776 (see for example Dobrizhoffer [1822] 1970, 345). However, none matched Dobrizhoffer's own exemplary "experience" (Dobrizhoffer [1822] 1970, 1: 680; Erfahrung [Dobrizhoffer 1783b, 1: 345]), which he underlines in numerous passages of his work.

It can be argued that Dobrizhoffer's work provides the most extensive and detailed ethnographical description concerning South America in the eighteenth century, totaling three volumes in octavo and seventeen hundred pages. It contains ten illustrations and three maps (of the Rio de la Plata region and of Mission Rosario) and is divided into three main parts, each of which comprises nearly six hundred pages. The first part covers the geography and natural environment of Paraguay and the wider Gran Chaco Region, including a historical perspective spanning the discovery and conquest of the Rio de la Plata Region from the beginning of the sixteenth to the mid-eighteenth century. The second part of Dobrizhoffer's study is focused specifically on the people of the Abiponi, among whom Dobrizhoffer spent approximately seven of his eighteen years in South America. The third part furthers the ethnographic description of the Abiponi nation and tries to explain why they, together with the Araucanians in Southern Chile, represented the only people in South America to have successfully resisted Spanish conquest for more than one and a half centuries, until the 1730s. Dobrizhoffer dedicates several chapters of this third part of his account to the history of the submission of the Abiponi, and their social integration into the Jesuit State of Paraguay. This integration, which appeared somewhat questionable after the expulsion of the Jesuits in 1767, was, according to Dobrizhoffer, in large part due to the winning personality of the Guaraní chief, Ycholay, who played an important political role; his biography receives substantial treatment in Dobrizhoffer's account, as do the skilful politics of the Jesuit fathers in Paraguay.

Dobrizhoffer's account, based on notes taken during his stay in South America, but only recorded during his exile in Vienna in the years 1772 to 1774, is characterized by his great precision in the description of the social structures, rituals, customs, and languages of the different peoples of Paraguay. In contrast to other Jesuit accounts, such as Johann Jakob Baegert's description of Lower California, *Nachrichten aus Californien*, published in 1772,[5] its structure of representation was not determined by a predominant logic of religious schemes and forms of perception. In some Jesuit accounts, derogatory comments about indigenous religious and social practices hinder a deeper intercultural understanding of those indigenous societies and cultures. Such negative judgment and criticism is marginal if not rare in Dobrizhoffer, whose account (especially the second part) attacks the persisting negative stereotypes of and prejudices about the American Indians found in the works of Spanish historians, such as Francisco López de Gómara's *Historia de las Indias* (1552) which, at the time, was one of the principal reference works on the conquest of South America:

> You cannot imagine in what dark colours the Europeans, who first entered these provinces, described the stupidity of the Americans. Brother Thomas Ortiz, afterwards Bishop of Sta. Martha, intimates in his letters to the Court of Madrid, that the Americans are foolish, dull, stupid, and unreasoning like beasts, that they are incapable of understanding the merits of religion, and devoid of human sense and judgment. Some of the Spaniards thought the Americans so stupid, that they wished to exclude them, even after they were grown up, from baptism, confession, and other sacraments, as being in the condition of infants who are not yet possessed of reason (Dobrizhoffer [1822] 1970, 1: 345).

Unlike, for example, Lópes de Gómara, Dobrizhoffer calls attention to the solemn and dignified appearance of the Abiponi; he describes the complexity of their language and social structures, pointing out their capacity for intellectual and cultural development, both in his discourse and in the illustrations that accompany it. Almost against his will (see Lüsebrink 2004),[6] writes Dobrizhoffer, he has been forced to admit the "naturally good qualities" ("natürlich guten Eigenschaften" [Dobrizhoffer 1783b, 2: 60]) of the Abipones.[7] He considers their violence and their occasional brutality not as inherent characteristics, but as genuine forms of resistance against the far more brutal violence of the Spanish conquerors.

It may seem astonishing, and even paradoxical, that Dobrizhoffer's discourse, which is characterized by scrupulous attention to native societies and cultures, is at the same time interspersed with numerous comparisons, not only to other cultures of the American continent, but also, and above all, to cultures and societies of Greek and Roman antiquity, especially through references to Plutarch, Tacitus, Titus Livy, Tertullian, Cicero, and Plato. For example, when describing in a very detailed manner the food of the Abipones, he adds the following reference to Tacitus: "The food also to which the Abipones are accustomed, in my judgment contributes not a little to prolong their lives. What Tacitus said of the ancient Germans is applicable to them" (Dobrizhoffer [1822] 1970, 3: 181).

Dobrizhoffer pays particular attention to social and cultural rituals and habits such as food practices, not to mention the language of the Abipones. His extensive description of the Abipone language constitutes one of the pioneering works on the study of the grammar, semantics, and syntax of American Indian languages. Dobrizhoffer did not have any dictionary or grammar for reference, such as already existed for other Indian languages like the Guaraní language in Peru in the eighteenth century. He was thus obliged to learn it for himself, in a largely autodidactic way, establishing his own dictionary and his own grammar through his contacts with the Abipones and with the help of older priests like Friar Brigniel, who transmitted to him a certain basis of knowledge. Dobrizhoffer describes quite precisely his own process of learning the Abiponi language, combining observation, improvised learning, and autodidactic appropriation:

> I do not deny that, by daily conversation with the Indians, I learnt the names of those things which are present to the eyes; but invisible things, which relate to God and the soul, can only be learnt by conjecture and very long use. When horses, tigers, or arms, are talked of, you will find any of the Abipones a Demosthenes or a Tully: if the question turn on the affections and functions of the mind, and the practice of virtue, they will either give you answers darker than night, or remain silent (Dobrizhoffer [1822] 1970, 3: 181).

Romantic Re-appropriations: Robert Southey's *A Tale of Paraguay*

The impact of Dobrizhoffer's work can be observed essentially in two quite different cultural fields. On the one hand, it had an important impact on the development of the anthropology and ethnography of native South American cultures and societies. The reception of the Spanish translation of *History of the Abipones*, as well as the critical appendix that accompanied it in its 1970 edition (Dobrizhoffer [1822] 1970 2: 47), proves the interest of South American ethnographers, linguists and anthropologists in Dobrizhoffer's work. On the other hand, we can observe the important influence Dobrizhoffer had on several outstanding protagonists of the Romantic movement in England, especially Sara Coleridge, who translated his work from Latin into English at the age of twenty (see 2: 202, as well as Coleridge 1873, 1: 33) in order to assist one of her brothers with his college expenses (see Dobrizhoffer and Brigniel 1896; Dobrizhoffer 1967). Robert Southey (1774–1834), one of the main representatives of Romanticism in England, came across Dobrizhoffer's work while composing his epic poem *A Tale of Paraguay* between 1810 and 1819. He himself probably suggested a translation of Dobrizhoffer's work into English to Sara Coleridge, who lived in his London neighbourhood at Greta Hall. Southey paid very delicate and enthusiastic homage to the young translator in his *Tale of Paraguay*, which was based on *The Account of the Abipones* (see Bernhardt-Kabisch 1974; Storey 1997, 236–9):

In Latin he composed his history;
A garrulous, but lively tale, and fraught
With matter of delight and food for thought.
And, if he could in Merlin's glass have seen
By whom his tomes to speak our tongue were taught,
The old man would have felt as pleased, I ween,
As when he won the ear of that great Empress Queen (Southey 1909, 680).

Dobrizhoffer, whose work also served as a source for Southey's poetic *History of Brazil*, is himself portrayed as follows in *Canto* 3 of *A Tale of Paraguay*, with a mistake concerning his birthplace (which was not Graz, Austria, but Friedberg, Bohemia):

He was a man of rarest qualities
Who to this barbarous region had confined
A spirit with the learned and the wise
Worthy to take its place, and from mankind
Receive their homage, to the immortal mind
Paid in its just inheritance of fame.
But he to humbler thoughts his heart inclined;
From Gratz amid the Styrian hills he came,
And Dobrizhoffer was the good man's honour'd name (Southey 1909, 680).

Southey's epic poem *A Tale of Paraguay*, which is divided into four *Cantos* and written in *Stanzas*, is based on a very precise narrative in Dobrizhoffer's work, which contains, besides the descriptive passages, numerous narrative episodes. One short episode, in the first volume of the *Account of the Abipones* (see Dobrizhoffer [1822] 1970, 1: 87–95; Dobrizhoffer 1783, 1: 113–22),[8] tells how during an expedition in the interior of Paraguay, in the years following the violent resistance of the Guaraní against the cession of their territory by the king of Spain to Portugal in 1750, Dobrizhoffer discovered a surviving family of Guaraní Indians living in complete isolation in a forest after their ethnic group had been almost completely decimated by illness and disease (see Dobrizhoffer [1822] 1970, 1: 92). This family, which consisted of a mother and her two children, a son and a daughter of fifteen and sixteen, lived there in penury, but without discontent, vexation, or disease. Dobrizhoffer affirms this as he describes in detail their lifestyle, their clothing, their food, and their physical appearance. He succeeded in persuading them to give up their isolation and to move with him to the Jesuit missions after they had been converted to Christianity. The new proselytes were "quickly clothed in town, and served with the daily allowance of food" (1: 93). They became slowly accustomed to civilized life, but at the same time they succumbed to an inexplicable disease which seemed to be related to their passage from the state of nature to the state of civilization: "A few weeks after their arrival they were affected with a universal heaviness and rheum, to which succeeded a pain in the eyes and ears, and not long after, deafness. Lowness of spirits, and disgust to food at length wasted their strength to such a degree that an incurable consumption followed" (1: 94). One after another the mother, the daughter, and the son faded away and died, the latter by "the melancholy remembrance of his mother and sister, with whom he has lived all his life" (1: 93),[9] and whose death now haunted his dreams.

Robert Southey transformed this melodramatic and ethnographic narrative into a versified Romantic epic, focused on the tragic dimension of the definite end of the state of nature having come in contact with civilization (see Fulford 2001). The first two of the four *Cantos* of the poem are thus dedicated to a mythological evocation of the state of nature, which is associated with the notions of "Eden" and "Paradise"; whereas the last two *Cantos* narrate the rapid descent of the small American Indian family, representing the natural world, through a semantic field of notions linked to disease and sickness on both a physical and psychological level. Southey amplified the central motifs of Dobrizhoffer's narrative – the forest, the innocence of childhood, the exaltation of feminine purity, the magnificence of nature – by integrating them in a Romantic mythology where the expulsion from paradise inevitably implies disease and death (see Southey 1909, 678). Southey also gave a new dimension to this narrative episode, which associated in its very structure colonialism with disease, epidemic, and death, an association which we can find in other discourses of the late Enlightenment period and the Romantic era; for example, in Diderot's *Supplément au voyage de Bougainville* (1771). Developing this critical perspective based on Dobrizhoffer's account, Southey also attacks, for example, in *Canto* 2 (*Stanza* 3), Spain's "fatal thirst of gold" (679) which had led to enslavement and disease, and reminds him of England's new "commercial slavery" (67), which represents for him a kind of epidemic disease (see also Southey 1822, 311).

Southey's *A Tale of Paraguay* and its Romantic rereading and rewriting of Dobrizhoffer's *Account of the Abigoni* represents one side of Dobrizhoffer's reception and re-appropriation in the nineteenth and twentieth centuries. The other side, focused on the ethnological and anthropological dimensions of his work, as well as on his biography, can, surprisingly, also be found in Southey's work, which is often labelled as "Romanticism." The forty-seven-page review article Southey published in 1822 on the English translation of the *Account of the Abipones* illustrates his intense preoccupation with Dobrizhoffer's works, its sources, and the biography of the author, who apparently fascinated him. In paying particular attention to the actions of the Jesuits in Paraguay and their attitudes towards indigenous societies, Southey defended them against the Spaniards, whom he believed responsible for the major negative effects of conquest and colonization – violence, slavery, disease and death. "Such a man," Southey writes in his review article on Dobrizhoffer,

> was worthy to take his place in civilized society; and undoubtedly, by his example and influence the Abipones might have been brought up to the highest standard of Civilisation that Paraguay afforded, if the whole superintendence of these, as of the Guarani Reductions, had been left to the Jesuits; or if the civil authorities, within whose jurisdiction they were placed, had acted more wisely and less penuriously (Southey 1822, 285).

Southey, who also highlights Dobrizhoffer's excellent knowledge of indigenous languages (see Southey 1822, 277), considers his *Account* as a pioneering work, superior for example to Clavijero's *History of Mexico* "which is most known in this country; but the work before us is that which contains the most original and curious information. Perhaps there is no other which gives so full and picturesque an account of savage life; it has a liveliness, an originality, a freshness which makes even garrulity attractive" (286).[10]

Whereas Southey's discourse, even if it also focused on the ethnographical and biographical issues of Dobrizhoffer's work, glides quite rapidly towards his fascination for the "beautiful story of a solitary family" (Métraux 1944, 185) which will constitute the frame for his own *Tale of Paraguay*, other critics focus more explicitly on Dobrizhoffer's impact on the development of ethnography and anthropology in South America. In an article published in 1944, Alfred Métraux, who was working as an ethnologist at the Smithsonian Institute in Washington, DC, in the 1940s, called Dobrizhoffer's work "one of the most often quoted sources in the field of the new science of anthropology and sociology," remaining "one of the few excellent monographs on any South American tribe" (185):

> His statements on the material culture are precise and fairly complete. They have been amply verified by observations among modern Indians of the Chaco. His account becomes invaluable when he deals with religion and social institutions. For no modern tribe of the Chaco we have such a wealth of detail on ceremonies, etiquette and beliefs. He devotes many pages to descriptions of social groups, such as military societies, which today have vanished. He is one of the first to have observed that Indian chieftainship was based mainly on continual acts of generosity. Modern anthropology has grown increasingly interested in social psychology and in collective neuroses. On these subjects little is to be found in the literature, and therefore it is a real surprise to discover that Dobrizhoffer describes at length a special type of insanity which assumed academic proportions (185).

According to Angela Blankenburg, who published a study on German missionary writers in Paraguay, Dobrizhoffer's work "was quite ahead of his time in the use of the procedures in ethnology" (Blankenburg 1947, 123). She cites "seven authoritative spokesmen for ethnology who say openly or in effect that Dobrizhoffer must be considered a pioneer or a founder of the science of comparative ethnology" (123). And Ricardo Rojas characterizes Dobrizhoffer in his *Historia de la Literatura argentina* as follows: "[A] book of great historical and scientific for the Argentinians" ([U]n libro de gran interés histórico y científico para los argentinos [Rojas 1918, 2: 363]).

Conclusion: Rethinking Knowledge Transfer in South America in the Eighteenth Century

Placing Dobrizhoffer's work, like that of other Jesuits, in the perspective of the history of knowledge by considering them as pioneers or predecessors of modern ethnology and anthropology, and founding fathers of modern Latin American identities, is both correct (or at least not false) and extremely problematic. If one looks more closely at the intercultural transfer and the Latin American appropriation of Dobrizhoffer's work, one can indeed observe that they are based on a quite selective and partial reading of it, a reading which is not founded on the original Latin or German versions, but on the English translation from the beginning of the nineteenth century, which had been adapted for modern readers. First, this version was far more elegant because it simply suppressed most of the erudite comparisons Dobrizhoffer introduced between the Abiponi and Guaraní societies on the one hand, and ancient or contemporary societies on the other hand, comparisons in which he had quoted freely from authors like Tacitus, Herodotus, Livy, Lafitau, or Charlevoix. Second, the translation omitted almost all of the polemics and controversies between Dobrizhoffer and other writers who had published on Paraguay in the sixteenth, seventeenth, and eighteenth centuries, such as Bougainville, whom he refuted radically for the most part, and with precise criticism. Both the Romantic and the ethnological appropriations and rereadings of Dobrizhoffer, which transformed him into a very modern, pioneering, and even anti-colonialist figure, thus overshadowed his more complicated and ambivalent eighteenth-century dimensions: first, his relation to the Jesuit theory of cultural adaptation, necessary to understand Otherness, but above all necessary to convert the Other to Christianity; next, his numerous and sometimes confusing references to and comparisons with modern and especially ancient Greek and Roman authors; and finally, the penchant, typical of both the Jesuits and eighteenth-century *philosophes*, to seek, even to desire, criticism, controversy, and polemic.

Dobrizhoffer's work must be viewed as a part of a complex network of intercultural knowledge transfers between the Americas and Europe in the eighteenth century. The Jesuits, especially the exiled Jesuits, played an important, if not decisive, role in the process of the production and diffusion of new anthropological, cultural, and political knowledge about pre-Columbian and colonial societies, which has been largely neglected by a historiographical discourse that has been far too focused on the so-called Enlightened, and European, side of the anthropological discourse. The critical edition of the Spanish translation of the *History of the Abipones*, published in 1967 in Argentina, recognized explicitly the pioneering role of exiled Jesuits like Dobrizhoffer in the process of renewing and revising the knowledge on early colonial South America. The phenomenon of "writing back," conceptualized in the postcolonial era by Ashcroft, Griffith, and Tiffin in their emblematic book *The Empire Writes Back* (1989), must thus systematically be traced back to the seventeenth and eighteenth centuries, the Jesuits having been among the main spokesmen of a counter-discourse to the hegemonic colonial discourses in Spain and other European countries. If we look more closely at these processes and phenomena, things become even more complex in terms of translation and intercultural transfers between very different cultural areas. Dobrizhoffer's work was, in fact, read and used in South America after having been published in German and Latin, and then in a largely modified English translation in Europe. Clavijero's famous and influential *History of Ancient Mexico* was published first in Italian, then in German and English, and was widely read in the intellectual spheres of late eighteenth-century Europe, before it was translated into Spanish, provoking an enduring echo in nineteenth-century Mexico and Central America.[11] The complex, ramified reception of Jesuit writing reflects thus, in some way, the international network of the Jesuit society itself, which may be seen as the first global intellectual network in the history of mankind.

NOTES

1 See also Furlong [1933] 1994, 52–3.

2 On Dobrizhoffer's life, see Benitez Jump 1991–1992; Kratochwill 1967–1969; Jacobsen 1947; and Hauff 1928, 5–17.

3 The English translation is unfortunately incomplete, the numerous notes concerning other sources on Paraguay having been suppressed by the translator who argued: "In the course of the work, Dobrizhoffer frequently takes occasion to refute and expose the erroneous statements of other writers respecting the Jesuits in Paraguay, and the malignant calumnies by which the ruin of their institutions in that country was so unhappily effected" (see "Preface," in Dobrizhoffer [1822] 1970, 1: vii).

4 See the passage in the original Latin and German versions: "Pluris est oculatus testis unus, quam auriti decem; Qui audiunt, audita dicunt, qui vident, plane seiunt"; "Ein Augenzeuge gilt mehr, als zehn Ohrenzeugen. Der etwas

höret, sagt blos, was er gehöret hat; der es sieht, weiß es gewiß" ("Preface," in Dobrizhoffer 1783a, 1: 2).

5 Dobrizhoffer 1783a, 1: 21.

6 For more general information on this issue, see Gerbi [1955] 1973.

7 In the original edition, Dobrizhoffer indicated that the reference to Father Ortiz has been drawn from the work of Lópes de Gómara.

8 "Being asked where the other Indians were to be found, the mother replied that no mortal besides herself and her two children survived in these woods; that all the rest, who had occupied this neighbourhood, had died long ago of the small-pox" (Dobrizhoffer [1822] 1970, 88).

9 See the following commentary by the narrator: "For we found by experience, that savages removed to towns often waste away from the change of food and air, and from the heat of the sun, which powerfully affects their frames, accustomed, as they have been from infancy, to moist, cool, shady groves. The same was the fate of the mother, son, and daughter in our town" (Dobrizhoffer [1822] 1970 1: 93).

10 See also p. 287, where Southey characterizes this story as follows: "In the whole annals of Paraguay there is not a more singular and impressive tale than this in all its circumstances."

11 See Clavijero 1780–1, as well as the German translation in 1789 and 1790 (after a first but partial translation published in the periodical *Der Deutsche Merkur*), the English translation in 1789, and the Spanish translation in 1826.

BIBLIOGRAPHY

Ashcroft, Bill, Gareth Griffith, and Helen Tiffin. 1989. *The Empire Writes Back: Theory and Practice in post-Colonial Literatures.* London: Routledge.

Bachleitner, Norbert. n.d. *Kapitel aus der Geschichte der Buchkultur in der Habsburger Monarchie 1700–1918.* Available at: http://www.kakanien.ac.at/mat/NBachleitner1.pdf. Accessed October 2013.

Benitez Jump, Hernan. 1991–1992 "Der Ethnograph Martin Dobrizhoffer aius Friedberg im Böhmenwald. Sein Leben und sein Werk über die Abiponer in Paraguay." *Jahrbuch für sudentendeutsche Museen und Archive* 36–7: 217–24.

Bernhardt-Kabisch, Ernest. 1974. "Southey in the Tropics: *A Tale of Paraguay* and the Problem of Romantic Faith." *The Wordsworth Circle* 5: 97–104.

Blankenburg, Angela. 1947. "German Missionary Writers in Paraguay." *Mid-America* 29 (1–2): 34–68.

Clavijero, Francisco Xavier. 1780–1. *Storia antica del Messico.* Cesena: Gregorio Biasini.

Coleridge, Sara. 1873. *Memoir and Letters of Sara Coleridge*, ed. Edith Coleridge, 2 vols. London: Henry S. King.

Dobrizhoffer, Martin. 1783a. *Historia de Abiponibus Equestri, Bellicosaque Paraquariae Natione Locupletata Copi osis Barbararum Gentium, Urbium, Fluminum, Ferrarum, Amphibiorium, Insectorum, Serpentium Praecipuorum, Oiscium, Avium, Arbroum, Plantarum, Aliarumque Eiusdem Provinciae Propietatum Observationibus*, 3 vols. Viennæ: Kurbeck.

Dobrizhoffer, Martin. 1783b. *Geschichte der Abiponer, einer berittenen und kriegerischen Nation in Paraguay. Bereichert mit einer Menge Beobachtungen über die wilden Völkerschaften, Städte, Flüsse, vierfüßigen Thiere, Amphibien, Insekten, merkwürdigsten Schlangen, Fische, Vögel, Bäume, Pflanzen, und andere Eigenschaften dieser Provinz. Verfaßt von Martin Dobrizhoffer, achtzehn Jahre lang gewesenen Missionär in Paraguay. Aus dem Lateinischen übersetzt von A. Kreil*, 3 vols. Wien: Joseph Edlen von Kurzbek.

Dobrizhoffer, Martin. 1967. *Historia de los Abipones*, trans. Edmundo Wernicke. Resistencia: Universidad Nacional del Nordeste.

Dobrizhoffer, Martin. [1822] 1970. *An Account of the Abipones, An Equestrian People of Paraguay*, 3 vols., trans. Sara Coleridge. Reprint, London: Johnson Reprint Corporation / London: John Murray.

Dobrizhoffer, Martin and Joseph Brigniel. 1896. *Lenguas americanas. Idioma Abipon. Ensayo fundado sobre el "De Abiponibus" de Dobrozhoffer y los manuscritos del Padre J. Brigniel, S. J.*, ed. Samuel A. Lafone. Buenos Aires: Imprenta de Pablo E. Coni e Hijos.

Fitzpatrick, Martin, Peter Jones, Christa Knellwolf, and Iain McCalman, eds. 2004. *The Enlightened World*. London: Routledge.

Fulford, Tom. 2001. "Blessed Bane: Christianity and Colonial Disease in Southey's *Tale of Paraguay*." *Romanticism on the Net* 24. Available at: http://id.erudit.org/iderudit/005998ar. Accessed October 2013.

Furlong, Guillermo. [1933] 1994. *Los Jesuitas y la cultura rioplatense*. Reprint, Buenos Aires: Editorial Biblios.

Gerbi, Antonello. [1955] 1973. *The Dispute of the New World: The History of a Polemic, 1750–1900*, trans. Jeremy Moyle. Reprint, Pittsburgh: University of Pittsburgh Press.

Hauff, Walther von. 1928. *Pater Martin Dobrizhoffer, S. J. Auf verlorenem Posten bei den Abiponen*. Leipzig: Brockhaus.

Jacobsen, Jerome V. 1947. "Dobrizhoffer: Abipón Missionary." *Mid-America* [new series] 18 (3): 139–84.

Kratochwill, Max. 1967–1969. "Martin Dobrizhoffer. Zu seiner Lebensgeschichte." *Jahrbuch des Vereins für Geschichte der Stadt Wien* 23–5: 198–205.

Lafone Quevedo, Samuel Alexander. 1896. *Lenguas argentinas. Idioma abipón: ensayo fundado sobre el "De Abiponibus" de Dobrizhoffer*. Buenos Aires: Imprenta de Pablo E. Coni e Higos.

Lüsebrink, Hans-Jürgen. 2004. "Missionarische Fremdheitserfahrung und anthropologischer Diskurs. Zu den *Nachrichten von der Amerikanischen Halbinsel Californien* (1772) des elsässischen Jesuitenmissionars Johann Jakob Baegert." In *Lateinamerika. Orte und Ordnungen des Wissens. Festschrift für Birgit Scharlau,* eds. Sabine Hofmann and Monika Wehrheim, 69–82. Tübingen: Gunter Narr Verlag.

Métraux, Alfred. 1944. "The Contribution of the Jesuits to the Exploration and Anthropology of South America." *Mid-America* 26: 183–91.

Raynal, Guillaume-Thomas. 1783. *Histoire philosophique et politique des établissemens et du commerce des Européens dans les deux Indes.* Neuchâtel: Pellet.

Rojas, Ricardo. 1917–1922. *Historia de la Literatura argentina.* 8 vols. Buenos Aires: La Facultad.

Southey, Robert. 1822. "*An Account of the Abipones, an Equestrian People of Paraguay,* trans. from the Latin of Martin Dobrizhoffer, Eighteen Years a Missionary in that Country. London, 3 vols." *The Quarterly Review* January: 277–323.

Southey, Robert. 1909. "A Tale of Paraguay." In *Poems of Robert Southey, Containing "Thalaba," "The Curse of Kehama," "Roderick," "Madoc," "A Tale of Paraguay" and Selected Minor Poems,* ed. Maurice H. Fitzgerald, 657–97. London: Henry Frowde.

Storey, Mark. 1997. *Robert Southey: A Life.* Oxford: Oxford University Press.

Tietz, Manfred, ed. 2001. *Los Jesuitas españoles expulsos. Su imagen y su contribución al saber sobre el mundo hispánico en la Europa del siglo XVIII.* Frankfurt am Main: Vervuert.

chapter six

From Sacred Rhetoric to the Republic of Letters: Jesuit Sermons in Seventeenth-Century New Spain[1]

PERLA CHINCHILLA PAWLING

Sacred Jesuit oratory in the seventeenth century constituted the very bedrock of Jesuit conversion practice; indeed, it was the frontline weapon in the struggle for souls. During the course of the seventeenth century, however, and into the eighteenth century, the demand for written transmission of oratorical content ultimately transformed the genre of the sermon. Though these changes to the canon were minute, imperceptible, and gradual, it is precisely within these changes that the emergence of modernity may be charted in Jesuit discourse, the roots of the very discourse that informs the Jesuit accounts, which are the focus of this volume. Indeed, the genealogy of the resulting change is ultimately as important as the transformed genre itself. To this end, I will explore both the process and the outcome of the transformation of sacred Jesuit oratory. In particular, I will focus on the sermon, and in the course of this essay, show how under the rubric "sermon" we can find, at least in the Catholic world during the second half of the seventeenth century, artistic features that will push this form of discourse towards literary art. In a masterful paragraph, Michel de Certeau describes this form of displacement, which occurred in the dimensions of both practice and discourse:

> Divisions are converted into classifying and manipulative operations that redistribute the traditional elements and that will give rise, later, to "theoretical figures" that specify their principles. Behind the conducts or the religious convictions, the possibility to make another thing with them and to use them in the service of different strategies is created – a possibility whose equivalent is found in the same epoch, in the most manageable fields of the writing or the aesthetic, with the art (baroque or rhetorical) of treating and displacing images or commonplaces to obtain new effects (Certeau 1993a, 32).

The Jesuits would be the best seventeenth-century spokesmen of such displacement. In this article, therefore, I discuss and locate part of "the seventeenth-century sacred oratories" in the Jesuit space. Since virtually all of the access we have to lost worlds is mediated by text, genres are, for all intents and purposes, Jesuit spaces.[2]

Preaching and Sacred Oratory: Orality and Literacy

A crucial step in the move from orality to literacy in Jesuit discourse can be found in the increasing application of conceptism, that is, the baroque literary "conceit" that defined the writing of Francisco de Quevedo. Characterized by simple, direct language formed into witty metaphors and puns, the style also appealed to Spanish mystics and appears in their writings as well. For the Jesuits, conceptism became a device used by the sacred orators of the seventeenth century as a last-ditch attempt to avoid communicative rejection. Indeed, conceptism, I argue, functioned as a form of communicative *amplificatio*, an innovation in the form of traditional "amplification" (discussed infra in the quotation from the fourth point of Book 3), which was largely rhetorical in scope, intended, as it was, to move the passions, either to persuade or dissuade through intensely performative rhetoric. Instead, conceptism appealed more to the intellect than to the affections and rose in tandem with the publishing of sermons, where the most noteworthy examples reflect the powerful influence of conceptism.

Although the Latin word *sermo* can be associated with many semantic fields, the most stable characteristic is informality, that is, an oral allocution which, since the times of the church fathers, came to be understood as the deliverance through a talk of God's word to the faithful. Since then it underwent a series of subtle changes and specifications. For the seventeenth century, the most frequent term for designating sermons was "preachable speeches." If we try to define the principal characteristics of this genre, we come to face an evident problem: although most were commonly delivered orally, sermons are only accessible to us thanks to their printing. If we focus on this variable to distinguish sermons from other forms of printed religious texts of the time, it is important to notice whether what we are reading has a unified thematic structure. Such appears to be, indeed, what places a sermon apart from texts such as treatises or homilies, for instance – this and a certain length; a sermon is always shorter than a treatise. For sermons of earlier times, it is very difficult to say anything, since the press is the only possibility we have for accessing the genre.[3]

While it was becoming increasingly difficult for a preacher to conceal the lack of information in his sermons while preaching orally, it became even harder to hide this gap in printed texts, where the ability to revise and omit repetition left no excuses for empty rhetoric. Therefore sacred orators, the composers of sermons, had to look for ways of provoking pleasure without distorting the already very narrowly defined content standards to which they were expected to adhere. Thus, required to leave the content intact, they had to innovate with the form. The result is a highly complex style of composition that appears distant and strange to the eyes of today's readers. To synthesize, *amplificatio* initially worked to persuade, especially during the first half of the seventeenth century, through its use of the "movimiento de los afectos" (movement of the affections) or "movimiento de las pasiones" (movement of passions), directed at the emotions of the audience, to stir them for or against a character, a virtue, a vice, a situation, and so forth. However, as the century moved forward, in the emerging courtly society this "affective oratory" began to be regarded as appropriate only for the moralization of the common people, and, as such, it no longer appealed to the elite, whose constant aim was to distinguish themselves from the common people. It is in this way that what I propose as a "second moment" of *amplificatio* surfaced (see Chinchilla Pawling 2009). In such a moment we observe the conceptist rhetoric as the last stronghold of *amplificatio*, and the qualities of an "acute," "witty," and "conceitful" oratory began to be praised more and more towards the second half of the century, persuading audiences through "admiration" (*admiratio*) or an appeal to the intellect.

The following fragment from Juan Pimental dedication for the *Sermón, que en la solemne fiesta, que celebró Al humano Seraphin llagado imagen viva de Christo* (printed in New Spain in 1683, and therefore presumably composed and pronounced not long before that time), apart from constituting a remarkable sample of baroque "conceptism" (see Chinchilla Pawling 2009, 81), shows the acuteness of the problem that the emergence of a culture of the printed word represented for a world based on a culture of orality:

> What can I say about a rough draft, or a sermon that is the same thing, which I pronounced compelled out of obedience? For whereas the subject offered me unlimited matter of which to speak, the limits of my impoverished talent remained with the crowd, since, for as much as I pondered it, I could never utter more than a few naked phrases, which, lacking the life of conceit, can say nothing when they sound so soulless. So much so, that when I wanted

to execute Your Excellency's orders to write them, since they were merely echoes that were animated with the fantastic life of their pronunciation when sounded, I find nothing left there; to obey I must write, and bound by obedience I scribble drafts, for I have nothing to say with the pen ("Que dirè yo de un borron, ó de un sermon que es lo mesmo, que à impuloso de la obediencia llegué à hablar? En donde quando el asumpto me ofreció casi innumerable materia, para dezir quedando con la muchedumbre la cortedad de mi talento empobrecido, por mas que lleguè à pensar, nunca lleguê â proferir mas que unas desnudas vozes que por carecer de la vida del concepto, nada dizen, quando tan sin alma suenan. Tanto que al querer executar elmandato de Vuestra Reverendisima en escrivirlas, como fueron unos ecos solos, que con la phantastica vida de su pronunciacion como animadas sonaron: hallo que nada es ya, lo que debo para obedecer escrivir, y ceñido a la obediencia borrones formo, por no tener con la pluma que dezir" [Pimental 1683, s. p.]).

"No tener con la pluma que dezir" ("not having anything to say with the pen") is a good metaphor for the fate that was awaiting the oral world as "what was said" began to be transferred onto paper, but for people living in the seventeenth century, the impossibility of "saying with the pen" was yet to become apparent. For them, the rhetorical vision of the world implied in these words was still functioning. They could not see that the whole edifice of rhetoric was going to contract until it became a part of the whole that we today designate, not in the plural, as "arts," but in the singular, as "art."

Viewed from this perspective, sacred oratory finds itself at the point of convergence of a complex textual world – both oral and written – from which it departs and to which it returns, having gathered social experience from those who exercise the occupation of preaching, who, in turn, are situated between two spaces: the religious-catechistic and the religious-artistic. In the course of the seventeenth century, the latter would place itself above the former, almost to the point where it interrupted the channel of communication between sacred oratory and audience (a congregation of the faithful). The result by the end of the century was a closed place of the "culture of the printed letter," in which specialized orators ("oradores") known as preachers of "villa and court" (so called because they preached in urban centres and the court), talked to each other, or rather *wrote* to each other, and audiences admired their rhetorical feats.[4] These sacred orators were integrated into the discourse of an urban courtly society; in the process, they left behind their former pedagogical-doctrinal functions and assumed new pedagogical-literary ones, vis-à-vis the public acquisition of the public's own space of distinction through the refinement of taste (see Bourdieu 1991, 259ff.; Elias 1982). This development marks the division of preaching within Catholicism into two distinct types carried on by different kinds of preachers. The function of evangelizing (here including catechizing) was henceforth left to "unofficial" (non-professional) preachers despised by the "villa and court" orators. These preachers of "town square and passion" were the silent heirs of the original function that the Council of Trent had assigned to all preachers: the reconquest of the Catholic faithful. Their counterparts in the city, in contrast, would embark on quite new paths and come to embody distinctively different functions.

Whenever an attempt is made to give an account of changes that denote a step towards modernity like the ones described above, we run into a complex and almost impenetrable set of phenomena. Two of these phenomena are especially relevant since, at their intersection, the sermon becomes a privileged place of observation, in which the aporia of religious society, in the face of modern society and their eventual consequences for culture, become visible.[5] On the one hand, the wholeness of the religious experience was challenged, as intimate religious experience began to collide with the exteriority of religious practices, thereby leading to the gradual divorce of externally practiced religiosity, that is, baroque piety, from internally focused spirituality; on the other hand, the integrity of the world of communication was fractured in the increasingly urgent confrontation between the world of oral culture and the world of print culture.[6]

How should we approach the subject of orality and writing in relation to the sermon? Let us first briefly locate the discussion with respect to the changes brought about in this period by writing, and in particular by the press. David Olson has summarized the approaches to this problem very lucidly by distinguishing between the views of two distinct sets of critics: "A group of authors attributes cultural changes associated with changes in the forms of communication to a transformation of the social and institutional practices, estimating that the cognitive processes of the individuals practically continue being the same" (Olson 1995, 203). Emphasizing social and institutional factors and leaving little room for psychological ones, Olson places Elizabeth Eisenstein, a pioneering voice in the study of the transition between orality and the published, written world in this group. Olson continues: "The other group associates these same cultural changes with psychological changes, with an alteration in the forms of representation and the forms of consciousness" (203; see also Eisenstein 1994). Olson places his own work in this second category, along with that of Eric A. Havelock. Despite the difficulties inherent in this dense discussion, it is possible to assert that in the seventeenth century, a historical conjuncture of the two coordinates occurred: transformations in social practices and cognition took place, from which a series of changes originated that would not become fully visible until the Enlightenment.

It is important to clarify a number of points bearing on orality and writing. Olson's proposal that writing systems were created to communicate information rather than to represent speech is particularly relevant. His position contravenes traditional hypotheses, which assert that writing arises as a representation of verbal language (see Havelock 1996). He affirms that the conceptualization of the word, as such, is only possible through writing; that in oral space the name *is* the thing (see Olson 1998, 100, as well as Harris 1986, and Gaur 1992); that in consequence, it is only in the world of writing that the distinction between reality and the arbitrary act of naming becomes possible. From this derives the most important characteristic of writing: its potential analytical capacity, as opposed to the fundamentally cumulative characteristic of orality. Writing's elements do not tend to be simple organizations, such as individual words, but rather groups of simple organizations, such as terms, locutions, or epithets. Writing's analytical capacity would propitiate the disarming of the expressions constructed throughout many years, since outside orality there is no place to preserve such expressions. Olson affirms that the relationship of writing with speech is, in every case, indirect (see Olson 1998, 91). Thus I can conclude that from their beginnings, orality and writing possessed distinctive qualities, which over time would be transformed until today, where we tend to relate orality with "art" and writing with "science." It is important, nevertheless, to stress, as Olson does, that written culture and oral culture are not necessarily opposed, that highly educated cultures have been, at the same time, extremely oral (see 86).

The second half of the seventeenth century can be described as a society of "secondary orality," where writing and orality coexist (see Ong 1999). By tracking the particular characteristics of primary oral communication throughout the seventeenth century, then, it is possible to identify its limitations and continuities through points of contact with the world of writing, keys to understanding the highly complex and unique historical period under investigation here. According to Ong, the world of orality depends on the "formulary constitution of thought." Once acquired, knowledge will have to be frequently repeated or it will be lost, for the "fixed and formulary patterns of thought" are vital to the preservation of memory: "The extensive thought of oral bases, although not of formal verse, tends to be extremely rhythmical, because rhythm helps the memory, including physiologically" (32–100). Consciousness of the mnemonic base of expression in primarily oral cultures allows comprehension of other characteristics. In addition to its formulary condition:

1. "Orality culture" is cumulative, before subordinated;
2. It is redundant or "copious": "The redundancy, repetition of what just has been said, maintains effectively both the speaker as the listener in the same syntony" (Ong 1999, 46). The voice fills the space, "the spoken word invades, affirms itself, and pretends to have preeminence. In a measure greater than that of written text, it is identical to the situation, but for that reason it cannot not last beyond the situation" (Luhmann and Georgi 1993, 111–2), and "sight isolates: ear unites [...] sound surrounds the listener" (Ong 1999, 75);
3. "Oral cultures stimulate fluidity, excess, wordiness. The rhetoricians would call this *Copia*" (Ong 1999, 46);
4. Oral cultures do not produce dictionaries. Words acquire their meaning at the actual moment of their enunciation, in which gestures, as well as vocal modulations, and facial expression participate in creating meaning, thereby establishing human and existential frames of reference. The meanings of words arise in the present, although the previous ones had already moulded the actual sense in many varied, non-perceivable forms (Ong 1999, 52).

While these characteristics of oral communication have been isolated for analytical reasons, it is a fact that in the West, since the time of the Greeks, they have coexisted with written communication; for this reason, it is important to delineate the relationship between the two forms of communication. Certainly, the first thing that must be established is the distinction between an *oral society* and a *scriptorial society* (as discussed infra). In the first, writing operates as a support system for orality. The point of union between the two lies in rhetoric. As a stylization of the faculties of a completely oral culture, rhetoric cannot exist in the absence of writing. Let us reflect on Aristotle's organizational view: the art of rhetoric, though related to oral discourse, as were the other arts, necessarily entailed writing. It conserved a fundamental relation with orality as far as its agnostic and formulary load were concerned: the objective of all rhetorical speech was to refute a point of some opposite opinion through the resource of invention, which consisted in tending to common places on which the arguments for all types of subjects were founded; it was, however, crucial that this complex structure be written down (see Ong 1999, 109–10 and 119).

Seventeenth-century sermons represented the last vestiges of this world of rhetoric, of orality conceived as art, and concomitantly, as a means for the reproduction of society. When working on its possibilities and limitations in that era, it is therefore useful to give an account of the fractures from which the scriptorial world, and especially the world of print, or modernity, would emerge. In the sermon, the characteristics of orality mentioned previously were conserved, even as the impact of the world of the book began to be felt. How can we conceptualize the process that produced this result?

Amplification and Novelty

The rhetorical resource used to obtain cumulative redundancy in orality is known as amplification, which I have discussed to some extent already and will expand upon here.[7] Niklas Luhmann has convincingly suggested that *amplificatio* "turns problematic if it is treated in terms of truth, whereas if its communicative function is seen, its importance is comprehended" (Luhmann and Georgi 1993, 130). It is precisely by means of *amplificatio,* in its paradoxical relationship with truth, that we can in some way penetrate the changes that took place in early modern European society. Amplification – rhetorical procedure for some, rhetorical figure for others – was always present in classical rhetoric (see Beristáin 1995, 44). Engaged to enhance and emphasize an idea, or to develop and extend a subject, the process had a function which was both aesthetic and argumentative, consisting of ornament as well as explanation. In the Renaissance, and most of all in the post-Tridentine Catholic sphere, the figure acquired an unprecedented importance. If we accept the implications of Luhmann's suggestion, we may be able to find an open way to elaborate the connections between the communicative function of rhetoric, a particular code of "truth," and society.

The Tridentine church was forced to secure "orthodoxy," yet, amidst the danger represented by the Protestant Reformation, going about this through a public debate of theological points was out of the question. Divine truths were not to be open for discussion within the space of the congregation, and actually questioning dogma was even more strictly prohibited. The space of the congregation was explicitly restricted to the catechization of the faithful, rather than dedicated to the plumbing of theological depths. Preaching was meant to teach without probing or questioning in ways that might endanger the faith. The rhetorical resource for this would be amplification, since it allowed for elaborating a text without engaging in judgment of its revealed truth. Sermons are a good indication of this (despite the fact that the sermon is a difficult genre to trace), since amplification can only be done by analysing their structures and the small, yet specific differences that distinguish them from other genres. As I state in my book *De la Compositio Loci a la República de las Letras. Predicación jesuita en el siglo XVII novohispano,* "we must take into account that, generally speaking, preaching was meant to standardize the faithful, and that the precepts dictated for the composition of sermons prescribed avoiding deviations from the accepted conciliar principles, so consequently the normative variations in the Catholic spaces seem minimal" (Chinchilla Pawling 2004, 54).

Symptomatically, and in contrast to earlier norms, texts on rhetoric written after the Council of Trent and the Catholic and Protestant Reformations dwell at length on sacred oratory as a mode of argumentation and on the special role of amplification in such forms of communication. Certainly the most extensive, and in this sense significant, text on *amplificatio* is Friar Luis de Granada's *Rhetorica Eclesiastica Ecclesuastocæ rhetoricæ libri,* written in the sixteenth century. Granada dedicates Books 2 and 3 of his work to the oratory mode of argumentation, which he carefully distinguishes from logic as such. Book 3, "Libro tercero de la Rhetorica Eclesiástica, o de la manera de predicar: en que se trata del modo de amplificar, y de los Afectos," treats amplification as a type of *probatio.* Marc Fumaroli summarizes Granada's text as follows:

> [Amplification] consists essentially in figures of thought, affective movements, and speaking paintings. These last ones are also adequate to awaken, by means of imagination, the affection of the audience. Description of habits (happiness of the contemplative life, corruption of lascivious women, etc.), description of characters (strong virgin, crazy virgin, etc.) of shows with entertainment purposes (combats that represent the spiritual combat, etc.). These descriptions of characters could be animated by *prosopopeias* that are borrowed (Fumaroli 1994, 212).[8]

In other words, Granada centres himself around amplification, the emotions and figures that raise "passions." While the classic organization of his work as a whole is obvious, it is significant that he breaks the old pattern of dividing rhetoric into five parts by adding two more parts – *amplificatio* and *emotio* – and at the same time eliminating *compositio* and *memoria*: "The change indicates a withdrawal from the Ciceronian emphasis on aureate rhythm and periodicity, in order to emphasize emotional expressiveness" (Shuger 1993, 126). The fourth point of Book 3 is of particular interest, where Granada enumerates these changes, by clearly denoting the shift towards a more intellectually based notion of amplification:

> The invention of things that lend themselves to Amplification can be found in the same places from which the arguments are taken. Because if Amplification, as we recently stated, is like a certain kind of Argumentation, one can infer that the Invention of both Amplification and Argumentation proceeds from the same places. Nevertheless, some of these places are more suitable to amplifying [...].
>
> We often make use then of this place brought forth from the Effects, through which we refer the advantages or disadvantages that may ensue, especially in persuasive or dissuasive sermons. Because through them we intend to prove that we must embrace the thing we are addressing if we exhort others to do so, or avoid it, if we advise against it.
>
> Until now, what was spoken belonged to the art of invention, that is, the place from which arguments must be drawn, with which we are able to amplify what we wish ("La Invencion de las cosas, que sirven para la Amplificacion, se tomarà de los mismos lugares, de donde se sacan los argumentos. Porque, si la Amplificacion, como poco ha digímos, es como cierta especie de Argumentacion, se infiere que la Invencion de entrambas proceda de los mismos lugares. Sin embargo, algunos lugares de estos sirven mas para amplificar [...].
>
> Nos servimos pues en muchas veces de este lugar trahido de los Efectos, por el qual vamos refiriendo las conveniencias, ò desconveniencias que se subsiguen; principalmente en los sermones suasorios, ò disuasorios. Porque dellos pretendemos probar, que de la cosa que tratamos, devemos abrazarla, si exhortamos; ò evitarla, o disuadimos.
>
> Lo dicho hasta aqui pertenece al artificio de inventar, esto es, de donde devan tomarse los argumentos, con que podamos amplificar lo que deseamos" [Granada (1770?), fol. 142–4, 159–60, and 163]).

By the end of the sixteenth and the beginning of the seventeenth century, passions acquired unprecedented weight in preaching, as we can see in the following paragraph, where Luhmann stresses the reflections on the concept of *admiratio* by two authors from the seventeenth century:

> "To amplify and to illustrate are both the main adornments of the eloquence that provide for the minds of men the greatest advantages: admiration and faith," wrote John Hoskins, in his *Directions for Speech and Style* (1599), and here *admiratio* is a sort of passion (and, therefore, a factor of motivation) that corresponds to the hierarchical structure of the society. Descartes emphasized: "[I]t is a passion that unlike the others, does not contain in itself any opposite impulse, that is to say, can be activated before each binary codification." Meaning that, it is a premise that guarantees the acceptance and avoids the communicative rejection. "A communication that provokes *admiratio* produces an understanding that is not separated from the acceptance" (Luhmann and Georgi 1993, 133).

Where did this *admiratio* come from? Communicative acceptance, as I have already mentioned, was granted to preachers according to their perceived "knowledge" and "virtue." It was believed that knowledge was obtained by an individual preacher through the workings of grace, by means of which God allowed him to read between the lines of sacred texts. His illumination was presumed to be a reflection of his moral virtue, which in turn derived from the moral code that he followed as a consecrated priest. Little by little, however, a preacher's ability to elicit admiration from his audiences would replace his evident knowledge as the sign of his virtue. This transformation can best be documented by comparing a quote from the chronicle of the Jesuit Francisco Xavier Alegre, which narrated the missionary activity in 1574 of Father Suárez de la Concha in the north of New Spain with a remark a century later by Jesuit José de Ormaza, recorded in his *Rhetoric* from 1648. Father Alegre wrote:

> To be charitable, on some holy days we decided to say mass in nearby villages where mass was seldom heard for lack of ministers. The good Father Concha remarked on the crowd that turned up and the devotion reflected on their countenance. Keenly grieved by the inability to make the most of this opportunity due to the foreignness of their tongue, he looked for a book from which to read to them, and despite the fact that he understood not one word, he did so with such great emotion and fervour, that, the Lord cooperating with his industrious zeal, the Indians who were listening to him

> experienced very positive effects ("Algunos días de fiesta se repartían, por caridad, a decir misa en los pueblos vecinos, que de otra suerte no la oyeran por la cortedad de ministros. Notó el buen Padre Concha la muchedumbre que acudía, y la devoción que mostraban en sus semblantes. Vivamente condolido de no poderles aprovechar, por ser extraño su idioma, buscó un libro en que leerles, y lo hacía con tanto afecto y fervor, aunque sin entender una palabra, que, cooperando el Señor a su industrioso celo, no se dejaron de experimentar muy Buenos efectos en los indios que le escuchaban" [Alegre (1751) 1957–1959, 1: 148–9]).

On the other hand, Father José de Ormaza indicated in his *Censura de la elocuencia para calificar sus obras y señaladamente las del Púlpito*, published under the name of Gonzalo Pérez de Ledesma in 1648:

> Is devotion any less because it is well expressed? [...] It is natural to brandish the well-wrought sword, display one's best arms, and they'll be doubled if they combine elegance and spirit. God wants us to use natural means; for though he has inspired some saints to cross the river's surface, should all attempt this, He'd be inflamed, and with shipwreck they would purchase punishment ("¿Pierde acaso la devoción con lo bien dicho? [...] Lo natural es herir la espada acicalada, vencer las armas de prueba, y serán dobles si se junta la elegancia y el espíritu. Quiere Dios nos valgamos de los medios naturales, que aunque a algunos Santos ha inspirado pasen en la capa del río, si todos lo intentaran hazer así le tentaran, y con el naufragio compraran el escarmiento" [quoted in Herrero Salgado 1996, 264]).

As these quotes demonstrate, *admiratio* began to be related to pure virtuosity, at least in oratory pieces and sermons. Hence the fracture of the union between knowledge and motivation in its traditional formula began. Moral virtue could no longer be derived "automatically" from one's clerical rank, and since the doctrinal function of the sermon began to lose weight with audiences' expectations in favour of more sophisticated rhetorical feats, moral virtue could no longer guarantee acceptance. Given that acceptance had been obtained through the moral authority of the preacher, and that moral authority had been undermined by the Protestant Reformation, preachers would henceforth have to develop to the fullest their rhetorical instruments of persuasion: as a result, amplification would be exploited to its greatest possible extent.

In addition, sacred preachers faced two problems, both arising from precisely the type of audience they addressed: urban elites. The traditional functions of preaching were to catechize and to moralize, but as the seventeenth century advanced, neither could be used as effective tools within this sector of society. Elites knew the dogmas ad nauseam, and began recognizing their reiteration. Furthermore, urban society had become more complex and heterogeneous, less open to moral exhortations in the traditional style. Both factors rendered audiences more difficult to impress than before. Responding to this set of conditions, and perhaps to the fact that the Catholic Church was becoming ever more dependent on the state, preaching became more courtly in nature. It is symptomatic that the gradual disconnection between moral virtues and the oratorical virtues of the preacher, imposed by the very authors of sacred rhetoric, made way for an asymmetry that valued the latter more highly than the former, in consonance with the *admiratio* manifested by urban congregations; this seems to confirm the point about the dislocation between the doctrinal and aesthetic standards of sermons. How, then, did preachers attempt to meet their Tridentine obligation to reiterate dogma according to the liturgical calendar in a congregational environment permeated by courtly values and mores?

A first movement towards that goal can be asserted if we reach for an analogical example. In a text on publicity, Luhmann discusses how the reflective value of information is used as an indicator of its importance in the operation of mass media: what needs to be remembered is repeated. The reader who perceives this repetition of information associates quality and value with the number of times something is repeated (see Luhmann 1995a, 21). With a bit of extrapolation, we can find an illustrative analogy with preaching. In this case – similar to how publicity works to induce the consumer to buy something – given the increasing consciousness of repetition and supply of sermons during the seventeenth century, the confirmation of the esteem for a piece of oratory was based less upon the catechetic content and more upon the fame and style of the preacher. The believer was compelled to hear the sermons, but the tediousness brought about by repetition and reiteration of the catechetical contents became increasingly evident. Whether boring or not, the message was the word of God, hence highly important, and congregations needed to remember it, permanently. Therefore, as we have seen, knowledge within oral culture had to be repeated so that it would be remembered; otherwise it would be lost. In a culture in which both oral communication and revealed truth bore so much weight, repetition of the doctrinal contents was mandatory regardless of the contingent situation of an unreceptive audience. In other words, being unable to switch contents that were fully known by the audience, preachers had to employ the most refined rhetorical tools within their reach. Thus, the purpose of the sermon had to remain that of recalling (renewing the memory of) the divine message. This brought about a situation in which the standards by which a sacred orator became renowned were rendered alien to his capacity to convey the pious message.

In the following approval for the publication of a sermon, the relationship between memory and ear elaborated by the author demonstrates awareness of the function that reiteration fulfils in the communicative space of orality: "[A]nd thus I estimate that our Lord's Glory, the Saint's virtue, and common edification will grow with publication, *in such a way that the memory of those who heard it is refreshed*, and those who shall read it will become impassioned with devotion to the Saint" ("Y assí juzgo redundarà en Gloria de nuestro Señor, honra del Sancto, y edificacion comun al imprimirse, *para que los que lo oyeron renueven la memoria*, y los que le leyeren se afficionen à la devocion del Santo" [Vaca Salasar 1638, fol. 192]). In the above quote, it is interesting to note the order in which the censor provides the motives for his approval. What comes first is not the possibility of sharing the doctrinal contents of the sermon with more people, but that of serving as a mnemonic device for those who were present during the preaching of the sermon. This shows to what extent reiteration was an indispensable component of sacred oratory.

How can reiteration be achieved without boring or alienating one's audience? How to suture, at least for a while, wounds deadly to the whole preaching enterprise? Preaching, as I argue, or at least sacred rhetoric, found a means of survival in art. I maintain this affirmation, conceptualizing art in the same terms employed by Luhmann, in order to explain the passage of traditional society into modernity:

> Art is a medium of communication generalized symbolically that corresponds [...] to the constellation of attributes within which the acting of Alter is experienced by Ego. The artist who acts and takes into consideration the work of art undergoes a determined experience [for these purposes: the preacher and the congregation] [...]. An object is perceived as a work of art when distinguishing it from *natural* objects when it is recognized that it is the result of someone's actions, and as such, artificial. The work of art possesses something surprising that cannot be explained as chance, and therefore it leads to ask with what aim was it made. The question of the reach of the work of art becomes particularly loaded with meaning given the differentiation of art as an autonomous system of functions, with the following resignation to external motivations or aids. The object of art is no longer to

> delay something not accessible directly [the space of the divine in the case of sermon], nor the limitation of nature, but simply to experience the combinations of unexplored forms [the Baroque is a forceful example of this]. In a way opposite to other artificial objects, works of art do not have any external use: they are aims in and of themselves (Luhmann 1995b, 23–4).

But to affirm that a sermon is a work of art is to create a paradox and a provocation: a work of art is created for its own sake; a sermon, for the religious purposes of catechizing and moralizing, which exist outside of itself. A sermon lacking religious functions would have been inadmissible in post-Tridentine, Old Regime Europe, and in the era of the Baroque, when art had a divine purpose and served the greater glory of God. Art as a closed, circular, or self-referential system – art for art's sake – would not appear until the nineteenth century. Thus the Baroque form can be seen as unstable and being so, expressing a paradox between the already evident opaqueness of art's purpose, as art itself embarks on a path towards autonomy, and the excessive and exacerbated insistence on its religious purpose in the post-Tridentine environment.

The concept of "fashion" was introduced as an answer to the challenges of the paradox. Meanwhile the questioning of the value of novelty that had begun in the sixteenth century was settled in the seventeenth century squarely in favour of the new or modern. Taste and esteem for novelty became commonplace: only what was "new, surprising, artificial" (Luhmann 1995a, 41) was followed and appreciated. I again quote Luhmann, who clearly describes this transition:

> Whether art can or cannot motivate the acceptance of its selected offer depends on whether the individual work of art manages to convey that it itself (unlike the world) has to be just as it is, since it has been produced like this and it has not had a model at its side. In this sense, from the Seventeenth Century on, the originality of the work of art is sought out.
>
> What now decides over originality is not the confrontation with nature, and definitely not the quality of imitation, but the confrontation with other works of art. In the form of a requirement that must be satisfied by the particular work, art differentiates itself as independent and refers to itself. And the reference to the particular work of art is explained because only in this way the paradox of the need of what is only possible can be developed (Luhmann 1995a, 157–8).

The sermon would become a work of art, in the terms I have discussed here, only slowly, in a process that would enhance the place of rhetoric.

This "pagan" art, with which the *ars praedicandi* had always had a love-hate relationship, now actually became the nucleus of "good preaching," its pertinence no longer questioned in any way. We can follow the evolution of sacred rhetoric by comparing the words of Friar Luis de Granada with those of seventeenth-century counterparts. In his 1655 *Apología de la predicación*, Friar Pedro de Miranda observed, for example:

> Wits have advanced so much, they are so lively and subtle, that if sermons were to be preached in the vast and coarse manner used in centuries past, there would be no one who would wait them out, and thus, so as not to upset and repel the congregation, it is useful to season the sermons with some conceits and facts of preachable and expressive topics ("Se han adelantado ya tanto los ingenios, están tan vivos y sutiles, que si se predicaran los sermones tan bastos y broncos cuanto en los siglos pasados, no habría quien los esperara, y así, por no desazonar y ahuyentar a los oyentes, conviene sazonar los sermones con algunos conceptos y realces de puntos predicables y lenguaje" [quoted in Herrero Salgado 1996, 258]).

As Miranda's words make clear, by the seventeenth century the controversy had already gone beyond arguments about the propriety of rhetoric to preaching, to address instead the question of excesses and transgressions in sacred rhetoric. Criticism of Baroque preachers, coming from traditional clerical sectors, is very revealing, for it charges that Baroque orators had abandoned moralizing and teaching in favour of self-promotion. Suddenly it seemed that doctrinal topics, once the cornerstone of preaching, had become an arduous obligation, abandoned at the slightest excuse. In his *Guía de la virtud* (1642), Father Alonso de Andrade, for example, warned that excesses from the pulpit deserve "eternal condemnation":

> A priest of the Jesuit order advised his very close friend, a cultivated and erudite preacher of our times, one who conveyed refined discourses and exquisite thoughts with great discretion in a carefully crafted language, to drop that way of preaching and to preach sincerely on Jesus Christ crucified, looking for the soul's profit. However, since those who engage in this weakness are educated men of genius, they disregard such counsel ("A un predicador de nuestros tiempos, de los que llaman cultos y galantes, persona que hablava muy a lo discreto, el lenguaje peinado, los discursos puldios y pensamientos exquisitos, avisó un Religioso de la Compañía, con quien profesava amistad estrecha, que dexase aquel modo de predicar y predicase llanamente a Jesu-Christo Crucufucado, poniendo la mira en el provecho

de las almas. Pero como son Letrados y personas de ingenio los que dan en esta flaqueza, no hazen caso de semejantes avisos" [quoted in Herrero Salgado 1996, 434; note how the preacher is referred to as a lettered man]).

Along these lines, it seems important to me to relate the discussion on *imitatio* within the space of preaching that occurred at that time with the rise of the autonomy of art and its connection with sacred oratory. The problem of exceeding and transgressing the limits of good preaching was taken up within the Jesuit order in a significant discussion, or debate, about the form of *imitatio* known as "adult" *imitatio.* Orthodox Ciceronians thought this form was excessively lax. The debate engendered a variety of positions, couched sometimes in polemical and unflattering terms, on the degrees and types of novelty permissible in *imitatio.* The case of Father Petau, which is discussed by Fumaroli, represents a Ciceronian Jesuit reaction against the excesses of adult *imitatio* in the Company of Jesus, especially in its northern European schools, "submissive to Spanish influence" (Fumaroli 1994, 345).[9] Note here the accusation associating this form of rhetoric particularly with Hispanic Jesuits. Fumaroli claims that in his *Theologica dogmata,* Petau affirmed that "modern Christian eloquence must be the flower of the style of the two Antiquities, rather than the fruit of servile imitation of this or the other ancient thinker" ("el aticismo cristiano moderno debe ser la flor del estilo de las dos Antigüedades, y no el fruto de la imitación servil de tal o cual Antiguo" [quoted from Fumaroli 1994, 345]). The influential Father Caussin offered a different point of view, favouring originality and personal genius: "'There are spirits who arrive in the world held by the spider's web on the fragile precipice, and they have filled the centuries with the admiration of their greatness; others who have been received (into the world) with pomp and purple are nevertheless stupid and dumb'" ("'Hay espíritus que llegaron al mundo entre las arañas de una endeble barranca, y que han colmado los siglos con la admiración de su grandeza; otros han sido recibidos en el oropel y la púrpura que no han dejado de ser estúpidos y tontos'" [quoted from Fumaroli 1994, 345]).

Another reaction, this one of Hispanic origin, can be appreciated in Baltazar Gracián's work on the talents of "acuteness" and "wit," which scorn servile imitation and glorify the artist's genius:

> If perceiving wit credits one an eagle, then producing it will by and by an angel prove: toil of cherubim and ennoblement of men, which brings us aloft amid such unparalleled rank. As far as being one of those who are better known in general terms and less in precise ones, let them be perceived,

not defined; in such far removed matters, let any description of mine be deemed true: as fair sights are to the eyes and harmonious sounds to the ears, such are conceptions to the intellect ("Si el percibir la agudeza acredita de águila, el producirla empeñará en ángel: empleo de querubines y elevación de hombres, que nos remonta a extravagante jerarquía. En este ser uno de aquellos que son más conocidos a bulto, y menos a precision, déjase percibir, no definir; y en tan remoto asunto, estímeseme cualquiera descripción: lo que es para los ojos la hermosura, y para los oídos la consonacia, eso es para el entendimiento el concepto" [Gracián 1960, 237]).

Under these postulates, and in spite of recriminations, it is understandable that "novelty" was particularly sought after in spaces of preaching, as in other artistic spaces of the seventeenth century: in order for audiences to receive sermon messages as "original" rather than tedious or boring, preachers had to innovate. Over the course of the seventeenth century in a variety of documents relative to preaching, the actual word "novelty" appears frequently:

> And now that the sermon contains no particular novelty since the Holy Fathers have already said it all [...] it is enough as far as novelty goes to concentrate a great deal in a brief amount of space and time ("Y ya que no tenga otra *novedad* el Sermon, aunque, todo lo tengan dicho los Santos Padres [...] bastale por *novedad* la de acumular mucho en corto espacio, y poco tiempo" [Millán de Pobrete 1696, s. p.]).

> Consider attentively the subtlety of the concepts, *the novelty of place*, and the erudition of reasoning ("Considerè atento lo sutil de los conceptos, *la novedad de los lugares*, lo erudito de la inteligencia" [Torre y Castro 1656, fol. 2–3; the comment is included not in the sermon as such, but in the approval of the sermon given by Friar Juan de Herrera]).

> [H]e has always preached with accuracy about everything, and about this with most veracity, since *the idea being very rare*, such that there was no model, since it was about the Holiest Mary, as her following in these kingdoms was so intense, her prayer *so rare*, erudite, solemn and unique, that with it, by giving a great deal of news about the miraculous apparition of Our Lady of Pilar of Zaragoza, his text could serve as a fortifying wall, strengthening devotion to her ("[H]a predicado siempre con acierto en todos, y en este acertadissimo; pues siendo *la idea rarissima*, assi por ser sin exemplar siendo de MARIA Santissima, como por exquisita su advocacion en estos Reynos, fue su oracion *tan rara*, docta, grave y singular, que con ella dando tantas

noticias de la Apparicion milagrosa de N. Señora de Pilar de Zaragoza, puede su escrito ser muro para que la devocion se fortifique" [Manuel José Villegas on a sermon by Friar Alonso de Avila, a *sentir* (kind of review) quoted in Torre y Castro 1656, fol. 2–3]).

Etymology (says Cicero) is the interpreter of the truth of words, whether in diction or in any letter of its phases […]. It was accompanied by ancient letters and hieroglyphs in modern style declaimed, and which make it very plausible to the erudites, because (as Quintillian says) ancient words give a sermon majesty with delight, because they lend authority by virtue of their antiquity […]. Engaging them in discourse about them *in a new way* is the diligence that exalts them ("La Etimologia (dize Ciceron) es interprete de la verdad de las palabras, yà en la diccion, yà en qualquier letra de sus peirodods […] Estaba compañada con letras antiguas de Hyeroglificos à los moderno discurridos, que la hazen para los doctos muy plaudisble, que las palabras antiguas (dize Quintiliano) dan à la oracion magestad con deleyte, porque tienen la autoridad de ser antiguas: […] El discurrirlas *à lo nuevo* es diligencia que las realza" [Ávila 1684, s. p.; quoted from a *parecer* (type of review) by Friar Agustin de Vetancurt on Avila]).

But the great challenge for preachers seeking to introduce novelty still lay, of course, in finding ways to do so within the limitations imposed by dogma and liturgy; altering the form, or perhaps the style, of a sermon was really the only available strategy.

In Conclusion: The Press and Amplification

In order to better understand the transformations that sermons underwent in their movement from doctrine to art, I must address the effects of another phenomenon: the press. Paradoxically the press would insert itself in the most important public oral practice of the seventeenth century: preaching. Where oral sermon making would adopt novelty of form in the battle against the boredom brought about by reiteration, in the presence of a public eager for the "wit and art of creativity," the printed version would actually continue to exploit the powers of amplification as a method for transmitting revealed truths. It would take a century or more for the consequences of this exploitation to completely manifest themselves in the urban world, where this way of communicating the "truths" of religion would become convoluted and tedious, in other words, "noisy."

For the famous preachers of the time – who were often also published authors – the ultimate goal of their sermons began to be the printing press. This transformed the process of production of sacred oratory, enhancing the value of the sermon in print over the one delivered from the pulpit. In order to support this disconcerting affirmation, I reproduce here fragments of the opinions, feelings, judgments, dedications, and censorships that were sometimes bundled together as front matter in printed sermon editions. Valuing print over the spoken word could be justified by means of diverse arguments, but the most persuasive strategies emphasized the permanence of the printed text and the vastness of its potential audience. It is interesting, however, that in these examples, the qualities of printed text are praised through metaphors taken from the world of voice; the texts offer evidence of some nostalgia for the disappearing world of orality:

> [S]o, generally speaking, as far as sermons go, after they have been spoken, only mere corpses remain; because when the speaking that gave them life in the pulpit is lacking, they die: the sermon [we have just spoken about] [that has not even enjoyed this short life] has only enjoyed or acquired the short life given to it by its orator; emerges so weak with imperfections and gaps that it needs more than anything else miraculous obscurity rather than publicity ("[P]ues, si por lo general en lo Sermones, despues de dichos, quedan unos meros cadaveres; porque en faltandoles el habla de quien les dió aliento en el pulpito, luego aspiran: este, que sobre no haver gozado, ni aquessa corta viveza, que no le pudo dar su orador, sale tan achacoso de imprefecciones, y faltas, necesita mas que todos, que en la plaza la publicidad, le toque su milagrosa sombra" [Florencia 1680, s. p.]).

> [T]his Sermon deserves first place among the most admired sermons by this Author, and it is worthy of being remembered by everyone, which will be accomplished through the impression it leaves, because it (memory) finds no obstacle ("[Y] digno de la memoria de todos, en que merec este Sermon el primer lugar entre los mas celebrados de el Author, y la conseguira mediante la impression, para que no hallo inconveniente" [Millán de Pobrete 1696, s. p.]).

Nevertheless, no contemporary could have known the radical consequences that the press would have, from which it follows that if communication is the way in which a society understands itself, the press must have had quite a profound effect during this time in which the very concept of communication was in the process of being transformed (see Luhmann and Georgi 1993, 116–17 and 121–2).

Critiques of amplification – with which rhetoric was identified – became more frequent as the seventeenth century went on:

> The fourth rule: The style should be oblique, haughty, and swollen with Latin or Greek, grandiloquent and, if possible, cadenced. Eschew if you can common and vulgar voices, despite their suitability; for if the preacher speaks from a lofty position and in a lofty voice, it stands to reason that the forms of expression be lofty as well. An illustrious model is found in the author of the famous *Florilegio*, and only by carefully studying his sentences will you acquire a style that lulls or astounds your listeners. Call silence a *sullenness of the lips*; call praising, *to panegyrize*, seeing, *the visual correlation of the objects*; never say *room*, which any rustic says, say *chamber* and leave it to me; *to exist* is vulgar, *existential nature* a great thing is ("Cuarta regla: Sea siempre el estilo crespo, hinchado, erizado de latín o de griego, altisonante y, si pudiere ser, candenciosos. Huye cuanto pudieres de voces vulgares y comunes, aunque sean propias; porque si el predicador habla desde más alto y en voz alta, es razón que también sean altas las expresiones. Insigne modelo tienes en el autor del famoso *Florilegio*, y solo con estudiar bien sus frases harás un estilo que aturrulle y atolondre a tus auditorios. Al silencio llámale *taciturnidades del labio*; al alabar, *panegerizar*; al ver, *atingencia visual de los objetos*; nunca digas *habitación*, que lo dice cualquier payo, di *habitáculo* y déjalo por mi cuenta; *existir* es vulgaridad, *existencial naturaleza* es cosa grande" [Isla 1960, 227–8]).

The paradox here lies in the fact that the very act of publishing seventeenth-century sermons containing amplification made the structural problems of amplification, when used in a scriptorial context, more readily apparent. Thus the attempt to preserve some sort of continuity of practice in the context of a transformation in the basic forms of communication had unintended consequences. The very same sacred preachers who were so eager and proud to publish their sermons, so that these works might transcend the time-space boundaries of oral communication, made the limits of *amplificatio* more evident and, consequently, intolerable. Seeking admiration, these preachers received ridicule; they themselves dug the grave of sacred rhetoric. The purpose of this essay has been to give an account of this paradoxical process

Despite its problems, sacred rhetoric would find two shelters that prevented it from disappearing completely: the sermon that I have called "of missions," which still survives today, and art, the only place, nowadays, in which one is allowed to say the same thing in several ways. It is clear that in this postmodern world we are aware of the content of the form that has been made notable by some theoreticians, in addition to being aware of the intrinsic impossibility of saying the same thing more than once, as the North American poet T. S. Eliot reminds us:

> You say I am repeating
> Something I have said before. I shall say it again.
> Shall I say it again? In order to arrive there,
> To arrive where you are, to get from where you are not,
> You must go by a way wherein there is no ecstasy.
>
> In order to arrive at what you do not know
> You must go by a way which is the way of ignorance.
> In order to possess what you do not possess
> You must go by the way of dispossession.
> In order to arrive at what you are not
> You must go through the way in which you are not.
> And what you do not know is the only thing you know
> And what you own is what you do not own
> And where you are is where you are not (Eliot [1943] 2000, s. p.).

NOTES

1 All the translations of the texts cited in this article are mine.

2 I have further developed the arguments presented in this paper in Chinchilla Pawling 2004.

3 See Chinchilla Pawling 2004, pt. 1 ("¿Qué es un sermón?"): 51–89. For further reference see Herrero Salgado 1996.

4 Towards the eighteenth century the relative unity of the Catholic world becomes increasingly fractured; yet it is possible to observe a more pronounced continuity in the Hispanic world of the so-called Asianist (or Asiatic) rhetoric than in France, for example, where a change towards the "attic" style can be observed.

5 "When I make this distinction, I visualize it departing from de Certeau's proposal that speaks of a 'theological' code of intelligibility, related to the oral society, and a 'sociological' (scientific) one, related to the scriptorial society. In essence, every society is oral; only an elite society – and then only in the field of its scientific activity – is actually 'scriptorial'" (Chinchilla Pawling 2004, 19–20, n. 15, quoting Certeau 1993a).

6 For the majority of the faithful this meant adhering to external practice to the detriment of internal spirituality. The latter would undergo a process of marginalization which led to highly specialized forms of religiosity, of which mysticism is a good example.

7 The practice of amplification expands the information provided by an adjectival description of an object without changing the original postulate. As Helena Beristáin notes in her dictionary of rhetoric, amplification's specificity is rendered in a "direct relation to the procedures applied to the expansion of the initial idea with the object of augmenting it gradually" (Beristáin 1995, 33). In this way, it facilitates efforts to protect the truth of original statements from challenges.

8 For the subject of the "passions" and the importance that they acquired in preaching during the last decades of the sixteenth and the first decades of the seventeenth century, see Chinchilla 1996.

9 Imitation – *imitation* – of the classics would have been the accepted manner. The discussion on "imitation" shows a symptomatic nuance, as you can see in the following quote: "Conceived by the regime of adult imitation, therefore eclectic, the *Cour Sainte* reveals the fusion and amalgamation of the Jesuit genius. Without breaking the notion of adult imitation, Rev. Schott has taken the trouble of insisting on the fact this could only make sense from the notion of 'imitation.'" See Fumaroli 1994, 345.

BIBLIOGRAPHY

Alegre, Francisco Xavier. 1957–1959. *Historia de la Provincia de la Compañía de Jesús de Nueva España,* 1751. Rome: Bibliotheca Instituti Historici.

Ávila, Alonso de. 1679. *Sermón, que predicó [...] a la aparición milagrosa de Nuestra Señora del Pilar de Zaragoza.* Mexico: Francisco Rodríguez Lupercio.

Beristáin, Helena. 1995. *Diccionario de retórica y poética.* Mexico: Porrúa.

Bourdieu, Pierre. 1991. *La distinction. Criterio y bases socials del gusto.* Madrid: Taurus.

Burrus, Ernest J., and Félix Zubillaga, eds. *Nueva España.* 4 vols. Rome: Institutum Historicum SJ.

Certeau, Michel de. 1993a. *La Fábula Mística. Siglos XVI–XVII.* Mexico: Universidad Iberoamericana (Departamento de Historia).

Certeau, Michel de. 1993b. "Etnografía. La oralidad y el espacio del otro: Léry." In *La escritura de la historia,* 203–33. Mexico: Universidad Iberoamericana.

Chinchilla Pawling, Perla. 1996. "La retórica de las pasiones. La predicación en el siglo XVII." *Historia y Grafía* 7: 93–124.

Chinchilla Pawling, Perla. 2004. *De la Compositio Loci a la República de las Letras. Predicación jesuita en el siglo XVII novohispano.* Mexico: Universidad Iberoamericana.

Chinchilla Pawling, Perla. 2006. "Presentación." In *La construcción retórica de la realidad. La compañía de Jesús*, eds. P. Chinchilla, Leonor Correa Etchegaray, and Alfonso Mendiola. Mexico: Universidad Iberoamericana.
Chinchilla Pawling, Perla. 2009. "La república de las letras y la prédica jesuita novohispana del XVII. Los paratextos y la emergencia del arte como sistema." *Estudios de historia novohispana* 41: 79–104.
Eisenstein, Elizabeth. 1994. *La revolución de la imprenta en la edad moderna Europea.* Madrid: Akal.
Elias, Norbert. 1982. *La sociedad cortesana.* Mexico: Fondo de Cutura Económica.
Eliot, Thomas Stearns. [1943] 2000. "East Coker." In *Four Quartets*, ed. 1943, Tristan Fecit. Available at: http://www.davidgorman.com/4Quartets/2-coker.htm. Accessed June 2000.
Florencia, Francisco de. 1680. *Sermón que predico [...]. A la solemne festividad del Principe de los Apostoles N. P. S. Pedro.* Mexico: Francisco Rodríguez Lupercio.
Fumaroli, Marc. 1994. *L'âge de l'éloquence. Rhétorique et "re litteraria" de la Renaissance au seuil de l'époque classique.* Paris: Albin Michel.
Gaur, Albertine. 1992. *A History of Writing.* New York: Cross River Press.
Gracián, Baltasar. 1960. *Obras completas.* Madrid: Aguilar.
Granada, Luis de. [1770?]. "Libro Tercero de la Rhetorica Eclesiastica, o de la manera de predicar: En que se trata del modo de amplificar, y de los Afectos Capitulo Primero. En que se diferencia la Amplificacion de la Argumentacion, in Los seis libros de la Rhetorica Eclesiastica." In *Los seis libros de la Rhetorica Eclesiastica.* Barcelona: Imprenta de Juan Solís and Bernardo Pla.
Greer, Allan. 2000. *The Jesuit Relations: Natives and Missionaries in Seventeenth-Century North America.* Boston: St. Martin's.
Harris, Roy 1986. *The Origin of Writing.* London: Duckworth.
Havelock, Eric. 1996. *La musa aprende a escribir. Reflexiones sobre oralidad y escritura desde la Antigüedad hasta el presente.* Barcelona: Paidós.
Herrero Salgado, Félix. 1996. *La oratoria sagrada en los siglo XVI y XVII.* Madrid: Fundación Universitaria Española.
Isla, José Francisco de. 1960. *Fray Gerundio de Campazas*, 2 vols. Madrid: Espasa Calpe.
Luhmann, Niklas. 1995a. *Die Realität der Masen medien.* Opladen: Westdeutscher Verlag.
Luhmann, Niklas. 1995b. "Autores, Textos y Temas." In *Glosario sobre la teoría social de Niklas Luhmann*, eds. Giancarlo Corsi, Elena Esposito and Claudia Baraldi, 11–14. Mexico: Universidad Iberoamericana / Instituto Tecnológico y de Estudios Superiores de Occidente / Anthropos.
Luhmann, Niklas and Raffaele de Georgi. 1993. *Teoría de la sociedad.* Mexico: Universidad de Guadalajara / Universidad Iberoamericana / Instituto Tecnológico y de Estudios Superiores de Occidente.
Millán de Pobrete, Juan. 1696. *Primacia de la iglesia santa. En oposición de la Ingrata Sinagoga delineada en la entrada de Christo Nuestro en la Casa de Nuestro Padre Señor San Pedro.* Mexico: Francisco Rodríguez Lupercio.

Nicolas, Juan Antonio, and María José Frápolli, eds. 1997. *Teorías de la verdad en el siglo XX.* Madrid: Tecnos.

Olson, David R. 1998. *El mundo sobre el papel. El impacto de la escritura y la lectura en la estructura del conocimiento.* Barcelona: Gedisa.

Olson, David R. 1995. "Cultura escrita y objetividad: el surgimento de la ciencia moderna," In *Cultura escrita y oralidad,* eds D. Olson and Nancy Torrance, 203–222. Barcelona: Gedisa.

Ong, Walter J. 1999. *Oralidad y escritura. Tecnologías de la palabra.* Mexico: Fondo de Cultura Económica.

Peace, Thomas G. M. 2006. "Deconstructing the Sauvage/Savage in the Writing of Samuel de Champlain and Captain John Smith." In *French Colonial History* 7: 1–20.

Pimental, Juan. 1683. "Dedicatoria." In *Sermón, que en la solemne fiesta [...] en México,* s. p. México: Francisco Rodríguez Lupercio.

Shuger, Debora. 1993. "Sacred Rhetoric in the Renaissance." In *Renaissance Rhetoric,* ed. Heinrich F. Plett, 121–42. Berlin: Walter de Gruyter.

Torre y Castro, Juan de. 1656. *Sacra dedicacion del templo de la Concepción purissima de Maria.* Mexico: Hipólito de Rivera.

Vaca Salasar, Luis. 1638. *Sermon predicado en la santa iglesia cathedral metropolitana de Mexico, a la fiesta del glorioso S. Felipe de Iesus.* Mexico: Juan Ruyz.

chapter seven

The Role of Culture and Art in France's Colonial Strategy of the Seventeenth Century

SARA E. MELZER

The *Jesuit Relations* were a series of reports written by Jesuit missionaries, published annually in Paris between 1632 and 1673, to chronicle their progress in converting the Native Americans to Christianity. However, as Alan Greer has noted, these reports include much more than simple accounts of evangelization. They offer detailed descriptions of the diverse Native American peoples of eastern Canada and the Great Lakes. But more importantly for my present concerns, they are also "crammed with news about the progress of colonization" in the New World. The Franco-Amerindian encounter in the *Jesuit Relations*, wrote Greer, "must always be seen as one aspect of a wider process of colonization" in which many of their narrators' most basic assumptions reveal their "colonialist colors" (Greer 2000, 1–9). More broadly, the church's evangelizing goal was in many instances inseparable from the nation's colonizing goal (see Belmessous 2005; Jaenen 1976; Goddard 2004; Havard and Vidal 2003; and Melzer 2012). The aim of this essay is to deduce the nation's implied colonial theory from the stories and rhetoric of the *Jesuit Relations*, bringing out some of its unstated assumptions. I centre my analysis on the role of culture to show how its discursive structures shaped how the French church and state conceptualized the nation's colonial endeavour and ideologically enabled it.

Assimilation was the dominant colonial strategy that both the church and state adopted in the seventeenth century, and it posed a particular set of challenges. Unlike the state's nineteenth- and twentieth-century versions of this basic policy, this earlier version fostered an unusually close level of contact between the French and the Native Americans. Ideally, they would all form "a same people and a same blood" ("un mesme peuple et un mesme sang"),[1] as Colbert, Louis XIV's minister, had phrased it (Colbert [1667] 1930–1931, 67). This policy essentially promoted communal living arrangements so that the French and the Native Americans would live together, work together, pray together, and be educated together. Moreover, both the church and state (despite their many conflicts) aggressively promoted intermarriage, although often at different times (see Aubert 2004; Belmessous 2005; and Jaenen 1976). The motivation for such unusually close contact between colonizer and colonized was to help transform the Amerindians so that they could be assimilated into the French Catholic community.

This assimilation policy had an expansionist goal that sought to open the nation's boundaries to include Native Americans. This openness is surprising given that the missionaries called them *sauvages* and portrayed their differences from French Catholics as so extreme that they seemed to inhabit the edge of civilization. (Although the term *sauvages* is objectionable, I use it, and adopt its French spelling, for reasons that will become clear shortly.) Describing the Amerindians as cruel, flesh-eating creatures, Jesuit missionary Father Paul Le Jeune reported that the Amerindians would eat the French raw, without even bothering to roast them (*JR* 5: 29).[2] And yet, the missionaries believed that these so-called cannibals could be transformed so fully that they could form "a same people and a same blood" with the French. Upholding an Amerindian girl who could pass as French as exemplary, Le Jeune wrote: "[T]his child has nothing savage about her except her appearance and color; her sweetness, her docility, her modesty, her obedience, would cause her to pass for a young well-born French girl" ("[C]et enfant n'a rien de *sauvage* que le teint et la couleur, sa douceur, sa docilité, sa modestie, son obeisance la ferait passer pour une petite Francaise bien née" [*JR* 9: 104, my emphasis]).

Delighted that this girl could successfully cross the cultural boundaries to become like those in the French Catholic world, Le Jeune presented assimilation as a willed crossing of the civilized/*sauvage* divide. Boundaries, then, were a major issue for assimilation for both the colonized and the colonizer, as the French understood it (see Melzer 2012, ch. 4). Regarding the colonized, this policy had to justify opening the boundaries to incorporate such an extreme form of Otherness within the civilized world of Catholic France.

However, the assimilation policy also presented a conflicting boundary need that focused on the colonizer: how to protect the identity of the French, Catholic community from being influenced by the Other it was assimilating? How to assure that the colonizer's community remained pure and unchanged, not giving way to a hybridized mix of both worlds? In sum, assimilation had two contradictory goals.

My aim is to show how the work of culture helped negotiate these competing needs. I, of course, do not mean to suggest that culture alone was sufficient. Other factors came into play. Most obviously, this policy reflected great confidence in the ability of the Catholic faith both to transform outsiders through conversion and at the same time to preserve the integrity of the insiders' community (see Goddard 2004, 57–77). But faith alone was not sufficient either. Culture played a key role.

Culture as Agriculture

At the most basic level, the seventeenth-century French understanding of culture provided an ideological underpinning for both the expansionist goal of including *sauvages* and for the protectionist goal of insulating the community from the colonized Other it was including. The term "culture" existed in the seventeenth century, although it had a very different meaning from our current usage (see DeJean 1997). Culture designated the world of agri*culture* and meant primarily "the effort necessary to render the land fertile through plowing," as Furetière's 1690 *Dictionnaire universel* defined it. The missionaries used what I call an agricultural discourse to frame their understanding of Amerindians, viewing them metaphorically as soil in which seeds could be planted, or as young plants, capable of growth and transformation through cultivation. Significantly, Paul Le Jeune filtered his first encounter with the indigenous people in the New World through an agricultural lens. Describing the abundant fruit trees of the New World, he wrote: "In a short time the leaves, the buds, the flowers and their fruit appear here and ripen; I mean the wild fruit, as there is no other" ("En fort peu de temps les feuilles, les boutons, les fleurs et les fruits paroissent icy, et meurisssent, j'entends les fruicts *sauvages,* car il n'y en a point d'autres" [*JR* 5: 25, my emphasis]). He then used this wild fruit as a frame to present his "discovery" of the Amerindians: "It was here that I saw Savages for the first time" ("Or c'est icy que j'ay veu des *Sauvages* pour la premiere fois" [25]), he wrote. His agricultural lens suggested that the same qualities characteristic of plant life also applied to the Amerindians.

Indeed, this Jesuit and many other missionaries used this agricultural discourse to frame their perceptions of the Amerindians:

> [T]heir soul is a soil which is naturally good but loaded down with all the evils that a land abandoned since the birth of the world can produce ("[L]leur ame est un sol tres bon de la nature, mais chargé de toutes les malices qu'une terre délaissée depuis la naissance du monde peut porter" [*JR* 6: 228]).

> [A]lthough the Savages are nomadic, the good seed of the Gospel will not fail to take root and bring forth fruit in their souls ("[E]ncor que les *Sauvages* soient errants, que la bonne semence de l'Evangile ne laissera pas de germer et de fruictifier en leur ame" [*JR* 6: 150]).

> It is from these young plants that one is to expect good fruits. God be forever blessed for the care he takes of this new Colony ("[C]'est de ces jeunes plantes qu'on doit esperer de bons fruicts. Dieu soit à jamais beny du soin qu'il a de cette nouvelle Colonie" [*JR* 8: 227]).

The image of the Amerindian as seedling was also framed as a young child:

> [I]f [the savages] have until now profited little, it is no wonder, for it would be too much to expect fruit from this grafting and to demand reason and maturity from a child ("[S]i [les *sauvages*] ont jusqu'ici peu profité, ce n'est merveille, ce seroit rigueur d'exiger si tost fruict d'un gref, et demander sens et barbe d'un enfant" [*JR* 1: 182]).

This agricultural discourse helped justify the French colonial strategy of including *sauvages* in two key ways. First, by framing the Amerindians as soil, seeds, and children, this discourse suggested that they were malleable, with the capacity for growth and change. It imagined them on a continuum in which these primitive beings were simply at the most elementary stage of a human being and contained the ability to develop and evolve into higher states of being, with proper cultivation. Second, this discourse set up a hierarchy in which the French were on top as farmers who were cultivating the Amerindians, who existed only in an incipient form. With attention and care, these seeds would grow to reach their highest potential – the French Catholic ideal. This discourse placed the Amerindians in a position of pure receptivity and passivity, much like women who wait openly to be impregnated by the active agent, which will shape the nature of their growth. As mere soil, the Amerindians were pure potential, with no predispositions, nor wills of their own, docile and eager to be cultivated. Moreover, the Amerindians' childlike statuses permitted the French to conceptualize them as not possessing the independent identity of an Other, which might potentially lead to a confrontation between colonized and colonizer. Furthermore, the future-oriented nature of agricultural cycles permitted the Jesuits to overlook the crude, primitive behaviour of the present moment, given the promise of fruit that would grow in a later era.

This agricultural discourse illuminates the implied assumptions of the term *sauvage*, which was the designation the French travel writers used the most commonly to refer to the indigenous population.[3] In English, this term is entirely derogative, conveying a subhuman, cruel, animal-like creature. In seventeenth-century French, however, this term had a different meaning, which has presented a big dilemma for the translators of the *Jesuit Relations*, some of whom have (understandably) chosen not to use this term in their translated texts (see Greer 2000 and Peace 2004). But to comprehend the historical context, it is important to note that while the seventeenth-century French term *sauvage* had negative meanings similar to our current English usage, these meanings were often overshadowed by their positive ones, which contributed to the underlying ideology supporting assimilation (see Sayre 1997). Furetière's *Dictionnaire universel* reminds us that the term comes from the Latin, "salvaticus," meaning "of the woods," or "wild." This etymology highlighted the meaning of uncultivated, as did the Académie's 1694 dictionary, which defined *sauvage* as the qualities associated with "certain plants, certain fruits which grow naturally, without the care of grafting or cultivation" ("certaines plantes, de certains fruits qui viennent naturellement, sans qu'on prenne soin de les greffer, de les cultiver"). Both the Académie and Furetière's dictionaries expanded this term's meaning to include animals, insisting that animals are *sauvage* only when they "dwell in the woods" ("habitent les bois") or when they "inhabit deserts, or remote places far from human society" ("se tiennent dans les deserts, dans les lieux esloignez de la frequentation des hommes" [*Le Dictionnaire de l'Académie française*, 1st ed., s. v. "Sauvage"]). However, animals can all be cultivated or domesticated. Even the most ferocious of beasts can be tamed according to Furetière: "There is hardly any animal so *sauvage* that it can't be tamed with skill and patience, if one begins when it is young" ("Il n'y a guerres de bête si *sauvage*, qu'on n'apprivoise avec de l'adresse et de la patience, quand on les élève de jeunesse" Furetière 1690, s. v. "Sauvage," my emphasis). These definitions expressed strong belief in the power of "culture" to transform the *sauvage* into civilized creatures. By cultivating and harnessing the wilder aspects of nature, humans can, in effect, colonize nature, making it serve human needs. This cultivating process is a form of colonization. As David Spurr noted, this understanding of "culture" is etymologically linked to colonization (see Spurr 1993, 10). The Latin word *colonus* is at the root of "colonization," designating a farmer or a husbandman in addition to its more conventional meaning, "a member of a settlement of Roman citizens or

COLONIA, in a hostile or a newly conquered country" (*Oxford English Dictionary*, s. v. "Colonization"). This term is linked to the Latin word *colere*, which means to cultivate, to till, to inhabit, or to take care of land or a place. Akin to agriculture, colonization takes a seed or plant from the mother country and transplants it in the "virgin" soil of another place, to cultivate it to become like the mother plant, but with roots in a new land.

The positive meaning of *sauvage* supported the assimilationist ideal by, paradoxically, diminishing the gap between colonizer and colonized, weakening its boundaries to promote the belief that the Amerindians, despite all their differences, could someday be made the same as French Catholics. (Obviously, the negative meanings of this term also widened the divide by highlighting the Amerindians' status as Other. But I do not have space to discuss this aspect.) This concept's positive meaning of uncultivated lessened the gap by suggesting that the Amerindians were not fundamentally of a different order of being. Their cruelty, their odd practices that were incomprehensible to French Catholics, did not inhere in their nature; rather, they resulted from external circumstances that could be altered. Their defining external circumstance was a lack of cultivation because they lived in remote places such as the woods, far from the civilizing effects of the human, for they "live ordinarily in the woods, without Religion, without laws, and without police, without fixed dwellings" ("vivent ordinairement dans les bois, sans Religion, sans Loix, et sans Police, sans habitations fixes" [Furetière 1690, s. v. "Sauvage"]). Their isolation from human society made them wild. However, once the *sauvages* were removed from their conditions of lack and associated with civilized humans who were both Catholic and French, they would imitate these models and become like them. This assumption was behind the policy of having the French and Amerindians live together in close proximity with each other.

Reducing further the boundaries between the *sauvage* and civilized worlds, this agricultural discourse slipped into an evolutionary discourse which positioned the Amerindians on the same continuum as the French and their Gallic ancestors, whom the Ancient Greeks and Romans had characterized as barbaric. Of course, the Amerindians and French occupied different stages in their evolutionary development, but each followed the same path. Le Jeune wrote: "I think it is Cicero who says that all nations were once vagabond" ("Il me semble que Ciceron dit qu'autrefois toutes les nations ont este vagabondes" [*JR* 5: 194]). The Amerindians represented what all nations looked like at the primitive stages of their evolution, and they resembled the Gauls at an earlier point in their history. Describing how the Amerindians constructed beds out of an animal skin spread out upon the ground to serve as a mattress, Marc Lescarbot articulated this line of thought when he observed: "And in this we have nothing to jest about, for our old Gallic ancestors did the same thing, and even dined from the skins of dogs and wolves, if Diodorus and Strabo tell the truth" ("Et en cela n'avons dequoy nous mocquer d'eux, par ce que nos vieux peres Gaullois en faisoient de meme, et dinoient aussi sur des peaux de chiens et de loups, si Diodore et Strabon dissent vray" [*JR* 1: 84]).

Even the civilized nations of other European nations were once in a similar state, as Le Jeune noted: "[B]efore the faith was received in Germany, Spain or England, those nations were not more civilized" ("[A]vant que la foy fut receue en Allemagne, en Espagne, en Angleterre, ces peoples n'estoient pas plus polis" [*JR* 5: 32]). Many missionaries attenuated the strangeness of the Amerindians by suggesting that they were embarking on the same journey as the French but were just at a more elementary stage in their evolution.

In sum, a root meaning of culture supported the nation's colonization agenda through its agricultural discourse that slipped into an evolutionary discourse, in which the *sauvage* characterized the first stage in a progressive movement towards a telos. Civilization was that telos. Only one model of civilization existed and France embodied this concept, although the term "civilization" did not yet exist (see DeJean 1997 and Starobinski 1989). The French in turn modelled their understanding of this ideal on Greek and Roman civilization. If the *sauvage* plants in the New World were cultivated religiously, politically, and socially, they would flower into civilized beings who could become members of civilization at some indeterminate moment in the future. "Savagery," then, was not outside of "civilization," but existed on the same continuum, albeit on opposite ends. While this continuum reduced the alien qualities of the Amerindians, it also affirmed a hierarchy. Those on the lowest end recognized the superiority of those on top and aspired to become like them by imitating them.

Art as a Cultivating Process

Imagining that the Amerindians were seeds, the missionaries thought that the culture of Catholic France would cultivate them, nurturing these *sauvages* to grow into civilized beings. In this context, culture takes on an additional meaning and shifts from the natural world to that of human artifice; culture assumes the form of art and material constructs, designed to attract attention. Artfulness played a pivotal role in determining the evolutionary stages of human society. Father Le Jeune divided that evolution into three stages in his *Relation* of 1634 and 1635:

> It was the opinion of Aristotle that the world had made three steps, as it were, to arrive at the perfection which it possessed in his time. At first men were contented with life, seeking purely and simply only those things which were necessary and useful for its preservation. In the second stage, they united the agreeable with the necessary, and politeness with necessity. First they found food, and then the seasoning. In the beginning, they covered themselves against the severity of the weather, and afterward grace and beauty were added to their garments. [...] In the third stage, men of intellect, seeing that the world was enjoying things that were necessary and pleasant in life, gave themselves up to the contemplation of natural objects and to scientific research ("C'estoit la pensée d'Aristote, que le monde avoit fait comme trois pas, pour arriver à la perfection qu'il possedoit de son temps. Au premier les hommes se contentoient de la vie, ne recherchants purement & simplement que les choses necessaires & utiles pour sa conservation. Au second ils ont conjoint le delectable avec le necessaire, & la bienseance avec la necessité. On a trouvé premierement les vivres, puis les assaisonements, on s'est couvert au commencement contre la rigueur du temps, & par après on a donné de la grace & de la gentillesse aux habits. [...] Au troisiéme pas les hommes d'esprit voyans que le monde jouyssoit des choses necessaires & douces pour la vie, ils se sont adonnez à la contemplation des choses naturelles, & à la recherche des sciences" [*JR* 7: 7]).

The Amerindians were at the lowest stage because they lived without art and were as close to nature as one could get. In fact, their existence resembled that of animals, using "the skin of Elk, Bears, and other animals" to clothe themselves. Guided by necessity, the Amerindians let nature dictate what they wore and how they wore it: "They only clothe themselves according to the exigencies of the weather, as soon as the air becomes warm or when they enter their Cabins, they throw off their garments and the men remain entirely naked, except a strip of cloth which conceals what cannot be seen without shame" ("Comme ils ne se couvrent que contre l'injure du temps, si tost que l'air est chaud, ou qu'ils entrent dans leurs Cabanes, ils jettent leurs autours à bas, les hommes restans tous nuds, à la reserve d'vn brayer qui leur cache ce qui ne peut estre veu sans vergogne" [*JR* 7: 7]).

Their harmony with nature was not a virtue, but the mark of their *sauvagerie*, since it meant that they gave no thought to art. Their primary goal was utilitarian – to defend against the natural elements: "There are some [American Indians] who wear sleeves, stockings, and shoes, but in no other fashion than that which necessity has taught them" ("Il y en a néanmoins qui portent des manches, des chausses, et des souliers, mais sans autre façon que celle que la nécessité leur a appris" [*JR* 5: 25]). Le Jeune disdained the fact that "they cover themselves to keep off the cold, and not for the sake of appearance" ("ils se couvrent pour banir le froid, non pour paroistre" [*JR* 7: 11]), and that "nature and not art set the fashion for them [...]. Their stockings are made of Moose skin, from which their hair has been removed [...] and they are considered well made if the feet and legs go into them, no ingenuity being used in making corners ("la nature & non l'art, qui en a trouvé la façon [...]. Leurs bas de chausse sont de poil [i. e. peau] d'Orignac passée sans poil, ils sont tout d'une venue, suffit que le pied & la jambe y passent, pour estre bien faits, ils n'ont point l'invention d'y mettre des coins" [15]). Their lack of art made the Amerindians appear primitive, barbaric, and animal-like in Le Jeune's eyes, for they were concerned only with survival. Their ideals were based on asocial, utilitarian practices.

Art produced a civilizing effect, propelling humans forward into the second stage of the evolutionary continuum because it encouraged them to live in the eyes of their neighbours: "In the early ages, houses were simply to be used, and afterward they were made to be seen" ("On a fait des maisons aux premiers siecles simplement pour s'en servir, & par apres on les a fait encore pour estre veuës" [*JR* 7: 7]). The concern with appearances and with praise from others was positive since this behaviour helped transform *sauvages* into more sociable creatures. Cultivating artistic appearances that were designed to be seen helped constitute the community and its social laws. Artistic surfaces, visible to all, forged social bonds by providing a shared sense of what was worthy of attention. In order for an object or behaviour to be deemed praiseworthy or foolish, the community members had to have a hierarchy of values that grounded any given judgment. To belong to the community was to know what those values and standards were and to abide by them. Artistic surfaces established boundaries, demarcating those who followed the proper art forms as insiders and those who did not as outsiders. When civilized people did things in order to be noticed, they did not isolate themselves in the particularized needs of mere convenience or comfort but turned towards a collective set of values, imitating the commonly accepted notions of the good.

Because the *sauvages* lacked art, they had no distinctions or boundaries to delineate and structure their community; everything was acceptable. Le Jeune disdainfully described their lack of sartorial distinctions: "During the winter all kinds of garments are appropriate to them, and all are common to both women and men, there being no difference at all in their clothes; anything is good, provided it is warm" ("Pendant l'hiver toutes sortes d'habits leurs sont propres, & tout est commun tant aux femmes comme aux hommes: il n'y a point de difformité en leurs vestemens, tout est bon, pourveu qu'il soit bien chaud" [*JR* 7: 9]). Not only did men and women wear the same clothes, but young girls wore the same clothes as old men. Le Jeune bemoaned their lack of tailors to adjust a man's coat to a young girl's size; the mass of material was simply gathered around the young girl's body "like one fastens twigs" ("[c]omme un fagot" [9]). No one cared how they looked, so long as they were warm: "Give them a hood, and a man will wear it as well as a woman; for there is no article of dress, however foolish, which they will not wear in all seriousness if it helps to keep them warm" ("Donnez leur un chaperon, un homme le portera aussi bien qu'une femme, il n'y a habit de sol dont ils ne se servent sagement, s'ils s'en peuvent server chaudement" [9]). No sartorial codes kept them in check:

> In Europe, if a boy should dress up like a girl, he would be a masquerader. In New France, a woman's dress is not improper for a man. The Ursuline Mothers having given a dress to a young girl who was leaving their seminary, the man who married her wore it soon afterward, with as much grace as did his wife; and, if the French made fun of him, he only laughed, taking their raillery for approval ("Si un garçon se vestoit en fille dans l'Europe, il feroit une mascarade. En la nouvelle France, la robe d'une femme n'est point mal-seante à un homme. Les Meres Ursulines, aiant donné une robe à une jeune fille, qui sortoit de leur seminaire, le mary qui l'espousa, s'en servit bientost après, aussi gentiment que sa femme; & si les François s'en mocquoient, il n'en faisoit que rire, prenant leur gausserie pour une approbation" [*JR* 44: 288]).

Le Jeune ridiculed this cross-dressed husband for not even understanding that the French were ridiculing him. The husband should have felt shame, in which case he would have changed his behaviour. Had he realized he was being ridiculed, he would have conformed to the conventional codes. His obtuseness suggested there were few social boundaries to differentiate insiders from outsiders.

Without any distinctions – aesthetic, social, or moral – the world of the *sauvage* had no inside or outside. If all garments were appropriate and no social laws regulated daily behaviour and social practices, then no one was stylish or foolish; they just simply were. For the French seventeenth-century way of thinking, there could be no real community until meaningful distinctions organized the collective. Without distinctions they were just a group of people who temporarily banded together like nomads and would disband as soon as convenience required. Leading a nomadic life, *sauvages* were guided by private asocial goals rooted in individual needs. So long as the Amerindians had no concern for art and the approval of others, they would have no real social bonds and would thus remain uncivilized, at the lowest rung on the continuum.

Art and Imitation as Protective Mechanisms for the Community

Needless to say, elite France cultivated a dazzling artfulness in its world and this was what gave the French a cultural authority over the Amerindians – or so thought the French elite. One goal of this art was to seduce outsiders into imitating it, shaping their desires to become like French Catholics and to become part of their world, sharing in the benefits of their material culture and ways of life. Reflecting the fact that imitation played a pivotal role in the nation's colonial policy (see Melzer 2012), many missionaries insisted (erroneously) that the Amerindians were eager to be like their colonizers and resembled "little monkeys, [...] they imitate everything they see done" ("de petits singes, [...] ils imitent tout ce qu'il voyent faire" [*JR* 32: 224]). Imitation was essential to France's colonial discourse because, from the French perspective, the Amerindians' mimetic relationship was a sign of their progress on the evolutionary continuum. Moreover, imitation implied a hierarchical dynamic that functioned like a boundary; it protected the colonizer's community by giving it a cultural authority that insulated it from the *sauvages*' influence. From the French perspective, imitation meant that the *sauvages* recognized the superiority of French ways and, correspondingly, the inferiority of their own. Thus, they would not hold on to their own customs and beliefs, but shun them, preventing the creation of a hybridized culture.

The *Jesuit Relations* told many stories about how the Amerindians felt the force of the implied boundaries as part of a natural order and respected them. These stories reassured the French readers that although the Amerindians were lawless, they nevertheless obeyed the seemingly natural law of their feelings that their contact with French culture supposedly produced. The effects of French culture created an implied divide in which the Amerindians voluntarily sided with their colonizers. For example, Father Le Jeune described a young Amerindian girl who was now living with the French and had been brought up "à la françoise." When she "goes back to the Cabins of the Savages, her father, very happy to see his daughter well clothed and in very good condition, does not allow her to remain there long, sending her back to the house *where she belongs*" ("s'en retourne par fois [aux] Cabanes des *Sauvage*, son père extremement aise de voir sa fille bien couverte, et en fort bon point, ne lui laisse pas demeurer longtemps la renvoyant en la maison, *où elle demeure*" [*JR* 11: 93, my emphasis]).

The girl's clothes and appearance constituted an implied boundary, since even her father felt their effects and accepted that his own daughter belonged on the opposite side of the imagined divide. In another example, Le Jeune highlighted the seductive force of French food and clothes. Once the Amerindians had experienced their benefits, they would not turn back to their own world. They

> will become so accustomed to our food and our clothes, that they will have a horror of the Savages and their filth. We have seen this exemplified in all the children brought up among our French. They get so well acquainted with each other in their childish plays, that they do not look at the Savages except to flee from them or mock them ("s'accoutumeront tellement à nos vivres, et à nos habits, qu'ils auront horreur des *Sauvages* et de leurs saletez. Nous avons vu l'exemple de cecy en tous les enfans nourris parmy nos François; ils font telle connaissance les uns avec les autres dans leur jeux d'enfants, qu'ils ne regardent les *Sauvages* que pour les fuir, ou se mocquer d'eux" [*JR* 9: 106]).

In these vignettes, the effects of French culture worked like a magic shield, drawing an imaginary, protective circle to shelter insiders from outsiders. Its power derived from the feelings that its material objects and practices stirred up, causing the Amerindians to be magnetically drawn towards French life and repelled by their own. The superiority of French culture, then, was so strong that the Amerindians respected its top-down hierarchy and did not seek a reciprocal exchange of both worlds.

Many stories, however, revealed that, in point of fact, the French did not possess the cultural authority that they claimed but were forced into accommodating the Amerindians who pressed for reciprocity. In reality, the colonial encounter stimulated a hybridized blend of both worlds, as numerous historians have pointed out (see Havard and Vidal 2003, as well as White 1991). However, had the French church and state fully realized this truth, they would not have been able to pursue such a policy. (At the end of the century when this truth could no longer be denied, many aspects of this assimilation policy were forbidden.) It is here that we see how the work of culture functioned in yet another way to promote the nation's colonial enterprise. The story form was itself a product of French culture, and the Jesuits were well skilled in the arts of writing and of rhetoric. The *Jesuit Relations* were a particularly fine example of the broader genre of the *relations de voyage* (see Melzer 2006; Pioffet 2008; Poirier and Gomez-Geraud 2011), because they offered many entertaining and amusing stories which helped make their reports bestsellers in France. These stories provided master narratives which served as filters to make sense of the Franco-Amerindian encounters. These narratives functioned to help deny the reality of a hybridized mix. And yet these narratives also revealed what they were denying, but in a veiled way that probably would not have been very evident to the seventeenth-century readers. Many of the stories unwittingly contained a double logic. In a first and dominant logic, the missionaries offered what they saw as examples of the Amerindians' progress due to their desire to imitate the greatness of Catholic French culture. But in an alternative, second logic, these stories about imitation could be reframed as evidence of an emerging cultural *métissage*. This double logic often emerged through amusing anecdotes that the missionaries told about the "cute mistakes" of the Amerindians, similar to what some parents tell about their children who imitate the adult world but misunderstand a key element of it. For example, Le Jeune, after detailing the three stages of evolution, described the Amerindians' progress, as evidenced by their imitation of the French; they no longer went naked but were wearing French shirts. However, he chuckled with a condescending irony that they "wear them *in the new fashion*" ("s'en servent *à la nouvelle facon*" [*JR* 7: 16–18, my emphasis]). His irony presupposed a hierarchy in which the French set the fashion and the Amerindians looked to them as models but did not quite get the style thing right. They wore these shirts, not under their clothes as do the French, but rather on top. Consequently, the shirts became "in no time as greasy as dishcloths" ("en moins de rien grasses comme des torchons de cuisine" [16–18]) since they never washed them. Assuming that over time the Amerindians would understand the proper French style, Le Jeune was amused by what he saw as their "cute mistake," because this incorrect fashion was promising. At least they were on the right track – the civility track. They were wearing clothes. And the clothes were French. And they were imitating the French, or so he thought.

However, Le Jeune's story revealed a second logic, pointing to the kind of cultural exchange that he, and the French colonial endeavour, wanted to deny. In describing their greasy shirts, he observed: "[T]his is just as they wish them to be, for the water, they say, runs over them and does not penetrate into their clothes" ("[C]'est ce qu'ils demandent, car l'eau, disent-ils, coule là-dessus, et ne pénètre pas jusqu'à leurs robes" [*JR* 7: 16–18]). In this alternative logic, the Amerindians developed a "new fashion" that was not a mistaken imitation; rather it was a deliberate, new invention: a cloth that became impermeable to rain – a raincoat. Le Jeune failed to see the cleverness of the Amerindians who created a new sartorial synthesis of the two worlds, adapting French clothing to their own environment. Instead, he saw a misguided imitation, which he found cute and comical. His amusement was predicated on one key assumption – that the Amerindians did not exhibit an independent will but were imitating the French, eager to assimilate and abandon their own customs and ways of being. Such an assumption presumed a hierarchical structure that placed the French on top as models and the Amerindians below as imitators. But this assumption was itself mistaken.

Looking at this story through a second, alternative logic, it is clear that the Amerindians were not seedlings or children, but fully grown and intelligent adults. Their new shirts reflected a clever invention created out of their intercultural contact, a hybridized article of clothing suitable to their life together. In this logic, the Amerindians were ingenious and independent, and did not regard themselves as inferior. Since this interpretation punctures the French myth of hierarchy, it would have been threatening, rather than amusing, to French readers. In sum, this vignette reveals two contrary logics at work, both impermeable to the other; it both revealed the reality of a hybridized world and also blinded the French observers and readers of these stories to this truth.

As twenty-first-century readers, we can clearly see what the seventeenth-century narrators most probably did not, at least not fully, because their master narratives largely blinded them to the evidence of a cultural *métissage.* Our insight and their blindness result from the ideological assumptions implicit in our respective notions of culture. Webster's second unabridged dictionary defines the meaning of culture for our modern era as "the concepts, habits, skills, art, instruments, institutions, etc. of a given people in a given period." This definition seems completely neutral to us now, devoid of the sharp edge it would have carried in the early modern era. This definition would have been shocking from a seventeenth-century perspective because it assumes that the important differences amongst peoples are simply value free and do not connote moral differences. They exist on a horizontal plane without referring to a teleological end. They simply *are*; they do not get translated into hierarchical notions of higher or lower forms of social evolution on a single scale of values and being. The variations amongst peoples are not viewed as corruptions of an ideal, be it a Christian ideal, a social ideal, an aesthetic ideal, or whatever other kind of ideal. However, such a hierarchy was built into the seventeenth-century French concepts of culture and civilization. The hierarchical implications of both concepts worked in tandem to form the ideological underpinnings for France's colonial endeavour, a structure so solidly constructed that it blinded the French elite in the seventeenth century to the fact that what they viewed as assimilation was, in fact, often a blending of two different worlds.

NOTES

1 "[S]'il se peut les y mesler, afin que par la succession du temps, n'ayant qu'une mesme loy et un mesme maitre, ils ne fassent plus ainsy qu'*un mesme peuple* et *un mesme sang*" (my emphasis). Also see: "[I]nstruits dans les maximes de notre religion et dans nos mœurs" so that "ils puissent composer avec les habitants de Canada *un mesme peuple* et fortifier, par ce moyen, cette colonie là" (Colbert [1671] 1930–1931, 14). Colbert also wrote Governor Frontenac: "Sa Majesté m'ordonne particulièrement de vous dire que [...] seulement il faut travailler à y attirer de nouveaux Français du Royaume et à prendre soin de la conservation de ceux qui y sont par les marriages [...] mais mesme en attirant les *sauvages* dans la société et dans la forme de vivre des Français; et comme jusque à présent il paraist que les Jésuites ont eu des maximes contraires que les prestres de Seminaires habituez à Montréal ne

s'y sont pas appliquez" (Colbert [1673] 1926–1927, 25). For more information on this policy, see Jaenen, Belmessous, Melzer.

2 All references to *The Jesuit Relations and Allied Documents,* ed. Reuben Gold Thwaites, will be designated as *JR*, followed by the volume number and then the page number.

3 "Barbarian" was the second most common term. The missionaries used their tribal names infrequently.

BIBLIOGRAPHY

Aubert, Guillaume. 2004. "The Blood of France: Race and Purity of Blood in the French Atlantic World." *William and Mary Quarterly* 61 (3): 439–78.

Belmessous, Saliha. 2005. "Assimilation and Racialism in Seventeenth- and Eighteenth-Century French Colonial Policy." *The American Historical Review* 110 (2): 322–49.

Colbert, Jean-Baptiste. [1667] 1930–1931. Lettre du Ministre Colbert à Talon, 5 April. *Rapport de l'Archiviste de la Province de Québec* 10: 67.

–. [1671] 1930–1931. Lettre du Ministre Colbert à Talon, 11 February. *Rapport de l'Archiviste de la Province de Québec* 10: 147.

–. [1673] 1926–1927. Lettre du Ministre Colbert à Buade de Frontenac, 13 June. *Rapport de l'Archiviste de la Province de Québec* 7: 25.

DeJean, Joan. 1997. *Ancients Against Moderns: Culture Wars and the Making of a Fin de Siècle.* Chicago: University of Chicago Press.

Goddard, Peter. 2004. "Two Kinds of Conversion ('Medieval' and 'Modern') among the Hurons of New France." In *Spiritual Conversion: the Christian Mission in the Colonial Americas,* ed. James Muldoon, 57–77. Gainesville: University of Florida Press.

Greer, Allan, ed. 2000. *The Jesuit Relations: Natives and Missionaries in Seventeenth-Century North America.* Boston: Bedford/St. Martin's.

Havard, Gilles, and Cécile Vidal, 2003. *L'histoire de l'Amérique Française.* Paris: Flammarion.

Jaenen, Cornelius J. 1976. *Friend and Foe: Aspects of French-Amerindian Cultural Contact in the Sixteenth and Seventeenth Centuries.* Toronto: McClelland and Stewart.

Melzer, Sara E. 2006. "The *Relation de Voyage:* A Forgotten Genre of the Seventeenth Century." *Biblio* 17(166): 33–52.

–. 2012. *Colonizer or Colonized: The Hidden Stories of Early Modern French Culture.* Philadelphia: University of Pennsylvania Press.

Peace, Thomas G. M. 2004. Adventurers and Authors. *An Examination of Samuel Champlain's and Capt. John Smith's Writings about the Aboriginal Peoples of North America.* Master's thesis, Saint Mary's University, Halifax.

Pioffet, Marie-Christine. 2008. *Écrire des récits de voyage (XVe - XVIIIe siècles). Esquisse d'une poétique en gestation.* Québec, Presses de l'Université Laval.

Poirier, Guy, and Marie-Christine Gomez-Geraud. 2011. *De l'Orient à la Huronie. Du récit de pèlerinage au texte missionnaire.* Québec, Presses de l'Université Laval.

Sayre, Gordon M. 1997. *Les Sauvages Américains: Representations of Native Americans in French and English Colonial Literature.* Chapel Hill: University of North Carolina Press.

Spurr, David. 1993. *The Rhetoric of Empire: Colonial Discourse in Journalism, Travel Writing and Imperial Administration.* Durham: Duke University Press.

Starobinski, Jean. 1989. "Le mot Civilisation." In *Le remède dans le mal. Critique et légitimation de l'artifice à l'âge des lumières*, 11–57. Paris: Gallimard.

Thwaites, Reuben Gold, ed. 1896–1901. *Jesuit Relations and Allied Documents: Travels and Explorations of the Jesuit Missionaries in New France, 1610–1791.* Cleveland: The Burrows Brothers.

White, Richard. 1991. *The Middle Ground: Indians, Empires, and Republics in the Great Lakes Region, 1650–1815.* Cambridge: Cambridge University Press.

PART II

INTELLECTUAL DISPUTES

chapter eight

José Basílio da Gama's Epic Poem *O Uraguay* (1769): An Intellectual Dispute about the Jesuit State of Paraguay

WIEBKE RÖBEN DE ALENCAR XAVIER

The polarizing transatlantic discourse about the so-called Jesuit state of Paraguay (1609–1768) in the eighteenth century was mainly based on knowledge gained from chronicles, accounts, travelogues, letters, and reports by real and alleged eyewitnesses from the New World, which had a lasting formative influence on the European conception of the missions and the Jesuits' missionary activities in Paraguay. The Brazilian poet José Basílio da Gama (1741–1795) belonged to those authors from the New World who participated in this discussion, and who increasingly did so from a non-European perspective. At the beginning of 1760, Gama lived for almost seven years in Rome and, after a short return to Brazil at the end of 1766, he came back to Europe in 1768. He spent the rest of his life in Lisbon, where he was first imprisoned because of his history in the Jesuit order, then rehabilitated for becoming an anti-Jesuit author; towards the end of his life, he was even elected corresponding member of the Academia Real das Ciências de Lisboa. During this turbulent life, Gama had the opportunity to critically compare his own experiences in Brazil and Europe with the philosophy and literature of the Enlightenment, as well as with Enlightenment conceptions of the New World.

His famous epic poem *O Uraguay*,[1] which is written in blank verse and comprises five *Cantos* composed of *Stanzas* unequal in length, appeared in Lisbon in 1769, two years after the disintegration of the Jesuit state of Paraguay and one year after the definite expulsion of the Jesuits from the Guaraní reductions, which occurred only in 1768 because of their localization in a jungle area and the difficulties to substitute the Jesuits from these villages by other fathers (see Hartmann 1994, 58).

In his poetic text, Gama paints an individual, albeit fragmentary, picture of the tragic events during the last stage of the realization of the military mission led by Portuguese and Spaniards between 1752 and 1756 to enforce the clauses of the Treaty of Limits (1750). In this Treaty, the colonial powers Spain and Portugal decided to exchange the Spanish and Jesuit-led territory of the Tupí-Guaraní Indians, the Colônia do Sanctíssimo Sacramento (Colony of the Most Blessed Sacrament of the Missions of Uruguay), bounded north and west by the Paraná River and east by the Uraguay, for the Portuguese Colônia do Santíssimo Sacramento (Colony of the Most Blessed Sacrament), near Buenos Aires. However, the Tupí-Guaraní Indians in the seven missions refused to comply with this decision and the Jesuits, in majority, passively tolerated their armed resistance (see Hartmann 1994, 56–7); therefore, military action was taken in 1752 that ultimately ended in a victory for the forces of Portugal and Spain, but not until 1756.

As a consequence of these events, it was no longer the Jesuit achievements, but the worldwide despotic missionary and power politics of the Society of Jesus that became the focal point of the discussion among intellectuals of the European Enlightenment. Basílio da Gama participated as a non-European within this dispute and in this context. *O Uraguay* is a criticism of the abuse of power by the Jesuits in the seven Tupi-Guaraní reductions and is also a general criticism against the abuse of power by the Jesuits in other regions of the world. It is also a paean to the anti-Jesuit policy of the Portuguese prime minister Sebastião José de Carvalho e Melo, also known as Marquês de Pombal. During his office as prime minister in the government of Dom José I of Portugal from 1750 to 1777, Pombal introduced many fundamental administrative, educational, economic, and ecclesiastical reforms justified in the name of enlightenment. Having lived in Vienna and London during his formative period, he was especially familiar with anti-Jesuit traditions, and as prime minister he launched a number of conspiracy theories regarding the order's desire for power.

In the poetic text of his epic poem, Gama shows compassion for the Tupí-Guaraní Indians and is critical of the Jesuits as well as of the conquering soldiers. Following the examples of Bayle and Voltaire, he restricts his polemical and sarcastic comments to the footnotes. The following essay will present a thorough analysis of the paratextual interrelations between the poetic text and the author's annotations.[2] This study reveals on various levels Gama's polemical and critical, although fragmentary, judgment of the various European views of the

Jesuit state of Paraguay, especially those concerning the Guaranític War of the Seven Reductions along the left or eastern bank of the Uruguay River, and the worldwide missionary activities of the Jesuit order.

On the initiative of Pombal, the Jesuits were banished from Portugal in 1758 and from Brazil in 1759 because they were suspected of having been involved in the assassination of the Portuguese King Dom José I. However, Gama, who at that time took his first vows as a novice of the Society of Jesus after his education at the Colégio dos Jesuítas in Rio de Janeiro, was allowed to stay in Portuguese territory after leaving the order.[3] Nevertheless, a short time later he travelled to Rome via Lisbon. In Rome he was, with the help of Jesuit friends, admitted in 1763 to the Arcadia Romana under the pseudonym of Termindo Sipílio. His literary works showed a predilection for pastoral poetry in the manner of *arcadismo* and *neoclassicismo*, and his satirical allusions soon revealed his "espirito americanista" within the context of Brazilian topics. At the end of 1766, he again spent some time in Brazil, but had to return to Lisbon in June 1768 owing to the king's expulsion decree concerning all former Jesuits. Upon his arrival in Lisbon, he was arrested and sentenced by the Suprema Junta de Inconfidência to be exiled to Angola within six months.[4] Before going into exile he wrote the *Epitalâmio* (1769) and dedicated it to Dona Maria Amália, the daughter of the Marquês de Pombal. In this text he explicitly condemned the machinations of the Jesuits for the first time. Simultaneously, his epic poem *O Uraguay*, which deals with the same topic, was published; he dedicated it to Pombal's brother, Francisco Xavier de Mendonça Furtado, Governor of Grand Para and Maranhão (1751–1759) and Minister of Marine and Overseas Colonies (1760–1769).[5] As a consequence, Gama's banishment was revoked. From 1774 to 1787, Gama even occupied an administrative function at the Portuguese court in Lisbon.

Because of its subject, *O Uraguay* was published and read in the eighteenth century more often than any other poem in the Portuguese language. But its first critical reception in Portugal was characterized by an exclusively formal comparison with Virgil's epic poems, with Camões's *Os Lusíadas*, and with the rules of Aristotle's *Poetics*. As Gama's epic poem had not been written in total accordance with classical rules, it was judged rather negatively at that time. It was the reception of the text in Brazil in the context of the Inconfidência Mineira (Minas Gerais Conspiracy)[6] in 1788, and especially its later reception by the Romantics in the nineteenth century, dominated as it was by the "espirito americanista," that made *O Uraguay* one of the most important texts with regard to the formation of a national basis for a Brazilian (literary) history.[7] In the nineteenth century, the text was for the first time translated into English by Sir Richard Francis Burton, the famous English translator who served as Her Majesty's consul in the Brazilian town of Santos between 1865 and 1868. This translation was published in Berkeley, Los Angeles, and London as late as 1982 (see Gama [1769] 1982).

The Historical Subject Matter and Gama's Literary Transposition

As a unique historical phenomenon, the Jesuit state of Paraguay provoked much discussion, particularly during the last stage of its existence in the eighteenth century (see Hartmann 1994). Montesquieu, for example, still defended the missions of Paraguay against all critical opinions in the 1748 *De l'Esprit des Lois*:

> Paraguay can offer us another example. The *Society* views the pleasure of commanding as the only good in life, and there were those who wished to make this a crime; but it will always be noble to govern men while making them happier. It is glorious for it (the Society) to have been the first to introduce in these countries the idea of religion joined to that of humanity. By repairing the devastation wreaked by the Spanish, it began to heal one of the greatest wounds ever inflicted on mankind ("Le Paraguay peut nous fournir un autre exemple. On a voulu en faire un crime à la *Société*, qui regarde le plaisir de commander comme le seul bien de la vie; mais il sera toujours beau de gouverner les hommes en les rendant plus heureux. Il est glorieux pour elle d'avoir été la première qui ait montré dans ces contrées l'idée de la religion jointe à celle de l'humanité. En réparant les dévastations des Espagnols, elle a commencé à guérir une des plus grandes plaies qu'ait encore reçues le genre humain" [Montesquieu (1748) 1951, 268–9]).

He glorified the Paraguay missions as a utopia already realized and as an alternative model for society which had succeeded in overcoming prejudices and passions. But despite his esteem for the Jesuits' achievements, he also qualified his praise for this form of government by stating that it could only be realized under the natural and social conditions of this region:

> An exquisite feeling that this society has for all that is called honour, its zeal for a religion that humiliates those who heed it far more than those

who preach it, has led it to undertake great things; and in this it has succeeded. They took dispersed peoples from the woods; they gave them an assured subsistence; they clothed them: and, if in so doing all they did was to increase industry among the men, then they accomplished a great deal. Those who wish to create similar institutions will establish the community of goods of Plato's Republic, this respect that he demanded for the gods, this separation from strangers with a view to preserving customs, and trade that was conducted by the city, not the citizens; they will transmit our arts without our luxuries, and our needs without our desires ("Un sentiment exquis qu'a cette société pour tout ce qu'elle appelle honneur, son zèle pour une religion qui humilie bien plus ceux qui l'écoutent que ceux qui la prêchent, lui ont fait entreprendre de grandes choses; et elle y a réussi. Elle a retiré des bois des peuples dispersés; elle leur a donné une subsistance assurée; elle les a vêtus: et, quand elle n'auroit fait par là qu'augmenter l'industrie parmi les hommes, elle auroit beaucoup fait. Ceux qui voudront faire des institutions pareilles, établiront la communauté de biens de la République de Platon, ce respect qu'il demandoit pour les dieux, cette séparation d'avec les étrangers pour la conservation des mœurs, et la cité faisant le commerce, et non pas les citoyens; ils donneront nos arts sans notre luxe, et nos besoins sans nos désirs" [Montesquieu (1748) 1951, 269]).

A short time after the publication of Montesquieu's *De l'Esprit des Lois*, a decisive turning point in public opinion and policy in relation to the Jesuit missions was introduced by the reception of and reaction to the military mission led by Portuguese and Spaniards to enforce the clauses of the Treaty of Limits (1750). The intellectuals of the European Enlightenment formed their opinions about the war events mainly on the basis of a contemporary polemical source book on the history of the War of the Seven Reductions and on the realization of the Treaty of Limits. The text in question, which is usually ascribed to Pombal, was published anonymously in Lisbon in 1757 and bears the title *Relação Abreviada da República, que os religiosos jesuitas das províncias de Portugal e Hespagna estabeleceram nos domínios ultramarinos das duas monarchias.*[8] This *Relação Abreviada* is a summary of the *Diário da Expedição de Gomes Freire de Andrade às Missões do Uraguay* by Capitão Jacinto Rodrigues da Cunha,[9] and has an anti-Jesuit tendency. Besides excerpts from the latter's diary entries, it contains two further important documents concerning the military events: first, a copy of the Jesuit regulations for the Tupi-Guaraní Indians doing military service, called *Instruções, que os Padres que governam os Indios lhe deram quando marcharam para o exercito, escriptas na lingua Guarany, e d'ella traduzidas fielmente na mesma fórma em que foram achadas aos referidos Índios*; second, a translation of the Indian chiefs' letter to the governor of Buenos Aires in which they asked him not to put the Treaty of Limits into effect. The second document is entitled *Copia da Carta sediciosa e fraudulenta, que se fingiu ser escripta pelos Caciques das aldêas rebeldes ao Governador de Buenos Ayres; sendo que é inverosimil que se mandasse ao dito Governador, e que o mais natural é que se compôz debaixo d'aquelle pretexto para se espalhar entre os Indios, ao fim de lhe fazer criveis os enganos, que n'ella se contém: escripta na língua – Guarany – e d'ella traduzida fielmente na língua Portugueza.* Very shortly after its publication, the *Relação Abreviada* was translated into other languages and also into German (see Anonymous [1760] 1892). The *Dedução Cronológica e Analítica* (1767) by José de Seabra da Silva, which was written by order of Pombal, also belonged to the category of anti-Jesuit "guidance writings" coming from Pombal's confidants. It is a juridical text listing all crimes in the Kingdom of Portugal in which members of the Society of Jesus were supposed to have been involved. But in later times, the *Relação Abreviada* was more frequently cited because it included translated sources pertaining to the historical war events that had originally been written in the language of the Indians and were therefore regarded as trustworthy. Gama himself uses these translated pieces of documents from the *Relação Abreviada* for his literary adaptation of this historical subject matter.

Up to the time of the events described in Gama's epic poem, the Spanish Jesuits dominated the aforementioned Sete Povos das Missões along the left or eastern bank of the Uruguay River. According to the Treaty of Limits, Spain granted these seven missions, which seemed to threaten Portuguese control of Rio Grande do Sul, to Portugal. Until the ratification of this border treaty in January 1750, the Portuguese held the Colônia de Sete Povos das Missões do Uruguai, a fort south of the Spanish territories on the mouth of the Rio de La Plata, ten miles away from Buenos Aires. The controversy over this strategically important place had for a long time been the cause of various conflicts between the Portuguese and Spanish forces, during which the Tupi-Guaraní Indians from the seven missions had repeatedly been brought into action as Spanish soldiers fighting against the Portuguese. Through the Treaty of Limits, Portugal ceded the Colônia do Sanctíssimo Sacramento to the Spanish, as compensation for the area of the seven Tupi-Guaraní missions organized by the Spanish Jesuits. Thus, the European borders in the Spanish part of America had to be drawn anew in order to enact these regulations. For this purpose two commissioners, who had been fully authorized by their kings, were sent to the south of the continent: General Gomes Freire de Andrade, Conde de Bobadela and Governor of Rio de Janeiro, Minas Gerais, and Sacramento on the part of Portugal, and the Marquêz de Valdelírios on the part of the Spanish crown.

From the *Relação Abreviada*, the contemporary reader is led to comprehend that the Treaty of Limits forced the handing over of those regions which the Society of Jesus considered its own in colonial South America to the Portuguese. Therefore, the Jesuits decided not to comply with the demands of the two kings. On the contrary, the fathers armed the Tupi-Guaraní Indians and placed them under obligation to stop the advance of the Portuguese army that had left the coast and was moving inland. In view of this surprising act of resistance near the River Pardo, the Portuguese general Andrade halted all activities in support of the new drawing of the borders; since both kingdoms were interested in the realization of the treaty, he ordered his men to wait for the Spanish forces so that together they could fight against the rebellious Indians. Yet before the two armies could unite in January 1756, the Jesuits forced the Indians to attack the Portuguese position. The battle that ensued was won by the Portuguese (see *Relação Abreviada* [1757] 1863, 264–75).

Referring to the *Relação Abreviada*, Voltaire also comments on this part of the War of the Seven Reductions in his 1756 *Essai sur les Mœurs et l'Esprit des Nations*, namely in chapter 154, entitled "Du Paraguai. De la domination des jésuites dans cette partie de l'Amérique; de leurs querelles avec les espagnols et les portugais" ("Of Paraguay: The domination of the Jesuits in That Part of America; Their Quarrels with the Spanish and Portuguese"). At the same time, however, Voltaire uses pro-Jesuit writings to obtain the knowledge he needs to reflect critically on the rule of the Jesuits in Paraguay and their praiseworthy administration of the missions. It is only regarding the war events that he quotes with skepticism from the polemical *Relação Abreviada*; he does so in French translation:

> "*The Jesuits are the only rebels. Their Indians have twice attacked the Portuguese fortress on the Pardo with a very well served artillery.*" The same account adds that these Indians cut off the heads of their prisoners and took them to their Jesuit commanders. This accusation may be true, but it is highly improbable ("'*Les jésuites sont les seuls rebelles. Leurs Indiens ont attaqué deux fois la forteresse portugaise du Pardo avec une artillerie très-bien servie.*' La même relation ajoute que ces Indiens ont coupé les têtes à leurs prisonniers, et les ont portées

> à leurs commandants jésuites. Si cette accusation est vraie, elle n'est guère vraisemblable" [Voltaire (1756) 1967, 429]).[10]

In regard to trade, Voltaire also has a subtly differentiated idea of the missionary activities of the Jesuits in Paraguay. He seems to comment on Montesquieu's idea of the Jesuit state as an alternative model for society. He compares the Jesuits with the Quakers in North America. In his opinion, both groups had given the world a new "spectacle." On the one hand, the Quakers educated the savages to trade with other people solely by means of their exemplary lives and without depriving them of their liberty. On the other hand, the Jesuits used religion

> to deprive the populations of Paraguay of their freedom: but they civilized them: they rendered them industrious and managed to govern a vast country, the way a convent is governed in Europe. It appears the natives were more just, and the Jesuits more political. The former viewed the idea of subduing their neighbours as an attack; the latter made a virtue of subduing the savages through instruction and persuasion ("pour ôter la liberté aux peuplades du Paraguai: mais ils les ont policées; ils les ont rendues industrieuses, et sont venus à bout de gouverner un vaste pays, comme en Europe on gouverne un couvent. Il paraît que les primitifs ont été plus justes, et les jésuites plus politiques. Les premiers ont regardé comme un attentat l'idée de soumettre leurs voisins; les autres se sont fait une vertu de soumettre des sauvages par l'instruction et par la persuasion" [Voltaire (1756) 1967, 424]).

Basílio da Gama was himself torn between two worlds. In *O Uraguay* he deals with the European idea of the New World at the precise moment in history when people in Europe were deeply divided on this very question. On the one hand, there were the supporters of the Jesuits, who saw them as individuals inspired by the mission of imparting knowledge to the world and civilizing the "savages." On the other hand, there were the anti-Jesuits, the opponents of the Society of Jesus, an organization they regarded as having been much too powerful for too long a time. The latter fanatically denounced this unjustified increase in power in view of the rebellion of the Tupi-Guaraní Indians in the seven reductions.

Against this background, *O Uraguay* is an original mixture of fiction, historical poetry, and discourse along the lines of the Enlightenment, which paints quite an individual, albeit fragmentary, picture of the tragic events during the last stage of the realization of the Treaty of Limits. Thus, Gama draws in miniature a problematic sketch of the cohabitation of Indians, Jesuits, soldiers, and white settlers in this region, that is to say a sketch of the formation of Brazilian colonial society (see Teixeira 1996, 54). Gama dissociates himself from positive concepts of the Jesuit state, considered by some to be a utopia already realized and thus an alternative model for society according to the spirit of Montesquieu. On the whole, he is quite disappointed with the way in which European intellectuals of the Enlightenment discuss the most recent events, including, no doubt, Voltaire's focus on the successful history of Jesuit power politics and military-type administration in the Paraguay missions, rather than on the then-recent military activities of the Indians under Jesuit command during the War of the Seven Reductions (see Gama [1769] 1996, 201, and Voltaire [1756] 1967, 423–9). But even in Gama's poetic presentation, the Tupi-Guaraní Indian, depicted according to the prevailing European concept of the "noble savage" with his natural virtues, takes precedence over the war events. Gama is not interested in the positive character traits of the war heroes, but in the tense relations between Indians, Jesuits, and European settlers in the missions, in the lack of communication, and particularly in the inappropriate behaviour of the Europeans in the New World.

As a consequence, in *Canto* 1 of *O Uraguay*, he criticizes the fact that contemporary European debate focuses only on the war events and condemns the Jesuits solely for inciting the Indians to offer resistance. Apart from that, however, the European view of the Jesuits' administration of the missions is still influenced by chronicles and letters written by Jesuits and their friends. Gama refers mainly to the following texts: the *Histoire du Paraguay* (1756) by Father Pierre-François-Xavier de Charlevoix, which has often been cited, the *Relation des missions du Paraguai* (1754) by Ludovico Antonio Muratori, the 1711–1743 *Lettres édifiantes et curieuses écrites des missions étrangères par quelques missionaires de la Compagnie de Jésus* ("Edifying and Curious Letters Written From Foreign Missions by Missionaries of the Society of Jesus"), edited by Jean-Baptiste Du Halde, and Jacques Vanière's new edition of the 1750 *Praedium Rusticum* ("The Rustic Farm"). It is especially the latter of these texts that Gama repeatedly cites to show the deficiencies of the discussion influenced by Jesuit and pro-Jesuit texts. In view of his own experiences, he believes that it is no longer possible to support the widely held but overly simplistic view of the Jesuits' building of the missions as an exemplary work of humanism, a model experiment aimed at civilizing the dependent Indian populations of the New World in order to better their lives. Being an eyewitness from the region, he promises not to write a chronicle of the War of the Seven Reductions, but to paint a more realistic view of the administrative structures in these missions, on which their power structures are based.[11] Yet this only means that in his capacity as an intellectual of the Enlightenment he complies with the public's desire for the "true" story:

> The Jesuits have had the gall to deny throughout all Europe what has just occurred in America in our time within the sight of two armies. The author experienced this in Rome, where many persons sought him out expressly to learn well-founded news of Uruguay; evidencing a strange contentment in finding an American who could inform them minutely of what had happened. The wonder, caused by the strangeness of facts so well known among us, brought forth the first ideas of this poem ("Os Jesuítas têm tido a animosidade de negar por toda Europa o que se acabou de passar na América nos nossos dias à vista de dois Exércitos. O autor o experimentou em Roma, onde muitas pessoas o buscavam só para saberem com fundamento as notícias do Uraguay; testemunhando um estranho contentamento de encontrarem um Americano, que os podia informar miudamente de tudo o sucedido. A admiração, que causava a estranheza de fatos entre nós tão conhecidos, fez nascer as primeiras idéias deste Poema" [Gama (1769) 1996, *Canto* 1: 201, n. to v. 156; trans. Gama (1769) 1982, 117]).

Gama then translates his intention into fiction, thematically complemented by critical annotations. Thus, the interrelation between poetry and paratexts, which could also be seen as a demonstration of his knowledge and erudition, is an individualized way of dealing with the European commentaries, reports, diaries, and documents related to the New World that he has encountered.

A Fragmentary Dispute Combining Historical Poetry and Commentary

Despite its concrete subject matter, the chronology of the five *Cantos* and the paratextual interrelations give a fragmentary and discursive quality to the epic poem. Against the background of the historical subject matter being addressed, this structural principle not only has a deep impact on the audience, but also is likely to prompt discussions. At the same time, it maintains a good balance between the presentation of the war events in the manner of Virgil, the anti-Jesuit polemic in the form of eyewitness accounts, quotations from ancient and contemporary sources which seem arbitrary at first glance, comparisons with the method of accommodation[12] characterizing the Jesuits' missionary work in China, and a brief outline of the history of the Jesuit order marked by a series of crimes.

On the one hand, Gama repeatedly quotes verbatim from the *Relação Abreviada* to depict the historical war events and the relations between Jesuits, soldiers, and Tupi-Guaraní Indians. On the other hand, his individual selection and arrangement of commentary on pieces of information from historical, politically polemical, philosophical, and literary sources, as well as his commentary on them, mainly serves the purpose of critically interpreting favourable assessments of the Jesuits' achievements and organizing principles since the foundation of the missions, assessments widely known in Europe through letters and chronicles. Instead of assuming that the Guaraní missions are in perfect condition, which is the ideal of the achievements of civilization in the New World, and that the crown profits financially from the missions, Gama stresses the missionaries' attitude in terms of power and profit.

Thus, he paints another stereotyped picture of the Jesuits and their organizing principles; this portrait encompasses the following aspects: the ambition of the fathers, the ban on verbal communication and independent trade between Indians and white settlers, slavery under the guise of the religion and goodness of the "holy fathers," the exploitation of the Indians' agricultural work, the enrichment of the Jesuit order in Rome, the Jesuit intolerance towards the social customs of the Indians, the lack of respect for the social system and religious rites of the Indians, the dangerous military organization, and the sexual exploitation of the Indian women in the missions. On the whole, he attributes the insufficient communication between European soldiers, white settlers, and Indians to the despotic power politics of the Jesuits.

Heroic Achievements of the Portuguese, Flawed European-Indian Communication and Jesuit Mediation

In *Canto* 1 of *O Uraguay*, General Gomes Freire de Andrade, who leads the Portuguese forces, describes in broad outline the history of the Guaraní missions since their foundation in 1609 and the contemporary events concerning the realization of the Treaty of Limits. But Gama dedicated the epic poem to Francisco Xavier de Mendonça Furtado, who, as Governor of Maranhão and Grão-Pará in the north of Brazil, freed the Indians of these regions from their "subjugation" by the Jesuits. Thus, the

Indians owe their freedom to Furtado despite severe fights and much bloodshed: "Hero of heroes, brother! If in grief / Your fair America still yearns for you, / Favour my lay" ("Herói, e Irmão de Heróis, saudosa, e triste / Se ao longe a vossa América vos lembra, / Protegei os meus versos" [Gama (1769) 1996, *Canto* 1: 197, v. 12–14; trans. Gama (1769) 1982, 48, v. 12–14]). The Indians were finally liberated by him from the captivity and political passiveness inflicted upon them by the Jesuits and "ennobled and admitted to the duties of the Republic. This procedure honors the humanity" ("nobilitados e admitidos aos cargos da Républica. Este procedimento honra a humanidade" [197, n. to v. 11]). In this passage, Gama makes a direct comparison between the heroic achievements of the Portuguese commanders and Pierre Corneille's heroic man of willpower, embodying man's claim to autonomous and self-determined behaviour. He quotes from Curiace's speech in act II, Scene I of Corneille's classical tragedy *Horace* (1640): "And whilst before all, she you three prefers, / She all our Houses braves with one of hers / [...] / By this, three Families must raise their Name"[13] ("Et son illustre ardeur [celle de Rome] d'oser plus que les autres / D'une seule maison brave toutes les nôtres. / [...] / Ce choix pouvoit combler trois familles de gloire" [198, n. to v. ; quoted from Corneille (1640) 1950, 796]).

In addition to the heroic achievements of the Portuguese commanders in helping to liberate the Indians, lack of communication between the two cultures and descriptions of how the Indians organized their lives in order to adapt to the peculiarities of nature in the New World play an important role in Gama's discourse. It is only owing to these adaptation techniques and the help of the Indians that the European soldiers manage to survive. For example, in *Canto* 1 Gama describes the soldiers' difficulties surviving in a foreign natural environment for several months during the flooding of the Jacuí River. They only succeed in doing so because they build tree houses like the Indians. Gama admires the Indians' natural way of living, which he says is wonderfully adapted to nature and to the climate, the "shape of the land" ("forma do terreno" [Gama (1769) 1996, *Canto* 1: 203, v. 212]). Due to the enormous amount of water in the region around the Uruguay River, there are whole Indian peoples that build their thatched huts in trees. In contrast to the soldiers, these Indians are very proficient in climbing up and down the trees without ropes or steps, although the trees are very high and their roots remain under water for most of the year (see *Canto* 1: 203, n. to v. 212). In another passage, Gama describes how the European soldiers move in so-called *balsas e pelotas*, that is, special Indian river boats. Once again, it becomes clear how much the European soldiers depend on the adaptation to the Indians' way of life, because these boats are pulled on both sides by swimming horses, which are led by strong Indians (see *Canto* 1: 203, n. to v. 199). He refers readers unfamiliar with the natural conditions of this region to scientific literature in which European authors systematically recorded the Brazilian fauna and flora. To explain the meaning of the word *jacaré* (cayman), for example, he refers to Georg Markgraf's *Historia Naturalis Brasiliae* (1648) and to Carl Linné's *Systema Naturae, Amphibia, Reptilia, Draco* (see *Canto* 2: 213, n. to v. 273). To show the meaning of the word *urucú* (fruit of the annatto tree), he makes use of Henrik van Reede tot Draakstein's *Hortus Malabaricus* (*Garden of Malabar*) (1679) and Carl Linné's *Species plantarum* (*Species of Plants*) (1753 [see *Canto* 4: 229, n. to v. 64]).

In *Canto* 2, the problematic encounter between soldiers and Indians becomes visible in the insufficient communication between the two Tupi-Guaraní chiefs, Cacambo and Cepé, and the Portuguese General Andrade. During the march of the soldiers towards the seven reductions, these two chiefs come into the soldiers' camp aiming, for the last time, at a peaceful solution to the conflict over the Indians' resettlement. In their speech, which they deliver in their native Tupi-Guaraní language, they condemn the cruelty of the white people. Nevertheless, they are prepared for reconciliation, even though the Jesuits have taught them not to trust white people. On the one hand, Cacambo turns to the Portuguese king, represented by General Andrade, and says that the latter shall not put the Treaty of Limits into effect because the region affected by it belongs to the Indians, and additionally does not offer the wealth of gold and precious stones that the Europeans usually prefer; trade is done only with the help of the "good Fathers" ("bons Padres" [Gama (1769) 1996, *Canto* 2: 209, v. 141]). General Andrade, on the other hand, argues according to his Pombalian view of political freedom and state reason, and informs him of the king's wish to free the Indians from the despotism of the Jesuits, which, however, includes the exchange of the seven Guaraní missions on the Uruguay River for the Colônia do Sanctíssimo Sacramento near Buenos Aires. No agreement is reached and Cacambo, expresses his resignation along with the wish that the Europeans had never crossed the sea. He thinks it was no accident that nature separated both continents by such an enormous amount of water (see *Canto* 2: 210). Cacambo realizes that both Jesuit missionaries and white settlers have destroyed the natural order of the Indians and that there has been no going back for quite some time. In the passage where Cacambo denounces the cruelty of the whites to the Indians throughout the history of colonization, Gama quotes directly from the Jesuit *Instruções* for the Indians doing military service.[14] Cacambo condemns "the prey / Of fraudful Europe and from this spot" ("perfidia de Europa e daqui mesmo" [*Canto* 2: 207, v. 52; trans. Gama (1769) 1982, 59, v. 51–2]), but at the end of his speech he nevertheless agrees to deal peacefully with the difficult situation. To prove that the Jesuits are to be blamed for the insurmountable conflict, Gama quotes once again directly from the *Instruções*. According to these regulations, the Indians avoided communicating with the whites. If they happened to come into contact with a white person, they would ask the fathers to act as sole interpreters so that everything could be arranged in accordance with God's will. Thus, the Jesuits were a monitoring body in regard to the communication between Europeans and Indians.

In *Canto* 2, Cepé, the second Indian chief, emphasizes the special quality of the Indian property situation to justify the Indians' military rebellion against the realization of the Treaty of Limits. Corresponding to the ideal of the "noble savage," he explains that the Indians have no private property, but have, as a community, inherited the land from their ancestors. At the same time, they also accept the religious guidance of the Jesuits. Parallel to this speech, the Jesuit Balda, who is in charge of the seven Tupi-Guaraní missions, is introduced. His character is modeled on the historical Spanish Jesuit Father Lourenço Balda. In the epic poem, he and an Indian woman have a son called Baldetta, who provokes the Portuguese soldiers while the above-mentioned conversation takes place in the soldiers' camp. It is only at this point that bloody fighting breaks out in which Cepé and many Tupi-Guaraní warriors as well as Portuguese soldiers die heroically or are injured. The Portuguese win a military victory and again the Jesuits have to be blamed for the bloody outcome, because Baldetta, the son of a Jesuit living between two cultures, interferes, unasked, in the dialogue intended to solve the problems between the soldiers and the Indians. Without his interference, the conflict might not have ended in bloodshed.

In *Canto* 3, the soldiers arrive on the bank of the Uruguay River after the end of the fight. Thereupon Cacambo, who earlier was called upon by Cepé in a vision to carry on fighting against the soldiers, sets fire to the soldiers' camp and returns to his reduction. Balda, who now wants to marry his son Baldetta to Lindoya, Cacambo's wife, to extend his power among the Indians, has Cacambo arrested for arson and poisons him.

Meanwhile, Lindoya, who knows nothing of the matter, goes to the Indian seer Tanajura to find her husband Cacambo with the help of a vision. She is, however, not successful because instead of her husband, she sees in the spring water the Lisbon earthquake and Pombal's famous measures to rebuild the town. In the end, she commits suicide because she cannot find her husband again and does not understand, from the perspective of Indian life, this vision that presents a European achievement. Balda, who in the meantime has prepared the wedding by means of a military parade, then shows relentless severity towards the religious rites of the Indians, sentences the seer Tanajura to be burnt at the stake, and denies Lindoya a Christian burial. In this passage, Gama reveals most clearly how the Jesuits' religious intolerance and their ban on verbal communication lead to a cultural misunderstanding on the part of the Indians. As the Jesuits neither teach the Indians how to use the language of the Europeans nor arrange any cultural contacts between them and the Europeans, the Indians do not understand the foreign images and the foreign way of thinking, in this case the vision of the Lisbon earthquake and Pombal's politics.

The Jesuit State and the Bee Colony

In his *Essai sur les Mœurs*, Voltaire describes, on the basis of historical sources, the fundamental organizing principles of the Jesuit state of Paraguay as an astonishing achievement. This includes the ban on having any contact with Spanish settlers, which was imposed for the protection of the Indians, the Jesuits' role in regard to the successful trade in natural products, especially *maté* (yerba mate herb), first used and cultivated by the Guaraní people, the political organization and administration, the mechanisms of self-supply, and the way in which the Indians are trained militarily:

> The Jesuits distributed goods, and used silver and gold for decorating churches and for governing. They kept an arsenal in every township; on specific days they gave weapons to the inhabitants. One Jesuit was assigned to the exercise; following this the weapons were replaced in the arsenal, and no citizen was allowed to keep any at home. The same principles which made these peoples the most submissive made them very good soldiers; they believed it was their duty to obey and to fight ("Les jésuites distribuaient les denrées, et faisaient servir l'argent et l'or à la décoration des églises et aux besoins du gouvernement. Ils eurent un arsenal dans chaque canton;

> on donnait à des jours marqués des armes aux habitants. Un jésuite était préposé à l'exercice; après quoi les armes étaient reportées dans l'arsenal, et il n'était permis à aucun citoyen d'en garder dans la maison. Les mêmes principes qui ont fait de ces peuples les sujets les plus soumis en ont fait de très-bons soldats; ils croirent obéir et combattre par devoir" [Voltaire (1756) 1967, 427]).

In *Canto* 4, Gama uses such a military ceremony to show how dangerous the military organization of the Jesuit state of Paraguay was. Before the news of Lindoya's suicide arrives, Balda, in preparation for the marriage of his son Baldetta, has the characteristic types of Indian warriors march past in a parade: Kobbé, whose face is coloured red by means of *urucú*, followed by wild cannibals, young Pindó, who succeeds the late Cepé as chief, Caitutú, Lindoya's brother and a brilliant archer, Baldetta himself, and Tatú-Guaçú, with his disordered group of fighters whose chests are protected by the skins of caymans. They do not fight when the Portuguese soldiers intrude, but by order of Balda they destroy the whole mission, including the temple, and flee to the neighbouring settlements. On arriving, General Andrade and his soldiers are horrified by the destruction, but in the temple they still find traces of the sacristy art characteristic of the Indians and thus astonishing proof of the refinement of the supposedly "uneducated" Indians. Although this may sound like a positive assessment of the fact that the Jesuits supported artistic talent, Gama, against the background of the war events, particularly condemns Jesuit militarism as well as the denial of Jesuit militarism by contemporary pro-Jesuit reports:

> Deny they now as treacherous Calumny / That to the barbarous Gentile host they taught / Our drill and discipline: deny they now / That traitor hands to savage distant tribes / By rugged paths thro' desert lands they brought / The sulphur dust, the hissing ball, the tube / Of bronze that roared its thunders from their walls ("Que negue agora a pérfida calúnia, / Que se ensinava aos bárbaros gentios / A disciplina militar, e negue / Que mãos traidoras a distantes povos / Por ásperos desertos conduziam / O pó sulfúreo, e as sibilantes balas / E o bronze, que rugia nos seus muros" [Gama (1769) 1996, *Canto* 4: 227, v. 9–15; trans. Gama (1769) 1982, 84, v. 9–15]).

In his commentary on this denial in the historical poem, Gama specifically accuses the Jesuits in Europe of continuing to boast about the fundamental organizing principles of the Jesuit state of Paraguay, as they had in former times, instead of recognizing the negative consequences of their activities in the New World (see Gama [1769] 1996, *Canto* 4: 227, n. to v. 9). But between the lines, Gama in this commentary also criticizes pro-Jesuit views that present the Paraguay missions as an astonishing achievement, as does Voltaire in his *Essai sur les Mœurs*. To corroborate his critical opinion, Gama quotes from chapter XIV, entitled "De apibus" ("On Bees"), of the previously mentioned *Praedium Rusticum* by the French Jesuit Jacques Vanière (1664–1739), who is also called the "Virgile de France." In his poetical text on work and life in the country, Vanière applied the fable about the bee colony from Book IV of Virgil's *Georgica* to the conditions in Paraguay. He used Jesuit sources for his description of the perfect organization of the Jesuit state. In contrast, Gama quotes in *O Uraguay* passages from Vanière's idealized depiction of the military training by the Jesuits to uncover the latter's dangerous machinations and to refute the concept of a peaceful Jesuit state. In his opinion, Vanière, and consequently Voltaire, had already drawn a wrong analogy with regard to the Indians' former military activities in the service of the Spanish king:

> [T]hey always have an ordnance depot / and generals and [train] they train in the cruel art of Mars, / [not because they are keen on wars, / but because they aim at reaching a stable and permanent peace] / After divine service on feast days / their relaxation consists in watching the exercises of the armed infantry and cavalry marching past to the sound of drums and trumpets ("[A]rma ducesque paratos / Semper habent, Martisque truces formantur in usus, / [Non belli studio, longae sed pacis amore] / Haec operum requies, sacris jam rite peractis, Tympanaque & lituos festis audire diebus, / et peditum turmas equitumque videre sub armis" [Gama (1769) 1996, *Canto* 4: 227, n. to v. 9; quoted from Vanière (1706 and 1750) 1788, 136–7]).

Gama introduces another fundamental issue, the question of inequality, by describing and assessing the different property conditions of the Jesuits and the Indians. In his speech in *Canto* 2, the chief Cacambo condemns the "great wealth" ("fantásticas riquezas" [Gama [1769] 1996, *Canto* 2: 208, v. 101]) of the white settlers. In order to be viewed as more credible in his criticisms of these property conditions, Gama makes use of an eyewitness account that focuses on the fortune made by the Jesuits on their plantations in Brazil, and in particular on the miserable conditions of the Indians working on these plantations (see *Canto* 2: 208, n. to v. 90 and 208–9, n. to v. 102). He enumerates several examples of the riches belonging to the Jesuits in Rio de Janeiro and Salvador. He says that one can see more than a thousand slaves and huge numbers of cattle on their plantations. To verify the exploitation of the Brazilian Indians by the Jesuits, Gama describes how he himself saw the Indians in Brazil working extremely hard for the Jesuits. He mentions a plateau between Santos and São Paulo so steep that one cannot climb up to it on horseback. Everybody has to go up on foot and walk beside the horses. But the fathers, he remarks cynically, who took the vow of poverty and have no horses, did not go on foot, but had themselves carried up and down in hammocks by the poor Indians. This might seem unbelievable in Europe, but he, Basílio da Gama, says he can confirm it as an eyewitness (see *Canto* 2: 209, n. to v. 102).

Another organizing principle of the Jesuit state that Gama particularly criticizes is the ban on independent trade between Indians and white settlers and its incorrect presentation in Jesuit writings, where this regulation is also justified by the culturally different property conditions of the Indians. In a commentary on the speech of the Indian chief Cepé in *Canto* 2, in which he justifies the Indian rebellion against the soldiers, Gama first quotes from the *Copia da Carta sediciosa e fraudulenta*, which is printed in the anti-Jesuit polemical source book *Relação Abreviada* and is said to have been written by the chiefs of the rebellious Tupi-Guaraní and sent to the Governor of Buenos Aires during the military mission led by Portuguese and Spaniards to enforce the clauses of the Treaty of Limits: "God gave us this land, and to our forefathers, and therefore we alone own it for the love of God" ("Estas terras no-las deu Deus, e a nossos Avós, e por isso só as possuímos em amor de Deus" [Gama (1769) 1996, *Canto* 2: 210, n. to v. 178; quoted from *Copia da Carta sediciosa*, in *Relação Abreviada* (1757) 1863, 291; trans. Gama (1769) 1982, 122]). But in the passage where Cepé in his speech accepts the religious guidance of the Jesuits, Gama quotes from the French Jesuit Vanière, not to praise the fighting strength of the warring nation, but to emphasize from his own anti-Jesuit perspective the dangerous strategy of the Jesuit missionary activities in the New World:

> This mixture of sacred and profane, or better said, the use of Religion for personal ends, has always been a Jesuit trait. Consider with care the following line: *We do not rule the people due to the right to give orders, but by means of religion* ("Esta mistura do sagrado com o profano, ou para melhor dizer, aquele fazer servir a Religião aos seus fins particulares, foi sempre o caráter dos Jesuítas. Considere-se atentamente este verso: *Non gentem imperio, sed relligione tenemus*" [Gama (1769) 1996, *Canto* 2: 183, n. to v. 183; Vanière

(1706 and 1750) 1788, 139; trans. Gama (1769) 1982, 122; my translation and emphasis]).

Gama especially points to the incorrect information on the Paraguay missions concerning the healthy profit made by trading in yerba mate herb, the product which has made the wealth of the Jesuits possible. To refute this claim in Jesuit writings, that the legal tax relief facilitates self-supply in the Paraguay missions, Gama makes his first comparison with the Chinese tea trade and once again stresses the fact that, according to the *Instruções*, it is only the Jesuits who are growing the yerba mate herb at the expense of the poor Indians, and selling it all over Spanish America, who profit by the trade in this product. That is the reason why he judges the trade in yerba mate herb solely as a source of enrichment for the Society of Jesus and not as an admirable masterpiece of organization on the part of the latter. In order to further reduce to absurdity the image of the charitable Jesuits in these writings and to emphasize the fact that the Indians do not all profit from the yerba mate herb trade and the ban on independent trade between Indians and white settlers, Gama quotes two more passages from Vanière's chapter "On Bees": "We take care of the seeds / we sow on blessed fields" and "[Everybody obeys no other law than their own wills, guided by the love of justice; people having no private property, but the right of usufruct / are not [attracted by the glitter of gold]" ("Semina nos colimus faustis, quae / jecimus agris" and "[Unaque lex est juris amans sua cuique voluntas. Non homines] proprium qui nil potiuntur, et usu / Cuncta tenent [auri fulgor capit]" [Gama (1769) 1996, *Canto* 2: 208, n. to v. 93; quoted from Vanière (1706 and 1750) 1788, 136]).

There is one more organizing principle of the Jesuit state with which particularly Gama finds fault, namely the ban on verbal communication between Indians and white settlers. What annoys him the most is the fact that the Jesuits in Europe even boast about how this tyranny of language protects the Indians: "And, what is worse, the Jesuits flaunted this kind of tyranny all over Europe" ("E o que é mais, é que os mesmos Jesuitas se jactavam desta espécie de tirania na face de toda Europa" [Gamma (1769) 1996, *Canto* 2: 206, n. to v. 48; trans. Gama (1769) 1982, 119]). On this occasion, he once again quotes from Vanière:

> These people do not know our people. They protect their coast against foreign religions / rather than against an enemy. / They built dwellings by

> the seashore; / if foreign ships reach their harbours, they receive them with benevolent hospitality, but / they prevent curious people from going into the interior / to see with their own eyes what they heard about it ("Nescia gens nostri vivit; [nec ab hoste tuetur, / Sed magis externis a relligionibus oras: / Appositas struxere domos ad littora; portus / Ut peregrina suos intret si navis, amice / Hospitio excipiant, sed] ad interiora venire / Regna vetent homines cupidos audita videndi" [*Canto* 2: 206, n. to v. 48; trans. Gama (1769) 1982, 119]).

As seen in the previous passage, Gama regards this categorical walling off and the consequent lack of communication between Europeans and Indians as the main cause of their conflicts. Another fundamental criticism in Gama's poem directly concerns the discrepancy between, on the one hand, the religious intolerance towards Indian religious rites and, on the other hand, the method of accommodation which even includes sexual relations with the natives, as is shown by the example of Baldetta (see Gama [1769] 1996, *Canto* 2: 212). In this passage, however, Gama points to an important transatlantic difference, namely the fact that the Jesuits in America and Asia have fewer scruples than those in Europe. This time, Gama uses the letter by the Austrian Jesuit Father Gottfried Xavier von Laimbeckhoven (1707–1787), bishop of Nanjing and administrator of the diocese of Beijing, to Pope Benedict XIV, as a piece of evidence.[15] Gama criticizes this form of adaptation, because he regards it as further evidence of the Jesuits' dishonesty and even hypocrisy.

The History of the Jesuit Order Seen as a Series of Crimes

Canto 5 of *O Uraguay* can be considered a kind of key to the understanding of the paratextual interrelations between the poetic text and the author's annotations concerning the supposed worldwide abuse of power by the Jesuits. It contains probably the most polemical anti-Jesuit passages ever written by Basílio da Gama. His polemic is mirrored by a multitude and variety of allusions to political crimes in the history of the order. This *Canto* comments on the history of the Jesuit missions worldwide and is deeply influenced by Gama's reading of Voltaire.

In the poetic text, General Andrade and his soldiers are in the destroyed Jesuit temple in the conquered Tupi-Guaraní mission São Miguel and look at the preserved ceiling fresco. Gama's description of this fresco, which in reality did not exist, can be considered as a parody of the famous, and for contemporary readers recognizable, ceiling fresco *The Triumph of Saint Ignácio de Loyola* in the Saint Ignacius Church in Rome, made by the Jesuit architect Andrea Pozzo (see Teixeira 1999, 494–9). In Gama's description of this allegory of the Society of Jesus, on one side, it appears to be some kind of an institution on a throne that is surrounded by villages, towns, provinces, and kingdoms, each submitting to it. Here a series of historical events from all over the world are shown or, to put it more precisely, indications are given of the crimes and the corruption the Jesuits have been responsible for worldwide, like the deaths of Henri III and Henri IV, both kings of France. The fathers of the Society of Jesus are always shown in twos in the painting, and they are always mirrored by the four ends of the world, from the Tejo to the Amazon, from the Ganges to the Nile. The following deeds are hinted at: their participation in the enslavement of the Indian population in America to get access to precious metals and stones, their domineering role regarding the trade and seafaring activities of the inhabitants, their toleration of the Confucian cult among Chinese Christians, their encouragement of political rivalry in Japan, which leads to their expulsion, their participation in a conspiracy in England and in the preparations for the assassination of the Portuguese king Dom Sebastião in the African territory of Alcáçar-Quibir, and the ensuing rule of Spain over Portugal in the sixteenth and seventeenth centuries.

The interrelation between the poetic text and the paratextual elements in the annotations begins with a reference to similar ceiling frescos in the church of the Colégio Romano and in the Casa Professa of the Jesuits in Rome which, in his opinion, however, preserve the mask of religion much more effectively (see Gama [1769] 1996, *Canto* 5: 237, n. to v. 1). This is followed by an enumeration of all instances in which Jesuits are supposed to have been involved in the murders of historical personalities. For this accusation, he probably uses José de Seabra da Silvas' *Dedução Cronológica e Analítica* (1767), but he completes his reference to the murder of the two French kings by giving detailed information on their assassinations. In view of his predilection for the writings of Voltaire, and considering the chronology, it seems reasonable to assume that he had also gained his knowledge from the latter's *Précis du Siècle de Louis XV* (see Voltaire [1768] 1967, ch. 37 ["Attentat contre la personne du Roi"]: 389–94). First, Gama condemns the crimes of the French Jesuits and their cover-up in history. He mentions the threadbare trial of the politically active Father Guignard as well as the involvement of Father Varade, superior of the Jesuit order in Paris, in the assassination of Henry IV (see Gama [1769] 1996, *Canto* 5: 237–8, n. to v. 13 and 15). Then he alludes to the latest crime directed against the Portuguese king Dom José I, supposed to be committed by the Jesuits Malagrida, Alexandre and Mathos on 3 September 1758, which finally led to the Jesuits' banishment from Portuguese territory. The Jesuits were banished from France due to a further incident in which Father La Valette, the superior of the Jesuit order in Martinique, was involved.[16] After a scandalous bankruptcy, the Parliament of Paris accused him of having despotically administered the property of the order in Martinique from Rome. The Society of Jesus had to pay for the total amount of damages. Against the background of these "pieces of evidence" for the Jesuits' criminal activities and despotism, in fact mostly allegations, Gama criticizes the contemporary attitude towards power on the part of the Jesuits and their worldwide corporation, whose "throne" and thus power centre is in Rome. He pleads for a rapid dissolution of the order, because he fears the worldwide abuse of power and political influence by the Jesuits' general in Rome. Gama's strongest argument against them refers to the danger of the powerful network within the Society of Jesus, the utmost despotism in which the general sends his orders to the Jesuit fathers, and the great extent to which he gets information, especially through letters written by the Jesuit fathers, on everything happening in all parts of the world. That is also Gama's argument of why banishing the Jesuits from the other provinces would be only a superficial solution. On the contrary, in his opinion, one must cut off their roots. But he is convinced that, considering the contemporary general mood, there is fortunately every reason to believe that the Society of Jesus would soon be dissolved (see Gama [1769] 1996, *Canto* 5: 238, n. to v. 21), which actually happened in 1773, although only temporarily.

On this occasion, Gama clearly condemns the power of the letters, chronicles, and travelogues of the Jesuits from all parts of the world, which for many years had strongly influenced positively the image of their activities around the globe, and had thus been a powerful factor in the Roman Catholic Church's policy. This point is underlined by Gama's vicious assumption that the Jesuits had even boasted about having discovered the source of the Nile. He points to the sad situation of the Indians in Paraguay by once again referring to the letters of General Gomes Freire de Andrade printed in the *Relação Abreviada*, which at this time had been published, translated and republished several times, and thus had been made accessible to a relatively large public. He emphasizes the Jesuits' abuse of power, by means of their writings, in presenting a further eyewitness account, which revealed the despotic trading principles of the Jesuits in Brazil. With regard to their trade in and transport of goods on their own frigate, they perfidiously used an acknowledged *Profecia* (Prophecy) by Father Anchieta in their illegal attempts to enrich themselves (see Gama [1769] 1996, *Canto* 5: 238–9, n. to v. 42). With the help of the *Profecia*, they claimed that their ship could not sink; in this way, they justified higher carriage for commodities. To prove this misuse of power and of the people's faith in the prophecies of Anchieta's old Jesuit sermons, Gama stresses that he also speaks from personal experience. He says he often saw and entered this frigate himself, which in all harbours enjoyed the honours of a royal vessel.

Next, Gama uses the history of the Jesuits' missionary activities in China in his criticism of intolerance towards other religions. He does so according to the prevailing taste of his time, and is most probably oriented towards Voltaire's *Précis du Siècle de Louis XIV*.[17] Gama outlines the most important stages of their activities in China, particularly the consequences of the accommodation method which was established in the *Decretos das Sagradas Congregações* (1645), despite the scepticism of the Jesuit power centre in Rome, and which can also be found in the *Proëmialis Declaratio* to the book *Confucius Sinarum Philosophus* (1687). According to Claudia von Collani, who studied the Jesuits' adaptation in China, Jesuit probabilism in China was based on the premise that contemporary Confucianism was a philosophy of state and not a religion. Therefore, the Chinese could be Confucians and Christians at the same time. For a long time, ancestor worship and Confucian worship were not regarded as religious acts, but as civil acts (see Collani 2000, 107). It was the Italian Humanist Matteo Ricci in particular who shaped the successful symbiosis between Jesuits and Chinese scholars, between missionary work, dissemination of knowledge, and cultural exchange, including relations with the court of the Chinese emperor to which admittance was extremely rare. The Jesuits even accepted Chinese names for God, like *Xamti* (Highest Emperor) and *Tien* (Heaven), which Gama also mentions (see Gama [1769] 1996, *Canto* 5, 239, n. to v. 52). Gama's description of the Jesuits in China is based on the *Catalogo degli ordini religiosi della chiesa militante. Espressi con imagini e espiegati con una breve narrazione* (1706–1707), a register of the religious and secular orders of knights compiled by the famous Father Filippe Buonanni from Rome. The end of Ricci's success, which Gama presents, at least in principle, in a positive light because of Ricci's tolerant attitude towards the traditional rites of a different culture, was initiated by the apostolic vicar of the province of Fujian, Charles Maigrot (1655–1730). In this province, Maigrot prohibited the ancestor and Confucius cult as well as the use of all Chinese names for God, except that of *Tianzhu* (Lord of the Heavens). In 1693, he even obtained permission from Rome to extend these bans all over China. In 1704, Charles-Thomas Maillard de Tournon (1668–1710) also travelled to China and openly denied, in front of the emperor, that Christianity and Confucianism were compatible with each other. He wanted to forbid Chinese Christians from participating in their traditional rites, which were regarded as rebellious and led to the Jesuits' temporary expulsion from China (see *Canto* 5: 239, n. to v. 52; as well as Collani 2000, 110–16). Apart from this misjudgment by the Roman Catholic Church, Gama enumerates some corresponding ones by the popes Clement XI in 1710, Benedict XIII in 1712, Clement XII in 1734, and Benedict XIV in 1742, but he also mentions that missionaries in China continued to use the accommodation method.

Considering the behaviour of the Jesuits in China, and other incidents in the history of the order, Gama is surprised that the Jesuits can still be the pope's "guarda pretoriana" (Gama [1769] 1996, *Canto* 5: 239, n. to v. 52). In order to show that this is a potentially dangerous situation, Gama quotes a passage from the *Epître à Darget* by Frederick II of Prussia, whom, like Voltaire, he calls the "Philosophe de Sanssouci" ("The Philosopher from Sansouci", namely "Carefree"): "Rome had as many traitors as Praetorian Guards, / They haggled over the Empire, and gave it masters" ("En ses Pretoriens Rome eut autant des traitres, / Ils marchandaient l'Empire, et lui donnaient des maîtres" [*Canto* 5: 239, n. to v. 52; quoted in Friedrich II of Prussia 1805, Épître 19: 155]). This refers to the fact that Frederick II of Prussia in particular, guided by his idea of religious tolerance, accepted the Jesuit fathers as well as the Calvinists and Lutherans as teachers, as long as they imparted their classical knowledge to him.

After these remarks about the history of the Jesuit order – seen as a series of crimes in Europe, America, Africa, and Asia – as well as remarks about the Jesuit mission in China as compared with the Jesuits' missionary activities in the seven Tupi-Guaraní reductions of the Uruguay River, reference shall now be made to the Caribbean expansions in the age of Louis XIV. With regard to these, Gama recommends reading Abraham Duquesne's 1692 *Journal du Voyage [...] aux Indes Orientales*:

> The Jesuits, with their mental reservations, did not doubt at first to trample the crucifix in order to retain that extremely lucrative trade. Anyone who may desire to be more informed on this matter, read the travels of Mr. Duquesne, sent to the East Indies by Louis XIV, vol 3, p. 81 ("Os Jesuítas

com as suas restrições mentais não duvidaram ao princípio calcar o crucifixo, por não perderem aquele riquissimo comércio. Quem quiser fazer conceito da extenção deste, e de outras curiosidades nesta matéria, leia as viagens de Mr. Duquesne, mandado por Luís XIV às Índias Orientais Tom.3, pág. 81" [Gama (1769) 1996, *Canto* 5: 240, n. to v. 60]).

According to Ivan Teixeira, the "architectonical essence" ("essência arquitetônica") of the text, especially in *Canto* 5 of *O Uraguay*, has to be seen not only as a parody of Andrea Pozzo's ceiling fresco, or as criticism of the worldwide abuse of power by the Jesuits, but also as an allegorical "staging" of an ambitious praise to the policy of the Marquês de Pombal (see Teixeira 1999, 498).

The paratextual interrelations between the poetic text and the author's annotations reveal also Gama's polemical and critical, although fragmentary, judgment of the various European views of the Jesuit state of Paraguay, especially concerning the Guaranític War of the Seven Reductions. Concentrating on the structural principle of *O Uraguay*, namely the dialogue between poetical text and annotations, it becomes clear, that, along the lines of the Enlightenment, this epic poem – written by a Brazilian with "espirito americanista" living in Europe – contains quite an original treatment not only of the Jesuits' missionary activities and their abuse of power and political influence, but also of the impact of their writings in Europe, which was equally important to Basílio da Gama, because he knew how powerful a developing public could be. This also applies to the future impact of his own text, which self-confidently and full of hope ends with the following verses:

Uruguay! Men shall read thee. Veil some day / To come mine eyed black shades of night eterne. / Live thou and joy the light serene and pure. / Hie to the groves of Arcady nor fear / To step a stranger on an unknown shore. / There mid the sombre myrtles shedding shade / No funeral urn shall all Mireo hold: Raise from the foreign sky and o'er it spread / With pilgrim hand the wreath of barbarous flowers / And seek thy follower who shall guide thy steps / Unto that place which long thy coming waits ("Serás lido Uraguay. Cubra os meus olhos / Embora um dia a escura noite eterna. / Tu vive, e goza a luz serena, e pura. / Vai aos bosques de Arcádia: e não receies / Chegar desconhecido àquela areia. / Ali de fresco entre as sombrias murtas / Urna triste a Mirêo não todo encerra. / Leva de estranho Céu, sobre ela espalha / Co'a peregrina mão bárbaras flores. / E busca o sucessor, que te encaminhe / Ao teu lugar, que há muito que te espera" [Gama (1769) 1996, *Canto* 5: 241, v. 140–50; trans. Gama (1769) 1982, 100, v. 140–50]).

Conclusion

José Basílio da Gama's hope that *O Uraguay* would make a deep impact on a wide audience came true only to a certain degree. The text provoked severe criticism among the Jesuits living in exile, including the German Jesuit Father Lourenço Kaulen, who wrote as a former eyewitness in exile a drastic refutation replying to *O Uraguay*. Until 1759, Kaulen worked as a missionary in Maranhão, but then he had to go into exile and serve a prison sentence in Lisbon until 1777. His text appeared in Lugano in 1786 under the title of *Reposta Apologética ao Poema Intitulado O Uraguay*. Although the *Real Mesa Censória* prohibited the distribution of the *Reposta Apologética*, it was circulated both in Portugal and in Brazil under the modified title of *Refutação das Calúnias Contidas no Poema "O Uraguay" de José Basílio da Gama* (see Kaulen [1786] 1907, 93–224). Kaulen mainly criticized Gama's anti-Jesuit comments for their lack of authenticity. He reproached him for having never been to the seven Guaraní missions; thus he could not have known the people and the region. In his opinion, Gama used incorrect sources such as the *Relação Abreviada* and the *Dedução Cronológica e Analítica*. He refuted Gama's descriptions of the coexistence of Jesuits and Indians by recounting his own experiences. Particularly, he found fault with the episode in which Father Balda denies the Indian woman Lindoya a Christian burial and has Tanajura burnt alive. This also applies to the military parade and the alleged Jesuit conspiracy in connection with the death of Dom Sebastião in North Africa in the sixteenth century. The Indian chief Cacambo, however, was a historical person even according to Kaulen, although he was not a hero, but just an average Indian. Moreover, Kaulen reproached Gama with weakness of character because, even though the latter enjoyed the protection of the Jesuits in times of crisis and entered the *Arcadia Romana* with their help, his epic poem was full of ingratitude and betrayed his former brother members. Kaulen's *Reposta Apologética* was the main reason for the negative tendency in the reception of Basílio da Gama's biography, as well as of *O Uraguay*, forced by Jesuits and pro-Jesuit intellectuals (see Chaves 1997, 65–74).

O Uraguay was later positively received by the Brazilian Romantics in the nineteenth century, dominated as it was by the "espirito americanista." In this national context, the polarizing European intellectual dispute about the advantages and disadvantages of the Jesuit state of Paraguay continued with a non-European view, with regard to the formation of a national basis for a Brazilian history as an important part for developing the national identity. This different, guided Brazilian interest is attested by a paralleled variety of other anti-Jesuit and Jesuit published writings, such as excerpts of chronicles, travelogues, and collections of letters, drawing a picture of Jesuits as successful civilizers of the New World. The critical dispute about these writings happened especially in the intellectual circle of the national Instituto Histórico e Geográfico Brasileiro, but also, again, in paratextual interrelations between the poetic text and the author's annotations in works of the Brazilian Romantics.

NOTES

1 The following quotations are taken from Gama [1769] 1996, 191–262.

2 See Genette 1987, especially the chapter "Les notes" (293–315) concerning fictitious texts. The present study of the paratextual interrelations in *O Uraguay* is premised on the assumption that the text of a literary work can be regarded as the generic term, whereas the paratext can be seen as the subsumable concept. It is exactly the schematic reading of the paratext which leads to a more precise understanding of the text from a historical and systematic perspective. In this way, it opens up a new look at an indefinite zone between the inside and outside, which itself does not have fixed limits to the inside (the text) and the outside (the discourse of the world about the text). As a consequence, perspectives are refracted, multiplied, and diffused. See Stanitzek, 2004, 8.

3 As regards the biography, see Chaves 2000, 9ff.

4 Officially, the Junta de Inconfidência was constituted on 4 January 1759 in Lisbon, during Pombal's absolutist regime. It was widely publicized as a legal instrument to fight crimes of conspiracy against Portugal, especially those committed by Jesuits. The prime minister instructed the Junta to carry out the trials in secret, but to impose the sentences, either death or exile to Angola, in public.

5 As governor of Grand Para and Maranhão in the north of Brazil, Furtado put into effect the first decree concerning the banishment of Jesuits from the colony.

6 The Minas Gerais Conspiracy of 1788 was at the beginning an unsuccessful Brazilian independence movement, but in the nineteenth century, in the

context of the developing national identity during the Brazilian Romanism, it was considered as the first conspiracy that aimed at independence, proclamation of a republic, and abolition of slavery.

7 On the history of reception in Brazil, see Chaves 1997.

8 Cf. Anonymous [1757] 1863, 265–94. In Brazil, the *Relação Abreviada* was published for the first time only in October 1842 in the *Revista Trimensal de História e Geografía ou Journal do Instituto Histórico e Geográfico Brasileiro* in Rio de Janeiro.

9 Cf. Cunha [1852] 1894. The *Diário* was published in Brazil also for the first time by the national press in the *Revista do Instituto Histórico e Geográfico do Brasil* in Rio de Janeiro in the second trimester of 1852.

10 Voltaire's quotation from the *Relação Abreviada* can be seen as a proof for the perception and discussion of this polemical anti-Jesuit text in French among intellectuals of the European Enlightenment before its Portuguese publication in Lisbon.

11 In the course of the reception of *O Uraguay* as a national epic in the nineteenth century, the historian Francisco Adolfo de Varnhagen defines it in his *História Geral do Brasil* as a chronicle of the War of the Seven Reductions. Furthermore, Gama is evoked several times in Southey's discussion of nascent hostilities on the Rio Pardo and Portuguese General Gomes Freire de Andrade's wartime deeds. While Gama is referenced along with other published Jesuit sources, it is clear that Southey considers him unreliable.

12 By adapting to the leading cultural elite, that is by an indirect mission with the help of science and art, the Jesuits were very successful in their missionary work in China, particularly in the seventeenth century. But soon the Jesuits were reproached for this adaptation according to the Biblical principle "to become everything to everybody" (de devenir tout à tous) because it was said that it distracted them from their missionary activities. See Collani 2000, 99–119, here 115–17 in particular.

13 Translation from Philips 1668, 79–80.

14 Cf. Gama [1769] 1996, *Canto* 2: 206, n. to v. 51; quoted from *Instruções*, printed in *Relação Abreviada*, [1757] 1863, 286.

15 As early as 1758, Laimbeckhoven wrote in one of his letters: "I have forgotten the European way of life to a large degree, and among the Chinese I have already become almost a Chinese man myself" (Der europäischen Lebens-Art habe ich ziemlich vergessen, und ich bin unter denen Chinesern nunmehro auch schon bald ein Chineser geworden [quoted from Stöcklein 1758, letter 673: 36, probably printed before in his *Reisebeschreibung*, and possibly in Jean-Baptiste Du Halde's *Lettres édifiantes et curieuses*, which were very successful before the Jesuits were also banished from France in 1764]).

16 Cf. Gama [1769] 1996, *Canto* 5: 238, n. to v. 18. Gama based his knowledge most probably on Voltaire [1768] 1967, especially ch. 38 ("Assassinat du Roi de Portugal, Jésuites chassés du Portugal, et ensuite de la France"): 395–400.

17 Voltaire [1752] 1967, ch. 39 ("Disputes sur les cérémonies chinoises. Comment ces querelles contribuèrent à faire proscrire le christianisme à la Chine"): 76–86.

BIBLIOGRAPHY

Chaves, Vania Pinheiro. 1997. *"O Uraguay" e a Fundação da Literatura Brasileira.* Campinas: Editora da UNICAMP.

–. 2000. *O Despertar do Gênio brasileiro. Uma leitura de O Uraguay de José Basílio da Gama.* Campinas: Editora da UNICAMP.

Collani, Claudia von. 2000. "Aspekte und Problematik der Akkommodation der Jesuiten in China." In *"[...] usque ad ultimum terrae". Die Jesuiten und die transkontinentale Ausbreitung des Christentums 1540–1773*, ed. Johannes Meier, 99–119. Göttingen: Vanderhoeck & Ruprecht.

Corneille, Pierre. 1950. *Horace.* In *Théâtre complet*, 1640, ed. Pierre Lièvre, vol. 1: 777–843. Paris: Gallimard.

Cunha, Jacínto Rodrigues da. 1894. "Diário da Expedição de Gomes Freire de Andrade às Missões do Uraguay," 1852. *Revista do Instituto Histórico e Geográfico do Brasil* 3: 10 (2nd trimester 1852).

Friedrich II of Prussia. 1805. *À Darget. Apologie des Rois.* In *Oeuvres primitives de Frederic II, Roi de Prusse; ou Collection des Ouvrages qu'il publia pendant son règne.* Vol. 3. Potsdam: Aux dépens des associés.

Gama, José Basílio da. 1769. *O Uraguay. Na Arcádia de Roma Termindo Sipílio dedicado ao Ill.mo e Exc.mo Senhor Francisco Xavier de Mendonça Furtado, Secretário de Estado de S. Magestade Fidelíssima.* Lisboa: Na Régia Officina Typográfica.

–. 1982. *The Uruguay (A Historical Romance of South America). The Sir Richard Burton Translation. Huntington Library Manuscript HM 27954*, 1769, eds. Frederick C. H. Garcia and Edward F. Stanton. Reprint, Berkeley: University of California Press.

–. 1996. *O Uraguay.* In *Obras poéticas de Basílio da Gama. Ensaio e edição crítica*, 1769, ed. Ivan Teixeira, 191–262. São Paulo: Editora da Universidade de São Paulo.

Genette, Gérard. 1987. *Seuils.* Paris: Editions du Seuil.

Hartmann, Peter Claus. 1994. *Der Jesuitenstaat in Südamerika 1609–1768. Eine christliche Alternative zu Kolonialismus und Marxismus.* Weissenhorn: Konrad.

Kaulen, Lourenço. 1907. "*Reposta Apologética ao Poema Intitulado "O Uraguay" Composto por José Basílio da Gama*, Lugano 1786. Refutação das Calúnias Contídas no Poema *O Uraguay* de José Basílio da Gama," 1786. *Revista do Instituto Histórico e Geográfico Brasileiro* 68 (1a): 92–224.

Kurtze Nachricht von der République, so von den R.R.P.P. der Gesellschaft Jesu in den Portugiessisch – und Spanischen Provinzen in den über Meer gelegenen diesen zweien Mächten gehörige Königreiche aufgerichtet werden. [1760] 1892. Reprint, Lissabon: H. Baumgartner and Wiener Neustadt.

Montesquieu, Charles-Louis de Secondat. 1951. *De l'Esprit des Lois ou Du rapport que les Lois doivent avoir avec la constitution de chaque gouvernement, les mœurs, le climat, la religion, le commerce, etc.* In *Oeuvres complètes,* 1748, ed. Roger Caillois, vol. 2. Paris: Gallimard.

Philips, Katherine. 1668. *Poems [...] To which is added Monsieur Corneille's "Pompey" & "Horace".* London: H. Herringman.

Relação Abreviada da República, que os Religiosos Jesuítas das Províncias de Portugal e Hespanha estabeleceram nos Domínios ultramarinos das duas Monarquias: Formada pelos registros das Secretarias dos dous respectivos principaes Commissarios e Plenipotenciarios, e por outros documentos authenticos. [1757] 1863. In *Revista Trimensal de História e Geografía ou Journal do Instituto Histórico e Geográfico Brasileiro* 15 (2): 265–94. Rio de Janeiro: Tipografia de Inácio da Silva.

Southey, Robert. 1822. *History of Brazil.* Second Edition. London: Longman, Durst, Kees, Orme, and Brown.

Stanitzek, Georg. 2004. "Texte, Paratexte in Medien: Einleitung." In *Paratexte in Literatur, Film, Fernsehen,* eds. Georg Stanitzek and Klaus Kreimeier, 3–19. Berlin: Akademie-Verlag.

Stöcklein, Joseph, ed. 1758. *Der Neue Welt-Bott mit allerhand nachrichten deren Missionarien Soc. Iesu.* Wien: P. Propst and F. Keller.

Teixeira, Ivan. 1996. *Obras poéticas de Basílio da Gama. Ensaio e edição crítica.* São Paulo: Edusp.

–. 1999. *Mecenato Pombalino e Poesia Neoclássica.* São Paulo: Edusp.

Vanière, Jacques. 1788. *Praedium Rusticum,* 1706 and 1750. Paris: Poinçot.

Voltaire, François-Marie Arouet. 1967. *Précis du Siècle de Louis XIV.* In *Œuvres complètes.* Vol. 15: 1–152, 1752. Nendeln: Kraus Reprint [Paris: Garnier Frères].

Voltaire, François-Marie Arouet. 1967. *Essai sur les Moeurs et l'Esprit des Nations.* In *Œuvres complètes.* Vol. 11–13, 1756. Reprint, Lichtenstein: Kraus Reprint [Paris: Garnier Frères].

Voltaire, François-Marie Arouet. 1967. *Précis du siècle de Louis XV.* In *Œuvres complètes.* Vol. 15: 153–435, 1768. Nendeln: Kraus Reprint.

chapter nine

Changing Perspectives: The Other, the Self, the In-Between of the Jesuit Experience in the Eighteenth Century

UTE FENDLER

In a recent book entitled *Visión de los Otros y Visión de Sí Mismos. ¿Descubrimiento o Invención entre el Nuevo Mundo y el Viejo?*, edited by Fermín del Pino and Carlos Lázaro, there are a few articles that analyse the narrations of Jesuit missionaries in the eighteenth century. Of particular interest in these articles is the discussion of how the Jesuit missionaries constructed their vision of themselves and how they constructed their vision of the Other. Héctor Sáinz Ollero speaks of the "culture shock" (Sáinz Ollero 1995, 96) those missionaries must have experienced, especially in the missions of the "selva," that is, the wooded regions of the Orinoco and the Amazon – in sharp contrast with the missions in the great plains of Paraguay (i.e., the "open, cultivated land" in opposition to the "selva"), as José A. Ferrer Benimeli has observed in his article, "La expulsión de los jesuitas de las reducciones del Paraguay" (Ferrer Benimeli 2001, 310).

Most critics agree that Jesuit discourse is the precursor to modern anthropological discourse, as the Jesuits lived the experience of "participating observation," or as Beatriz Vitar expresses it, of "the close look" ("la mirada cercana" [Vitar 1995, 117]). Sáinz Ollero has emphasized that in spite of their "culture shock" (being isolated and being the only Europeans), the Jesuits reached an empathic perception of the Indians characterized by the development of a modern sensibility for the other.[1] María Cipolletti takes into consideration the temporal dimension, in that she describes the exceptional merit of the Jesuits in transferring anthropological, botanical, and zoological information in a more differentiated way, drawing attention to the changing presentation of the collected data. Considering the standardized education of the Jesuits and the structured template or standardized "cuestionarios" (see Solano and

Pilar 1988; Figueroa et al. 1986) originally provided to them for reporting on their missionary work, the individual's perspective only emerges in the eighteenth century; thus Jesuit narration no longer adhered to the highly codified structure of the sixteenth- and seventeenth-century *relation,* but rather evolved as a more differentiated perception and description of the experience of the foreign, particularly in the New World (Cipolletti 2001, 240). The Jesuit accounts are therefore always part of a missionary discourse, which is again embedded in a larger colonial one (see Vitar 1995).

Elena Altuna also speaks of this colonial discourse in her book *El discurso colonialista de los caminantes. Siglos XVII–XVIII.* She characterizes the authors of the travelogues of the eighteenth century as "intercultural mediators" or "agents" who transmit information about unknown and remote regions and peoples (Altuna 2002, 165). Adrien Pasquali has proposed the discussion of discourses when analysing travelogues, so that the mosaic nature of the texts can be taken into consideration. He speaks of the "totalizing discourse of knowledge" ("discours totalisateur de savoirs") in the eighteenth century (see Pasquali 1994, 127). But beneath the prevailing idea of the mission with respect to the Jesuit accounts, or of the collection of knowledge in a wider sense with respect to the eighteenth century, the Jesuit texts are in fact collections of various fragmentary discourses: anthropological, botanical, geographical, religious, and so forth; these fragments are then put together to present a more or less coherent text. Pasquali draws attention to the boundaries, the passages between those fragments, which might allow for individual perspectives in spite of the dominating colonial and missionary discourses; those fragments very often correspond to anecdotes that interrupt the dominant discourse.[2] With this in mind, an analysis of the construction of the narration might bring forth, on the one hand, the individual experience within the dominating missionary discourse and, on the other hand, it might allow the reader to consider the hypothesis of the Jesuit travellers as the predecessors of modern anthropologists as well as other intercultural mediators who succeeded in overcoming a "culture shock" to establish an empathic relationship with the natives.

I propose to analyse the account of Joseph Gumilla, written and published in the 1740s, and the account of Manuel Uriarte, written in Ravenna from 1771 to 1773 as a reconstruction of the diaries of his missionary work in the Maynas region from 1750 to 1767. This choice is motivated by the common experience of the "selva" and by the chronological order in which these texts were written, so that the two periods – the ones preceding and following the expulsion of the Jesuits – might be studied so as to reveal the Jesuits' changing perspective on their experience as missionaries following the expulsion (see Cipolletti 2001; Ferrer Benimeli 2001; and Sáinz Ollero 1995).

Joseph Gumilla, *El Orinoco Ilustrado, y Defendido*

Joseph Gumilla (1686–1750) was born in Valencia and came to America in 1705. He studied in Santa Fe de Bogotá and began his missionary career in 1715. Ángel Santos mentions Gumilla as the major missionary of the Orinoco, in that he succeeded in founding various settlements in this region after previous missionary work had been interrupted for about 20 years due to attacks by the "Caribs" (Santos 1992, 255).[3] Gumilla's book, *El Orinoco ilustrado, y defendido*[4] was first published in 1741 and then a second and enlarged edition followed in 1745. The title gives an initial idea of the subjects Gumilla will deal with and reflects the concept of the "totalizing discourse of the transfer of knowledge" mentioned above:

> The Orinoco enlightened and defended, the natural, civil and geographical history of this "great river," and its mighty tributaries: government, habits and customs of the Indians, its inhabitants, with new and useful information about animals, trees, fruits, oils, resins, herbs and medicinal roots; and above all you will find extraordinary accounts of conversions in N. Santa Fé and highly exemplary cases ("El Orinoco ilustrado, y defendido, Historia Natural, civil, y geographica de este rio, y de sus caudalosas vertientes, govierno, usos, y costumbres de los indios, sus habitadores, con nuevas, y utiles noticias de animales, arboles, frutos, aceytes, resinas, yervas, y raíces medicinales; y sobre todo se hallarán conversiones muy singulares à N. Santa Fé, y casos de mucha edificación" [Gumilla [1745] 1954]).

In the preface, Gumilla insists on two aspects of his text:

> 1) the fact that the whole text is based on his personal experience: "I declare that that which was not collected here in the two manuscript Histories by Fathers Mercado and Ribero, both men of heroic virtue and well respected throughout my Province, is the daughter of my own experience, of what has passed through my hands, and of what I have seen with my own eyes, not without careful observation ("Protesto que lo que no fuere recogido

aquí de las dos Historias manuscritas por los Padres Mercado y Ribero, ambos varones de heroica virtud y venerables en toda mi Provincia, serán noticias hijas de mi experiencia, y de aquello mismo que ha pasado por mis manos y he visto por mis ojos, no sin cuidadosa observación" [Gumilla (1745) 1954, 32]);

2) the novelty of the information he will deliver about the New World.

Both aspects come together when he emphasizes that his narration is not fantastic and, by doing so, refers implicitly to imagined journeys and descriptions of the New World. It seems important to him to stress the verisimilitude of his narration, as the world he will describe is so novel that it might seem invented:

> [S]eeing with clarity the undeniable existence of the new American world, they see that, all of that being new, its component parts must also be new, because it is not only called the new world on account of its recent discovery, but also because, compared to this old World, that one is altogether new and different. Thus new ideas are also necessary for your complete understanding [of it], ideas born of new types of people for the New World, and for every part in and of itself ("[V]ista con claridad la existencia innegable del Nuevo Mundo americano, vean que siendo nuevo aquel todo had de ser también nuevas las partes de que se compone porque no sólo se llama Mundo Nuevo por su nuevo descubrimiento, sino también porque, comparado con este Mundo antiguo, aquél es del todo nuevo y en todo diverso. De aquí es que para su cabal comprehensión son precisas también ideas nuevas, nacidas de nuevas especies para el todo nuevo, y para cada parte de por sí" [Gumilla (1745) 1954, 33]).

At the same time, he argues in favour of the type of close observation that was such a crucial aspect of the Enlightenment approach to the experienced world.

The novelty of the New World distorts perceptions of the Indians as well; at first sight, they appear to be part of the natural landscape, but they begin to appear less strange or foreign to the reader as Gumilla recognizes them as human beings with intellectual capacities, so that they become identifiable as a part of mankind (see Gumilla [1745] 1954, 34). At first, the description of the Indians seems to repeat various topoi from preceding texts, that is, assigning them to the categories of noble savages, already civilized peoples, or barbarians exhibiting the respective, desultory characteristics:

> The Indian in general (I speak of those who live in the woods and of those who start to become sedentary) is certainly a human being; but the lack of education has affected their rational capacities so much that in a moral sense, I dare to say that the Indian is barbarian and wild, an unseen monster that has a head of ignorance, a heart of ungratefulness, a breast of instability, shoulders of laziness, feet of fear, and his belly for drinking and inclination towards drunkenness are two bottomless abysses ("El Indio en general (hablo de los que habitan las selvas y de los que empiezan a domesticarse) es ciertamente hombre; pero su falta de cultivo le ha desfigurado tanto lo racional, que en el sentido moral me atrevo a decir que el indio es bárbaro y sílvestre es un monstruo nunca visto, que tiene cabeza de ignorancia, corazón de ingratitud, pecho de inconstancia, espaldas de pereza, pies de miedo, y su vientre para beber y su inclinación a embriagarse son dos abismos sin fin" [Gumilla (1745) 1954, 103]).

Further on, Gumilla differentiates between Indians who are civilized and Indians living in the jungle who would need moral and religious instruction to become "human beings." In this context, he describes himself as an artist who will form the raw material to get a perfect statue (see Gumilla [1745] 1954,103).

His narration is in large part a mise en scène of nature[5] in which the civilizing labour of the missionaries transforms savages into sedentary and Christianized men and nature into landscape. In the summary for chapter 8, Gumilla describes the beauty of the vast regions of the Orinoco, where rocks shaped like balconies or benches invite the wanderer to rest and enjoy the beautiful sights. In this almost pre-romantic arrangement, Gumilla describes the landscape as a sort of paradise with biblical reminiscences by evoking the successful campaigns of settlement by various priests.[6] In the context of the Enlightenment, Michael Bravo has called this style of writing by travellers "stage settings in the *theatrum mundi*": "They [the enlightened explorers] entertained and they edified, reinforcing for the reader the categories of 'explorer,' 'native,' 'map,' 'progress'" (Bravo 1999, 211). Christopher Balme goes even further, as he establishes parallels between theatricalization and colonialism, referring to Said's Orientalism[7] and to aesthetic reflections of the eighteenth century, for example, in the analysis of a text written by a member of the first Cook expedition, Sir Joseph Banks: "This act of staging the landscape, of making it conform to the controlling optic of a central perspective, could then be interpreted as the aesthetic precondition of the colonial enterprise. Not only is nature framed in terms of

European perceptual categories, but it is also controlled in Said's sense and made to look more like the stage that the European mind apparently required as a prerequisite for actual conquest and control" (Balme 2001, 229).

The mise en scène, by combining the picturesque and the spectacular as well as the theatrical, is also present in Gumilla's text, as can be seen in the choice of narration from the perspective of the river or of a traveller on a boat. At the same time, it reveals the specific attitude of a missionary such as Gumilla, who has established a close relationship over the years with this region and its people. This thesis is supported by the author's preface, when he apologizes for any aspects of his style that might reflect the influence of native languages:

> Regarding style, I will only try to make myself understood as clearly as I can; and it will be no small thing if I succeed in doing so; because after all these years of having grown accustomed to the barbarous pronunciation, to the arrangement and the sentences of the harsh languages of those Indians, it would be mere chance if my narration were to flow without a mistake, either in the style of speech, or in the correctness of the words themselves: nevertheless, I will try to make my quill amble at times and run at others at the pace of the Orinoco River and its tributaries ("En el estilo solo tiraré a darme a entender con la mayor claridad que pueda; y no será poca dicha si lo consiguiré; porque acostumbrado largos años a la pronunciación bárbara, a la colocación y cláusulas de los lenguajes ásperos de aquellos indios, será casualidad si corriere mi narración sin tropiezo, ya en la frase, ya en la propiedad de las palabras: no obstante, procuraré que mi pluma unas veces ande y otras veces corra al paso del río Orinoco, cuyas vertientes sigue" [Gumilla (1745) 1954, 31–2]).

Gumilla's text oscillates between the mise en scène and the empathic experience. In this way, Gumilla constructs the community of the missionaries and the people entrusted to them.

So far we have seen that the different steps taken, from culture shock to approximation to empathy, are present in the narrations of the missionary experience. When Gumilla relates various historical examples of Spaniards captured by Indians who then underwent a certain process of "going native," for example Alvar Nuñez Cabeza de Vaca, he adds to them the case of a Jesuit father whose experience serves as an example for the work accomplished by the Jesuit order. Father José Cabarte spent nine years in remote areas, and when he finally found his way back to the outposts of the mission, he looked so much like an Indian that he would have been killed if he had not been able to prove himself to be a Christian (Gumilla [1745] 1954, 192).

By telling a multitude of anecdotes, Gumilla presents the missionary work of the Jesuits as a network that allows for pushing the frontier a little further every time, both metaphorically and literally. The Jesuits appear therefore as frontiersmen, as "mediators" between two worlds, that is, the civilized world and the New World that is still waiting to be civilized, so that the New World may become part of the paradise that the Jesuits were establishing on earth. This slow but steady process manifests itself in the dialogue between Gumilla and his priest collaborators and colleagues on the one side, and the Indians on the other. While describing rituals dealing with death, he tells one anecdote that illustrates the ways in which ideas and concepts were negotiated between the missionaries and the natives: Indians would bury their dead in the house where the family of the dead lived, so that the whole family had to move after each burial because they were afraid of the return of the dead. Instead of indoctrinating European and Christian ideas, Gumilla reports how a priest succeeded in changing this ritual by reasoning with the Indians, so that they might recognize their error by experience:

> "Tell me, where did death take the soul of the dead?" The Indian answered that death took the soul around the corner, indicating an angle of the house. "Alas, – answered the priest very seriously – if this is the path of the death, the death would not recognize the path if you took away some of the leaves and put some new ones. So, death will pass in a greater distance." "That's true – said the Indians who heard this –, the priest said this very well; and we, simple ones that we are, tire ourselves making new houses every day" ("'Dime, por dónde se llevó la muerte el alma del difunto?' El indio respondió que por aquella esquina, señalando un ángulo de la casa. 'Pues, bobo, – replicó el padre con mayor seriedad –, si ése es el camino de la muerte, con quitar esa poca hoja de palma y poner otra nueva desconocerá el camino y pasará de largo la muerte.' 'Es verdad – dijeron otros indios que estaban oyendo –, dice muy bien el padre; y nosotros, bobos, nos cansamos haciendo casas nuevas cada día'" [Gumilla (1745) 1954, 174]).

This anecdote serves as an exemplary case of the missionaries' use of the value systems of the Indians in order to facilitate communication.

Even if this case seems to illustrate a dialogue with one-sided interests, the idea of mutual learning in a process of empathy becomes more evident in other anecdotes, for example, when Gumilla tries to explain to the Indians that the eclipse of the moon does not mean the death of the moon. He demonstrates what happens during the lunar eclipse using a mirror, a candle, and an orange (Gumilla [1745] 1954, 459). In this way, Gumilla transfers astronomical knowledge that helps to remedy fear caused by ignorance. On the other hand, Gumilla admits his own ignorance as a foreigner in this new world. To illustrate this, he relates one exemplary case, when some soldiers, another priest, and he himself are awakened in the middle of the night by a frightening sound resembling thunder. They begin to prepare themselves for enemy attack, when the local chief comes to explain that the sound was actually funeral music and dances. Gumilla admits, at this moment, that being afraid was ridiculous and a result of his ignorance, and was therefore his own fault (see 166–7). He then goes on to describe the instruments, dances, and ceremonies of the funeral in an ethnographic mode. But it is obvious that he is concerned not only with the transmission of new anthropological knowledge and the necessity of extending his description of the other world beyond external observations, but also of understanding it from the inside.

Gumilla's empathic vision of the New World becomes more evident when we compare his account with a contemporary one by Juan Magnin, a Jesuit of Swiss origin working in the missions of the Mainas during the same period. Both men described their work along similar lines by defining it against the prevailing historical model of the day. Gumilla presented his text as a collection of minor facts that could not compete with a full history, but that nevertheless would allow for the transmittal of useful knowledge (Gumilla [1745] 1954, 30). Magnin also presented his book as a "small description of customs of simple and uncivilized nations" ("pequeña descripción de costumbres de naciones sencillas e incultas" [Magnin (1771) 1998, 127]), or a history of the common people, and not as a history of monarchs and kingdoms:

> Otherwise, it doesn't deal with the big history of great monarchs and powerful kingdoms, but just with a small description of customs of simple and uneducated nations, and, in a word, uncivilized Indians, born and raised as animals in the middle of dense forests and dark jungles ("Por lo demás no se trata aquí de una gran historia de grandes monarcas y poderosos reinos

> sino solamente de una pequeña descripción de costumbres de naciones sencillas e incultas y, para decirlo en una palabra, de indios no civilizados, nacidos y educados como animales en medio de los densos bosques y oscura selva" [Magnin (1771) 1998, 127]).

The difference between Gumilla and Magnin lies not in the conception of Indians as barbarians, which was also present in Gumilla's text, although in a rudimentary way, but in the underlying deception about the minimal gain in light of the enormous effort of missionary work. This becomes evident in Magnin's explanation of the surname "hunters of souls" ("cazadores de almas") for the priests:

> Authentic hunters of souls! Because, if missionaries have sometimes deserved to be called by this name, never were they more aptly called in this way than in these regions. In fact, taking risks in forests and brambles, with hardly a guide, wandering in mud and swamps for five, eight, ten days like people who are lost in a desert without seeing anything but birds, tigers and similar animals, carrying their masato liquor and yuka flour on their shoulders ("[¡]Auténticos cazadores de almas! Porque si los misioneros han merecido a veces este nombre, nunca lo fueron con tanta razón como en estas comarcas. En efecto, el arriesgarse así por bosques y espinos con tan débil escolta, andando en el fango y los pantanos, cinco, ocho, diez días como gente extraviada en un desierto, sin ver otra cosa que aves, tigres y animales semejantes, llevando ellos mismos en sus espaldas su masato y su harina de yuca" [Magnin (1771) 1998, 196]).

Magnin's jungle is a hostile environment that causes suffering to human beings who inhabit it. There is no beauty in the descriptions of nature as in Gumilla, nor enthusiasm for the novelty of the information delivered. For example, in his treatment of crocodiles, Magnin gives just a brief description: "The alligator or the crocodile is the enemy of the lagoons and the rivers. Its form and corpulence are well known and make it misshapen, as do its scales, its fangs, feet and hands and its being amphibian at home on land and in water" ("El lagarto o cocodrilo es el enemigo de las lagunas y ríos. Conocida es su hechura y corpulencia que los hay disformes, como así mismo sus escamas, colmillos, pies y manos y el ser anfibios de tierra y agua" [(1771) 1998, 175]).

On the contrary, Gumilla's description is vivid and creates an image of the beast:

> It is the embodiment of ferocity itself and the awful miscarriage of the worst monstruosity, horror of every living thing; so formidable, that if ever the caiman were to see itself in a mirror, it would flee trembling in fear from itself. Not even the most lively fantasy could imagine a more accurate picture of the demon than by painting the caiman with all of its features. This wild, warty snout, all black and made of hard bones, with jawbones that I measured to be four palms long [...]; this labyrinth of grinders, with identical rows of teeth above and below [...]; those eyes bulging from the skull, perspicacious and malicious, with such cunning, that when the corpulent beast is completely submerged, it needs only to raise the top of its eyes from the water to take in everything without being seen ("El es la ferocidad misma y el aborto tosco de la mayor monstruosidad, horror de todo viviente; tan formidable, que si el caimán se mirara en un espejo, huyera temblando de sí mismo. No puede idear la más viva fantasía una pintura más propia del demonio que retratándole con todas sus señales. Aquella trompa feroz yberrugosa, toda negra y de duro hueso, con quijadas, que las he medido, de cuatro palmos [...]; aquel labirinto de muelas, duplicadas las filas arriba y abajo [...]; aquellos ojos, resaltados del casco, perspicaces y maliciosos, con tal maña, que sumida toda la corpulenta bestia del agua, saca únicamente la superficie de ellos para registrarlo todo sin ser visto" [Gumilla (1745) 1954, 420]).

Once again Gumilla uses mise en scène in order to present a phenomenon of the New World that will cause wonder, and invites the reader to identify with the narrator. Magnin, on the contrary, always keeps a certain rhetorical distance from his reader, which may be attributed to the fact that, as a friend of Charles de La Condamine, member of the first Spanish scientific expedition to Ecuador, and later a correspondent of the Académie Française in Paris, he considered himself to be a scientist. This distancing on the part of Magnin might also be due to personal difficulties in overcoming the culture shock of being in the New World. The dialogue that is an important and vivid rhetorical device in Gumilla's report is lacking in the account of Magnin, whose commentary on language is revealing in this regard:

> The variety and the complexity of the languages of the country is a further cause of affliction. What can a lone missionary do with people he doesn't understand and who don't understand him and to whom he can't even make his most urgent needs understood through gestures, trying in vain to make them evident ("La variedad y la complejidad de las lenguas del país es

otra causa de aflicción. Qué puede hacer un misionero solo, con gente a la que no entiende y que no le entienden y a quien no puede ni siquiera hacer comprender por señas sus necesidades más urgentes y que trata en vano de volverlas evidentes" [Magnin (1771) 1998, 259]).

This complaint shows the despair and isolation of the European, in a new world that remains strange to him. The wider reliance upon description might therefore also be due to the fact that the narrator cannot communicate or ask questions, so that his narrative is based on pure observation from the outside.

A comparison of these two texts makes clear that there are a certain number of elements that commonly appear as parts of histories and descriptions of the time, but that the narration itself is highly individualized. Both authors construct continuity in the history of the Jesuit missions by mentioning the work and experiences of other priests, but even at this crucial point of the construction of one's own identity as a community, the two texts differ considerably; where Gumilla invokes anecdotes so that the other priests and their work are present and that the net of their missionary work is filled with life, Magnin closes his account with a chapter on the priests who had died as martyrs. In the last paragraph, he praises the glory of those missions where the Jesuits carried the cross while enduring a multitude of sufferings.

Gumilla, on the contrary, ends his narrative with practical advice for new missionaries, those who would replace the Jesuits, based on his own experience. He explains the native ceremonies of reception using anecdotes, provides a translation of the first questions that will be asked of the missionaries and gives examples of arguments used to convince Indians to accept a new missionary among them, as well as the gifts the missionary should offer (Gumilla [1745] 1954: 241ff.). He concludes his history by giving eighteen maxims that the missionary should respect, along with reflections on the spiritual rewards that might encourage him to endure the difficulties of this hard but fascinating life in the wilderness. So it is possible to conclude that this text constitutes an invitation to missionary work with a prospective perspective.

Manuel Uriarte, *Diario de un Misionero de Maynas*

Manuel Uriarte (1720–1790) arrived in America from Granada, Spain, in 1742. Upon completion of his studies in Quito, he worked as a teacher before he was being sent to the missions of Maynas in 1750, where he stayed till the expulsion of the Jesuits. From 1771 to 1773, he reconstructed his diaries with the help of a short summary that he had succeeded in hiding during the long trip to Ravenna, Italy. Uriarte's style and tone differ significantly from those of Gumilla's text. First of all, it is striking that there are very few detailed descriptions of nature, botanical phenomena, or anthropological specimens. This type of information is instead embedded in the narration of episodes or in the descriptions of daily life, so that it might be viewed as part of a viable whole. This indicates that the author himself feels personally engaged in the life of the missions and of the Indians. The enumeration of episodes might, however, also be due to the retrospective nature of the narrative, in which events related within a context may have been easier to remember as life experiences, as opposed to the initial impressions that miraculous nature in the New World made upon those whose sojourns took place over brief spans of time. This is to be expected, considering that they had become part of the author's daily routine over the course of eighteen years. Along with this, there is also no need for Uriarte to transmit detailed information necessary for the survival of future missionaries, as the Jesuits had been expelled at the time he was rewriting his diaries, but rather a need to preserve the memory of the Jesuits' work.

Nature is presented as dangerous and wonderful at the same time in Uriarte's text. When the author narrates his journey to the river Nanai, this double signification becomes evident in the description of nature:

> Via Hayai, avoiding the dangers of the Marañon, I arrived in Nanai, where it is deep, but not very wide. And I am telling you that said Maranon branched off at the Itayai and flowed into the Nanai, a considerable arm, [...] so that you will see how enormous this king of the rivers is. To say nothing of the scrublands over here that fill when it floods [...]. As the Nanai flows through such flat terrain, it makes immense turns and curves, and if you travel during the night, you can see the moon [...], and there are abundant lagoons with fish; and the turtles are extremely large, the water is fresh and the fruit, which you can see on the trees from the water, is abundant and varied, and I saw one acorn-like fruit that I didn't dare try because the Indians didn't eat them. They looked for elevated places to sleep because of the tigers, and sometimes they put their hammocks in the tree tops above the water. They trapped wild boar, parakeets, jaguars, and small turtles. You will also find cacao, and something whiter, that resembles it, but if the

Indians don't hurry to pick it once it is ripe, the monkeys will finish it off. It was a sight that made you praise God to see so many different species of those monkeys playing, flying like kites through the trees, and to hear so many songs of different birds, to see ducks and white swallows like canaries that flew in formation from one side of the river to the other ("Por Hayai, evitando los peligros del Marañon, salí a Nanai, que es profundísimo, mas no muy ancho. Y advierto que dicho Marañon después ha roto por Itayai y echó al Nanai un brazo condiserable [...] para que se vea qué monstruo es este rey de los ríos. Y no digo nada de los montes que llena por aquí con sus inundaciones [...]. [C]omo el Nanai corre por tan llano terreno, hace inmensos rodeos y vueltas y caminando de noche se ve a la luna [...], y hay abundantes lagunas de pescados; y las charapas son grandísimas, y el agua fresca, las frutas diversas y regladas, que se ven en los árboles dentro del agua, y vi una como bellota que no me atrevi a probar porque no comían los indios. Buscaban para dormir algunos sitios altos, por los tigres, y a veces ponían sus hamacas en lo alto de los árboles sobre el agua. Cogieron puercos, pericos, ligeros, charapillas. Y hay también cacao, y otro que se parece, más blanco, pero si no se dan prisa los indios al madurar, ya los monos lo acaban. Era cosa de alabar a Dios ver tanta especie de éstos jugando como volatines por los árboles, y oír tantos cantos de pájaros diferentes, ver patos y golondrinas blancas, como canarios, que hacían sus cursos de una vuelta a otras del río" [Uriarte (1771) 1986, 190]).

This is one of the rare examples wherein Uriarte describes the abundance and variety of nature – and it is telling that his description is concentrated on survival rather than on aesthetics. Uriarte is much more preoccupied with people than with descriptions of the environment. While there is no formal definition of the Indian, the dichotomy between the Christianized Indian and the still-wild one is a repeating motif throughout his diary. When referring to Indians living in the missions, he always calls them "my Indians," and insists that there exists between them a cordial, sort of father-child relationship; he gives as an example the welcome extended to him by the Indians when he returns from a journey:

The reception was delightful: we all sat down on large palm leaves that look like small planks with five fingers. They continuously tapped me on the shoulder and said to the whole community: Rai qué? (Have you come?), and I answered each: rayé (I have come); then they plied us with *pates* [gourds] with some two liters of their corn spirits ("Fué cosa gustosa el

> recibimiento: todos nos sentamos en unos tarapotos largos, como tablilas de cinco dedos, y me iban tocando el hombro, y a toda la comitiva, diciendo: Rai qué? (Has venido?), y a cada uno respondía: rayé (He venido); luego nos llenaron de *pates* [calabazas] de a dos azumbres, con su chicha" [Uriarte (1771) 1986, 108]).

One can feel the joy that Uriarte must have experienced at being received as a member of the community. This is also an opportunity to describe the way the reception of a traveller is organized within the community. His intimate knowledge of the rituals is strengthened by his linguistic performance in adding whole sentences in the local language followed by his translation into Spanish. This is how he is painting the scene, letting the participants speak for themselves.

Nevertheless, the dangers of treachery are also present in the missions. Uriarte relates how he fell victim to an ambush by Indians who were afraid of being punished for quarrelling with another group. The narration here is very vivid, almost like the sequence of a film. Uriarte describes the situation, the comings and goings of the persons involved, quoting them directly, building suspense up to the moment when he attempted to translate in order to bring the groups together and the assailant hit him with an axe. Although he was seriously injured, so much so that he had to be treated in Quito afterwards and suffered from headaches for the rest of his life, Uriarte did not grow bitter against the Indians. This episode clearly shows that Uriarte usually describes his own personal experiences. The transmission of his knowledge passes through experiences that serve as examples, and not through abstractions and distant accounts.

In spite of his love for the Indians, the dichotomy of the noble savage and the barbarian is also present in Uriarte's description, though less so than in Gumilla's text. The author, as well as the Christianized Indians, differentiate between the civilized and the savage Indians by calling the latter *brujos* ("magicians") – as we see in the rare ethnographic descriptions we find in the diary, where the Otherness of those Indians living in remote parts is striking because of the author's long experience of living with Indians:

> How slovenly and lazy is this nation of Mayorunas, and since they only eat tree seeds or people [...]; since their appearance is awful, because from childhood on, they pierce the skin around their lips, nostrils, arms and cheeks, and they adorn themselves with feathers and small sticks so that

they look like hedgehogs. But now, thank God, through comunication with the missionaries, they have been leaving behind such brutal customs and have even started cultivating sweet corn, plantains and manioc ("[Q]ué dejada y perezosa es esta nación de mayorunas, y cómo sólo comen pepitas de árboles o gente [...]; cómo su aspecto es terrible, porque desde niños se agujerean alrededor de los labios, narices, brazos y mejillas, y se meten por gala plumas y palillos que parecen erizos. Pues ahora, gracias a Dios, con la comunicación de los misioneros, iban dejando esas brutalidades, y hasta iban haciendo chagras de maíz, plátano y yuca" [Uriarte (1771) 1986, 466]).

The characteristics of the "savage barbarian" are all present in the description of the Indians living in the forest: they are naked, nomads, and often cannibals; any changes in their lives are due to the missionary work of the Jesuits.

The civilized regions dominate Uriarte's discourse, so that the savage Indians appear rather rarely and always as a threat to the domesticated Indians or the settlements. This Christianized world in the forests becomes visible in his descriptions of the multitude of travels and visits of various missionaries, as a part of the network of missionaries from Quito to the remotest Jesuit settlement. Besides this macrostructure, so to speak, Uriarte also constructs a microcosm through his descriptions of the church as the heart of every mission, the decorations such as paintings and carvings often fabricated by priests or Indians themselves (see Uriate [1771] 1986, 421), and other religious utensils like crosses and silver candelabras sent by the headquarters in Quito (see 285):

The goodhearted H. Pedro arrived with his Christians from Santa Bárbara and some from Santa María. I found much solace in learning that they were all doing well in the two villages. Being a good architect, the above mentioned brother helped me attach two cedar retablos to the two sides of the presbytery, and arranging the beautiful custom made paintings that Father Bizoqui brought from Quito, the altars were greatly improved, with their tables, altar hangings, benches and candelabras, etc. ("Vino el buen H. Pedro con sus cristianos de Santa Bárbara y algunos de Santa María, con quienes me consolé mucho por saber se mantenían todos con salud de los dos pueblos. Ayudóme dicho Hermano, que es buen arquitecto, a poner abajo, en los dos lados del presbiterio, los dos retablos de cedro qe él había hecho, y acomodando los bellos cuadros, que dejó el P. Bizoqui a medida, traídos de Quito, quedaron perfeccionados los altares, con sus mesas, frontales, banquetas, candeleros, etc." [450]).

The intensive work in the missions that transforms wilderness into civilization is based, in Uriarte's work, as well as in the case of Gumilla's, on understanding and mutual learning. On the one hand, the misfortune of one Indian can serve as an example to the others, allowing them to conclude for themselves that the changing of certain habits would be favourable to them, as in the case of the Indian who gets drunk regularly and beats his wife. Although this man promises to change his life, he doesn't, and when he dies in a tiger trap, his death is interpreted as a punishment sent by God, causing the inhabitants of the village to promise never to get drunk again.[8] On the other hand, Uriarte learns how to fish like the Indians, and transmits this knowledge through an exact description of the process as well as of the construction of various models of fishing nets (see 379).

Besides this type of learning, on the level of an exchange of ideas and practices between the Indians and the missionary, there exists the transfer of knowledge by the missionary network: Uriarte mentions that having read Gumilla's text, he learned about the gathering of turtle eggs in order to assure provisions (see 177). He himself provides a catalogue of advice for new missionaries who will come to the Amazon regions; for example, there is rule number seven: "[B]e very friendly and patient with the Indians, never raise your hand against them, unless the need is very great, and even then, do it sparingly with the elder ones; and never with the young ones" ("[S]er muy amable y paciente con los indios, nunca castigarlos por su mano, ni sin mucha necesidad, y eso poco con los antiguos; con los nuevos, nada"), and rule number eleven: "Taking some pains to learn the language inga [*sic*] and the characteristics of the people, which can be best achieved through listening and speaking practice, even if one makes mistakes" ("[A]plicarse aprender la lengua inga [*sic*] y particulares del pueblo, lo que más se consigue con el ejercicio de oír y hablar, aunque sea errando" [223–4]). He advises the superiors of the Jesuit missions that the choice of missionaries suited to this important and delicate work should be considered carefully, "so that the Superiors will think carefully about those whom they send to the Missions" ("para que los Superiores miren bien a quiénes envían a las Misiones" [332]).

In the third part of his four-part diaries, Uriarte starts making comments in brackets that represent his own retrospective view on his narration of the events during his stay in the Amazon region. This is also the case in the bits of advice he is eager to offer for new missionaries, if the Jesuit order were ever to be re-established:

> Here is another warning that I would like the Superiors to consider, if ever the Company were to be reestablished and they were to go to Mainas again: don't separate the people from the missionaries who diligently apply themselves to learning the language until they know it well, and before calling them back, give them a partner for a few years, as they used to do in other Missions; it is assumed that they enjoy full confidence and that both they and the Indians are happy ("Y esta es otra advertencia que deseo que tengan los Superiores, si vuelve otra vez la Compañía a instituirse, y vayan a Mainas: no apartar de los pueblos los Misioneros que con gusto se aplican a aprender la lengua hasta que la sepan bien, y antes de sacado, ponerle el compañero un par de años, como se hacía en otras Misiones; se supone, siendo de confianza y estando contentos ellos y los indios" [353]).

The announcement of the expulsion of the Jesuits, written between the lines, and the consequences (see 473) of this expulsion, are more explicit in the fourth and last part of the diaries, where Uriarte describes the preparations for leaving, and the handing over of the missions to Franciscan priests ("we are not worthy to succeed the Jesuits" ["no somos dignos de suceder a los jesuítas" (505)]), who feel helpless in face of this giant task.

Another important aspect of the expulsion discussed in the fourth part of the diaries is the defence of the Jesuits against the accusations brought forward against the Company, regarding, in particular, the accumulation of wealth by the Jesuit order. After having handed in an inventory of the churches, in which they appear rather poor (see 509–11), the difference between the outside image of the Jesuits and their daily life becomes obvious in a dialogue between Uriarte and another priest: "Alluding to the few things that they saw in the house, the good clergy men said: [']And where are the rich ornaments that they told you that they had acquired in Portugal? These are the riches we were often told they had in the Mission[']" ("Los buenos clérigos, unos decían, aludiendo a las pocas cosas que veían en la casa: [']Y dónde están las ricas alhajas que nos decían tenían Vs. Rs. Adquiridas en Portugal? Estas son las riquezas que tanto nos decían tenían en la Misión[']" [513]),

And further on:

> It was engrained in the minds of the clergy to never think of acquiring personal gain in the Mission. [...]
>
> – And what do I gain from all this work?, he would say.
>
> – Well, sir, this is what it means to be a missionary in Mainas; God will pay you a hundred times over if you work for his Majesty.
>
> – Thus went his deliberations: And this is what Your Reverences spent so much time considering? What did they really possess? Mosquitoes, heat, chiggers, bad food; there is nothing else; and the people, so aloof, etc.
>
> ("En lo que inculqué más con el clérigo, fué que no pensase sacar ganancias de la Misión. [...].
>
> – Y qué saco yo de tanto trabajo?, decía.
>
> – Pues, señor, esto es ser misionero de Mainas; dios le pagará cien doblado, si trabaja usted por su Majestad.
>
> – Aquí sus ponderaciones: Y esto era lo que tanto ponderaban de Vs. Rs. [Vuestras Reverencias] Que tenían tanto? Mosquitos, calor, niguas, mala comida; ho hay otra cosa; y la gente, tan esquiva, etc." [524]).

When Uriarte finally has to leave his mission, his narration becomes almost pathetic, which reveals the deep sorrow he feels when he is obliged to leave behind his beloved Indians. He confesses to the reader that even at the death of his parents, he did not feel this deep a pain, nor did he weep as he did on his expulsion from his home (527). In this way, his description of the departure turns almost into an ode:

> I extended my gaze up the river as far as I could, and with my eyes bathed in tears, I pulled myself away: Farewell, Napo, where I took my first steps in missionary work; and why didn't you leave me buried on your shores during the rebellions? Or drowned in your waters during the shipwrecks of Rumituñisca and San Miguel? Oh, a thousand times blessed Padre Francisco Real, you who deserved, to leave behind to the violence of the machetes that killed your body as a permanent pillar of this Mission! Farewell, my treasures, more than mines of gold, the tributes that await me above! Farewell, my sons and heirs, Aguaricos, Quajoyas, Uncuyés Ancuteres, Payaguas, Tirirés! I can do nothing but consider my great sins because of which I have to leave you and, who knows, may never see you again. Oh, Most Holy Name of Jesus, my first nation! Oh, Name of Maria, my second! Oh, San Luis Gozanga, my third! Oh, San Francisco de Icaguates, my fourth! Oh, San Miguel, my church and my fifth! Oh, San Pedro de

Payaguas, my sixth!, intervene with all the Holy Guardian Angels in favour of these poor helpless creatures, more than ever ("Extendía cuanto podia la vista río arriba, y bañados los ojos en lágrimas me desahogaba así: ¡Adiós, Napo, primicias de mi apostolado; ¿y por qué no me dejaste sepultado en tus orillas cunado las rebeliones? ¿O sumergido en tus aguas cuando los naufragios de Rumituñisca y San Miguel? ¡Oh, mil veces dichoso Ven. P. Francisco Real, que mereciste dejar à la violencia de las macanas tu mismo cuerpo por firme columna de la Misión! ¡Adiós, riquezas mias, más que las minas de oro que arriba tributas! ¡Adiós, mis hijos primogénitos, aguaricos, quajoyas, uncuyés, ancuteres, payaguas, tiriríes! No tengo más que considerar mis grandes pecados por los que os debo dejar y quizás no os volveré a ver. ¡Oh, Nombre Santísimo de Jésus, mi primer pueblo! ¡Oh, Nombre de María, el segundo! ¡Oh, San Luis Gonzaga, el tercero! !Oh, San Francisco de Icaguates, el cuarto! !Oh, San Miguel, mi anejo, y el quinto! !Oh, San Pedro de Payaguas, el sexton!, interceded con todos los Santos Angeles Custodios or esos pobres desamparados, más que nunca" [528–9]).

For Uriarte, the Amazon region was his homeland, and even if he seemed to be imperturbable in all his adventures, the tenderness he felt for "his Indians" was perceptible throughout his entire narration. The episodic structure of his narrative could therefore also be due to his intense nostalgia for his home and the world from which he was expelled. The lack of detailed description that one can observe in comparison with Gumilla might be explained by his familiarity with this new world that had become his home during the eighteen years he had lived there, so that, when he arrived in the Mediterranean region, he was reminded of the Marañon (589). In this way, in the retrospective on the one hand, but also in the longing for a lost home on the other hand, he stresses the missionary network and its sentimental boundaries.

Conclusion

These two Jesuit accounts reflect a certain colonial discourse that aims at establishing new settlements, and thus at civilizing the people and the land in order to make each settlement a profitable colony. Mary-Elizabeth Reeves describes the Spanish colonial expansion as a three-part process: "[*E*]*ntradas* (expeditions), the establishment of towns and *encomiendas* (grants of indigenous tribute-payers) pertaining to them, and finally, the establishment of missions along major rivers" (Reeves

1994, 114). She emphasizes that the aim of the missionary work of the Jesuits was the development of self-sufficient settlements, so that the Indians could live in a non-nomadic way. The civilizing process via sedentary settlements is extended into a Christianizing one as the regular instruction and control by the missionary is assured, so that the missionary discourse gains the upper hand when an establishment is successful (see 118 and 124). In the case of the two examples I have discussed, the missionary discourse turns into an intercultural one, as the missionaries go beyond culture shock, and even the status of a comparative approach, to eventually achieve an empathic perspective. This latter perspective is based on mutual learning and reference to both cultural code systems, so that the missionaries and Indians will assimilate one another's values.

This gradual approach from both sides to a mutual understanding manifests itself in the anecdotes that interrupt the official discourse – the missionary and the colonial one. For Stephen Greenblatt, anecdotes represent the telling of the history of the common people (Greenblatt 1991, 2). In this context, the differentiation that Elizabeth Wright makes between "to see" and "to look" is rather interesting: "There is a difference between (conscious) seeing and (unconscious) looking. To see concerns the image which gives us pleasure: to look has a relation to the object which is lacking. This search produces anxiety instead of pleasure, because the real object is unrepresentable. It cannot be represented by an image, since it is what is lacking in the image" (Wright 1999, 61).

Following her reflections, the Jesuit accounts seem to use both the mise en scène and the "seeing" (Balme 2001), the procedures and techniques that reflect the encounter with the Other in a colonial context; but at the same time the anecdotes permit a glimpse at the "looking" as well. Elena Altuna described these pieces of the narration as "the edges of testimony" ("franjas testimoniales" [Altuna 2002, 25]). The multitude of anecdotes in both texts allows us to consider Gumilla and Uriarte as missionaries who seem to be examples of the "intercultural mediators" who cross borders and yet report back to their culture of origin. As a consequence, they live in between the two worlds which they relate to each other. Sáinz Ollero called them "citizens of nowhere" ("ciudadanos de ninguna parte" [Sáinz Ollero 1995, 98]), and as "straddling both worlds" ("a caballo entre dos mundos" [98]). The Spanish expression seems to be more appropriate in its idiomatic image than the English translation, as the missionaries do not find themselves between two positions, rather they come and go, as travellers, between two worlds.

NOTES

1 Sáinz Ollero writes: "This defense of the Indian and the feelings of empathy allow us, in my understanding, to consider the works of the Jesuits of this period as real predecessors of contemporary anthropological thinking. Independently of the testimonial worth that the precious 'noticias' contain about indigenous groups that have disappeared today or are in the process of disappearing, the works of the Jesuit missionaries of the 18th century in Paraguay express a 'modern anthropological sensibility' at the moment of discovering the indigenous groups with whom they were in contact" (Esta defensa del indio y esos sentimientos muy claros de empatía son los que hacen, a mi juicio, que podamos inscribir a las obras jesuitas de este periodo como verdaderos antecedentes del pensamiento antropológico actual. Independientemente del valor testimonial que poseen al ofrecernos noticias preciosas sobre grupos indígenas hoy desaparecidos o inmersos en procesos de desaparición, las obras de los misioneros jesuitas del siglo XVIII en el Paraguay manifiestan una "sensibilidad antropologica moderna" a la hora de describir a los grupos indígenas con los que estuvieron en contacto [Sáinz Ollero 1995, 95–6]).

2 See Stephen Greenblatt, and also Enrique Pupo Walker who speaks of "cuentecillos," in Stolley 1996, 358.

3 In chapter 9, entitled "Daños gravissimos de las misiones que causan las Armadas de los barbaros Indios Caribes, que suben de la Costa del Mar," Gumilla refers to repeated attacks in the years 1684–1693 that destroyed most missionary stations.

4 The title of the first edition (1741) is slightly changed for the second one (1745). To the original title *El Orinoco ilustrado* is added "y defendido."

5 "This notion of theatricality designates a particularly Western style of thought which ultimately was brought to bear on most of the colonized world. Taking Said's use of the term one step further, we can postulate that theatricalization and colonialism are related phenomena and that theatricalization is, as Said suggests, closely connected with containment and circumscription, the essential perceptual prerequisites for power and control" (Balme 2001, 228).

6 "Tomemos aquí nuestros asientos, y a todo placer, y sin dudar un paso, vamos registrando con la vista terrenos poblados de gentiles y de cristianos nuevos, tantos cuantos no pudiéramos visitar en muchas semanas de camino" (Gumilla [1745] 1954, 201).

7 "The discourse of Orientalism, according to Said, 'theatricalizes' the East in the sense that it reduces and defines it, rendering it observable as though the East or Orient were a stage on which the basically finite set of dramatic figures peopling the Orient made their exits and entrances for the delectation and edification of the Western beholder. This notion of theatricality designates a particularly Western style of thought which ultimately was brought to bear on most of the colonized world. Taking Said's use of the term one step further, we can postulate that theatricalization and colonialism are related phenomena and that theatricalization is, as Said suggests, closely connected with containment and circumscription, the essential perceptual prerequisites for power and control" (Balme 2001, 227–8).

8 "[I] told them that God is just and punishes the sinners; and that I had confidence in his Majesty, and if I had time [...] I would really do repentant acts. All of the people were full of admiration for the divine judgment which was more useful for the changing of some of them than a lot of instructive talking that I could give them. While drinking they would say 'we are not getting drunk, so that the devil will not catch us, as he did with Juanico, Amaonos [ethnic group]'" ("[D]iciendoles que Dios era justo y catigaba a los pecadores; mas que confiaba en Su Majestad que si tuvo tiempo [...] haría actos de contrición verdadera. Todo el pueblo quedó admirado de este juicio divino, y sirvió más para la enmienda de algunos que muchas pláticas que les pudiera hacer. En sus bebidas decían: 'No nos emborrachemos, para que el diablo no nos coja, como al Juanico, amaono'" [Uriarte (1771) 1986, 334–5]).

BIBLIOGRAPHY

Altuna, Elena. 2002. *El Discurso colonialista de los caminantes. Siglos XVII–XVIII.* Berkeley: Latinoamericana Editores / Centro de Estudios Literarios Antonio Cornejo Polar.

Balme, Christopher. 2001. "Metaphors of Spectacle. Theatricality, Perception and Performative Encounters in the Pacific." In *Wahrnehmung und Medialität*, eds. Erika Fischer-Lichte, Christian Horn, Sandra Umathum, and Matthias Warstat, 215–31. Tübingen: Francke.

Bravo, Michael T. 1999. "Ethnographic Navigation and the Geographic Gift." In *Geography and Enlightenment*, eds. David N. Livingstone and Charles W. J. Withers, 199–235. Chicago: University of Chicago Press.

Cipolletti, María Susana. 2001. "Fruto de la melancolía, restos del naufraio: el Alto Amazonas en los escritos de los jesuitas expulsos." In *Los jesuitas españoles expulsos. Su imagen y su contribución al saber sobre el mundo hispánico en la Europa del siglo XVIII*, ed. Manfred Tietz, 237–63. Frankfurt: Vervuert.

Ferrer Benimeli, José A. 2001. "La expulsión de los jesuitas de las reducciones del Paraguay." In *Los jesuitas españoles expulsos. Su imagen y su contribución al saber sobre el mundo hispánico en la Europa del siglo XVIII*, ed. Manfred Tietz, 295–321. Frankfurt: Vervuert.

Figueroa, Francisco de, Cristobal de Acuna et al. 1986. *Informes de Jesuitas en el Amazonas 1660–1684.* Iquitos: IIAP/CETA.

Greenblatt, Stephen. 1991. *Marvelous Possessions: The Wonder of the New World.* Oxford: Clarendon Press.

Gumilla, Joseph. [1745] 1954. *El Orinoco ilustrado, y defendido, Historia natural, civil, y geographica de este gran río y de sus caudalosas vertientes*, ed. Constantino Bayle, SJ. Reprint, Madrid: Aguilar.

Magnin, Juan. [1741] 1998. *Descripción de la provincial y misiones de Mainas en el Reino de Quito*, eds. Julián G. Bravo, SJ, and Octavio Latorre. Reprint, Quito: Biblioteca Ecuatoriana Aurelio Espinosa Pólit / Sociedad Históricas y Geográficas.

Pasquali, Adrien. 1994. *Le tour des horizons. Critique et récits de voyage.* Paris: Klincksieck.

Reeves, Mary-Elizabeth. 1994. "Regional Interaction in the Western Amazon: The Early Colonial Encounter and the Jesuit Years: 1538–1767." *Ethnohistory* 41 (1): 106–38.

Sáinz Ollero, Hector. 1995. "Comprensión del otro y asimilación del otro. El reto de los chaquños y el problema de la resistencia indígena en los textos jesuitas del siglo XVIII." In *Visión de los Otros y Visión de Sí Mismos. ¿Descubrimiento o invención entre el Nuevo Mundo y el Viejo?*, eds. Fermín del Pino and Carlos Lázaro: 89–105. Madrid: Consejo Superior de Investigaciones científicas.

Santos, Ángel. 1992. *Los jesuitas en América.* Madrid: Mapfre.

Solano, Francisco, and Pilar Ponce, eds. 1988. *Cuestionarios para la formación de las Relaciones geográficas de Indias Siglos XVI/XIX.* Madrid: CSIC.

Stolley, Karen. 1996. "The 18th century: narrative forms, scholarship, and learning." In *The Cambridge History of Latin American Literature*, eds. Roberto González Echevarria and Enrique Pupo-Walker, vol. 1, ch. 10. Cambridge: Cambridge University Press.

Uriarte, Manuel J., SJ. [1771] 1986. *Diario de un misionero de Maynas.* Reprint, Iquitos: IIAP / CETA.

Vitar, Beatriz. 1995. "Mansos y salvajes. Imágenes chaqueñas en el discurso colonial." In *Visión de los Otros y Visión de Sí Mismos. ¿Descubrimiento o invención entre el Nuevo Mundo y el Viejo?*, eds. Fermín del Pino and Carlos Lázaro, 107–26. Madrid: Consejo Superior de Investigaciones científicas.

Wright, Elizabeth. 1999. *Speaking Desires can be Dangerous: The Poetics of the Unconscious.* Stafford, Australia: Polity Press.

chapter ten

East from Eden: Domesticating Exile in Jesuit Accounts of Their 1767 Expulsion from Spanish America[1]

KAREN STOLLEY

In the historical imaginary of Spain and Spanish America, 1767 is a date that represents a turning point – like 1588, or 1898, or even 1492 – a moment when history swerved from its path to follow a new trajectory. The tangled web of political, economic, and ecclesiastical factors that led to the expulsion of the Jesuits – first from Portugal in 1759, then from France in 1764, and finally from Spain and its territories in 1767 – is far too complex to address adequately in these pages. Among those factors, however, one might include concern in Spain about Jesuit ultramontanism, Bourbon regalist reforms aimed at centralizing political and economic power, and rivalries with Jansenists and others leading to charges of Jesuit laxity in moral and theological matters. In the Americas, there was increasing resentment over wealthy Jesuit missions and the Jesuits' insistence on managing those missions without interference from local authorities.[2] Popular riots in Madrid in March of 1766 – known as the Motín de Esquilache – further exacerbated the situation. The riots were ostensibly set off by a decree issued by the much-reviled Italian minister Leopoldo de Grigorio, Marquis of Esquilache, banning the use of long capes and hats. In fact, they reflected a broad range of economic and political complaints. In the ensuing chaos, Esquilache and other foreign ministers were forced from office, but even after order was restored, questions lingered about possible conspiracies by the Jesuits and others against royal sovereignty.[3] The commission of inquiry appointed by Charles III to investigate the riots issued a detailed report, written by Pedro Rodríguez de Campomanes, that "placed the blame squarely on the Jesuits" (Lynch 1989, 282). As Lynch sums it up, "[t]he Jesuits had been too successful for their own good" (282).

Charles III's 1767 expulsion edict makes no reference to any of these factors:

> Motivated by grave causes related to my obligation to maintain my People in subordination, tranquility and justice, as well as other urgent, just and necessary causes that I reserve to my Royal self: [...] I have decided to order removed from all my dominions in Spain and the Indies, and the Philippine Islands and adjacent dominions, all members of the Company [of Jesus], as well as Priests, coadjutors or lay brothers who have made their first vows, and any Novices who wish to follow them ("[E]stimulado de gravísimas causas, relativas a la obligación en que me hallo constituido, de mantener en subordinación, tranquilidad y justicia mis Pueblos, y otras urgentes, justas y necesarias, que reservo en mi Real ánimo: [...] He venido en mandar extrañar de todos mis dominios de España, e Indias, e Islas Filipinas, y además adyecentes a los Regulares de la Compañía, así Sacerdotes, como Coadjutores o Legos que hayan hecho la primera profesión, y a los Novicios que quisieren seguirles" [Díaz-Plaja 1986, 208–9]).

The document does not offer a lengthy narrative of historical cause and effect, as does, for example, the 1492 edict on the expulsion of the Jews. Rather, it emphasizes and legitimizes a deliberative decision-making process. The edict begins by referring to prior consultations with the proper administrative bodies and invokes the sovereign's divine authority to take whatever means necessary to protect his subjects. It then empowers administrators – governors, magistrate, *alcaldes*, military and civilian troops – to carry out the expulsion order. Charles III's reticence in the relatively brief edict is striking. Some historians argue that he originally wished to write a "memoria" explaining in greater detail his reasons for expelling the Jesuits, but decided against it in order not to further incite public sympathy for the order (Vaca de Osma 1997, 192).

If the document does not deal with the "why" of the expulsion, it is obsessive in terms of the "how." An accompanying missive signed by Pedro Pablo Abarca de Bollea, Conde de Aranda, laid out the particulars of the expulsion.[4] Every detail concerning the execution of the expulsion edict is spelled out: the means of transporting the Jesuits from their communities into exile, the amount of luggage they would be permitted to carry, the designated ports of embarkation and destination, the escorts who would accompany the exiles, the amount of the pensions to be allotted to the Jesuits, and the disposition of any holdings left behind (Díaz-Plaja 1986, 209–10).[5] All members of the community were to be accounted for. It is as though the author (or, more probably, authors) were attempting to contain the strong reactions certain to be unleashed by the publication of the expulsion edict by prescribing its contingencies to the letter.

One of the most chilling details of the document would have been the proscription against any sort of written commentary or protest regarding the expulsion: "I expressly prohibit that anyone write, declaim or move either for or against these provisions; rather, I impose silence regarding this material on all my vassals, and I order that those who disobey this order be punished as criminals guilty of high treason" ("Prohibo expresamente que nadie pueda escribir, declamar o conmover con pretexto de estas providencias en pro ni en contra de ellas; antes impongo silencio en esta material a todos mis vasallos, y mando que a los contraventores se les castigue como reos de lesa Majestad" [Díaz-Plaja 1986, 210]).

This proscription may have been due in part to Campomanes's conviction that anonymous writings by the Jesuits had played a key role in the Motín de Esquilache (Cejudo and Egido 1977, 13). In addition, the instructions called for the confiscation of all papers, books, and archives belonging to the exiles[6]:

> Once this has been done, the judicial occupation of archives, all order of papers, common library, private books and desks will be carried out in the company of the father superiors and procurer of the house: distinguishing those which belong to each Jesuit, gathering them in one or more places, and turning the keys over to the judge of the commission ("Hecha la intimación, procederá sucesivamente en compañía de los padres superiores y procurador de la casa a la judicial ocupación de archivos, papeles de toda especie, biblioteca común, libros y escritorios de aposentos: distinguiendo los que pertenecen a cada jesuita, juntándolos en uno o más lugares, y entregándose de las llaves el juez de la comisión" [Rionda Arreguín 1996, 423]).

Thus the 1767 expulsion represents a dilemma for eighteenth-century Jesuit historians of Spanish America. They are faced with an event that can only be inscribed with difficulty in the historical record it had been their life's work to create: first, because the expulsion edict itself expressly prohibits them from writing about it in their personal correspondence or scholarly works, and second, because of the extraordinarily disruptive effect the expulsion had on their lives, health, working conditions, archives, and libraries. This explains why many Spanish American

Jesuit histories end abruptly in 1767, either immediately before or after describing the circumstances of the expulsion, leaving a gap that could only be bridged later, when Jesuits wrote from the relative stability and obscurity of their exiled communities in Italy.[7]

I propose here to look at a number of narrative accounts written by Jesuits caught up in the maelstrom of events, exploring the narrative strategies they used to circumvent or even subvert the expulsion edict in order to tell their untellable tale.[8] Narratives by Francisco Javier Alegre and Carlos Bustamante (on the expulsion from New Spain), Francisco Javier Clavigero and Juan Jacobo Baegert (on the expulsion from Baja California), José Manuel Peramás (on the expulsion from Paraguay), and Manuel Uriarte (on the expulsion from the upper Amazon regions) inscribe the promulgation and execution of the expulsion edict in the historical imaginary of Spain and Spanish America, moving beyond the "how" in ways that implicitly address and challenge the "why."[9]

One of the most compelling accounts is Francisco Javier Alegre's *Historia de la Compañia de Jesús en la Nueva España.*[10] Alegre was part of an important group of Jesuit humanists living in eighteenth-century New Spain. Known for his encyclopedic knowledge and erudition, he has been called "Mexico's first literary critic" (Deck 1976, 1; see also Maneiro and Fabri 1951, 211–46). Alegre had almost finished writing the *Historia* in 1767 but was obliged to leave all of his papers behind and recreate the text later from memory. One of his biographers marvels:

> It is no small praise to note that Alegre, having left behind in Mexico the *Historia* and all the documents used in writing it, and motivated by the insistence of his friends, devoted his leisure time in Bologna to the redaction of a compendium of the history; all were astonished, and with good reason, that it preserved not only the facts, but even dates and many details, with no other assistance than Alegre's stupendous memory ("No es pequeña alabanza de Alegre decir, que habiendo dejado en México la *Historia* y cuantos documentos le sirvieron para escribirla, movido de las instancias de sus amigos, empleó sus ocios en Bolonia en redactar un compendio de ella; admirando todos, con razón, que conservara no solamente los hechos, sino hasta las fechas y muchos pormenores, sin otro auxilio que su estupenda memoria" [Maneiro and Fabri 1951, 11]).

In describing the days before the expulsion order was made public, Alegre creates for his readers a feeling of suspense and impending doom with frequent references to "pliegos misteriosos" and "despachos secretos" referring to the Jesuits (207). Alegre may be attempting, in this way, to counter earlier accusations of Jesuit complicity in spreading pernicious rumors against the crown during the Esquilache uprising. As a narrative strategy, the references to mysterious notes and secret missives serve to highlight the great uncertainty surrounding an outcome which was, perhaps, not entirely unanticipated by the Jesuits, but was nevertheless beyond their control or design. They also suggest that the Jesuits are the victims, rather than the agents, of any plotting.

Once the expulsion order had been made public, the Jesuits' response was, according to Alegre, characterized at all times by resignation, modesty, and meekness (see 14). Indeed, the Jesuits' calm and willing cooperation with royal officials was so striking that it led to speculation about whether they might have been given advance warning of their impending exile, despite the fact that Charles III had issued his edict with elaborate instructions to maintain absolute secrecy in order to coordinate its simultaneous execution throughout his realm (see Rionda Arregúin 1996, 442).[11] In Alegre's account the description of extreme Jesuit humility at times verges on irony. In one telling anecdote Alegre quotes a conversation between a Spanish official and a group of Jesuits who respectfully inquire if his Majesty's orders will allow them time to take communion prior to their forced departure:

> "What?" he replied, astonished. "Are you ready to take communion?" They responded that affronts and temporal concerns should never perturb the spirit of a Christian, and much less that of a member of a religious order, to the degree that one neglected divine matters, the source from which emanates the only solid comfort in times of adversity! ("'Y qué, respondió admirado, estarán para comulgar?' Se le respondió, que las afrentas y los trabajos temporales, nunca debían perturbar tanto el ánimo de un cristiano, y mucho menos de un Religioso, que no le dejasen atender primeramente a las cosas divinas, fuente de donde mana únicamente el sólido consuelo en las adversidades!" [Rionda Arregúin 1996, 209]).

This humble explanation of the role of Christian faith in the faith of adversity stands in marked contrast to the incredulous attitude of the official, although an explicit evaluation of the relative merit of each attitude is left to the reader. In Alegre's history any expressions of protest – tears, lamentations, or questions – are voiced not by the Jesuits themselves but rather by the lay townspeople and the indigenous population who are the reluctant witnesses to their unjust expulsion (see Andrés-Gallego 2000, 161). In a move reminiscent of Las Casas's geographically organized accounts of Spanish abuses in the *Brevísima relación*, Alegre describes how, in one instance, "the natives [...] in the dark of night surrounded the College with furious howls" ("naturales [...] a deshoras de la noche cercaron con furiosos alaridos todo el Colegio") and reiterates this point by describing similar incidents of protest in towns and settlements all over New Spain (see Rionda Arregúin 1996, 453ff.).

Alegre describes the Jesuits' arduous journey to the port of Veracruz, from which they were to embark, as a *via cruces*, a trajectory of pain and humiliation offered up by the Jesuits in sacrifice: "[T]he roads impassable because of continuous rain, days of either burning sun or pernicious showers, uncomfortable lodging made even worse by the number of passengers and infested with bugs that made it impossible even to rest briefly during the night" ("[L]os caminos intransitables por las continuas lluvias, los días o con el sol abrasador o con aguas perniciosas, las posadas incómodas por sí, y estrechas por tanto número de pasajeros e infestadas de insectos, que negaban aún el corto descanso de la noche" [Alegre (1841–1842) 1956–1960, 1: 223]).

And just in case the reader should consider these to be insignificant inconveniences, a few pages later he makes the *imitatio Christi* narrative strategy even more explicit: "It would be redundant to mention the shameful minutia with which the Jesuit prisoners were mortified every day, offering up to the Lord very painful sacrifices" ("Sería muy prolijo referir las menudencias vergonzosas en que cada día tenían que mortificarse los reclusos jesuitas, y que ofrecer al Señor muy dolorosos sacrificios" [Alegre (1841–1842) 1956–1960, 1: 227]). Alegre explains that in their overly zealous search for any documents, notes, or other writings the Jesuits might have attempted to carry with them, the authorities wreaked havoc on the Jesuits' few possessions, heightening their sense of vulnerability and humiliation:

> The inventory was carried out in such a haphazard and disorderly way that it caused horror: broken chests, unlocked trunks, mattresses ripped open, clothes strewn about, mistreated and even notably reduced, many small pieces of furniture and jewelry stolen or not accounted for later among the belongings of these poor religious men. May God be blessed, as by so many ways and means he has wanted to humiliate and mortify us, in order to remove from our hearts all vestiges of temporal concerns ("Este registro se ejecutó con una irregularidad y un desorden, que causa horror: las cajas

quebradas, los baúles descerrajados, desliados los colchones, las ropas confundidad, maltratadas y aun notablemente disminuídas, robados no pocos de aquellos mueblecillos o alajuelas, que no podían hallarse entre el equipaje de unos pobres religiosos. Sea Dios bendito, que por tantos medios y caminos ha querido humillarnos y mortificarnos, para despegar de todo lo temporal nuestros corazones" [237]).

Alegre concludes his account of the expulsion with a numerical accounting of the priests who died en route to exile, and their numbers stand out as a stark coda to the impassioned story he has just offered the reader.

Jesuit historians writing later were in a position to refer more openly to the politically charged atmosphere of the expulsions. Andrés Cavo (1739–1803), a Jesuit historian who spent many years in the Nayar region of northern New Spain before being exiled to Italy, wrote a history of Mexico that was unpublished at the time of his death. Carlos Bustamante published Cavo's manuscript with the title *Tres siglos de México* in 1836, adding a supplement that continued the story where Cavo had left off. Bustamante explained: "I found it convenient to continue that work, taking it beyond the year 1767 in which the expatriation of the Jesuit fathers occurred, a memorable event that Father Cavo chose not to mention, being a Jesuit and not wishing to appear overly impassioned" ("[C]reí conveniente continuar aquella obra tomándola desde el año 1767 en que se verificó la expatriación de los padres jesuitas, de cuyo suceso memorable no quiso hacer mención el padre Cavo por ser jesuita y no presentarse con el carácter de apasionado" [Bustamante 1836, editor's note, s. p.]).

The final chapters of Cavo's history, however, had included a description of the exiled Jesuits' arrival in Xalapa that reads like a baroque *entrada* turned upside down. In this ritualized procession, viceregal authorities arriving from the metropolis traditionally made their way from a landing point on Mexican *tierra firme* through a succession of towns and villages towards Mexico City, ceremoniously performing en route their assumption of secular or ecclesiastical power. In Cavo's account the Jesuits also make their way through an admiring throng that has gathered to witness their procession. But they are moving away from a locus of power and influence towards an uncertain future. Cavo remarks:

Their arrival in the village of Jalapa was like a triumphal entry, though mixed with bitterness; windows, balconies, streets and terraces were all full of people who showed in their faces what they felt in their hearts: it was necessary for the troops who escorted the exiles to open a path with their whips ("Su llegada a la villa de Jalapa parecía una entrada en triunfo, aunque mezclado con amargura; ventanas, balcones, calles y azoteas todo se veía lleno de gentes que bien mostraban en sus semblantes lo que pasaba en sus pechos: necesitóse que la tropa que escoltaba aquellos desterrados se abriera paso a culatazos" [132]).[12]

The Jesuit expulsions are implicitly represented as a distortion of the principles of good governance based on Christian virtues of piety and religion. The reference to "an entry in triumph, though mixed with bitterness" ("una entrada en triunfo, aunque mezclado con amargura") underscores an ironic contrast of which both the crowds of onlookers and the historian himself are only too aware.

The issue of the supposed wealth of the Jesuits is another recurring theme in these expulsion accounts.[13] In the *Dictamen fiscal de expulsion,* Campomanes had stressed the conflict between the Jesuits' vow of poverty and their temporal interests in the Indies – pearl fishing in California, sugar *ingenios* in Quito, or the Paraguayan *reducciones* (see Campomanes 1977, 106ff.) – and the expulsion edict included provisions for the confiscation of all Jesuit possessions, including tillable lands. Jesuits responded vehemently to Campomanes's accusations that they were amassing vast fortunes in the Americas, pointing to the many personal sacrifices they made in establishing missions in far-flung and isolated areas completely devoid of any source of material wealth. Their narrative accounts of events leading up to the expulsion are marked by what might be called a discourse of misery that enumerates the privations and hardships they willingly endured as soldiers of the Jesuit order.

In this highly contested spiritual and material economy, the region now known as Baja California stands out as a particularly barren Eden.[14] Francisco Javier Clavigero's *Historia de la antigua o Baja California* (1789), one of the first accounts of the Jesuits' missionary efforts there, is often overlooked by Latin Americanists. Perhaps this is because its portrayal of indigenous culture is radically different from the discussion of the rich cultural legacy of ancient Mexico included in Clavigero's best-known work, *Historia Antigua de México* (1780–1781). The Indians of Baja California could claim no such legacy, and Clavigero in the *Historia de la antigua o Baja California* focuses on the primitive conditions and grueling deprivation of the missionaries' daily lives. His account of the expulsion of the Jesuits from Baja California comprises the final chapter of his history and repeats many of the same themes we have seen in Alegre's account:

> The missionaries, after carrying out punctually what the superior and commissary demanded of them, set off for Loreto. The neophytes, seeing the departure of those who had educated them in Christian life and who had taken such care for their well-being, sobbed disconsolately, and the missionaries, turning their eyes to those dear children in Jesus Christ to whom they had given birth with such pain and whom they were leaving so afflicted, could not contain their tears. As they said goodbye in order to embark, the soldiers, even those who accompanied the commissary, were moved to kneel in his presence to kiss the feet of the missionaries and bathe them with their tears ("Los misioneros después de haber ejectuado puntualmente lo que les exigieron el superior y el comisario, se pusieron en camino para Loreto. Los néofitos viendo partir a los que los habían educado en la vida cristiana y tanto se habían afanado por su bien, lloraban sin consuelo, y los misioneros volviendo los ojos a aquellos sus caros hijos en Jesucristo, los que habían parido con tantos dolores y dejaban ya tan afligidos, no podían contener sus lágrimas. Al despedirse para embarcarse, enternecidos los soldados, aun los que habían ido con el comisionado, se hincaban a presencia de éste a besarles los pies y bañarlos con sus lágrimas" [Clavigero (1789) 1933, 248]).

Clavigero notes the meek obedience with which the missionaries comply with the expulsion order and the anguish of those left behind. But for Clavigero, what makes the expulsion especially unjust is the harshness and cruel poverty of the land itself. A recurring theme in his account is the misery in which the Californian Jesuits and their indigenous charges lived. His emphasis on the Jesuits' anguish at the prospect of abandoning their flock undermines any possible accusation that they have been principally occupied with the acquisition of wealth for themselves. Clavigero explains that when the Franciscans charged with replacing the exiled Jesuits in the California missions reached their destination, they were astonished and dismayed by the inhospitable landscape:

> [T]he new missionaries had barely seen with their own eyes that California was not what they expected, when they abandoned the missions and the peninsula and returned to their monasteries, spreading the word everywhere that the land was inhabitable and that the Jesuits should give

great thanks to the King for having removed them from such great misery ("[A]penas los nuevos misioneros vieron con sus propios ojos que la California no era como la ponderaban, cuando abandonaron las misiones y la península y se volvieron a sus conventos, publicando por todas partes que aquel país era inhabitable y que los jesuitas debían agradecerle mucho al rey el que les hubiera sacado de aquella grande miseria" [248–9]).[15]

While Clavigero's discourse of misery marks the entire *Historia*, in the final chapter it functions as an implicit rebuttal of the accusations by Campomanes and others of Jesuit greed and unchecked acquisition of wealth.

Johann Jakob Baegert's account of the seventeen years he spent as a missionary in Baja California, the *Noticias de la peninsula americana de California* (first published in German in 1772), strikes a similar tone as Clavigero's work. Baegert stressed the hardships suffered by the Jesuit missionaries and began his final chapter, on the departure of the Jesuits from California, with a resounding rejection of the suggestion that the Jesuits had anything to gain materially by their missionary efforts:

> The fate encountered by the Jesuits of Spain was, naturally, the same one encountered by those of the Americas and California. Examining this fact merely from a temporal point of view, one might say that no greater favor could have been granted these missionaries, and many others, than that of removing them by this forced retirement from so much misery and returning them to their home ("La misma suerte que tocó a los jesuítas de España, la tuvieron que correr, naturalmente, también los de América y por ende, los de California. Mirando este hecho únicamente desde el punto de vista temporal, quizá se diría que no se hubiera podido hacer otro favor más grande a esos misioneros, así como a otros muchos, al sacarlos, por medio de su retiro forzoso, de tanta miseria y mandarlos de nuevo a su patria" [Baegert (1772) 1942, 213]).

In this account the exiles are forced to travel through pouring rain, in mud up to their knees, to reach the port of disembarkation. Many eventually succumb to fevers during the long ocean voyage from Veracruz to Cadiz. Rather than focus on the Jesuits' own sense of desperation, however, Baegert (like Alegre) prefers to suggest the depths of despair of the indigenous parishioners they must leave behind: "Here much could be said about the lamentations of the Californian Indians as the missionaries abandoned the missions; to them this retreat seemed like a punishment, which it truly was, in spite of the fact that there were no crimes that preceded it" ("Aquí habría mucho que escribir sobre las lamentaciones de los californios al abandonar los misioneros sus misiones; a ellos, esta retirada les parecía un castigo, lo que realmente era, a pesar de no saberse nada de crímenes que la hubieran precedido" [219]).

Baegert adds two appendices to his principal text (like the lengthy dissertations that conclude Clavigero's *Historia Antigua de México*) in which he systematically refutes the false accusations made about the Californians and the Jesuits who had gone there to evangelize them. Vehemently rejecting the charge that the Jesuits had attempted to install themselves as kings among the indigenous inhabitants, Baegert scoffs: "Fine kings! Those who, to tell the truth, drank with the horses, ate corn with the chickens and many times had to sleep on the ground with the dogs. Great honor! That which might be found in California and could be expected from the Indians" ("Unos bonitos reyes! Quienes, para decir la verdad, bebieron con los caballos, comieron maíz con las gallinas y muchas veces tuvieron que dormir con los perros en el suelo pelón. Mucha honra! La que se podia entrojar en California y que podía esperarse de los indios!" [240]).

Like Clavigero, Baegert offers a discourse of misery in response to those who accused the Jesuits in the Americas of appropriating Spanish wealth and passing it on to Rome. As a parting shot, he challenges the reader to answer the following question: "Besides, if so many millions flew each year from California to Rome, why then were the Californian and Paraguayan missionaries not held accountable for such exorbitant sums?" ("Además, si volaron tantos millones, cada año, de California a Roma, porqué, entonces, no se exigieron responsabilidades a los misioneros californianos y paraguayos por sumas tan exorbitantes?" [253]).

The Jesuit missionaries in Paraguay were also reported to control vast treasures of hidden gold and agricultural holdings. Indeed, among the possible motives for the expulsion edict (in addition to those mentioned earlier) were growing concerns about plans for a "Jesuit State of Paraguay" ("estado jesuítico del Paraguay" [Ferrer Benimeli 2001, 295; also see Campomanes 1977, 128ff.]).[16] The Paraguayan expulsions were thus characterized by significant military involvement, stemming in part from memories of earlier Jesuit resistance to the Treaty of Madrid. Many of the same themes we have seen in Alegre, Clavigero, and Baegert figure in accounts written by the Paraguayan Jesuit exiles, such as the *Diario del destierro* by José Manuel Peramás (1732–1793).[17]

Peramás spent a brief sojourn as a missionary among the Guaraní Indians before being recalled to the city of Córdoba to fill a teaching position at the university there. In subsequent years, however, he returned to missionary work regularly during his vacations. Thus, he was in a unique position to refute the slanderous charges that the Paraguayan Jesuits were slaveholding traitors determined to use the Guaraní missions for their own political and economic ends. Peramas's story, written as an epistolary response to an unnamed superior, begins in medias res and narrates the events from July 1767 to September 1768. Despite the retrospective nature of his account, Peramás creates a sense of immediacy through the use of details – names of local authorities such as Governor Bucareli, snippets of dialogue – and through the repetition of the shifter "at this point" ("en este punto") as he takes the reader through those tumultuous months from July 1767 to September 1768 (see Perrén de Velasco 2004, 14, and Ferrer Benemeli 2001, 301ff.).[18] He also includes in their entirety a number of letters written to and by the exiled Jesuits as a means of demonstrating their unimpeachable comportment (see Peramás 1952, 104–5). He makes reference to several instances in which news of the shocking injustice of the edict leads to the death of a parishioner who hears it: "When a lady from Cordoba heard what was happening, that our Church was closed, the College sacked and the Fathers taken prisoner, she was so affected by sentiment that, clutching her heart, she gave her soul up to God" ("A una señora de Córdoba le contaron luego lo que pasaba, cómo nuestra Iglesia estaba cerrada, el Colegio saqueado y los Padres presos; fué tan grande el sentimiento que concibió, que encogiéndosele el corazón entregó el alma al Señor"[97]). At the close of his narrative Peramás turns to a valedictory description of Paraguay, La Plata, and Tucumán, offering a "a brief summary of the great vineyard in which the Jesuits labored so gloriously" ("breve reseña de tan grande viña, en que tan gloriosamente trabajan los Jesuitas" [143]), reminding readers of how brutally that vineyard has been uprooted.

The Jesuit missions in the upper Amazon regions were perhaps the most isolated and dangerous of all, due to the linguistic and cultural diversity of the local indigenous groups and the dense jungle surroundings (see Ferrer Benemeli 2001, 308–10). For these reasons, news of the expulsion edict was slow to arrive, and the challenge of recruiting and training acceptable replacements for the exiled Jesuits from other missionary orders was almost insurmountable, as we see in Manuel Joaquín Uriarte's *Diario de un misionero de Maynas.* Uriarte (1720–1802) was born into a prominent Basque family and joined the Jesuit order in 1737. After spending a number of years in Quito, he realized his dream of being sent to do missionary work in Mainas in the upper Amazon, where he was living at the time of the expulsion edict. Uriarte wrote lengthy letters about his experiences to his brother and kept a diary as well (Marzal, 1994, 2: 134–7). Like Alegre, Uriarte had to recreate his diary from memory years after the expulsion, having made heroic attempts at the time to save his notes and selections from his diaries from being burned (see Uriarte [1952] 1985, 13 and 49).[19] In his *Diario* Uriarte gives a vivid account of the hardships and humiliations suffered by the Jesuits as they travel by canoe down the Marañon and Amazon rivers (a journey lasting, like Lenten penitence, forty days) and then by ship across the sea to Portugal.[20] He also emphasizes Jesuit exemplarity in the face of unjust persecution and includes quotes from impartial observers who protest on behalf of Jesuit innocence. For example, Uriarte recounts the following encounter with the missionaries who arrived to replace the exiles:

> But the good clergy surrounded me humbly saying, Father, we are not worthy to succeed the Jesuits; but since this is what is ordered, we will take care of things as best we can until you return, because it seems to us that this cannot last long. God will discover the innocence of the Company ("Pues los buenos clérigos me rodearon diciendo humildes: Padre, no somos dignos de suceder a los jesuítas; pero, pues así lo mandan, atenderemos como mejor podamos a mantener esto hasta que F. Rs. vuelvan, pues nos parece que esto no puede durar. Dios descubrirá la inocencia de la Compañía" [505]).

As we have seen, there are a number of recurring themes in the writings of Spanish American Jesuits on the expulsion: the *imitatio Christi,* the *via cruces,* the inversion of the baroque *entrada,* and the use of a discourse of misery to counter rumors about the supposed wealth of the Jesuits. In the narrative accounts examined in this essay, Campomanes's accusations of Jesuit "despotism" and the related charges of seditiousness and regicide are undercut by repeated anecdotes demonstrating Jesuit humility and obedience to viceregal authorities. But there is a deeper meaning that links them as well.

According to Miguel Batllori, the New World historiography produced by the Jesuits, tinged with nostalgia and ambivalently positioned between Europe and America, served as a foundation for an emerging sense of criollo identity:

> They were no longer pure Spaniards nor yet pure Americans: they represent a prenationalist regional phase in which the nostalgia of exile played the role that historical romanticism would play in similar situations that would arise in Europe more than a century later, in states lacking ethnographic and linguistic homogeneity ("[N]o eran ya españoles puros ni todavía americanos puros: representan una fase regionalista prenacional, en la que la nostalgia de desterrados representó el papel que el romanticismo histórico había de ejercer en las situaciones similares que en Europea conocerán, más de un siglo después, los Estados faltos de homogeneidad etnográfica y lingüística" [Batllori 1966, 578]).

It's worth noting that the term *extrañar* is often used to refer to the expulsion, both in the official documents and in the Jesuit narratives. Literally, *extrañar* means: to exile someone to a foreign country. The word conjures up the range of emotions we see in these accounts by Alegre, Clavigero, Baegert, Peramas, and Uriarte: the sense of strangeness or disbelief, the violence of the forced separation from country and community, the nostalgia that was an almost immediate response to the edict (even as many Jesuits hoped and firmly believed that it would eventually be rescinded and they would be able to return). This is what I mean to suggest with the reference to "domesticating exile" in the title of this essay. In the Jesuit histories I've examined, exile is inevitably and paradoxically connected with domestication – with the creation of a sense of place or home. Moreover, the inevitability of exile is countered with a narrative "homecoming," in which the Jesuits lay claim through their written accounts to territories – "homelands" – from which they have been forever expelled.

In the 1767 expulsion edict, Charles III had declared: "I prohibit by law and general regulation that any individual from the Company [of Jesus] or member of the Community be permitted to return to any part of my realm for whatever purpose or intention whatsoever" ("Prohibo por la ley y regla general, que jamás pueda volver a admitirse en todos mis Reinos en particular a ningún individuo de la Compañía, ni en cuerpo de Comunidad, con ningún pretexto ni colorido que sea" [Díaz-Plaja 1986, 210]).

Confronted with this barrage of negatives, the exiled Jesuits recreate Spanish America in their writings as both a "place-that-was" and a "place-to-come" (Casey 1993, ix). Spanish America is represented as a lost paradise from which the Jesuits have been expelled and also as the possibility of a utopian future, sharply differentiated from their present circumstances in Europe. In what is expressed in these narratives and also in what is silenced, the 1767 expulsion continues to resonate.

NOTES

1 I would like to thank all the presenters and members of the audience at the conference "Jesuit Accounts of the Colonial Americas. Textualities, Intellectual Disputes, Intercultural Transfers" (William Andrews Clark Memorial Library, University of California, LA, 8–9 April 2005), who shared thought-provoking papers and provided helpful comments and questions. Special thanks go to the conference organizers: Clorinda Donato, Marc André Bernier, and Hans-Jürgen Lüsebrink.

2 The bibliography on the possible causes leading up to the expulsion is vast: see Herr 1958, 14–27; Lynch 1989, 280–90; Andrés-Gallego 2000, 491–528; Andrés-Gallego 2001, 78–102; Noel 2001; Rico González 1949, 1–9; Vaca de Osma 1997, 1916; and Andrien 2011. For original documents related to the expulsion, see Díaz-Plaja 1986, 208–27. See also the extensive introduction to Campomanes's *Dictamen fiscal* by editors Cejudo and Egido.

3 For a brief overview, see Lynch 1989, 261–8; for an exhaustive treatment of the topic, see Andrés-Gallego 2003; for documents related to the uprising see Macías Delgado 1988.

4 The various documents are included in Rionda Arreguín 1996, 421–37; see also Díaz-Plaja 1986, 208–26; Cejudo and Egido in Campomanes 1977, 5–40. The Conde de Aranda was president of the Council of Castille from 1766–1773. See Lynch 1989, 291–8 and Andrien 2011.

5 This is a subject of particular interest for historians of colonial Spanish America and is further elaborated in documents written by viceroyal authorities. See Aguirre Beltrán 1999 and Pastells 1949.

6 For a balanced discussion of the practical effects of this censorship, see Domergue 2001. In contrast, an aggrieved and elegiac tone permeates Eguía Ruiz's essay on the dispersion of Spanish Jesuits' papers, in which he condemns "appropriations and thefts, plagiarism and adulterations, and in other cases, arbitrary repartitions of the sweat and labor of others" ("las

apropriaciones y rapiñas, los plagios y adulteraciones, y en otros casos, las reparticiones arbitrarias de los sudores y trabajos ajenos" [Eguía Ruiz 1951, 680]).

7 Materials confiscated from the Jesuits often served later as a foundation for national archives and libraries, and their writings – fomented in part by an offer from the Count of Floridablanca, Spain's ambassador to Rome, to increase the pension of any Jesuit who had authored a work while in exile – were enormously important: "It has been justly affirmed that the work of the exiled Jesuits contributed in a decisive manner to making Spanish America known in European cultural centers (and also contributed to highlighting American singularity, and with that, to creating a national identity, not American but rather of the diverse regions of America) ("Se ha podido afirmar con razón que la obra de los expulsos contribuyó de forma decisiva a dar a conocer la Hispanoamérica real en los medios cultos centroeuropeos (y también a contribuir a poner de relieve la singularidad Americana y, con ello, a crear una identidad nacional, aunque no americana sino de los diversos ámbitos de América") [Andrés-Gallego 2000, 169–70]). See also Batllori 1966.

8 There are, of course, other kinds of texts that refer to the expulsion: official documents, inventories, anonymous satire, and occasional poetry. Vargas Ugarte quotes several verses inspired by the expulsion edict, penned by the poet Constantino Carrasco: "So that sorrow does not grow / if silence adopts it / let me declare it / in these pale verses" ("Porque no crezca la pena / si la prohija el silencio / permitid que la declare / en éstos pálidos metros" [*Trabajos poéticos*, 1878, 109, quoted in Vargas Ugarte 1934, vi–vii]).

9 See Andrés-Gallego 2000 for a recent assessment of the impact of the Jesuit expulsions in America.

10 For a discussion of the life and works of the Jesuits exiled from New Spain to Italy, see Vargas Alquicira 1989; Maneiro and Fabri 1951; and Méndez Plancarte 1941. For examples of a regional history approach to the Jesuit expulsion, see Recéndez Guerrero 2000 and Rionda Arreguín 1996.

11 For details on how the expulsion order was executed in New Spain, see Aguirre Beltrán 1999, 116–23, and Rionda Arreguín 1996, 432ff.

12 For a discussion of triumphal arches as a reflection of viceregal power, see Cañeque 2004, 26–36.

13 For differing perspectives on the economic issue, see Ferrer Benimeli 2001 and the introduction by Cejudo and Egido to Campomanes 1977, 23–4.

14 For a recent (and highly sympathetic account), see Martinez 2001, 235–46. A more balanced and scholarly perspective on the Jesuits in Baja California may be found in Dunne 1968, and several books by Ernest J. Burrus, SJ, including his 1967 and 1984 works (see bibliography).

15 The unwillingness or inability of other orders to replace the exiled Jesuits is a recurring theme in these accounts and can be read as a response to Campomanes's manipulation of inter-order rivalries (see Cejudo and Egido, in Campomanes 1977, 37).

16 Ferrer Benimeli reminds us that the Paraguayan missions were located across vast territories that at one point corresponded to what are today parts of Argentina, Uruguay, Paraguay, Chile, Bolivia, and Brazil (see Ferrer Benimeli 2001, 296–7). Portions of these territories had been under dispute between Spain and Portugal, temporarily resolved by the Tratado de Límites in 1750 (which was later revoked by Charles III in 1760). For background on the Paraguayan expulsions, see Astrain 1995, 365–408; Ferrer Benimeli 2001; and Hernández 1908, 306.

17 The diary (originally written in Spanish in Turin and dated Christmas Eve, 1768) was published in 1952 with an extensive introduction by Guillermo Furlong. A later, slightly expanded version also exists in Latin. A 2004 edition by the Universidad Católica de Córdoba includes a brief introduction and literary analysis of the diary by Lila Perrén de Velasco and reproduces the text of the 1952 edition (all quotations come from this edition).

18 Bucareli appears as a central figure and villain in the documents of the expulsions from Paraguay; see Hernández 1908.

19 The recent reissue of the diary (based on an earlier edition prepared by Constantino Bayle) by Monumenta Amazónica includes a lengthy introductory study on missionary efforts in Maynas and on various Jesuit memoirs, including those of Velasco, Chantre, and Uriarte.

20 Another fascinating account of the expulsions, written by a Spaniard who never traveled to the Americas, drawing heavily from Uriarte's writings, is José Chantre y Herrera's *Historia de las misiones de la Companía de Jesús en el Marañón español.*

BIBLIOGRAPHY

Aguirre Beltrán, Cristina. 1999. *La expulsión de los jesuitas y la ocupación de sus bienes.* Puebla: Benemérita Universidad Autónoma de Puebla / Archivo Histórico Universitario.

Alegre, Francisco Javier. 1956–1960. *Historia de la Provincia de la Compañía de Jesús de Nueva España* [*Historia de la Compañia de Jesús en la Nueva España*], 1841–1842, eds. Ernest J. Burrus, SJ, and Félix Zubillaga, SJ, 4 vols. Reprint, Rome: Institutum Historicum SJ.

Andrés-Gallego, José. 2000. "Consecuencias de la expulsión de los jesuitas en América: primer balance," In *Jesuitas. 400 años en Córdoba,* vol. 2, 149–75.

Córdoba: Facultad de Derecho y Ciencias Sociales de la Universidad Nacional de Córdoba.

–. 2001. "1767: Por qué los jesuitas." In *Los jesuitas españoles expulsos. Su imagen y su contribución al saber sobre el mundo hispánico en la Europa del siglo XVIII*, ed. Manfred Tietz, 78–102. Madrid / Frankfurt: Iberoamericana / Vervuert.

–. 2003. *El motín de Esquilache, América y Europa.* Madrid: Fundación Mapfre Tavera / Consejo Superior de Investigaciones Científicas.

Andrien, Kenneth J. 2011. "Clerical Reform under Charles III: The Expulsion of the Jesuits, 1762–1773." Paper presented at the TePaske History Seminar, Emory University, Atlanta, GA, 25 March.

Astrain, Antonio. 1995. *Jesuitas, Guaraníes y Encomenderos. Historia de la Compañía de Jesús en el Paraguay.* Asunción del Paraguay: Centro de Estudios Paraguayos Antonio Guash.

Baegert, Juan Jacobo. 1942. *Noticias de la península americana de California,* 1772, trans. Pedro Hendrichs. Reprint, Mexico: Antigua Librería Robredo de José Porrúa e Hijos.

–. 1952. *Observations in Lower California,* trans. M. M. Brandenburg and Carl L. Baumann. Berkeley: University of California Press.

Batllori, Miguel. 1966. *La cultura hispano-italiana de los jesuitas expulsos. Españoles, Hispanoamericanos, Filipinos (1767–1814).* Madrid: Gredos.

Burrus, Ernest J. 1967. *Ducrue's Account of the Expulsion of the Jesuits from Lower California, 1767–1769.* St. Louis: St. Louis University Press.

–. 1984. *Jesuit Relations, Baja California, 1716–1762.* Los Angeles: Dawson's Book Shop.

Bustamante, Carlos María. 1836. *Los tres siglos de México [...] por el Padre Andrés Cavo. Notas y Suplemento.* Mexico: Luis Abadiano y Valdés.

Campomanes, Pedro R. de. 1977. *Dictamen fiscal de expulsión de los jesuitas de España (1766–1767),* eds. Jorge Cejudo and Teofanes Egido. Madrid: Fundación Universitaria Española.

Cañeque, Alejandro. 2004. *The King's Living Image: The Culture and Politics of Viceregal Power in Colonial Mexico.* New York: Routledge.

Carrasco, Constantino. 1878. *Trabajos poéticos.* Lima: Imprenta del Estado.

Casey, Edward S. 1993. *Getting Back into Place: Toward a Renewed Understanding of the Place-World.* Bloomington: Indiana University Press.

Cejudo, Jorge, and Teofanes Egido, eds. 1977. "Introduction." In *Dictamen fiscal de expulsion de los jesuitas de España (1766–1767),* 5–40. Madrid: Fundación Universitaria Española.

Chantre Y Herrera, José. 1901. *Historia de las misiones de la companía de Jesús en el Marañón español, 1637–1767.* Madrid: Imprenta de A. Avrial.

Clavigero, Francisco Javier. 1933. *Historia de la antigua o Baja California,* 1789. Reprint, Mexico: Imprenta del Museo Nacional de Arqueología, Historia y Etnografía.

–. 1987. *Historia antigua de México,* 1945. Reprint, México: Porrúa.

Deck, Allan Figueroa. 1976. *Francisco Javier Alegre: A study in Mexican literary criticism.* Rome/Tucson: Jesuit Historical Institute/Kino House.

Díaz-Plaja, Fernando. 1986. *La historia de España en sus documentos. Siglo XVIII.* Madrid: Cátedra.

Domergue, Lucienne. 2001. "Les jésuites espagnols écrivains et l'appareil d'Etat (1767–1808)." In *Los jesuitas españoles expulsos. Su imagen y su contribución al saber sobre el mundo hispánico en la Europa del siglo XVIII,* ed. Manfred Tietz, 265–94. Madrid / Frankfurt: Iberoamericana / Vervuert.

Dunne, Peter Masten. 1968. *Black Robes in Lower California.* Berkeley: University of California Press.

Eguía Ruiz, Constancio. 1951. "Dispersión total de los papeles jesuíticos en España." *Hispania. Revista española de historia* 9: 679–702.

Ferrer Benimeli, José A. 2001. "La expulsión de los jesuitas de las reducciones del Paraguay y de las misiones de Amazonas. Paralelismo y consecuencias humanas." In *Los jesuitas españoles expulsos. Su imagen y su contribución al saber sobre el mundo hispánico en la Europa del siglo XVIII,* ed. Manfred Tietz, 295–321. Madrid / Frankfurt: Iberoamericana / Vervuert.

Hernández, Pablo. 1908. *El extrañamiento de los jesuítas del Rió de la Plata y de las misiones del Paraguay por decreto de Carlos III.* Madrid: Victoriano Suárez.

Herr, Richard. 1958. *The Eighteenth-Century Revolution in Spain.* Princeton: Princeton University Press.

Lynch, John. 1989. *Bourbon Spain 1700–1808.* Cambridge, MA: Basil Blackwell.

Macías Delgado, Jacinta, ed. 1988. *El motín de Esquilache a la luz de los documentos.* Madrid: Centro de Estudios Constitucionales.

Maneiro, Juan Luis, and Manuel Fabri. 1951. *Vidas de mexicanos ilustres del siglo XVIII,* ed. Bernabé Navarro. México: Universidad Nacional Autónoma de México.

Martinez, John J. 2001. *Not Counting the Cost: Jesuit Missionaries in Colonial Mexico – a Story of Struggle, Commitment, and Sacrifice.* Chicago: Loyola Press.

Marzal, Manuel M. 1994. *La utopia posible. Indios y jesuitas en la América colonial (1549–1767).* 2 vols. Lima: Pontificia Universidad Católica del Peru.

Méndez Plancarte, Gabriel. 1941. *Humanistas del siglo XVIII.* México: Universidad Nacional Autónoma de México.

Morner, Magnus, ed. 1965. *The Expulsion of the Jesuits from Latin America.* New York: Knopf.

Noel, Charles C. 2001. "Clerics and Crown in Bourbon Spain, 1700–1808: Jesuits, Jansenists, and Enlightened Reformers." In *Religion and Politics in Enlightenment Europe,* eds. James E. Bradley and Dale K. Van Kley, 119–53. Notre Dame, IN: University of Notre Dame Press.

Pastells, R. P. Pablo. 1949. *Historia de la compañía de Jesús en la provincia del Paraguay.* Vol. 18, pt. 2. Madrid: Consejo Superior de Investigaciones Científicas. Instituto Santo Toribio de Mogrovejo.

Peramás, José Manuel. 1952. *José Manuel Peramás y su "Diario del Destierro" (1768)*, ed. Guillermo Furlong. Buenos Aires: Librería del Plata.

–. 2004. *Diario del destierro.* Córdoba: Editorial de la Universidad Católica de Córdoba.

Perrén de Velasco, Lila. 2004. "Prólogo." In Peramás 2004, 7–16.

Recéndez Guerrero, Emilia. 2000. *Zacatecas. La expulsión de la Compañía de Jesús (y sus consecuencias).* Zacatecas: Universidad Autónoma de Zacatecas.

Rico González, Victor. 1949. *Documentos sobre la Expulsión de los Jesuítas y Ocupación de sus Temporalidades en Nueva España (1772–1783).* Mexico: Publ. Del Instituto de Historia.

Rionda Arreguín, Isauro. 1996. *La Compañía de Jesús en la provincia guanajuatense 1590–1767.* Guanajuato: Centro de Investigaciones Humanísticas, Universidad de Guanajuato.

Ronan, Charles E. 1977. *Francisco Javier Clavigero, S.J. (1731–1787), Figure of the Mexican Enlightenment. His Life and Works.* Rome: Institutum Historicum, SJ / Chicago: Chicago University Press.

Santos Hernández, Angel. 1992. *Los jesuítas en América.* Madrid: Editorial Mapfre.

Subirats, Eduardo. 1981. *La Ilustración insuficiente.* Madrid: Taurus.

Tietz, Manfred, ed. 2001. *Los jesuitas españoles expulsos.* Madrid / Frankfurt: Iberoamericana / Vervuet.

Uriarte, Manuel J. 1985. *Diario de un misionero de Maynas,* 1952. Reprint, Iquitos: Monumenta Amazónica.

Vaca de Osma, José Antonio. 1997. *Carlos III.* Madrid: Rialp.

Vargas Alquicira, Silvia. 1989. *La singularidad novohispana en los jesuitas del siglo XVIII.* Mexico: Universidad Nacional Autónoma de México.

Vargas Ugarte, Rubén. 1934. *Jesuitas peruanos desterrados a Italia.* Lima: El Arzobispo.

chapter eleven

"Ils estoient si subjects à leur bouche": la *Relation* de 1616 face à la topique antijésuite

ISABELLE LACHANCE

> [D]evant que d'entrer au recit d'une si funeste Tragedie: Je proteste en foy & parole d'homme de bien, & d'honneur […] que je ne diray rien par invectives, ains par une pure verité, & qui ne soit à dire par un fidele sujet amateur de la vie de son Roy, & desireux de la conservation de sa Patrie, & manutention de la Paix, & je prie Dieu qu'il me confonde si ce que je diray pourvient d'autre zele, que du devoir d'un bon François de la Religion Catholique, Apostolique, & Romaine […], & sur l'opinion que je dois avoir que toutes personnes qui dissimulent ou déguisent la verité quand il y va de la conservation du Roy, sont traistres à sa Majesté & à leur Patrie, Pestes de l'Estat, plusque Heretiques, & Diables incarnez (Legrain 1614, 290–1).

C'est en ces termes, à la fois sibyllins et transparents, que Jean-Baptiste Legrain, dans la *Decade contenant la vie et gestes de Henry le Grand* qu'il fait imprimer à ses frais, entreprend de narrer au jeune Louis XIII le meurtre de son père par François Ravaillac. Or, l'année même où Legrain interpelle de manière si véhémente ces "pestes" et ces "diables," sous la figure desquels le lecteur devine sans peine les pères jésuites, paraît le *Factum du procès entre messire Jean de Biencourt, sieur de Poutrincourt, baron de S. Just, appelant, d'une part, et Pierre Biard, E[n]emond Massé et consorts, soit disant prêtres de la société de Jésus, intimés.* Cet opuscule, qui met manifestement au jour un procès fictif – il n'est que d'observer la construction proprement hallucinante des personnages et de leurs plaidoyers pour s'en convaincre –, vise avant tout à défendre les intérêts des Biencourt, père et fils. Mais la cause sert par la bande à diffuser un antijésuitisme virulent et, en même temps, à atténuer les soupçons qui pesaient sur l'implication de marins protestants dans l'échec que représente la brève expérience coloniale de Port-Royal en Acadie (cet établissement, rappelons-le, est fondé en 1605 et tombe sous les feux anglais en 1613). Parmi tant d'autres railleries, le *Factum*, en accusant évidemment la Compagnie de Jésus de troubler la paix religieuse retrouvée en France après la proclamation de l'Édit de Nantes, va jusqu'à offrir à Marie de Médicis, par le biais du discours rapporté de matelots dieppois, de "freter les vaisseaux et [...] passer tous [les jésuites] à leurs despens" afin de la "desfaire de tous ceux qui sont en France" ([Poutrincourt] [1614] 1887, 9).

Soupçons d'incitation au régicide, crainte de l'intrusion trop forte d'un ordre relevant directement de Rome dans les affaires de l'Église gallicane, voire dans celles de l'État français lui-même, volonté de dénoncer dans le jésuite un cancer social: le *Factum* décline sur tous les tons une topique qui s'était fixée en France dès 1602, deux ans avant la réinstauration de l'ordre, dans le *Catéchisme des Jésuites*, paru anonymement mais vite attribué à Étienne Pasquier. Sur ce point, il est remarquable que, dans ce faux rapport, Gilbert du Thet, missionnaire somme toute assez marginal dans les entreprises acadiennes, soit celui qui, au beau milieu de la transcription du supposé procès, cristallise cette topique pour mieux l'incarner: "[C]e Jesuite commença à dire que c'estoit un grand coup que l'assassinat du Roy, que sans cela la Chrestienté estoit perdue, [...] & que la France ne seroit jamais subjecte à autre qu'à l'Espagnol" (35).

Néanmoins, il n'est pas certain qu'en 1614, ces propos malveillants – comme la prise de position de Legrain, d'ailleurs – bénéficient d'un droit de cité indiscuté en France; rappelons seulement que la royauté comptait sur les services de confesseurs membres de l'ordre de Loyola depuis Henri III. Mais encore, la polémique suscitée par un supposé aval de l'appel au tyrannicide de Juan Mariana par des jésuites français, ainsi que par le cosmopolitisme (forcément malsain) des membres d'un ordre sans feu ni lieu, et surtout sans allégeance nationale envers la France, témoigne d'une position culturelle et politique excentrée. De fait, le confesseur de la famille royale depuis Henri IV, Pierre Coton, dédie en 1610 à la régente une *Lettre declaratoire de la doctrine des peres jesuites* dans laquelle il prend soin de réfuter les positions du *De regis and rege institutione* (1598) de Mariana:

> Mais toy pauvre Societé qui ne subsistois que par le benefice de ce Monarque, qui t'a ainsi desolee! si deplorablement abaissee! si miserablement accablee! [...] O combien il est vray, & combien sensiblement tu l'experimentes, que la douleur qui se peut dire, ne se peut dire douleur (Coton 1610, 27)!

La même année, l'*Anticoton ou refutation de la lettre declaratoire du pere Coton* dénonce le procédé en interpellant lui aussi la régente: "[L]'opinion commune, tant de vos sujets que des estrangers, est que les Jesuites sont autheurs [du] damnable parricide" d'Henri IV ([Plaix] [1610] s. d., 3), puisqu'ils auraient sinon commandité, du moins moralement avalisé le sombre dessein de Ravaillac. Le parodique *Advis sur le sujet de l'Anticoton* qui paraît en 1611 sous le nom de Maître Guillaume, pseudonyme de Guillaume Marchand,[1] dévoile quant à lui l'obsolescence dont témoigne la polémique. L'opuscule souligne à larges traits l'aberration qui consiste à considérer que la réinstauration de la Compagnie marque l'intrusion d'une force étrangère dans les affaires nationales. Les membres français de l'ordre, y lit-on en substance, "pour estre entrez en ceste societé, [n'ont pas] entierement despoüillez le naturel François, pour ne respirer que l'Espagne" (Marchand 1611, 15). "[C]et ordre celebre, ajoute-t-il, [est] composé de nos freres, de nos enfans, de nos oncles, de nos cousins, de nos parens & alliez, tous François comme nous" (15). "Par quelle regle, par quelle loy," demande enfin le narrateur sous les traits d'un fou du roi, "les Pretendus reformez" (62) sont-il plus français que les jésuites de France? Pierre Biard ne dira pas autre chose dans sa *Relation de la Nouvelle France*, publiée à Lyon en 1616: "[V]rayement [ce serait] bien estre malheureux, si les François courants au bout du monde pour convertir les Sauvages, y venoyent perdre leurs propres concitoyens" (Biard [1616] 1972, 30: 2e col.). Dans son récit, c'est par la bouche même de celui qui, en Nouvelle-France, mit Sainte-Croix, Port-Royal et Saint-Sauveur à sac, l'Anglais Samuel Argall, que sera confirmée l'allégeance à leur identité nationale des membres français de la Société de Jésus. En effet, non seulement les missionnaires en Nouvelle-France n'auraient pas servi de guides aux saccageurs – ce dont les accuse le *Factum* –, mais encore ce serait "par l'exemple [...] qu[e] [ce capitaine] avoit du P. Biard' qu'il 'n'osoit attendre qu'aucun François [...] voulust [le] conduire ou conseiller sincerement" (53: 2e col.).

Mais revenons au *Factum*, auquel répond, après tout, la *Relation* de Biard. L'opuscule, qui se donne à lire, comme nous l'avons dit, sous l'apparence de la transcription fidèle d'un procès, se livre à une représentation littéralement réductrice des missionnaires jésuites, qui s'y voient diminués au point de perdre tout être propre. Rejetés dans une altérité absolue, les pères de la Compagnie y deviennent un repoussoir dont la fonction est de circonscrire une identité française en péril, dans le Nouveau comme dans l'Ancien Monde. En imaginant une créature insaisissable, le texte donne du jésuite un portrait dont les contours se réduisent, singulièrement, à ceux de sa bouche. Double d'Homenaz, papimane de la fiction rabelaisienne, fainéant, mangeur et buveur invétéré, son rôle consiste essentiellement à discourir, en cultivant une parole fourbe et ambiguë. Ce glissement du physique au moral s'opère partout dans le plaidoyer, mais il culmine dans la réitération d'une accusation, déjà obsolète, faisant des pères de la Compagnie de "[s]ubtils Regnards & grands mangeurs d'Images," portrait que le *Factum* tirerait de "vers en vieil Roman" ([Poutrincourt] 1614, 80); en fait, il s'agit de l'un des quatrains "sur les abuz de ce monde"[2] de Guillaume Crétin, mort près d'un siècle plus tôt. Mais il n'était pas besoin d'aller chercher si loin: le *Catéchisme des Jésuites* comparait de manière encore plus convaincante ces derniers à des "renards [qui] se repeurent, comme bestes assouvies, du sang des François" ([Pasquier] 1602, fol. 104 v°). Ce procédé de déshumanisation constitue, en fait, l'amorce même du *Factum*. Les citations données dès la page de titre comme dans l'exorde – véritable "fil dans la main du juge" (Martineau 1994, 23) dans le cas d'un discours polémique – inscrivent déjà l'opuscule dans un processus explicitement réducteur. Entre le vers "Cælum, non animum mutant, qui trans mare currunt,"[3] tiré d'une épître d'Horace, et les vers "Accipe nunc Danaum insidias, & crimine ab uno / Disce omnis,"[4] tirés de l'*Énéide*, le ton est donné et peu de latitude subsiste pour appréhender avec quelque objectivité le rôle des missionnaires qui s'embarquèrent pour la Nouvelle-France. Suivant cet esprit, on nous livre le portrait d'un Pierre Biard métamorphosé en "pourceau" ([Poutrincourt] 1614, 14) – encore une fois, Rabelais n'est pas loin – se vautrant dans sa vomissure dès avant le départ de Dieppe ou, à destination, "couché le ventre en haut derrière un coffre" (51), s'abîmant dans un délire d'excommunication collective à l'endroit de toute la petite colonie.

De passage à la cour avant son départ pour la Nouvelle-France, Poutrincourt aurait d'ailleurs averti en personne le père Coton que ces jésuites-bouches ne pouvaient vraisemblablement prendre part à l'expédition, puisque "la cuisine n'estoit encores bastie' (4) à Port-Royal. Loin de se présenter comme une simple boutade, cette allusion à la gourmandise ou, pour parler la langue du *Factum*, à la 'sobrieté Jesuitique" (14) des missionnaires, constitue non seulement une manière de les tenir à distance du reste des voyageurs, supposément prêts à endurer des privations de toutes sortes pour assurer le succès de l'entreprise, mais elle est surtout le signe extérieur et visible du péché (contrairement à l'envie, par exemple, qui peut se dissimuler). "[S]i subjects à leur bouche" (33), les jésuites auraient pareillement voulu assujettir les autres membres de l'expédition en s'arrogeant le pouvoir de les nourrir ou de les laisser mourir de faim. Une lettre de Charles de Biencourt à son père, transcrite dans le *Factum* à titre de preuve, rapporte ainsi les paroles de Biard: "[N]ous vous nourrissons tous & parcon[se]quent [...] vous & vos gens estes nos subjects" (41). "Parl[ant] en plurier," ce dernier aurait considéré que les missionnaires "avoient nourris" tous les membres de l'équipage, "que [les] gens [de Biencourt] estoient leurs serviteurs, & eux leurs maistres, & par conséquent que [la colonie de Port-Royal] leur appartenoit" (49).

Indice de la voracité insatiable des Jésuites, ces paroles rapportées prennent tout leur sens dans un contexte de remise en question des pouvoirs temporels accordés par Rome à la Compagnie; mais les *Exercices* de Loyola n'invitaient-ils pas déjà les membres de l'ordre à vivre en chrétiens *dans le monde*? Pareil programme demandait en effet, en marge de la vie religieuse, d'investir les différentes sphères de l'activité politique et économique. Dans cette vision de la relation du spirituel au temporel – qui unit le bien et l'utile –, le mercantilisme, que le *Factum* reproche aux hommes ayant participé à la première mission en Nouvelle-France, était conçu par eux – ainsi que par les États où, sous l'impulsion de la *Ragion di Stato* de Botero, ils exerçaient une influence –, comme "un moyen moralement acceptable" et "recommandable pour fortifier l'état" (Bireley 1996, 237). Le *Factum*, en prêtant au capitaine Argall des dires qui attaquent avec virulence "ceux qui entrent par la fenestre, [...] mangent & escorchent & se paissent eux-mêmes" de leurs victimes ([Poutrincourt] 1614, 71), montre en cela aussi (et non seulement dans sa prise de position en faveur des huguenots), qu'il émane d'une sphère politiquement excentrée.

Fortement dominés par une conception étroite de la prédestination, ces énoncés englobants s'opposent d'évidence à la formulation du rôle de la grâce divine – ce que Biard nomme "la lumière et l'engin" (Biard 1972 [1616], 42: 2e col.) –, rôle que la théologie jésuite cherchait à illustrer et dont elle faisait l'instrument premier de la Contre-Réforme. En effet, cette théologie suppose un exercice du libre-arbitre s'ouvrant sur la possibilité d'influencer le jugement de l'autre et, en conséquence, sur une revalorisation de la rhétorique dans sa relation au religieux et ce, précisément après les doutes que la Réforme avait fait peser sur cette relation. Ce sont d'ailleurs ces doutes auxquels Pierre Coton veut donner l'impression de souscrire en écrivant, dans sa *Lettre* à Marie de Médicis citée plus haut, que la Compagnie de Jésus, en sol français, "experiment[e], que la douleur qui se peut dire, ne se peut dire douleur" (Coton 1610, 27), formule dont le succès a peut-être justifié sa reprise dans ses *Sermons sur les principales et plus difficiles matières de la foy* (1617).

Cette reprise témoigne d'une tentative de séparer l'expression religieuse de l'art de bien dire, en essayant de disqualifier cette relation, le plus artificieusement du monde dans le cas du père Coton (il va sans dire), puisque la formule, en parfait accord avec la tradition oratoire, permet de mieux dissimuler l'art sous une nature prétendue. En donnant l'exemple d'un chrétien qui, priant sans savoir qu'il prie, converse d'autant mieux avec Dieu qu'à l'image de l'orateur peu soucieux d'éloquence, il ne se trouve pas en situation autoréflexive, le jésuite soutient qu'il n'est d'expérience authentique que séparée de la conscience de celui qui la vit:

> Saint Antoine le Grand, fort expérimenté en telles affaires disait, au rapport de Cassien, que l'oraison ne se peut dire parfaite quand celui qui prie s'aperçoit qu'il prie: d'autant que si elle est parfaite, elle ravit tellement l'esprit en Dieu qu'il ne fait aucune réflexion et ne se souvient d'autre chose sinon de Dieu avec lequel il traite et converse. L'Orateur romain, en chose semblablement dissemblable, a laissé par écrit qu'il ne faut estimer l'éloquence laquelle donne loisir aux auditeurs de remarquer qu'on dit bien. Quelque autre quasi en même sens estimait que la douleur qui se peut dire, ne se peut dire douleur (Coton 1617, 391).

On peut en outre mesurer la fortune de cette formule auprès du public visé dans sa première mouture, celle de la *Lettre* dédiée à la Régente, en songeant qu'elle sera reprise à l'identique dans les *Eloges et vies de reynes, des princesses, et des dames illustres* d'Hilarion de Coste, qui la fait suivre d'une paraphrase forgée à partir d'un vers de l'*Hippolytus* de Sénèque:[5]

> Quand Louyse de Savoye Comtesse d'Angoulesme demeura veuve du Comte Charles son mary, chargée de deux petits enfans, elle n'estoit aagée que de 18. ans. Ce coup inopiné, pareil à un foudre qui frappe en esclairant, surmonta et estonna ce grand courage, qui avoit assez de pieté pour supporter un tel accident, mais non pas assez de vigueur pour soustenir un assaut si brusque et si violent: c'est pourquoy elle demeura fort triste [...]. La douleur qui se peut dire, ne se peut dire douleur; les petits déplaisirs donnent place à la plainte, mais les grands accablent l'esprit, et l'assoupissent. C'est pourquoy les anciens ont estimé que l'insensibilité et le

> silence estoient les seules couleurs qui pouvoient bien dépeindre une juste et incomparable affliction (Coste 1647, 161).

Cela dit, si cet *excursus* pseudo-néo-stoïcien est digne d'intérêt pour l'histoire de l'art oratoire jésuite, c'est avant tout le doute qu'elle fait planer sur la légitimité de la rhétorique dans son rapport au religieux qui doit retenir l'attention, dans la mesure où la défense de la renommée de la Compagnie de Jésus dépend bel et bien de la capacité de ses auteurs à réunir expression de la foi et foi en l'éloquence, même si, en consacrant plusieurs paragraphes de sa *Lettre* à une longue plainte sur la situation des Jésuites de France, Coton lui-même n'obéit pas au principe qu'il énonce. Et pour cause!

Il n'est que d'entendre le personnage du père Biard tel que dépeint dans le *Factum* pour concevoir que la *Relation* de 1616 se devait de revaloriser cette relation, ne serait-ce que pour rétablir sa réputation en même temps que celle de son ordre, dans un contexte qui, faisant de la renommée "un concept central [de] la pensée politique du baroque" (Bireley 1996, 234), érige le rapport de l'apparence à la réalité au sommet des préoccupations des agents politiques. Personnage du *Factum*, Biard est évidemment toujours prêt à décocher quelques "blandices & attraicts selon [l']inclination" ([Poutrincourt] 1614, 35) de ses semblables; par exemple, lorsqu'il s'offre pour régler un litige entre Poutrincourt et des pêcheurs maloins en "us[ant] [...] de sa rhetoricque" (23), il finira par tromper tout le monde. On entend poindre sous le décit le gentilhomme mis en scène dans le *Catechisme* de Pasquier, qui affirme que la "doctrine" jésuite et "le haut Alemand" ([Pasquier] 1602: fol. 8 v°) sont pour lui une seule et même chose. Pour sa part, le *Factum* accuse encore les jésuites de tenir un "discours pedantesque" ([Poutrincourt] 1614, 57).

Au centre de la démarche de Pierre Biard relationnaire se trouvent donc non seulement l'impérieux devoir de défendre sa renommée en même temps que celle de la Compagnie, mais également celui de transformer ces insultes (qui sont en fait des lieux communs) en vertus, si l'on peut dire. Aussi choisira-t-il judicieusement d'attaquer le *Factum* sur le terrain du discours. D'évidence, pour le jésuite, s'appuyer sur une diffamation publiée constitue un atout. En effet, la médiation du papier, en plus de jouer au désavantage d'un accusateur qui se cache derrière elle, offre une prise exceptionnelle à celui qui doit se défendre: il peut, grâce à elle, mettre à distance le contenu de l'accusation. Ainsi, tout en ne manquant pas de confondre le plaidoyer et "son Escrivain" (Biard [1616] 1972, 24: 2e col.), cité explicitement dans la *Relation* de 1616 à titre de "factieux," Biard situe son travail d'écriture à un niveau supérieur, rabaissant l'objet de la polémique au statut d'anecdote. Aussi inscrit-il son entreprise de réfutation dans le genre noble de l'histoire, et convoque-t-il à cet effet un bestiaire beaucoup moins flamboyant que celui qu'appliquent ses adversaires à ses confrères et à lui-même, bestiaire, nous l'avons vu, peuplé de renards et de loups enragés: "[J]e raconte la verité du faict, écrit Biard, sans perdre le temps à combattre des larves" (33: 2e col.), c'est-à-dire des fantômes. En outre, si "l'Escrivain" du *Factum* a décidé de "sortir au monde" (24: 2e col.) en publiant une querelle d'intérêt limité, la *Relation de la Nouvelle France*, elle, serait d'intérêt véritablement public, puisqu'elle sort cette querelle du domaine privé et ce, afin de lui conférer un sens universel, ce qu'exigent aussi bien le précepte cicéronien de l'*historia magistra vitae* que la théorie oratoire, encore là cicéronienne, qui invite à s'élever d'une *causa* particulière à une *quaestio* d'intérêt général.[6]

En valorisant "la lumière et l'engin," le jésuite fonde de surcroît son plaidoyer sur une défense du libre-arbitre qui, en plus de s'inscrire d'emblée dans le mouvement de la Contre-Réforme et, en conséquence, de discréditer à la base la partie adverse, qui représente, en plus des intérêts des Biencourt, celui des protestants impliqués dans l'entreprise coloniale acadienne, suppose que, s'"il existe des œuvres naturellement bonnes" dont, au premier chef et dans le cas qui nous concerne, les missions des membres de la Compagnie, "l'histoire propose des *exempla* positifs à imiter" (Chédozeau 1999, 16). Ainsi, bien qu'il se voit "contraint souvent de particulariser plusieurs petites affaires, non guiere bien convenables à la gravité d'une histoire, ny à la dignité d'un Lecteur honorable," Biard assure le lecteur que "sa prudence pourra beaucoup [se] former" à la fréquentation de son récit (Biard [1616] 1972, 25: 1e col.). Mais, on le devine, bien qu'elle constitue pour lui un moyen commode, la défense de l'*ars historica* n'est pas ce qui intéresse au premier chef notre auteur; pour lui, le récit créant un intérêt pour ses propres ressorts renforce la figure de ses protagonistes et se trouve, en ce sens, plus convaincant que la démonstration argumentée, toujours susceptible d'entraîner une démonstration opposée.

Au reste, je ne reviendrai pas sur la querelle qui oppose les missionnaires jésuites au parti de Poutrincourt quant à la conversion des Sauvages (voir Carile 2000); rappelons seulement qu'en 1610, ce dernier avait fait traverser en Nouvelle-France un prêtre du nom de José Fléché, qui y célébra quelque quatre-vingts baptêmes. Pour Biard, qui défend l'idée d'une pastorale catéchétique et, partant, d'une conversion progressive, l'action spectaculaire du baptême collectif est proprement contre-nature, "fai[sant] naistre des enfans avec les dents et la barbe, et introdui[sant] des meres sans mammelles et sans laict" (Biard [1616] 1972, 21: 2e col.). Mais afin de "fermer la bouche au mensonge" (29: 1e col.) et de désarmer la charge de ceux dont le discours, excessif et servant des intérêts particuliers, s'avère inconsistant – un "grand bruit" (27: 2e col.), un cri poussé "jusques à l'enrouëment" (28: 1e col.) –, Biard oppose à une représentation du jésuite réduite à un organe buccal hypertrophié (qu'il lui serve à se goinfrer des pauvres vivres nécessaires au voyage, à boire jusqu'à l'ivrognerie ou à parler en vain) une entreprise qui rend visible la maîtrise raisonnée du corps missionnaire. Au "pourceau" informe ou au corps jésuite agi par une colère insensée, tel qu'il se lit partout dans le *Factum*, l'auteur de la première relation des missionnaires de la Compagnie de Jésus en Nouvelle-France réplique par le spectacle d'un corps rationnel, quitte, pour reprendre son mot, à "particulariser" beaucoup et à trouver le moyen de justifier ses excès passionnels.

Par exemple, devant le refus du chef souriquois Membertou, agonisant, d'accepter une sépulture chrétienne, Biard écrit s'être emporté, avoir "denonç[é] que cest enterrement se feroit sans luy" et "protest[é] qu'il renonçoit" à donner son accord à une sépulture païenne (33: 2e col.). Cependant, se ravisant à l'idée que "le malade ne pensast que ce qui estoit devoir de charité ne fust cholere" (33: 2e col.), il serait revenu auprès de lui, pour constater cependant que cette démonstration aura, au final, réussi: Membertou aurait, au final, "chang[é] d'advis" (33: 2e col.). Quel est le sens de cette sainte et, surtout, très démonstrative colère? De la part de Biard, ce choix, a priori douteux, semble judicieux, puisque, dans le texte d'une réponse à un libelle diffamatoire, cette représentation de lui-même implique que les autres voyageurs, pécheurs comme lui sinon plus, n'ont pas à porter un jugement sur ses actions et, par extension, sur ses paroles.

Ce procédé de reformulation du corps jésuite est systématique et se remarque de manière plus générale à travers plusieurs accumulations rhétoriques, où le nombre des actions entreprises est, bien évidemment, inversement proportionnel aux moyens dont on dispose dans la petite colonie, qu'il s'agisse de tâches ménagères, de construction navale ou d'effort de conversion: "[S]'il falloit laver leur linge, si netoyer leurs habits, si les rapiecer, si pourvoir à aultres necessités, [les jésuites] avoyent privilege," ironise-t-il, "de le faire eux-mesmes aussi bien que le moindre" (29: 1e col.). Veulent-ils forger des termes équivalents dans "la langue du pays" pour des termes "abstracts et universels, comme croire, douter, esperer, discourir, apprehender, un animal, un corps, une substance, un esprit, vertu, vice, peché, raison, justice"? "[E]n cela, précise l'auteur, il falloit ahanner et suer" (31: 1e col.). "[L]à estoyent les tranchées de [notre] enfantement" (31: 1e col.), ajoute-t-il, en reprenant une image déjà employée en début de chapitre pour conférer aux "contradictions et difficultés qui s'éleverent à Dieppe" (Biard [1616] 1972, ch. 12) – c'est-à-dire les tentatives par lesquelles les matelots protestants auraient fait pression pour empêcher l'embarquement des missionnaires jésuites –, une dimension providentielle, conforme à ce qu'exprime l'*Apocalypse* de Jean (12, 2): "L'Eglise de Dieu [...] *Cruciatur ut pariat*" (27: 1e col.), elle s'accouche dans la douleur. Mais les actions des missionnaires ont parfois des fins beaucoup plus terrestres. Ainsi, la représentation du père Énemond Massé, relativement effacée, se construit-elle de manière à concentrer les manifestations les plus physiques de l'activité que déploie le duo qu'il forme avec Pierre Biard. Cet homme "qui sçait tout faire" (43: 1e col.), insiste l'auteur, est celui qui s'inscrit le plus dans la participation des missionnaires à la matérialité de l'entreprise coloniale. Sciage, rabotage, calcul des courbes, fabrication des étoupes, fabrication et application de résine, rien ne manque à l'épisode qui décrit, étape par étape, la construction d'une barque de fortune. Épisode prodigieux, au figuré comme au propre d'ailleurs, puisque, au final, le bâtiment sauvera la vie des accusateurs des jésuites eux-mêmes!

La *Relation de la Nouvelle France* condense, en somme, certains moyens mis de l'avant par Pierre Biard pour répondre au *Factum* comme à l'antijésuitisme français dont il se fait l'écho: réhabilitation de la rhétorique et foi dans le libre-arbitre, moyens qui réussissent même, ici, à convaincre un hérétique brutal et sanguinaire, du moins si l'on en juge par une conversation que l'auteur rapporte avoir eue avec le capitaine Argall. L'équipage de Biencourt, on ne manquera pas de l'observer, s'y voit écorché au passage et, de surcroît, par la bouche même de ce personnage décidément très commode pour l'un comme pour l'autre parti:

> Mais, dit [Argall] en dissimulant, je m'estonne fort que vous autres Jesuites, qu'on tient communement pour hommes de conscience et religion, vous vous trouviez icy en compagnie de forbans et picoteurs, gens sans aveu et sans

loy ny honneur. Le Pere Biard respondit et prouva avec tant d'argument, que toute leur troupe estoit de gens de bien et recommandez par sa Majesté tres chrestienne, et refuta si peremptoirement toute objection contraire, que le Capitaine Anglois fut constrainct de faire semblant qu'il s'y accordoit, vaincu par ses raisons (49: 1e col.).

NOTES

1 "[F]ol en titre d'office sous Henri IV et sous Louis XIII, [il] s'appelait de son vrai nom Guillaume Marchand ou Le Marchand. [...] C'est à Louviers que naquit Maître Guillaume [...]. Une fois sa formation [de cuisinier] achevée, on le fit entrer au service du cardinal de Bourbon [qu'il] aurait quitté en 1589, profitant de la présence d'Henri IV en Normandie pour entrer à son service. Mais selon d'autres sources, il n'aurait fait partie de la maison du roi qu'à partir de 1594" (Lever 1985, 235–8). À propos des opuscules publiés sous ce nom, notons qu' "[o]n recense actuellement près de soixante-dix brochures attribuées à Maître Guillaume, mais il dut en paraître au moins trois fois plus. [I]l s'agissait bien, en fait, de bulletins d'information de caractère satirique, souvent féroces et cela [...] une trentaine d'années environ avant que Renaudot ne crée sa fameuse *Gazette*, autrement dit avant l'apparition d'une presse périodique. [C]es opuscules paraissaient sans privilège ni permission d'aucune sorte [...]. [I]ls étaient imprimés en secret [...] et vendus sous le manteau" (240–1). Voir également Savare 1969.

2 Voir le trente-quatrième des quatrains rassemblés sous le titre "S'ensuivent aulcuns quatrins faictz par ledict Cretin sur les abuz de ce monde": "Subtilz regnars et grans mangeurs de ymages / Pour hault monter contrefont des bigotz, / Puys quant il sont juchez sur leurs argotz, / Au monde font de merveilleux dommaiges" (Crétin [après 1515] 1932, 93–94).

3 Il s'agit du v. 27 de l'Épître XI (à Bullatius). François Richard le traduit ainsi: "[À] traverser la mer, on change de pays, on ne change pas d'âme" (Horace 1967, 227).

4 Il s'agit des v. 65 et 66 du Livre II de l'*Énéide*. Traduction d'Anne-Marie Boxus et Jacques Poucet: "Écoute maintenant les fourberies des Danaens, et connais-les tous à partir du crime d'un seul" (Virgile 2011: http://bcs.fltr.ucl.ac.be/Virg/V02-001-267.html).

5 Sénèque, *Hyppolytus*, Acte III, Scène 1, v. 607: "Les douleurs faibles font discourir, les importantes rendent muet" ("Curae leves loquuntur, ingentes

stupent"). On retrouve également au ch. 30 du *De finibus bonorum et malorum* de Cicéron: "Si la douleur est le plus grand mal, il est impossible de rien dire d'autre" ("Si dolor summum malum est, dici aliter non potest").

6 Voir Cicéron, *De l'orateur,* Livre III.

BIBLIOGRAPHIE

Biard, Pierre. [1616] 1972. *Relation de la Nouvelle France,* dans *Relation des Jésuites contenant ce qui s'est passé de plus remarquable dans les missions des Pères de la Compagnie de Jésus dans la Nouvelle-France,* 6 vol., vol. 1: 1–76. Montréal: Éditions du Jour [facsim. de l'éd. Québec: A. Côté, 1858].

Bireley, Robert. 1996. "Les jésuites et la conduite de l'état baroque." In *Les jésuites à l'âge baroque (1540–1640),* éd. Luce Giard et Louis de Vaucelles, 229–42. Grenoble: Jérôme Millon.

Carile, Paolo. 2000. "Lescarbot et Biard. La première querelle sur l'évangélisation en Nouvelle-France." In *Le regard entravé. Littérature et anthropologie dans les premiers textes sur la Nouvelle-France,* 129–50. Québec / Rome: Septentrion / Aracne.

Chédozeau, Bernard. 1999. "Les jésuites et l'histoire au XVIIe siècle." *Littératures classiques* 30: 9–19.

Coste, Hilarion de. 1647. *Eloges et vies des reynes, des princesses, et des dames illustres en pieté, en Courage & en Doctrine.* Paris: Sébastien et Gabriel Cramoisy.

Coton, Pierre. 1610. *Lettre declaratoire de la doctrine des peres jesuites conforme aux decrets du Concile de Constance, adressee à la Royne mere du Roy Regente de France.* Paris: Claude Chappelet.

Coton, Pierre. 1617. *Sermons sur les principales et plus difficiles matières de la foi.* Paris: Sébastien Huré.

Crétin, Guillaume. [après 1515] 1932. "S'ensuivent aulcuns quatrins faictz par ledict Cretin sur les abuz de ce monde." In *Œuvres poétiques,* éd. Kathleen Chesney: 93–4. Paris: Firmin-Didot et Cie.

Horace. 1967. *Œuvres,* trad. et éd. François Richard. Paris: Garnier Frères.

Legrain, Jean-Baptiste. 1614. *Decade contenant la vie et gestes de Henry le Grand roy de France et de Navarre IIII. du Nom.* Paris: Jean Laquehay ["Imprimé aux despens de l'Autheur"].

Lever, Maurice. 1985. *Le sceptre et la marotte. Histoire des fous de cour.* Paris: Fayard.

Maître Guillaume [Marchand, Guillaume]. 1611. *Advis de Maistre Guillaume nouvelle retourne de l'autre monde, sur le sujet de l'Anticoton, composé par P.D.C. c'est à dire, Pierre du Coignet, jadis mort & depuis n'agueres resuscité.* S. l.: s. n.

Mariana, Juan. 1598. *De rege & regis institutione.* Tolède: Petrum Rodericum.

Martineau, François. 1994. *Lè discours polémique. Essai sur l'ordre du discours judiciaire.* Paris: Quai Voltaire.

[Pasquier, Étienne]. 1602. *Catechisme des Jesuites: ou examen de leur doctrine.* Villefranche [Paris]: Guillaume Grenier.

[Plaix, César de]. [1610] s. d. *Anticoton ou refutation de la lettre declaratoire du pere Coton.* S. l.: s. n.

[Poutrincourt, Jean de Biencourt, sieur de]. [1614] 1887. *Factum du procès entre Jean de Biencourt, sieur de Poutrincourt et les pères Biard et Massé, jésuites,* éd. Gabriel Marcel. Paris: Maisonneuve et Charles Leclerc.

Savare, Jean. 1969. "Maître Guillaume, fils d'apothicaire et bouffon de roi (XVIIe siècle)," *Revue d'histoire de la pharmacie* 57 (202): 401–10.

Virgile. 2011 [document consulté le 28 janvier]. *Énéide,* Livre II, dans *Bibliotheca classica selecta,* trad. et éd. Anne-Marie Boxus et Jacques Poucet: http://bcs.fltr.ucl.ac.be/Virg/V02-001-267.html.

chapter twelve

Les *Relations* des jésuites et la construction de l'observateur européen face au monde indigène

KLAUS-DIETER ERTLER

Les *Relations de la Nouvelle-France* constituent un ensemble de textes extrêmement complexe et riche en informations sur les nouvelles colonies françaises de l'Amérique septentrionale. Elles sont considérées comme une source précieuse en ce qui concerne les us et coutumes des autochtones, la vie quotidienne de la mission ainsi que les régimes de discursivité spécifiques que pratiquent les différents groupes sociaux. Dans la mesure où elles jettent les bases ethnographiques d'une étude authentique d'un grand nombre de groupes indigènes établis dans le nord-est du continent américain, on peut les lire comme le premier grand panorama de la fondation de la colonie française boréale. Mais elles donnent également naissance à un genre aux "frontières de l'historiographie" (Le Bras 1993), proche même d'une narration totalisante sur l'entreprise jésuite de cette époque. Le récit de "ce qui s'est passé en la Nouvelle France" de 1632 et 1673, pour paraphraser le titre le plus commun des *Relations*, constitue ainsi une large fresque qu'anime un dessein de propagande, au sens étymologique du terme, préfigurant en quelque sorte l'espace public proprement dit.

Il est évident que, pour atteindre ce but, la construction discursive d'une telle œuvre suppose une entreprise de grande envergure, dont la vaste architecture polyphonique prend pour objet les colonies de la Nouvelle-France, puis se déploie afin de célébrer le mouvement de réforme catholique lancé un siècle plus tôt par Ignace de Loyola et ses compagnons, qu'il s'agisse de François Xavier en Chine ou, plus tard, de Manoel da Nóbrega au Brésil. Mission première du dicastère de la *Propaganda Fide*, fondé au début des années 1620, pareille entreprise de glorification de la foi et de sa diffusion, construite selon un modèle préétabli et suivant une structure discursive bien ordonnée, permet de mieux comprendre la portée de ces écrits au XVIIe siècle. Si les pères jésuites se voient contraints de fournir des rapports détaillés de leurs activités à un supérieur qui transmettra les manuscrits à Paris pour les faire imprimer, le processus de production des *Relations* comme de celui de leur réception est d'une complexité dont il importe de prendre d'emblée la mesure en en rappelant le programme:

> Donnez toutes les nouvelles dont la connaissance en Europe doit porter à glorifier Dieu à ceux qui les recevront. Dans ces lettres, vous devrez apporter un discernement et un choix dans les faits; qu'elles passent sous silence ce qui peut atteindre indirectement les personnes ou les offenser par une allusion téméraire. Toute la substance et le style doivent être conformes à la gravité comme à la prudence ecclésiastiques. Que vos écrits soient de telle nature qu'étant portés en Europe, ils puissent passer de mains en mains et même être communiqués au public par la voie de l'impression. Vous ne devrez pas perdre de vue que les mémoires de ce genre qui proviennent de pays si éloignés sont curieusement recherchés et lus avidement en Europe, en Italie et ailleurs. Et nous devons par là même écrire avec plus d'attention et de réserve les lettres que nous envoyons. Elles ne doivent pas seulement être remises dans les mains de nos amis, mais elles doivent passer en celles de personnes souvent injustes, et souvent jalouses et malveillantes. Il faut donc que ces lettres satisfassent tout le monde, si c'est en effet possible, et qu'elles portent chacun à rendre hommage à Dieu et à la sainte Église (François Xavier à Jean de Beira. In Martin 1974, x–xii).[1]

Abstraction faite de la dimension religieuse, l'ordonnance du jésuite-voyageur ne manque pas d'insister sur le caractère polyvalent de ces écrits qui, d'une part, s'inscrivent à l'intérieur de la logique propre à la Compagnie, mais qui, d'autre part, s'adressent à un grand public de lecteurs, préfigurant ainsi non seulement la presse moralisatrice naissante des *Spectateurs*, mais aussi des œuvres de grande envergure, comme le *Journal des savants* ou le *Dictionnaire de Trévoux*, qui paraîtront quelques décennies plus tard. Le corpus des *Relations* prélude, en quelque sorte, à la pratique d'une communication à grande échelle, dans la mesure où il s'ouvre partiellement au public pour lui fournir des textes non seulement brefs et segmentés, mais encore enrichis d'une panoplie de curiosités. La multitude de ces lettres et de ces rapports venant d'outre-Atlantique suivent les méthodes ignaciennes, si bien qu'ils observent une taxonomie rigoureuse, en particulier dans la *dispositio* des faits, relatés de façon chronologique, ou dans la comptabilité des âmes sauvées ou perdues. Ces *Relations* ne manquent pas de tisser un système de références, à interprétations multiples certes, mais dont les micronarrations ont généralement pour protagonistes les pères jésuites dans leur lutte héroïque contre l'environnement sauvage. Aussi ce discours met-il en scène un rapporteur écrivant en qualité de "civilisé" et dont les observations qu'il recueille sur le terrain de la conversion se moulent dans un texte spécifique et largement destiné au grand public (voir Parent 1993). Dès le départ, les rapports rédigés font également partie d'un ensemble dans lequel les intertextes et les interdiscours fleurissent, afin de leur conférer la marque d'une identité commune et d'un esprit de corps dont l'homogénéité et le rayonnement mondial deviennent proverbiaux. En même temps que la personnalité du rapporteur se met en scène pour fournir un exemple des faits racontés, le texte est susceptible de subir des corrections et des retouches au niveau supérieur de la hiérarchie. Ainsi l'individu et la collectivité agissent-ils de concert, ce qui confère aux relations jésuites les caractéristiques d'un premier réseau de dimension mondiale.

Les *Exercices spirituels* d'Ignace de Loyola fournissaient à ces prêtres militants et à ces missionnaires les principales idées à partir desquelles ils pouvaient entreprendre de traduire en texte narratif les expériences de leur vie active et contemplative. Il est surprenant de constater à quel point le fondateur de l'ordre insiste sur le fait que la dimension méditative de la vie spirituelle doit privilégier la médiation des sens, afin d'agrémenter la narration, dont la fonction ne cesse de prendre de l'importance en se chargeant d'une dimension personnelle et vivante:

> [L]a personne [...] doit narrer l'histoire de telle contemplation ou méditation de manière fidèle, et discourir en rappelant seulement les points essentiels, de manière à ce que le propos soit bref ou sommaire; parce que la personne qui contemple, tirant cette histoire de sa source véritable, discourant et raisonnant par elle-même, [...] inspire plus de goût et de plaisir spirituel que celle qui procure des exercices accompagnés de grandes déclarations et d'amplifications sur le sens de cette histoire: car ce n'est pas la grandeur du savoir qui remplit et satisfait l'âme, mais le sentir et le goûter des choses éprouvées dans son for intérieur ("[L]a persona [...] debe narrar fielmente la historia de la tal contemplación o meditación, discurriendo solamente por los puntos, con breve o sumaria declaración; porque la persona que contempla, tomando el fundamento verdadero de la historia, discurriendo y raciocinando por sí mismo, [...] es de más gusto

> y fruto espiritual que si el que da los ejercicios hubiese mucho declarado y ampliado el sentido de la historia; porque no el mucho saber harta y satisface al ánima, mas el sentir y gustar de las cosas internamente" [Loyola [ca. 1527] 1990, 43]).

Ce passage montre avec éloquence toute l'importance que prend le fait narratif dans les modes de transmission du savoir et des expériences personnelles chez les jésuites. Dans un contexte où l'écrivain en appelle à l'expérience sensible et où le narré devient plus authentique de ce fait, il faut aussi souligner plus particulièrement la promotion que connaît le sens de la vue, qui prime désormais sur l'ouïe dans l'observation du monde et de soi-même. Rappelons que l'ouïe avait dominé l'imaginaire jusque-là, car elle semblait refléter plus fidèlement la perception du monde que la vue, celle-ci étant trop connotée par la dimension sensuelle. Quoi qu'il en soit, c'est en regard de cette promotion de l'expérience sensible que l'instance narrative s'institue en tant qu'exemple, les estimations personnelles que procure l'ensemble de ces narrateurs jésuites jouant dès lors un rôle important dans la modélisation complexe du monde de leur époque.

De ce point de vue, les *Relations* s'offrent donc tel un texte polyphonique, formé d'une marqueterie de réflexions elles-mêmes marquées par la diversité des expériences quotidiennes à la faveur desquelles chacun, à la fois observateur et participant, essaie de narrer sa vie active et contemplative. C'est par le "narrat" que la réalité intérieure et extérieure est prise en charge: l'observateur participant ne cherche pas à s'exclure, mais à faire participer son lectorat jésuite ou non jésuite au vécu de la situation coloniale. Par un procédé d'exemplification, il se met en scène pour illustrer ses conditions de survie ainsi que ses perceptions intérieures dans un cadre de vie étranger. De même, lorsque le fondateur, Ignace de Loyola, évoque trois dimensions dans la mémorisation des péchés, il se réfère également aux éléments-clés d'une telle mise en scène, éléments qui deviendront constitutifs dans la description de la Nouvelle-France:

> [S]e remémorer d'année en année, ou de temps en temps; en cela, elles servent à trois choses: la première, regarder le lieu et la maison où j'ai habité; la seconde, la conversation que j'ai eue avec d'autres; la troisième, le service dans lequel j'ai vécu ("[T]raer a la memoria de año en año o de tiempo en tiempo; para lo cual aprovechan tres cosas: la primera, mirar el lugar y la casa adonde he habitado; la segunda, la conversación que he tenido con otros; la tercera, el oficio en que he vivido" [73]).

Multiples sont les préceptes qui se trouvent dans les *Exercices* afin d'ériger les observateurs à la fois en sujet et en objet de leurs histoires, et de les présenter comme des exemples *ad majorem Dei gloriam* fournis à l'intention du lectorat de leur époque. N'oublions pas qu'outre les préceptes rappelant l'importance de la description des lieux ou, si l'on préfère, de la "composition de lieu," le texte fondateur fournit aussi des indications précises sur la mémorisation du temps et de son organisation. En effet, Loyola rappelle maintes fois que le cadre chronologique de la répétition possède une fonction essentielle dans l'organisation du récit, ce qui constitue finalement la base discursive des *Relations de la Nouvelle-France.* C'est, en somme, le récit comme moyen d'expression ainsi que la mise en exergue de la vie intérieure et extérieure du narrateur qui fournissent les éléments-clés à ce genre particulier de l'écriture missiologique canadienne.

Si l'auto-représentation de l'observateur jésuite caractérise donc généralement les *Relations*, celles-ci se trouvent également intégrées dans un cadre épistémologique, que fixe notamment la mention du destinataire et du destinateur, qui ne manquent pas d'être indiqués par le paratexte. Ainsi, habituellement, les textes portent-ils des indicateurs bien ordonnés suivant le modèle d'une lettre officielle. À titre d'exemple, nous citerons la première *Relation* de 1632, intitulée *Brieve Relation du Voyage de la Nouvelle France fait au mois d'Avril 1632 par le P. Paul Le Jeune, de la Compagnie de Jésus, envoyée au R. P. Barthélemy Jacquinot, Provincial de la même Compagnie en la Province de France.* D'emblée, le narrateur s'y pose en exemple pour raconter les circonstances qui l'ont mené à effectuer son voyage en Nouvelle-France. Le message est ambivalent car, bien qu'il semble s'agir d'une lettre privée et intime rédigée à l'intention du supérieur hiérarchique de la Compagnie, celle-ci vise également un large public, dans la mesure où elle est manifestement écrite pour servir la propagande en faveur de la cause de la colonisation. Le rédacteur s'y présente comme un sujet obéissant, dont les sensations intimes se déclinent au fil de l'écriture. On y apprend non seulement la satisfaction de Paul Lejeune à prendre le large, mais on y découvre aussi une sorte de mise en abyme, qui intègre une première lettre dans la lettre en en faisant une "marque de distinction"[2] dans la vie du jeune jésuite:

> Estant aduerty de vostre part, le dernier iour de Mars, qu'il falloit au plus tost m'embarquer au Haure de grace, pour tirer droict à la Nouvelle France, l'aise et le contentement que i'en resenty en mon ame fut si grand, que de

> vingt ans ie ne pense pas en auoir eu vn pareil, ny qu'aucune lettre m'ayt esté tant agreable (Lejeune 1632, 3).

La lecture de la lettre inespérée du provincial a soulevé l'enthousiasme du jeune homme, pareil témoignage correspondant entièrement à l'esprit des directives d'Ignace de Loyola. Du même souffle, Lejeune fait état à son supérieur de ses sentiments personnels et des événements relatifs à l'entreprise missionnaire et coloniale. La mise en scène du narrateur, véritable "sonde" chargée d'explorer du Nouveau Monde, passe par une narration organisée selon les principes ignaciens. Remarquons aussi l'obéissance avec laquelle Lejeune répond à l'injonction que formule le texte de la *Brieve Relation*, ainsi que la satisfaction de pouvoir réaliser les plans que l'on a conçus pour lui.[3]

Dans le même esprit, le narrateur se met en scène en tant que représentant subalterne qui, en *miles Christi*, prépare le terrain en faveur de ceux qui le suivront: "[A]ussi m'est-il aduis [par l'Évangile] que ie viens icy comme les pionniers, qui marchent les premiers pour faire les tranchées, et par apres les braues soldats viennent assieger et prendre la place" (3). Le concept de soldat fait partie de l'auto-construction narrative de ce genre de textes. Les jésuites recourent volontiers à de telles métaphores pour manifester leur organisation stricte et hiérarchique, ce qui est particulièrement le cas dans les écrits de Paul Lejeune (voir Pioffet 1993).[4] Ainsi la narration est-elle sous-tendue par un système de valeurs formant une topique destinée à soutenir entièrement un plaidoyer en faveur de l'entreprise de colonisation, qui est lui-même lié à la défense et illustration de la religion. Au reste, nous savons que cette apologie de l'action militaire exprime et magnifie également le rôle de la Compagnie de Jésus, fondée précisément pour être le fer de lance de la Contre-Réforme.

En conséquence, il semble que le sous-texte dont se nourrit ce thème, véritable foyer du discours jésuite, renvoie à la vocation d'un ordre cultivant lui-même une mise en scène militaire de son action et développant un discours de conquête mondiale que des martyrs, si besoin est, viendront assurer. Les *Exercices spirituels* – une fois de plus – en fournissent le sous-texte argumentatif:

> [C]'est une chose plus digne de considération de voir le Christ, notre Seigneur, roi éternel, et devant lui, tout l'univers qu'il interpelle, disant à chacun en particulier: "Ma volonté est de conquérir le monde entier et tous les

> ennemis, et d'entrer ainsi dans la gloire de mon Père; qui veut venir avec moi doit donc travailler avec moi, parce que celui qui me suit dans la peine, me suit aussi dans la gloire ('[E]s cosa más digna de consideración ver a Cristo nuestro Señor, rey eterno, y delante dél, todo el universo mundo, al cual y a cada uno en particular llama y dice: "Mi voluntad es de conquistar todo el mundo y todos los enemigos, y así entrar en la gloria de mi Padre; por tanto, quien quisiere venir conmigo ha de trabajar conmigo, porque siguiéndome en la pena también me siga en la gloria'" [88]).

Dans les *Relations*, les narrations sont teintées, pour ne pas dire générées, par cet intertexte qui rappelle précisément les intentions missionnaires de la *militia Christi* d'Ignace de Loyola. L'entreprise jésuite cultive donc le discours de la conquête spirituelle, au sein de laquelle s'inscrivent les relations particulières avec leurs nombreuses narrations et récits à l'appui.

Mis à part l'aspect martial de l'entreprise missionnaire, nous trouvons dans les *Relations* un trait bien particulier de la représentation de la violence et du supplice. C'est avec force détails que les scènes de torture et de douleurs sont racontées par les pères, si bien qu'on se demande les raisons d'une telle acribie. Dans les *Exercices spirituels*, les références à la pénitence font partie intégrante du texte:

> La troisième [...] châtier la chair, c'est-à-dire lui procurer une douleur sensible, ce qui s'obtient lorsqu'on porte sur soi des cilices, des cordes ou des barres de fer, lorsqu'on se flagelle ou s'impose des blessures ou des rigueurs d'autres sortes ("La tercera [...], castigar la carne, es a saber, dándole dolor sensible, el cual se da trayendo cilicios o sogas o barras de hierro sobre la carne, flagelándose o llagándose, y otras maneras de asperezas" [81]).

Suivant l'approche systémique qui est la nôtre, il faut donc présumer un lien essentiel entre la perception de la pénitence chez Loyola et sa représentation dans les *Relations*, en particulier lorsqu'il s'agit d'évoquer les fonctions du châtiment corporel chez les autochtones. Le supplice faisant partie de son quotidien, le père jésuite, qui enregistre les châtiments avec soin, en saisit les particularités pour, en tant que "civilisé," marquer sa différence par rapport aux excès qu'il observe. Dans l'ensemble des écrits, nous trouvons maintes références à de tels châtiments, relatés sous forme d'intenses dramatisations qui s'appuient sur des descriptions détaillées. L'ensemble des récits atteint une sorte de paroxysme de la complexité, lorsque le rapporteur d'horribles châtiments, le père

Brébeuf, sera torturé à son tour, événement raconté dans la *Relation* de 1649 et largement diffusé dans le monde catholique. Par ce procédé est créée une véritable auto-référence narrative qui ouvrira l'ensemble de l'entreprise littéraire à d'autres textes et à d'autres lecteurs.

Au reste, c'est dans la première *Relation* de Lejeune, récit homodiégétique, que le narrateur se décrit comme le représentant d'un ordre où le monde s'organise autour d'une dichotomie entre le Bien et le Mal, suivant en cela une conception conforme aux préceptes ignaciens. De fait, Lejeune décrit ses relations avec les peuples autochtones de manière à mieux faire valoir le processus de conversion à ce Bien qu'il représente. "Or, c'est icy que j'ay veu des Sauuages pour la premiere fois" (Lejeune 1632, 4). Avec cette phrase commence, en effet, une série de descriptions de l'Autre, dont le lecteur européen semble être curieux de connaître les coutumes, mais se dessine aussi une ligne de démarcation déterminant une posture narrative où écriture et fictionnalisation vont de pair. C'est ainsi que Lejeune manque sans cesse de catégories pour appréhender – du moins de façon adéquate – la fonction culturelle de ce qui se déroule devant ses yeux, chaque signe se découvrant dès lors une valeur qui, certes, ne manque pas de couleur, mais qui se trouve en porte-à-faux par rapport à ce qui se passe réellement sous ses yeux. Par exemple, faute de repères culturels adéquats, il recourt à des images connues, importées de sa France natale, lorsqu'il met en scène le jeu des masques autochtones:

> [I]l me sembloit, les voyant entrer dans la chambre de nostre Capitaine, où i'estois pour lors, que ie voyois ces masques qui courent en France à Caresme prenant. Il y en auoit qui auoient le nez peint en bleu, les yeux, les sourcils, les iouës peintes en noir, et le reste du visage en rouge, et ces couleurs sont viues et luysantes comme celle de nos masques (4).

Lejeune réagit au spectacle des masques comme s'il s'agissait d'un événement familier survenant au sein de la culture catholique, car même en se décrivant comme un observateur qui participe à la scène, il n'arrive pas à inscrire les coutumes indigènes dans leur propre contexte culturel. Certes, si la narration avait été hétérodiégétique, la distance par rapport au monde observé aurait été encore plus grande, et donc moins révélatrice, puisque l'observation externe crée par définition une distance plus marquée. Mais si le seul fait de rendre compte du monde autochtone par écrit lui permet de valoriser ces peuples, il ne peut toutefois éviter que ces derniers ne soient renvoyés à une autre sphère, laquelle relève d'une axiologie européenne proche des références des missionnaires. La *Relation* introduit donc un écart par rapport à la sphère culturelle du monde observé, qui sera surdéterminé par une dimension métaphysique propre à la pensée jésuite, dans la mesure où les pères perçoivent les coutumes des peuples autochtones en fonction d'une axiologie dont les principes directeurs s'adossent non seulement à leur structure de pensée européenne, mais aussi spécifiquement aux préceptes de Loyola.

Mais la construction de l'observateur européen ne passe pas seulement par la description de sa présence dans le Nouveau Monde, avec tout ce que cela suppose. Lecteurs habitués aux *Exercices spirituels* d'Ignace de Loyola, dont Michel Foucault et Roland Barthes ont analysé les implications communicationnelles, nous savons que les Pères avaient maîtrisé aussi une série de techniques d'interlocution qui reposaient surtout sur une structure dramatique, modèle rhétorique qui fait partie des codes essentiels des *Relations* (voir Foucault 1991, 91; Barthes 1997, 62). Chez Lejeune, le lecteur découvre ce procédé herméneutique lorsqu'il s'agit de transmettre les discours indigènes et leur logique particulière. À titre d'exemple, nous citerons les harangues d'un chef autochtone, qui ne manquent pas d'intérêt et que le jésuite n'hésite pas à mettre en parallèle avec les discours de l'Antiquité classique européenne: "[C]e Capitaine prend la parole pour respondre, mais avec vne rhetorique aussi fine et deliée, qu'il en sçaurait sortir de l'escolle d'Aristote, ou de Ciceron" (Lejeune 1632, 26). Le narrateur ou rapporteur jésuite se pose en arbitre afin de transmettre mot pour mot les arguments coloniaux et indigènes, dont les deux isotopies se heurtent et s'affrontent inlassablement. Selon la représentation qu'en donne Lejeune, le discours du capitaine possède tous les éléments d'un discours raisonnable. Ainsi sera-t-il érigé en exemple par l'observateur européen, qui se trouve à inscrire dans la parole sauvage son propre système de valeurs, apparemment aussi universel qu'irréfutable.

Un jour, Lejeune se voit confronté à des autochtones du camp ennemi, qu'il range d'entrée de jeu dans le monde du Diable: "Ces sorciers, c'est ainsi que les François appellent ceste nation, pource qu'elle fait vne particuliere profession de consulter leur Manitou, ou parler au Diable; ces sorciers, dis-ie, sont venus iusques à Kebec" (29). Le père suit les préceptes de Loyola, fondés sur l'idée d'une dichotomie morale partageant le monde entre deux principes, afin de mieux marquer la complicité entre les colons français et les groupes indigènes amis. L'ennemi se voit relégué au rang de "sorcier," ce qui l'exclut d'emblée de l'univers culturel de Lejeune et de tout effort pour l'accueillir à l'intérieur de son système. Nous trouvons là un exemple de la construction dichotomique sous-tendant un discours qui se veut toujours exemplaire, c'est-à-dire susceptible de fournir – au jour le jour – une comptabilité de l'œuvre apostolique réalisée dans les colonies, sans pour autant renoncer à la narration détaillée et agréable des travaux qu'exige l'entreprise de conversion. Le récit privilégie donc les dichotomies connues de la structure anthropologique de l'Imaginaire (voir Durand 1984 [1969]), en insistant sur les oppositions ignaciennes, qui reconduisent la confrontation entre le Bien et le Mal, le Paradis et l'Enfer, voire la civilisation et la sauvagerie. Établies sur ce schéma antithétique, ces dichotomies acquièrent une logique narrative qui structurera – en particulier au niveau de l'exemplification – les rapports quotidiens entre les autochtones et les colonisateurs, que surdétermine le texte de base auquel ils sont censés faire référence, c'est-à-dire les préceptes d'Ignace de Loyola. Mais la narration et ses effets de mise en scène, chez les jésuites, n'ont pas toujours eu le privilège d'une réception favorable. Leurs vertus pédagogiques et exemplaires ont été de plus en plus récusées comme une déformation de la réalité, surtout au XVIIIe siècle, alors que les critiques se multiplient à l'encontre de leurs récits (voir Gerbi [1955] 2000).

Certes, nous savons que, par leurs récits si fortement marqués par la personnalité de leurs auteurs, les *Relations* ont largement influencé l'imaginaire européen. À l'époque, si elles circulaient bien sûr dans les réseaux de la Compagnie, elles ont été aussi utilisées à des fins de propagande dans le but d'intéresser les contemporains à l'entreprise coloniale de la France. Ainsi construisirent-elles une image du Nouveau Monde qui marque encore les œuvres postérieures, en particulier celles du baron de Lahontan, de Lafitau et de Charlevoix. D'une part, ces narrations homodiégétiques seront appelées à devenir autant de matériaux mis à la disposition des travaux d'une recherche anthropologique encore à venir et qui sera plus objective et plus scientifique. D'autre part, elles feront leur entrée, dès l'âge classique, dans le système littéraire européen proprement dit et marqueront les discours fictionnels mettant en scène des autochtones.

Mais l'auto-construction de l'*ethos* jésuite aura perdu de sa vigueur dans l'intervalle, dans la mesure où l'ordre fera l'objet d'une répression de plus en plus vigoureuse au cours du XVIIIe siècle et jusqu'à son expulsion finale de la plupart des royaumes catholiques. Les *Recherches philosophiques sur les Américains* (1768) de Cornélius De Pauw marquent, à cet égard, un moment déterminant dans la critique de ses missions américaines, alors que le savant d'origine hollandaise y développe une thèse selon laquelle l'homme américain était si “dégénéré” que sa chute était irrémédiable. De Pauw réfute la mise en scène des jésuites, qui lui paraît être à l'opposé de ses propres conjonctures sur les Amérindiens. Convaincu que les autochtones sont réfractaires à toute forme de civilisation, il fait preuve à leur endroit d'une hargne devenue proverbiale. Il considère même les jésuites comme des usurpateurs qui ont mis leurs récits au service de leurs intentions politiques et apologétiques, afin de tromper le monde et de maintenir leur pouvoir:

> [N]ous savons qu'il y a d'autres contrées dont on a soustrait à dessein la connaissance au public. Ceux qui, en abusant à la fois de la sainteté de leur ministère & de la confiance d'un peuple bon & malheureux, se sont érigés en petits tyrans sous les deux tropiques du nouveau monde, ont cru qu'il n'étoit ni de leur gloire, ni de leur intérêt de donner des relations trop sincères de leurs conquêtes (De Pauw [1768] 1990, vol. 1: 149).

Le philosophe y développe des arguments qui ne sont pas plus tendres envers ces relations qu'envers leurs auteurs. Il dénonce ainsi ces mises en scène de soi auxquelles se livre le narrateur dans ces textes, de même que le caractère dépravé des autochtones de tout le continent. Mais à son avis, ce qui nuit le plus à la compréhension de la nature véritable des Amériques, “ce sont des espèces de légendes” (149) propagées par les *Relations*, quelle que soit leur provenance. Pour De Pauw, il est inconcevable de donner crédit à ces relations du Nouveau Monde et de croire sur leur foi en la capacité de ses habitants à se civiliser. À l'exemple de Buffon, qui avait réduit la faune du continent à un niveau bien inférieur à celui de l'Europe (voir 149 et suiv.), De Pauw renchérit en appliquant la même méthode à ses habitants. Dans ce contexte peu propice aux jésuites, leurs écrits de propagande, qui semblaient de moins en moins mériter les égards dus à un témoignage authentique sur l'Amérique, avaient perdu tout crédit, jugement qui sera porté aussi sur leurs narrations à vocation pédagogique. Cette fois, la mise en scène de l'observateur européen ne se heurte pas aux arguments d'un sorcier hostile, mais aux critiques acerbes d'un philosophe européen, dont les paramètres, pourtant difficiles à soutenir, arrivèrent néanmoins à se maintenir dans le discours des sciences naturelles.

Inlassablement, la critique de De Pauw se porte contre les effets de mise en scène discursive des narrateurs jésuites, dont il ne manque pas de souligner le côté fantasque, se félicitant au passage qu' "[a]ujourd'hui [...] cette société ne subsiste plus, & que son esprit de vertige & d'inévitables malheurs l'ont précipitée dans le néant" (157). La critique touche particulièrement les successeurs des *Relations* au XVIIIe siècle, les Lafitau et Charlevoix, dont les thèses et la manière de les présenter sont violemment prises à partie par De Pauw: "D'ailleurs le voyage des Cariens aux isles Caraïbes n'a pu venir dans l'esprit que d'un écrivain qui sans respect pour la vérité, & pour la vrai-semblance, prodiguait à chaque page les paradoxes & les fables les plus maladroitement imaginées" (vol. 2: 55). Une fois de plus, le système narratif propre aux Jésuites est remis en cause. Et De Pauw de renchérir:

> Charlevoix, qui n'a pu se dispenser d'abandonner en partie les opinions de son confrere [Lafitau], qu'il ose nommer un homme docte, n'a pas été plus heureux dans ses propres conjectures; au moins est-il difficile de se contenter de ce qu'il a écrit à ce sujet dans son style missionnaire' (55).

À examiner son argumentation de près, l'on se rend compte que c'est la narration et ses effets de mise en scène qui sont critiquées avec le plus de sévérité. L'illusion, voire les chimères produites par de tels procédés mis en œuvre dans la représentation de l'Amérique, se voient récusées par le philosophe qui, lui, n'avait pourtant jamais mis les pieds sur le continent américain. Son système d'analyse est donc contraire à celui des Lafitau et des Charlevoix qui, eux, puisent des connaissances de première main sur le continent et ses habitants dans les narrations des missionnaires du siècle précédent.

Certes, les analyses de De Pauw constituent un cas extrême de la critique du Nouveau Monde tel que les jésuites le donnaient à voir, et il est vrai que d'autres auteurs s'expriment d'une façon plus nuancée. La première œuvre à se réclamer d'une ambition ethnologique, *L'esprit des usages et des coutumes des différents peuples* (1776), de Jean-Nicholas Demeunier, traite l'information transmise par les voyageurs et les missionnaires jésuites avec plus de détachement. Il ne cherche pas à désavouer les *Relations*, mais abandonne résolument l'aspect narratif et trop personnel pour construire une sorte de science comparatiste. Pour lui, il importe surtout de ne plus présenter les usages ou coutumes extra-européens comme s'il s'agissait de quelque chose de curieux ou d'étrange. Demeunier adopte plutôt une stratégie comparatiste, selon laquelle le fait doit primer sur la narration qui, elle, se voit mise en examen. Dans son

"Avertissement," il met le lecteur en garde contre toute forme de narration, essentiellement susceptible d'être biaisée par la culture de leur auteur:

> Après tant de livres sur l'homme, on n'a point rapproché les Moeurs, les Usages, les Coutumes & les Loix des différens Peuples: on veut réparer cette omission. Nous connaissons presque toutes les nations, policées ou sauvages, il est tems de les comparer; & comme le genre humain offrira désormais un spectacle monotone, on tâche de conserver les vestiges des premiers tems. Les Ecrivains ne presentent guères les usages étrangers que sous un point de vue bisarre ou ridicule; on change ici de méthode, & on en cherche l'esprit (Demeunier [1776] 1988, v).

Dans sa première comparaison d'ordre ethnologique, Demeunier ne s'attaque pas directement à l'œuvre des *Relations*, bien qu'il questionne leur méthode. Les auteurs de référence sont plutôt Lahontan, Lafitau et Charlevoix; il s'intéresse donc aux héritiers directs des *Relations de la Nouvelle France* plutôt qu'à celles-ci. Avec *L'esprit des usages* naît un nouveau genre de discours, qui s'élève contre la manière de "narrer" l'autre culture comme un objet rare et inaccessible, dans un contexte où la mise en scène de l'observateur européen jouait un rôle non négligeable dans ce genre de récit. Pour Demeunier, l'interprétation de la culture passe par une comparaison rigide et substantielle plutôt que par une mise en scène narrative foisonnante telle que les auteurs des *Relations* l'avaient pratiquée. À la fin du XVIIIe siècle, le sens à donner aux us et coutumes de l'Autre semble être plus accessible à la faveur d'une comparaison que d'une rhétorique théâtralisée à vocation apologétique et herméneutique. Alors que le narrateur jésuite cherche à intéresser son lecteur – en ne le reléguant pas au dernier plan, comme le voudrait Cornélius de De Pauw – Demeunier semble être conscient du fait que la compilation de toutes les expériences personnelles représente néanmoins une condition *sine qua non* du développement de l'ethnologie moderne.

En ce sens, concluons en observant que la rhétorique fortement narrativisée des missionnaires, avec ses mises en scène exemplaires, constituait à la fois leur force et leur faiblesse: leur force, en raison de la valeur littéraire des récits, de leur plausibilité et de leur caractère pédagogique; leur faiblesse, en raison de la distorsion qu'introduit une isotopie axiologique et religieuse par rapport aux valeurs des autochtones, ce qui a provoqué l'ire des lecteurs philosophes. Si les *Relations* ont connu un impact extraordinaire auprès du lectorat de leur temps, elles ont également subi les critiques sévères de plusieurs représentants des Lumières. Leur œuvre a pourtant joué un rôle de catalyseur, fixant même un système important de représentation littéraire qui, par la suite, n'a cessé d'être admiré et dénoncé en même temps.

NOTES

1 Cité d'après Le Bras 1993, 64.
2 Par "marque de distinction," nous entendons la ligne de différentiation qui, selon la théorie de la complexité, fournit le cadre de perception à un observateur dans un entourage complexe (voir Bateson 1972).
3 Lorsque Lejeune se référera au monde américain, le texte comportera aussi des éléments de fiction. Les repères culturels de son nouvel environnement ne lui sont pas accessibles par les instruments de l'observation traditionnelle.
4 L'auteure souligne, entre autres, l'admiration des missionnaires pour les actions militaires (*militia Christi*).

BIBLIOGRAPHY

Barthes, Roland. 1997. *Sade, Fourier, Loyola.* Madrid: Cátedra.
Bateson, Gregory. 1972. *Steps to an Ecology of Mind. Collected Essays in Anthropology, Psychiatry, Evolution and Epistemology.* New York: Chandler.
De Pauw, Cornélius. 1990 [1768]. *Recherches philosophiques sur les Américains,* éd. Michèle Duchet, 3 vol. Paris: Jean Michel Place.
Demeunier, Jean-Nicholas. 1988 [1776]. *L'esprit des usages et des coutumes des différents peuples,* éd. Jean Puillon. Paris: Jean Michel Place.
Durand, Gilbert. 1984 [1969]. *Les structures anthropologiques de l'Imaginaire.* Paris: Dunod.
Foucault, Michel. 1991. *Tecnologías del yo y otros textos afines.* Barcelona: Paidos.
Gerbi, Antonello. 2000 [1955]. *La disputa del Nuovo Mondo. Storia di una polemica (1750–1900).* Milano: Adelphi.
Le Bras, Yvon. 1993. "Les *Relations* de Paul Lejeune: aux frontières de l'historiographie." In *Rhétorique et conquête missionnaire. Le jésuite Paul Lejeune,* éd. Réal Ouellet: 53–65. Québec: Septentrion.
Lejeune, Paul. 1632. *Brieve Relation du Voyage de la Nouvelle France fait au mois d'Avril 1632 par le P. Paul Le Jeune, de la Compagnie de Jésus, envoyée au R.P. Barthélemy Jacquinot, Provincial de la même Compagnie en la Province de France.* Paris: Sébastien Cramoisy.

Loyola, Ignace de. [ca. 1527] 1990. *Ejercicios espirituales*, éd. Cándido de Dalmases. Santander: Sal Terrae.

Martin, Félix. 1974. "Introduction." In *Relations inédites de la Nouvelle-France (1672–1679)*, 2 vol. Montréal: Éditions Élysée.

Parent, Marie. 1993. "Restriction de validité et héroïsation du protagoniste dans le *Grand voyage du pays des Hurons* de Sagard et la *Relation* de 1634 de Lejeune." In *Rhétorique et conquête missionnaire. Le jésuite Paul Lejeune*, éd. Réal Ouellet, 67–87. Québec: Septentrion.

Pioffet, Marie-Christine. 1993. "L'arc et l'épée: les images de la guerre chez le jésuite Paul Lejeune." In *Rhétorique et conquête missionnaire. Le jésuite Paul Lejeune*, éd. Réal Ouellet: 41–65. Québec: Septentrion.

chapter thirteen

Une rhétorique du silence: l'œuvre jésuite dans la *Description de la Louisiane* du récollet Louis Hennepin

CATHERINE BROUÉ

À son retour en France à la fin de 1682, après un séjour de six ans en Nouvelle-France et un périple dont on n'a pas encore bien circonscrit les limites dans la région du Mississipi, Louis Hennepin, missionnaire récollet et aumônier des troupes de l'explorateur Cavelier de la Salle, se fait semble-t-il le porte-parole de son ordre et de Frontenac en rapportant à la Cour les griefs circulant dans la colonie contre les missionnaires jésuites, dont la rigueur morale est jugée excessive. Son premier récit de voyage, la *Description de la Louisiane*, qui paraît en 1683, relance d'ailleurs la critique sur le travail de la Compagnie de Jésus en Nouvelle-France, en affirmant que l'évangélisation des peuples de l'Amérique est impossible sans une colonisation du territoire et leur assujettissement à grande échelle.

De fait, dans le débat visant à établir lequel des ordres installés en Nouvelle-France est le plus apte à établir des missions, la *Description de la Louisiane* souligne le désintéressement, la popularité, la prudence des disciples de saint François, ainsi que la fiabilité de leurs écrits. Du travail et de la présence jésuite en Nouvelle-France, nulle mention dans ce récit: mais l'implicite du texte fait progresser le lecteur vers des conclusions peu tendres à l'endroit des missionnaires de la Compagnie de Jésus.

Contexte historique

L'année 1670 marque le retour en Nouvelle-France, après plus de quarante ans d'absence, des frères mineurs de saint François, communément appelés récollets. Évincés des missions canadiennes au profit des jésuites en 1632, malgré un début d'apostolat entre 1615 et 1629, les récollets se rétablissent en effet sur les terres qui leur appartiennent à Québec à partir de cette date. À la cour, on espère que leur présence tempèrera l'influence jugée embarrassante de la Compagnie de Jésus (voir Louis XIV [1672] 1927, 6). L'appui inconditionnel que leur accorde, dès le début de son mandat, le gouverneur Frontenac[1] n'empêche pas ces récollets de se sentir exclus d'un territoire dont ils se considèrent pourtant les apôtres.[2] Jusqu'à la fin des années 1680, de nombreux conflits les opposeront en effet à l'évêque de Québec, François de Laval, dont l'autoritarisme heurte de plein fouet leur zèle missionnaire (voir Dubé 1995, 20–3). Dans la lutte de pouvoir qui se joue entre les autorités ecclésiastiques et les autorités coloniales (manifeste notamment à propos de la "querelle de l'eau-de-vie" qui bat son plein durant les années 1670), les récollets, pris à parti par le gouverneur, seront tenus à l'écart des missions par l'évêque.

À Catarackoui,[3] chasse gardée du gouverneur, deux récollets pourront exercer les fonctions d'aumôniers dès 1675 (voir Jouve 1912, 38). En 1679, trois religieux prêteront leur concours à l'entreprise pour laquelle La Salle vient de recevoir des lettres-patentes: Louis Hennepin, Zénobe Membré et Gabriel de la Ribourde suivront l'explorateur. Arrivé à Québec en 1675, Louis Hennepin ne semble pas se contenter, comme l'évêque l'en aurait prié, "de prêcher l'Avent et le Carême au Cloitre des Religieuses de St. Augustin de l'Hopital dudit Québec" (Hennepin 1697, 17), mais aurait sillonné raquettes au pied le territoire habité le long du littoral laurentien (voir 17 et Dubé 1997, 201–31), avant d'exercer les fonctions de chapelain au fort Frontenac aux côtés de Luc Buisset de 1676 à 1678 (Jouve 1912, 41) et de participer, de 1679 à 1681, à la première expédition officielle de La Salle vers l'embouchure du Mississipi.[4] De retour en France vers la fin de 1681, le récollet rédige, à l'intention de Louis XIV, un rapport de son expédition. Soucieux de produire sur la cour une impression favorable à son ordre, il utilise le canevas narratif que constitue la *Relation des découvertes* de Claude Bernou[5] et l'agrémente d'observations et d'opinions personnelles susceptibles de mettre en valeur son rôle dans l'expédition. Ce rapport (ou une partie de ce rapport) recevra, en juillet 1682, un permis d'imprimer[6] et paraîtra sous le titre de *Description de la Louisiane, Nouvellement découverte au Sud de la Nouvelle-France* en 1683.

La *description de la louisiane*: une rhétorique du silence

Les récits de voyage de la Nouvelle-France s'inscrivent dans la tradition du discours rhétorique classique dont le but était "le transfert de la volonté du locuteur à son interlocuteur" par trois moyens obligatoires: "instruire, émouvoir et plaire, c'est-à-dire satisfaire la raison, susciter des passions et contenter les exigences esthétiques de l'auditeur" (Vigh 1979, 12–13).[7] Leur ambiguïté – et leur intérêt – réside dans la multiplicité des causes défendues (religieuse, commerciale, coloniale, personnelle) et des interlocuteurs visés, comme en témoigne généralement leur paratexte liminaire, qui s'adresse d'abord au Roi (ou à une personnalité influente), puis au lecteur. Les enjeux de la persuasion dans la *Description de la Louisiane* sont particulièrement nombreux à cet égard: luttes d'influence qui opposent les trois ordres ecclésiastiques (jésuites, récollets et sulpiciens) en Nouvelle-France; conflits territoriaux entre les grandes puissances européennes; clivages culturels entre Amérindiens et explorateurs;[8] concurrence commerciale; conflits de personnalité. Les textes du récollet réclament de leurs lecteurs qu'ils prennent position contre d'autres discours qu'on ne leur signale que par allusions, négations, distorsions ou surenchères. Les procédés persuasifs appuyant les divers arguments ou contre-arguments invoqués par le texte ne s'arrêtent pas aux figures classiques de la rhétorique, mais convoquent aussi les structures narrative, descriptive ou temporelle. Ainsi, il n'est pas difficile de relever, dans la *Description de la Louisiane*, des indices du parti-pris pro-récollet du narrateur. Le débat opposant l'ordre de saint François à celui de la Compagnie de Jésus comporte en effet, dans la *Description de la Louisiane*, de nombreuses ramifications.

On le sait, les jésuites font, en cette fin de XVIIe siècle, l'objet de vives critiques. À son retour en France, Hennepin, semble-t-il, se fait le porte-parole de son ordre et de Frontenac en rapportant les griefs circulant dans la colonie contre les jésuites (voir Dudouyt 1995 [1682], 164–5). La *Description de la Louisiane* porte ainsi de nombreuses traces des arguments ou contre-arguments employés par les récollets dans cette polémique, en ne donnant jamais à lire, toutefois, que l'aboutissement d'un raisonnement qu'il appartient au lecteur de reconstituer à rebours.[9] De fait, dans le débat visant à établir lequel des ordres installés en Nouvelle-France est le plus apte à établir des missions, la *Description de la Louisiane* souligne d'abord le désintéressement des disciples de saint François. L'Amérindien – ou du moins sa figure – semble à cet égard un outil privilégié.[10] Iroquois, Illinois ou Sioux, tous s'accordent, si l'on en croit le texte, à louer le dénuement absolu et volontaire des frères mineurs. La métonymie récurrente de "pieds nus" sert d'ailleurs à faire valoir ce désintéressement:

> [L]e premier Capitaine de ces Sauvages se retournant du costé des Recolets, voila dit il des Robes grises dont nous avons bien de l'estime, ils vont

> nuds pieds, comme nous, ils mesprisent les Robes de Castors que nous leurs voulons donner, sans aucune esperance de retour (Hennepin 1683, 100).

> [P]our nous autres pieds nuds, c'est ainsi que l'Iroquois nous appelle, nous ne voulions recevoir ny Castor ny pelleteries [...]; ce chef Iroquois fut surpris du refus que je fis de son present, & disoit à ceux de sa Nation que les autres François ne faisoient pas de même (299–300).

Habilement, le récit oppose en effet les "pieds nus" aux "autres Français" engagés dans le commerce des fourrures; mais comment ne pas inclure dans ces "autres Français" les jésuites, dont Frontenac prétend qu'ils "songent autant à la conversion du castor qu'à celle des âmes" (Frontenac 1861 [1672], 247–8)? Le glissement de "Français" à "jésuites" est d'autant plus facile à faire que l'expression "robes grises" proposée comme synonyme de "pieds nus" fait écho à une autre métonymie, bien connue des lecteurs des *Relations* jésuites, celle de "robes noires," et s'oppose dans le texte aux "robes de castor" tant convoitées en Nouvelle-France, mais méprisées par les frères mineurs. Rapprochées, ces allusions disséminées ça et là font ainsi progresser la lecture vers une conclusion bien incriminante pour les missionnaires de la Compagnie de Jésus.

Par ailleurs, la même métonymie de "pieds nus" offre l'avantage de prêter à l'Amérindien une préférence. Entre les deux ordres, le cœur de l'Amérindien ne balance pas:

> [I]ls nous dirent que la seule envie qu'ils avoient d'arrester nostre Capitaine, avec les Robes grises, ou pieds nuds (comme tous les Sauvages de l'Amerique appellent nos Religieux de Saint François) pour rester avec eux, les avoit obligez à nous cacher la verité (Hennepin 1683, 180).

Cette métonymie, associant *récollets, pieds nus, vie communautaire* et *amérindiens*, apparaît révélatrice de l'intention polémique du narrateur, désireux de faire valoir non seulement l'abnégation des récollets, mais aussi la popularité de leur ordre, qui fait contraste avec l'austérité que ferait peser la présence jésuite sur les habitants du Canada.

La prudence des récollets dans l'exercice de leurs fonctions sacerdotales constitue, chez Hennepin, un troisième argument en leur faveur. Alors que certains missionnaires de la Compagnie de Jésus ont déjà été sévèrement critiqués pour avoir administré trop rapidement le baptême à des Amérindiens insuffisamment préparés – par exemple, le sulpicien Galinée laisse entendre que les jésuites de Sainte-Marie-du-Saut auraient administré le baptême dans des cas discutables (voir Galinée [env. 1670] 1903, 70) –, les récollets garderaient une extrême prudence dans l'administration du baptême, soutient la *Description de la Louisiane*, puisque les frères débattent des cas litigieux entre eux et en confèrent même avec des "civils" (voir Hennepin 1683, 256–7). À côté des listes de baptêmes d'Amérindiens que dressent chaque année les *Relations* des jésuites – listes parfois impressionnantes –, l'unique baptême d'une petite Dakota, morte d'ailleurs peu après, que signale la *Description de la Louisiane*, constitue la preuve la plus probante de la conscience professionnelle des frères mineurs.

Enfin, un dernier argument plus subtil met en parallèle l'honnêteté de l'ordre de saint François et la partialité de la Compagnie de Jésus. On est d'abord surpris, en lisant Hennepin, de ne pas retrouver cet enthousiasme autochtone pour l'entreprise d'évangélisation, dont font état si amplement et si régulièrement les *Relations* des jésuites. Bien au contraire, la *Description de la Louisiane* affirme haut et fort la profonde indifférence des "Sauvages" pour la religion chrétienne – thème par ailleurs développé dans les *Mœurs des Sauvages*, opuscule publié à la suite de la *Description de la Louisiane* (voir Tremblay 1995):

> [L] a plus grande partie des Sauvages, de tous ceux que j'ay bien examinez, font connoistre que l'indifférence qu'ils ont pour toutes les maximes de nostre Religion Chrestienne, comme pour toute autre chose, est le plus grand obstacle à la Foy que j'ay connu parmy ces Barbares (Hennepin 1683, 39).

Ce discours désabusé dénigre l'un des fondements des *Relations* des jésuites: la confiance dans l'efficacité du travail missionnaire.[11] Pour Hennepin, l'évangélisation des peuples de l'Amérique est impossible sans une colonisation du territoire et leur assujettissement à grande échelle. Cette indifférence des Amérindiens aux efforts évangélisateurs, qui reviendra d'ailleurs en force dans les écrits subséquents de Louis Hennepin,[12] constitue un contre-argument à la foi des jésuites et mine la crédibilité de leur travail d'écrivains.[13]

Des *relations* exagérées?

Ce n'est d'ailleurs pas tant le travail sur le terrain des missionnaires de la Compagnie de Jésus qui est en cause que leurs *Relations* mêmes: on pourrait considérer la *Description de la Louisiane* dans son ensemble comme un vaste argument à l'appui du "on-dit" qui circule à la cour de France sur le fait que les *Relations* seraient fausses ou exagérées à bien des égards.[14] En effet, le récit fait tout de même l'apologie de la colonisation (voir Vachon 1977, 188) et la description du territoire sert d'alibi à l'action missionnaire.[15] Toutefois, le silence qu'oppose le texte à la présence jésuite en Nouvelle-France constitue en termes rhétoriques une façon de dénigrer l'autre par effacement:[16] ils n'y étaient pas, ou leur présence est insignifiante, puisque le récit ne les montre pas.[17]

Il s'agit là de l'une des nombreuses ramifications à ce même argument voulant que le travail des jésuites n'a que peu d'effet sur l'avancement de la foi en Nouvelle-France, alors que celui des récollets promet de nombreux fruits:

> [I]l y a lieu de croire qu'il s'y formera une Colonie considérable [au fort Frontenac], y ayant déjà treize à quatorze familles, & une maison de Mission, que j'y ay establie avec nostre cher Pere Luc Buisset Recollet [...]. [S]es envieux jugeans par de si beaux commencemens ce qu'il pourrait faire dans la suite avec nos Missionaires Récolets qui attiroient par leur vie desinteressée, plusieurs familles qui venoient demeurer au fort (Hennepin 1683, 12–13).

En effet, devant l'intransigeance de l'évêque de Québec, qui multiplie les vexations pour obtenir la soumission des frères de saint François, une voie s'ouvre à ces derniers que seule l'entreprise de La Salle semble pouvoir assurer: la création d'un nouvel évêché en Amérique du Nord, dans un territoire qu'il s'agit de bien distinguer (par l'éloignement, par les caractéristiques morphologiques et climatiques, par les nations qui l'occupent) de celui de l'évêché de Québec. Naît ainsi la Louisiane, "partie de la Terre arrosée d'un Fleuve de plus de huit cens lieues, & beaucoup plus grande que l'Europe, que nous pouvons appeller les Delices de l'Amerique" ("Epistre au Roy." In Hennepin 1683, s. p.)

L'image paradisiaque cristallisée dans cette métaphore hyperbolique des "Délices" déplace le "Paradis terrestre" autrefois situé par Lejeune le long du "premier de tous les fleuves" (Lejeune [1636] 1895, 158 et 190). Le nouveau territoire n'a rien à voir avec les terres froides du fleuve Saint-Laurent où d'aucuns disent que même les arbres ne valent rien:

> [C]e sont des Prairies sans bornes meslées de Forests de haute-fustaye, où il y a de toute sorte de bois à bâtir, & entr'autres d'excellent chaine plain

> comme celuy de France, & bien different de celuy du Canada; Les arbres sont d'une grosseur & d'une hauteur prodigieuses, & l'on y trouveroit les plus belles pieces du monde pour construire des Vaisseaux que l'on peut faire sur les lieux, & amener le bois qui serviroit de Leste aux Navires, pour la construction de tous les Vaisseaux de France, ce qui seroit d'une grande épargne à l'Etat (Hennepin 1683, 132).

Pour revendiquer ce territoire, il faut prouver d'abord l'antériorité de la présence des récollets, et donc minimiser l'importance de la descente du Mississippi effectuée par Marquette et Jolliet en 1673. À cet égard, la parole indigène rapportée sert visiblement à éluder certaines réalités gênantes que le récit ne peut pourtant éviter de passer sous silence. Coup sur coup, la *Description de la Louisiane* dénie explicitement aux jésuites les trois phases qui président habituellement à l'établissement d'un droit territorial: exploration, occupation, inscription (voir 13). Plus insidieuses sont les marques de toutes sortes qu'inscrit la relation à la fois sur le papier et dans le paysage: ainsi les croix laissées par le supérieur d'Hennepin, le père La Ribourde, au portage de la Kankakee effacent-elles peut-être d'autres croix, dessinées des années auparavant par un premier missionnaire – le père Marquette, par exemple, aurait utilisé ce portage au retour de son dernier voyage chez les Illinois Kaskakia en 1675 (voir Baker 1899, 22). Hennepin seul le sait: le récit n'en garde pas de traces.

Enfin, l'apprentissage des langues amérindiennes constitue un autre *topos* permettant au père Hennepin d'afficher une compétence qui tranche avec les tâtonnements et les ânonnements étalés dans certaines *Relations* jésuites:[18]

> D'abord que je pû attraper ce mot de Taketchiabihen, qui signifie en cette langue comment appelle-tu cela?, je fus dans peu de temps en état de raisonner des choses familieres avec eux; il est vray qu'au commencement pour demander le mot de courir dans leur langue, j'estois obligé de redoubler mes pas d'un bout de leur grande Cabanne à l'autre: Les Chefs de ces Barbares voyans l'inclination que j'avois d'apprendre, me faisoient souvent écrire, me nommant toutes les parties du corps humain, & comme je ne voulois point mettre sur le papier certains mots honteux, dont ces Peuples ne font point de scrupule, ils se divertissoient agreablement entr'eux, ils m'interogeoient souvent, mais comme j'estois obligé de regarder mon papier pour leur répondre, ils disoient entr'eux, quand nous interrogeons le Pere Loüis (c'est ainsi qu'ils m'avoient entendu appeller par nos deux

> François) il ne nous repond pas, mais d'abord qu'il a regardé ce qui est blanc, (car ils n'ont point de mot pour nommer le papier) il nous répond, & il nous fait entendre ses pensées (Hennepin 1683, 248–51).

La description des efforts déployés par le récollet pour apprendre la langue ne laisse transparaître ni le sens du ridicule, ni le sentiment d'humiliation que certains textes jésuites antérieurs laissaient filtrer. En effet, d'enseignants et rhétoriciens réputés et respectés qu'ils étaient en France, plusieurs de ces ecclésiastiques se sentaient devenir "petits Escoliers" quand il s'agissait d'apprendre les langues amérindiennes, si l'on en croit les *Relations* jésuites.[19]

Conclusion

En somme, à l'instar d'un négatif en photographie, la *Description de la Louisiane* révèle une lecture critique des représentations du travail missionnaire et des habitants du Nouveau Monde que contenaient les *Relations* jésuites ou que le public imputait à ces dernières. On lit entre les lignes de l'œuvre du récollet Hennepin les principaux reproches adressés par une partie de la bonne société française à la Compagnie de Jésus: esprit de lucre imputé à ses missionnaires, impopularité auprès des habitants ou des autochtones, baptêmes précipités de ces derniers n'aboutissant qu'à leur apostasie subséquente, exagération manifeste des résultats de l'évangélisation conduite par les jésuites, enfin, incompétence globale de ces derniers, qui seraient peu doués pour l'apprentissage des langues amérindiennes et peu présents sur le territoire.

Ce constat peu amène à l'égard des jésuites et de leurs *Relations*, la *Nouvelle Découverte*, deuxième récit du même voyage publié par Hennepin quinze ans plus tard, le nuancera néanmoins en faisant réapparaître certains jésuites (le père Pierson et le père Garnier lors de l'ambassade chez les Sénécas). Leur présence explicite dans ce deuxième récit dénote par ailleurs un changement considérable dans les enjeux polémiques sous-jacents aux deux récits. Alors que la *Description de la Louisiane* avait effacé la présence jésuite en Nouvelle-France et vantait le désintéressement, la popularité, la prudence et la fiabilité des récollets par des arguments sous lesquels un lecteur malveillant pouvait reconnaître des accusations contre la Compagnie de Jésus, la *Nouvelle Decouverte* semble vouloir revenir sur cette polémique entre les deux ordres en affirmant la solidarité de Louis Hennepin envers ses confrères, si jésuites soient-ils. Mais cela, c'est une autre histoire…

NOTES

1 Eustache Maupassant, supérieur des récollets du Canada, écrit à Colbert: "Nous recevons de tres grandes charités et une tres forte protection de Monsieur le comte de Frontenac. Je ne scais si l'honneur qu'il nous fait de nous aymer n'a point attiré sur nous la jalousie de certaines gens, mais nous nous sommes aperceu que ceux qui ont la direction de l'Eglise font soubs main ce qu'ils peuvent pour decrier nos ministeres et pour nous rendre inutiles dans ce pays" (Maupassant [1679] 1931, 602).

2 Des récollets accompagnent Champlain en Nouvelle-France dès 1615. L'*Histoire chronologique de la Nouvelle France ou Canada* revendique pour eux la primeur de l'installation en Nouvelle-France et souligne que les disciples de saint François ont été les premiers à y "jetter les fondements de la Religion dans les habitations françaises & sauvages" (Le Tac [1689] 1980, 129).

3 Appelé aussi Frontenac, ce fort était situé à l'embouchure de la rivière Catarakoui, en amont des Mille-Îles, à l'extrémité nord-est du lac Ontario, là où s'élève aujourd'hui la ville de Kingston. Voir Lorin 1885, ix et 90; Shea 1861, 264–5 et Frontenac [1673] 1926–1927, 37–8.

4 Ses incursions depuis le fort Frontenac dans les missions iroquoises sont signalées dans le *Premier Établissement de la foy dans la Nouvelle-France* attribué à Chrétien Le Clercq. Voir [Le Clercq] 1691, vol. 2: 114.

5 L'accusation de plagiat portée jusqu'à tout récemment contre le récollet ne tient plus, désormais, à la lumière des recherches de Louant (1980, 73–77), selon qui la *Relation des Découvertes* aurait été le résultat d'une véritable collaboration entre Claude Bernou et Louis Hennepin. L'examen des premières pages de la *Relation des Découvertes* (fol. 51–2) m'a permis de confirmer cette collaboration. Voir Broué 1999, vol. 1: 25–34.

6 La Chambre syndicale des libraires ([1704], fol. 85) consigne, pour l'année 1682, la "*Description de la Loüisiane par le P. Loüis henpin*, chez la veuve Huré."

7 Voir également Reboul 1991, 7.

8 Signalons à ce propos l'étude d'Hélène Vachon sur le rôle de la métaphore temporelle dans la *Description de la Louisiane*: "[À] coups de métaphores temporelles, un plan de colonisation s'échafaude à demi-mot" (Vachon 1977, 189). Parmi les arguments où s'exprime la domination, l'auteure souligne également l'importance du fort, qui "offre une maîtrise du sauvage par une maîtrise du lieu" (189); de la ruse, qui souligne les points faibles des Amérindiens et "indique à qui veut l'entendre des moyens de nuisance" (190); et, enfin, de la raillerie, qui renvoie l'Amérindien à l'insignifiance (189).

9 On pourrait en effet caractériser les arguments présentés dans la *Description de la Louisiane* comme des propositions doubles, du type P/NP, P/NP' ou P/P,' qui ne donnent jamais à lire que le second élément de la proposition. C'est, en d'autres mots, ce que souligne Dominique Maingueneau à propos du discours polémique, qui serait un "processus réglé d'exclusion de l'autre" (Maingueneau 1983, 16) posant en négatif un autre discours.

10 Réal Ouellet souligne la manipulation des dialogues dans les relations de voyage, notamment celle de la parole donnée aux Sauvages: "Ce subterfuge rhétorique culmine dans les scènes d'adieu pathétiques où la voix collective des Sauvages clame les louanges d'une figure tutélaire, capable de repousser les assauts du diable et d'assurer aux Amérindiens un commerce avec les Blancs dont ils affirment ne pouvoir se passer" (Ouellet 1993[b], 239).

11 L'intention édificatrice des *Relations* des jésuites ne fait aujourd'hui guère de doute. Rachel Ferland relève dans les *Relations* de Lejeune divers procédés rhétoriques visant à susciter un appui au développement de la Nouvelle-France, dont les citations bibliques (voir Ferland 1993, 25). De même, Yvon Le Bras souligne le 'souci de l'énonciateur [...] de faire voir à partir d'exemples précis que tous les espoirs sont permis' (Le Bras 1994, 60) en matière d'évangélisation.

12 La *Nouvelle Decouverte* nie toute intervention de la Providence en matière de lutte contre l'Infidélité: "Je ne dirais rien ici de la conversion des Sauvages de l'Amerique, par ce que j'en feray un ample recit dans un troisiéme Tome de cet Ouvrage, qui desabusera bien des gens de plusieurs opinions fausses, dont ils sont prevenus. Autrefois les Apôtres n'avoient qu'à ouvrir la bouche dans les pays, où la providence conduisoit leurs pas [...]. Mais il faut avoüer, que Dieu n'attache plus la grace ni l'onction de son Esprit à nos Ministères modernes pour esperer ces conversions miraculeuses, comme dans les premiers Siecles" (Hennepin 1697, 308–309).

13 On trouve le même motif d'écriture dans le *Mémoire sur le Canada* attribué par Armand Yon à Fénelon: "Il y a quarante ans qu'on travaille à la conversion des sauvages sans néanmoins avoir faict de grands progrès [...]. Les hurons sont plus dociles, moins débauchés et plus sédantaires [*sic*], mais avec tout cela il se commet parmi eux beaucoup de désordres de vin et d'impureté, quelque soin et quelque précaution que prennent pour l'empêcher les pères Jésuites qui les gouvernent. [...] Il faut croire leurs relations puisqu'elles sortent de personnes sincères et vertueuses, mais je suis fort asseuré que ce que nous avons veu durant deux ans dans les missions des Iroquois du nord du lac Ontario ne nous a pas trop édifiés" ([Fénelon] [1670] 1970, 184–5).

14 Frontenac, dont l'antijésuitisme était notoire, aurait été pour quelque chose dans la cessation, en 1673, de la parution annuelle des *Relations* jésuites (voir Thwaites 1896–1901, 41.)

15 Pour Pierre Berthiaume, la réalité amérindienne s'inscrit "à l'intérieur d'une vision anagogique qui allégorise le monde, les hommes et leurs gestes pour leur faire signifier la lutte du bien et du mal, de façon à légitimer l'apostolat missionnaire" (Berthiaume 1990, 119).

16 Le même raisonnement rend énigmatique le silence du texte sur l'un des confrères récollets d'Hennepin, Zénobe Membré, qui n'apparaît nommément qu'à la p. 140 (soit environ au tiers du récit) de la *Description de la Louisiane*, alors qu'il faisait partie de la même expédition.

17 Ainsi Marie de l'Incarnation s'objecte-t-elle aux conclusions qu'un lecteur pourrait tirer du silence des *Relations* de Lejeune sur le travail des Ursulines: "Si on nous dit que nous sommes icy inutiles, parce que la relation ne parle pas de nous, il faut dire que Monseigneur notre Prélat est inutile, que son séminaire est inutile, que le Séminaire des Révérends Pères est inutile [...] et enfin que les Mères Hospitalières sont inutiles, parce que les relations ne disent rien de tout cela. Et cependant, c'est ce qui fait le soutien, la force et l'honneur même de tout le païs" (Marie de l'Incarnation 1971 [[9 août 1668] 1971, 802–3).

18 Réal Ouellet remarque à ce propos que "l'apprentissage des langues sauvages est [dans les relations de voyage] à la fois indice d'adaptation au monde étranger et moyen d'agir,' et qu'il n'est donc pas surprenant que glossaires et dialogues attestent de cette compétence et héroïsent le protagoniste 'par une mise en scène textuelle qui choisit habilement les verbes déclaratifs (rétorquer, répartir, répliquer), donne "le dernier mot" à l'Européen ou fait avouer au Sauvage lui-même la supériorité de son interlocuteur" (Ouellet 1993[a], 20).

19 Victor E. Hanzeli souligne le sentiment d'humiliation transparaissant dans les écrits de Brébeuf, par exemple. Voir Hanzeli 1969, 47.

BIBLIOGRAPHIE

Baker, George A. 1899. *The Saint-Joseph-Kankakee Portage. Its Location and Use by Marquette, La Salle and The French Voyageurs.* South Bend: Northern Indiana Historical Society.

Bernou, Claude. [1681]. *Relation des decouvertes et des Voyages du Sieur de La Salle, seigneur et gouverneur du Fort de Frontenac, au delà des grands Lacs de la*

Nouvelle-France, faits par l'Ordre de Monseigneur Colbert 1679, 80 et 81. Archives nationales de France, Marine, 3JJ 271, 67, nº 4.

Berthiaume, Pierre. 1990. *L'aventure américaine au XVIIIe siècle: du voyage à l'écriture.* Ottawa: Presses de l'Université d'Ottawa.

Broué, Catherine. 1999. *Édition critique de la* Description de la Louisiane *et de la* Nouvelle découverte *du père Louis Hennepin,* thèse, 2 vol. Québec: Université Laval.

Enregistrement des Privilèges. [1704]. *Extrait des Registres de la Chambre syndicale des Libraires contenant les Livres des Privileges, imprimés depuis le mois de novembre 1663 jusqu'en 1703.* Bibliothèque nationale de France: NAF 2490.

Dubé, Pauline. 1995. *Les frères insoumis ou L'ombre d'un clocher.* Québec: Nuit Blanche Éditeur.

Dubé, Pauline. 1997. *Édition critique de* La morale pratique du jansenisme ou appel comme d'abus, à notre souverain seigneur le pape Innocent XII: interjetté par le R. P. Louis Hennepin, missionnaire recollect, notaire apostolique, & chapelain de son altesse electorale de Baviere, thèse, 2 vol, Québec: Université Laval.

Dudouyt, Jean. [1682] 1995. "Lettre de Dudouyt à Laval, 9 mars 1682." In *Les frères insoumis ou L'ombre d'un clocher,* éd. Pauline Dubé, 164–5. Québec: Nuit Blanche Éditeur.

[Fénelon, François Salignac de la Mothe]. [1670] 1970. "Description du canada [*sic*] et de ce que l'on trouve d'advantageux, tant pour les interets de Sa majesté que pour ceux des colonies françoises qui y sont establies." In Armand Yon, "François de Salignac-Fénelon, sulpicien: son Mémoire sur le Canada." *Les cahiers des dix* 35: 141–90.

Ferland, Rachel. 1993. "La citation biblique comme procédé conatif dans les *Relations* du père Lejeune." In *Rhétorique et conquête missionnaire: le jésuite Paul Lejeune,* éd. Alain Beaulieu et Réal Ouellet, 25–39. Québec: Septentrion.

Frontenac, Louis de Buade, comte de. [1672] 1861. "Extrait d'une lettre du Comte de Frontenac à Colbert, en date du 2 novembre 1672." In *Découvertes et établissements des français dans l'ouest et dans le sud de l'Amérique Septentrionale (1614–1754). Mémoires et documents originaux recueillis et publiés par P. Margry,* vol. 1: 247–8. Paris: Maisonneuve et Cie.

Frontenac, Louis de Buade, comte de. 1861 [1673]. "Lettre de Frontenac à Colbert, datée du 13 novembre." *Rapport de l'Archiviste de la Province de Québec* 7: 26–52.

Frontenac, Louis de Buade, comte de. [1674] 1861. "Lettre du Gouverneur Frontenac au ministre Colbert, 14 novembre 1674." *Rapport de l'Archiviste de la Province de Québec* 7: 60–78.

Galinée, René de Bréhant de. [env. 1670] 1903. "Voyage de MM. Dollier et Galinée." In *Exploration of the Great Lakes 1669–1670 by Dollier de Casson and De Bréhant de Galinée,* éd James H. Coyne. Toronto: Ontario Historical Society Papers and Records.

Hanzeli, Victor E. 1969. *Missionary Linguistics in New France. A study of Seventeenth and Eighteenth-century Descriptions of American Indian Languages.* La Haye: Mouton.

Hennepin, Louis. 1688 [1683]. *Description de la Louisiane, nouvellement découverte au Sud'Oüest de la Nouvelle France, par ordre du Roy. Avec la Carte du Pays: Les Mœurs & la Maniere de vivre des Sauvages. Dediée à sa Majesté.* Paris: Amable Auroy.

Hennepin, Louis. 1697. *Nouvelle découverte d'un très grand pays situé dans l'Amérique, entre le Nouveau Mexique et la mer Glaciale, Avec les Cartes, & les Figures necessaires, & de plus l'Histoire naturelle & Morale, & les avantages, qu'on en peut tirer par l'établissement des Colonies. Le tout dedié à Sa Majesté Britannique. Guillaume III.* Utrecht: Guillaume Broedelet.

Jouve, Odoric-M. 1912. *Le père Gabriel de la Ribourde, récollet.* Québec: Couvent du Saint Stigmate.

Le Bras, Yvon. 1994. "L'Amérindien dans les *Relations* de Paul Lejeune (1632–1641)." In *Études sur la relation de voyage en Nouvelle-France,* éd. Yvon Le Bras et Pierre Dostie, 7–157. Sainte-Foy: Éditions de la Huit.

[Le Clercq, Chrétien]. 1691. *Premier établissement de la foy dans la Nouvelle-France.* Paris: Amable Auroy.

Le Tac, Sixte. 1980 [1689]. *Histoire chronologique de la Nouvelle France ou Canada depuis sa découverte (mil cinq cents quatre) jusques en l'an mil six cents trente deux,* éd. Eugène Réveillaud. Montréal: Leméac.

Lejeune, Paul. 1895 [1636]. "Relation de 1636." In *The Jesuit Relations and Allied Documents,* éd. Reuben G. Thwaites, vol. 8: 201–vol. 9: 315. Cleveland: The Burrows Brothers.

Lorin, Henri. 1885. *Le comte de Frontenac. Étude sur le Canada français à la fin du XVIIe siècle.* Paris: Armand Colin, 1885.

Louant, Armand. 1980. *Le cas du Père Louis Hennepin, récollet, missionnaire de la Louisiane (1626–170?) ou Histoire d'une vengeance.* S. l.: s. d.

Louis XIV. [7 avril 1672] 1927. "Mémoire du Roi pour servir d'instruction au sieur Comte de Frontenac." *Rapport de l'Archiviste de la Province de Québec* 7: 3–6.

Maingueneau, Dominique. 1983. *Sémantique de la polémique. Discours religieux et ruptures idéologiques au XVIIe siècle.* Lausanne: L'âge d'homme.

Marie De L'incarnation. 1971 [9 août 1668]. "Lettre 235 de Québec, à son fils." In *Correspondance,* éd. Guy Oury, 800–3. Solesmes: Abbaye Saint-Pierre.

Maupassant, Eustache. [1679] 1931. "Lettre du R. P. Eustache Maupassant, supérieur des Recollets du Canada, au ministre Colbert, 12 septembre 1677." *Bulletin des Recherches Historiques* 37 (2): 602–3.

Ouellet, Réal. 1993[a]. "La Nouvelle-France." *La Licorne* 97 ("Littérature de langue française en Amérique du Nord"): 11–31.

Ouellet, Réal. 1993[b]. "Qu'est-ce qu'une relation de voyage?" In *La recherche littéraire. Objets et méthodes,* éd. Claude Duchet et Stéphane Vachon, 235–46. Montréal / Paris: XYZ / Presses de l'Université de Vincennes.

Reboul, Olivier. 1991. *Introduction à la rhétorique.* Paris: Presses Universitaires de France.

Shea, John G. 1861. *Early Voyages up and Down the Mississipi by Cavelier, St. Cosme, Le Sueur, Gravier and Guignas.* Albany: Joel Munsell.

Thwaites, Reuben Gold, éd. [1896–1901] 1959. *The Jesuit Relations and Allied Documents. Travels and Explorations of the Jesuit Missionaries in New France, 1610–1791.* New York: Pageant Book.

Tremblay, Mylène. 1996. "L'image de l'Amérindien chez Louis Hennepin: méthodologie, perception et référence." *Folklore canadien* 18 (2): 111–27.

Vachon, Hélène. 1977. "L'implicite comme langage publicitaire: étude de la syntaxe temporelle dans la *Description de la Louisiane.*" *Études littéraires* 10 (1–2): 175–194.

Vigh, Arpad. 1979. "L'histoire et les deux rhétoriques." *Revue d'esthétique* (1–2): 11–37.

PART III

TEXTUALITIES

chapter fourteen

L'héritage de José de Acosta

PIERRE BERTHIAUME

Au cours de leur apostolat en terre canadienne, les jésuites français ont été peu portés à définir leur doctrine évangélisatrice ou, si l'on veut user d'un néologisme, à produire un traité missiologique. Aussi est-ce un événement particulier qui a déterminé Pierre Biard, le rédacteur de la "relation" de 1611, à exposer les principes sur lesquels a reposé sa pratique évangélisatrice au cours de son séjour en Acadie entre 1611 et 1613. Ce sont même, sans doute, les accusations contenues dans le *Factum du procez*, qui a opposé Jean de Biencourt, sieur de Poutrincourt, aux jésuites, qui expliquent que la relation ait été imprimée, ces derniers ayant senti le besoin de riposter aux attaques dont ils étaient l'objet.

Comme le rappelle Lucien Campeau, le mémoire n'est pas un véritable factum puisqu'il ne s'adresse à aucun tribunal et qu'il n'est lié à aucune "action légale dont il aurait été un préliminaire" (Campeau, dans [Poutrincourt] [1614] 1967, 321). Attribué à Poutrincourt,[1] l'opuscule, publié en 1614, reproche notamment aux missionnaires de n'avoir baptisé "les sauvages qu'ils ne fussent catéchisez à leur mode et duits à leurs façons de faire" (343)[2] et les accuse de n'avoir adopté cette attitude "que pour ce qu'ils [étaient] venus après que le commencement en a[vait] esté faict" (374). Non seulement, soutient le rédacteur du factum, Pierre Biard et Énemond Massé refusèrent-ils d'administrer le sacrement aux "grands qui [n'étaient] pas catéchisez à leur mode,' mais aussi aux "petits naiz de chrestiens," si bien qu'ils laissèrent "tourmenter au diable les pauvres sauvages non receus en l'Eglise" (374). C'est à ces accusations que répond Pierre Biard dans le chapitre de sa relation qui porte sur "la nécessité qu'il y a de bien catéchiser ces peuples avant que les baptiser."[3] Mais force est de constater que son discours n'est pas sans entretenir des liens avec le *De Procuranda Indorum Salute O predicacion del evangelio en las Indias* de José de Acosta.[4]

Persuadé que le message évangélique s'adresse à l'ensemble de l'humanité, le missionnaire espagnol aborde dans son ouvrage tous les aspects de l'évangélisation des païens et produit un véritable traité missiologique. Or, constate-t-il, l'évangélisation des "barbares" est d'autant plus difficile que les missionnaires ont affaire à un nombre élevé de peuples aux mœurs fort différentes.[5] Aussi convient-il d'adapter la pratique missionnaire à chacun pour mieux atteindre l'objectif poursuivi, encore que lui-même s'en tienne surtout au cas des Péruviens, qu'il connaît mieux.[6] Pour ce, il distingue trois catégories de païens, ou trois "classes," pour reprendre sa terminologie.

"La première comprend ceux qui ne s'écartent "pas trop de la droite raison et des us communs du genre humain" ("La primera es la de aquellos que no se apartan demasiado de la recta razón y del uso común del género humno" [Acosta [1588] 1954, 392]). Aussi, tout barbares qu'ils sont, ils ont su créer des "institutions politiques, définir des lois et bâtir des villes afin de vivre sous l'autorité de magistrats" ("epública estable, leyes públicas, ciudades fortificada, magistrados obedecidos y lo que más importa" [392]). À l'instar des Européens, ils ont inventé une forme d'écriture et "cultivent les lettres" ("conocimiento de las letras" [392]). José de Acosta pense ici aux Asiatiques, plus précisément aux Chinois, aux Japonais et aux nations des Indes orientales.[7] La seconde catégorie comprend les peuples qui,

> bien qu'ils ne connaissent pas l'usage de l'écriture et qu'ils n'aient développé ni connaissances philosophiques ni civilité, vivent toutefois dans des états constitués, dans lesquels on trouve des magistrats et où les hommes sont soumis à des règles sociales. En outre, ces peuples ont imaginé une forme de culte religieux ("En la segunda clase incluyo los bárbaros, que aunque no llegaron a alcanzar le uso de la escritura, ni los conocibientos filosóficos o civiles, sin embargo tienen su república y magistrados ciertos, y asientos o poblaciones estables, donde guardan manera de policia, y orden de ejércitos y capitanes, y finalmente alguna forma solemne de culto religioso" [392]).

Témoins les Mexicains et les Péruviens qui, à défaut de connaître l'écriture, ont inventé les *quipos*, c'est-à-dire des cordelettes nouées, pour conserver la mémoire du passé et pour répertorier leurs lois (voir 392).

Dans la dernière catégorie, on trouve les "sauvages" qui, semblables aux fauves, ont

> à peine accès à des sentiments humains, qui vivent sans loi, sans organisation sociale, sans roi, sans magistrats ni république, qui n'ont pas de demeure fixe, sauf à s'assembler dans des grottes ou près des animaux ("apenas tienen sentimiento humano; sin ley, sin rey, sin pactos, sin magistrados ni república, que mudan la habitación, o si la tienen fija, más se asemeja a cuevas de fieras o cercas de animales" [393]).

Dans ce groupe, on trouve non seulement les Caraïbes, "toujours assoiffés de sang, cruels aux étrangers, anthropophages, qui vont nus ou qui couvrent à peine leurs parties honteuses" ("siempre sedientos de sangre, crueles con los extraños, que devoran carne humana, andan desnudos o cubren apenas sus vergüenzs" [394]),[8] mais aussi beaucoup d'autres "barbares" qui, "s'ils ne sont pas aussi assoiffés de sang que les tigres ou les panthères, ne se distinguent guère des animaux, puisqu'ils sont nus et qu'ils sont portés à la luxure et aux vices, dont la sodomie" ("aunque no son sanguinarios como tigres o panteras, sin embargo, se diferencian poco de los animales: andan también desnudos, son timidos y están entregados a los más vergonzosos delitos de lujuria y sodomía" [394]).

À défaut de reprendre les catégories définies par son prédécesseur espagnol, Pierre Biard semble parfois penser à celui-ci lorsqu'il décrit les "sylvicoles" (Biard [1616] 1967, 486) de l'Acadie. Ainsi signale-t-il discrètement certaines caractéristiques des "Souriquois" et des "Eteminquois," qui les excluent en partie de la troisième catégorie des "barbares" recensée par José de Acosta. Non seulement ne logent-ils pas dans des grottes comme les animaux,[9] mais, en plus, ils "ont l'esprit assez gaillard et net, quant à l'estime et jugement des choses sensibles et communes, et deduisent fort gentiment leurs raisons, les assaisonnant tousjours avec quelque jolie similitude" (480). À défaut d'avoir accès à l'écriture, ils connaissent l'art de la rhétorique. Sans doute n'ont-ils pas développé une "grande police" parmi eux, puisqu'ils sont peu nombreux et qu'ils vivent "espars et vagabonds," mais ils "ne peuvent [...] s'en passer, puis qu'ils sont hommes et associés" (487). Loin d'être assoiffés de sang, les Amérindiens ont un "naturel" qui est "de soy libéral, et point malitieux" (480). Mieux, leur générosité ne s'adresse pas seulement à leurs proches,[10] mais aussi aux étrangers, comme le montrent leur "amitié et fidélité" à l'endroit des Français après la défaite de ceux-ci aux mains des Anglais.[11] Enfin, “ils croyent un Dieu,” encore qu’ils “ne sçavent le nommer” (507–8). En somme, les “Sauvages” ne diffèrent pas des autres hommes: si leur évangélisation est remplie d’obstacles, il “ne faut jà en accuser le sol ou malignité de la terre, l’air ou les eaux, les hommes ou leurs humeurs. Nous sommes tous faicts et relevons de mesmes principes” (461), conclut Pierre Biard, qui range résolument les Amérindiens de l’Acadie parmi l’ensemble des “hommes” et qui exclut toute distinction de nature entre eux.

La question de l’aliénation des païens se pose aussi en des termes différents chez les deux missionnaires. Dès l’avant-propos de sa relation, Pierre Biard oppose le “paradis de délices,” que représente tout lieu où s’épanouit la foi, à la “solitude d’un désert,” où Dieu n’a pas encore laissé son empreinte.[12] Dans cette perspective, teintée de militantisme,[13] Lucifer devient l’ennemi à abattre:

> [T]oute ceste région, quoy que capable de mesme félicité que nous, toutefois, par malice de Satan qui y règne, n’est qu’un horrible désert, non guière moins calamiteux pour la malencontreuse disette des biens corporels que pour celle qui absolument rend les hommes misérables, l’extrême nudité des parements et richesses de l’âme (461).

Aussi Pierre Biard voit-il partout l’empreinte du diable: dans les rites chamaniques de guérison,[14] dans la religion des Amérindiens, qui “n’est autre qu’ès sorcelleries et charmes des autmoins” (506), qui ne sont eux-mêmes que de “vrais sorciers,” des “triacleurs mensongers et trompeurs” (500). D’ailleurs, les Amérindiens eux-mêmes reconnaissent la présence de Satan sur le continent. Ils lui auraient “souvent dit que, du temps de leurs pères et avant la venue des François, le diable les mastinoit fort” (507) et Membertou lui aurait avoué que “le diable s’estoit apparu souventes fois à luy” (507). Enfin, au cours de leur apostolat, les jésuites ont bien senti que le diable s’opposait à leur action (524)[15] et que c’est lui qui “est venu de malice à mettre le feu à [leurs] travaux et [les] emporter hors du champ” (603).

Certes, José de Acosta estime lui aussi que le démon tient un rôle non négligeable dans l’idolâtrie des Péruviens et des Mexicains, qu’il croit sous le “joug […] des lois de Satan” (Acosta [1589] 1979, 398), mais jamais il ne dénonce la présence concrète du Malin, comme le fait Pierre Biard. Son approche du problème du mal est davantage métaphysique. D’une part, l’existence du paganisme s’inscrit dans le mystère des desseins de Dieu,[16] de l’autre, le mal tire sa source de l’orgueil de l’ange déchu: "[L]'orgueil du démon est si grand et si opiniâtre que toujours il séduit et s'efforce de se faire passer pour Dieu et d'être honoré comme tel," écrit José de Acosta en tête du livre de son *Histoire naturelle et morale des Indes occidentales* dans lequel il analyse les différentes formes de superstition que l'on trouve chez les Amérindiens (235). Le missionnaire espagnol s'intéresse moins à la présence concrète du diable au sein des communautés amérindiennes qu'il n'expose les fondements de son activité (son orgueil) et qu'il ne rappelle que le diable trompe les hommes depuis toujours, comme le montrent les textes sacrés (235–6). Au vrai, les difficultés rencontrées proviennent moins du diable que des hommes, plus précisément des chrétiens eux-mêmes: "[S]i on employait à les aider dans leur salut seulement la moitié du soin qu'on met à profiter de leur pauvre sueur et de leur peine, ce serait la chrétienté la plus paisible et la plus heureuse du monde. Mais bien souvent nos péchés ne nous permettent pas de passer outre" (398). Puisque le problème de l'aliénation des Amérindiens se pose en des termes différents chez le jésuite espagnol et chez son confrère français, la problématique évangélisatrice défendue par l'un et par l'autre sera aussi marquée par des différences. Dans le *De Procuranda*, José de Acosta s'interroge longuement sur l'administration du baptême aux Amérindiens et fait appel à nombre de docteurs de la loi avant d'arrêter sa position. Selon les canons et la tradition de l'Église, rappelle-t-il, tout païen, "avant d'être baptisé, doit manifester sa volonté de recevoir le sacrement, montrer qu'il a la foi et manifester un net repentir de ses fautes passées" ("[a] tres cosas debe atender en la bautismo principalmente de los bárbaros le fiel dispensador de los misterios de Dios: la voluntad, la fe y la penitencia" [Acosta 1954 [1588], 581]).[17] Non seulement le ferme désir du catéchumène d'être baptisé est-il nécessaire parce que la foi est exigeante,[18] mais le plein consentement de celui-ci est indispensable pour éviter que le sacrement ne soit profané, ce qui constituerait un crime grave.[19] Quant à la "contrition" ("penitencia") elle implique une solide volonté de la part du futur chrétien de s'amender et de "détester véritablement sa vie passée et la ferme intention de ne pas retomber dans ses anciennes fautes" ("la verdadera detestación de la vida pasada y firme propósito de enmendarla para adelante" [584]).

Ces exigences impliquent que le catéchumène comprenne clairement le sens de son geste et qu'il ait une bonne connaissance de la foi chrétienne: il "ne peut être baptisé qu'à la condition qu'il sache ce dans quoi il s'engage" ("[q]ué medida de la fe se ha de hacer para que se acerque a las aguas des bautismo suficientemente instruído y firme"] [584]). Aussi

José de Acosta suggère-t-il la rédaction de deux catéchismes: le premier, destiné aux "disciples" ("discípulos"), ne serait qu'un "compendium" ("uno breve y compiendioso") des principaux points de la doctrine; le second, qui s'adresserait aux "catéchumènes" serait beaucoup "plus long et plus complet" ("más extenso [y] más copiosamente" [568]). Tout cela ne va pas sans difficultés, l'absence de grâce divine, la perversion de la nature et des mœurs chez les "barbares," la différence de langues et les difficultés inhérentes aux endroits où les missionnaires doivent pratiquer leur apostolat ne facilitant pas leur tâche.[20] Tout en opérant une distinction entre "la dépravation de la nature et de la culture" ("la depravación de la naturaleza y las costumbres"), José de Acosta constate que c'est surtout l'éducation et le mode de vie des Amérindiens qui rendent difficile leur évangélisation:

> Outre ce qui a été dit, il faut ajouter une chose fort importante: le manque de perspicacité mentale et la brutalité des mœurs chez les Indiens ne trouvent pas leur origine dans la naissance, la condition sociale ou la nature de l'environnement, mais dans leur éducation plutôt et leur genre de vie proche de celui des bêtes[21] ("A lo dicho hay que añadir una cosa muy importante, y es que la incapacidad de ingenio y fiereza de costumbres de los indios no proviene tanto del influjo del nacimiento o la estirpe, o del aire nativo, cuanto de la prolongada educación y del género de vida no muy desemejante al de las bestias" [412]).

Aussi, pour aider les Amérindiens à trouver le chemin du salut, convient-il de modifier leurs mœurs en réformant leurs "condition et coutumes" ("la condición y costumbres de los bárbaros"). C'est pourquoi il estime nécessaire de regrouper les Amérindiens dans des *encomiendas*, dans lesquelles ils seraient sous tutelle administrative et religieuse et dans lesquelles leur mode de vie pourrait être radicalement changé:

> Si on peut leur enseigner la vérité en les y attirant, tant mieux, mais s'ils résistent, cela ne doit pas les faire abandonner, sinon qu'ils se rebellent contre leur bien et salut, et s'emportent contre leurs remèdes et leurs maîtres, il faut les contenir avec force et pouvoir convenable, et les obliger à laisser la forêt [sauvagerie] et les réunir dans des villages, encore contre leur volonté d'une certaine façon, user de force pour les faire entrer dans le règne du ciel[22] ("Y i atrayéndolos con halagos se dejan voluntariamente enseñar, mejor sería; mas si resisten, no por eso hay que abandonarlos, sino que si

se rebelan contra su bien y salvación, y se enfurecen contra los médicos y maestros, hay que contenerlos con fuerza y poder convenientes, y obligarles a que dejen la selva y se reúnan en poblaciones y, aun contra du voluntad en cierto modo, hacerlez fuerza [en note: "L[u]c., 14, 23"]. Para que entren en el reino de los cielos' [393]).[23]

Puisque ce qui s'oppose le plus à la christianisation des Amérindiens, partant ce qui lui semble être le "plus grave" ("más grave" [393]), ce sont leurs "vices enracinés et leurs coutumes invétérées" ("vicios tan arraigados y costumbre inveteradas" [393]), il faut donc modifier le comportement des Amérindiens pour qu'ils adoptent un mode de vie différent, et par là des mœurs différentes qui finissent par amenuiser leurs vices jusqu'à les faire disparaître:

> Aussi sera-t-il très profitable de mettre en valeur les rites, les symboles et toutes les cérémonies ayant lieu à l'extérieur [il s'agit des rites cultuels catholiques] étant donné que ces hommes-animaux y prennent plaisir, faisant en sorte que la mémoire de ces choses-là [leurs habitudes passées] finisse peu à peu par s'estomper[24] ("Será también muy provechoso poner toda diligencia en los ritos, señales y todas ceremonias des culto externo, porque con ellas se deleitan y entretienen los hombres animales, hasta que poco a poco vaya borrándose la memoria y gusto de las cosas pasadas" [458]).

Créés pour les néophytes ("neófitos"), les *encomiendas*, qui incluent aussi les catéchumènes qui attendent le baptême, forment un espace dans lequel les missionnaires peuvent à la fois instruire leurs ouailles et modeler leur comportement:

> Par conséquent, outre que c'est le soin du prince de les régir et de les défendre de la même façon que les autres; c'est le métier propre et particulier des *encomendores* et curés de paroisses de s'occuper sérieusement de leur salut. Les appeler avec diligence à la grâce de l'évangile, les instruire en la foi, corriger leurs coutumes, admettre avec plaisir au sein de l'Église ceux qui le désirent et qui en sont dignes, les secourir avec les eaux baptismales s'ils se trouvent en grave péril, comme l'enseignent les décrets des saints Pères[25] ("Por tanto, además de que es cuidado del principe regirlos y defenderlos lo mismo que a los demás; es oficio proprio y peculiar de los encomenderos y párrocos tratar seriamente de su salvación. Llamarlos con diligencia a la

> gracia del evangelio, instruirlos en la fe, corregirlos en las costumbres, a los que lo desean y son dignos admitirlos gustosos al seno de la Iglesia, si se encuentran en grave peligro socorrerlos con el agua del bautismo, como enseñan los decretos de los santos Padres" [480]).

Vivant dans les bois, l'Amérindien ne peut être qu'un *homo sylvestris*, un homme des bois, pour tout dire, un être proche de l'animalité. Pour en faire un *homo sapiens*, puis un *homo catholicus*, il faut le retirer de son milieu et modeler son comportement sur celui des chrétiens (457–8).[26] Aux yeux de José de Acosta, les conditions matérielles de vie des êtres humains exercent une influence considérable sur leurs mœurs, sinon sur leur nature. À la limite, la culture transforme la nature.

Dans sa relation, Pierre Biard souscrit en partie aux thèses défendues par José de Acosta, mais en les infléchissant. Après avoir observé qu'un être humain doit prendre des forces avant de pouvoir se passer d'aide (Biard [1616] 1967, 510),[27] le missionnaire français explique que les jésuites ont d'autant plus insisté pour "bien catéchiser, instruire, cultiver, et accoustumer les sauvages, et avec longue patience, et n'attendre pas que d'un an ny de deux ils deviennent chrestiens qui n'ayent besoin ny de curé, ny d'évesque" (511), que les "Canadiens sont vagabonds" (511)[28] et qu'ils sont appelés à vivre éloignés de tout secours spirituel.[29] D'ailleurs, l'exemple des Péruviens et des Mexicains, qui ont continué à marmotter "leurs anciennes idolâtries" à l'église et à faire leurs anciens "sacrifices, danses et superstitions" lors des "festes commandées" (512), donne raison au missionnaire français.[30] C'est pourquoi les jésuites venus en Acadie se sont soumis à "l'ancien usage de l'Eglise de donner le baptesme reservément, ayant premièrement des postulants et requérans, et puis des catéchumènes, et à la parfin des baptisés" (512).

Pour asseoir sa thèse et riposter aux accusations du factum, Pierre Biard a recours à trois autorités. La première, attendue, est celle du "maistre de toute Sapience" qui a dit: "Que la terre fructifie premièrement l'herbe, puis l'espy, et en fin le plein froument en l'espy" (512).[31] La seconde est précisément celle de José de Acosta, qui a "très bien remarqué la faute" qui a consisté à donner le baptême à des Amérindiens sans les avoir bien préparés à la vie de chrétien (513).[32] La dernière est celle du droit canon, qui prescrit qu'il faut s'assurer que le catéchumène adhère aux rudiments de la foi avant d'être baptisé, qu'il reconnaisse l'incarnation du Christ, qu'il comprenne ce qu'est le sacrement du baptême, ainsi que la grâce qu'il reçoit.[33] D'ailleurs, comme le constate le relationnaire, les Amérindiens baptisés avant l'arrivée des jésuites ignoraient tout de la foi (513).[34] Certains se moquaient même des cérémonies religieuses chrétiennes.[35] Cela explique que les jésuites n'administrèrent le sacrement du baptême qu'en suivant de près les "saincts canons," c'est-à-dire, dans le cas d'un adulte, qu'après l'avoir "bien initié et catéchisé," à défaut de quoi l'administration du sacrement était "non seulement une prophanation du christianisme, ains aussi un'injustice enuers les sauvages" (514),[36] puisqu'il est injuste "de pousser un homme de sens et d'aage compétent à faire profession solemnelle de la loy de Dieu—ce qui se faict par le baptesme—sans qu'il ait esté jamais au paravant novice, ny qu'on luy ait donné à entendre les règles et devoirs de saditte profession" (514).[37] Aussi, avant d'administrer le baptême aux adultes, les missionnaires préférèrent-ils attendre de les "instruire en leur langage" et s'assurer qu'ils puissent "respondre. Car, précise Biard, il faut que le baptisé adulte responde luy-mesme, et non le parrain pour luy" (515). Dans le cas des enfants, les jésuites ne les ont baptisés qu'après en avoir obtenu l'autorisation de leurs parents, dans l'espoir de pouvoir les initier plus tard à la foi chrétienne[38]:

> Partant, conclut Pierre Biard, vous voyez que la première chose que nous taschons de leur apprendre, c'est la manière de se convertir à Dieu de tout leur cœur par vraye contrition et désir de s'unir et incorporer avec nostre Sauveur Jésus-Christ. Car c'est une disposition pour recevoir le baptesme mesme. Et elle est telle qu'elle suffit à salut, quand on ne peut recevoir le sacrement par effect (515–16).[39]

À lire la relation de Pierre Biard, on a le sentiment qu'il partage les mêmes préoccupations que José de Acosta et qu'il propose les mêmes solutions que celui-ci aux problèmes posés par l'évangélisation des "Sauvages." Toutefois, alors que le jésuite espagnol fonde surtout l'espoir de convertir les Amérindiens sur une contrainte qui les amène à réformer leurs mœurs, Pierre Biard croit davantage à l'efficacité de l'exemple et de la parole pour arriver au même résultat.[40] N'écrit-il pas que les missionnaires français ont "catéchisé tat qu'ils ont peu et par les yeux et par les oreilles" (602)? Par les yeux, précise-t-il, en "leur faisant voir [les] us et cérémonies [des chrétiens] et les y accoustumants" (602).[41] C'est d'ailleurs parce qu'il croit à la valeur pédagogique de l'exemple qu'il souhaite la fondation d'une "peuplade chrestienne et catholique ayant suffisance de moyens pour vivre" en terre canadienne (509), afin "d'aider ces nations à leur salut éternel" (id.). L'exemple des Français servirait à influer sur les Amérindiens, en même temps que les pratiques cultuelles des chrétiens les acclimateraient à la foi.[42]

Second volet de son programme missionnaire: le recours au verbe. Mais comme le reconnaît Pierre Biard, une difficulté, et non des moindres, a surgi, qui a souvent empêché les missionnaires de s'adresser aux "oreilles" de leurs ouailles: leur ignorance des langues amérindiennes. "Il falloit ahanner et suer," rappelle-t-il, pour apprendre les "mots qu'on appelle abstracts et universels, comme croire, douter, espérer, discourir, appréhender, un animal, un corps, une substance, un esprit, vertu, vice, péché, raison, justice, etc." (534). Et comme si cela n'était pas suffisant, non seulement les langues amérindiennes ne possèdent-elles pas de termes qui renvoient à la religion,[43] mais en plus les Amérindiens "se mocquoyent libéralement" des missionnaires (534), si bien que très souvent, après s'être "rompu le cerveau à force de demandes et recherches, comme l'on se pensoit enfin d'avoir bien rencontré la pierre philosophale, on trouvoit néantmoins puis après que l'on avoit pris le phantosme pour le corps, et l'ombre pour le solide, et que tout ce précieux élixir s'en alloit en fumée" (535). Malgré tout, les jésuites parvinrent à composer un "catéchisme en sauvageois" et purent "jargonner" avec leurs "catéchumènes" (603).[44] Mais c'est sur la traduction "en canadois [de] l'oraison dominicale et [de] la salutation de l'Ange, [du] symbole, et [des] commandements de Dieu et de l'Eglise, avec une petite explication des sacremens et quelques oraisons" que compte Pierre Biard pour préparer les Amérindiens à recevoir la foi: "[C]'estoit toute la théologie de laquelle ils avoyent besoin" (514), estime-t-il. Le projet des jésuites français est de faire réciter ces prières à leurs ouailles avant même qu'elles ne soient baptisées et de leur faire faire par là l'exercice de la foi pour la leur inculquer. Comme il l'explique dans sa lettre du 31 janvier 1612 à Christophe Baltazar, son provincial, même si les jésuites n'ont guère pu "converser avec ces pauvres gentilz," ils ont tout de même "tasché de leur imprimer quelques premières conceptions de la grandeur et vérité du christianisme, autant que les moyens s'en addonnoyent" (Biard [1612] 1967, 249). Ainsi les "Sauvages" ont-ils vu les missionnaires "prier, célébrer, prescher, et par [leurs] discours, les images et croix, la façon de vivre et choses semblables, ont receu les premières appréhensions et semences de [la] saincte foy, lesquelles s'esclorront et germeront abondamment s'il plaist à Dieu, quelque jour, y survenant un plus long et meilleur cultivage" (249). Comme dans le cas des "petits sauvagins" à qui les jésuites faisaient porter "les cierges, les clochettes, l"eau bénite et autre chose, marchants en bel ordre aux processions et enterremens [...]. Ainsy [les autres "Sauvages"] s'accoustument-ils à estre chrestiens, pour en son temps le bien estre' (249).

Si le jésuite espagnol insiste sur la nécessité d'imposer une réforme des mœurs et l'enseignement religieux pour inscrire le païen dans une problématique qui l'amène à s'humaniser et à se convertir, Pierre Biard croit plutôt à l'efficience du verbe et du geste pour transformer le Sauvage en chrétien. Chez lui, réciter les prières, mimer la conduite des chrétiens conduisent le païen à la foi: dire, c'est faire; imiter, c'est devenir.

Au lieu de cloîtrer les Amérindiens dans des *encomiendas* pour les contraindre à adopter des *habitus* qui modifient leur nature, le relationnaire français croit pouvoir investir l'esprit des Amérindiens en l'enveloppant dans les mailles d'un verbe et d'une gestuelle qui sécrètent la signification dont ils sont porteurs. Il s'agit d'incorporer un sens, selon les deux acceptions du substantif, qui travaille l'esprit de l'autre pour qu'il se transforme en même. En cela, Pierre Biard s'inscrit bien dans le classicisme: plus qu'à la contrainte physique, il croit à l'efficacité de la parole, du verbe, et rejoint par là les assises mêmes du livre fondateur de sa foi: il a suffi à Dieu de dire pour que l'univers fût; il suffit de faire prier les Amérindiens et de leur faire une place dans les cultes chrétiens pour qu'advienne en eux la foi. À l'orée de l'engagement missionnaire jésuite au Canada est ainsi définie une pédagogie sous l'ombre portée de José de Acosta. Fondée sur l'*imitatio* plutôt que sur la *contentio*, elle a engagé toute l'action à venir de la Compagnie de Jésus en Amérique du Nord et, si elle a permis la création de communautés chrétiennes au sein de tribus amérindiennes, elle a aussi été à l'origine d'une méprise, les relationnaires ayant parfois pris le simulacre, l'*imitatio*, pour la réalité.

NOTES

1 On y lit en effet que "le sieur de Poutrincourt [a] cependant baillé ce factum pour le faire voir à ses amis et disposer ses juges à luy rendre justice" (Poutrincourt [1614] 1967, 396).

2 Plus bas, le rédacteur du factum accuse Pierre Biard d'avoir refusé de baptiser une femme et une petite fille, "tenant ceste maxime que les sauvages doivent estre instruicts et catéchisez à leur mode" (355).

3 Il s'agit du titre du ch. 10 de Biard [1616] 1967, 510–16. Pierre Biard eut même à défendre la politique des jésuites auprès des colons: "Cecy n'est point tolérable, disoient-ils, ainsi que le Factum le professe; ces gens-cy

sont inutiles; il en faut escrire en France; et autres menaces lesquelles ils vindrent faire au Père Biard, lequel tascha de les appaiser" (510–11). L'observation fait problème puisque, si l'on se fie à la date indiquée sur le factum, 1613, il aurait vraisemblablement été rédigé après le départ des missionnaires du Canada.

4 José de Acosta (1540–1600) aurait commencé dès 1576 à rédiger son ouvrage, qui subit la censure. Voir Lopetegui 1942, 207–11 et 217–20; Lopetegui 1943, 120, n. 9 et Mustapha 1989, 415–23. Arrivé au Pérou en 1571, José de Acosta a été recteur du collège de Lima (1575–1576), puis provincial de la province du Pérou (1576–1581). Après son retour en Espagne (1587), il a mené une bataille contre Claudio Aquaviva, le général des jésuites, ce qui lui a valu d'être emprisonné (1592–1593). Après sa soumission au général (1594), il a pu reprendre ses fonctions au sein de la Compagnie de Jésus et être nommé supérieur des jésuites de Valladolid et recteur du collège de Salamanque (1598). En plus de l'ouvrage déjà signalé, il a rédigé un catéchisme, *Doctrina cristiana y catecismo para instrucción de las Indias*, publié à Lima en 1585, et une *Historia natural y moral de las Indias* (1590). Sur la biographie de José de Acosta, voir Burgaleta 1999, 3–69 et Lopetegui 1942, 3–203.

5 Voir Acosta [1588] 1954, 390: "Cosa harto dificil es tratar con acierto del modo de procurar la salvación de los indios. Porque, en primer lugar, son muy varias las naciones en que están divididos, y muy diferentes entre si, tanto en le clima, habitación y vestidos, como en le ingenio y las costumbres; y establecer una norma común para someter al evangelio y juntamente educar y regir a gentes tan diversas, requiere un arte tan elevado y recóndito, que nosotros confesamos ingenuamente no haberlo podido alcanzar."

6 Voir 391: "Y por ser las naciones de indios innumerables, y cada una con sus ritos proprios, y necesitar ser instruída de modo distinto, y no sentirme yo con disposición para tanto, por serme desconocidas muchas de ellas, y aunque las conociera todas, sería trabajo interminable; por todo eso he preferido ceñirme principalmente a los indios des Perú; la otra, porque siempre he creído que estos indios ocupan como un lugar intermedio entre los otros, por donde con más facilidad se puede por ello hacer juicio de los demás." Sur le classement des différents païens, voir Burgaleta 1999, 92–4 et Mustapha 1989, 468–73.

7 "Les Chinois [...] les Japonais et ceux de plusieurs autres provinces de l'Inde orientale" ("Los chinos [...] los japoneses y otras muchas provincias de la India oriental" [Acosta [1588] 1954, 392]).

8 José de Acosta inclut aussi dans cette catégorie les Chundos, les Chiriguanás, les Mojos, les Yscaycingas et les Amérindiens du Brésil et de la Floride (voir Acosta [1588] 1954, 393).

9 Pierre Biard observe que la première chose que font les Amérindiens en arrivant quelque part, "c'est de faire du feu et de se cabaner" près de "quelque bonne eau et en lieu de plaisant aspect" (Biard [1616] 1967, 482–3). D'ailleurs, il décrit précisément la construction des "logis" des Amérindiens (483).

10 "Ils ne sont nullement ingrats entr'eux; ils s'entredonnent tout. Nul oseroit esconduire la prière d'un autre, ny manger sans luy faire part de ce qu'il a," observe Biard (491).

11 "Ceste amitié et fidélité desdits peuples envers les François a paru remarquablement après nostre desroute faicte par les Anglois, ainsi qu'ouyrez. Car eux l'ayants sceu s'en vindrent à nous de nuict et nous consoloyent au mieux qu'ils pouvoyent, nous présentants leurs canots et leur peine pour nous conduire où nous voudrions" (479–80).

12 Voir 460. Pierre Biard cite le livre de Joël (2, 3): "La campagne qu'il a trouvée comme un jardin de délices n'est après lui qu'un désert affreux, et nul n'échappe à sa violence" (*Sainte Bible* 1990).

13 C'est son "ardent désir et zèle de voir ceste Nouvelle-France [...] conquise à Nostre-Seigneur" (Biard [1616] 1967, 462) qui lui a fait prendre la plume, soutient-il.

14 Tout en adoptant un ton ironique, Pierre Biard note que l'activité du chaman vise à "tuer Belzébut" (501). Dans sa description de la guérison, il fait sans cesse allusion à "Satan," que le guérisseur essaie d'extirper de dessous une cheville plantée dans le sol. À ce terme s'ajoutent l'expression "ennemy d'enfer," le substantif "diable" (trois fois) et le nom "Lucifer." Voir 501–2.

15 "Mais quand ce vient à esclorre le bon œuvre, je veux dire, quand le terme de ce pieux enfantement de vertu approche, lors il semble que tout conspire à la suffocation de ceste divine créature, lors faut-il sentir les douleurs et transes que Satan suscite et craindre plustost d'un avortement infructueux qu'avoir espérance d'un heureux accouchement. Les jésuites ont expérimenté cecy par tout, et nommément aux effets salutaires qu'ils ont désiré produire à la conversion de la Nouvelle-France."

16 Traduction de Isabelle Lachance: "Nous ne pouvons nier qu'il y ait beaucoup d'hommes qui, en raison des jugements secrets de Dieu, sont laissés dans l'obscurité, et je parle tant des hommes particuliers, que des familles, des villes, des provinces entières et des nations" ("No podemos negar que hay muchos hombres que por ocultos juicios de Dios, están abandonados en las tinieblas, y qué digo hombres particulares, familias y ciudades y aun provincias y nationes enteras" [Acosta [1588] 1954, 404]).

17 Sur l'importance de cette question aux yeux de José de Acosta (voir Lopetegui 1942, 281–90).

18 Comme “le poids de la religion est lourd à supporter” (“peso de la religión cristiana, grandes las expensas de la torre evangélica”), “il ne faut pas imposer un pareil fardeau à des êtres faibles comme le sont les êtres humains” (“no se podia imponer tal carga a la flaqueza humana” [Acosta [1588] 1954, 581]).

19 Après s’être appuyé sur la doctrine du pape Innocent III pour exiger un consentement pleinement volontaire du catéchumène avant de le baptiser, puisque c’est un crime grave de profaner le sacrement, José de Acosta se demande “si des lacunes sur le plan de la volonté invalident le baptême” (“si faltando las dos clases de voluntad será válido le bautismo” [582]). Sa réponse se fonde sur les idées développées par Augustin dans le second de ses *Traités anti-donatistes*, plus précisément sur les § 101 et 102 de la section 53 du Livre VII (voir Augustin 1964, 569–72). Comme l’explique Claudio Burgaleta (1999, 91–2), José de Acosta exige des catéchumènes une “foi explicite dans le Christ” (“explicit faith in Christ”), sans laquelle il n’est pas de salut possible à ses yeux.

20 Ce qui nuit à l’évangélisation des Amérindiens, ce sont “la sustracción de la gracia de Dios, la depravavación de la naturaleza y las costumbres, la dificultad del lenguaje y la molestia de los lugares y habitación” (Acosta [1588] 1954, 404).

21 Trad. de Daniel Castillo Durante, professeur au Département des lettres françaises de l’Université d’Ottawa.

22 Trad. de D. Castillo Durante.

23 Comme on s’en doute, José de Acosta fait allusion au passage de l’évangéliste Luc dans lequel le maître de la maison demande à son serviteur de forcer les gens qu’il a invités à entrer: “Le maître dit au serviteur: ‘Allez dans les chemins et le long des haies, et forcez les gens d’entrer afin que ma maison se remplisse’” (*Sainte Bible* 1990). Comme le rappelle Feliciano Cereceda (1941, 245), José de Acosta n’est pas l’inventeur des *encomiendas*. En revanche, il “proclame la légitimité de la fondation et de la continuation des *encomiendas*, dans une forme atténuée [cependant], imposée depuis le concile de Valladolid en 1542, corrigé par une ordonnance de 1543” (“proclama la licitud del origen y de la continiación de las encomiendas en su forma mitigada, impuesta después de la memorable junta de Valladolid en 1542, rectificada por las *Ordenangas* en 1543” [245]); trad. de I. Lachance. Pour Monique Mustapha (1989, 494), José de Acosta se rallie à cette institution, dont il connaît les faiblesses et les inconvénients, “parce qu’elle garantit à ses yeux l’évangélisation des Amérindiens.” Voir 483–95 et Lopetegui 1942, 359–62.

24 Trad. de D. Castillo Durante.
25 Trad. de Rainier Grutman.
26 José de Acosta expose, du reste, les assisses du "gouvernement et de l'administration" des *encomiendas* au Livre III de son ouvrage, intitulé "Del gobierno y administración de los indios en lo politico y civil" (Acosta [1588] 1954, 459–503), ainsi que Leon Lopetequi, qui écrit (trad. de I. Lachance): "Je dois accomplir le travail varié que se propose le missionnaire dans ce domaine, en substituant immédiatement les cérémonies chrétiennes aux païennes, méthode qui fut si féconde entre les mains de saint Patrick, saint Martins de Tours et de tant d'apôtres" ("Hay que completar la variada labor que se proponia el misionero en este campo con la inmediata sustitución de ceremonias criatianas a las paganas, método tan fecundo en manos de San Patricio, San Martin de Tours y tantos apóstoles" [1942, 295]).
27 "C'est contre nature, en quelque espèce que vous le voudrez prendre, que l'enfant aussi tost né, aussi tost se nourrisse et soustienne de soy-mesme. Car en fin, ce n'est pas en vain que les mamelles grossissent aux mères pour un temps."
28 "Comment est-ce donc que vous voulez qu'ils se puissent entretenir en la foy et grâce de Dieu, s'ils ne sont bien instruits, et au double des autres?"
29 Mais en même temps, "si par tout il faut diligemment catéchiser les peuples autant que les introduire dans l'Eglise et leur communiquer le sacrement de régénération, c'est en ces lieux où sur tout il le faut," écrit le jésuite (Biard [1616] 1967, 511).
30 Pourtant, au contraire des Amérindiens de l'Acadie, c'était "gent [qui] n'estoit point sauvage, ains civile; non coureuse, mais arrestée" (512).
31 Pierre Biard reprend en partie le texte de la parabole du grain qui pousse tout seul, tirée de l'évangile de Marc (4, 28): "Car la terre produit d'elle-même premièrement l'herbe, ensuite l'épi, puis le blé tout formé qui remplit l'épi" (*Sainte Bible* 1990). On le constate, Pierre Biard interprète librement le texte car la parabole signifie, pour reprendre une note de la traduction de l'École biblique de Jérusalem (*Sainte Bible* 1961, 1335, n. b), que "le royaume de Dieu porte en lui-même un principe de développement, une force secrète qui l'amènera à son complet achèvement." Peut-être le texte de l'épître de saint Jacques (5, 7) eût-il mieux convenu: "Mais vous, mes frères, persévérez dans la patience jusqu'à l'avènement du Seigneur. Vous voyez que le laboureur, dans l'espérance de recueillir le fruit précieux de la terre, attend patiemment que Dieu envoie les pluies de la première et de l'arrière-saison" (*Sainte Bible* 1961).

32 Dans son *De Procuranda Indorum salute*, l'auteur observe en effet qu'il n'est pas facile d'extirper la superstition chez les Amérindiens, même baptisés: "D'aucuns, depuis, se découragent ou implorent le ciel, parce que les Indiens baptisés conservent de nombreux reliquats de leurs anciennes sauvagerie, superstition et vie bestiale" ("No hay, pues, que desanimarse ni levantar le grito al cielo, porque todavía los indios bautizados conservan muchos resabios de su antigua fiereza y superstición y vida bestial" [Acosta [1588] 1954, 414]); trad. de I. Lachance. Mais il ajoute que leurs mœurs se sont améliorées petit à petit.

33 Comme l'indique Lucien Campeau (Biard [1616] 1967, 513, n. 7), Pierre Biard renvoie ici au *Decretum Gratiani*, Livre III, dist. iv, § 54, intitulé "Officium baptizandi catechumeni preueniant": "Avant le baptême, l'homme doit être préparé par le catéchisme, afin de recevoir les rudiments de la foi. [...] Jésus a d'abord redonné la vue à un aveugle de naissance en lui enduisant les yeux d'argile et de salive, avant de l'envoyer aux eaux de Siloé, parce qu'il convient d'être instruit avant d'être baptisé dans la foi en l'incarnation du Christ et d'être admis au baptême des fidèles, dont la grâce est de savoir qu'il en fait partie et qu'il est désormais débiteur [du Christ]" ("Ante baptismum catechizandi debet hominem prævenire officium, ut fidei primum catechumenus accipiat rudimentum. [...] Prius ipse Iesus cæci nati oculos luto ex sputo facto superlinivit et sic ad aquas Siloe misit: quia prius debet baptizandus fidei incarnationis Christi instrui et sic ad baptismum iam credulus admitti, ut sciat cuius gratiæ eo est particeps et cui iam debitor fiat deinceps"); trad. de I. Lachance. Le texte, rappelle Lucien Campeau, provient de Raban Maur et a été inclus dans le *Decretum Gratiani*.

34 "Ils ne sçavoyent pas mesme faire le signe de la croix." Pierre Biard avait déjà fait une observation semblable dans sa lettre du 10 juin 1611 à Christophe Baltazar. Voir [1611] Biard, 141.

35 "Quelques François nous rapportoyent que quand ils estoyent à part, ils se mocquoyent insolemment de nos cérémonies" (513).

36 Dans sa lettre du 31 janvier 1612, adressée à Christophe Baltazar, Pierre Biard énonçait la même règle de ne baptiser les adultes qu'après les avoir bien catéchisés. Voir 229–30.

37 Selon Pierre Biard, l'argument vient même des Amérindiens, qui justifiaient par là leur abandon de la foi: "Les sauvages n'ont point esté si hébétés, qu'ils n'ayent fort bien sceu nous reprocher cest injustice" (514). À noter que les jésuites baptisèrent aussi les adultes à l'article de la mort: "[L]es aagez qui meurent, nous les baptisons aussi, les catéchisants du mieux que nous pouvons et que le temps le permet" (515).

38 Les missionnaires baptisèrent “les petits enfans, comme vous voyez, de la volonté de leurs parens, et soubs l'esperance que nous aurons moyen de les instruire, quand ils viendront à l'usage de raison” (515). La pratique n'est pas sans faire problème, puisque l'autorisation demandée aux parents ne peut être valide que si ceux-ci savent à quoi ils engagent leurs enfants en permettant aux missionnaires de les baptiser.

39 Pierre Biard prend alors la peine d'insister à nouveau sur la prudence des missionnaires: “Il est vray, nous avons la jambe fort pesante pour monter mesme ce premier degré” (516).

40 Sans doute ne reprend-il pas l'idée de sédentariser les Amérindiens de l'Acadie, parce qu'il est conscient que l'opération serait vouée à l'échec, compte tenu des conditions de la colonisation et des mœurs des Amérindiens de la région.

41 D'ailleurs, note Pierre Biard, les jésuites faisaient participer les enfants aux cérémonies chrétiennes et ces derniers, dit-il, “y prenoyent du plaisir, comme s'ils eussent esté vrayment chrestiens” (603).

42 Dans son édition de la “relation,” Lucien Campeau écrit: “On ne saurait dégager des écrits du P. Biard une théorie de la colonisation. Ce que le jésuite en dit ici, il paraît le tenir en commun avec ses contemporains, spécialement avec Lescarbot. Colonisation et évangélisation doivent aller de pair. Elles se feront par la fondation d'un établissement français, ravitaillé d'abord de la France par les navires, puis, de plus en plus, par la culture du pays lui-même. Autour de ce poste, on établira les Indiens convertis, qu'il faudra nourrir, du moins aussi longtemps qu'ils n'auront pas appris à se subvenir à eux-mêmes par l'agriculture, plus que par la chasse et la pêche” (509, n. 1). Rien dans le texte de Biard ne permet de lui prêter l'intention d'établir des Amérindiens convertis autour des postes français. Certes, c'est ce que feront plus tard les jésuites, mais L. Campeau projette sur Biard des pratiques ultérieures des jésuites que celui-ci ne propose aucunement ici. Si l'on se fie à la fin de son texte, c'est par l'exemple, par “les yeux” qu'il entend influencer les Amérindiens. En cela, il s'oppose à Samuel de Champlain, dont les idées sur l'évangélisation des Amérindiens se rapprochent de celles de José de Acosta: en effet, Champlain estime que “la reduction en la cognoissance de Dieu [serait] plus facille, si leur pays estoit habitué de personnes qui prissent la peine, & le soing, de leur enseigner” (Champlain [1619] 1973, 575). “[C]e n'est pas assez d'y enuoyer des Religieux, ajoute-t-il, s'il n'y a des gens pour les maintenir, & assister: car encores que ces peuples ayent le desir auiourd'huy de cognoistre que c'est que Dieu, le lendemain ceste volonté leur changera, quand il conuiendra oster, &

suprimer, leurs salles coustumes, la dissolution de leurs mœurs, & leurs libertez.inciuilles: De façon qu'il faut des peuples, & des familles, pour les tenir en debuoir, & auec douceur les contraindre à faire mieux, & par bons exemples les esmouuoir à correction de vie" (575).

43 "Comme ces sauvages n'ont ny religion formée, ny police, ny villes, ny artifices, les mots aussi et les paroles propres à tout cela leur manque: sainct, bien-heureux, ange, grâce, mystère, sacrement, tentation, foy, loy, prudence, subjection, gouvernement, etc." (535).

44 Pourtant, selon l'aveu même du père Biard, il ne put bénéficier de l'aide d'un "maistre en langue sauvagine" que pendant "trois semaines durant" (557). Compte tenu des difficultés qu'implique l'apprentissage d'une langue amérindienne, on peut s'interroger sur la connaissance réelle qu'en avait le missionnaire.

BIBLIOGRAPHIE

Acosta, José de. [1588] 1954. *De Procuranda Indorum salute O predicacion del evangelio en las Indias.* In *Obras del P. José de Acosta de la Compañia de Jesus,* éd. Francisco Mateos, S. J.: 387–608. Madrid: Atlas.

Acosta, José de. [1589] 1979. *Histoire naturelle et morale des Indes occidentales,* trad. Jacques Rémy-Zéphir. Paris: Payot.

Augustin. 1964. *Traités anti-donatistes* [*De baptismo libri VII*]. In *Œuvres,* trad. Guy Finaert, éd. Yves Congar, vol. 29: 53–665. Paris: Desclée de Brouwer.

Biard, Pierre. [1611] 1967. Le P. Pierre Biard au P. Christophe Baltazar, Prov." In *Monumenta Novæ Franciæ,* éd. Lucien Campeau, vol. 1 ("La première mission d'Acadie (1602–1616)"): 123–51. Rome / Québec: Monumenta Historica Soc. Iesu / Presses de l'Université Laval.

Biard, Pierre. [1612] 1967. "Le P. Pierre Biard au P. Christophe Baltazar, Prov." In *Monumenta Novæ Franciæ,* éd. Lucien Campeau, vol. 1 ("La première mission d'Acadie (1602–1616)"): 225–50. Rome / Québec: Monumenta Historica Soc. Iesu / Presses de l'Université Laval.

Biard, Pierre. [1616] 1967. "Relation de la Nouvelle-France, de ses terres, naturel du païs et de ses habitans; item du voyage des Pères jésuites ausdictes contrées et de ce qu'ils y ont faict jusques à leur prinse par les Anglois. Faicte par le P. Pierre Biard, Grenoblois, de la Compagnie de Jésus." In *Monumenta Novæ Franciæ,* éd. Lucien Campeau, vol. 1 ("La première mission d'Acadie (1602–1616)"): 456–637. Rome / Québec: Monumenta Historica Soc. Iesu / Presses de l'Université Laval.

Burgaleta, Claudio M. 1999. *José de Acosta, S. J. (1540–1600). His Life and Thought.* Chicago: Loyola Press.

Cereceda, Feliciano. "Le Padre José de Acosta y le origen de las encomiendas americanas." *Razón y fe* 124 (3): 240–50.

Champlain, Samuel. [1619] 1973. *Voyages et descovvertvres faites en la Novvelle France, depuis l'année 1615. iusques à la fin de l'année 1618*, dans *Les voyages de Champlain*, éd. par Charles Honoré Laverdière, vol. 2: 481–631. Montréal: Éditions du Jour.

Lopetegui, León. 1942. *Le Padre José de Acosta, S. I. y las misiones.* Madrid: Consejo superior de investigaciones científicas.

Lopetegui, León. 1943. "¿ Cómo debe entenderse la labor misional del P. José de Acosta S. I.?." *Studia missionalia* 1: 115–36.

Mustapha, Monique. 1989. *Humanisme et Nouveau Monde. Études sur la pensée de José de Acosta.* Lille: Atelier national de reproduction des thèses.

[Poutrincourt, Jean de Biencourt, sieur de]. [1614] 1967. "Factum du procez entre messire Jean de Biencourt, chevalier, sieur de Poutrincourt, baron de Sainct-Just, appellant, d'une part, et Pierre Biard, Enemond Massé et consorts, soy-disant prestres de la Société de Jésus, intimez. *Coelum, non animum, mutant qui trans mare currunt.* M. DC. XIIII." In *Monumenta Novæ Franciæ*, éd. Lucien Campeau, vol. 1 ("La première mission d'Acadie (1602–1616"): 320–406. Rome / Québec: Monumenta Historica Soc. Iesu / Presses de l'Université Laval.

Sainte Bible, La. 1961. Trad. par l'École biblique de Jérusalem. Paris: Éditions du Cerf, 1961.

Sainte Bible contenant l'Ancien et le Nouveau Testament, avec des notes courtes pour l'intelligence des endroits les plus difficiles, La. 1990 [1696–1702], trad. par Louis-Isaac Lemaître de Sacy. Paris: Robert Laffont.

chapter fifteen

La Nouvelle-France dans l'imaginaire jésuite: *terra doloris* ou Jérusalem céleste?

MARIE-CHRISTINE PIOFFET

La vallée laurentienne est, au XVIIe siècle, entachée d'une fort mauvaise réputation. En 1609, Antoine Du Périer, le premier auteur à notre connaissance à avoir introduit ce vaste territoire dans une œuvre de fiction, *Les amours de Pistion et de Fortunie*, la perçoit comme une terre ingrate "où aucun ne vient et n'y vit que par force" ([1609] 1973, 61). Conscient de sa hardiesse, il multiplie au début du récit les formules d'excuses, de crainte de rebuter la dédicataire, Marguerite de Valois, avec le choix de ce cadre géographique: "[S]i ma plume n'est assés douce, vous excuserés le pays d'où je l'ay tirée & l'affection que j'ay voüée à vostre service" (53). Bien que certains apôtres de la colonisation se soient efforcés d'atténuer cette impression négative et de montrer que l'Amérique septentrionale est un lieu parfaitement habitable pour peu que l'on en défriche les terres, cette opinion défavorable perdure au milieu du siècle. En 1662, Desmarets de Saint-Sorlin imagine un jeu de cartes récréatif sur lequel sont gravés les noms de divers continents et pays. La Nouvelle-France, incarnée par le dix de trèfle, s'y définit comme un "Pays couvert d'arbres, et mal cultivé" (Saint-Sorlin 1662, s. p.). À cette image d'un terroir étouffé par d'épaisses forêts, on ne trouve que peu de démentis. Autant que les échecs successifs de Cartier au Cap-Rouge et du marquis de La Roche à l'île de Sable, l'image terrifiante du Canada véhiculée dans les *Relations des Jésuites* n'est pas étrangère à cette désaffection populaire.[1]

Ces "derniers confins du monde"[2]

Avant d'aborder la représentation du sol canadien dans l'imaginaire des jésuites, j'aimerais dire un mot sur leur conception du monde. François de Dainville a montré l'importance de la géographie dans la formation des missionnaires de la Compagnie de Jésus (Dainville 1940, 105–13) et Paul Lejeune n'est pas en reste. À défaut d'avoir lui-même arpenté le globe,[3] le missionnaire a d'évidence étudié les cartes. Il connaît non seulement la configuration des vieux pays mais aussi celle des terres situées au-delà de l'Atlantique, comme le suggère la leçon qu'il donne à son hôte Mestigoit[4] au cours de l'hiver 1634:

> [M]on hoste [...] me demanda un jour comme la terre estoit faite, et m'apportant une écorce et un charbon, il me la fit décrire. Je luy despeins les deux Hemispheres, et apres luy avoir tracé l'Europe, l'Asie et l'Afrique, je vins à nostre Amerique, luy montrant comme elle est une grande Isle; je luy décrivy la coste de l'Acadie, la grande Isle de Terre-neufve, l'entrée et golfe de nostre grand fleuve de sainct Laurens, les peuples qui habitent ses rives, le lieu où nous estions pour lors (Lejeune [1635] 1972, 82–3).[5]

L'ordre dans lequel sont énumérés les quatre continents n'est pas indifférent. Que le missionnaire commence par l'Europe et l'Asie, avant de s'attarder à la terre de son hôte, peut sembler tout naturel pour un homme tributaire des valeurs de son temps, qui ne tenait pas en égale estime toutes les régions de la planète. Toutefois, sa vision n'est pas complètement dépourvue d'originalité. En représentant l'Amérique comme une "grande Isle," il se démarque des conjectures du jésuite Joseph Acosta, de François de Belleforest et de Marc Lescarbot, qui la rattachent tous trois par quelque détroit à l'Europe septentrionale.[6] Il suit de là que la Nouvelle-France, bien que située au même parallèle que la France, présente un hiatus par rapport aux autres grandes aires géographiques. Lejeune considère en effet l'un, puis l'autre hémisphère, au sens étymologique du terme,[7] soit la partie orientale formée des trois continents connus des Anciens aux Indes occidentales. Entre ces deux moitiés du globe, il existe dans son esprit une nette démarcation. C'est pourquoi il insiste sur la barrière atlantique, "cette grande mer qui environne vostre pays" (17), dit-il aux Sauvages, s'inscrivant en faux contre leur opinion voulant que leurs "terres sont conjointes en quelque endroit" (17) avec le reste du monde. Par ailleurs, gardons-nous bien de voir une marque d'affectivité dans l'expression "nostre Amérique" utilisée par le jésuite.

Un autre extrait de la même relation montre bien qu'il ne s'y considère nullement chez lui: "Tout vostre pays, leur dis-je (sçavoir est l'Amérique), est une grande Isle" (17). Ailleurs, pour montrer la force de son amour envers ses hôtes, Lejeune leur rappelle la grandeur du sacrifice qu'il fit en s'arrachant à son terroir natal: "Vous voyez, disois-je, de quel amour je suis porté en vostre endroit: j'ay non seulement quitté mon pays, qui est beau et bien agreable, pour venir dans vos neiges et dans vos grands bois" (64). La mappemonde imaginaire de Lejeune n'est pas complètement imperméable à l'a priori idéologique faisant de l'Europe et de l'Asie le berceau de la civilisation et le fief des nations les mieux nanties. Par-delà ces substrats historiques et culturels, la cosmographie jésuite bipolaire se construit à partir de considérations théologiques ou, plus exactement, sur un double antagonisme entre chrétienté et paganisme,[8] civilisation et sauvagerie. Il est significatif que, dans la *Relation de ce qui s'est passé en la Nouvelle-France en l'année 1636*, le même missionnaire, saluant les efforts de construction, décrive la ville de Québec comme un autre monde: "Kébec me semble un autre Païs" (Lejeune [1637] 1972, 41). Le regard missionnaire porté sur le Nouveau Monde porte les stigmates d'une aversion marquée pour les mœurs amérindiennes décrites sans aménité. Dans l'esprit des hommes du Grand Siècle, l'environnement est le miroir des êtres qui y vivent. Louis Van Delft a mis au jour la "caractériologie" de l'espace établie par les sujets du Roi-Soleil, qui "associent des propriétés morales à des lieux géographiques" (Van Delft 1993, 91). Mais il ne s'agissait pas d'une hypothèse nouvelle. "Dans un pays heureux, tout concourt à la paix, tandis que dans un pays misérable, tout conduit à la guerre et au mâle courage," écrivait déjà Strabon (1969, 109). Or l'Amérique appartient, selon les disciples d'Ignace de Loyola, à la deuxième catégorie, celle des nations défavorisées vouées à une existence âpre et sans joie.

Le mal du pays

Paul Lejeune, qui est venu au Canada par vœu d'obéissance, n'éprouve manifestement pas beaucoup de sympathie pour ces peuples, comme en témoignent ses aveux: "[J]e ne pensois nullement venir en Canada quand on m'y a envoyé: je ne sentois aucune affection particuliere pour les Sauvages" ([1632] 1972, 6). Tout au long de la célèbre *Relation* de 1634, il grossit le cliché de l'Amérindien immonde, en rappelant constamment son manque d'hygiène, ce qu'il considère comme sa perversité. Pas plus que ses habitants le paysage canadien ne l'enthousiasme. On perçoit aisément sa déception peu après avoir atteint ces "miserables contrées" (3), comme il les appelle de manière fort significative à son arrivée. Semblable désappointement gagne Jérôme Lalemant au terme d'un épuisant voyage vers la mer du Nord:

> On ne voit rien icy de si beau, rien d'attrayant; c'est un sol sec, aride et sablonneux; les montagnes n'y sont couvertes que de rochers, ou de petites pointes d'arbres, qui ne trouvent pas assez d'humeur dans les crevasses où ils naissent, pour grossir. L'on n'y voit ny beaux bois, ny belles terres. [...] Les oiseaux semblent s'estre retirez de ces solitudes, tant on en voit peu (Lalemant [1662] 1972, 18).

Pour peindre leur nouvel habitat, les relationnaires émaillent leur discours d'adjectifs dysphoriques: ainsi les glaces charriées sur le Saint-Laurent sont "horribles" (Lejeune [1634] 1972, 13) tout comme les rochers qui bornent ce même fleuve (Lejeune [1635] 1972, 81); d'autres plus au nord "sont épouvantables à voir, tant pour leur hauteur que pour leur grosseur" (Quen [1657] 1972, 38). "Prodigieux" sont aussi les monts enneigés des Laurentides qu'on aperçoit non loin de Québec (Lejeune [1634] 1972, 22), "affreux" les chemins (ibid.: 2) et les rochers (Lejeune [1634] 1972, 62), tandis que les forêts sont "capables d'effrayer les voyageurs les plus asseurez" (Lalemant [1662] 1972, 13). Il me paraît inutile de multiplier les exemples pour montrer que l'exotisme canadien ressortit à l'expression d'une frayeur irrépressible, celle que procure la contemplation des grands espaces, la menace d'un vide.

L'empire de thanatos[9]

La densité des bois comme l'immensité des glaces qui dérivent aux abords de Terre-Neuve rappellent au missionnaire la précarité de la condition humaine: "Quand on en rencontre quantité, et qu'un navire se trouve embarrassé la dedans, il est bien-tost mis en pieces" (Lejeune [1632] 1972, 2–3). L'Amérique sauvage se révèle donc un *locus horribilis.* Les relationnaires évoquent inlassablement les dangers de toutes natures qui les guettent – ici des précipices, là des collines escarpées, là-bas de redoutables rapides. Avant même de débarquer à Québec, Paul Lejeune envisage les eaux du fleuve comme son sépulcre: "[I]l me semble que je me voyois mourir" (14). Égaré au milieu de la forêt de Charlevoix, il entrevoit derechef l'image de la mort: "Le froid estoit si violent que je m'attendois infailliblement de mourir la nuit" (Lejeune [1635] 1972, 73).[10] Cette obsession macabre, qui fait des serviteurs du Christ les martyrs de la conquête des âmes, prend dans l'idéologie jésuite une résonance toute particulière, comme le prouve cette nouvelle déclaration de Lejeune: "Quand je me veois assiégé de flots homicides, de forests infinies, il me vient à l'esprit ceste riche parole de St. Ignace, martyr; *nunc incipio esse Christi discipulus*, c'est aujourd'huy que je commence d'estre de la Compagnie de Jesus" (Lejeune [1637] 1972, 47). Réal Ouellet a relevé la présence de tentations suicidaires chez le même auteur (voir Ouellet, 1990). Mais la nature canadienne ne se montre guère plus clémente envers les autochtones: Mestigoit[11] sera "estouffé" dans les eaux du fleuve à la marée montante (Lejeune [1637] 1972, 11). Quiconque s'aventure en ces déserts s'expose à tous les périls. En certains endroits, "les oyseaux s'elevent en si grand nombre qu'ils renversent les personnes" (Lejeune [1632] 1972, 2); dans les bois, les "maringoins" "mettent un homme en sang quand ils l'abordent: ils font la guerre aux uns plus qu'aux autres" (7).[12] La violence profuse va souvent de pair avec l'utilisation d'un lexique guerrier pour suggérer la poursuite importune des éléments. Le sentiment d'agression atteint son paroxysme dans la représentation du tremblement de terre de 1663. Nous avons déjà montré dans une étude antérieure (voir Pioffet 1997, 181–5) comment Jérôme Lalemant, qui fait dans son journal de l'événement un incident sans gravité qui eut pour seule conséquence d'endommager "certaines cheminées" et d'entraîner d'"autres legeres pertes" matérielles (Lalemant [1663] 1871, 316), donne au séisme des proportions apocalyptiques dans sa relation. Un simple échantillon de la version qu'il livre à l'imprimeur suffira à s'en persuader:

> Un tremblement de terre de plus de deux cents lieuës en longueur, et de plus de cent en largeur, qui font en tout vingt mille lieües, a fait trembler tout ce païs, où l'on a veu des changemens prodigieux: des Montagnes abysmées, des Forests changées en des grands Lacs, des Rivieres qui ont disparu, des Rochers qui se sont fendus, dont les debris estoient poussez jusques au sommet des plus hauts arbres; des tonnerres qui grondoient sous nos pieds, dans le ventre de la terre, qui vomirent des flammes; des voix lugubres qui s'entendoient avec horreur; des Baleines blanches et Marsoüins qui hurloient dans les eaüx; enfin tous les elements sembloient armez contre nous, et nous menaçoient d'un dernier malheur (Lalemant [1664] 1972, 2).

Ce séisme spectaculaire prend l'allure d'une lutte à finir entre ce pays rebelle qui résiste à la doctrine chrétienne et les propagateurs de la foi.[13] Les images du registre guerrier qui ferment la citation et la métaphore filée qui suit confirment cette interprétation. La bataille, amorcée sur les eaux, se transporte aux forêts: "[I]l sembloit qu'il y eust un combat entre les arbres qui se heurtoient ensemble; [...] on eut dit que les troncs se destachoient de leurs places pour sauter les uns sur les autres, avec un fracas et un bouleversement qui fit dire à nos Sauvages que toute la forest estoit yvre" (3–4). Bientôt le conflit, qui prend de l'ampleur, atteint les montagnes: "[L]es unes se deracinoient pour se jetter sur les autres, laissant de grands abysmes au lieu d'où elles sortoient et tantost enfonçoient les arbres dont elles estoient chargées bien avant dans la terre jusqu'à la cime" (4). Enfin, le narrateur rapporte que certains témoins ont vu "des picques et des lances de feu voltiger" (id.). Jérôme Lalemant, d'abord soucieux de donner à son rapport des assises historiques – "Ce fut le cinquiéme Fevrier 1663, sur les cinq heures et demie du soir" (3), écrit-il –, s'abandonne dans une sorte de transe à une rêverie aux accents eschatologiques. Tout se passe comme si ce "desordre" apocalyptique servait d'exutoire au jésuite, qui cherche à déverser sur ces contrées toute sa hargne devant les insuccès de l'entreprise missionnaire. Curieusement, la main du Tout-Puissant aplanit le relief, brouille les saisons, décolore les eaux du fleuve, mais laisse les hommes indemnes. Mais que la secousse présentée comme un châtiment de Dieu épargne les habitations françaises n'a rien pour surprendre.[14] Dans la rhétorique jésuite, la description hyperbolique du séisme de 1663 correspond à la fin du règne de Satan: "Les Trembles-terre ont fait paroistre la Foy de nos Neophytes, et l'apprehension qu'ils ont des jugements de Dieu, aux bontez duquel ils ont eu recours avec une confiance extraordinaire" (9).

On cherchera en vain à travers les mailles de leur récit les germes d'un eldorado mythique, si courant dans les écrits du Nouveau Monde.[15] Certes, tout n'y est pas négatif: les jésuites louent la frugalité des Amérindiens qui leur rappelle l'âge d'or.[16] Mais cette idéalisation utopique présuppose comme condition *sine qua non* la christianisation de ces peuples.[17] Au lieu de sublimer les vertus du pays et de ses habitants, les relationnaires ont choisi une stratégie opposée: mettre au jour les périls de leur pénible labeur pour attiser la sympathie. La *Relation* de 1634 en fournit une illustration: "J'ay bien voulu descrire ce voyage, pour faire voir à V. R. les grands travaux qu'il faut souffrir en la suite des Sauvages" ([1635] 1972, 87). Il est en outre frappant de constater que l'œil du missionnaire, qui inventorie la faune et toise non sans répugnance les Amérindiens, ne se pose que furtivement sur le décor canadien. Sans doute celui-ci n'offre pas la diversité souhaitée. Point d'allées, de jardins, de vergers, de fontaines qui caractérisent le paysage idéal de l'époque (voir Niderst, 1992). Du reste, la visée apologétique des comptes rendus de missions s'accommode difficilement du pittoresque paysager. Est-il séduit par les environs de Trois-Rivières qu'il compare, dans une autre relation, à l'Anjou (voir Lejeune [1637] 1972, 46), Lejeune en esquive aussitôt la description: "Je décrirois volontiers la beauté de ce lieu, mais je crains d'être long" (13). Les jésuites font d'ordinaire peu de cas des territoires sauvages, à moins qu'ils ne soient habités ou propres à l'érection de bâtiments. Le chapitre 8 de la *Relation* de 1637, intitulé "De l'estat present de la Nouvelle France sur le grand Fleuve de S. Laurens," est éloquent à cet égard. Après avoir évoqué la situation générale du pays, le missionnaire change brutalement de propos pour s'attarder aux habitations: "Ce preambule est long, entrons en nos demeures" (41); à vrai dire, le souci de fidélité à l'environnement n'engendre qu'une topographie sommaire. On retrouve bien quelques considérations sur la largeur du Saguenay—"[C]e fleuve est aussi beau que la Seine, quasi aussi rapide que le Rosne, et plus profond que plusieurs endroits de la mer" (Lejeune [1632] 1972, 3)—, sur l'étendue des neiges, sur le dédale des sentiers forestiers, mais très peu de considérations sur le panorama, qu'on ne semble pas voir, si l'on peut dire. Amplifiées fréquemment par le *topos* de l'ineffable, les aspérités du décor résistent à toute représentation: "De vous depeindre la difficulté des chemins, je n'ay ny plume ny pinceau qui le puisse faire [...]. Nous ne faisions que monter et descendre," dira Paul Lejeune ([1635] 1972, 67) pour résumer son odyssée montagnaise, qui prend l'allure d'une course à obstacles. Bref, je ne pense pas m'égarer en affirmant que la vision négative du Canada exerce dans les rapports annuels des missionnaires une fonction encomiastique inversée: elle participe du rejet des mœurs sauvages.

Mais il y a plus. Cette représentation terrifiante du pays permet encore la sublimation des épreuves au moyen desquelles le missionnaire peut espérer s'élever au rang de "soldat du Christ." Les disciples de saint Ignace de Loyola voient leur séjour en Nouvelle-France comme une longue purgation pour gagner des âmes. Claude d'Ablon résume ainsi les périls de ce métier: les conversions, écrit-il,

> ne s'achettent que par des famines, qui reduisent quelquefois le Missionnaire au gland et à la mousse; par des travaux qui l'épuisent de sueurs depuis le matin jusqu'au soir, et par des périls de mort presque continuels, soit qu'il faille courir aprés la brebis égarée dans ces vastes forests, sur les

> neiges et sur les glaces, soit qu'on soit obligé de voguer dans de fresles canots d'écorce sur des Lacs qui ne sont pas moins orageux que la mer ([1672] 1972, 2).

Sur ce théâtre instable et houleux qu'est l'Amérique septentrionale s'affirme la certitude que la rédemption de ces peuples ne s'obtiendra qu'au prix de force souffrances: "Si nos Peres qui iront en ces païs là, ont de la peine, Dieu les sçaura fort bien recompenser," conclut encore Lejeune ([1634] 1972, 3) après quelques mois de séjour.

Glaces et frimas

Plus encore que les forêts labyrinthiques et les chutes d'eau du Canada, l'hiver terrifie. Les "hauts et prodigieux glaçons nageants" dérivant du fleuve Saint-Laurent impressionnent manifestement Pierre Biard ([1616] 1967, 529), saisi par ce spectacle. Paul Lejeune sera aussi ébloui par les icebergs qui, telles de véritables forteresses de glace, gardent l'entrée du golfe. Mais ce sont surtout les rigueurs du climat qui importunent les missionnaires. Un an après son arrivée au Canada, Paul Lejeune note ceci: "Le froid estoit par fois si violent, que nous entendions les arbres se fendre dans le bois et en se fendans faire un bruit comme des armes à feu" ([1634] 1972, 10).[18] Ce dernier entretient, du reste, des rapports ambivalents avec la neige comme avec l'hiver canadien. Lui qui aimait naguère se rouler sur les collines enneigées aux abords de Québec (15), lui qui affirme que le climat est tout à fait supportable,[19] éprouvera, au cours de son hivernement avec les Montagnais, le pouvoir aveuglant de cet élément: "[L]e mal estoit que la neige n'avoit pas plus de pitié de mes yeux que la fumée" ([1635] 1972, 53). Le jésuite est ainsi partagé devant l'hiver canadien: d'une part, il tente de rassurer les craintifs peu enclins à quitter le confort de leur maison; d'autre part, il se décrit avantageusement comme un martyr de l'évangélisation. Dans cette dialectique, c'est sans aucun doute la deuxième polarité qui pèse le plus, soit le souvenir des tourments et des intempéries.

Dans ce désert de givre, la glace recouvre tout, même les fenêtres des maisons: "[C]'est au travers ce crystal que le Soleil nous communique sa lumiere," précise encore Paul Lejeune ([1634] 1972, 10). Mais nulle épreuve ne peut surpasser ces pénibles sorties hivernales au cours desquelles le marcheur, s'"engageant [...] dedans les neiges jusques aux genoux et parfois quasi jusques à la ceinture" ([1635] 1972, 55), se voit contraint à une pénible gymnastique. Lors des redoux qui rendent les glaces friables, ces escapades paraissent plus hasardeuses encore: "[I]l me sembloit que je marchois sur des chemins de verre qui se cassoit à tous coups soubs mes pieds," note encore Lejeune (67).

Un pays satanique?

Mais où faut-il chercher la cause de ces rigueurs? La Nouvelle-France ne se situe-t-elle pas au même parallèle que la France? Dès 1616, Pierre Biard, qui soupèse toutes les causes possibles, invoque un argument religieux:

> [E]n pure vérité, toute ceste région, [...] par malice de Satan qui y règne, n'est qu'un horrible désert, non guière moins calamiteux pour la malencontreuse disette des biens corporels que pour celle qui absolument rend les hommes misérables, l'extrême nudité des parements et richesses de l'âme. Et ne faut jà en accuser le sol ou malignité de la terre, l'air ou les eaux, les hommes ou leurs humeurs (461).

Le jésuite établit ici une adéquation entre l'indigence matérielle et la disette spirituelle. La malignité de la terre, pour reprendre son expression, découle en réalité de tares morales. Ce pays, privé des lumières de l'Évangile et donc de Dieu, ne peut qu'engendrer pour ceux qui en foulent le sol de multiples tribulations.

Paul Lejeune rappelle au lecteur les "croix" ([1640] 1972, 48) que les missionnaires doivent supporter dans ces contrées boisées. Curieusement, un voile de fumée vient souvent tamiser la lumière du soleil, comme l'enregistre l'auteur de la *Relation* de 1661:

> L'air est icy presque tousiours embruny des fumées que causent les embrasemens des forests circonvoisines, qui s'allumant à quinze et vingt lieuës à la ronde tout ensemble, nous ont jetté leurs cendres de plus de dix lieuës loin; c'est ce qui a fait que nous n'avons que rarement jouy de la beauté du soleil à descouvert: il nous a paru voilé de ces nuages de fumée, et quelque fois avec tel excès, que les plus grandes esclipses de soleil ne rendent point l'air, la terre et les herbes plus tristes, ny plus sombres. Ces embrasements [...] sont icy fort ordinaires pendant un mois ou deux de l'Esté ([1662] 1972, 18).

Derrière ce pays propice aux incendies, on peut aisément décoder le paradigme de la géhenne. L'adéquation entre le Canada et la terre des réprouvés semble prégnante sous la plume des relationnaires.[20] Cette malédiction transparaît encore dans les désordres climatiques dont "ces quartiers" deviennent la proie (Lejeune [1637] 1972, 36). Peu après le tremblement de terre, Jérome Lalemant rapporte entre plusieurs événements singuliers qu'une "pluye de cendre" a traversé le Saint-Laurent non loin du cap Tourmente ([1664] 1972, 5), comme si le créateur voulait châtier ce territoire rebelle. L'onomastique renforce le rapprochement. La métaphore "l'empire de Sathan" (Lejeune [1639] 1972, 2) utilisée par les jésuites n'est pas que symbolique; elle a des retombées sur la vision de cette région, comme le prouve la suite du passage: "Ce pais si disgracié de la nature ne laisse pas d'avoir ses habitants, qui, ayans part à la Rédemption de Jésus Christ aussi bien que nous meritent bien que nous leur procurions, pour les faire jouir d'un repos éternel, après tant de peines dans lequelles ils traisnent leur miserable vie" (19). Aux yeux des disciples de saint Ignace, ce pays est fâcheux non pas tant en vertu de son âpre climat, mais parce que plongé dans les ténèbres. L'aversion de Lejeune pour ce qu'il considère comme un château fort de Lucifer est à ce point perceptible qu'au cours de son difficile hivernement, Mestigoit[21] lui dit, pour l'encourager: "Considere que voicy un beau pays, ayme-le: si tu l'aymes, tu t'y plairas; si tu t'y plais, tu te resioüiras; si tu te resioüis, tu guariras" ([1635] 1972, 83). Mais le visiteur ne semble pas avoir retenu ce conseil.

Châteaux de cartes

Le rejet des vastes espaces va de pair avec une volonté de les apprivoiser, voire de les civiliser.[22] Lejeune, pétrifié devant le spectacle que lui révèle le sorcier sur un des sommets de Charlevoix, se plaît à reconnaître sous ses pieds de petites tours ou des châteaux:

> Je voyois au dessous de moy avec horreur des precipices, qui me faisoient trembler; j'appercevois des montagnes au milieu de quelques plaines qui me paroissoient comme des petites tours, ou plustost comme de petits chasteaux, quoy qu'en effet elles fussent fort grandes et fort hautes. [...] la pente estoit si roide, qu'il estoit fort aisé de rouler à bas, et de s'aller fendre la teste contre un arbre (81).

La comparaison, bien qu'assez stéréotypée, est lourde de signification. La vue aérienne exemplifie la propension qu'il a d'investir le vide canadien de constructions ou de fortifications imaginaires. La fréquence dans les *Relations* des images appartenant au registre architectural en fait foi. Saisi d'effroi devant les imposants icebergs qui émergent du golfe du Saint-Laurent, Pierre Biard se rappelle la cathédrale Notre-Dame de Paris: "[V]ous diriés [...] l'église nostre Dame de Paris, avec une partie de son Isle, maisons et palais, [....] flottant dessus l'eau" ([1616] 1967, 529). Paul Lejeune les assimile à des "Eglises" ([1632] 1972, 2). Un peu en amont de Montréal, Jean de Quen signale des rochers "grands comme des villes" ([1657] 1972, 9), d'autres "hauts comme des tours" (37). Davantage qu'un effet d'amplification ou qu'un simple ornement rhétorique, l'intrusion de ces bâtiments de papier coïncide avec une volonté de rendre prospère le "pays le plus malheureux du monde" (Lemercier [1666] 1972, 2), de transformer ces terres de "Barbares" en "un beau Royaume François"; bref, "d'en faire un grand Empire Chrestien" (2).[23]

En effet, les relationnaires réaffirment à quelques reprises leur souhait d'assister à la naissance prochaine de belles cités. Quelques années après son arrivée, Lejeune caresse le désir de voir ces peuples sédentarisés et policés: "[L]es plus grandes villes et les plus celebres ont commencé par un ramas de vagabons" ([1637] 1972, 5). C'est pourquoi il envisage comme de bons augures toutes les entreprises de construction, qu'elles soient laïques ou religieuses: les Européens, se plaît-il encore à rêver, "meditent diverses demeures ou habitations, jusques au Grand Sault de sainct Louys, qui seront peut estre un jour autant de Villes" (42). À défaut de pouvoir décrire un pays attrayant, Lejeune y prophétise avec une foi inébranlable la fondation prochaine d'un vaste royaume:

> [N]on seulement nous rendrons nostre Amerique Françoise, mais encore nous la ferons toute Chrestienne; et d'une vaste solitude, nous en ferons un Sanctuaire, où la divine Majesté trouvera des adorateurs de toutes les Langues et de toutes Nations [...]. Enfin cette derniere guerre plantera la Paix et les Lys dans toutes nos forests, pour en faire des Villes, si l'on veut, et d'une terre de Sauvages, en faire une Conqueste pour Jesus-Christ et pour la France ([1662] 1972, 40–1).

François Lemercier renoue, dans sa relation des événements de 1664 et 1665, avec la même promesse: "[N]os plaintes ont touché le cœur de sa Majesté, qui va faire un Royaume de nostre Barbarie et changer nos forests en villes, et nos deserts en provinces" ([1666] 1972, 2). Les jésuites, comme tous les esprits cultivés de leur temps, ne s'émeuvent non pas tant de la beauté naturelle que de la magnificence urbaine. L'éloge des villes est d'ailleurs un lieu commun de la littérature géographique de la Renaissance, comme le rappelle Jean-Claude Margolin (1987, 10). La chorographie jésuite, qui privilégie les bâtiments au détriment des vastes solitudes, dérive d'une "géographie de l'homme," selon l'expression de François de Dainville (1940, 121).[24]

Conclusion

Malgré la fermeté de telles prédictions, les Français bouderont dans une large mesure l'Amérique. Leur émigration somme toute modeste se limitera aux rives du Saint-Laurent et au littoral acadien. Les relationnaires, ardents défenseurs de la cause missionnaire, se révéleront en fait de piètres apôtres de la colonisation. En magnifiant le culte du héros martyr, peinant sous le poids de nombreux travaux et errant dans des sentiers impraticables, ils découragèrent sans aucun doute les éventuelles recrues, peu enclines à se rallier à cet idéal du sacrifice. Leurs projections et leurs désirs de conquêtes ne suffirent pas à calmer les craintes suscitées par certaines images effroyables du pays.

La rémanence du *locus horribilis* stérile et désolé n'est pas là seulement pour rendre hommage aux "ouvriers évangéliques" qui en foulent le sol, mais aussi pour servir de ferments aux futures républiques qui n'auront rien à envier à celles d'Europe. Sur cette sombre esquisse de l'Amérique sauvage se déploie une vision prospective du pays, fondée sur une herméneutique incertaine de quelques versets bibliques prédisant le ralliement de toutes les nations à la foi.[25] Le *locus horribilis* cède ainsi le pas à l'uchronie. Sur les rives du Saint-Laurent, les jésuites prophétisent l'émergence d'une "Hierusalem celeste" (Lejeune [1637] 1972, 33).[26] À l'aide de comparaisons et de conjectures, Paul Lejeune fait, à l'image de son Dieu, "éclorre un Monde du fond du Neant" ([1662] 1972, 30). Dépassant les frontières du visible, les missionnaires sèment sur ce champ d'orties un jardin de délices, faisant germer des "roses" au milieu des épines ([Lejeune] [1642] 1972, 31). Les oppositions foisonnent sur leur écritoire, suggérant qu'il faut regarder au-delà des apparences. Lejeune, malgré la lenteur de la colonisation, envisage une issue favorable: "[I]l me semble qu'en contemplant le progrez des affaires de la Nouvelle France, je voy sortir une Aurore des profondes tenebres de la nuict" ([1637] 1972, 40). Le relationnaire cultive et aplanit les antithèses pour mieux esquisser la transfiguration virtuelle du pays opérée avec l'aide de Dieu: "[L]a Nouvelle France sera un jour un Paradis terrestre si nostre Seigneur continue de la combler de ses benedictions tant corporelles que spirituelles" (52). Mais ce rêve impossible réitéré avec force se révèle tout aussi factice que les descriptions cauchemardesques que nous livrent ailleurs les jésuites de leur nouvel environnement, la vallée laurentienne à travers le prisme du regard missionnaire restant une fiction paradoxale, issue d'un amalgame de deux modèles eschatologiques: la terre des réprouvés et un lieu de bénédictions à venir. En projetant sur l'axe temporel tous leurs rêves déçus, les disciples d'Ignace de Loyola espèrent racheter leurs insuccès auprès de ces peuples rétifs. Leur plaidoyer équivoque, teinté par une mystique de la souffrance, ne pouvait toutefois masquer complètement les traces de leur amertume.

NOTES

1 Les *Relations* des Jésuites n'étaient pas seulement lues par les membres de la communauté, mais elles étaient aussi, au dire de Paul Lejeune, attendues par une "grande partie de la France [...] avec quelque passion" ([Lejeune] [1641] 1972, 1).

2 Voir Lejeune [1640] 1972, 6.

3 À ceux qui veulent connaître la distance entre les colonies espagnoles et la Nouvelle-France, Paul Lejeune formule la réplique suivante: "Je responds qu'il n'est pas besoin de Chorographie pour cognoistre cét éloignement; adjoustez que je n'en sçaurois faire que sur les cartes qui ont desja cours, n'en ayant ny le temps, ny le loisir, ny les moyens de me transporter en tant d'endroits pour prendre les hauteurs necessaires" ([1637] 1972, 44).

4 "Brave chasseur" et d'un "bon naturel," selon le portrait que brosse Paul Lejeune ([1635] 1972, 58). Le jésuite le prit pour hôte durant son périple de 1634. Il mourra l'année suivante (11).

5 Les références bibliographiques des *Relations* citées se trouvent à la fin de cet article. Elles comportent à la fois la date de publication de chacune et la période qu'elles recouvrent. Par exemple, la *Relation* publiée par Lejeune en 1635 traite de l'année 1634, alors que celle publiée par d'Ablon en 1672 porte sur les années 1670 et 1671.

6 Sur l'hypothèse d'un passage nordique entre l'Europe et l'Amérique, voir Acosta [1589] 1979, 60–61, Belleforest 1575, vol. 1: 2035 et Lescarbot 1618, 47.

7 "Hémisphère" désignait alors "une moitié quelconque du globe" (*Dictionnaire historique* 1992, vol. 1: 953).

8 Réal Ouellet a déjà montré que cette dichotomie régit l'imaginaire jésuite. Voir Ouellet, 1994.

9 Dans la lettre au père provincial qui suit la *Relation* de 1638, qui rapporte les événements de l'année 1637, Paul Lejeune ([1638] 1972, 97) appréhende le Canada comme le "païs de la mort."

10 Sur le même thème, Paul Lejeune décrit l'une de ses promenades le long du cap Diamant en ces termes: "Ces chemins sont affreux: j'allois des pieds et des mains, avec belle peur de me laisser tomber. Je passay par des endroits si estroits, que la marée montant, et m'empeschant de poursuivre mon chemin, je ne pouvois retourner en arriere, tant le passage me sembloit dangereux. Je grimpay au dessus des rochers, et m'agraffant à une branche qui arrestoit un arbre abbattu, cet arbre s'en vint rouler sur moy avec une telle impetuosité, que si je n'eusse esquivé son coup, il m'eût tout brisé, et jetté dans la riviere" (Lejeune [1634] 1972, 2).

11 Voir n. 5.

12 Sur le même thème: "[J]'ai coustume d'appeler ces contrées là, le pays d'importunité envers les estrangers, pour ce que les mouches, qui en sont le symbole et le hieroglyphique, ne vous laissent reposer ny jour ny nuict; [...] elles nous assaillent avec telle furie [...] tout le monde paye de son sang ce tribut" (Lejeune [1635] 1972, 33).

13 Pierre Berthiaume (1982, 336) note la même inflation verbale dans la description du jésuite Charlevoix, largement redevable à la *Relation* de Jérôme Lalemant: "Charlevoix amplifie le phénomène et il lui confère finalement une dimension qui le soustrait aux lois de la nature [...] les lois physiques ne paraissent plus respectées et l'univers se trouve investi par le sacré."

14 On lit, chez Lalemant: "[N]ous voyons proche de nous de grandes ouvertures qui se sont faites, et une prodigieuse estenduë du païs toute perduë, sans que nous y ayons perdu un enfant, non pas mesme un cheveu de la teste. Nous nous voyons environnez de bouleversemens et de ruïnes, et toutefois nous n'avons que quelques cheminées demolies, pendant que les montagnes d'alentour ont esté abysmées" ([1664] 1972, 5).

15 Par exemple, Brébeuf conclut à propos de la Huronie: "Il est certain que ce Pays [...] est beaucoup plus propre à engraisser une âme des fruicts du Ciel, que de ceux de la terre" ([1640] 1972, 97).

16 On lit chez Lejeune que "[l]a foy s'estend et jette de profondes racines parmy les Sauvages; ces [...] paroles suffiroient pour monstrer que nous vivons dans un siecle d'or. Ceux qui ont parlé des siecles dorés, ne les embellissent pas des mines du Perou, mais d'une innocence preferable aux richesses de l'un et de l'autre hemisphere" ([Lejeune] [1642] 1972, 5).

17 J'ai abordé brièvement la question de l'idéalisation du mode de vie sauvage dans la *Nouvelle relation de la Gaspesie* du récollet Chrétien Leclercq. Voir Pioffet 1999.

18 L'année suivante, Lejeune développe la même métaphore guerrière: "[L]'air estoit ordinairement en ce temps-là si froid, que les arbres, qui ont la peau plus dure que celle de l'homme et le corps plus solide, ne luy pouvoient resister, se fendans jusques au cœur, faisans un bruit comme d'un mousquet en s'éclatans" ([1634] 1972, 53).

19 "[Q]uoy que le froid surpasse de beaucoup les gelées de France, il n'y a rien d'intolerable [...] la nature s'habituë à cela, la nature et la grace pourront bien nous donner assez de cœur et de force pour le supporter joieusement" (10).

20 Les images des enfers essaiment aussi chez Brébeuf, qui assimile le pays des Hurons tantôt à un "donjon des Demons" ([1640] 1972, 77), tantôt à une "fournaise" (79).

21 Voir n. 5.

22 "Peuplement français et puissance militaire française sont, selon Denys Delâge (1991, 176), indissociables et constitutifs" de l'entreprise de conversion des Amérindiens. Shenwen Li insiste sur la mission éducatrice dont les jésuites se voient investis: "Considérant leur civilisation comme supérieure, les Français cherchent à civiliser de force les barbares et à les intégrer de force à la civilisation française. Les jésuites, premiers artisans de cette tentative, tâchent de remodeler les autochtones en chrétiens idéaux, et en sujets français soumis, conformément aux valeurs européennes" (Li 2001, 75).

23 Il ne me semble pas non plus tout à fait anodin que Paul Lejeune apparie encore l'évangélisation des Indiens d'Amérique à la construction de la cathédrale Sainte-Sophie (voir Lejeune [1637] 1972, 33). N'est-ce pas là une preuve supplémentaire que les missions, présentées symboliquement comme une œuvre de maçonnerie, doivent s'accompagner par des signes extérieurs de puissance et d'éclat? Pour dresser cette "Hierusalem celeste" (id.) annoncée, l'éloquence ne suffit pas. Aussi le jésuite affirme-t-il que les futurs missionnaires doivent apprendre à manier "la truelle d'une main, et l'espée de l'autre" (31), double métaphore qui exemplifie assez bien les projets caressés en Nouvelle-France.

24 François de Dainville justifie cette orientation humaniste de la façon suivante: "[L]es Jésuites concentrent leur observation et leur intérêt sur les renseignements utiles à la propagation de la foi, essentiellement donc, sur les hommes avec qui ils ont à vivre et à traiter et sur les genres de vie auxquels ils devront s'adapter" (1940, 121).

25 "Et il me semble que le temps viendra et qu'il est desja venu auquel Dieu se veut faire cognoistre à une partie de ces nations: on ne peut revoquer en doute que le Pere eternel ne veuille mettre son Fils en possession de l'heritage qu'il luy a promis, dabo tibi gentes hereditatem tuam [je te

donnerai les nations en héritage]" (Lejeune [1640] 1972, 36, d'après les Psaumes 2, 8). Rémi Ferland a montré que les citations bibliques permettaient au jésuite Paul Lejeune de prendre "sa revanche sur la réalité" (1992, 121).

26 Lejeune prophétise encore: "[I]l se dressera ici une Hierusalem benite de Dieu, composée de Citoyens destinez pour le Ciel" (Lejeune [1637] 1972, 5).

BIBLIOGRAPHIE

Ablon, Claude d'. [1672] 1972. "Relation de ce qui s'est passé de plus remarquable aux missions des pères de la Compagnie de Jésus en la Nouvelle France, ès années 1670 et 1671." In Jésuites 1972, vol. 6.

Acosta, Joseph de. [1598] 1979. *Histoire naturelle et morale des Indes occidentales*, trad. Jacques Rémy-Zéphyr. Paris: Payot.

Belleforest, François de. 1575. *La cosmographie universelle de tout le monde*, 4 vol. Paris: Michel Sonnius.

Berthiaume, Pierre. 1982. "Le tremblement de terre de 1663: les convulsions du Verbe ou la mystification du logos chez Charlevoix." *Revue d'histoire de l'Amérique française* 36 (3): 375–87.

Biard, Pierre. [1616] 1967. "Relation de la Nouvelle-France, de ses terres, naturel du païs et de ses habitants." In *Monumenta Novæ Franciæ*, éd. Lucien Campeau, vol. 1 ("La première mission d'Acadie (1602–1616)"), 456–637. Rome / Québec: Monumenta Historica Soc. Iesu / Presses de l'Université Laval.

Dainville, François de, S. J. 1940. *La géographie des humanistes*. Paris: Beauchesne.

Delâge, Denys. 1991. *Le pays renversé. Amérindiens et Européens en Amérique du Nord-Est, 1600–1664*. Montréal: Boréal.

Desmarets De Saint-Sorlin, Jean. 1662. *Les jeux de cartes des roys de France, des reines renommées, de la géographie et des fables*. Paris: s. n.

Dictionnaire historique de la langue française, éd. Alain Rey. 1992. Paris: Dictionnaires Le Robert.

Du Périer, Antoine. 1973. *Les amours de Pistion et de Fortunie*, éd. Roméo Arbour. Ottawa: Éditions de l'Université d'Ottawa.

Ferland, Rémi. 1992. *Les* Relations *des Jésuites: un art de la persuasion. Procédés de rhétorique et fonction conative dans les* Relations *du Père Paul Le Jeune*. Québec: Éditions de la Huit.

Jésuites. 1972. *Relation des Jésuites contenant ce qui s'est passé de plus remarquable dans les missions des Pères de la Compagnie de Jésus dans la Nouvelle-France*, 6 vol. Montréal: Éditions du Jour [facsim. de l'éd. Québec: A. Côté, 1858].

Lalemant, Jérôme. [1663] 1871. "Febvrier." In *Journal des jésuites*, éd. Henri-Raymond Casgrain et Charles-Honoré Cauchon dit Laverdière, 316–17. Québec: Léger Brousseau.

Lalemant, Jérôme. [1664] 1972. "Relation de ce qui s'est passé [...], ès années 1662. et 1663." In Jésuites 1972, vol. 5.

Lejeune, Paul. [1632] 1972. "Brieve relation du voyage de la Nouvelle France fait au mois d'Avril 1632." In Jésuites 1972, vol. 1.

Lejeune, Paul. [1634] 1972. "Relation de ce qui s'est passé en la Nouvelle France en l'année 1633." In Jésuites 1972, vol. 1.

Lejeune, Paul. [1635] 1972. "Relation de ce qui s'est passé en la Nouvelle France sur le grand fleuve de S. Laurens en l'année 1634." In Jésuites 1972, vol. 1.

Lejeune, Paul. [1636] 1972. "Relation de ce qui s'est passé en la Nouvelle France en l'année 1635." In Jésuites 1972, vol. 1.

Lejeune, Paul. [1637] 1972. "Relation de ce qui s'est passé en la Nouvelle France en l'année 1636." In Jésuites 1972, vol. 1.

Lejeune, Paul. [1638] 1972. "Relation de ce qui s'est passé en la Nouvelle France en l'année 1637." In Jésuites 1972, vol. 2.

Lejeune, Paul. [1639] 1972. "Relation de ce qui s'est passé en la Nouvelle France en l'année 1638." In Jésuites 1972, vol. 2.

Lejeune, Paul. [1640] 1972, "Relation de ce qui s'est passé [...], en l'année 1639." In Jésuites 1972, vol. 2.

[Lejeune, Paul].* [1641] 1972. "Relation de ce qui s'est passé en la Nouvelle France en l'année 1640." In Jésuites 1972, vol. 2.

[Lejeune, Paul].** [1642] 1972. "Relation de ce qui s'est passé en la Nouvelle France en l'année 1641." In Jésuites 1972, vol. 2.

Lejeune, Paul. [1662] 1972. "Relation de ce qui s'est passé [...], ès années 1660. et 1661." In Jésuites 1972, vol. 5.

Lemercier, François. [1666] 1972. "Relation de ce qui s'est passé en la Nouvelle France ès années 1664 et 1665." In Jésuites 1972, vol. 5.

Lescarbot, Marc. 1618. *Histoire de la Nouvelle-France.* Paris: Adrian Périer.

Li, Shenwen. 2001. *Stratégies missionnaires des jésuites français en Nouvelle-France et en Chine au XVIIe siècle.* Québec / Paris: Presses de l'Université Laval / L'Harmattan.

Margolin, Jean-Claude. 1987. "Voyager à la Renaissance." In *Voyager à la Renaissance*, éd. Jean Céard, 9–34. Paris: Éditions Maisonneuve et Larose.

Niderst, Alain. 1992. "Nature et préciosité." *Littératures classiques* 17 ("L'idée de nature au début du XVIIe siècle"): 193–7.

Ouellet, Réal. 1990. "Projet missionnaire et hantise du pouvoir chez le jésuite Paul Lejeune en Canada (1632–1640)." In *Les productions symboliques du pouvoir (XVIe-XXe siècles)*, éd. Laurier Turgeon, 111–23. Sillery: Septentrion.

Ouellet, Réal. 1994. "Monde sauvage et monde chrétien dans les *Relations* des jésuites." *Littératures classiques* 22 ("La notion de "monde" au XVIIe siècle"): 59–72.

Pioffet, Marie-Christine. 1997. *La tentation de l'épopée dans les relations des jésuites.* Québec: Septentrion.

Pioffet, Marie-Christine. 1999. "Entre nature et culture: les ambiguïtés du discours utopique de Chrestien Leclercq." *Études francophones* 14 (2): 83–98.
Pouliot, Léon. 1940. *Étude sur les Relations des Jésuites de la Nouvelle-France (1632–1672)*. Montréal / Paris, Imprimerie du Messager / Desclée de Brouwer.
Quen, Jean de. [1657] 1972. "Relation de ce qui s'est passé en la mission [...] ès années 1655 et 1656." In Jésuites 1972, vol. 5.
Strabon. 1969. *Géographie*, éd. et trad. Germaine Aujac. Paris: Belles Lettres.
Van Delft, Louis. 1993. *Littérature et anthropologie. Nature humaine et caractère à l'âge classique*. Paris: Presses universitaires de France.

* Publiée sous le nom de Barthélemy Vimont, cette relation fut probablement en grande partie rédigée de la main de Paul Lejeune. Sur la question des attributions des relations, voir Pouliot 1940, 18–19.

** Id.

chapter sixteen

The Legacy of Joseph Gumilla's *Orinoco Enlightened*

MARGARET R. EWALT

Recent books such as *The Insufficient Enlightenment* and *Truncated Modernity in Latin America* participate in the time-honoured description of a limited or failed Hispanic Enlightenment.[1] As Jorge Cañizares-Esguerra has discussed, historians and scholars have excluded Catholic Spain and Spanish America from narratives of the origins of modernity since the eighteenth century.[2] A longstanding presumption maintains that Northern Europe exported any traces of modernity to Iberia. This suggests that signs of modernity originated solely outside of Spanish America, which instead imported Enlightenment culture in the same way that Creole[3] society imported fine French cloth or British soaps into the land of "barbarians." Despite early efforts to illustrate Enlightenment culture in Spain and Spanish America, most discussions of Spanish America's modern era postpone it to the very end of the eighteenth century.[4] This is precisely when the prototypical European Enlightenment intellectual, Alexander von Humboldt, travelled to South America. Humboldt gathered ethnographic and botanical information, measured geographies, then retired to "civilized" Paris and published copious volumes that informed both Europeans and Americans of both the Northern and Southern Hemispheres about the emerging new republics' peoples, politics, nature, and geographies. Although immediately regarded as a "re-discoverer" of South America, and then celebrated as a father of its Enlightenment, Humboldt, in fact, compiled knowledge from Amerindians, Creoles, and clerics who continue to be insufficiently cited, as their contributions to modernity have been eclipsed by Humboldt's international fame.[5] Recently, historians and literary critics have been revealing the Prussian adventurer-scientist's intellectual and stylistic debts. One important source for Humboldt was the Jesuit Father Joseph Gumilla, who, over fifty years before Humboldt's famous Orinoco journey, culminated his own twenty-three-year journey to learn about and catalogue the Orinoco by publishing a natural history in Madrid. By focusing on how Gumilla informed not only Humboldt but also a host of other readers, this study reveals the Jesuit's scientific and non-scientific legacy, and situates these particular origins of Enlightenment culture in Spanish America.

First published in 1741, with an expanded second edition appearing in 1745, *El Orinoco ilustrado* (hereafter, *Orinoco Enlightened*) put the Jesuit missions within the Spanish viceroyalty of New Granada on the map.[6] Gumilla marketed this challenging region to missionaries and politicians, and tied their financial and evangelical support to securing a river route with great commercial potential. The Jesuit missions along the Orinoco River and its "abundant branches" had recently suffered attacks by Carib cannibals, supported by Dutch "heathens" of Surinam, so Gumilla in turn sought strategic support. In addition to arguing for an increased missionary and military presence to improve opportunities for evangelizing, trade, and immigration, he also narrated the Jesuit Enlightenment (both spiritual and scientific) of this previously untamed "peripheral region."[7]

Orinoco Enlightened enjoyed immediate popularity inside and outside the Jesuit community, from Bogotá, Quito, and Santo Domingo to Barcelona, Madrid, and Rome. Before it was translated into French, several periodicals such as the *Mémoires de Trévoux* (1748) and the *Journal Étranger* (1756) favourably reviewed *Orinoco Enlightened.* Later, *L'Année Littéraire* praised the translation's importance for "philosophers and non-philosophers alike."[8] These first editions reached the libraries of cosmopolitan Enlightenment figures such as Thomas Jefferson, and late eighteenth-century encyclopedia entries on the Orinoco invariably cited Gumilla.[9] *Orinoco Enlightened* has enjoyed a remarkable print run, with five European editions in the eighteenth and nineteenth centuries, and nine twentieth-century editions, including two published in Spain and the rest in Venezuela and Colombia. Despite such widespread circulation and appeal beyond its Catholic readership, criticism has underestimated Gumilla's contributions to the Hispanic Enlightenment. *Orinoco Enlightened* has been categorized merely as an account of the Jesuit missions and as a catalogue of curious indigenous customs and spectacles of nature. Gumilla's ornate style, replete with astonishing anecdotes about the marvels of the Orinoco region, has limited some readers' abilities to appreciate the legacy of this Jesuit's religious and scientific contributions to the Enlightenment, a legacy that refutes stereotypes of Spanish America's delayed entrance into modernity.

Enlightenment in Western Europe has traditionally been defined as a period of critical reform facilitated by the secularization and rationalization of culture, and by the application of mathematics and experimentalism in the "new" sciences. However, this paradigm leaves behind Catholic Spain and her colonies (see Pimental 2001, 24). If we accept the notion that enlightened science does not adhere to a universal characterization and that we must instead consider its individual cultural constructions, we can expand restrictive and Eurocentric definitions. In the case of Spain and her South American colonies, we must consider the role of Jesuit science and of missionary naturalists in the development of a modern scientific identity. Historians of science have detailed "Jesuit visions" of New World knowledge that incorporated modern empiricism with local cultures, and new scientific theories from Europe with anecdotal evidence from mission cultures (see 27, as well as Harris 2005, 71–9). Recent scholarship in studies of Hispanic modernity suggest that if we challenge narrow perceptions of what Enlightenment means, we can better appreciate how texts like *Orinoco Enlightened* indeed "enlightened" many in diverse fields of knowledge.

Orinoco Enlightened was widely read and highly regarded throughout the eighteenth century as the key source of information about the Orinoco River region. Wonder-provoking rhetorical strategies that attracted readers to Gumilla's lively prose would eventually cause some to question his credibility, yet *Orinoco Enlightened* continued to be cited, weathering the paradigm shift that discredited missionary and traveller tales in favour of philosophical history writing and secular scientific narrative.[10] Thus, instead of classifying the Jesuit's natural history as "pre-" or "unmodern," we should view Gumilla's recourse to wonder, and his combination of sentiment and reason in the accumulation, enumeration, and dissemination of knowledge, as the hallmarks of an alternative pathway to modernity. To this end, I clarify the legacy of *Orinoco Enlightened*, in both its scientific and literary dimensions, in order to contribute to recent studies that question the notion of a truncated or non-existent Hispanic Enlightenment, a perception which limits Enlightenment culture to a foreign import for Spain and Spanish America.

By considering various readings of *Orinoco Enlightened*, this study underscores possibilities for wider definitions of Enlightenment. That Gumilla's text found a diverse readership demonstrates its multifaceted contribution to the Enlightenment. The following examples focus on how *El Orinoco ilustrado* was read by two distinct classes of readers: first by non-scientific American readers, and second by scientific European readers. The first series of examples demonstrates ways that Alejo Carpentier, José Eustasio Rivera, and Jorge Isaacs informed their novels with Gumilla's scientific observations. The second series examines how Charles Marie de La Condamine, Jorge Juan, Antonio de Ulloa, and Alexander von Humboldt borrowed literary strategies for their scientific interpretations of the flora, fauna, and peoples in under-explored areas. The legacy of Joseph Gumilla's *Orinoco Enlightened*, as revealed in the appropriation not only of specific facts about Orinoco nature and peoples, but also of the wonder-provoking rhetoric with which the Jesuit presented them, shows how Gumilla influenced Europeans and Americans many years before and after Humboldt. It also indicates ways that "peripheral" eighteenth-century Catholic cultures were in fact central to the making of modernity. The novelists' use of scientific data and the earlier scientific travellers' appropriation of Gumilla's literary discourse demonstrate that traditional definitions of the Enlightenment are too restrictive.

Gumilla's Legacy for Novelists

Well after the eighteenth-century peak of Jesuit mission culture, *Orinoco Enlightened* found mainstream readers during and beyond the nineteenth- and early twentieth-century vogue of natural history writing.[11] Novelists would take from Gumilla rhetorical strategies that employed vivid descriptions of the region and included tropical standards such as the abundance of multicoloured birds and verdant vegetation. Renowned authors from various literary movements have borrowed literary techniques and at times even lifted entire descriptions from early modern chronicles to add authority to their jungle representations.[12] Literature written about and within Latin America continues this tradition today. Even more interesting, however, than Gumilla's influence on the literary descriptions of Carpentier, Rivera, and Isaacs, is how these novelists were informed by his facts. In the following examples, I will discuss the scientific legacy of *Orinoco Enlightened*, first in the details about Orinoco peoples in *Los pasos perdidos* ("The Lost Steps"), next through facts about Orinoco flora and fauna in *La vorágine* ("The Vortex"), and finally in the echoes of both ethnographic and natural historical details in *María*.

Alejo Carpentier's *Los pasos perdidos* (1953) takes its readers on a myth-like journey into an Orinoco River region seemingly unaffected by time. Here, Carpentier has undoubtedly incorporated Gumilla's vivid river and jungle descriptions and wonder-provoking literary strategies.[13]

The Cuban-born novelist acknowledges his own debt to colonial sources through his narrator, also a writer, who self-consciously evokes the early chronicles that serve as pre-texts for his jungle descriptions: "Where the chronicler was amazed before the presence of gigantic trees, I have seen gigantic trees, the sons of those trees, born in the same place, inhabited by the same birds, struck by the same lightening bolts" ("Donde el cronista se asombraba ante la presencia de árboles gigantescos, he visto árboles gigantes, hijos de aquéllos, nacidos en el mismo lugar, habitados por los mismos pájaros, fulminados por los mismos rayos" [Carpentier (1953) 1985, 174]).[14]

Even though Carpentier's narrator gains his own first-hand knowledge of the region, by the end of *Los pasos perdidos* the rise of the river has restored his adoptive Orinoco village to "lost world" status, forcing him to leave the jungle for civilization and thus consult source texts to garner tribal information. Thanks to Gumilla's work with various tribes of the Arawak indigenous language group, the legacy of *Orinoco Enlightened* reveals itself not only as a pioneering chronicle of the Orinoco River, flora, and fauna, but also as a primary source for ethnographic details. In a passage at the end of chapter 2 of *Los pasos perdidos*, the narrator details the Saliva tribe's funeral ceremonies, evoking the musical instrument first described and illustrated in Gumilla's text: "the famous jar with two mouthpieces" ("a famosa jarra con dos embocaduras" [89]).[15] A year before publishing his novel, Carpentier had mentioned Gumilla as a source in newspaper articles describing the Orinoco as a "world of stopped time" ("mundo del tiempo detenido").[16] In short, far beyond his jungle descriptions, Carpentier borrows from Gumilla's field experience with Orinoco region tribes. In this way, the Jesuit missionary "enlightened" the novelist with data gleaned from his privileged access to cultures, practices, and human artefacts such as the above mentioned musical instrument described in part 1, chapter 13 of *Orinoco Enlightened*.

In contrast to Carpentier's ethnographic facts, José Eustasio Rivera borrowed jungle horrors from *Orinoco Enlightened* for the man-eating jungle he portrayed in *La vorágine* (1924).[17] So, while Gumilla does echo Columbus's theory that the Orinoco River region contains God's earthly paradise and offers several views of amenable places waiting to be mastered by civilization from the safety of watchtowers, he also provides fodder for Rivera's horrific sublime, built around an anthropophagic *locus terribilis* that intensifies as his landmark novel progresses and its characters travel deeper into Amazonia.[18] As legend has it, the same rainforest/vortex that swallowed the protagonist of *La vorágine* first devoured the poet Rivera's earlier literary efforts and later caused the untimely death of this author, who had temporarily escaped the jungle.[19] Rivera certainly focused on the hazards of nature. One jungle horror that he takes from Gumilla are the nearly invisible parasites lurking in swamp water, though he also echoes the Jesuit's remedy by providing details on how to strain swamp water two or three times with a handkerchief as a sieve to remove insects.[20] However, not even Gumilla could find a way to cleanse the waters of dangerous reptiles such as crocodiles and anacondas: the iconic South American boa figures prominently in Latin American literature from the era of the *Florentine Codex* all the way to Horacio Quiroga and beyond. Along these lines, part 2, chapter 14 of Gumilla's account provides a great deal of scientific information about giant serpents of the Orinoco River region. In "De las culebras venenosas de aquellos países" ("On the Poisonous Snakes of Those Lands") the Jesuit details the fatally attractive vapours that spring forth when a giant *buío* opens its jaws wide. Not only does Rivera refer to the anaconda's magnetic breath, but he also appropriates Gumilla's rarely used name for the giant boa: "[B]reaking off a limb, I bent down to sweep away the aquatic vegetation with it, but don Rafo stopped me, quickly like Alicia's scream. A *guío* snake, as thick as a trunk, had emerged yawning in order to trap me" ("[P]artiendo una rama, me incliné para barrer con ella las vegetaciones acuátiles, pero don Rafo me detuvo, rápido como el grito de Alicia. Había emergido bostezando para atraparme una serpiente guío, corpulenta como una viga" [Rivera (1924) 1998, 94]).

The novelist explains what the *guío* (*buío*) is in his regional glossary found at the end of the novel: "huge water snake" ("enorme serpiente acuática" [388]), and Rivera's most recent editor provides an explanatory footnote within the text: "[i]mmense" ("[i]nmensa") boa (94). *La vorágine* was clearly indebted to particular details from *Orinoco Enlightened*, especially for its natural history of jungle terrors.

This giant snake with attractive properties also appears in Jorge Isaacs's Colombian national romance *María* (1867). This novel has long been written off as a servile imitation of French Romanticism. However, far from limiting himself to echoes[21] of European works of fiction, Isaacs borrows heavily from the autochthonous discourse of natural history in vogue during the years surrounding the South American independence movements. In Isaacs's novel, the protagonist expresses a strong regional patriotism through romantic descriptions of the Cauca Valley region of Antioquia that are also tied to descriptions of the character María. His love of country and of the cousin who has shared his home(land) are equally passionate, and when "exiled" to London for medical school, he misses them both. Towards the end of the novel (chapters 57–60), he recreates his thrilling journey along the Dagua River, including a ride through the jungle, where a majestic and at times threatening nature leads him away from the coast towards his homeland (and fiancée), while at the same time delaying his return to Colombia's interior. It is here that Isaacs echoes scientific details about the ethnography, geography, flora, and fauna from Gumilla that are particular to Colombia. Some examples from *María* that echo *Orinoco Enlightened* include details about an underground cooking practice that caused some to believe that regional tribes were earth eaters, musical instruments, virgin forests of palm trees, unforgettable swarms of pesky mosquitoes, vampire bats, folkloric beliefs about crocodile fangs protecting against snakebites, and the "attractive properties" of the anaconda (Isaacs [1867] 1991, 300–6). The similarities between Gumilla and Isaacs in terms of the latter include some finer points on how to break the anaconda's invisible magnetic force:

> [T]hat viper harmed in this way: while the prey that it lies in wait for does not pass it at a distance such that the snake, only extended in all its length, can reach it, it stays still, and achieving this condition [...] the snake attracts the prey towards itself with an invincible force [...]. There have been cases in which hunters and oarsmen save themselves from this type of death [...] by hurling a poncho onto its head ("[A]quella víbora hacía daño de esta manera: mientras la presa que acecha no le pasa a distancia tal que solamente extendida en toda su longitud la culebra, puede alcanzarla, permanece inmóvil, y conseguida esa condición [...] la atrae a sí con una fuerza invencible [...]. Casos han ocurrido en que cazadores y bogas se salven de ese género de muerte [...] arrojándole una ruana sobre la cabeza" [303]).

Here and in other sections of his novel Isaacs clearly echoes *Orinoco Enlightened.*

Gumilla's natural history has had a lasting legacy in part because of the Jesuit's combination of missionary authority (having "been there" to accumulate data) along with the rhetoric of wonder to disseminate it. This combination provides a pathway to knowledge by blending empirical fact with wonder-provoking details that appeal to European expectations of New World curiosities. *Orinoco Enlightened* maintains its authority as an eighteenth-century biological-anthropological field report not only because of its wealth of information, but also due to

Gumilla's rhetorical skill for creating in readers the sense that they see, hear, and even feel these details almost as if they had "been there" too.[22] Gumilla's text continues to enlighten twentieth- and twenty-first-century anthropologists and ethnologists, who often borrow the same facts and details as novelists, further continuing a longstanding tradition of citing Jesuit natural histories published since the early modern period, which relay Amerindian customs, racial typologies, regional animals, and valuable details about plant products ranging from cinchona bark quinine to niopo powder snuff.[23] Because Gumilla presents these details within startling anecdotes that are meant to intensify his readers' wonder at the Orinoco River region, the scientific weight of his first-hand knowledge has at times been undervalued. Nonetheless, numerous readers absorbed these scientific facts from the poetic prose in which they were relayed, which resulted in their being educated indirectly about the region's flora, fauna, and Amerindian tribes. Novelists such as Carpentier, Rivera, and Isaacs availed themselves of Gumilla's scientific data to craft realistic descriptions in their fictional prose. This means of presentation, combined with earlier scientific travellers' appropriation of Gumilla's literary discourse, suggests alternative routes to Enlightenment that has implications for how we understand the production and dissemination of knowledge during the first half of the eighteenth century and beyond.

Gumilla's Legacy for Scientists

Perhaps more surprising than Gumilla's legacy among novelists, anthropologists, and ethnologists is his influence on some of the most famous scientific expeditions to South America.[24] To write their groundbreaking scientific travel accounts, Charles Marie de La Condamine and Alexander von Humboldt gathered data both in the field and from various sources such as *Orinoco Enlightened.* However, just as important as the details they borrowed from Gumilla's Orinoco region experience is how they presented these and other facts with rhetorical strategies that provoked a sense of wonder in their readers. We clearly see the Jesuit's legacy in these travellers' choices about which sights to bring before their readers' eyes. Even more fascinating is how they chose to make use of the still barely known (and therefore exotic) lands of South America to enlighten Europe through means similar to Gumilla. The French explorer La Condamine and his Spanish companions Jorge Juan and Antonio de Ulloa chose some of Gumilla's most unusual descriptions of Orinoco's nature, and placed their narrative within a traditionally marvellous framework while also buoying their scientific apparatus. The Prussian aristocrat Humboldt's famed synthesis of art and science – which blends imagination, reason, and emotion – also shares several literary strategies employed by Gumilla's travel narrative, while adding the instrumental precision of his own field experience.

La Condamine's quest to resolve one of the greatest scientific questions of the first half of the eighteenth century by measuring the circumference of the earth near the equator also exposed valuable South American secrets and resources to Europe.[25] Two reports – La Condamine's *Relation abrégée d'un voyage* (1745) and Juan and Ulloa's *Relacion historica del viage* (1748) – echo Gumilla's stories that personify Orinoco's plants and animals. Juan and Ulloa may question the reliability of local eyewitnesses as to the "attractive properties" of the anaconda's breath, but they still included four pages of details straight from Gumilla's narrative.[26] For example:

> The breath it discharges from itself is so harmful that, enrapturing with it the Person, or Animal, that is in the path on which it directs the breath, it forces it to move towards it involuntarily until, having it close, it swallows it. They say and promote that the way to free oneself from a similar trance is by cutting that breath, when it is first felt, with another Body, which by violently passing in between divides and breaks the breath: thus executed one who had started to suffer can take another route and get away from the danger. All of this when considered well has more appearance of a fable than reality, like the already cited *Mr. de la Condamine* implies in his Relation ("El aliento, que despide de sí es tan ponzoñoso, que embriagando con él a la Persona, o Animal, que está en el camino por donde lo dirige, lo hace moverse hacia ella involuntariamente hasta que teniéndolo cerca se lo traga. Esto dicen, y adelantan, que el modo de librarse en semejante trance es cortando el tal aliento, quando se empieza a sentir, con un otro Cuerpo, que passando violentamente por medio, lo divida, y rompa: lo que executado puede, el que empezaba a padecer, tomar otra senda, y salir del peligro. Todo esto bien considerado tiene mas viso de fabula, que apariencias de realidad, como el mismo ya citado *Mr. de la Condamine* da a entender en su Relacion" [Juan and Ulloa 1748, 539; cf. Gumilla [1745] 1963, 376–95]).

Later in this section, the Spaniards again clearly paraphrase Gumilla's text. While partially supporting and refuting the anaconda's ability to stun its victims, they take full advantage of the "strange but true" presentation of this same phenomenon that Gumilla described:

> We should not oppose the possibility that the quality of its breath could have such an effect, that it enraptures all that perceive it [...] in response to this I find no difficulty believing that the breath of this Snake would have this property that is attributed to it [...] since upon losing its senses the animal [...] having no means left to flee, nor freedom to continue on its path; but rather leaving it immobile, it is normal that the Snake would go, with its sluggish movement, approaching until it has the animal in range for grabbing and devouring it ("No debemos oponernos a que pueda ser de tal calidad el efecto de su aliento, que embriague al que lo perciba [...] a correspondencia pues de esto no encuentro yo dificultad, en que el aliento de esta Culebra tenga la propiedad, que se le atribuye [...] pues perdiendo los sentidos el Animal [...] y no quedándole arbitrio para huir, ni libertad para continuar su rumbo; antes bien dexandolo inmóvil, es regular vaya la Culebra con su tardo movimiento acercándose a él, hasta que lo tenga a tiro, para cogerlo, y engullirlo" [Juan and Ulloa 1748, 540]).

Even if the Jesuit's tales of cows, herons, and human victims being pulled into the mouth of the *buío* strike La Condamine, Juan, and Ulloa as "repugnant to credulity" ("repugnante a la credulidad" [Juan and Ulloa 1748, 538]), they still privilege Gumilla's wonder-provoking anecdotes and rhetorical strategies for this and other New World marvels.

La Condamine, Juan, and Ulloa borrowed a number of memorable stories from *Orinoco Enlightened*; so while they contested Gumilla, they also imitated him. Thus, assuming that La Condamine dismissed Gumilla's "views as those of a traveler who was both too skeptical and too credulous" (Cañizares-Esguerra 2001, 28; see also Cañizares-Esguerra 1998, 329–49), he limits any consideration of Gumilla's legacy to a geographical error the Jesuit had corrected and to some seemingly doubtful facts, such as his insistence on the existence of El Dorado and the aforementioned fantastic treatment of the anaconda.[27] Not only does this downplay the value of Gumilla's first-hand knowledge of the region, from which La Condamine and others benefited, but it misunderstands Gumilla's non-factual legacy. The travel writers both confirmed and rebutted Gumilla's scientific knowledge; but more striking is how Gumilla's literary legacy manifests itself, as when the travellers make use of unforgettable "characters" such as Gumilla's personified virgin plant, which flees from human touch or gaze. In this example, the travellers' delight at the reasonable modesty of the bashful *vergonzosa* or *doncella* plant (*mimosa pudica*), whose leaves are sensitive enough to evade men, supersedes other natural historical references to this South American native, the "sensitive plant":

> This one's [modesty] is so clear that as soon as one of its little Leaves is touched, it closes up all the leaves on that Branch, and they clench against the others with such speed, that it seems as if the springiness of all of them were waiting for that moment with precaution so that they all might make their move at the same time [...] and in this way they wonder at the fact that a Plant would have Sense and Instinct in order to manifest obedience at that which was commanded of it ("Es tan visible la de esta, que luego que se toca alguna de sus Hojitas, se cierran todas las de aquella Rama, y aprietan unas contra otras con tanta prontitud, que no parece sino que los resortes de todas ellas estuvieron esperando aquel instante con prevención, para jugar todos a un mismo tiempo [...] y así admiraban que en una Yerva huviesse Sentido, y Instinto para manifestar la obediencia a lo que se le mandaba" [Juan and Ulloa 1748, 70–1]).

Here the virgin plant's instinct for obedience alludes to its rational faculties, to which Gumilla added a moral aside, first commanding his readers to look into this "mirror of nature" ("mírense en el espejo de esta vergonzosa hierba"), and then placing these commandments in the mouth of hypothetical mothers and teachers: "Come, observe, attend to and learn from this bashful plant. Note that when she is touched, she gives herself for dead, fainting and wilting" ("Venid, observad, atended y aprended de esta hierba vergonzosa; reparad que en cuanto la tocan, se da por muerta, desfallece, se desmaya y se marchita" [Gumilla [1745] 1963, 444–5]).[28] Here there is certainly an overlap as to which Orinoco region topics Gumilla, La Condamine, Juan, and Ulloa privilege. However, to underscore the wonder of individual facts, the scientific travellers also borrowed Gumilla's literary strategies for personification and anecdotes.

Alexander von Humboldt's appropriation of Gumilla's rhetoric of wonder particularly demonstrates Gumilla's legacy. Humboldt famously explored the waterways from the Orinoco to the Amazon. His narrative of this journey is replete with the same wonder-provoking tropical biodiversity, vivid descriptions of virulent insects, electric eels, monstrous crocodiles, and both the Christian and cannibal natives who shoot poison arrows from blow guns, that are found in *Orinoco Enlightened.* Humboldt is said to have invented a "new literary genre": a modern travelogue that effects a happy union between literature and science.[29] Not only is Humboldt indebted to Gumilla for how he presents the Orinoco River region, but his purposeful use of imagination and wonder to lead his readers on pathways to knowledge echoes the Jesuit's epistemology as well.[30] *Orinoco Enlightened*'s synthesis of literary strategies and scientific elucidations prefigures Humboldt's writings, even though the latter used scientific measuring instruments for precise calculations and illustrations.[31]

Humboldt includes many individual facts from *Orinoco Enlightened*, and cites specific pages from its 1791 edition in his writings.[32] However, within a wider context of Humboldt's extensive opus, perhaps more important than the scientific data he borrows from Gumilla is the rhetoric he employs to inform and entertain readers. Both travelling naturalists' vivid descriptions of this "land worthy of a European's curiosity" (Humboldt [1805–1838] 1995, 177) delighted, educated, and persuaded their readers with wonder-provoking rhetorical constructs.[33] As a Catholic missionary on a spiritual journey, Gumilla constituted a different brand of natural traveller than the Protestant scientist-observer. His agenda served religious and political goals, exciting his fellow Jesuit readers' imaginations about travel to this distant land while convincing government representatives to support their Catholic civilizing mission. In addition to political consciousness, Humboldt's travelogues incited nineteenth-century gentlemen naturalists and ladies of means to repeat his journeys and write their own accounts.[34]

To clarify Gumilla's literary legacy, the last section of this study will examine a few of the rhetorical strategies that he and Humboldt shared. First, both authors kindled their readers' emotions by recording their own passionate responses to nature's sublimities.[35] Second, they depended on stirring rhetorical strategies, especially vivid description, or *ecphrasis*, which fixed images in the mind's eye of their readers. In order to do this, Humboldt borrowed the rhetorical technique of displaying individual specimens in a textual natural history cabinet from Gumilla, by echoing the author's selection of Orinoco objects (*inventio*), such as palm trees and curare poison, their arrangement (*dispositio*), and a hyperbolic style for their description (*elocutio*).

The first notable rhetorical strategy in Humboldt's text is his recreation of emotional responses to nature through poetic prose. While Humboldt does not tie the purpose of his natural history descriptions to worshipping God, he does invite his readers to join him in experiencing nature's sublimities, as in: "[F]ollow me in spirit with willing steps to the recesses of the primeval forests" (Humboldt 1850, vi).[36] On the other hand, the Jesuit seeks emotional reactions primarily to invite his readers to direct their wonder at the Creator, and the harmonious nature on display in Gumilla's "Orinoco cosmos" illuminates the mysteries of the divine order. Instead of echoing Gumilla's goal of expanding man's knowledge in order to better know God, however, Humboldt addresses late eighteenth-century readers' assumptions that an effusive style and an abundance of natural wonders precludes serious scientific intent. Humboldt's second preface (1849) to *Aspects of Nature* summarizes the difficulties involved with "the combination of a literary and of a purely scientific object – the endeavor at once to interest and occupy the imagination, and to enrich the mind with new ideas by the augmentation of knowledge" (vii). As his original preface had apologized:

> [S]uch an artistic and literary treatment of subjects of natural history is liable to the difficulties of composition [...]. The unbounded riches of Nature occasion an accumulation of separate images; and accumulation disturbs the repose and the unity of impression which should belong to the picture. Moreover, when addressing the feelings and imagination, a firm hand is needed to guard the style from degenerating into an undesirable species of poetic prose. But I need not here describe more fully dangers which I fear the following pages will show I have not always succeeded in avoiding (v).

Humboldt appealed to human pleasure and awe of nature, with vivid descriptions meant to inspire new awareness of little-known regions. This technique was an integral part of Jesuits' natural philosophy inquiries as well. Gumilla had already relied on poetic prose to stimulate man's imagination, awaken vivid enjoyments of nature, and increase natural knowledge. Even though Gumilla tied human wonder for nature to Christianity, both men saw scientific value in artistic strategies, and both men invited readers to view representations of Orinoco's grandeur and support investigation of its natural phenomena.

The key literary influence of Gumilla for Humboldt is his aforementioned use of *ecphrasis* as the most important strategy for displaying objects in a rhetorically constructed natural history cabinet. Familiar with rousing rhetorical strategies that invite visualization during sermons by painting colourful mental images, Gumilla preached to his readers' eyes, constructing a textual cabinet of curiosities to showcase diverse Orinoco region flora, fauna, and ethnography. In the introduction to *Orinoco Enlightened* Gumilla likened his natural history to "the most curious gallery" ("la más curiosa galería" [Gumilla [1745] 1963, 37]). If we view this frame within the context not only of Jesuit natural history displays in actual cabinets but also of the cabinets of amateur naturalists in Europe and Spanish America, we understand that Gumilla meant to evoke the gentleman's cabinet, which boasted spectacular wonders such as stuffed crocodiles or caimans, the enormous shed skin of an anaconda, and other rare fauna, flora, and curious human artefacts from diverse cultures and Amerindian nations. Humboldt also evoked actual cabinets, once even comparing a display of Carib cannibal skulls to their living Orinoco counterparts, marveling: "Having seen only skulls of these Indians in European collections, we were surprised to see that their foreheads were more rounded than we had imagined" (Humboldt [1805–1838] 1995, 187). At another point, Humboldt enthused that "we saw for the first time live animals that we had only previously seen stuffed in European cabinets" (196). In his *Personal Narrative* and *Aspects of Nature*, Humboldt borrows the literary strategy of a rhetorical cabinet display of Orinoco wonders. Naturally, both men choose the most vivid and memorable plants, insects, river creatures, and native men and women, from the bloody Carib cannibals to the peaceful, Christianized Saliva tribe.

Humboldt's treatment of the Orinoco palm provides a perfect example of how Gumilla's literary legacy goes beyond simply the selection of which objects to showcase, a process that corresponds rhetorically to the *inventio* stage. In addition to the subject matter of palms (*inventio*), Humboldt also borrows Gumilla's arrangement (*dispositio*) and style (*elocutio*). The order of things throughout Gumilla's textual natural history cabinet confirms the palm tree's importance. It is both the first and nearly the last plant treated in *Orinoco Enlightened*.[37] Humboldt follows an identical arrangement in his own textual cabinet: "We will begin with palms, the loftiest and noblest of all vegetable forms, that to which the prize of beauty has been assigned" (Humboldt 1850, 238–9).[38] Another aspect of the palm discourse that Humboldt borrows is the authority granted by eyewitness experience. Gumilla underscores the extensive detail he can offer from personal observation: "[S]omething of this can be read in some authors who have written about the Indians, but not as much as I have seen myself with the Guaraúnos" ("[A]lgo de esto se lee en algunos autores que han escrito acerca de los indios, pero no tanto como lo que he visto en los guaraúnos" [Gumilla [1745] 1963, 133]). Humboldt purposely builds upon Gumilla's authority when adding his own view of the Guarani tribe's tree houses: "The Padre José Gumilla, who twice visited the Guaranis as a missionary, says, indeed, that this people had their habitation in the *palmares* (palm groves) of the morasses; but he only mentions dwellings raised upon high pillars, and not scaffoldings attached to trees still in a growing state" (Humboldt 1850, 148–9).[39] Finally, to increase readers' wonder both Gumilla and Humboldt compare the palm tree with the banana, a well-established "tree of life" that was praised in Pliny's *Natural History* as well as the Bible.[40] Humboldt explains that "in all parts of the globe the palm form is accompanied by that of Plantains or Bananas" (239), while Gumilla's admiration for the banana knows no bounds: "[T]here is no healthier nor substantial and delicious fruit in the Americas [...]. In short, bananas are the relief of all the poor; in America bananas serve as bread, viands, drink, preserves and everything, because they take away hunger from all" ("[N]o hay fruta más sana en las Américas ni tan sustancial ni tan sabrosa [...]. En fin, los plátanos son el socorro de todo pobre; en la América sirven de pan, de vianda, de bebida, de conserva y de todo, porque quitan a todos el hambre" [Gumilla [1745] 1963, 436]). Both authors activate panegyrical strategies that favourably compare the Orinoco palm to this providential gift to the poor: the banana tree. Even the briefest comparison of Humboldt's treatment of the "lofty and noble palm tree" and Gumilla's lengthy palm panegyric reveals striking similarities in how these authors describe and privilege this wonder of nature.

To conclude our discussion of shared literary strategies we turn to perhaps the most famous example of Gumilla enlightening Humboldt. A quick comparison of their narrations about the most famous South American poison, curare, illustrates Gumilla's legacy in Humboldt's more famous synthesis of literary strategies with science despite fundamental differences in their scientific practices. If on the one hand Humboldt insists on efforts in the field to recreate the precision of European laboratories, on the other he borrows the anecdotal aside Gumilla first used to spark his readers' curiosity and then to interest them in appropriating Amerindian knowledge. Gumilla's version of the Caverre tribe's distillation of the liana root (*bejuco maracure*) made its way from *Orinoco Enlightened* first into several eighteenth-century encyclopedic and scientific journals published in French,[41] and then to Humboldt's *Aspects of Nature* and, more extensively, his *Personal Narrative.* Humboldt directly acknowledges his source ("Gumilla asserts that 'this preparation was enveloped in great mystery'" ["esta fabricación se ocultaba por un gran misterio"]) before quoting the Jesuit's story featuring ancient "women who (being otherwise useless) are chosen to watch over this operation" (Humboldt 1852–1853, 438–9).[42] As with the palm, Humboldt clearly borrows Gumilla's literary techniques to enlighten his reader. And in this case, Humboldt amplifies the Jesuit's story with his own first-hand experience in the mission town of Esmeralda in order to reveal his more meticulous scientific practices. At the same time that Humboldt plays up Gumilla's "mysterious Amerindian secrets" discourse, he also emphasizes that he saw a male who was not using a cauldron but instead a "chemical laboratory" to fabricate curare. This "chemist of the place [...] had that tone of pedantry of [...] the pharmacopolists of Europe" who performed "this chemical operation [...] [that] appeared to us extremely simple"; his description contrasts greatly with Gumilla's evocation of witchlike old hags (439–40). Humboldt underlines his view of "the greatest order and neatness [that] prevailed in this hut, which was transformed into a chemical laboratory" (439) as well as the simple chemist's desire for European knowledge:

> [His] funnel was of all the instruments of the Indian laboratory that of which the poison-master seemed to be most proud. He asked us repeatedly if, *por alla* (*out yonder*, meaning in Europe) we had ever seen anything to be compared to this funnel [...]. [He] seemed flattered by the interest we took in his chemical processes. He found us sufficiently intelligent to lead him to the belief that we knew how to make soap, an art which, next to the preparation of curare, appeared to him one of the finest of human inventions (441–7).

Finally, since the Esmeralda chemist's laboratory is grossly inferior, Humboldt proposes to relocate research: "[A]n interesting chemical and physiological investigation remains to be accomplished in Europe on the poisons of the New World, when, by more frequent communications, the *curare de bejuco*, the *curare de raiz*, and the various poisons of the Amazon, Guallaga, and Brazil, can be procured" (445–6); Gumilla, on the other hand, blends the artistic with the scientific – wonderful stories with narrations of experiments – and favourably compares the results of Jesuit "in-the-field" science to knowledge gained in "those European labs" with "the latest microscopes" (see Gumilla [1745] 1963, 384).[43]

By examining Gumilla's legacy on scientific travellers and how he enlightened La Condamine, Juan, Ulloa, and Humboldt with much more than individual Orinoco region facts, we can appreciate how the Jesuit's rhetoric of wonder first led these readers on pathways to scientific knowledge and then enhanced their own literary strategies. Gumilla in particular influenced Humboldt's more celebrated synthesis of literature and science. From actively involving readers in stirring representations of sublime nature, to privileging *ecphrasis* to create mental images of objects that are displayed in a rhetorically constructed cabinet of natural history, Humboldt's writings reveal the legacy of *Orinoco Enlightened.* Gumilla's artistic dissemination of knowledge about the mysterious curare poison production and a host of other Orinoco region topics prefigures Humboldt's more celebrated narratives. And despite Humboldt's displacement of Gumilla's Enlightenment to Europe, their wonder-provoking literary styles share fundamental goals such as capturing their readers' imaginations and transporting them to far-off lands in order to inform them about the unfamiliar. Humboldt's writings have been posited "not only as the product of a genius working in isolation but also as a summary of the Spanish American Enlightenment."[44] The legacy of Gumilla's *Orinoco Enlightened* helps us to expand our definition of Enlightenment, as it suggests new routes for understanding the first half of the eighteenth century and the Jesuit role in shaping scientific identity in Spain and Spanish America. Humboldt may have employed a more developed scientific apparatus; however, he maintained Gumilla's literary techniques. This legacy continues to enlighten twentieth- and twenty-first-century biologists, herpetologists, and pharmacologists who evoke Gumilla's "mythical anaconda" and curare narration alongside current discussion about these topics (e. g., see Thorbjarnarson 1995, 38–46; Bisset 1992, 1–26; and Lee 2005, 83–92).

Novelists writing about the Orinoco River region also availed themselves of Gumilla's rhetoric. However, by exploring how Carpentier, Rivera, and Isaacs inserted scientific information from *Orinoco Enlightened,* we gain a wider perspective on the nature of Enlightenment. The legacy of Joseph Gumilla's *Orinoco Enlightened* exemplifies an alternative pathway to an Enlightenment that does not conform to traditional, secular definitions. Further research into how cultural documents such as Gumilla's (which have not usually been examined as Enlightenment texts) are in fact enlightened can help us move beyond sweeping generalizations about Spanish America's tardy entrance into modernity and further our understanding of a successful Hispanic Enlightenment.

NOTES

1 Subirats' works *La ilustración insuficiente* (1981) and *Modernidad truncada de América* (2001) treat Spain and Spanish America respectively.

2 *How to Write the History of the New World* from Cañizares-Esguerra (2001) remains an essential study for understanding the long-standing commonplace

of "unenlightened" Spain and Spanish America and their supposed resistance to modernity. Ralph Bauer synthesizes Cañizares' examination of Spain and Spanish America's "making of modernity." Bauer summarizes the "Protestant philosophy of history" that wrote off Catholic cultures as "pre-"or "un-modern," and celebrates Cañizares' role in challenging this "Eurocentric bias in contemporary historiography that still treats Spain and Spanish America as outcasts from the history of modernity" (Bauer 2002, 976–77). Among other topics, in a 2004 article in *Perspectives on Science,* "Iberian Science in the Renaissance: Ignored How Much Longer?" Cañizares-Esguerra discusses Anglo-American scholarship's continued exclusion of Iberia.

3 By "Creole" I mean the standard definition for American-born Spaniards (criollos) that denies racial miscegenation.

4 See, for example, Whitaker 1942 and 1971.

5 As Roberto González Echevarría summarizes, nineteenth-century "scientific exploration brought about the second European discovery of America, and the traveling naturalists were the new chroniclers" (González Echevarría 1990, 11). For Humboldt's leading role in this rediscovery, see Mary Louise Pratt 1992, 111–43. To appreciate Humboldt's fame in his moment, we should recall that Simón Bolívar himself referred to Humboldt as "the true discoverer of South America" for exploring more of the continent's six million square miles than anyone before, for captivating the world with his depictions of the region's aesthetic and scientific wonders (see Helferich 2004, 303).

6 All quotes in this article are from the edition based on the 1745 version. The New Kingdom of Granada included territories found in modern-day Venezuela, Colombia, and Ecuador.

7 For placement of Spanish and Spanish American science within the centers and peripheries of modernity, see Pimental 2001, 17–30. For the theorization of the "peripheries" see Basalla 1993, 599–604; Chambers 1993, 605–17; and Dussel 1993, 65–76.

8 Fréron [1758] 1966, 350. Gumilla's French edition significantly widened his reading public to include philosophers such as the Abbé Raynal, who borrowed some passages from this work for his *Histoire du commerce des Europeens dans les deux Indes* (1770), and Adam Smith, who cited Gumilla in a footnote about El Dorado in Book 4, ch. 6 of *The Wealth of the Nations* (Smith [1761] 1776). As for "non-philosophers," Jules Vernes must have consulted Gumilla's *Histoire naturelle, civile et geographique de l'Orenoque* (1758) in addition to Humboldt's *Relation historique du voyage aux regions équinoxiales du nouveau continent* (1805–1838) when composing his novel, *Le Superbe Orénoque* (1898).

9 See, for example, the entry "Orinoco" in Alcedo 1967, 62–3. After listing many of the Orinoco tribes the Jesuits worked with along the banks of the Orinoco, this renowned encyclopedia laments the fate of the Society of Jesus's flourishing missions passing to the Capuchin Order after the Jesuit expulsion. A quick check of the most recent editions of classic encyclopedias (for example, the Grolier online encyclopedia) reveals the Jesuits Gumilla and Gilij as sources of eighteenth-century knowledge of the Orinoco and Humboldt as the nineteenth-century source.

10 On this shift, see Cañizares-Esguerra 1998, 329–49 and Cañizares-Esguerra 2001.

11 For more on readers' passion for natural histories, see Freedburg 2002 and Jardine, Secord, and Spary 1996.

12 For details on how narratives of colonial-era real-life experiences repeatedly found their way into nineteenth- and twentieth-century fictions, see, for example, Bost 1988, 34–44, as well as Bost 1996, 143–90.

13 González Echevarría notes that entire pages of *Los pasos perdidos* were lifted from *Orinoco Enlightened* (1972, 280).

14 Despite this indirect textual acknowledgement, however, Carpentier does not have his musicologist-narrator enumerate actual chronicles. Instead, he fabricates sources such as a seventeenth-century missionary whom readers might not recognize as an invention without González Echevarría's annotations. See Silva Cáceres 1967, 33–7, for the first hypothesis that this invented Friar Servando de Castillejos was actually the Jesuit Gumilla who, "as well as entirely describing the river, its flora, its fauna and many indigenous peoples that live along its banks, he [Gumilla] includes a precise design of the musical instruments sought by the main character" ("además de describir integramente el río, su flora, su fauna y muchos pueblos indígenas que viven en sus orillas, incluye un diseño preciso de los instrumentos musicales buscados por el personaje principal" [35]). Silva Cáceres compares two very similar descriptive passages of the Orinoco River taken from Gumilla and then from Carpentier.

15 In "Semejante a la noche" ("Such a Night") and in his introduction and notes to *Los pasos perdidos*, González Echevarría writes about general connections between Gumilla's facts and Carpentier's fiction. *Myth and Archive* assigns to twentieth-century Latin American novelists a self-consciously anthropological perspective and discusses the authority they sought "by mimicking the texts that constitute anthropological discourse" (González Echevarría 1990, 144). Here he includes Carpentier in this appropriation of a legitimizing "hegemonic discourse" backed by and embodying the system of anthropology: "The critic that the novelist becomes is essentially an

anthropologist, because anthropology furnishes the only discourse capable of authoritatively analysing and narrating the autochthonous, hence the fable of legitimation" (156). Lesley Wylie takes this one step further by applying the postcolonial theories of Homi Bhabha, Jean-François Lyotard, and Edward Said, and asserting that Carpentier's "colonial mimicry" of anthropological discourse constitutes a parodic appropriation of "imperial tropes" of travel writing in order to reclaim and then re-inscribe the South American rainforest in a manner demonstrating the limits of Western epistemology (Wylie 2005, 105–16). While this reading is compelling in the context of recent trends in literary criticism, and in fact the line between imitation and parody can be nebulous, I still prefer to read Carpentier's meta-textual moments not as postmodernism but instead as inserting himself within the historical, scientific, and literary clout accorded chronicles well into the twentieth century

16 "Los hombres llamados salvajes" ("The Men Called Savages") and "El mundo del tiempo detenido" ("The World of Stopped Time"), the two 1952 articles from *El Nacional* where Carpentier mentions Gumilla, *Orinoco Enlightened*, and the Saliva tribe's musical instrument with two mouthpieces, are cited by González Echevarría in a footnote (Carpentier [1953] 1985, 90). While positing the importance of anthropological discourse on twentieth-century novelists in *Myth and Archive*, González Echevarría includes among Carpentier's influences texts ranging from twentieth-century French anthropologists (Claude Lévi-Strauss and Michel Leiris) and Orinoco travelers (Alain Gheerbrant) to early modern chronicles by scientific travelers and missionaries.

17 At one point Gumilla even compares his accumulation of man-eating beasts to a "vortex": "all this whirlwind of deadly species" ("todo este torbellino de especies funestas" [Gumilla 1963, 394]).

18 A progression exemplified in brief when the protagonist (Cova) and his lover (Alicia) first flee to the Casanare region, where they are overcome by the beauty of the sun rising over the *llanos* (plains). As the Orinoco region grasslands turn to swamplands, however, both the narrator's foreboding and the actual dangers increase. See Rivera [1924] 1998, 91–6.

19 The Mexican poet Juan José Tablada called Rivera's death at forty, after he had worked with a commission to delimit the Colombian, Venezuelan, and Peruvian borders in the Orinoco and Amazon River regions, a mortal "revenge of the jungle," which shot a metaphorical curare-poisoned dart across the continent and killed him with malaria. Cited in the introduction to Rivera [1924] 1998, 14–16.

20 Editor Montserrat Ordóñez points out the similarities between Rivera's passage, "'Cover it with a handkerchief so that it serves as a sieve.' I did this various times, removing the little animals" ("'Tápelo con el pañuelo pa que le sirva de cedazo.' Así lo hice varias veces, sacudiendo los animalillos" [Rivera [1924] 1998, 166]) and what "father Gumilla already similarly notes, in the eighteenth century, this means of straining the water" ("ya el padre Gumilla registra así, en el siglo XVIII, esta manera de colar el agua"); that is, with a "folded handkerchief" ("pañuelo doblado") that strains "countless little animals, almost undiscernable to the eye, that if transferred to the stomach, anchor into it" ("innumerables animalejos, casi imperceptibles a la vista, que transferidos al estómago, se aferran de él" [166]). Montserrat Ordóñez provides two other footnotes that refer readers to Gumilla (107, 174).

21 See González Echevarría 1990, 40, for more on this categorization of Isaacs' foundational fiction. As he explains, "conventional literary history, which focuses on works that fall within the sphere of influence of European literature such as Jorge Isaacs' *María* [...] hardly take into account the powerful influence of scientific travel books on those very novels and on Latin American narrative of the nineteenth century in general" (103).

22 Here I echo a persuasion technique for creating rhetorical eyewitness status that reaches far back into classical rhetorical treatises, but was more recently appropriated into modern anthropological writing. As Clifford Geertz explains, "Ethnographers need to convince us [...] not merely that they themselves have truly 'been there,' but that had we been there we should have seen what they saw, felt what they felt, concluded what they concluded" (Geertz 1988, 16).

23 In addition to Spanish-language articles such as Suárez 1974, 309–35, Gumilla is cited as a reliable source in various articles from classic journals such as *American Anthropologist* (see Conzemius 1928, 183–205; and Gillin 1934, 331–44) and *Ethnohistory* (Navarrete 2000, 535–59).

24 For over two centuries Jesuits have continued to mine *Orinoco Enlightened* for facts and have praised Gumilla's missionary propaganda and religious enlightenment of the Orinoco River region as a source of pride, crafting hagiographic accounts of Gumilla's legacy. Gumilla's text clearly influenced exiled Jesuits such as Filippo Salvatore Gilij, Mario Cicala, and Antonio Julián. Beyond the Society of Jesus, however, his natural history has been lauded as "the genesis of national consciousness" in Venezuela while at the same time it has earned him fame as a patriotic "son of Colombia" (Fajardo Morón 1986, 1101–2). These comments point to late eighteenth- and early nineteenth-century appropriations of Gumilla in Colombia and Venezuela as regional pride took precedence over the Spanish Viceroyalty of New

Granada. The "proto-Creole" and "proto-nationalistic" status afforded Gumilla provides an interesting consideration for a different study that considers a transatlantic formation of "Creole subjectivity" and points to alternate and conflicting understandings of the politics and economics of Spain and America. Today, Gumilla's legacy includes *Centro Gumilla*, which was founded as an ecclesial base community in Venezuela in 1968 and is a supporter of Jesuit political activism and a proponent of social justice.

25 The Paris Royal Academy of Sciences managed to convince the Spanish government to allow La Condamine's expedition in order to resolve competing theories about the size and shape of the world proposed by Newtonians and Cartesians. Juan and Ulloa were sent along as Spanish emissaries and were supposed to guard against the theft of secrets. However, La Condamine managed to spirit away the seedlings of two extremely valuable trees: the *Cinchona officinalis* (a source of quinine) and the *caoutchouc* (rubber).

26 This disdain for the *savoir des gens* is evidenced in statements like the following conclusion to the section on the anaconda's breath: "The majority of this was assumed with commonness by those ignorant people, and believed with good faith by others; because nobody would have flung himself into the danger of testing it to satisfy their curiosity" ("Lo mas de esto fue con vulgaridad supuesto de aquellas incultas Gentes, y creído de los otros con buena fé; porque ninguno por satifacer la curiosidad se havrá arrojado al peligro del examen" [Juan and Ulloa 1748, 540]). Such disregard for regional "common sense," or as Foucault put it in his lectures on the relationship between power and knowledge, disregard for "a particular, local, regional knowledge" participates in an authority-building discourse that subjugates "naïve knowledges, located low down on the hierarchy, beneath the required level of cognition and scientificity" (Foucault 1980, 82).

27 La Condamine famously refuted Gumilla's initial denial of a connection between the Orinoco and Amazon Rivers in a *Philosophical Transaction* to the Paris Royal Academy of Sciences that was excerpted in the French translator's preface to the French edition of *El Orinoco ilustrado* (1758). However, as we know from vol. 1, Book 1, ch. 4 of the Jesuit Gilij's *Saggio di storia Americana*, Gumilla had revised this geographical error based on fellow Jesuit Manuel Román's daring 1744 voyage, not quite in time for the 1745 printing of his revised and expanded second edition, but according to Gilij, in 1749 Gumilla had read aloud these additions to him. See Gilij 1987, 53. Humboldt repeated this information. As for El Dorado, Gumilla's location of it actually included a realistic analysis instead of fabulous geography and was later praised by Antonio Julián and Adam Smith.

28 While Gumilla, Juan, and Ulloa take the rhetorical strategy of *prosopopoeia* much further, I would be remiss if I did not note here that Gumilla himself

modeled his plant personification after his Jesuit forefather's lengthy description, which attributed rational faculties to the virgin plant. See Rodríguez 1684, 376. See also a Dominican Friar's treatment of the "Sensitive plante," which shares much detail with Gumilla and Rodríguez (see Labat 1722, 200).

29 See Humboldt [1805–1838] 1995, xxxix. Unless specified, all quotes are from this abridged version of the *Personal Narrative.* Humboldt's writings famously detail the natural and civil (or political) histories of Mexico, Cuba, Peru, and Venezuela, and their importance to emerging American republics has been discussed since the early nineteenth century. As Pratt famously affirms, "Humboldt's writings [...] became essential raw material for American and Americanist ideologies forged by creole intellectuals in the 1820s, 1830s, and 1840s. His writings were a touchstone for the civic literature that claimed Spanish America's literary independence [...]. Over and over in the founding texts of Spanish American literature, Humboldt's estheticized primal América provided a point of departure for moral and civic prescriptions for the new republics. His reinvention of América for Europe was transculturated by Euroamerican writers into a creole process of self-invention" (Pratt 1992, 175).

30 The opening lines of Humboldt's *Personal Narrative* articulate an Aristotelian trope: "whatever is far off and suggestive excites our imagination; such pleasures tempt us far more than anything" (Humboldt [1805–1838] 1995, 15). Implicit in this is Aristotle's dictum that from wonder grows knowledge, as articulated in the classic paradigm of *admiratio-scientia.* See Ewalt 2005, 303–33, and 41–55 for more on this wonder-to-knowledge paradigm in Gumilla's natural history.

31 Humboldt's writings include the single-volume *Ansichten der Natur* (1808), simultaneously published as *Tableaux de la nature ou, considerations sur les desert, sur la physionomie des végétaux, et sur les cataracts de l'Orenoque* (1808) and later translated as *Aspects of Nature, in Different Lands and Different Climates; with Scientific Elucidations* (Philadelphia, 1850) and *Views of Nature, or Contemplation of the Sublime Phenomena of Creation* (London, 1850). His most famous work is perhaps the *Voyage aux régions équinoxiales de Humboldt et Bonpland,* or *Personal Narrative of a Journey to the Equinoctial Regions of the New Continent* ([1805–1838] 1995). The last part of the five volumes of the *Kosmos: Entwurf einer physischen Weltbeschriebung* (1845–1862), translated first in 1849 as *Cosmos: A Sketch of the Physical Description of the Universe,* was published posthumously. Although explicitly tied to his Catholic agenda, Gumilla was already striving for the kind of useful and pleasing text described by Humboldt in his *Ansichten der Natur* ("Aspects of Nature"): "I venture to hope that these

descriptions of the varied Aspects which Nature assumes in distant lands may impart to the reader a portion of that enjoyment which is derived from their immediate contemplation by a mind susceptible of such impressions. As this enjoyment is enhanced by insight into the more hidden connection of the different powers and forces of nature, I have subjoined to each treatise scientific elucidations and additions" (Humboldt 1850, vi).

32 Especially in vol. 2 of the *Relation historique du Voyage*, where in addition to indirectly alluding to Gumilla, Humboldt directly references the Spanish original of *Orinoco Enlightened* twenty-seven times as a source. See Humboldt 1970, 661. Some of the facts Humboldt borrowed from Gumilla included information on the Orinoco tortoise, its egg harvest, and the Otomac tribe's niopo powder snuff and earth eating. For the latter, Humboldt passes judgment on Gumilla: "It is curious that the usually credulous and uncritical Father Gumilla positively denies the earth-eating as such (*Historia del Rio Orinoco*, nueva impr. 1791, t. 1. p. 179.) He affirms that the balls of clay had maize-meal and crocodile fat mixed with them" (Humboldt 1850, 157). A few lines later, however, he excuses the Jesuit, "May Gumilla, by a confusion of things wholly distinct, have been alluding to the preparation of bread [...] which is previously buried in the earth in order to hasten the commencement of the first stage of decay?" (158). For slightly different versions of these same passages, see also ch. 2.24 of Alexander von Humboldt 1852–1853.

33 While Gumilla remained loyal to the king of Spain, Humboldt, as a foreign "outside observer" who wrote much of his *Personal Narrative* during the wars for South American independence, looked ahead to Spanish American economies. In fact, as the introduction to his *Personal Narrative* reveals, he envisioned a future political and even foundational role for his own writings: "I also venture to hope, once peace has been established, that this work may contribute to a new social order. If some of these pages are rescued from oblivion, those who live on the banks of the Orinoco or Atabapo may see cities enriched by commerce and fertile fields cultivated by free men on the very spot where during my travels I saw impenetrable jungle and flooded lands" (Humboldt [1805–1838] 1995, 13).

34 See Stepan 2001, 31–56 for an account of the fascinating power of Humboldt's tropical tropes, literary results of his own youthful "urge to travel to distant lands seldom visited by Europeans," a desire spurred on by the "special charm" of what Humboldt himself was able to "glean from travelers' vivid descriptions" (Humboldt [1805–1838]1995, 15).

35 As Humboldt explained early in his multi-year publishing process, "throughout the entire work I have sought to indicate the unfailing influence of

external nature on the feelings" (Humboldt 1850, vi). Later, in a chapter on plant physiognomy, Humboldt famously encouraged mining these feelings with an alliance between studying plants and painting them into landscapes, enthusing with a wonder-provoking blend of the visual and tactile, stating that "it is under the burning rays of a tropical sun that vegetation displays its most majestic forms" (244–5).

36 The vivid description of tropical majesties so integral to Humboldt's cosmos was already an integral part of Gumilla's.

37 Gumilla illustrates this marvel twice: first in part 1, ch. 9, and again among a more general description of trees in part 2, ch. 20.

38 By the eighteenth century, praise of the palm as manna sent to the Amerindians from God had appeared repeatedly in New World chronicles, letters, relations, and natural histories. But Humboldt clearly read Gumilla's chapter on the Orinoco palm entitled, "Temperament and strange life of the Guaraúna nation. Strange/Striking palm from which they dress, eat, drink and have everything they need." As Pratt and others have pointed out, the friendship between Humboldt and Andrés Bello, who took some field trips with the Prussian, resulted in Bello translating excerpts of Humboldt's writings into Spanish for the London-based *Repertorio Americano.* This suggests an important, indirect legacy of Gumilla. Bello takes the first part of his article "Palmas Americanas" directly from Humboldt, and states that his "Descripción del Orinoco" is from Book 7, ch. 23–4 of Humboldt. However, when he mentions Gumilla by name it is not exactly what Humboldt had written. See Bello 1872, 177–85 and 241–62.

39 Humbolt refers to "Gumilla, Historia natural, civil, y geografica de las Naciones situadas en las riveras del Rio Orinoco [*sic*], nueva imp. 1791, pp. 143, 145, and 163."

40 The first time Humboldt mentions Gumilla by name he writes, "Gumilla terms the Mauritia flexuosa of the Guaranis the tree of life, arbol de la vida" (Humboldt 1850, 149–50), echoing the Jesuit's description of the palm as a new tree of life: "[T]his wonder [...] a New Tree of Life, which is what it should be called" ("[E]sta admiración [...] un nuevo árbol de la Vida, que así se debe llamar" [Gumilla 1963, 135]). Later in *Orinoco Enlightened* Gumilla praises the banana's utility for Amerindian nations: "[T]hey have found [...] in a certain manner their tree of life in only the banana" ("[H]an hallado [...] en cierto modo su árbol de la vida en solo el plátano" [Gumilla 1963, 437]).

41 The lengthy section on curare from *Orinoco Enlightened* was also translated word for word into the *Mémoires pour l'Histoire des Sciences & Beaux-Arts* (1747, 2319–45, 2501–24), and this suspense-filled account enlightened many. Gumilla's curare fabrication details also made their way into several

other reviews of both the Spanish original and the French translation (1758) of *Orinoco Enlightened* in Switzerland, Holland, and Belgium. See *Journal étranger* (1756: 4–46), *L'Année littéraire* (Fréron [1758] 1966, 327–50, and 73–92), *Journal des savants combiné avec les Mémoires de Trévoux* (1758: 686–8), and *Journal encyclopédique* (1759: 73–99).

42. La Condamine gets credit for removing the first curare poison from South America, but Humboldt bragged that he was "first to bring a considerable quantity to Europe" (Humboldt 1850, 165). For their part, Juan and Ulloa's dread at the instantly lethal effects of the curare poison echo passages where Gumilla marvels at, for example, how man can eat the animals killed by curare-tipped arrows without being poisoned himself.

43 My perception of Gumilla's amateur scientist status owes much to sociological trends in the history of science. See, for example, Latour 1979 and Porter and Rousseau 1980.

44 Cañizares-Esguerra 2003, 737. Cañizares-Esguerra joins other scholars who are challenging traditionally hagiographic conclusions about Humboldt's role in South American identity formation and instead exploring the Prussian's dependence on Creole and Amerindian knowledge for his compilation of natural knowledge. For example, see Cañizares-Esguerra 2005, 148–68, for an example of such revisionist accounts' contributions to the history of science.

BIBLIOGRAPHY

Alcedo, Antonio de. 1967. *Diccionario geográfico histórico de las Indias Occidentales o América. Es a saber: de los Reynos del Perú, Nueva España, Tierra Firme, Chile, y Nuevo Reyno de Granada (1786–1789).* Madrid: Ediciones Atlas.

Basalla, George. 1993. "The Spread of Western Science Revisited." In *Mundialización de la ciencia y cultura nacional,* eds. Antonio Lafuente, Alberto Elena, and María L. Ortega, 599–604. Madrid: Doce Calles.

Bauer, Ralph. 2002. "The Postcolonial Origins of Modernity." *William and Mary Quarterly* 59 (4): 975–81.

Bello, Andrés. 1872. *Obras completas de don Andrés Bello Volumen XIV Opúsculos Científicos.* Santiago de Chile: Imprenta Cervantes.

Bisset, Normand Grainger. 1992. "War and Hunting Poisons of the New World." *Journal of Ethnopharmacology* 30 (1): 1–26.

Bost, David. 1988. "Historiography and the Contemporary Narrative: Dialogue and Methodology." *Latin American Literary Review* 16 (31): 34–44.

–. 1996. "Historians of the Colonial Period: 1620–1700." In *The Cambridge History of Latin American Literature,* eds. Roberto González Echevarría and Enrique Pupo-Walker, vol. 1, 143–90. Cambridge: Cambridge University Press.

Cañizares-Esguerra, Jorge. 1998. "Spanish America in Eighteenth-Century European Travel Compilations: A New 'Art of Reading' and the Transition to Modernity." *Journal of Early Modern History* 2 (4): 329–49.

–. 2001. *How to Write the History of the New World.* Stanford: Stanford University Press.

–. 2003. "Spanish America: From Baroque to Modern Colonial Science." In *Cambridge History of Science, Volume Four: Eighteenth-Century Science,* ed. Roy Porter, 718–38. Cambridge: Cambridge University Press.

–. 2004. "Iberian Science in the Renaissance: Ignored How Much Longer?" *Perspectives on Science* 12 (1): 86–124.

–. 2005. "How Derivative Was Humboldt? Microcosmic Nature Narratives in Early Modern Spanish America and the (Other) Origins of Humboldt's Ecological Sensibilities." In *Colonial Botany: Science, Commerce, and Politics in the Early Modern World,* eds. Londa Schiebinger and Claudia Swan, 148–68. Philadelphia: University of Pennsylvania Press.

Carpentier, Alejo. 1985. *Los pasos perdidos,* 1953, ed. Roberto González Echevarría. Reprint, Madrid: Cátedra.

Catrou, François, René Joseph de Tournemine, Claude Buffier, père Du Cerceau, Pierre Brumoy, Pierre Julien Rouillé, and Pierre-François-Xavier de Charlevoix et al. 1701–1767. *Mémoires pour l''histoire des sciences & des beaux arts [Mémoires de Trévoux].* Genève: Slatkine Reprints.

Chambers, David W. 1993. "Locality and Science: Myths of Centre and Periphery." In *Mundialización de la ciencia y cultura nacional,* eds. Antonio Lafuente, Alberto Elena and María L. Ortega, 605–17. Madrid: Doce Calles.

Conzemius, Eduard. 1928. "Ethnographical Notes on the Black Carib." *American Anthropologist* 30 (2): 183–205.

Dussel, Enrique. 1993. "Eurocentrism and Modernity (Introduction to the Frankfort Lectures)." *Boundary 2* 20 (3): 65–76.

Ewalt, Margaret. 2005. "Father Gumilla, Crocodile Hunter? The Function of Wonder in *El Orinoco ilustrado.*" In *El saber de los jesuitas, historias naturales y el Nuevo Mundo,* edited by Luis Millones Figueroa and Domingo Ledesma, 303–33. Madrid: Iberoamericana.

–. 2005. "Frontier Encounters and Pathways to Knowledge in the New Kingdom of Granada." *The Colorado Review of Hispanic Studies* 3: 41–55.

–. 2006. "Crossing Over: Nations and Naturalists in *El Orinoco ilustrado.* Reading and Writing the Book of Orinoco Secrets," *Dieciocho* 29.1: 1–25.

Fajardo Morón, Guillermo. 1986. "El escritor venezolano José Gumilla." *Boletín de la Academia Nacional de la Historia:* 1101–2.

Foucault, Michel. 1980. "Lecture One: 7 January 1976." In *Power/Knowledge: Selected Interviews and Other Writings, 1972–1977,* ed. C. Gordon, 78–92. New York: Pantheon Books.

Freedburg, David. 2002. *The Eye of the Lynx: Galileo, His Friends and the Beginnings of Modern Natural History.* Chicago: Chicago University Press.

Fréron, Elie. [1756] 1968. *Journal Étranger ou notice exacte et détaillée des ouvrages des toutes les nations étrangéres, en fait d'arts, des sciences, de littérature.* Reprint, Genève: Slatkine Reprints.

–. [1758] 1966. *L'Année Littéraire.* Reprint, Genève: Slatkine Reprints.

Geertz, Clifford. 1988. *Works and Lives: The Anthropologist as Author.* Stanford: Stanford University Press.

Gilij [Gilii], Filippo Salvadore. 1780–1784. *Saggio di storia americana; o sia, Storia naturale, civile e sacra de'regni, e delle provincie spagnuole di Terra-Ferma nell' America Meridionale.* Rome: L. Perego erede Salvioni.

Gilij [Gilii], Filippo Salvadore. 1987. *Ensayo de Historia Americana, Tomo I.* Caracas: Academia Nacional de Historia.

Gillin, John. 1934. "Crime and Punishment among the Barama River Carib of British Guiana." *American Anthropologist* 36 (3): 331–44.

González Echevarría, Roberto. 1972. "*Semejante a la noche* de Alejo Carpentier: *Historia/Ficción.*" *MLN* 87 (2): 272–85.

González Echevarría, Roberto. 1990. *Myth and Archive: A Theory of Latin American Narrative.* Cambridge: Cambridge University Press.

Gumilla, Joseph. 1741. *El Orinoco ilustrado, historia natural, civil y geographica de este gran río, y de sus caudalosas vertientes; govierno, usos, y costumbres de los Indios sus habitadores, con nuevas, y utiles noticias de animales, arboles frutos, aceytes, resinas, yervas, y raíces medicinales.* Madrid: Manuel Fernandez.

Gumilla, Joseph. 1745. *El Orinoco ilustrado, y defendido, historia natural, civil y geographica de este gran río, y de sus caudalosas vertientes; govierno, usos, y costumbres de los Indios sus habitadores, con nuevas, y utiles noticias de animales, arboles frutos, aceytes, resinas, yervas, y raíces medicinales.* Madrid: Manuel Fernandez.

Gumilla, Joseph. 1758. *Histoire naturelle, civile et geographique de l'Orenoque, et des principales rivieres que s'y jettent [...].* Avignon: Chez la Veuve de F. Girard.

Gumilla, Joseph. 1963. *El Orinoco ilustrado y defendido,* ed. Demetrio Ramos. Caracas: Fuentes para la Historia Colonial de Venezuela.

Harris, Steven. 2005. "Jesuit Scientific Activity in the Overseas Missions, 1570–1773." *ISIS* 96: 71–9.

Helferich, Gerard. 2004. *Humboldt's Cosmos: Alexander von Humboldt and the Latin American Journey that Changed the Way We See the World.* New York: Gotham Books.

Humboldt, Alexander von. 1995. *Personal Narrative of a Journey to the Equinoctial Regions of the New Continent,* 1805–1838, trans. Jason Wilson. Reprint, London: Penguin Books.

–. 1850. *Aspects of Nature, in Different Lands and Different Climates; with Scientific Elucidations,* trans. Mrs. Sabine. Philadelphia: Lea and Blanchard.

–. 1852–1853. *Personal Narrative of Travels to the Equinoctial Regions of America, during the years 1799–1804,* ed. and trans. Thomasina Ross. London: Henry G. Bohn.

–. 1970. *Relation historique du Voyage aux régions équinoxiales du Nouveau Continent.* 3 vols. Stuttgart: F.A. Brockhaus.

Isaacs, Jorge. 1991. *María,* 1867, ed. Donald McGrady. Reprint, Madrid: Cátedra.

Jardine, Nicholas, James A. Secord, and Emma C. Spary. 1996. *Cultures of Natural History.* Cambridge: Cambridge University Press.

Journal des savants combiné avec les Mémoires de Trévoux. 1758. Amsterdam: Rey.

Journal Encyclopédique. 1759. Liège: Bouillin.

Juan, Jorge, and Antonio de Ulloa. 1748. *Relacion historica del viage a la America Meridional hecho de orden de S. Mag. para medir algunos grados de Meridiano Terrestre e, y venir por ellos en conocimiento de la verdadera Figura, y Magnitud de la Tierra, con otras varias Observaciones Astronomicas, y Phisicas: Por Don Jorge Juan, Comendador de Aliaga, en el Orden de San Juan, Socio correspondiente de la Real Academia de Ciencias de Paris, y Don Antonio de Ulloa, de la Real Sociedad de Londres; ambos Capitanes de Fragata de la Real Armada.* Madrid: Antonio Marin.

La Condamine, Charles Marie de. 1745. *Relation abrégée d'un voyage fait dans l'interieur de l'Amérique Méridionale. Depuis la côte de la Mer du Sud, jusqu'aux côtes du Brésil & de la Guiane, en descendant la riviere des Amazones.* Paris: Veuve Pissot.

Labat, Jean-Baptiste. 1722. *Nouveau voyages aux isles de l'Amerique. Contentant L'histoire naturelle de ces pays, l'Origine, les mœurs, la Religion & le Gouvernement des Habitans anciens & modernes [...] Avec une Description exacte & curuiese de toutes ces Isles.* Paris: Chez Pierre-Francois Giffart.

Latour, Bruno. 1979. *Laboratory Life: The Social Construction of Scientific Facts.* Beverley Hills: Sage Publications.

Lee, Michael Radcliffe. 2005. "Curare: the South American Arrow Poison." *Journal of College Physicians of Edinburgh* 35 (1): 83–92.

Navarrete, Rodrigo. 2000. "Behind the Palisades: Sociopolitical Recomposition of Native Societies in the Unare Depression, the Eastern Venezuelan Llanos (Sixteenth to Eighteenth Centuries)." *Ethnohistory* 47 (3–4): 535–59.

Pimental, Juan. 2001. "The Iberian Vision: Science and Empire in the Framework of a Universal Monarchy, 1500–1800." *Osiris* 15: 17–30.

Porter, Roy, and George Sebastian Rousseau. 1980. *The Ferment of Knowledge: Studies in the Historiography of Eighteenth-Century Science.* Cambridge: Cambridge University Press.

Pratt, Mary Louise. 1992. *Imperial Eyes: Travel Writing and Transculturation.* New York: Routledge.

Raynal, Abbé [Guillaume-Thomas-François]. 1770. *Histoire Philosophique et politique, des etablissemens & du commerce des Europeéns dans les deux Indes.* Amsterdam: s.n.

Rivera, José Eustasio. 1998. *La vorágine,* 1924, ed. Montserrat Ordóñez. Reprint, Madrid: Cátedra.

Rodríguez, Manuel. 1684. *El Marañon y Amazonas. Historia de los descubrimientos, entradas, y reducción de naciones. Trabajos malogrados de algunos conquistadores, y dichosos de otros, así temporales, como espirituales, en las dilatadas montañas, y mayores rios de la America.* Madrid: Antonio Gonzalez de Reyes.

Silva Cáceres, Raul. 1967. "Una novela de Carpentier." *Mundo nuevo* 17: 33–7.
Smith, Adam. 1776. *An Inquiry into the Nature and Causes of the Wealth of the Nations,* 1761. Reprint, London: W. Strahan and T. Cadell.
Stepan, Nancy Leys. 2001. "Going to the Tropics." In *Picturing Tropical Nature.* Ithaca: Cornell University Press.
Suárez, María Matilde. 1974. "El contenido etnográfico del *Orinoco Ilustrado.*" *Montalban* 3: 309–35.
Subirats, Eduardo. 1981. *La ilustración insuficiente.* Madrid: Taurus.
–. 2001. *Modernidad truncada de América Latina.* Caracas: CIPOST, Centro de Investigaciones Postdoctorales.
Thorbjarnarson, John. 1995. "Trailing the Mythical Anaconda." *Americas* 47 (4): 38.
Vernes, Jules. 1898. *Le Superbe Orénoque.* Paris: J. Hetzel.
Whitaker, Arthur P. 1942. *Latin America and the Enlightenment.* New York: D. Appleton-Century Co.
Whitaker, Arthur P. 1971. "Changing and Unchanging Interpretations of the Enlightenment in Spanish America," In *The Ibero-American Enlightenment,* ed. A. Owen Aldridge, 21–57. Urbana: University of Illinois Press.
Wylie, Lesley. 2005. "Hearts of Darkness: The Celebration of Otherness in the Latin American *novela de la selva.*" *Romance Studies* 23 (2): 105–16.

chapter seventeen

Pierre Pelleprat's *Accounts of the Jesuit Missions in the Antilles and in Guyana* (1655)[1]

RÉAL OUELLET AND MARC ANDRÉ BERNIER

Part I: The Telling of an Adventure and the Detailed Account of a Territory

Born in Bordeaux in 1606, Pierre Pelleprat, Jesuit novice at seventeen years of age, taught for some years and then was ordained a priest in 1633. College regent, army chaplain, and preacher, he was an exorcist in Loudun in 1638 (until 1641), four years after Grandier was burned at the stake. Once more a preacher, minister, and college rector, in 1651 he obtained a mission on St. Christopher Island (also known as St. Kitts) to convert the Indians of the Caribbean. Disappointed by the poor results achieved by missionaries on the islands, he dreamed of grander projects on "the mainland of meridional America," as he referred to this geographical area in the title of his *Relation* (Pelleprat [1655] 2009). After six months in the region of Guarapiche ("Oüarabiche" in his *Relation*), Pelleprat returned to France to publish with Cramoisy, in 1655, his *Relation des missions des PP. de la Compagnie de Jesus dans les Isles et à la Terre Ferme de l'Amerique Meridionale.* The publication, first written in Latin[2], aimed at enhancing a project for a vast Jesuit mission on the continent, supported by a powerful colonizing company. The latter was formed and a ship, under the direction of La Vigne, left Paimbœuf in 1656, carrying onboard Pelleprat and his colleague Boislevert. The expedition turned into a disaster when the future settlers found no place to land, and were shipwrecked on the Jamaican coast. Pelleprat subsequently found himself in New Spain (now Mexico) and requested in vain to return to Europe. He died in Puebla on 21 April 1667.

Pelleprat the Writer

Pelleprat's *Relation* is part of a long Jesuit tradition. In the mid-sixteenth century, Ignatius of Loyola and Francis Xavier were already ordering that missionaries write to their superiors on a recurring basis. This regular correspondence allowed the scattered Jesuits to keep in touch, to encourage one another, to support one another mutually, and to better understand explored regions and evangelized populations. With the rapid development of the Society after the death of its founder in 1556, each Jesuit provincial sent an annual missive to Rome, which reported on the state of the missions that had been placed under his jurisdiction. An annual synthesis of all the letters received was subsequently distributed to the members of the order; as of 1583 this synthesis appeared in a published form. Gradually, these *Relations* were distributed by publishing houses that targeted an even broader readership. The incentive to do so served both the public and Jesuits alike. With regard to the public, these writings interested both the devout as well as those eager for exotic knowledge; as far as the Jesuits were concerned, they constituted an effective propaganda device for their missions. From the beginning, the *Relations* made up a type of literary subgenre, with their alternating narrative and descriptive sequences. Indeed, very early on, the *Relation* recounted an adventure on foreign soil, spreading before readers' eyes a geographical and ethnographical encyclopedia (of topography, flora and fauna, and the practices and customs of indigenous populations).

If the *Relations* that came from the Orient and South America consolidated the style and technique of the annual letter and, up to a certain point, its thematic and factual contents, the forty-one volumes of the *Relations de la Nouvelle France*, published between 1632 and 1673, constituted the model Pelleprat used. Before him, only Jacques Bouton (1640) had published a very short account of the Lesser Antilles. Published by missionaries who were stationed in Canada, and who had served as college professors in France, these *Relations de la Nouvelle France* were the work of intellectuals and men of action who were deeply engaged in the field, as shown by the long series published by Paul Lejeune from 1632 to 1642.

A mere glimpse of its contents shows that Pelleprat's *Relation* is made up of three distinct parts: the first section dealing with the "Islands of America," where various religious orders had been established for twenty years; the second section on the attempts to establish missionaries on "the

Firm Land" ("la Terre Ferme") or the continent, where Spaniards were solidly implanted; and finally, the third section, in the form of an appendix, bearing a title page and independent pagination, which proposes an "Introduction à la langue des Galibis, Sauvages de la Terre Ferme de l'Amerique meridionale" ("Introduction to the Language of the Galibis, Savages of the Mainland of Meridional America"). While the last section is exclusively encyclopedic, the main body of the *Relation* is divided into chapters that alternate between the narrative and the descriptive, as is suggested by the table of contents. On one hand, action words proclaim events: "First Voyage of Our Fathers to the Islands" (Pelleprat [1655] 2009, pt. 1, sec. 2), "Massacre of Fathers Aubergeon and Gueimu" (pt. 1, sec. 8); on the other, several titles indicate an encyclopedic development: "Of the Advantages and Marvels of This Country" ("Des avantages et des merveilles de ce pays" [pt. 2, sec. 4 and 5) and "Customs and Ways of Doing [of Savages]" ("Coutumes et façons de faire [des Sauvages]" [pt. 2, sec. 7 and 8]).

The Telling of an Adventure

Faithful to the Ignatian directive to relate the facts and actions of its order, Pelleprat devoted the entire first part of his *Relation* to the Jesuit's Antilles mission: their beginnings (Pelleprat [1655] 2009, pt. 1, sec. 2), among the Protestants (pt. 1, sec. 3), the French (pt. 1, sec. 4), Irish Catholics (pt. 1, sec. 5), Negro and Savage slaves (pt. 1, sec. 6), "Savages of Martinique and Saint Vincent" (pt. 1, sec. 7). In part 2, the territory represented is increased to include a vast portion of the continent. However, the action is reduced to that of two adventurous missionaries, Denys Mesland and Pierre Pelleprat himself.

Relating the Jesuit missionary adventure in the islands was a difficult task. Although devoted to the conversion of Caribbean Savages, the missionaries baptized very few.[3] Furthermore, two of them, Guillaume Aubergeon and François Gueimu, were massacred by the aboriginals of St. Vincent a few months before the publication of the *Relation*. It was therefore necessary to orchestrate the narration of the Jesuit enterprise in such a way as to obscure this failure by enhancing the sum of their actions. Narrative, which is able to create suspense and enhance the character profiles of its player protagonists, is more convincing than demonstration, which is always susceptible to rational opposition. Obviously, Pelleprat sought to give the impression of an enormous worksite buzzing with activities of all kinds: the Jesuit missionaries moving from one island to another to catechize, hear confessions, assist the dying – in short, to respond to demands made upon them from all sides, selflessly expending themselves for the salvation of souls. A mere tally of the people affected is impressive: 15,000 or 16,000 "French Established in the Islands" (without counting those passing through), "more than twelve or thirteen hundred" Protestant converts (including 400 by John Stritch), a "considerable" number of Irish Catholics served, and 600 Christianized black slaves each year. How not to admire the work accomplished by these "evangelical workers" (Pelleprat [1655] 2009, pt. 2, sec. 8: 78)?

But this accounting, on its own, would not be nearly as eloquent if the author had not used exempla to illustrate the actions of missionaries who literally toiled to death, such as Father Conard and La Vallière, who "gloriously ended their days" during an epidemic' (pt. 1, sec. 4: 85–6). Thus, La Vallière, after

> assisting these poor people while they were alive, took their bodies on his shoulders and buried them with his own hands. Nothing repulsed him, on the contrary, the stench of the corpses and the malignity of the disease, from which he saw so many people die everyday, was an attraction rather than an impediment to their zeal ("avoir assisté ces pauvres gens pendant leur vie, il prenoit encore soin de leurs corps après leur mort, & les chargeoit sur ses épaules, les portant au cemetiere commun avec une ferveur incroyable; & là les enterroit de ses propres mains, & leur rendoit ce dernier devoir avec une tres-grande charité. La puanteur de ces cadavres, & la malignité de la maladie dont ils voyoient tous les jours mourir tant de personnes, estoient plûtost un attrait qu'un retardement à leur zele" [Pelleprat (1655) 2009, pt. 1, sec. 4: 34]).

The dramatic intensity reaches its apex before the final chapter of part 1 of the *Relation*, which recounts the "massacre of Fathers Aubergeon and Gueimu," presented less as an act of revenge against the French who were invading the Caribbean than as a martyrdom for the cause. While the theme of revenge is only suggested – the Savages "sought revenge from the French of Sainte Alousie, whom they claimed had stolen their land" ("Tandis que ceux-là se vengeoient des François de Sainte Alousie, qu'ils pretendoient avoir usurpé leurs terres" [pt. 1, sec. 8: 85–6]) – the theme of the martyr is carefully constructed in previous chapters (especially chapter 7). To obscure the failure of the mission among the Caribbean Savages, the narrator focuses all his attention on the missionary Aubergeon, presented as a man always on the lookout for "the salvation of souls": travelling from one multi-family hut to another, preaching and catechizing without respite. In particular, he introduces a crowd of aspiring converts gathered before the missionary who insistently plead to be baptized: "'Father, you must come with us, to teach those of our nation how to pray to God.' 'When will you baptize us?' asks a great number of people of every age and sex" ("'Père, il faut que tu viennes avec nous, pour apprendre à prier Dieu à ceux de nostre nation.' [...] 'Quand serace que tu nous baptiseras?'" [pt. 1, sec. 7: 71–6]).

But as conversion "in three months' time" would be suspect, the narrator reminds us that the missionary could sorrowfully not confer baptism "except with all the necessary precautions, for fear of risking it at the wrong time" (pt. 1, sec. 7: 71–6). He then ends his chapter with a passage reminiscent of the Passion of Christ offering his life to save humanity: "[H]ands joined and raised to the sky, eyes filled with tears, [...] he offered to God, with the precious blood of his son Jesus Christ, his very own that he was to shed a few months hence" ("[L]es mains jointes, & elevées vers le ciel, les yeux baignez de larmes, [...] il offroit à Dieu, avec le precieux sang de son fils Jesus-Christ le sien propre qu'il devoit repandre quelques mois après" [Pelleprat (1655) 2009, pt. 1, sec. 7: 111]). Once the scene and main character have been established, the drama of the eighth chapter may be presented to the reader as "The Massacre of Fathers Aubergeon and Gueimu."

The heroization of missionary work was not solely accomplished through the use of spectacular exempla. It was also carried out through multiple anecdotes that sought to illustrate effective action in the field and, especially, to dramatize a meeting or a situation, as when a group of children literally assaulted Pelleprat with cries of "Baptize me, Father, baptize me" (Pelleprat [1655] 2009, pt.1, sec. 7: 111). Another anecdote seeks to lend credibility to an unlikely story that the author himself qualifies as "marvelous," when a "poor dying man" finds health after receiving extreme unction. Even if he alleges "several witnesses able to testify in favor of the truth of this story" (pt. 1, sec. 3: 82), the narrator appears so uncertain of being able to convince his readers that he follows with another conversion recital, this time multiplying the rapid biological features and space-time references to create an effect of truth:

> Let us end with the conversion of a German who arrived last year on the same island: he was a man of spirit who had been raised with much care in his religion and who acted as a sermon reader for the Dutch in Brazil; he took refuge in Martinique when the Dutch were chased from Brazil by the Portuguese, and had brought into this country a Negro woman whom

he had kept for a long time and with whom he had had two children. Father Schemel, like him, a German, made such an impression on his spirit that not only was he obliged to leave heresy behind, but also to marry his concubine ("Finissons par la conversion d'un Allemand, arrivée l'année passée dans la méme Isle: c'estoit un homme d'esprit qui avoit esté élevé avec beaucoup de soin dans sa Religion, & qui faisoit l'office de Lecteur dans un des Presches que les Hollandois avoient dans le Brasil; celuy-cy s'estoit refugié dans la Martinique depuis que les Hollandois avoient esté chassez du Brasil par les Portugais: & avoit ammené de ce pays une femme Negre qu'il entretenoit depuis long-temps, & dont il avoit eu deux enfans. Le Pere Schemel, Allemand comme luy, fit tant d'impression sur son esprit, que non seulement il l'obligea de quitter l'heresie: mais aussi d'épouser sa concubine" [Pelleprat (1655) 2009, pt. 1, sec. 3: 83]).

The dramatization of missionary action manifested itself even more strongly in the insertion of textual sequences featuring a strong coefficient of suspense as events unfold. A good example is provided by a highly cinematographic scene in which a group of Indians in their pirogues, bows arched, are making ready to fire poisoned arrows at the almost defenseless French (Pelleprat [1655] 2009, pt. 1, sec. 8: 117). Although not as gripping, other passages maintain a climate of suspense by mentioning, in passing, a rumor (a story circulated that the Jesuit Mesland had died [pt. 2, sec. 3: 142]), a news brief ("The Caribbeans have made several outings [...] pillaging and burning caves" ["Les Caraïbes ont fait plusieurs courses [...] pillant et brûlant les cases" (pt. 1, sec. 8: 118)]), or a realization after the fact ("The danger we risked had been greater than we thought" ["le danger que nous avions couru avait été plus grand que nous n'avions pensé" (pt. 1, sec. 8: 117)]).

As a writer, when he records a defence and illustration of his order in the Caribbean region, Pelleprat is also making himself into his own apologist. Even as he boasts of the work of his colleagues, events are narrated in such a way that we feel he is somehow tied to the action being related. With the clever skill of a storyteller, he plays with the personal pronouns "I," "we," and "one." "We" designates the Jesuit collective of which Pelleprat is a part, even when he is not a prime actor: "the work that we have"; "we lost"; "we catechized them" (pt. 1, sec. 8: 117). This frequent use of the inclusive "we" gives the impression of continual participation in missionary action. The use of "I" is even more subtle, as it simultaneously refers to Pelleprat as a writer ("I would say that") and to Pelleprat the missionary protagonist ("I entered the chapel"). When these two uses of "I" rapidly alternate, the reader may be tempted to credit the protagonist with actions that may not correspond with his paltry participation in what is described: "I have already brought back an example [...]. A Negro [...] came to me one day to request baptism" ("J'en ay déja rapporté un exemple [...]. Un Negre [...] me vint un jour demander le Baptesme" [Pelleprat (1655) 2009, pt. 1, sec. 6: 102]). The heroization of the protagonist is so strongly ensured that the writer does not hesitate to narrate like a secret shared, such as an anecdote taken without credit from Carmelite Maurile de Saint-Michel[4]: "I would say on this subject that monsieur Giraud, a spirited man of recognized integrity, reported to me that one night the devil mistreated [...] one of his slaves" ("Je diray à ce sujet ce que monsieur Giraud homme d'esprit, & de probité connuë m'a rapporté, qu'une nuit le diable maltraita [...] une de ses Esclaves Sauvages" [pt. 1, sec. 6: 61]).

The making of Pelleprat the protagonist into a hero becomes even clearer in the second part of the *Relation*, when he accompanies his colleague Mesland onto the mainland. Following a period of initiation in the shadows of his colleague, who knows the region from previous travel, Pelleprat soon finds his own freedom to act when Mesland leaves the mission of "Oüarabiche" to start another mission in Saint-Thomas de Guyane. Remaining "alone with a boy of 16, without being able to speak or find an interpreter," Pelleprat sees himself immobilized where he is by "a prodigious swelling of the legs and feet" ("une enflure prodigieuse aux jambes et aux pieds" [Pelleprat (1655) 2009, pt. 1, sec. 9: 180]). However, this misfortune, in addition to crowning the protagonist with a halo of suffering, affords self-actualization in another respect, when Pelleprat applies himself to methodically learning the Galibi language to the degree that he can soon "be understood," "teach Christian doctrine" (pt. 1, sec. 9: 180), and even hold a sustained conversation on a point of dogma or on the motivations that prompted him to come "save" the Galibis, rather than to do business with them like the other French. Even the weakness of his language skills becomes an asset to him, because he knows how to play with words and, with his ignorance, how to maintain an upper hand over the Savages:

> As I was still rather new to the language, I didn't quite distinguish the words *Ouclian*, which means man, and *Ouclian*, which means woman, and answered yes; but having immediately noticed the ensuing doubt, I asked her if she had said *Ouclian* or *Ouclian*. She replied that she had always said *Ouclian*; I took forthwith the word and made everyone understand that the Son of God was made a man for men and women, and that it was not necessary that he be a woman to save women, because men and women were of the same

> nature though of a different sex ("Comme j'estois encore assez nouveau en la langue; je ne distinguay pas suffisamment les mots d'*Ouclian* qui signifie un homme, & *Oulian*, qui veut dire une femme, & lui répondis qu'oüy; mais m'étant aussi-tost apperçeu de l'equivoque, je luy demanday si elle disoit *Ouclian* ou bien *Oulian*? elle me repartit qu'elle avoit toûjours dit *Oulian*; je pris incontinent la parolle, & fis entendre à tout le monde que le Fils de Dieu s'estoit seulement fait homme pour les hommes, & pour les femmes, & qu'il n'estoit pas necessaire qu'il se fit femme pour sauver les femmes, puis que l'homme & la femme estoient de méme nature, bien que de sexe different" [Pelleprat (1655) 2009, pt. 2, sec. 9: 183–4]).

The fact that dialogue became a means of heroization for the missionary, because he used it to convert – that is, to *conquer*[5] through the word – is clearly shown elsewhere, as when the teller adopts his own version of a common component of the traditional missionary recital: the supplication of Indians who ask the Jesuit not to abandon them. As soon as Macau, "the captain of the large, multi-family hut," learns of Pelleprat's departure, he runs to him:

> My friend, what have I done to you? Why do you want to leave me? You want to return to the Islands: have I angered you in any way? Has one of my people displeased you? Do you fear our enemies? Tell me, I beg you, why do you want to abandon us? ("Mon compere que t'ay-je fait? pourquoi me veux-tu quitter? tu veux retourner aux Isles: t'ay-je fâché en quelque chose? quelqu'un de mes gens t'a-t'il déplu? crains-tu nos ennemis? Dis moy je te prie pourquoy tu nous veux abandonner?" [Pelleprat (1655) 2009, pt. 2, sec. 7: 194]).

While sparing us, however slightly, the grand scenes of leave-taking found, for example, among the works of Recollets Sagard (1632) and Leclercq (1691), we nevertheless see that such highly dramatic supplications aim at making us forget the missionary's ineffectiveness by enhancing his person through rhetoric. Here, as in the majority of the accounts of missionaries who are not able to make themselves heroes on the battlefield, literary address replaces the penury of action. If one wants to enliven not the adventure, but the narration of the adventure, another literary ruse may also be employed: the micro-account of hypothetical heroics,[6] a subterfuge used to evoke all sorts of dangers that, while possible, are never met, such as the mention of the "furious hurricane that would have meant our certain death if we had still been at anchor" ("furieux houragan qui nous eût fait périr irrémissiblement si nous eussions encore été à l'ancre" [Pelleprat (1655) 2009, pt. 2, sec. 2: 134–5]). Why bring up a misfortune that did not occur if not to make the reader sympathize with the plight of the protagonist? Sometimes, the micro-account develops to suggest an action that takes on the attributes of an anecdote in which the missionary was, we are told, "favored by a special protection of God" ("favorisé d'une particuliere protection de Dieu"), as when three hundred Caribbean warriors are made to flee by a handful of French armed only with "nasty stone-throwing cannons" ("deux méchans pierriers" [pt. 2, sec. 8: 117]). The protagonist here wins on two fronts simultaneously, because he appears both as chosen by God and as the hero who has no fear that anything will detract from his missionary ideal.

The Detailed Account of a Territory

While telling an adventure, the missionary account is also the detailed account of a territory, as was required not only by Jesuit custom but also by the royal power that sought knowledge of the region in order to colonize it.

But how can one give an account of a human and physical reality in which everything abounds? The most attentive observation would initially only reveal a number of references difficult to position with respect to the partial and disparate knowledge gleaned by one's predecessors. From raw perception to verbal representation, a considerable gap must be breached to turn a traveller into a relator. The latter has chosen and classified a certain amount of data – on ethnography, zoology, botany, and physical geography – from everything the first has understood through observation, oral testimony, and reading. For every new reality, one had to find points of comparison familiar to one's eventual reader. Thus, the manatee, unknown in France, "is a big and powerful fish, fifteen to twenty feet long, that has the muffle of a cow; we catch it like a whale; the flesh is as agreeable as that of veal when it is freshly eaten" ("est un grand & puissant poisson, de quinze ou vingt pieds de longueur, qui a le mufle de Bœuf: on le prend comme la Balene: la chair en est aussi agréable que celle du Veau, quand elle est mangée fraîche" [Pelleprat (1655) 2009, pt. 2, sec. 4: 152]).

"The Oulana" is "a type of hare that is much bigger than ours; although it has shorter legs, it has scarcely less bulk than a one-year old lamb" ("une espece de lievre qui est beaucoup plus grand que les nostres; bien qu'il aye les jambes plus petites, il n'a gueres moins de corps qu'un Agneau d'un an" [Pelleprat (1655) 2009, pt. 2, sec. 5: 154]). The exotic repertory therefore adopts the tried and true formula of the comparative parataxis, largely used to describe hybrid beings that, from the Bible to our time, have populated mythologies, science fiction stories and fantastic writings: dragons, centaurs, and other fabulous teratological creatures.

The author was a missionary in the service of a cause (the Christianization of Indians and the colonization of America); we suspect, therefore, that his representation of reality would indicate as much. Although contenting himself with a few lines to evoke the excessive climate of the islands and their "repelling" character (Pelleprat [1655] 2009, pt. 1, sec. 1: 3), the relator devotes two enthusiastic chapters to the continental territory: "Of the Advantages and Marvels of This Country" ("Des avantages et des merveilles de ce pays" [pt. 2, sec. 4 and 5]) and "Customs and Ways of Doing [of Savages]" ("Coutumes et façons de faire [des Sauvages]" [pt. 2, sec. 7 and 8]). Of the five encyclopedic chapters that make up the second part of the *Relation*, one pair addresses the "advantages" and "marvels of this country," while the other three are on the "Savages of these countries," their "customs," "police," and "disposition to receive the faith" (pt. 2, sec. 7 and 8). The missionary and colonial endeavour, we observe, is what orients the portrayal. From the first paragraph on the "marvels of this country," the tone is set: despite certain "inconveniences" similar to those of the islands, the mainland "bears tobacco, sugar cane, indigo, cotton, cassia, ginger, and generally everything that makes a stay on the Islands either pleasant, or profitable, in addition to many other commodities not found there" ("porte le pétun, les cannes de sucre, l'indigo, le coton, la casse, le gingembre, et généralement tout ce qui rend le séjour des Îles ou agréable, ou profitable, et de plus beaucoup d'autres commodités dont elles sont dépourvues" [pt. 2, sec. 4: 143]). The second paragraph, which at first glance would appear to present nature as a landscape pleasing to the eye (one thinks of the *locus amœnus*), quickly remedies this impression by emphasizing the practicality of a generous natural world:

> This land is irrigated by several large rivers that beautify it and make it fruitful. It is adorned with beautiful landscapes that the Spanish name *savanes*, full of pasturage for livestock, but useless for Savages who do not eat domestic animals. I have seen some of such broad range that I could not discover the end. They are bordered by high clusters of woods of several varieties unknown in Europe, and of a prodigious height and size, that are green in all seasons of the year and that bear aromatic gums for various usages

("Cette terre est arrousée de plusieurs grandes rivieres, qui l'embelissent, & qui la rendent feconde. Elle est ornée de belles campagnes que les Espagnols nomment *Savanes*, pleines d'herbage pour le bestail: mais inutiles aux Sauvages qui ne nourrissent point d'animaux domestiques. J'en ay veu d'une si grande étenduë que je n'en pouvois pas découvrir le bout. Elles sont bordées de bois de haute fûtaye de plusieurs especes inconnuës en Europe, & d'une hauteur, & grosseur prodigieuse; qui sont verds en toutes les saisons de l'année, & qui portent des gommes aromatiques propres à divers usages" [Pelleprat (1655) 2009, pt. 2, sec. 4: 143]).

The rest of the chapter and the following merely develop, in a manner akin to long musical variations, the themes of abundance and utility already set forth: "The Senna grows in the fields of this country without being sown or cultivated" ("Le Sené croist dans les campagnes de ce pays, sans y être semé, ny cultivé"); "We find in these countries a number of reptiles excellent to eat" ("On trouve en ces contrées quantité de reptiles excellens à manger"); "One encounters frogs of such a prodigious size that a single one fills an entire plate" ("Il s'y rencontre des Grenoüilles d'une si prodigieuse grandeur qu'une seule est capable de remplir un plat tout entire"); "[O]ne is sometimes pleasantly deceived, by mistaking its flesh for that of chicken" ("[O]n y est quelquefois agréablement trompé, en prenant la chair pour celle d'un poulet" [Pelleprat (1655) 2009, pt. 2, sec. 4: 146]).

The reference when speaking of the richness of local fare is not to the Antillean archipelago, but to France, and because of the extent to which everything grows and bursts on the continent, often "without being sown or cultivated," it suffers from the comparison: "The ducks have one time again as much girth as those of France" ("Les canards ont une fois autant de corps que ceux de France"); the reeds "become big trees"; "The Fern, which in France is but a small plant, grows like a tree to the size of a thigh" ("La Feugere qui n'est en France qu'une petite plante, y croît en arbre de la grosseur de la cuisse, & de dix-huit et vingt pieds de hauteur" [Pelleprat (1655) 2009, pt. 2, sec. 4: 144–5]). We see that moving from the islands to the mainland is to shift from understatement to hyperbole.

The same "advantages" and "marvels" are laid down by the relator when he wants to describe the "great number of Savages" of the Guyanese coast (Pelleprat [1655] 2009, pt. 2, sec. 6: 157–9). While the first part of the *Relation* hardly presents a rough ethnographical account of the Caribbeans, reducing their function to making heroes of the missionaries, the second devotes three chapters to the Galibis, ending with a grandiloquent apology borrowed from the Spanish Dominican Las Casas:

> God created these people infinite in every way, very simple, without finesse or guile, without malice, very obedient, very loyal, very humble [...]. They have very clear and alert understanding, being docile and capable of every good doctrine, suitable for receiving our holy Catholic faith ("Dieu crea ces gens infinis de toute sorte, tres simples, sans finesse ou cautele, sans malice, tres obeyssants, & tres fideles; fort humbles [...]. Ils ont l'entendement tres net et vif, estans dociles & capables de toute bonne doctrine, tres propres à recevoir nostre sainte Foy Catholique, & à estre enseignés en bonnes & vertueuses mœurs" [Pelleprat (1655) 2009, pt. 2, sec. 8: 158]).

This favourable judgment, which the author dare not pronounce in his own voice, is further underscored by a paradoxical comment that borders on heresy: "[O]ne would almost say upon seeing them that they had not in them the sin of Adam, like other men, because one notices in them but little or no inclination toward vice" ("[O]n diroit à les voir qu'ils n'ont pas peché en Adam comme les autres hommes, parce qu'on ne remarque en eux que peu, ou point d'inclination au vice" [Pelleprat (1655) 2009, pt. 2, sec. 8: 173]).[7]

Such a panegyric, placed under the guarantee of an incontestable authority, would not have been admissible had it not been preceded by two semi-descriptive, semi-argumentative chapters that seek to exonerate the Galibis of accusations of inhuman barbarism carried out against the Savages of Canada and of the Caribbean region. At first, the relator nuances and relativizes, even if it means accusing other indigenous groups: the Savages of the mainland "are not cruel" even towards "their greatest enemies, whom they do not torment and whom they do not make languish like the Canadois" ("Les Sauvages de ce pays ne sont pas cruels, non pas méme envers leurs plus grands ennemis, qu'ils ne tourmentent pas, & qu'ils ne font point languir comme les Canadois") on the pole of torture. Nor do they eat them: at most they cut "sometimes a hand or a foot off the corpse of their enemy, that they roast on a low fire, [...] to conserve them without decay. This they do rather for spectacle and to show their valor, than for greed or cruelty" ("quelque fois une main ou un pied du corps mort de leur ennemy, qu'ils font rostir à petit feu, [...] pour les conserver sans putrefaction. Ce qu'ils font plûtost par parade, & pour faire montre de leur valeur, que par gourmandise ou par cruauté" [Pelleprat (1655) 2009, pt. 2, sec. 6: 162]).

Gradually, the exoneration becomes an apology on clichés, such as non-compliance or harshness of children towards their parents, which Pelleprat transforms into qualities:

> Children obey their parents only inasmuch as it pleases them, because they exercise no chastisement upon them.[...] [T]hey make them obey through gentleness and love rather than through fear. Their obedience and their respect toward them is nevertheless so great that I do not believe there are any more obedient or respectful in the world ("Les enfans n'obeïssent à leurs parens qu'autant qu'il leur plaist; car ils n'exercent aucun châtiment sur eux [...]: ils les font obeïr par douceur et par amour plûtost que par crainte. Leur obeïssance, & leur respect envers eux est neantmoins si grand, que je ne crois pas qu'il y en ait de plus obeïssans, ny de plus respectueux dans le monde" [Pelleprat (1655) 2009, pt. 2, sec. 8: 160]).

As well, their belief "that the world has never had a beginning" is not presented as contemptible nor is attributed to superstition, because it brings them closer to "a few ancient philosophers" ("Ils se sont persuadés aussi bien que quelques philosophes anciens, que le monde n'a jamais eu de commencement" [Pelleprat (1655) 2009, pt. 2, sec. 6: 174]). With this chapter on their "mores," all the faults that are usually considered obstacles appear rather like "dispositions to receive faith": if they have "superstitions," they

> will be advantageous to evangelical workers who will use them in their teaching: because they already believe in spirits, it will be easy to persuade them that there are good, as well as bad, and particularly one who is supremely good and the creator of all things, who gave Christians the power to chase devils ("seront avantageuses aux ouvriers Evangéliques qui s'employeront à leur instruction: puis qu'ils croyent déja qu'il y a des esprits, il sera aisé de leur persuader qu'il y en a de bons, aussi bien que de mêchans; et particulierement un qui est souverainement bon, & createur de toutes choses, qui a donné aux Chrestiens le pouvoir de chasser les diables" [Pelleprat (1655) 2009, pt. 2, sec. 8: 175]).

When Paul Lejeune in his 1632 *Relation* devoted a chapter to "Good Things Found in Savages" (subtleness of mind and generosity), he followed it with another entitled "Of Their Vices and Their Imperfections" (pride, incivility and cruelty). With Pelleprat, the affirmation of a quality is not usually balanced with a negative side: the defect is mentioned only to be contested or made relative.

As we see, it is not the ethnographer that is manifested in Pelleprat's work, but the propagandist, the bearer of a project that sees "la Terre Ferme" – the continental land – as a kind of El Dorado of colonization and missions. With this hyperbolization of the territory, the author has abandoned the register of fact for the literary portrayal of the exotic.

Réal Ouellet (Université Laval)

Part II: From the Spectacle of Nature to a New Form of Moral Sentiment

In his *Elements of Literature* published in the second half of the eighteenth century, Jean-François Marmontel, a brilliant student of the Jesuits but a disciple of Voltaire as well, observed that rather than debate theological issues, a preacher should in his sermons plead "the cause of a people and of humanity" ("la cause d'un peuple et de l'humanité" [Marmontel (1787) 2005, 244]). That Marmontel recommends duty to humanity as a fitting subject for the pulpit, and for religious discourse in general, is hardly a surprise, since the author drew his inspiration from the Enlightenment and, therefore, rejected the absolutism of an intransigent theology. But Enlightenment philosophers were not alone in holding this view. Throughout the Enlightenment, religious orators and the religious sensibility also turned away from a theology based on fear. As Marc Fumaroli underscores, the Catholic eighteenth century "no longer wishes to terrorize with vehemence" ("ne souhaite plus faire peur par la vehemence" [Fumaroli 2004, 791]). What it cultivated, rather, was "an aesthetics of grace" ("une esthétique de la grâce" [792]), which preferred the benevolent moral lessons of a kindly religion or even "the imaginative description of the sublime beauties of the created world" ("la description imaginative des sublimités du monde créé" [790]) to the radical severity of classical Catholicism, whose harsh spirit had dominated the seventeenth century. The merit of a beautiful work on classical Catholicism published a few years ago by Jean-Louis Quantin lies precisely in this – that it demonstrates the extent to which the second half of the seventeenth century in France witnessed the affirmation, and later the triumph, of a Christianity of intransigence which, in his words, "preaches penitence under the sign of the Cross" ("qui prêche la pénitence sous le signe de la Croix" [Quantin 1999, 591]). This Christianity of atonement, whose influence extended well beyond the narrow circles of a militant Jansenism, combined rigid moral standards and a patristic theology and ministry with recourse to the Church Fathers, notably Saint Augustine. The effect was to nurture both a glorified memory of the early Church and the ideal of "an austere Christianity, which does not spare sinners the sense of terror" ("un christianisme sévère, qui ne ménage pas l'effroi aux pécheurs" [455]).

How can we explain the transition from a seventeenth century haunted by a nostalgia for the purity of Church origins to an eighteenth century that favoured a religion eager to inspire humane benevolence? How can we understand this apparently striking discontinuity, which I have deliberately emphasized, between these two moments in the history of religious sensibility? In fact, as of the seventeenth century, the austere ideal of a return to the sources of Christian spirituality, which relied on the authority of the Church Fathers to better combat the corruption of the time, already coexisted with another kind of Catholicism. This other face of classical Catholicism was, to quote Jean-Louis Quantin once again, "more Jesuitical, less exclusively French, more oratorical than historical, more liturgical than erudite" ("plus jésuite, moins exclusivement français, plus oratoire qu'historique, plus liturgique qu'érudit" [Quantin 1999, 462]): it is "a Catholicism of the present" (462) – a "religion of the poor, [...] of home missions, of devotion to Mary, of the worship of the Sacred Heart and of a relative forgiveness for sin" ("religion des pauvres, [...] des missions intérieures, de la dévotion mariale, du culte du Sacré Cœur et d'une relative indulgence pénitentielle" [585]).

I would like to demonstrate that the spirit of this religion of the poor and of home missions that Quantin evokes was often the very spirit that presided over the foreign missions operated throughout the seventeenth century by the Society of Jesus. In this context, even the patristic tradition so dear to classical Catholicism can be seen in a different light. At least, this is what can be inferred from a late nineteenth-century comment by Paul Jacquinet, who wrote concerning the *Relations* of the Jesuit Paul Lejeune in New France that "practical advice, authentic descriptions of customs, commonsense moral lessons – it is in these particular ways that Father Lejeune imitates the Fathers" ("raisonnements pratiques, tableaux de mœurs pris sur le vif, leçons morales d'une application directe, voilà ce que le Père Le Jeune imite surtout des Pères" [Jacquinet 1885, 164; quoted by Quantin 1999, 463]). This observation is valid for other writers as well. Another work in the Jesuit tradition that was certainly influenced by the accounts of New France likewise provides a good deal of practical advice, lifelike descriptions of customs, and moral lessons. This was the *Relation des missions des PP. de la Compagnie de Jesus dans les Isles et à la Terre Ferme de l'Amerique Meridionale*, published by Father Pierre Pelleprat. If this *Relation* may be considered an example of the method and style of the Jesuits, the same can be said for Pelleprat's itinerary. Trained in the Jesuit colleges in which he later taught, Father Pelleprat was an educated man who, before going to America in 1651, had worked in the home missions operated by the Society of Jesus in France (Societatis Jesu 6 [1], fol. 210 v°, 215 v° and 227; 6 [2]: fol. 293 and 318 v° 227). Exemplary account, exemplary itinerary – the term "exemplary" aptly describes both the text and its author. My aim here is to demonstrate that the account and itinerary of this French Jesuit priest in South America reveals the hallmarks of a sensibility that began to flourish within European Catholicism during the age of reason. Whether, as we shall gradually see, it is through the heavy promotion of moral exempla or the often lyrical descriptions of the spectacle of a bountiful nature, an indication emerges with each example, almost as a foreshadowing, of the expression religious sensibility would assume in the following century. In short, if we now know the extent to which the exotic nature of the Jesuits' travel accounts encouraged the cultural relativism of militant philosophers during the eighteenth century, I hope through my examination of Pelleprat's *Relation* to offer a glimpse of another aspect of the Society's heritage – a religion less harsh than in its classical form, a religion that focused on ethics, the spectacle of nature and sensitivity – in short, a Catholicism of the Enlightenment (see Fumaroli 2004, 800), still to be discovered.

The Spectacle of Nature

A skilful prose narrator who sprinkled his text with scholarly references without lapsing into pedantry and a favourite object of mockery in the seventeenth century, Pelleprat evokes the "advantages" and "wonders" of Guyana, a description of which opens the fifth chapter of the second part of his *Relation*:

> I would have to build an amphitheatre much larger than those of the ancient Romans to have sufficient room to display the innumerable multitudes of animal species that have never existed in our Europe; [...] Aristotle was right when he said that a sovereign intelligence has created the work of nature. [...] God is wonderful in all of His works ("Il me faudroit dresser

> un amphitheatre beaucoup plus grand que ceux des anciens Romains, pour y faire voir cette innombrable multitude d'especes d'animaux qui ne parurent jamais dans nostre Europe [...]. C'est avec raison qu'Aristote a dit qu'une souveraine intelligence avoit mis la main à l'ouvrage de la nature. [...] Dieu est merveilleux en toutes ses œuvres" [Pelleprat (1655) 2009, pt. 2, sec. 5: 153–5]).

In this passage, Pelleprat celebrates nature not only by mentioning Aristotle, a conventional reference for a Jesuit, but also by using the metaphor of the ancient amphitheatre, which adds a note of dramatic appeal to the description of nature's wonders. Having become a *theatrum mundi*, that is, a "stage of the world," to use an expression dear to the hearts of seventeenth-century Jesuits and moralists (see Van Delft 2005), nature was then transformed into a spectacle whose beauties were to be admired. This perspective implied at least two fundamental outcomes.

The first outcome was to turn nature into a theatre, which revealed a taste for the spectacular, itself governed by an oratorical ambition – to celebrate the world and its creator so as to better act upon the senses, heart, and mind of the reader. This, at least, is what I infer from the sequel to the passage I have just quoted, wherein Pelleprat provides a lengthy description of the animal life of Guyana. Here is his depiction of the flying fish:

> The flying fish we see in these waters have the shape and size of herrings; the author of nature, seeing they could not defend themselves from attacks by other fish, gave them wings to avoid persecution; [...] their wings are not made of feathers like those of birds, but of the same substance as that of the tip of fishtails.
>
> The wonders one observes in the sky are all the more admirable in that they are not common to other climates ("Les poissons volans qu'on voit en ces mers sont de la forme, & de la grandeur des harengs; l'Auteur de la nature voyant qu'ils ne se pourroient pas deffendre des attaques des autres poissons, les a pourveus d'ailes pour en éviter la persécution: [...] leurs ailes ne sont pas de plume comme celles des oiseaux; mais de la méme matiere que l'extremité de la queuë des poissons.
>
> Les merveilles qui concernent le Ciel sont d'autant plus admirables, qu'elles ne sont pas communes aux autres climats" [Pelleprat (1655) 2009, pt. 2, sec. 5: 155]).

Here again, nature multiplies the wonders that attest to the goodness of God and that offer themselves for the reader's admiration. An even more striking detail is that Pelleprat then rewrites this passage with a description by the Dominican priest Jean-Baptiste Dutertre[8] who, in a work entitled *Histoire generale des Isles* published in 1654, observed about these same flying fish:

> I never think about these little fish without remembering the miserable state of Man before the Fall, against whom it appears that all of the elements conspire to avenge his insult to their common creator and procure for him the death he has deserved for his crime ("Je ne pense jamais à ces petits poissons, qu'il ne me souvienne du miserable estat de l'homme depuis le peché, contre lequel il semble que tous les élements conspirent pour vanger l'injure par luy faite à leur commun Createur, & luy procurer la mort qu'il a merité par son crime" [Dutertre 1654, pt. 4, sec. 1: 276]).

As we see, flying fish make wonderful apologists. For Dutertre, their weakness is a manifest sign of the corruption of nature and of man's fallen state due to original sin; for Pelleprat, these same fish have their place within the vast amphitheatre of nature, where each of us is invited to stand in awe before the spectacle of wonders. The Dominican recalls Pascal, who wrote during the same period in France: "Nature has some perfections to show that she is the image of God and some defects to show that she is only His image" ("La nature a des perfections pour montrer qu'elle est à l'image de Dieu et des défauts pour montrer qu'elle n'en est que l'image" [Pascal 1958, 249, frag. 934]). The Jesuit, however, gives voice to a sensibility that will triumph in the following century with the publication of the *Spectacle de la Nature* (1732–1742), a famous work by Abbot Noël-Antoine Pluche.

A New Form of Moral Sentiment

Pelleprat, therefore, does not describe the world in a way that emphasizes its corruption, but views it instead as the stage of a vast theatre, not only for an astonishingly diversified fauna – but for human beings as well. And this brings us to the second outcome. The New World that Pelleprat describes is also a theatre presenting a succession of short scenes whose sequence organizes the narrative, and which represent moral exempla illustrating the benefits of religion and the missionary efforts of the Jesuits. Out of a large number of examples, I have chosen a passage typical of his point of view, which is moral rather than theological. This excerpt is from a chapter titled "First Voyage of Our Fathers to the

Islands and Their Labours" (Premier voyage de nos Peres aux Isles & leurs emplois):

> In the years 1652 and 1653, this island [St. Kitts] was afflicted with many dangerous diseases, and since there was at the same time an extreme shortage of food crops, many persons died for lack of food and assistance [...].
>
> This sight greatly distressed our fathers, who considered how to relieve such overwhelming suffering: each one did what he could, using every skill suggested by charitable impulse; they impressed upon individuals who had the power to help, through either their influence or their personal means, their obligation to assist these poor wretches; and they discussed the situation in their sermons with all the zeal merited by such enormous suffering.
>
> One of our missionaries made charity for one's neighbour the subject of his daily instructions and sermons; within a short time, his words had made such an impression that people could think of nothing except helping the sick: they ran to the countryside to wherever one of these poor abandoned beings could be found; there was hardly a cabin master who did not take one home and care for him as tenderly as for one of his own children. As soon as the person died or was cured, people immediately sought out another; and if there weren't enough needy persons to satisfy people's charitable impulses, they began a holy quarrel over who would get to bring home the one who was available. [...] What a change in individuals who had come to the islands for an entirely different purpose! ("Les années 1652. & 1653. cette Isle fut affligée de beaucoup de maladies tres-dangereuses: & comme il se rencontra en mesme temps une extréme nécessité de vivres, plusieurs personnes moururent faute de nourriture, & de secours [...].
>
> "Ce spectacle toucha sensiblement nos Peres, qui penserent efficacement à pourvoir à des maux si pressans: chacun fait de son costé ce qu'il peut, & se sert de toutes les industries que la charité luy suggère: on représente aux particuliers qui y pouvoient contribuer ou de leur credit, ou de leurs moyens, l'obligation qu'ils avoient de secourir ces pauvres miserables; & on en parle aux sermons avec tout le zele que demande une si grande nécessité.
>
> Un de nos Missionnaires prend pour sujet de ses instructions familiaires, & de ses exhortations la charité du prochain: il fait en peu de temps tant d'impression dans les esprits, qu'on ne pense plus qu'à l'assistance des malades: on court à la campagne, & en tous les lieux où on espère rencontrer quelqu'un de ces pauvres abandonnez; il n'y a quasi pas de maistre de case qui n'en retire au moins un chez soy, & qui n'en prenne autant de soin que d'un de ses propres enfans. Aussi tost que leur malade estoit ou mort, ou guery, ils en cherchoient incontinent un autre; & s'il ne s'en trouvoit pas

assez pour contenter la charité de tous, ils entroient en une sainte contestation à qui emporteroit chez soy celuy qu'ils avoient rencontré. [...] Quel changement en des personnes qui estoient venuës dans les Isles à tout autre dessein!" [Pelleprat (1655) 2009, pt. 1, sec. 2: 76–7]).

By insisting upon the missionary's power to inspire, this vivid description also illustrates an oratorical ideal long inherent in the Jesuit tradition, which made the power to move hearts and motivate action the very essence of pastoral discourse. If the aim of the oratory, taught so well in Jesuit colleges during the classical age, was to influence the will by stirring the emotions, the *Relation*, when reporting the triumphs of this art, emphasizes how Jesuit eloquence could be used to plead – and here we remember Marmontel's expression – "the cause of a people and of humanity" ("la cause d'un peuple et de l'humanité" [Marmontel (1787) 2005, 244]).

If this shift to feelings of humanity and loving-kindness foreshadowed the main characteristics of Catholic sensibility in eighteenth-century France, it presaged yet more. It also offered another sign of things to come through its generous view of the moral nature of man and its optimistic anthropology, which Enlightenment philosophers would later adopt. In fact, nature here is not entirely fallen. On the contrary, it preserves a trace of its original innocence, as shown by this passage on the natural goodness of the Galibis, the Amerindians in Guyana whom Pelleprat aspired to convert:

> I believe that after this account [he writes concerning Las Casas, whose *Destruction of the Indies* he has just quoted], [...] no one will have cause to suspect that I overstep the boundaries of truth when I say that these people live in a wondrous state of innocence, and that seeing them one would say that Adam's sin is not in them as in other men, because they show little or no inclination to vice ("Je crois qu'aprés ce témoignage [...] personne n'aura sujet de soupçonner que je passe les bornes, de la verité quand je diray que ces peuples vivent dans une merveilleuse innocence, & qu'on diroit à les voir qu'ils n'ont pas peché en Adam comme les autres hommes, parce qu'on ne remarque en eux que peu, ou point d'inclination au vice" [Pelleprat (1655) 2009, pt. 2, sec. 8: 173]).

What is important here is that the evocation of this "wondrous state of innocence" authorizes what Enlightenment philosophers would extol under the terms "morale naturelle":

> But I have great cause for concern that these poor infidels [Pelleprat continues regarding the Galibis] will rise up against many Christians on Judgment Day [...], because these barbarians, knowing nothing of the mysteries of our faith and without the light of the Bible to guide them, [...] nevertheless live more innocently than do most Christians ("Mais j'ay grand sujet d'apprehender que ces pauvres infideles ne s'élevent au jour du jugement contre plusieurs Chrestiens [...], pource que ces Barbares, sans sçavoir les mysteres de nostre Foy, & sans avoir les lumieres de l'Evangile [...] vivent neantmoins plus innocemment que la pluspart d'entr'eux" [Pelleprat (1655) 2009, pt. 2, sec. 8: 178]).

Of course, although the purpose of such comments was to shame Christians, we know that their main effect was to nurture the moral anthropology of the eighteenth century, since the "innocent life" of primitive peoples allowed philosophers to portray the natural, pagan virtues very favourably when compared with the so-called virtues of the Christians, seen as artificial and destructive. But if French free thought could find, and in fact *would* find, in such observations arguments in favour of a "natural morality" that were far more able to inspire a feeling of humanity than any revealed religion, it was precisely because the Jesuits' moral anthropology could be diverted to support an unorthodox interpretation. It was also because for Pelleprat, as for the Jesuits in general, the work of religion was not so much to root out of our hearts the inclinations of a nature that was by definition corrupt, but to perfect this same nature in ourselves, as he intimates in this passage: "The good character God has given them is a grace one can never value highly enough, since a good foundation is to a large and beautiful house, what nature is to grace, whose function is to perfect nature" ("Le bon naturel que Dieu leur a donné, est une grace qu'on ne sçauroit assés priser, puisque ce qu'est un bon fondement à une belle, & grande maison, la nature l'est à la grace, le propre de laquelle est de perfectionner la nature" [Pelleprat (1655) 2009, pt. 2, sec. 8: 178]).

In this context, the missionary acts upon the natural morality of peoples somewhat in the manner a painter, poet, or orator works, according to the precepts of classical doctrine: his material is nature herself, which he then perfects with the help of art. We may better judge this after reading another moral exemplum, so characteristic of Pelleprat's writings, where he relates the story, both odd and amusing, of a young girl disguised as a boy:

> I cannot leave out the victory of a young Irish girl over the weakness of her sex. This girl had come to America when very young, and to protect her, her

father had passed her off as a boy and dressed her in boy's clothes, believing she would be less vulnerable. After the father died, the girl [...] entered the service of a master who developed a particular regard for her [...]; but as this make-believe boy was loved by everyone, and particularly by his mistress, [...] the master grew jealous and suspected his wife of being [...] too familiar with this valet: upon which, having reproached his wife many times, he encouraged and even obliged her to lead the boy into sin, while he hid in a place where he could watch without being seen [...]. The servant, tempted [...] by his mistress, remonstrated with her about the crime she wished to commit; but seeing she refused to abandon her shameful pursuit [...] was obliged to reveal his sex. Which not only created massive confusion for the master [...], but also fostered a veneration for this virtuous girl, and the inhabitants of Gardeloupe have had a very special affection for her ever since. What I find admirable in the girl is not that she disguised herself as a boy, nor that she resisted the temptations of her mistress, since she was incapable of the sin she was tempted to commit, but that she preserved such a profound innocence, although she lived a very long time with vicious, dissolute young men, with whom she could have sinned without arousing anyone's suspicion ("Je ne puis omettre la victoire qu'une jeune fille Irlandoise remporta sur la foiblesse de son sexe. Cette fille estoit venuë fort jeune dans l'Amerique, & son pere pour la conserver l'avoit travestie, & élevée sous l'habit d'un garçon, croyant qu'elle y seroit moins exposée. Le pere estant mort, la fille [...] se met au service d'un maistre qui en faisoit une estime particuliere [...]; mais comme ce garçon pretendu estoit chery de tout le monde, & particulièrement de sa maistresse, [...] le maistre en entra en jalousie, & soupçonna sa femme d'avoir [...] trop de familiarité avec ce valet: sur quoy ayant fait à sa femme diverses fois des reproches, il la presse, & mesme l'oblige d'inviter ce garçon au péché: se cachant cependant dans un lieu d'où il les pouvoit voir sans estre veu [...]. Ce serviteur sollicité [...] par sa maîtresse luy remonstre l'horreur du crime qu'elle vouloit commettre: mais voyant qu'elle ne desistoit de sa honteuse poursuite [...], il fut contraint de se faire connoistre. Ce qui donna non seulement de la confusion au maistre [...]; mais encore de la veneration pour cette vertueuse fille, dont tous les habitans de la Gardeloupe firent depuis une estime tres-particuliere. Ce que je trouve de loüable en cette fille, n'est pas qu'elle se soit travestie; ny qu'elle n'ait pas consenty aux prieres de sa maistresse, puisqu'elle estoit incapable du mal auquel on la sollicitoit; mais de s'estre conservée dans une si grande innocence, quoy qu'elle ait demeuré fort long-temps avec de jeunes hommes vitieux & libertins, avec lesquels elle pouvoit pecher sans estre soupçonnée de personne" [Pelleprat (1655) 2009, pt. 1, sec. 5: 93–4]).

This colourful exemplum serves as the conclusion to chapter 5 on the Irish mission in the Antilles, in which the author extols the Catholic faith of the Irish persecuted by the English; this spirit pervades the *Relation* as a whole, namely, that religion, by sustaining and perfecting nature, has a primarily moral purpose. The apostolate for black slaves or primitive peoples testifies to this as well: "It is difficult," Pelleprat thus writes, "to speak of the change we notice in the customs of slaves after their Baptism, for [...] many are so chaste and so honest, when they are Christians, that they would prefer to die than perform the slightest act of dishonesty ("Il est difficile de dire le changement qu'on remarque dans les mœurs des Esclaves aprés leur Baptéme, car [...] plusieurs sont si chastes, & si honnestes, quand ils sont Chrestiens, qu'ils subiroient plustost la mort que de commettre la moindre deshonnesteté" [Pelleprat (1655) 2009, pt. 1, sec. 6: 103]). And the author concludes:

> Of a large number of examples, I shall content myself with recounting two: A native slave woman, upon being invited to sin by a Frenchman on the island of Saint Christopher, declared she would rather die than perform such a wicked act and, having no other way to defend herself from this libertine, struck him so hard with a branding iron that he was obliged to back away and renounce his evil plan. The virtue of another slave woman on the island of Martinique was no less admirable: this one was a Negro and was tempted to evil by her own master; finding herself assailed by his persistent entreaties, she gave him a stinging slap and hence protected herself from his shameful pursuits. The courage of these two women, born infidels, is remarkable in that, knowing that their happiness and life depended entirely upon those who wished to lead them into sin, they not only resisted them, but treated them in the manner I have just described: a fact that should shame Christians who behave so cowardly in similar situations ("D'un grand nombre d'exemples je me contenteray d'en rapporter deux. Une Esclave Sauvage se voyant sollicitée au mal, par un François, dans l'Isle Saint Christophle, luy declara qu'elle aimeroit mieux mourir que de commettre une si meschante action, & ne se pouvant autrement defendre de ce libertin, elle le frappa si rudement d'un tison de feu, qu'il fut obligé de se retirer, & de se déporter de son mauvais dessein. La vertu d'une autre Esclave ne fut pas moins loüable dans l'Isle de la Martinique, celle-cy estoit Negre, & fut invitée par son propre maistre à mal faire, & se trouvant violentée par ses instances, luy déchargea un grand soufflet, par lequel elle se garantit de ses honteuses poursuites. Le courage de ces deux femmes nées dans l'infidelité, est remarquable en ce que sçachant bien que leur bonheur, &

leur vie dépendoit entierement de ceux qui les portoient au mal, elles ne leur resisterent pas seulement, mais les traitterent de la maniere que je viens de dire: ce qui doit faire honte aux Chrestiens, qui sont si lâches en de pareilles occasions" [Pelleprat (1655) 2009, pt. 1, sec. 6: 104]).

In short, examples, anecdotes, and stories all helped prove more convincingly than any abstract preaching the moral benefits of the missionary policy of the Society of Jesus in the New World.[9] But if the main consequence of this rhetoric of the exemplum was to multiply, in the words of Jacquinet, "examples of practical advice, depictions of customs and moral lessons" ("raisonnements pratiques, tableaux de mœurs et leçons morales" [Jacquinet 1885, 164; quoted by Quantin 1999, 463]), its function was not limited to shifting apologetic discourse about concerns that were moral, rather than doctrinal, in nature. At the same time, I believe that this rhetoric extended into a pictorial style of writing; this is particularly evident in the second part of the *Relation*, where the narrative flow is interrupted in several passages to describe the marvels of Guyanese nature. In such a case, the purpose of the depiction is to "paint," that is, to place the represented landscape before the reader's eyes, and the description becomes at once an appeal to the sensibility, even the senses, of the reader and a manifest proof of the glory of God. As an example, I will refer to a very striking passage in which Pelleprat evokes the warm and shimmering colours of the birds of Guyana:

> I can include, among the things most delightful to the eye, that beautiful variety of feathers of the many species of birds who are perched in the trees and who form a kind of lovely diversified painting with colours of many kinds: the backdrop is a beautiful green that consists not only of the leaves of trees, which, as I have mentioned, are always a lush green in this country, but also of the feathers of parrots and birds that have a green plumage and are as common in this region as sparrows are in France; against this canvas, nature forms a second rainbow on earth, which has no less of a rapport with the heavens; here we see an array of dazzling colours made by the plumage of birds: red, red-orange, crimson, sky blue, orange, yellow, violet, white, black, the hue of autumn leaves and of other colours all very pleasing to the eye, insomuch as it is true that nature enjoys parading itself in these beautiful creations, and God takes delight in being admired through his creatures ("Je puis mettre au nombre des choses qui sont les plus agreables à la veuë, cette belle varieté de plumage de tant d'especes d'oiseaux qui sont perchés sur les arbres, & qui font comme un beau tableau diversifié de toute sorte

> de couleurs: le fons est d'un beau verd qui ne consiste pas seulement au feüilles des arbres, qui, comme j'ay dit, sont toûjours verdoians en ce climat; mais aussi aux plumes des perroquets, & des Pericles, qui ont le plumage verd, & sont aussi communs en ce pays que les moineaux en France: sur ce fons la nature forme un second Arc-en-ciel sur terre, qui n'a pas peu de rapport avec le Celeste; on y voit un mélange des éclatantes couleurs que fait le plumage des oiseaux, du rouge, du nacarat, de l'incarnat, du bleu celeste, de l'orangé, du jaune, du violet, du blanc, du noir, du feüille-morte, & d'autres couleurs toutes fort agréables à la veuë, tant il est vray que la nature se joüe dans ces beaux ouvrages, & que Dieu se plaist à se faire admirer dans ses Creatures" [Pelleprat (1655) 2009, pt. 2, sec. 4: 146]).

There is no obvious utilitarian intent here, no economic or colonial predictions, only a vision that represents space as a landscape, or better still, as a painting, with its various surfaces and masses of colours so perfectly harmonized and contrasted that it is no longer possible to distinguish animal from vegetable, or the earthly from the divine. Here, the *Relation* is less interested in describing a New World than in seducing the reader through an eloquent tableau that aestheticizes represented space. Here, the *locus amœnus*, that literary topos so dear to the Ancients, is reinvented in America with apologetic designs: *Cœli enarrant Dei gloriam*, the heavens speak the glory of God, as each page of Pelleprat's *Relation* appears to proclaim.

Pelleprat's Moral Sensibility and the Jesuit Rhetorical Tradition

In a text entitled *Dialogue entre le siècle de Louis XIV et le siècle de Louis XV*, published in 1751, almost a century after Father Pelleprat's *Relation*, the Oratorian Louis Antoine Caraccioli took on the task of defending the religious eloquence of his time. In an age when nothing was more banal than to lament the decline of religious eloquence in the absence of the great orators of the century of Louis the Great, Caraccioli insisted on the beauties of contemporary Catholic sermons, whose renewed inspiration, he claimed, had benefited from a strong sentiment for nature. Here, for example, is what he writes regarding a certain Jacques Joseph Duguet, a religious writer then in fashion and now largely forgotten:

> When he paints the Universe in its cradle, he opens before our eyes all the glories of Sky and Earth. At times he calls the firmament the original preacher of Truth and represents it as a Book written in characters of light in which primitive Man learns about the author of his being, at times he

assembles the waves of the sea, gathering together both foam and shells to portray the majesty of this proud element ("Nous peint-il l'Univers dans son berceau, il fait éclore à nos yeux toutes les richesses du Ciel et de la Terre. Tantôt il nomme le firmament le premier prédicateur de la Vérité, le représente comme un Livre écrit en caractères de lumières où l'homme sauvage apprend à connaître son auteur, tantôt il amoncelle les flots de la mer, il en rassemble et l'écume et les coquillages pour montrer la majesté de ce fier élément" [Caraccioli, *Dialogue entre le siècle de Louis XIV et le siècle de Louis XV*, 1751; quoted by Fumaroli 2004, 790]).

Judging by Pelleprat's work, this same firmament, conceived as "the first preacher of Truth," and this same Book, "in which primitive Man learns to know the author of his being" ("où l'homme sauvage apprend à connaître son auteur"), were how the accounts of the Jesuit fathers described the New World to readers beginning in the seventeenth century. Mission work, therefore, offered the Jesuits an opportunity to transform America into a vast *theatrum mundi* on whose stage, as we have observed, scenes illustrating moral values were alternately portrayed alongside eloquently coloured depictions celebrating the glory of God. As a result, an oratorical ambition took over historical, moral, colonial, and apologetic concerns, and flourished in writings where to instruct and seduce, to discover and persuade, to describe and move became inseparable terms.

Of course, the hold that rhetoric maintained on the very genre of the travel narrative was a response to the overriding desire of the time to reach a wider public than the religious or political authority who mandated the authors of such accounts. In this age of eloquence, who would willingly renounce an oratorical ideal inherited from the Ancients and be driven by the double aspiration to instruct (*docere*) and delight (*delectare*)? Samuel de Champlain, disturbed by Marc Lescarbot's accusation that he caused "disgust to the reader"[10] with his many topographical accounts, wrote in the dedication to his *Voyages* in 1613: "Your Majesty will take greater pleasure in this than in preceding accounts [...]. Here you will learn, more particularly, about the ways and customs of these peoples [...] through many details that will satisfy a curious mind" ("Votre Majesté prendra un plus grand plaisir qu'aux precedents [...]. En celuy-cy vous y pourrez remarquer plus particulierement les mœurs & façons de vivre de ces peuples [...] en plusieurs particularitéz, servant à contenter un esprit curieux" [Champlain 1619, n. p. ("Au Roy")]).

Even Jean de Léry, who waged a fierce battle against the "impostures" of the often inventive cosmographer André Thevet, wrote in the 1599 re-edition of his *Histoire d'un voyage en terre du Brésil* that he had adorned his text, "adding here and there the many beautiful flowers picked [...] to embellish it and please those who enjoy such things" ("y semant plusieurs belles fleurs cueillies çà et là [...] pour l'embellir, et satisfaire à ceux qui sont désireux de telles choses" [Léry (1599) 1994, 597]). In Pelleprat's account and, more generally, in the writings of the Jesuit missionaries in America, the rhetorical aspect of the travel narrative raised this ambition to its highest degree, in that it mobilized all the resources of oratorical art to develop an apologetics that celebrated both nature's wonders and examples of extraordinary virtue, thereby helping to transform religious sensibility in France.[11]

Contemporary university research has, we know, strongly emphasized the extent to which rhetoric, far from being "a trite technique of manipulation or pretence" or "a technique of speaking too well to be honest," was, for the Jesuits of the classical age, "the creative driving force of their ethics, spirituality, exegesis, anthropology, and theology" (Fumaroli 1999, 91–2). The same holds true for Pelleprat: rhetoric was not simply a writer's guide on how to entertain and instruct. As the picturesque scenes and charming tableaux demonstrate, it was, rather, the active principle of the mutation of a religion of intransigence into a religion of the heart, a religion less concerned with instilling terror in the faithful than in awakening a moral sensibility, even an enchantment of the senses, before the spectacle of nature.

Marc André Bernier (Université du Québec à Trois-Rivières)

NOTES

1 Translated from the French by Karen Pick and Eugenia Drolet.

2 This autograph manuscript, consisting of forty-four recto-verso folios (22.5 by 13.5 cm), is part of the Marcel Chatillon collection of the Bibliothèque Mazarine. It contains neither a title page nor the "Introduction à la langue des Galibis."

3 "The zeal that our Fathers have always had for the salvation of these Barbarians made them seek every opportunity to work toward their conversion, which was the principal motive that had brought them to America" ("Le zele que nos Peres ont tousjours eu pour le salut de ces Barbares, leur a fait rechercher toutes les occasions de travailler à leur conversion, qui estoit le principal motif qui les avoit attirez dans l'Amerique" [Pelleprat [1655] 2009, pt. 1, sec. 7: 106]). The difficulty appears even greater if one

remembers the deep divisions that separated Jesuit missionaries working in the Antilles, as witnessed by an accusatory letter written by Denis Mesland to Superior Lecase. See Mesland [1654] 1988–1991, 45–53.

4 "The sieur Girault, captain from Saint-Christophe, told me that one day he had residing with him a Savage who was often beaten by the *Maboyar*, and whose blows and screams he himself could hear, until one night this poor slave was dragged to the middle of the place, where *Maboyar* so mistreated him that he was found dead there" ("Le sieur Girault capitaine de Saint-Christophe, m'a dit qu'il avoit un jour un Sauvage chez lui, qui estoit souvent battu par le *Maboyar*, dont il entendoit luy-mesme les coups & les cris, jusqu'à ce qu'une nuit ce pauvre esclave fût traîné dans le milieu de la place, & là si maltraité par *Maboyar*, qu'il y fut trouvé mort" [Saint-Michel 1652, 134]).

5 It should not be neglected that the Jesuit is a "soldier of Christ" who wants to "conquer souls for Jesus Christ" (Pelleprat [1655] 2009, pt. 1, sec. : 73). Paul Lejeune expressed well this constraining power of the mastered Indian language in his "Brieve relation. Kebec, Aoust 28, 1632": "[A]ny one who knew their language perfectly would be powerful among them" ("[Q]ui sçauroit parfaitement leur langue, il seroit tout puissant parmy eux" [Lejeune[1632] 1896, 62).

6 This rhetorical ruse has been thoroughly studied by Vachon 1977.

7 Here, Pelleprat appears to recall Carmelite Maurile de Saint-Michel who wrote: "It seems [...] that the Savages do not have the sin of Adam, because they are not ashamed of their nudity" ("Il semble [...] que ces Sauvages n'ont pas péché en Adam, car ils n'ont point honte de leur nudité" [Saint-Michel 1652, 135]). But Pelleprat changes the meaning of the passage completely, for Saint-Michel added a blatant condemnation: "[O]n the other hand, this same sin has so blinded them that they are neither men of God nor men of heaven, but only men of the Earth, without knowledge of a first being, without lifting their eyes to the sky, no more than pigs, to see from whence comes the good that they enjoy" ("[D]'un autre côté, ce même péché les a tellement aveuglés qu'ils ne sont ni hommes de Dieu, ni hommes du ciel, mais seulement hommes de terre, sans connaissance d'un premier être, sans lever les yeux au ciel, non plus que des porcs, pour voir d'où leur vient le bien dont ils jouissent" [135]). In reality, Pelleprat retakes the opposition that his predecessor already posed between insular Indians and those of the mainland. Of the first, "more hostile" and "cruel," Saint-Michel wrote: "[I]t is difficult to convert them because of their libertinage, polygamy, drunkenness [...], nudity, cruelty, defiance, dissimulation, fickleness, laziness, mother of all vice, and impunity of vice, having at present neither

faith, nor law, nor king" ("[I]l est difficile de les convertir à cause de leur libertinage, polygamie, ivrognerie [...], nudité, cruauté, défiance, dissimulation, inconstance, oisiveté mère de tout vice, et impunité de vice, n'ayant à présent ni foi, ni loi, ni roi" [135]). Of the others, infinitely more numerous, we can hope for "easier and more ordinary conversions" ("conversions plus faciles et ordinaires"), because they "surpass the islanders in religion [and] in piety" ("surpassent les insulaires en religion [et] en piété"), feeding "their relatives in their extreme age with great charity" ("leurs parents dans leur extrême vieillesse avec grande charité" [135]).

8 On the Dominican priest Jean-Baptiste Dutertre, see in particular "Appendice IV. Jean-Baptiste Dutertre et Pierre de La Vigne" in Pelleprat [1655] 2009, 251–63.

9 "I used this method and noticed through its success that it was useful to free them from deception and persuade them of the mysteries of our faith. I brought back an example that I will use as proof" ("Je me servois de cette methode, & remarquois par le succés, qu'elle estoit efficace pour les détromper, & pour leur persuader les mysteres de notre Foy. J'en rapporteray un exemple qui me servira de preuve" [Pelleprat [1655] 2009, pt. 2, sec. 8: 175]).

10 "[C]onsidering that the descriptions by said Captain Quartier [Cartier] & Champlain are of the islands, ports, capes, rivers & places they have seen, which, as they are very numerous, the reader would find more tedious than enjoyable to read, given that I myself, similarly, have sometimes skipped over the descriptions of the provinces given by PLINY in books II.IV.V.&VI of his Natural History: something I would not have done if I had had the present geographic Map" ("[C]onsiderant que les descriptions desdits Capitaine Quartier [Cartier] & Champlein sont des iles, ports, caps, rivieres, & lieux qu'ils ont veu, lesquels étans en grand nombre apporteroient plutot un degout au lecteur, qu'un appetit de lire, ayant moy-méme quelquefois en semblable sujet passé par dessus les descriptions des provinces que PLINE faits és livres II. IV. V. & VI. de son Histoire naturelle: ce que je n'eusse fait si j'eusse eu la Charte geographique presente" [Lescarbot 1609, 229]).

11 Some years ago, Jean de Viguerie accurately revealed to what extent Catholicism, in eighteenth-century France, "est devenu jésuite" (Viguerie 1981, 369).

BIBLIOGRAPHY

Bouton, Jacques. 1640. *Relation de l'Establissement des François depuis l'an 1635 en l'isle de la Martinique, l'une des Antilles de l'Amerique.* Paris: Cramoisy.

Champlain, Samuel de. 1619. *Voyages et descouvertures faites en la Nouvelle France depuis l'annéee 1615 jusques à la fin de l'année 1618.* Paris: Claude Collet.

Dutertre, Jean-Baptiste. 1654. *Histoire generale des Isles de Saint-Christophe de la Guadeloupe, de la Martinique et autres dans l'Amerique.* Paris: J. et E. Langlois.

Fumaroli, Marc. 1999. "The Fertility and the Shortcomings of Renaissance Rhetoric: The Jesuit Case." In *The Jesuits: Cultures, Sciences and the Arts, 1540–1773*, ed. John W. O'Malley, 90–106. Toronto: University of Toronto Press.

–. 2004. "Une *terra incognita* de l'histoire littéraire: l'éloquence sacrée du siècle des Lumières." *Revue d'histoire littéraire de la France* 104 (4): 783–800.

Jacquinet, Paul. 1885. *Des prédicateurs du XVIIe siècle avant Bossuet.* Paris: Veuve Belin et Fils.

Lejeune, Paul. [1632] 1896. "Brieve Relation. Kebec, Aoust 28, 1632." In *The Jesuit Relations and Allied Documents* 5: 5–76. Cleveland: Burroughs.

Léry, Jean de. 1994. *Histoire d'un voyage fait en la terre du Brésil*, 1599, ed. Frank Lestringant. Reprint, Paris: Librairie générale française.

Lescarbot, Marc. 1609. *Histoire de la Nouvelle France.* Paris: Jean Millot.

Marmontel, Jean-François. [1787] 2005. *Éléments de littérature*, ed. Sophie Le Ménahèze. Reprint, Paris: Desjonquères.

Mesland, Denis. 1988–1991. "Une lettre du père Denis Mesland, 23 September 1654." *Annales des Antilles* 27: 45–53.

Pascal, Blaise. 1958. *Pensées*, ed. Louis Lafuma. Paris: Club du meilleur livre.

Pelleprat, Pierre. [1655] 2009. *Relation des missions des pères de la Compagnie de Jésus dans les îles et dans la Terre Ferme de l'Amérique méridionale*, ed. Réal Ouellet et al. Reprint, Québec: Presses de l'Université Laval.

Quantin, Jean-Louis. 1999. *Le catholicisme classique et les Pères de l'Église. Un retour aux sources (1669–1713).* Paris: Institut d'études augustiniennes.

Saint-Michel, Maurile de. 1652. *Voyage des Isles Camercanes en l'Amerique qui font partie des Indes Occidentales.* Le Mans: Hierôme Olivier.

Societatis Jesu. "Aquitania." *Archivum romanum* 6 (1) and 6 (2).

Vachon, Hélène. 1977. "L'implicite comme langage publicitaire." *Études littéraires* 1–2: 175–94.

Van Delft, Louis. 2005. "Du théâtre de l'univers au spectacle du monde." In *Les spectateurs de la vie. Généalogie du regard moraliste*, 37–45. Québec: Presses de l'Université Laval.

Viguerie, Jean de. 1981. "Quelques aspects du catholicisme des Français au XVIIIe siècle." *Revue historique* 265 (2): 335–70.

chapter eighteen

Dans le sillage du père Joseph-François Lafitau: les *Avantures* de Claude Le Beau[1]

ANDRÉANNE VALLÉE

Depuis sa publication en 1738, le *Voyage curieux et nouveau parmi les Sauvages de l'Amerique Septentrionale* de Claude Le Beau a été l'objet de sévères critiques, notamment en raison des emprunts que l'auteur fait aux textes d'autres voyageurs. D'après le rédacteur du *Journal de Trévoux*, cette relation de voyage aurait pu être écrite sans que l'auteur ne mette les pieds en Amérique tant elle reprend plusieurs pages d'auteurs connus (voir Anonyme 1738, 1947). Gilbert Chinard estimait que Le Beau était un "effronté pillard" (Chinard 1934, 307) qui copiait et imitait ses modèles, alors que Gustave Lanctôt accusait Le Beau d'avoir "pillé à pleines mains ses prédécesseurs [...] avec une abondance égale à son audace" (Lanctôt 1948, 169). À l'instar de ces critiques, plusieurs chercheurs ont remis en question l'originalité de la relation de voyage de Le Beau (voir Cliche 1978, 52 et Taillemite 1969, 389).

Le *Voyage curieux et nouveau parmi les Sauvages de l'Amerique Septentrionale* présente deux modes discursifs entrecroisés: un mode *descriptif et didactique*, dont les sources sont souvent tirées des textes de ses prédécesseurs et qui permet à l'auteur de produire des informations sur le Nouveau Monde et les Sauvages d'Amérique du Nord, et un mode *narratif*, qui propose une intrigue amoureuse et un récit d'aventures original.[2] Dès la préface, Claude Le Beau reconnaît que des emprunts nourrissent la partie descriptive et didactique de sa relation:

> Je n'ai pas cru devoir omettre entiérement[3] quelques articles raportés par differents Missionnaires, que j'ai trouvés si bien dits & si conformes à ce que j'ai vû, que j'aurois cru manquer à mon devoir si je n'en eusse fait mention dans les occasions où ils m'ont parus necessaires. C'est pourquoi le Lecteur me pardonnera, s'il lui plaît, quelques petites Digressions que je n'ai faites

qu'à dessein de l'instruire, en le divertissant de mes malheurs (Le Beau 1738, vol. 1: s. p. [Préface]).

Comme l'ont montré Gustave Lanctôt et Serge Trudel, parmi toutes les sources utilisées par Le Beau, le texte du père jésuite Joseph-François Lafitau, les *Mœurs des Sauvages ameriquains, comparées aux mœurs des premiers temps*, occupe une place particulière (voir Lanctôt 1948, 169 et Trudel 1989, 108–10). L'aventurier en tire des exemples, des phrases, voire des paragraphes entiers, mais sans nécessairement le reprendre textuellement. Par ailleurs, Claude Le Beau n'a presque jamais recours aux guillemets.[4] Aussi le repérage des emprunts nécessite-t-il une analyse comparative minutieuse. En effet, en plus de corriger le style de Lafitau, Le Beau inscrit souvent ses emprunts dans la trame narrative du récit en créant l'illusion de l'expérience vécue et du témoignage personnel. Parfois même, le texte de Lafitau devient une véritable source d'inspiration au service de l'humour et de l'imagination du relationnaire. Ainsi, l'analyse des stratégies discursives qui permettent au voyageur de transformer et de personnaliser le discours de son prédécesseur jésuite lève le voile sur le processus d'utilisation et de récriture des sources, mais aussi sur les particularités du texte car, bien qu'il s'inscrive dans le sillage de Lafitau, ce *Voyage* est original à plusieurs égards.[5]

Le "beau" pillard ou L'astucieux Le Beau

L'examen minutieux des emprunts tirés de l'œuvre de Lafitau prouve que Le Beau considérait le texte du jésuite comme un ouvrage de référence extrêmement fiable. Comme le remarque Serge Trudel, on "peut imaginer que l'œuvre de Lafitau constitue pour l'époque une espèce d'encyclopédie qui peut sembler complète, sérieuse, et surtout pratique pour l'ensemble des renseignements qui y sont consignés" (Trudel 1989, 61). Contrairement aux ouvrages de Lahontan, de Hennepin et de Moreri (que Le Beau cite, tout en les critiquant sévèrement),[6] le texte de Lafitau est repris, modifié et nuancé, mais Le Beau ne le contredit jamais directement. Par exemple, lorsqu'il emprunte presque textuellement le contenu de cinq pages sur le "caractère" des Amérindiens (cf. Lafitau 1724, vol. 1: 103–7 et Le Beau 1738, vol. 1: 305–10), Le Beau préfère gommer les mots qu'il juge inexacts et critiquer quelques jésuites anonymes, plutôt que de s'en prendre directement au père Lafitau:

> Je ne sai aussi si ce n'est point par un mouvement de Politique, que quelques Jesuites me paroissent [...] loüer un peu trop [les Amérindiens], quand

> ils disent qu'ils ont la conception aisée, la mémoire admirable; qu'ils sont dociles, &c. car lorsque je demeurois à *Quebec* dans le Couvent des R. R. P. P. Recollets, j'ai entendu dire tout le contraire (Le Beau 1738, vol. 1: 310–11).

Au reste, Claude Le Beau est presque toujours de l'avis du père Lafitau. Il arrive parfois qu'il nuance l'image que le jésuite donne des Amérindiens en ajoutant des adjectifs dépréciatifs ("grossier," "mauvais," "vilain," "ridicule") mais, dans la plupart des cas, s'il modifie le texte de son prédécesseur, c'est pour le personnaliser, pour changer l'ordre de présentation des idées ou pour alléger le propos en modifiant la ponctuation et en supprimant des archaïsmes, des répétitions, des imprécisions ou des références aux textes anciens.

Afin de s'approprier et de personnaliser le discours du père Lafitau, Le Beau introduit souvent dans les extraits qu'il emprunte des témoignages ou des commentaires qu'il juge pertinents et qui lui permettent de s'inscrire dans la trame narrative. Par exemple, lorsqu'il est question de la "simplicité des Sauvages en matière de religion," Le Beau emprunte plusieurs phrases à Lafitau (voir Le Beau 1738, vol. 1: 259–62 et Lafitau 1724, vol. 1: 111–12, 124, 126–7 et 132); il les amalgame en y opérant quelques modifications et le résultat forme un nouvel ensemble de phrases plus ou moins original. Le Beau ajoute ensuite un long commentaire qui lui permet d'inscrire ses péripéties dans le texte qu'il récrit tout en fondant sa crédibilité:

> Pour moi je puis dire qu'ayant eu l'avantage de courir parmi ces Barbares, j'ai encore eu celui de pouvoir converser avec eux, & de si bien étudier leurs mœurs, caractère & façons d'agir, dans le peu de tems que j'ai habité dans leurs Villages, que, joint aux Memoires que j'en avois reçus des autres, sur lesquels je m'étois déja formé des idées, que j'ai trouvées en partie fausses, en partie véritables, il me seroit impossible de les mieux connoître si je passois avec eux le reste de mes jours (Le Beau 1738, vol. 1: 260–1).

Dans cet extrait, le pronom personnel "je" renvoie à Claude Le Beau, mais les phrases qui précèdent et qui suivent ce commentaire sont tirées presque textuellement de l'ouvrage de Lafitau. L'absence de guillemets et de références bibliographiques, ainsi que l'insertion du commentaire personnel permettent à Claude Le Beau de s'approprier le discours de Lafitau.[7] Mais ce n'est pas là la plus astucieuse des stratégies de Le Beau.

La manipulation des pronoms est si importante et si audacieuse dans certains emprunts que seul un examen attentif permet de déterminer si le pronom personnel "je" renvoie à Lafitau ou à Le Beau. Prenons par exemple la description des vestales amérindiennes. Lafitau introduit ce sujet en précisant que ses connaissances sur cette question sont limitées: "Je ne connsois pas assez en détail les mœurs des differentes Nations de l'Amerique, même de la Septentrionale, pour dire avec certitude, si toutes ont eu leurs Vestales" (Lafitau 1724, vol. 1: 172). Le Beau, qui utilise le texte du jésuite comme une référence, gomme le pronom personnel "je" et récrit le texte en créant l'illusion qu'il a lu l'ensemble des relations missionnaires, et non pas seulement le texte de Lafitau: "Les Missionnaires n'ont pas encore pû savoir, si toutes les differentes Nations de *l'Amerique Septentrionale*, ont eu des Filles qui ayent fait vœu de leur virginité" (1738, vol. 1: 273). Le Beau emprunte ensuite les propos du père jésuite en modifiant les pronoms personnels:

Pour ce qui est des Iroquois, que je connois un peu mieux, ils ont eu certainement leurs Vestales, qu'ils nommoient *Ieouinnon*, & qui étoient Vierges par Etat. Je ne puis pas dire, quelles étoient proprement leurs fonctions de Religion. Tout ce que j'ai pû tirer des Iroquois, c'est qu'elles ne sortoient jamais de leurs Cabanes, qu'elles s'y occupoient à de petits ouvrages, uniquement pour s'occuper (Lafitau 1724, vol. 1: 173).	A l'égard des *Iroquois*, ils ont certainement eu leurs Vestales qu'ils nommoient *Ieouinnon*, & qui étoi ent établies Vierges. On ne peut dire quelles étoient proprement leurs fonctions de Religion. Tout ce que l'on en peut avancer, c'est qu'elles ne sortoient jamais de leurs Cabanes, & qu'elles y fabriquoient de petits ouvrages, uniquement pour s'occuper (Le Beau 1738, vol. 1: 273–4).

La disparition du pronom personnel confère une valeur objective et scientifique aux observations. Le Beau crée l'illusion que c'est la science et la vérité qui parlent. Dans la suite de l'emprunt, Le Beau continue de transcrire presque mot à mot les propos de Lafitau, mais, cette fois, sans modifier les pronoms:

Elles vivoient en Communauté, autant que j'en puis juger par la Rélation que fait Jacques Carthier. [...] C'est sans doute de ces Vestales Iroquoises, que Vincent le Blanc a voulu parler, quand il dit, qu'il y a [...] quelques Vierges dédiées à leurs Dieux, comme nos Religieuses (Lafitau 1724, vol. 1: 173–4)	Elles vivoient en communauté, autant que j'en puis juger par la Relation qu'en fait *Jaques Cartier*. [...] C'est sans doute aussi de ces Vestales *Iroquoises*, dont *Vincent le Blanc* veut parler, quand il dit qu'il y a [...] quelques Vierges vouées à leurs Dieux, comme nos Religieuses (Le Beau 1738, vol. 1: 274–5)

Le Beau suit scrupuleusement le texte de Lafitau, mais il est très peu probable qu'il ait véritablement lu le texte de Cartier et celui de Le Blanc.[8] Le résultat est tout à fait réussi: Le Beau s'approprie et personnalise le texte de son prédécesseur, tout en créant, dans l'esprit du lecteur, l'illusion d'une recherche savante et d'un savoir beaucoup plus vaste qu'il ne devait l'être en réalité.[9] La manipulation des pronoms rend le repérage des emprunts encore plus complexe.[10] Le lecteur de Le Beau doit être vigilant car, si l'aventurier n'hésite pas à s'approprier le savoir et la science du père Lafitau, il n'hésite pas non plus à masquer la voix de ce prédécesseur.

Dans le chapitre qu'il consacre à la médecine amérindienne, Le Beau ne se contente pas de citer le jésuite en modifiant quelques pronoms, il récupère littéralement ses mots et il les attribue à un missionnaire qu'il a rencontré au cours de son séjour:

> Ils [les Amérindiens] sont persuadez que l'amour de cette vertu [la virginité] s'étend jusqu'au sentiment naturel des plantes; de sorte que parmi elles, il y en a qui ont un sentiment de pudeur, comme si elles étoient animées; & que pour operer dans les remedes, [...] elles veulent être employées, & mises en oeuvre par des mains chastes, sans quoi elles n'auroient aucune efficace. Plusieurs m'ont dit souvent, au sujet de leurs maladies, qu'ils sçavoient bien des secrets pour les guérir; mais qu'étant mariez, ils ne pouvoient plus s'en servir (Lafitau 1724, vol. 1: 339–40).

> Ainsi que me l'a dit le *R. P. Cirene* [Sirême],[11] les Sauvages [regardent] toutes les Plantes pour animées, ils croyent superstitieusement qu'il y en a parmi elles qui ont un sentiment de pudeur, & prétendent par consequent, qu'elles doivent être employées & mises en œuvres par des mains chastes: sans quoi ils s'imaginent qu'elles ne peuvent avoir aucune force pour le remede. C'est pourquoi un chacun n'est point propre à les cueillir de peur de souiller leur virginité (Le Beau 1738, vol. 2: 100).

Même si Claude Le Beau modifie quelque peu les propos qu'il emprunte, l'information restituée demeure la même et la mise en scène du père Sirême ajoute réalisme et cohérence au récit de l'aventurier. Il est possible que Le Beau ait véritablement rencontré le père Sirême, comme il le prétend dans sa relation mais, à l'évidence, le discours qu'il rapporte ici est celui du père Lafitau. Une lecture systématique des textes de Le Beau et de Lafitau permet de relever une multitude de liens et de parallélismes comme ceux-ci, mais l'influence du père jésuite ne se limite pas aux emprunts textuels.

Lafitau, muse de Le Beau

Qui connaît l'austérité de l'œuvre du père jésuite sera étonné de constater qu'un texte aussi dense et aussi sérieux ait pu servir de source d'inspiration à la mise en scène d'épisodes drôles, voire burlesques.[12] Prenons par exemple la remarque de Lafitau à l'égard des clystères:

> [Les Amérindiens] ignorent l'usage des lavements, & je n'en sçache qu'un seul exemple que le Pere Garnier m'a dit avoir appris d'un Sauvage, des Païs d'enhaut vers les Outaouacs, qui faisoit de ces sortes de compositions. Il les mettoit dans une vessie à laquelle il attachoit une canule, & il faisoit entrer le remede, en comprimant la vessie fortement avec les mains (1724, vol. 2: 370).

Le Beau se contente de retenir les informations de la dernière phrase pour rédiger une scène amusante qui s'inscrit dans le récit de ses aventures personnelles:

> [Je] vis à mon reveil une chose assez singulière. Au bout de la même Natte où j'étois couché, il y avoit un pauvre Sauvage malade, qui [...] s'aprêtoit à recevoir un Clystère. Le Sauvage qui devoit lui servir d'Apotiquaire, tenoit en main pour Serringue, une Vessie dans laquelle étoit le remede preparé pour le Malade. Cette Vessie avoit une petite Cannule de bois. [...] [Le malade] remuoit tellement les fesses, que cet Apotiquaire mal armé, n'en seroit jamais venu à bout, sans le secours d'une Femme qui l'aida dans ce ministère. Tandis que cette Sauvagesse tenoit ferme la Cannule au bon endroit, & à mesure que ce Valet de la Pharmacie barbare, compressoit sa Vessie, le Malade levoit de plus en plus les fesses, en criant toujours: *Al, al, al,* & faisant des grimaces épouvantables. Enfin à peine avoit-il reçû la moitié du remede, qu'ayant le derrière fort élevé, les forces lui manquérent sans doute, & il tomba tout à plat sur le ventre. Alors le Clisteriseur extrèmement irrité de voir son bon office si mal reçû, se leva brusquement; puis déchargeant sa colère sur ce Demi-clisterisé, il lui donna quantité de coups de sa flasque Serringue, tant sur le corps que sur les fesses, après quoi il disparut en murmurant (1738, vol. 2: 362–4).

Cet exemple montre que le travail de récriture des sources ne se réduit pas à un simple processus de reprise d'information, d'imitation ou de critique. Claude Le Beau crée une scène originale à partir d'un fait qu'il estime sans doute véritable parce qu'il provient d'un ouvrage sérieux. Son intention ne se limite pas ici au désir d'instruire par le biais d'un projet encyclopédique; il s'agit bel et bien de divertir le lecteur, voire de l'amuser. Les scènes comme celles-ci ne sont pas rares dans les *Avantures* de Le Beau et plusieurs d'entre elles trouvent leur source dans le texte du père Lafitau. Le cas des vieilles Iroquoises fournit un autre excellent exemple.[13]

Lafitau rapporte qu'il a vu, dans la mission où il était, des Sauvagesses qui étaient parvenues à une vieillesse extrême:

> [L'une d'elle] avoit devant ses yeux les enfans de ses enfans jusqu'à la cinquiéme génération. [...] [Une autre était d'un âge] si avancé, qu'on n'en avoit point d'Epoque, si ce n'est que les plus anciens ne se souvenoient pas de l'avoir vûë autrement que vieille. [...] [Par ailleurs,] avant que de mourir, son corps sembla rentrer en lui-même, il se rappetissa, & se recoquilla tellement, que [...] son cercüeil [...] avoit à peine deux pieds & demi de long (1724, vol. 2: 361).

Le Beau, qui aurait lui aussi fait la rencontre de deux vieilles Amérindiennes, récupère l'information donnée par Lafitau et la prête au père Sirême[14]:

> Le *R. P. Cirene*, homme digne de foi, m'a assûré qu'elles étoient toutes les deux si vieilles, qu'on avoit point d'Epoque de leur âge & que les plus Anciens du Lieu, à qui il s'en étoit informé, n'en savoient rien autrement, si non qu'ils les avoient toujours vuës Vieilles, & que ce qu'il y avoit de certain, c'est que toutes deux voyoient dans ce Village leurs Petits-Enfans de la sixiéme génération (Le Beau 1738, vol. 2: 93).

Ce qui doit retenir l'attention ici dépasse largement le cadre de l'analogie, puisque Le Beau ne s'arrête pas là. Le désir d'amuser ou de divertir le lecteur prend visiblement le pas sur le projet didactique; en effet, Le Beau réinvestit l'information fournie par Lafitau en brossant un portrait des deux femmes qui est à la fois saisissant et digne d'intérêt sur le plan de l'intention récréative:

> [Je croyais avoir rencontré] deux affreux Animaux [mais] [...] les deux Portraits hideux, que j'avois pris pour celui de quelques Monstres, étoient deux Vieilles Femmes accroupies sur leurs genoux [...]. [Ces] deux Vieilles [...]

> étoient si rappetissées, arrondies, ou recoquillées en elles-mêmes, que, enveloppées comme elles étoient, elles auroient encore bien pû passer pour deux gros pelotons de laine, si elles n'eussent point remué de leur place. Leurs mammeles pendantes & allongées en forme de boyaux pouvoient facilement être jettées par dessus leurs épaules. La peau de leur visage entiérement semblable à celle d'un Crapaud verdier ou graisset, ridée en côte de Melon sur des os décharnés; leurs yeux renfoncés, bordés de rouge & de bleu, leurs lévres aussi de diverses couleurs & remplies de bave: en un mot tout sembloit former le Portrait le plus parfait de ce que la Nature humaine à de plus affreux. [...] Ces deux Vieilles m'apercevant, sortirent de dessous leurs couvertures leurs mains ou plutôt leurs pates d'Araignées, armées de griffes; car leurs ongles longs & crochus n'avoient peut-être jamais été rognés. Munies donc de pareilles armes, elles faisoient mine de vouloir venir à moi (91–2).

Il arrive aussi que l'influence du père jésuite s'inscrive plus subtilement dans le texte de l'aventurier. Prenons par exemple la question religieuse et, plus précisément, les informations données par le père Lafitau à l'égard des serpents et des dragons. Claude Le Beau a lu attentivement le chapitre que le père Lafitau consacre aux croyances religieuses des Amérindiens: il en tire d'ailleurs de nombreux emprunts littéraux. Aucun des emprunts ne concerne les serpents et les dragons, mais Claude Le Beau n'hésite pas à récupérer les informations qu'il juge pertinentes pour les réinvestir dans le récit de ses aventures personnelles.

Lorsqu'il décide de quitter Québec pour fuir vers la Nouvelle-Angleterre, Le Beau se déguise en Sauvage et se fait peindre un serpent sur le visage (vol. 1, 108–9). Plus tard, lorsqu'il fait la rencontre d'un sorcier amérindien, celui-ci porte un extraordinaire tatouage qui est aussi en forme de serpent (vol. 2, 376–7). Ces détails sont-ils réels ou fictifs? Une chose est certaine, Claude Le Beau a la caution du père Lafitau, qui rapporte qu'en dépit du fait que la plupart des Amérindiens ont horreur des serpents, "[il] n'est presque pas néanmoins de Sauvages qui n'en fassent peindre, ou graver quelques figures sur leur corps" (Lafitau 1724, vol. 1: 253). En fait, Claude Le Beau semble croire le père Lafitau sur parole. Pour preuve, il suffit d'examiner comment l'avocat récupère les informations fournies par le jésuite au sujet de l'image et des croyances liées à la figure du dragon.

Après avoir expliqué que les Chinois "font une Divinité du Dragon volant, qu'ils appellent, l'esprit, ou le génie de l'air & des montagnes,"

Lafitau explique que "[le] Serpent a quelque chose de mysterieux chez tous les Idolâtres des Indes Orientales, de la Chine & du Japon, comme [...] chez tous les Sauvages de l'Amerique" (100 et 247). Le jésuite ajoute ensuite que "les Sauvages Méridionaux ont à peu près les mêmes idées qu'on a dans les grandes Indes, touchant le Dragon qui veut dévorer la Lune pendant son éclypse" et qu'anciennement, les Hurons avaient eux aussi "les mêmes idées à peu près" sur cette question (248–9). L'explication est accompagnée d'une magnifique gravure d'un dragon ailé dévorant la lune (250bis, planche XIII).

Le Beau reprend toutes ces informations pour nourrir un autre épisode burlesque qu'il qualifie lui-même de scène "tragi-comique" (1738, vol. 1: 240). Alors qu'il se trouve en plein cœur de la forêt, les Amérindiens qui l'accompagnent lui demandent de les aider à affronter un manitou qui, disent-ils, les empêche de traverser un lac. Le texte de Lafitau est mis à contribution pour décrire la scène, mais le résultat n'a rien d'austère: le mauvais génie auquel Le Beau doit se mesurer est certes un "Manitou des Vents" qui habite entre quatre petites montagnes escarpées, mais l'arme choisie pour l'ultime combat n'est autre chose qu'un bâton au sommet duquel Claude Le Beau a accroché ses diplômes de bachelier et de licencié de la Faculté de Paris (226–8). Les Amérindiens (qui confondent ces diplômes avec des reliques sacrées) baisent dévotement les sceaux, entonnent quelques chants religieux, puis se mettent en route avec le voyageur vers la résidence du manitou, en formant une procession ridicule:

> *Antoine* & *Nicolas* marchoient à mes côtés; tenant chacun une hache à la main. [...] [L'un] d'eux ayant une couverture trouée par le milieu, me la mit dans le cou en forme de Chasuble. *Joseph* suivoit seul derrière moi, pas à pas, tenant d'une main son arc & de l'autre trois fléches; les quatre autres *Iroquois*, tenoient le devant, deux à deux & avançoient gravement, portant tous leur fusil en forme de cierge [...], les uns chantant toujours & les autres repondant (229).

Arrivé au lieu où sévit l'esprit malin, Le Beau reconnaît dans le roc quelques "caractères hiérogliphiques" qui ressemblent à des "écritures Chinoises"; il repère ensuite un rocher qui porte "assez distinctement, en bas relief, la Figure d'un Dragon aîlé d'une grandeur énorme" (230–1), puis il se trouve face à face avec le manitou, un serpent tout à fait extraordinaire:

> [C'était] un monstrueux Serpent, de la grosseur de la jambe [...]. [Il mesurait] douze pieds de longueur, [il avait] la tête presqu'aussi grosse que celle d'un Enfant, mais plus longue; sa gueule étoit garnie de deux rangées de dents fort pointus; sa langue en forme de dard avoit bien un pied & demi; & son col étoit couvert de poil (231 et 239).

Au terme d'un affrontement exceptionnel qui ne manque pas de rappeler le combat d'Héraclès contre l'Hydre,[15] Claude Le Beau jette le corps du reptile dans un énorme brasier et porte en trophée l'affreuse tête du serpent au bout du bâton porte-reliques (232–40).

Conclusion

L'analyse comparative des textes de Claude Le Beau et de Joseph-François Lafitau permet de repérer un nombre considérable d'emprunts, d'établir une somme impressionnante d'analogies et de parallélismes et de mettre en lumière l'influence que le texte du jésuite a exercée sur celui de l'aventurier. À l'instar de Pierre Laberge, nous croyons qu'il est "erroné et injuste de parler de plagiat, car les *Avantures* prêtent forme et sens à un ensemble dont les éléments constitutifs sont "régénérés," quelle qu'en soit la provenance" (Laberge 1987, 18–19). Lorsqu'il emprunte des informations pour la partie encyclopédique de son voyage, Claude Le Beau récrit ce qu'il emprunte au père Lafitau. Les aventures personnelles du fugitif prennent aussi pour cadre des observations du jésuite, mais elles demeurent tout à fait originales et elles répondent au désir d'amuser et de divertir le lecteur.

Inscrit dans le sillage du père Joseph-François Lafitau, le *Voyage curieux et nouveau* de Le Beau se situe dans l'ensemble des relations de voyage de la Nouvelle-France comme une œuvre intergénérique, qui hésite entre la relation de voyage traditionnelle et le roman exotique. Fidèle aux intentions qu'il annonce dans sa préface, Claude Le Beau *instruit* et *divertit* son lecteur. Le récit de ses aventures personnelles et l'intrigue amoureuse qui s'y insère sont originales. Par ailleurs, l'intention récréative, voire le désir de faire rire le lecteur, fait partie des plus intéressantes caractéristiques du texte. Enfin, les aventures de Claude Le Beau en Nouvelle-France sont en elles-mêmes originales, puisque parmi tous les fils de famille envoyés en Nouvelle-France par lettres de cachet, Claude Le Beau demeure, à ce jour, le seul exilé qui ait laissé derrière lui un témoignage de son expérience du Nouveau Monde.

NOTES

1 Cet article, publié avec la permission des Presses de l'Université Laval, reprend des commentaires déjà parus dans Lebeau [1738] 2011.

2 Il est souvent difficile de départager le réel et la fiction dans les *Avantures* de Claude Le Beau, car la biographie de l'auteur est imprécise et compte encore plusieurs lacunes. Nous savons que Le Beau est né le 29 mars 1704 à Lucienne (aujourd'hui Louveciennes), à quelques kilomètres de Versailles. Il était, comme il le dit lui-même dans son texte, le fils d'un cent-suisse du roi de France. Après avoir été reçu avocat au Parlement de Paris, le 8 août 1724, Le Beau est incarcéré par lettre de cachet à Bicêtre, l'une des maisons de l'Hôpital Général de Paris, le 1er juin 1728. Le 29 avril 1729, les autorités françaises prescrivent son transfert, avec plusieurs autres prisonniers, en Nouvelle-France. Les détenus arrivent dans la colonie le 1er septembre 1729, à bord de *L'Éléphant*, un navire du roi. Le printemps suivant, Claude Le Beau est encore en Nouvelle-France, puisqu'il est témoin du mariage du chevalier de Courbuisson à Québec, le 22 mai 1730. Nous perdons ensuite sa trace. Le 14 novembre 1730, un ordre d'arrestation est lancé contre Le Beau, mais le voyageur est sans doute déjà en fuite, puisque les autorités de la colonie décident finalement de le condamner par contumace et de le pendre en effigie pour "crime d'exposition frauduleuse de fausse monnoye de carte." Ce que nous savons de la fuite de Claude Le Beau en Nouvelle-Angleterre provient de ce qu'il en dit lui-même dans son récit de voyage. Après avoir surmonté des difficultés inouïes, Le Beau aurait gagné Boston et, au cours de l'été 1731, aurait trouvé l'occasion de rentrer en Europe. Il est possible que le fugitif ait trouvé refuge aux Pays-Bas, puisque c'est à Amsterdam qu'il publie ses *Avantures* en 1738. Quoi qu'il en soit, l'avocat refait surface en Allemagne: il se rend d'abord à Erfurt où il publie la *Gazette d'Erfort* (1752), puis il s'installe à Braunschweig (1753) et s'y marie (1754). Pendant vingt ans, il gagne sa vie dans cette ville en publiant la *Gazette de Brunswic*. Claude Le Beau est décédé à Braunschweig le 17 décembre 1779, à l'âge de 75 ans (voir Berg 1999 et les pièces d'archives mentionnées à la suite de la bibliographie).

3 Nous respectons intégralement la graphie et la ponctuation des textes originaux, mais nous remplaçons naturellement le "ſ" par le "s" moderne.

4 Au ch. 28, Le Beau utilise les guillemets à quatre reprises pour signifier qu'il s'agit de citations, mais il ne précise pas que les *Mœurs des Sauvages* de Lafitau en sont la source. Au ch. 13, Le Beau nomme le père Lafitau et il le cite (avec les guillemets), puis, au ch. 30, le procédé est repris une dernière fois: Le Beau nomme et cite le père Hennepin (avec les guillemets). Ces cas sont exceptionnels: en règle générale, Le Beau n'utilise pas les guillemets

et ne donne pas ses références. Voir Le Beau 1738, vol. 1: 215–16 et vol. 2: 145–52 et 188.

5 Trudel (1989, 66–78) produit une analyse très intéressante de la transformation des sources utilisées par Le Beau et du processus de fabulation qui en procède. Il montre que le travail de récriture entrepris par l'aventurier est subjectif et que l'encyclopédisme y joue un rôle déterminant, notamment sur le plan de la crédibilité et de la rhétorique de la vérité. On y lit aussi comment les sources "informent" et "inspirent" le récit et l'histoire, et comment les notes encyclopédiques influent sur l'ordre du récit.

6 Claude Le Beau juge que "*Moreri* se trompe [...] fortement" à l'égard de l'étymologie du nom "Québec" (1738, vol. 1: 71). Il critique aussi le père Hennepin sur l'article des canots et sur celui de l'anthropophagie: "Le P. *Hennepin* raporte qu'ils [les canots] sont ronds par dessous. Cependant je n'en ai jamais vû que de plats, & je n'ai point entendu dire, ni ne crois pas même qu'il y en ait d'une autre sorte. [...] [Le] *R. P. Hennepin* se trompe, quand il dit que de tous les Sauvages, il n'y a que les *Iroquois*, qui mangent de la chair humaine. Pour moi je crois que de toutes les differentes Nations qui habitent *l'Amerique Septentrionale*, sur tout du côté du Nord, il n'y en a point ou du moins très peu, qui soient scrupuleuses sur cet Article" (96 et vol. 2, 191). Plus nombreuses, les critiques adressées à Lahontan sont aussi plus cinglantes. Voir notamment vol. 1, 91, 153, 198 et 268, ainsi que vol. 2, 77 et 288.

7 La narrativisation des descriptions empruntées à Lafitau est un procédé discursif récurrent chez Le Beau; dans son mémoire, Serge Trudel (1989, 69–73) en cite de nombreux exemples.

8 Encore aujourd'hui, les critiques se font prendre au jeu de Claude Le Beau. Par exemple, au sujet des vestales amérindiennes, O'Meara (1992, 85) critique sévèrement Le Beau, parce qu'il cite un texte aussi peu sérieux que celui de Le Blanc et, dit-elle, parce qu'il ose ajouter un commentaire personnel au sujet des "Vierges folles." Or, dans cet exemple comme dans plusieurs autres, Le Beau se contente simplement de citer plus ou moins exactement ce qu'il trouve dans l'ouvrage de Lafitau.

9 Le séjour de Le Beau en Amérique fut très court et plusieurs chercheurs ont fait la preuve que ses connaissances à l'égard du Nouveau Monde étaient limitées. Il suffit notamment d'étudier les repères géographiques insérés dans sa relation pour comprendre à quel point Le Beau méconnaissait le territoire de la Nouvelle-France et de la Nouvelle-Angleterre.

10 La manipulation des pronoms est récurrente et elle se présente sous diverses formes. Serge Trudel remarque avec justesse que Claude Le Beau personnalise souvent les pronoms indéfinis utilisés par Lafitau. Ce faisant, l'aventurier s'approprie le texte de son prédécesseur et le narrateur

"actualise l'histoire de l'auteur-héros" (Trudel 1989, 68–9). Il ne faut donc jamais perdre de vue les sources utilisées par Le Beau pour mettre en perspective son "véritable" voyage.

11 Jacques de Sirême ou Syresme (1695–1747). Jésuite français ayant intégré la Compagnie en 1712, il arrive au Canada en 1716. On croit qu'il aura pu séjourner et finir ses jours dans le Maine. Il fut missionnaire à Narantsouak, comme Claude Le Beau l'explique dans ses *Avantures* (1738, vol. 2: 6). Voir Anonyme 1738, 1950; Melançon 1929, 69 et 79, ainsi que Jones 1901, 164.

12 L'intention récréative dans le récit des aventures personnelles de Le Beau demeure l'une des plus importantes particularités du texte. Dans une perspective comparatiste, le projet encyclopédique de Le Beau gagne aussi à être mis en relief. À ce sujet, on lira avec beaucoup d'intérêt la très convaincante démonstration de Serge Trudel (1989, 70–6).

13 L'analogie entre les vielles Iroquoises dont Lafitau parle dans son chapitre sur la médecine et les deux vieilles Iroquoises que Claude Le Beau rencontre à Narantsouak est mentionnée par Trudel (1989, 69–70).

14 Voir n. 10.

15 Après avoir été criblé de plombs, battu avec le bâton porte-reliques et transpercé d'une flèche, le serpent meurt finalement décapité par un coup de hache.

BIBLIOGRAPHIE

Anonyme. 1738. "Avantures du Sieur Claude Le Beau, avocat en parlement," *Journal de Trévoux* 38 (102): 1945–1953.

Berg, Britta. 1999. " 'Vor dieses mahl noch ...'": Claude Le Beau und die *Gazette de Brunswic* (1753–1773)." *Leipziger Jahrbuch zur Buchgeschichte* 9: 77–96.

Chinard, Gilbert. 1934. *L'Amérique et le rêve exotique dans la littérature française au XVIIe et au XVIIIe siècle.* Paris: Droz.

Cliche, Marie-Aimée. 1978. "*Aventures du Sieur Claude* Le Beau *avocat en parlement ou Voyage curieux et nouveau parmi les sauvages de l'Amérique septentrionale,* récit de Claude Lebeau." In *Dictionnaire des œuvres littéraires du Québec,* éd. Maurice Lemire, vol. 1: 51–3. Montréal: Fides.

Jones, Arthur Edward. 1901. "Catalogue of Jesuit Missionaries to New France and Louisiana, 1611–1800." In *The Jesuit Relations and Allied Documents,* éd. Reuben G. Thwaites, vol. 71: 119–217. Cleveland: Burrows Brothers Company.

Laberge, Pierre. 1987. *Analyse des* Avantures du Sr. C. Le Beau, *relation de voyage publiée en 1738,* mémoire de maîtrise. Québec: Université Laval.

Lafitau, Joseph-François. 1724. *Mœurs des sauvages ameriquains comparées aux mœurs des premiers temps,* 2 vol. Paris: Saugrain l'aîné et Charles-Estienne Hochereau.

Lanctôt, Gustave. 1948. “Les aventures imaginaires d’un fils de famille.” In *Faussaires et faussetés en histoire canadienne*, 148–70. Montréal: Variétés.

Le Beau, Claude. 1738. *Avantures du S^{R}. C.* Le Beau, *avocat en parlement, ou Voyage curieux et nouveau, Parmi les Sauvages de l’Amérique Septentrionale. Dans lequel On trouvera une Description du Canada, avec une Relation très particulière des anciennes Coutumes, Mœurs & Façons de vivre des Barbares qui l’habitent & de la manière dont ils se comportent aujourd’hui*, 2 vol. Amsterdam: Herman Uytwerf.

Le Beau, Claude. [1738] 2011. *Avantures du sieur Claude Le Beau, avocat en parlement. Voyage curieux et nouveau parmi les Sauvages de l’Amérique septentrionale*, éd. Andréanne Vallée. Québec: Presses de l’Université Laval.

Melançon, Arthur. 1929. *Liste des missionnaires jésuites. Nouvelle-France et Louisiane, 1611–1800.* Montréal: Collège Sainte-Marie.

O’Meara, Maureen F. 1992. “The Truth / Fiction of Encounter: *Avantures du Sr. Charles* [*sic*] *Lebeau ou Voyage curieux et nouveau parmi les Sauvages.*” *Romance Languages Annual* 3: 84–8.

Taillemite, Étienne. 1969. “Lebeau, Claude.” In *Dictionnaire biographique du Canada*, éd. Ramsay Cook et Réal Bélanger, vol. 2: 388–9. Québec: Presses de l’Université Laval.

Trudel, Serge. 1989. *Narration et encyclopédisme dans les “Avantures” du Sr Claude Le Beau*, mémoire de maîtrise. Montréal: Université de Montréal.

Pièces d’archives

Archives De L’assistance Publique—Hôpitaux De Paris: 4Q–5, *f.* 6.

Archives Départementales Des Yvelines: AD078–1080401: fol. 167 et 5MI1722: fol. 118.

Archives Nationales Du Canada: MG8–A6, bobine C-13589 (X): 366; MG1-série C11A, bobine F-55 (LV): fol. 5–7; MG1-série E (CCLXV), bobine F-708 (dossier Lebeau).

Archives Nationales Du Québec (Fonds Drouin), *Registre de la paroisse Notre-Dame de Québec*, bobine 3142: fol. 66 v°.

Centre Historique Des Archives Nationales De France: X^{1A} 9327: f. 94; COL. B53$^{2:}$ fol. 548 v°-549 et fol. 572–3 v°; COL. B53$^{1:}$ fol. 134 r° et v^{o}.

chapter nineteen

Postface: De l'usage de la comparaison dans les écrits des Jésuites sur les Amériques

HANS-JÜRGEN LÜSEBRINK

Comparer: retours et transformations d'un paradigme épistémologique

La comparaison comme acte de connaissance, après avoir connu une place épistémologique plutôt marginale dans le domaine des lettres et sciences humaines occidentales pendant ces 150 dernières années, vit actuellement une certaine renaissance, sous d'autres formes et à travers d'autres enjeux que ceux qui la caractérisaient pendant l'âge classique et l'époque des Lumières. Le romaniste Ulrich Schulz-Buschhaus, dans un article programmatique intitulé "Die Unvermeidlichkeit der Komparatistik" ("L'incontournabilité des études comparées"), paru en 1979, a précisément souligné, face au recentrement national des disciplines littéraires et historiques depuis la première moitié du XIXe siècle, la nécessité impérative de la démarche comparatiste pour toute analyse des phénomènes littéraires et culturels.[1] De récentes études, notamment en théorie de la communication interculturelle, en histoire et en études politiques, ont à la fois montré le caractère incontournable, sur le plan épistémologique, de la comparaison et la nécessité de questionner les fondements de ses usages traditionnels et ainsi de la repenser, notamment en relation avec les concepts de transculturalité et d'interculturalité, d'histoire croisée, de mémoire interculturelle et de transfert culturel (voir Matthes 1990, Osterhammel 1996, Middell 1999, Werner et Zimmermann 2002 et, au sujet des transferts transatlantiques dans la seconde moitié du XXe siècle, Rausch 2007). Michel Espagne, entre autres, a mis en garde contre l'aporisme voulant que "le comparatisme présuppose des aires culturelles closes pour se donner les possibilités d'en dépasser ultérieurement les spécificités grâce à des catégories abstraites" (Espagne 1994, 112; voir également Espagne

1999). Il critique en particulier le fait que le comparatisme ait tendance à "pétrifier les oppositions" et qu'il "oppose des groupes sociaux au lieu de mettre l'accent sur les mécanismes d'acculturation" (Espagne 1994, 115). De même, l'historien critique le fait que le comparatisme tend, depuis le XIXe siècle, à opérer à partir d'un "point de vue national," renforçant ainsi "le concept de nation" (115). Et, enfin, il souligne que le paradigme comparatif traditionnel "me[t] l'accent sur des différences avant d'envisager des points de convergences" et des "imbrications préexistantes" (118).

Jusqu'aux premières décennies du XIXe siècle, à travers la naissance de disciplines comme la linguistique générale et comparée, l'étude comparée des religions et des civilisations et la littérature comparée – disciplines émergeant aux alentours de 1830 –, on peut en effet observer la présence forte, voire centrale, de l'acte de comparer, qui s'enracine dans l'importance que lui accordait déjà la rhétorique classique. Dans le *Dictionnaire universel* de Furetière, qui constitue un ouvrage de référence pour la première moitié du XVIIIe siècle, le champ conceptuel du comparatisme se trouve ancré dans une série de notions qui cernent en même temps sa fonction au sein de l'*épistémè* classique et les procédés rhétoriques qui y furent associés. Le *Dictionnaire* donne au terme "Comparaison" le sens de "rapport de deux choses mises l'une devant l'autre, pour voir en quoy elles conviennent ou différencient" (Furetière 1690, s. p.), et précise qu'il s'agit aussi "d'une figure de Rhétorique et de Poésie qui sert à l'ornement et à l'éclaircissement d'un discours." L'article "Comparer" définit ce verbe, d'une part, comme l'acte de "conférer une chose avec une autre, [de] les faire voir ensemble, pour examiner en quoy elles se ressemblent, ou en quoy elles diffèrent" (Furetière 1690, s. p.), et cite l'exemple des *Hommes illustres* de Plutarque, renvoyant implicitement à l'article "Parallèle." D'autre part, le verbe "comparer" signifie aussi, d'après Furetière, "égaler, vouloir rendre semblable."

Le champ notionnel de la comparaison dans le *Dictionnaire* de Furetière renvoie ainsi aux fonctions mêmes que la comparaison a occupées dans la rhétorique classique. Celles-ci peuvent se résumer essentiellement à quatre. D'abord, la comparaison est sous-tendue par l'idée de *mesure*, qui peut s'énoncer par opposition, par ordination qualitative ou quantitative, permettant ainsi de situer des phénomènes par rapport à d'autres, par exemple à travers des degrés de différences, de perfection ou d'évolution culturels (voir Jouvancy [1712] 1892), idée dominée toutefois, à l'âge classique, par la comparaison omniprésente avec l'Antiquité.[2] Ensuite, la comparaison est, sous quelques aspects, disqualifiante ou, plutôt, *relativisante*: "Traiter sa patrie, sa famille, comme une patrie, une famille, c'est déjà la priver d'une partie de son prestige; de là le caractère quelque peu blasphématoire du rationalisme, qui se refuse de considérer les valeurs concrètes dans leur unicité," soulignent par exemple Perelman et Olbrechts-Tyteca ([1970] 1976, 332) en se référant à la rhétorique classique. Cette fonction de la comparaison peut aller de pair avec la réévaluation ou la légitimation de phénomènes soit nouveaux, soit sous-évalués ou encore marginalisés. La comparaison occupe, à cet égard, une place centrale dans les procédés oratoires par lesquels on montre, dans la rhétorique classique, "la grandeur d'une chose" qui peut s'effectuer, comme le formule Balthazar Gibert dans *La Rhétorique ou les règles de l'éloquence*, "par sa nature en elle-même, ou par comparaison" (Gibert [1729] 2004, 145).[3] En troisième lieu, la comparaison occupe dans la rhétorique classique une fonction d'*ornement*, susceptible, comme les métaphores, les hyperboles ou d'autres figures, de rendre les phénomènes décrits ou évoqués plus imagés, plus "palpables" et plus "vifs" (495). Les comparaisons insérées "ne sont pas," selon Nicolas Boileau, "simplement mises pour éclaircir et pour orner le discours, mais pour amuser et pour délaisser l'esprit du Lecteur, en le détachant de temps en temps du principal sujet, et le promenant sur d'autres images agréables à l'esprit" ([1693] 1810, 284). Enfin, la comparaison entre des événements et des personnages d'époques différentes, mais sous-tendus par un même esprit, un même mode de penser et d'agir, renvoie à la fonction de *connaissance historique* conçue comme *magistra vitae*, ainsi que le formule Séran de La Tour dans la préface au *Parallèle de la conduite des Cathaginois à l'égard des Romains, dans la seconde Guerre punique, avec la conduite de l'Angleterre à l'égard de la France dans la guerre déclarée par ces deux puissances en 1756*. Dans les collèges jésuites de l'époque, cette conception de l'histoire comme *magistra vitae* paraît fonder la pratique du registre comparatif et, plus particulièrement, du parallèle:

> La connoissance du passé est la règle de conduite la plus sûre pour l'avenir: elle fait voir les motifs, les desseins et les menées de chaque puissance. C'est l'unique objet de ce parallèle de la conduite des Anglois, dans la guerre de 1756, avec la conduite des Carthaginois dans la seconde guerre punique (1757, xix).[4]

La rhétorique des XVIe, XVIIe et XVIIIe siècles est ainsi ancrée, en ce qui concerne le recours à la comparaison, dans une conception cyclique de l'histoire. La mise en parallèle des événements et des personnages de l'Antiquité et de la modernité était à la base du genre des parallèles, né entre la fin du XVIe siècle (avec la réflexion théorique d'Henri Estienne) et le début du XVIIe, qui vit apparaître les premiers ouvrages portant dans leurs titres le terme de "parallèle."[5] Le genre littéraire et historiographique du parallèle devint ainsi "l'expression adéquate d'une conception cyclique de l'histoire" ("In diesem Sinn wird das historiographische Genre der 'Parallèle' im 17. Jahrhundert – am deutlichsten bei Perrault – zur adäquaten Ausdrucksform der zyklischen Geschichtsauffassung" [Schlobach 1980, 235]). Il impliquait, comme l'a notamment montré Jochen Schlobach dans *Zyklentheorie und Epochenmetaphorik*, une étude sur les modèles historiographiques du XVIIIe siècle, d'une part, un modèle de connaissance par analogie – en premier lieu entre l'Antiquité et le présent, mais qui fut successivement transposé à des comparaisons entre différentes nations, entre différentes institutions ou encore entre des monarques ou hommes d'État[6] d'époques et de cultures différentes – et, d'autre part, une conception cyclique de l'histoire supposant l'hypothèse fondamentale d'une répétitivité de l'évolution historique selon une logique de l'essor et de la décadence (voir Schlobach 1980, 235). "Sur son versant politique," le parallèle procède bien, comme le soulignent Thierry Belleguic et Marc André Bernier, "d'une logique du rapprochement analogique entre deux figures," la seconde tirant sa gloire de "se confondre et ne former qu'un tout" avec la première, qu'elle fait "renaître" (Belleguic et Bernier 2007, 9). En même temps, le XVIIIe siècle donne à voir, comme le corpus des *Relations* des Jésuites l'atteste également, un "paysage éclaté et parfois insolite, façonné par des temporalités diverses et incertaines" (16).

De la mise en parallèle à la comparaison: le cas de lafitau

L'œuvre du père Joseph-François Lafitau, en particulier son ouvrage programmatique *Mœurs des sauvages amériquains, comparés aux mœurs des premiers temps* (1724), représente, sans doute, au sein de toute la littérature des Jésuites sur le Nouveau Monde, l'ouvrage dont la structure est le plus étroitement construite autour de la comparaison, omniprésente dans cet ouvrage. En effet, la préface aux *Mœurs des sauvages* se fonde sur la tradition rhétorique, peu novatrice, du parallèle entre les Anciens et les Modernes: "L'Ouvrage que j'ai l'honneur d'offrir à votre Altesse Serenissime," écrit Lafitau dans son "Épître à Monseigneur le Duc d'Orléans" qui fait figure de préface, "est une peinture des Mœurs des Peuples du nouveau Monde. Ces Mœurs, et le Parallèle que j'en fais avec celles des premiers temps, ne présentent que des dehors Sauvages, et des Coutumes barbares, qui sont bien éloignées de la politesse de notre siècle et de notre Nation" (Lafitau 1724, vol. 1: s. p. [1]). À regarder de plus près la présence et les formes d'usage de la comparaison dans l'ouvrage même, on constate néanmoins que ces dernières vont bien au-delà du geste d'établir des degrés de civilisation à partir des valeurs posées d'emblée par l'Antiquité gréco-romaine et la culture classique française du XVIIe siècle. On trouve, en effet, deux fonctions dominantes de la comparaison: celle, d'une part, qui consiste à penser l'origine de l'humanité et le concept de nature humaine et, d'autre part, celle qui se présente comme un outil différencié de connaissance culturelle et anthropologique. Le fondement comparatif des concepts de "nature humaine" et d'"origine de l'humanité" se trouve, certes, à la base de cet ouvrage, qui perçoit essentiellement les civilisations américaines précolombiennes comme un stade antérieur du développement de l'humanité, appelé tour à tour "barbare," "sauvage," "naturel" et "originel." Le recours à la comparaison sert ici, comme dans d'autres écrits des Jésuites sur le Nouveau Monde, à retrouver, par-delà la christianité, une "origine adamique" de la civilisation (voir Détienne 1981, 20). Dans cette perspective, l'originalité de Lafitau résiderait, selon Marcel Détienne, dans sa capacité à "étendre la comparaison au plan intellectuel," en montrant l'étrange "conformité" des mœurs et coutumes entre les Sauvages de l'Amérique et les Anciens: dans "les pratiques d'abstinence, les codes de l'initiation, les gestes du sacrifice, la forme des cabanes, l'institution des Vestalines" (20).

Le frontispice de l'ouvrage (voir Annexe) présente, à travers son programme visuel, cette thèse fondamentale voulant que l'origine de l'homme et des civilisations soit aussi bien saisissable par la lecture des auteurs de l'Antiquité que par l'observation des peuples de l'Amérique. La connaissance est ici censée procéder par comparaisons, les deux civilisations, extrêmement distantes dans le temps et dans l'espace, paraissant à la fois très différentes – par exemple quant à leur rapport à l'écriture et à l'image –, mais en même temps foncièrement semblables et ce, singulièrement quant à certaines valeurs fondamentales et certains comportements humains s'exprimant, par exemple, à l'égard de la religion:

> Le Frontispice présente une personne en attitude d'écrire, et actuellement occupée à faire la comparaison entre plusieurs monumens de l'Antiquité,

> Pyramides, Obélisques, Figures, Panthées, Médailles, Auteurs anciens, et entre plusieurs Cartes, Voyages et autres curiosités de l'Amérique au milieu desquelles elle est assise. Deux génies rapprochent ces monumens les uns des autres, lui aident à faire cette comparaison, en lui faisant sentir le rapport qu'ils peuvent avoir ensemble. Mais le temps à qui il appartient de faire connoître toutes ces choses, et de les découvrir à la longue, lui rend ce rapport encore plus sensible en la rappellant à la source de tout, et lui faisant comme toucher au doigt la connexion qu'ont tous ces monumens avec la première origine des hommes, avec le fond de notre Religion, et avec tout le système de révélation faite à nos premiers Pères après leur péché, et qu'il montre dans une espèce de vision mystérieuse (Lafitau 1724, vol. 1: s. p. [première page de l'"Explication des planches et figures contenuës dans le premier tome"]).

L'exposition d'une thèse affirmant l'existence d'une civilisation des "premiers temps" commune aux sociétés occidentales et non occidentales, en l'occurrence américaines, paraît ainsi constituer l'intention première de l'ouvrage de Lafitau, porté par un usage rhétorique d'emblée très conventionnel de la comparaison, même si celui-ci finit par donner un statut culturel revalorisé aux sociétés amérindiennes. La méthode comparative y sert en premier lieu, comme l'ont montré les études sur Lafitau (Fenton et Moore 1974, Motsch 2001 et Lemay 1983), à établir que "les Amérindiens descendent des peuples barbares qui habitaient la Grèce avant l'arrivée des Grecs et qui avaient dû en partir pour échapper à la guerre et assurer leur survie. De la Grèce antique, ces peuples seraient passés par voie de terre en Amérique, où ils seraient arrivés peu de temps après le Déluge" (Motsch 2001, 61).[7] Même si les comparaisons entre les "premiers temps" de l'Antiquité, historiquement lointains, et ceux, géographiquement éloignés, des Amérindiens contemporains sont censées illustrer en premier lieu cette thèse fondamentale, elles semblent revêtir successivement, au cours de l'ouvrage et à la faveur de sa structure argumentative, d'autres fonctions, l'une d'entre elles consistant notamment à mettre l'accent sur les soubassements communs de la civilisation occidentale et judéo-chrétienne et des civilisations amérindiennes, que le discours culturel et religieux des XVIe et XVIIe siècles avait tendance à enfermer dans une altérité anthropologique et culturelle radicale.

Le second type d'usage de la comparaison, que l'on retrouve également dans les écrits de nombreux autres jésuites, reflète une toute autre dynamique de la connaissance. Celui-ci est ancré dans l'une des fonctions essentielles de cette figure telle que la définit la rhétorique classique, soit l'identification, au moyen de la méthode comparative, des phénomènes et des structures semblables, afin de pouvoir dresser un tableau différentiel des sociétés et des cultures. Le champ des comparaisons ne s'y limite pas aux seuls auteurs et sociétés de l'Antiquité, mais englobe d'autres sociétés non européennes, à partir d'observations personnelles de Lafitau ou, le plus souvent, de relations d'autres auteurs. Prenons deux exemples: les rites d'initiation du peuple des Gayanais, habitant en Guyane (île de Cayenne), que Lafitau tire en grande partie d'une relation du père jésuite Neuville, qu'il cite d'ailleurs *in extenso* (Lafitau 1724, vol. 2: 20–2).[8] Ces rites sont par la suite commentés à travers une série de comparaisons avec l'Antiquité (les soldats de Mithra, les Lacédémoniens), mais aussi à la lumière des coutumes des habitants des Caraïbes et de celles des Mexicains et des Péruviens, série qui débouche sur un tableau de similitudes et différences culturelles (23).

Le chapitre consacré aux divinations et à l'idée de l'âme, qu'il y voit associée, procède, en ce qui concerne sa structure argumentative, de manière inverse, tout en ayant recours aussi à toute une série de comparaisons. Lafitau part ici du constat suivant: "Bien que tous les peuples s'attachassent à la Divination, il y avoit cependant différentes manières d'y parvenir" (89), ainsi que de réflexions générales sur l'idée de l'âme, qu'il tire des Anciens – entre autres Plutarque et Virgile – et de Descartes. Ces réflexions se trouvent entremêlées d'observations personnelles ou de première main sur les formes de divination chez les Iroquois. Bref, comme le résume Edna Hindie Lemay, chez Lafitau, références à l'Antiquité classique, récits de voyageurs récents et observations personnelles s'entremêlent "pour alimenter cette nouvelle histoire de l'humanité qui commence à voir le jour au XVIIIe siècle" (Lemay 1983, 25). Toutefois, suivant les termes de François Hartog, par cette manière de rendre observations et réflexions,

> Lafitau ne vise nullement à fonder une ethnologie comparée, parce que la raison d'être de tout ce travail d'enquête comparative n'est pas à chercher ni du côté des Sauvages ni du côté des Anciens, mais chez les Modernes. L'ethnologie passe par la théologie. Le fondement de sa comparaison est proprement un article de foi. Par ce livre, il entend en effet réfuter les athées et les sceptiques, en démontrant que les Sauvages comme les Anciens "témoignent" de l'existence d'une religion primordiale (Hartog 2005, 209).

Dynamiques comparatives

Critique des sources et mise en perspective de l'observation empirique

La fréquence, la forme et la fonction des comparaisons employées dans les écrits des Jésuites des XVIIe et XVIIIe siècles dépendaient en premier lieu du genre textuel et discursif utilisé. Elles s'imposaient, dans l'optique des auteurs, dans les genres du traité, des Mémoires et de la description historique et naturelle, tandis qu'elles s'avéraient beaucoup plus rares dans le genre proprement dit de la relation, qui est sous-tendu par une trame axée autour d'un ordre chronologique et événementiel et un code d'écriture spécifique (voir Ferland 1992 et Thérien 1995). Le père Brébeuf a ainsi recours, dans sa *Relation de ce qui s'est passé dans le pays des Hurons en l'année 1636*, à des comparaisons avec l'Antiquité qui seront amplifiées ultérieurement, et notamment par Lafitau. Au sein d'une description détaillée de la mythologie des Hurons, Brébeuf utilise ainsi une comparaison avec le personnage ancien de la déesse romaine de l'agriculture et de la fécondité, qu'il rapproche de la figure mythologique d'Iouskeha, que les Hurons auraient considérée "comme faisait jadis l'antiquité profane une Cérès: à les entendre, poursuit le jésuite, c'est *Iouskeha* qui leur donne le blé qu'il mangent, c'est lui qui le fait croître et le conduit à maturité" (Brébeuf [1637] 1996, 113). Le père Lejeune a plus souvent recours à des comparaisons entre l'Ancienne et la Nouvelle-France, en décrivant des similitudes et des différences qu'il remarque sur le plan de la faune et de la flore, du climat, de la fertilité du sol, ainsi que des mentalités et des cultures. Ainsi compare-t-il, par exemple, la fertilité des sols en France et au Canada: "L'orge est plus beau qu'en France: et je ne doute point que si le pays estoit découvert qu'on ne rencointrast des vallées très fertiles" (Lejeune [1634] 1897, 28). Il établit également des similitudes entre des données géographiques:

> Les trois Rivières me semblent comme l'Anjou: c'est un païs sablonneux, je croy que la Voghne s'y plairoit [...]. Kébec est diversifié, [...] le seigle y vient fort bien; au moins je puis asseurer que j'ay veu croistre icy de tous ces grains aussi beaux comme en France. Les pois sont plus tendres et meilleurs que ceux qu'on y apporte par la navigation (Lejeune [1637] 1898, 162).[9]

En regard de la logique des parallèles entre l'Antiquité et l'époque moderne, et de celle de l'établissement des similitudes et des différences entre l'Ancien et le Nouveau Monde, l'analyse de l'usage des comparaisons chez Lafitau et certains jésuites de la seconde moitié du XVIIIe siècle s'inscrit dans un paradigme de connaissance très différent. En effet, chez Lafitau, on peut observer, d'une part, une tension entre l'usage de la comparaison comme une sorte de "rituel rhétorique" de la mise en parallèle et, d'autre part, son inscription dans une étude comparée des civilisations et des cultures amérindiennes. Cette étude allait avoir une influence certaine sur la naissance de l'anthropologie et de l'ethnologie modernes (voir Fenton et Moore 1969 et 1974, Certeau 1980 et Lemay 1983), ainsi que sur des disciplines-phares du tournant du XVIIIe siècle, telle l'étude comparée des langues, des religions et des littératures populaires, comme on le remarque dans l'œuvre de William Robertson et, surtout, chez Johann Gottfried Herder, qui fut fortement influencé par l'œuvre de Lafitau (Fenton et Moore 1974, cvi–cviii). Le père Pierre-François-Xavier de Charlevoix, dans sa volumineuse *Histoire du Paraguay* (1757), se proposant de dresser un tableau à la fois de l'histoire naturelle, civile et religieuse des établissements jésuites dans cette région, a très peu recours à des comparaisons, parce qu'il tient à souligner d'emblée le caractère *incomparable* et unique de l'entreprise jésuite, qu'il établit, singulièrement, sur une série de comparaisons qu'il développe dans la préface de son ouvrage:

> Je parle de ces Républiques chrétiennes, dont le Monde n'ait point encore vu de modèles, et qui ont été fondées dans le centre de la plus féroce barbarie, sur un plan plus parfait que ceux de Platon, du Chancelier Bacon et de l'illustre Auteur du Télémaque, par des Hommes, qui n'en ont cimenté les fondemens que de leurs sueurs et de leur sang, qui animés du seul glaive de la parole, et l'Évangile en main, ont affronté la fureur des Sauvages les plus intraitables et que les armes des Espagnols n'avoient fait qu'irriter; les ont civilisés et en ont fait des Chrétiens, qui depuis un siècle et demi font l'admiration de tous ceux qui les ont vus de plus près (Charlevoix 1757, vol. 1: 5).

En s'abstenant largement d'avoir recours, comme nombre de ses prédécesseurs et contemporains, aux comparaisons transhistoriques ou transculturelles, Charlevoix se limite, s'il utilise le registre comparatif, à des mises en parallèle succinctes afin de souligner le caractère singulier de certains événements ou personnages. Il évoque par exemple, au début de son *Histoire et description générale de la Nouvelle-France* et à la faveur d'une mise en parallèle entre les conquérants français et espagnols, le caractère unique de ces derniers:

> J'accorderai sans peine aux Espagnols que nous n'avons point eu dans le Nouveau Monde de Voyageurs, de Conquérans, de Fondateurs de Colonies, qu'on puisse mettre en parallèle avec ceux de leur Nation, qui ont paru avec plus d'éclat sur le théâtre du Nouveau Monde, si avec leur mérite personnel on met dans la balance la grandeur de leurs conquêtes et la richesse des Provinces, dont ils ont augmenté la Monarchie (Charlevoix 1744, vol. 1: 2).

L'œuvre ethnographique et anthropologique des jésuites exilés, publiant leurs ouvrages sur l'Amérique après leur expulsion des États de la couronne espagnole en 1767, notamment en Italie, en Autriche et en Allemagne, constitue un relais encore relativement peu exploré entre l'œuvre pionnière de Lafitau et l'anthropologie comparée du début du XIXe siècle. L'ouvrage monumental de Martin Dobrizhoffer, jésuite d'origine autrichienne ayant vécu comme missionnaire au Paraguay entre 1749 et 1768, en fournit un exemple parmi de nombreux autres. Son *Histoire des Abiponi, une nation guerrière à cheval au Paraguay*, parue en 1783 en latin et parallèlement en allemand, constitue, avec ses trois volumes totalisant 1 700 pages, l'ouvrage ethnographique le plus détaillé consacré à l'ethnologie des sociétés amérindiennes au XVIIIe siècle. Comme chez Lafitau, on relève chez Dobrizhoffer de nombreuses comparaisons avec l'Antiquité, notamment entre les Amérindiens et les Gaulois ou encore les ethnies germaniques décrites par Tacite.[10] Il compare ainsi les principes guidant l'élection des chefs militaires abiponi, parfois d'origine modeste, dans une société faisant, semble-t-il, abstraction de toute considération liée à la noblesse et à ses droits particuliers, avec ceux observés par Tacite chez "les anciens Germains" (Dobrizhoffer 1783, vol. 2, 2e part.: 138). Afin d'expliquer le sentiment fort d'attachement à la terre qu'il observe chez les Indiens du Paraguay, Dobrizhoffer fait notamment référence à Ovide – "L'agonie est plus douloureuse que la mort elle-même"[11] ("Morsque minus poenae / Quam mora mortis habet" [Ovide 1874, v. 82 et 92]) – et à Cicéron (*De oratore*). La coutume de certains peuples amérindiens de se couper la partie proéminente des cheveux est comparée par Dobrizhoffer avec la même coutume observée par Plutarque (*Vie de Thésée*) chez les peuples de l'ancienne Germanie (31). Le chapitre de son ouvrage consacré aux coutumes matrimoniales des Abiponi est introduit par un tableau comparatif succinct qui évoque, à partir de références puisées dans Plutarque, Tite-Live, Tacite et Pline, les différences et les particularités propres aux Amérindiens (251–3). La coutume, observée chez les Abiponi, consistant à utiliser les crânes d'adversaires tués comme des coupes à boissons, qui peut paraître un signe de barbarie propre aux peuples "sauvages," est mise en parallèle et ainsi relativisée par des références à de nombreux historiens de l'Antiquité ayant relevé la même habitude chez les Scythes, les peuples germaniques, les Hongrois, ainsi que les anciens Belges; Dobrizhoffer cite à ce propos Strabon, Hérodote et Diodore de Sicile (594–652). Le penchant des chefs abiponiens consistant à s'adonner à des excès d'alcool et de débauche lors des commémorations de leurs victoires est comparé à toute une série de comportements semblables, répertoriés chez plusieurs hommes de l'Antiquité gréco-romaine, comme Néron, Marc Antoine, Mithridate et Alexandre le Grand, évoqués dans cette perspective notamment par Horace, César et Strabon (575–95).[12] Et dans un des rares passages de son ouvrage qui décrit un dialogue interculturel, en l'occurrence entre un Cacique et lui-même, il compare sa propre rhétorique, non sans un clin d'œil ironique, au style oratoire véhément de Cicéron dans ses *Catilinaires* (104).[13] Dans sa préface, Dobrizhoffer légitime comme suit ce recours conventionnel à la figure du parallèle entre les Anciens et les Modernes, dont il semble avoir ressenti le caractère suranné:

> J'ai parfois inséré dans la narration des curiosités abiponiennes des exemples de l'Antiquité, et parfois des sentences (de la même manière que nous avons l'habitude d'épicer nos mets), nullement dans l'intention ridicule de me faire attribuer la gloire d'un philologue, mais afin de montrer clairement que les coutumes et les visions du monde des Abiponiens étaient déjà courantes en Europe et en Asie chez d'autres peuples dans les temps les plus reculés ("Ich habe in die Erzählung der abiponischen Merkwürdigkeiten manchmal Beispiele aus dem Alterthume, und manchmal Kernsprüche miteingestreuet (so ungefehr, wie wir unsere Speisen zu würzen pflegen) keineswegs in der lächerlichen Ansicht den Ruhm eines Philologen dadurch zu erhaschen, sondern um deutlich dazuthun, daß die Gebräuche und Meinungen der Abiponer bei andern Völker[n] in Europa und Asien schon in den ältesten Zeiten üblich waren" [5e p. de la préface s. p.]).

Ce "réflexe comparatif" qu'induit l'enseignement de la rhétorique avec sa forte mise en valeur des parallèles est néanmoins dépourvu, chez Dobrizhoffer, du soubassement idéologique situant l'origine des

Amérindiens dans l'Antiquité. Dobrizhoffer réduit également le nombre des comparaisons binaires entre l'Ancien et le Nouveau Monde, caractéristique des *Relations* jésuites. En revanche, il développe, dans le sillage de Lafitau qu'il cite également (553–4), la perspective d'une étude comparée des cultures, des sociétés et des civilisations, en mettant en regard les différentes sociétés amérindiennes sur la base de ses propres observations et expériences, mais aussi d'une mise en relation comparative des récits de voyage et relations qu'il avait lus. Ses réflexions sur les langues des peuples du Paraguay, qu'il accompagne d'un inventaire de particularités lexicales, sémantiques et syntaxiques, sont en partie fondées sur la comparaison avec d'autres langues amérindiennes, du Pérou, du Chili, de Nouvelle-Grenade ainsi que du Canada et de l'Acadie (247 et suiv.). On peut ainsi constater chez Dobrizhoffer, mais aussi chez d'autres jésuites exilés, comme chez le Mexicain Xavier Clavijero et l'Allemand Johann Heinrich Baegert,[14] à la fois une prise de distance par rapport au modèle rhétorique de la comparaison-parallèle dans sa structure classique, une "réinvention" du regard comparatiste dans la perspective d'une étude comparée des sociétés et des cultures humaines en germe à la fin du XVIIIe siècle, ainsi que l'introduction d'une perspective foncièrement critique (des sources et des auteurs antérieurs), également fondée sur des comparaisons systématiques impliquant l'observation empirique et la prise en considération de travaux antérieurs, examinés en vue de leur validité. En effet, Dobrizhoffer accompagne sa description et son analyse des sociétés et cultures amérindiennes du Paraguay, en particulier du peuple des Abiponi, d'une critique à la fois acerbe et minutieuse des publications existantes, en premier lieu du *Voyage autour du monde* (1769) de Louis-Antoine de Bougainville (Dobrizhoffer 1783, vol. 1: 1e part.).[15] Et il légitime le recours à des exemples pris dans l'Antiquité à la fois par des raisons stylistiques – celle d'embellir une matière qui, autrement, risquerait d'être aride, de même manière que l'"on a l'habitude d'épicer des mets" ("so ungefähr, wie wir unsere Speisen zu würzen pflegen" [vol. 1, s. p. (5)]) – et par la volonté de donner aux cultures amérindiennes qu'il décrit le statut d'une civilisation comparable, et foncièrement équivalente, aux civilisations occidentales ([5]).

Cette "réinvention" du regard comparatif dans les écrits ethnographiques des pères de la Compagnie, et notamment ceux des jésuites exilés, allait donc de pair avec un nouveau souci de précision dans l'observation empirique, permettant d'établir des paramètres précis de comparaison ainsi que d'afficher une volonté neuve de théorisation, visant à produire un tableau différencié des civilisations. Par exemple, les préfaciers des traductions anglaise et allemande de l'*Historia antigua de México*[16] (1780) de Clavijero soulignèrent le fait qu'il était natif de Vera Cruz au Mexique et, par conséquent, qu'il maîtrisait plusieurs langues du pays, compétence jugée désormais indispensable à une connaissance et une compréhension sérieuses des cultures décrites.[17] Davantage que Lafitau lui-même, des traducteurs et commentateurs, comme l'historien allemand Siegmund Jacob Baumgarten dans sa longue préface à la traduction allemande de l'ouvrage de Lafitau parue en 1752 à Halle,[18] entreprirent ce travail d'examen critique des sources, que Dobrizhoffer et d'autres jésuites exilés continuèrent, notamment en passant au crible les historiens et chroniqueurs espagnols, mais aussi des auteurs comme Charlevoix, jugés peu fiables à leur regard comparatif souvent très peu indulgent. La préface de Baumgarten contient ainsi un nombre impressionnant de références à des ouvrages sur les deux Indes. En intégrant également les traductions et en embrassant les différentes langues européennes, Baumgarten fait dès lors ressortir la dimension proprement transnationale et transculturelle du discours sur le monde non-occidental, impliquant que tout travail scientifique d'examen comparatif des sources et des références doit être ancré aussi bien dans une connaissance des langues pratiquées sur le terrain que dans la maîtrise des principales langues de la communauté académique internationale.

Les écrits des Jésuites sur le Nouveau Monde portent ainsi la trace d'un changement des fonctions du paradigme comparatif dans la connaissance historique et anthropologique: d'une mise en parallèle entre l'Antiquité et la modernité, sous-tendue par des visées de légitimation, le regard comparatif évolue vers un nouvel outil de connaissance, lié à la critique des sources et à une vision globale de l'histoire des civilisations mettant désormais l'accent non pas sur les figures de pensées que sont l'opposition, l'antinomie et la répétition, mais sur une vision différentielle des sociétés et des cultures.

NOTES

1 Sur la discussion autour de la méthodologie comparatiste en littérature comparée, voir Konstantinovic 1978 et, plus généralement, tout le dossier dirigé par Bleicher 1978.

2 Dans cette perspective, Jouvancy opère une distinction entre "Comparaison des majeures," "Comparaisons des mineures" et "Comparaisons des égaux." De manière générale, il définit la comparaison comme un "lieu commun

où l'on compare deux ou plusieurs choses qui ont quelques rapports communs" (Jouvancy [1712] 1892, 14).

3 Voir aussi les remarques succinctes qui sont relatives à cette question chez Quintilien 1728, Livre II, ch. vi: 96–97.

4 La première phrase reprend en partie un extrait du Livre III de l'*Histoire* de Polybe, cité en exergue à l'ouvrage de Séran de La Tour.

5 Jochen Schlobach (1980, 231) mentionne comme premier ouvrage comportant le terme dans son titre les *Parallèles de César et de Henry le Grand* de Sully, parus à Paris en 1615. Voir aussi Schlobach 1976.

6 Comme la comparaison entre Alexandre et César, exemple canonique dans les dictionnaires du XVIIIe siècle. Voir aussi Vaugelas [1634] 1981, 96–97.

7 Voir également Lafitau 1724, 40–41, Lemay 1983, 23, ainsi que Fenton et Moore 1969.

8 La *Relation* du père Neuville parut, comme Lafitau le précise dans une note (1724, vol. 2: 20), sous forme de "Lettres" dans *Mémoires de Trévoux*, en mars 1713.

9 Sur Lejeune et son usage de la comparaison, voir Ferland 1992, 169–172.

10 Ces comparaisons sont notamment reprises de l'*Histoire de la Nouvelle-France* (1609) de Marc Lescarbot, ouvrage synthétisé et traduit dès 1613, certainement à l'intention des jésuites allemands, sous le titre de *Nova Francia. Auss einem zu Pariss gedrukten Französischen Buch summarischer weiss ins Teutsch gebracht.* Augsbourg: Chrysostome Dabersshofer; je remercie Isabelle Lachance pour cette indication. Voir chez Lescarbot, par exemple, des comparaisons comme celle-ci, qui s'appuie par la suite sur des références à Diodore, Tite-Live et Strabon: "Nos anciens Gaullois ne faisoient pas moins de trophées que noz Sauvages des têtes de leur[s] ennemis" (Lescarbot 1609, 869–870).

11 Je traduis.

12 Voir tout particulièrement la p. 583. Le chapitre où sont décrits ces excès porte le titre de "Von den jährlichen Gedächtnissen ihrer Siege, und dem, was bei einem öffentlichen Trinkgeboth vorgeht" ("Des commémorations annuelles de leurs victoires et de ce qui se passe lors d'une incitation publique à boire").

13 "Jusques à quand encore, commençai-je, en imitant à cette occasion l'éloquence tonitruante de Cicéron contre Catilina" ("Wie lange noch, fieng ich an, indem ich bei dieser Gelegenheit die donnernde Beredsamkeit des Cicero wider den Catalina nachahmte").

14 Au sujet de Johann Heinrich Baegert, voir Lüsebrink 2004.

15 Voir également vol. 1: s. p. [9–11], 174, 175 et 227; vol. 2: 197 et 216, ainsi que vol. 3: 20. Voir aussi, à ce sujet, notre article "Between Ethnology and Romantic Discourse: Martin Dobrizhoffer's Account of the Abiponi in a

(post)modern perspective," figurant dans la première partie du présent ouvrage ("Intercultural Transfers").

16 L'ouvrage parut d'abord en italien en 1780, sous le titre *Storia Antica del Messico* (Cesena: Georgio Bisiani), et fut ensuite traduit en 1789 allemand et en 1826 en espagnol. Voir Clavijero 1991.

17 Ma traduction: "L'histoire de Mexico, par l'abbé Clavigero, natif de Veracruz, qui a habité près de quarante ans dans les provinces de la Nouvelle-Espagne, a examiné ses richesses naturelles, appris la langue des Mexicains et d'autres nations, décrit plusieurs de leurs traditions, étudié leurs peintures historiques, et leurs autres monuments anciens; l'on suppose qu'il a comblé leurs lacunes" ("The history of Mexico, by the Abbé Clavigero, a native of Vera Cruz, who resided near forty years in the provinces of New Spain, examined its natural produce, acquired the language of the Mexicans and other nations, gathered many of their traditions, studied their historical paintings, and other monuments of antiquity, it is presumed, has supplied their deficiencies" [Cullen 1817, viii]). Voir aussi la traduction allemande qui reprend la préface de Cullen ("Vorrede der englischen Übersetzung" ("Préface à la traduction anglaise"), dans Clavijero 1789).

18 "Geneigter Leser" ("Cher Lecteur"), dans Baumgarten 1752: s. p. *Allgemeine Geschichte der Länder und Völker von America* ("Histoire générale des terres et des peuples d'Amérique") présente une traduction de l'ouvrage de Lafitau.

BIBLIOGRAPHIE

Baumgarten, Jacob. 1752. "Geneigter Leser." In *Allgemeine Geschichte der Länder und Völker von America. Aus dem Französischen übersetzt von Johann Friedrich Schröter und herausgegeben von Siegmund Jacob Baumgarten*: vii–xxiv. Halle: Johann Justinus Gebauer.

Belleguic, Thierry et Marc André Bernier. 2007. "Le siècle des Lumières et la communauté des Anciens: rhétorique, histoire et esthétique." In *Parallèle des Anciens et des Modernes. Rhétorique, histoire et esthétique au siècle des Lumières*, éd. T. Belleguic et M. A. Bernier, 1–28. Québec: Presses de l'Université Laval.

Bleicher, Thomas, éd. 1978. *Konzepte der Komparatistik.* Mainz: Johannes Gutenberg Universität.

Boileau-Despréaux, Nicolas. 1810 [1693]. "Réflexions critiques sur quelques passages du rhéteur Longin." In *Œuvres complètes, contenant ses poésies, ses écrits en prose, sa traduction de Longin, des Lettres à Racine*, vol. 3: 243–316. Paris: Mame.

Brébeuf, Jean de. [1637] 1993. "Relations et Mémoires. Seconde partie: 'De la créance, des mœurs et des coutumes des Hurons'." In *Écrits en Huronie*, éd. Gilles Thérien: 107–95. Montréal: Bibliothèque québécoise.

Certeau, Michel de. 1980. "Writing vs. Time: History and Anthropology in the works of Lafitau." *Yale French Studies* 59: 37–64.

Charlevoix, François-Xavier. 1744. *Histoire et description générale de la Nouvelle France, avec le Journal historique d'un voyage fait par ordre du roi dans l'Amérique septentrionale.* Paris: Veuve Garneau.

Charlevoix, François-Xavier. 1757. *Histoire du Paraguay*. Paris: Desaint, David et Durand.

Clavijero, Francisco Javier. 1991. *Historia Antigua de México*, éd. Mariano Cuevas. Mexico: Editorial Porrua.

Clavijero, Franz Xaver. 1789. *Geschichte von Mexico aus spanischen und mexicanischen Geschichtsschrebern, Handschriften und Gemälden der Indianer zusammengetragen und durch Charten und Kupferstiche erläutert nebest einigen critischen Abhandlungen über die Beschaffenheit des Landes, der Thiere und Einwohner von Mexico. Aus dem Italienischen des Abts D. Franz Xaver Clavigero durch den Ritter Carl Cullen ins Englische, und aus diesem ins Deutsche übersetzt*, 2 vol. Leipzig: im Schwickerschen Verlage.

Cullen, Charles. 1817. "Translators Preface." In Francisco-Xavier Clavijero, *The History of Mexico, Collected from Spanish and Mexican Historians, from Manuscripts and Ancient Printings of the Indians, together with the Conquest of Mexico by the Spaniards*, trad. C. Cullen, vol. 1: vii–viii. Philadelphie: Thomas Dobson.

Détienne, Marcel. 1981. *L'invention de la mythologie*. Paris: Gallimard.

Dobrizhoffer, Martin. 1783. *Geschichte der Abiponer, einer berittenen und kriegerischen Nation in Paraguay*, trad. Antal Kreil. Vienne: Joseph Edlen von Kurzbek.

Espagne, Michel. 1994. "Sur les limites du comparatisme en histoire culturelle." *Genèses* 17: 112–21.

Espagne, Michel. 1999. "Au-delà du comparatisme." In *Les transferts culturels franco-allemands*, ch. 2: 35–49. Paris: Presses universitaires de France.

Fenton, William N. et Elizabeth L. Moore. 1969. "J.-F. Lafitau (1681–1746), Precursor of Scientific Anthropology." *Southwestern Journal of Anthropology* 25 (2): 173–87.

Fenton, William N. et Elizabeth L. Moore. 1974. "Introduction." In Joseph-François Lafitau, *Customs of the American Indians compared with the customs of primitive times*, éd. et trad. W. N. Fenton et E. L. Moore, vol. 1: xxix–cxix. Toronto: Champlain Society.

Ferland, Rémi. 1992. *Les* Relations *des Jésuites: un art de la persuasion. Procédés de rhétorique et fonction conative dans les* Relations *du Père Paul Lejeune.* Québec: Éditions de la Huit.

Furetière, Antoine. 1690. *Dictionnaire universel, contenant généralement tous les mots françois tant vieux que modernes, et les termes de toutes les sciences et les arts.* Paris: Arnout et Reinier Leers.

Gibert, Balthazar. 2004 [1729]. *La rhétorique ou les règles de l'éloquence*, éd. Samy Ben Messaoud. Paris: Honoré Champion.

Hartog, François. 2005. *Anciens, Modernes, Sauvages*. Paris: Galade Éditions.

Jouvancy, Joseph de. [1712] 1892. *L'élève de rhétorique* [*Candidatus rhetoricae*], trad. Henri Ferté. Paris: Hachette.

Konstantinovic, Zoran. 1978. "Der reflektierende Vergleich – Ein Beitrag zur Methodendiskussion in der 'Komparatistik.'" In *Konzepte der Komparatistik:* 6–14. éd. par Thomas Bleicher. Mainz: Johannes Gutenberg Universität.

Lafitau, Joseph-François. 1724. *Mœurs des sauvages amériquains, comparés aux mœurs des premiers temps*. Paris: Saugrain et Hochereau.

Lejeune, Paul. [1634] 1897. "Relation de ce qui s'est passé en la Nouvelle France, en l'année 1633." In *The Jesuit Relations and Allied Documents*, éd. Reuben Gold Thwaites, vol. 6: 5–32. Cleveland: Burrows Brothers.

Lejeune, Paul. [1637] 1898. "Relation de ce qui s'est passé en la Nouvelle France, en l'année 1636." In *The Jesuit Relations and Allied Documents*, éd. Reuben Gold Thwaites, vol. 9: 5–304. Cleveland: Burrows Brothers.

Lemay, Edna Hindie. 1983. "Introduction." In Joseph-François Lafitau, *Mœurs des sauvages amériquains comparés aux mœurs des premiers temps*, éd. E. H. Lemay, vol. 1: 5–38. Paris: Maspéro.

Lescarbot, Marc. 1609. *Histoire de la Nouvelle France, Contenant les navigations, découvertes, & habitations faites par les Français és Indes Occidentales et Nouvelle-France souz l'avœu & autorité de noz Rois Très-Chrétiens, & les diverses fortunes d'iceux en l'execution de ces choses, depuis cent ans jusques à hui. En quoy est comprise l'Histoire Moale, Naturelle & Geographique de ladite province*. Paris: Jean Milot.

Lüsebrink, Hans-Jürgen. 2004. "Missionarische Fremdheitserfahrung und anthropologischer Diskurs. Zu den Nachrichten von der Amerikanischen Halbinsel Californien (1772) des elsässischen Jesuitenmissionars Johann Jakob "Baegert." In *Lateinamerika. Orte und Ordnungen des Wissens. Festschrift für Birgit Scharlau*, éd. Sabine Hofmann et Monika Wehrheim, 69–82. Tübingen: Gunter Narr Verlag.

Matthes, Joachim. 1990. "Kulturvergleich: einige methodologische Anmerkungen," dans *Interamerikanische Beziehungen. Einfluß – Transfer – Interkulturalität*, éd. Helmbrecht Breinig: 7–12. Frankfurt / Main: Vervuert Verlag.

Middell, Matthias. 1999. "La Révolution française et l'Allemagne: du paradigme comparatiste à la recherche des transferts culturels." *Annales historiques de la Révolution française* 317 ("France-Allemagne. Interactions, références"): 427–54.

Motsch, Andreas. 2001. *Lafitau et l'émergence du discours ethnographique*. Québec / Paris: Septentrion / Presses de l'Université de Paris-Sorbonne.

Osterhammel, Jürgen. 1996. "Sozialgeschichte im Zivilisationsvergleich. Zu künftigen Möglichkeiten komparativer Geschichtswissenschaft." *Geschichtswissenschaft und Gesellschaft* 22 ("Erweiterung der Sozialgeschichte"): 143–64.

Ovide. 1874. "Epistola X. Ariadne Theseo." In *P. Ovidii Nasonis Heroides XIV*, éd. Arthur Palmer: 89–96. Londres: G. Bell and Sons.

Perelman, Charles et Lucie Olbrechts-Tyteca. 1976 [1970]. *Traité de l'argumentation. La nouvelle rhétorique.* Bruxelles: Éditions de l'Université de Bruxelles.

Quintilien. 1752. *De l'institution de l'orateur*, trad. Nicolas Gedoyn. Paris: Grégoire Dupuis.

Rausch, Helke, éd. 2007. *Transatlantischer Kulturtransfer im* "Kalten Krieg": *Perspektiven für eine historisch vergleichende Transferforschung.* Leipzig: Leipziger Universitätsverlag.

Schlobach, Jochen. 1976. "Pessimisme des philosophes? La théorie cyclique de l'histoire au XVIIIe siècle." *Studies on Voltaire and the Eighteenth Century* 155: 1971–1987.

Schlobach, Jochen. 1980. *Zyklentheorie und Epochenmetaphorik. Studien zur bildlichen Sprache der Geschichtsreflexion in Frankreich von der Renaissance bis zur Frühaufklärung.* Munich: Fink.

Schulz-Buschhaus, Ulrich. 1979. "Die Unvermeidlichkeit der Komparatistik." *Arcadia. Zeitschrift für Vergleichende Literaturwissenschaft* 14: 223–36.

Séran De La Tour, Louis-François, abbé. 1757. *Parallèle de la conduite des Carthaginois à l'égard des Romains, dans la seconde guerre punique, avec la conduite de l'Angleterre à l'égard de la France dans la guerre déclarée par ces deux puissances en 1756.* S. l.: s. n.

Thérien, Gilles. 1995. "L'Indien du discours." In *Figures de l'Indien*, éd. G. Thérien, 11–31. Montréal: Typo.

Vaugelas, Claude Favre, dit. [1634] 1981. "Parallèle." In *Remarques sur la langue française utiles à ceux qui veulent bien parler et bien écrire*, 96–7. Paris, Champ Libre.

Werner, Michael et Bénédicte Zimmermann. 2002. "Vergleich, Transfer, Verflechtung. Der Ansatz der *Histoire croisée* und die Herausforderung des Transnationalen." *Geschichte und Gesellschaft* 28 (4): 607–36.

Annexe

Gérard Jean-Baptiste Scotin. 1724. Frontispice. In Lafitau 1724, vol. 1. © Library of Congress. 2011. *France in America / La France en Amérique*. http://international.loc.gov/intldl/fiahtml.

Contributors

Beatriz de Alba-Koch is Associate Professor at the University of Victoria, the founding director of the Latin American Studies Program, the founding coordinator of the Latin America Research Group, and a member of the editorial boards of the *Revista Canadiense de Estudios Hispánicos*, *Textos Nómadas*, and *Cincinnati Romance Review*. Her research focuses on colonial and nineteenth-century Mexican literature. She has published on Enlightenment thought and sixteenth-century indigenous accounts of the conquest of México, particularly in the work of Francisco Javier Clavigero. She has also published on Enlightenment *novohispano* appropriations of Golden Age genres. *Ilustrando la Nueva España* (1999) explores the relationship between text and images in Lizardi's *El Periquillo Sarniento*; her edition of this novel is forthcoming.

Marc André Bernier est professeur de littérature française à l'Université du Québec à Trois-Rivières. Il est titulaire de la Chaire de recherche du Canada en rhétorique et président de la Société internationale d'étude du XVIIIe siècle. Il est l'auteur de *Libertinage et figures du savoir* (2001) et a dirigé ou codirigé plusieurs ouvrages collectifs, dont *La raison exaltée. Études sur* De la littérature *de Madame de Staël* (2011), *Les* Lettres sur la sympathie *(1798) de Sophie de Grouchy. Philosophie morale et réforme sociale* (2010), *Parallèle des Anciens et des Modernes* (2006) et *Portrait des arts, des lettres et de l'éloquence au Québec, 1760–1840* (2002).

Pierre Berthiaume est professeur émérite de l'Université d'Ottawa. Il est spécialiste de l'histoire des idées et des formes littéraires – plus spécifiquement de littérature française du XVIIIe siècle – et de littérature de voyage. Responsable de l'édition critique des *Mœurs, coutumes et religions des sauvages* de Nicolas Perrot (2004), du *Journal d'un voyage* de Charlevoix (1994) et des récits de Cavelier de La Salle (*Une épopée aux Amériques*, 2006), il est également l'auteur d'une monographie intitulée *Personae et personnages dans les récits médiévaux* (2008).

Catherine Broué est professeure de littérature à l'Université du Québec à Rimouski. Elle a obtenu un doctorat à l'Université Laval sous la direction de Réal Ouellet. Spécialiste des écrits du récollet Louis Hennepin, elle travaille actuellement sur la parole amérindienne dans les récits d'exploration et les textes missionnaires de la Nouvelle-France. Elle prépare également une édition critique de la correspondance de Cavelier de La Salle et de textes connexes. On lui doit notamment la traduction de *Les Nouvelles Frances* de Philip Boucher (2004).

Clorinda Donato is the George L. Graziadio Chair of Italian Studies at California State University, Long Beach, where she is Professor of French and Italian and a Chevalier dans l'Ordre des Palmes Académiques. Her co-edited volumes, articles, and book chapters span a wide range of disciplines including the history of encyclopedias, the Protestant and Catholic Enlightenments, gender studies, translation, and travel literature.

Klaus-Dieter Ertler est Professeur au Département de littératures romanes de l'Université de Graz (Autriche). Ses recherches portent sur le roman francophone, les *Relations* des Jésuites des Amériques, la littérature latino-américaine et la théorie des systèmes comme modèle épistémologique. Parmi ses publications récentes, notons : *Cultural Constructions of Migration in Canada – Constructions culturelles de la migration au Canada* (éd. avec Martin Löschnigg et Yvonne Völkl, 2011); *Canadian Studies. The State of the Art – Études canadiennes. Questions de recherche* (éd. avec Stewart Gill, Susan Hodgett et Patrick James, 2011); *Regards sur les "spectateurs"* (éd. avec Alexis Lévrier et Michaela Fischer, 2012).

Margaret R. Ewalt is Associate Professor of Spanish at Wake Forest University in North Carolina. She is the author of *Peripheral Wonders: Nature, Knowledge, and Enlightenment in the Eighteenth-Century Orinoco* (2008), and various articles on transatlantic eighteenth-century natural histories. Her current book project, tentatively entitled *Francis Bacon in Hispanic Science: Knowledge, the Nature of Modernity, and the Spanish World, 1539–1782*, analyses sixteenth- through eighteenth-century Spanish-language texts, both to reveal how natural philosophers conceived Bacon's influence and to recover Spain's influence on Bacon's construction of the "modern scientific method" by including non-European knowledge production and paradigms.

Ute Fendler est professeure à l'Université de Bayreuth. Elle est spécialiste des littératures et médias francophones et met de l'avant une approche comparatiste des corpus germanophone et francophone ainsi que de ce dernier et du corpus hispanophone. Ces travaux portent sur l'Afrique de l'Ouest, l'Océan indien, le Maghreb, les Caraïbes, l'Amérique latine et le Canada. Elle est coresponsable de la publication de *Francophonie et globalisation culturelle* (2008) et de *Littératures et sociétés africaines. Regards comparatistes et perspectives interculturelles* (2001). Elle est l'auteure de *Interkulturalität in der frankophonen Literatur der Karibik* (1994) et a préparé, en collaboration avec Susanne Greilich, une édition critique du Livre VI (« Découverte de l'Amérique ») de l'*Histoire des deux Indes*, dont la direction est assurée par Anthony Strugnell.

Girolamo Imbruglia is Professor at the University "l'Orientale" in Naples. His research interests include the religious history of the sixteenth, seventeenth and eighteenth century, especially the Catholic evangelization of the New World, as well as the political culture of the Enlightenment and the history of modern historiography and the contemporary publication of books. He is responsible for the edition of Muratori's *Relation des Missions du Paraguay* (1983). He is also the author of *L'invenzione del Paraguay* (1987), and editor of *Il razzismo e le sue storie* (1992), *Ragione e immaginazione. Edward Gibbon e la storiografia europea del Settecento* (1996), and *The Birth and Fall of a Nation* (2000, 2007). He also published a study entitled *Illuminismo e storicismo nella storiografia italiana*, in an appendix to his edition of F. Venturi and D. Cantimori's correspondence (2003).

Isabelle Lachance est professionnelle de recherche au Centre interuniversitaire de recherche sur la première modernité (XVIe-XVIIIe s.) et à la Chaire de recherche en rhétorique de l'Université du Québec à Trois-Rivières (sous la direction de Marc André Bernier), et chargée de cours dans la même université. Elle a complété une thèse de doctorat sur l'*Histoire de la Nouvelle-France* de Marc Lescarbot (2004) à l'Université McGill. Elle est l'auteure de plusieurs articles sur les récits de voyages et de missions en Amérique et sur l'écriture de l'histoire à la Renaissance, et elle prépare actuellement avec Marie-Christine Pioffet l'édition critique de textes brefs de Lescarbot.

Hans-Jürgen Lüsebrink est titulaire de la Chaire d'études culturelle et de communication interculturelle de l'Université de Saarbrücken. Il travaille principalement sur les littératures populaires et les médias, les transferts culturels transatlantiques et l'histoire conceptuelle. Il complète actuellement une édition critique de l'*Histoire des deux Indes* de l'abbé Raynal et est auteur ou coauteur de nombreux ouvrages, dont *Enlightenment, Revolution and the Periodical Press* (2004), *Interkulturelle Kommunikation. Interaktion – Kulturtransfer – Fremdwahrnehmung* (2005, 3ᵉ éd. 2012) et *Das Europa der Aufklärung und die außereuropäische koloniale Welt* (2006).

Sara E. Melzer is Professor at the University of California, Los Angeles. She is the author of *Colonizer or Colonized: The Hidden Stories of Early Modern French Culture* (2012), *Discourses of the Fall: A Study of Pascal's "Pensées"* (1986), co-editor of *From the Royal to the Republican Body: Incorporating the Political in Seventeenth- and Eighteenth-Century France* (1998), and co-author of *Rebel Daughters: Women and the French Revolution* (1992).

Réal Ouellet est professeur émérite de littérature française et québécoise à l'Université Laval. Il a été aussi professeur invité dans plusieurs universités en tant que spécialiste de l'édition critique et de la narratologie. Boursier Killam, il a publié plusieurs livres et études sur le roman, la nouvelle, le théâtre et la relation de voyage. Responsable de plusieurs éditions critiques de voyages en Nouvelle-France, il a également fait paraître un roman historique (*L'aventurier du hasard. Le Baron de Lahontan*, 1996) et deux recueils de nouvelles.

Perla Chinchilla Pawling is Doctor in History and Professor at the Universidad Iberoamericana. Her main areas of expertise are historiography, as well as discourse analysis from the perspective of rhetoric and social theory. Her principal research interest is the evolution of sermons from piety devices to works of art and then back to their pious background during the seventeenth and eighteenth centuries. Her publications include articles on the Mexican history of science, a book on Jesuit sermons in seventeenth-century New Spain (*De la* compositio loci *a la república de letras*, 2004), "La transmisión de la verdad divina" (*Renaissance Quarterly* 63 [1], 2012, *El sermón de misión y su tipología. Antología de sermons en español, náhuatl e italiano* (2013), and a monograph on Michel De Certau (*Michel De Certeau. Un pensador de la diferencia*, 2009). She is currently working on a lexicon of Jesuit forms of discourse in partnership with six research institutions from around the world.

Marie-Christine Pioffet est professeure à l'Université York, où elle enseigne la littérature française et, plus spécifiquement, celle des XVIIe et XVIIIe siècles. Elle est spécialiste de littérature de voyage. Ses principales publications comptent un *Dictionnaire analytique des toponymes imaginaires (1605–1711)* (2011), une édition critique de l'*Histoire de la Nouvelle-France* de Marc Lescarbot (2007), ainsi que deux monographies: *La tentation de l'épopée dans les* Relations *des jésuites* (1997) et *Espaces lointains, espaces rêvées dans la fiction romanesque du Grand Siècle* (2007). Elle a dirigé et co-dirigé plusieurs collectifs portant sur les voyages, historiques et imaginaires.

Wiebke Röben de Alencar Xavier has a Doctor of Philosophy (Germanist) from the University of Osnabrück and is currently Professor at the Federal University of Rio Grande do Norte (Natal, Brazil). She is working on the following topics in comparative literature: European Enlightenment and its reception in Brazil; cultural transfers; Salomon Gessner; and translations of the Brazilian Romantic author José de Alencar.

Karen Stolley is Professor at Emory University. Her areas of scholarly interest are colonial and eighteenth-century Latin America and Spain. She is the author of *El lazarillo de ciegos caminantes. Un itinerario critico* (1985), "Narrative Forms, Scholarship and Learning in the XVIII Century" in the *Cambridge History of Latin American Literature* (1996), and numerous articles on the Hispanic eighteenth century. Her most recent work, *Domesticating Empire: Enlightenment in Spanish America* (2013), explores the Ibero-American Enlightenment as a project that reflects key concerns of eighteenth-century Spain and its territories in the Americas.

Après avoir enseigné au Nunavik et en Ontario, **Andréanne Vallée** a terminé en 2008 des études doctorales en lettres françaises à l'Université d'Ottawa sous la direction de Pierre Berthiaume. Actuellement enseignante au secondaire, sa thèse, une édition critique des *Avantures du sieur Claude Le Beau*, a été publiée en 2011 aux Presses de l'Université Laval.

Eileen Willingham specializes in languages and cross-cultural communication. She is an independent scholar and translator. She has taught at universities in the United States and Australia. Her PhD thesis (2001) focuses on Juan de Velasco's *Historia del Reino de Quito.*

Index Nominum

www.ingramcontent.com/pod-product-compliance
Lightning Source LLC
LaVergne TN
LVHW090758070826
844660LV00022B/1020

* 9 7 8 1 4 8 7 5 4 9 7 7 0 *